Artistic Exchange and Cultural Translation in the Italian Renaissance City

This book considers the reception of the early modern cultures of Florence, Rome, and Venice in other centers of the Italic peninsula, such as Ferrara, Bologna, Ancona, San Gimignano, and Pistoia, which had flourishing local cultures of their own. Offering a perspective that focuses on dialogue and exchange among various urban centers and cultural groups, it also involves a reexamination of the Renaissance itself as a form of translation of a past culture, one that attempted to assimilate the lost or fragmentary world of the Roman emperors, the Greek Platonists, and the ancient Egyptians. Collectively the essays examine how the processes of cultural self-definition varied among the Italian urban centers in the early modern period, well before the formation of a distinct Italian national identity. Exploring how artistic forms made the transition from one Italian city to another, the contributors also focus attention on the subtle modification of practice that local conditions and priorities required.

Stephen J. Campbell is a professor in history of art at The Johns Hopkins University. The author of *Cosmè Tura of Ferrara: Style, Politics and the Renaissance City, 1450–1495* and the forthcoming *Painting, Humanism, and the Studiolo of Isabella d'Este,* he has received fellowships from the Metropolitan Museum and the Harvard University Center for Italian Renaissance Studies at Villa I Tatti in Florence.

Stephen J. Milner is a senior lecturer in Italian at the University of Bristol. Editor of *Niccolò Machiavelli: The Prince and Other Political Writings* and the forthcoming *At the Margins: Minority Groups in Premodern Italy,* he has received a fellowship from the Harvard Center for Italian Renaissance Studies at Villa I Tatti in Florence.

Artistic Exchange and Cultural Translation in the Italian Renaissance City

EDITED BY

STEPHEN J. CAMPBELL
The Johns Hopkins University

STEPHEN J. MILNER
University of Bristol

CAMBRIDGE
UNIVERSITY PRESS

PUBLISHED BY THE PRESS SYNDICATE OF THE UNIVERSITY OF CAMBRIDGE
The Pitt Building, Trumpington Street, Cambridge, United Kingdom

CAMBRIDGE UNIVERSITY PRESS
The Edinburgh Building, Cambridge CB2 2RU, UK
40 West 20th Street, New York, NY 10011-4211, USA
477 Williamstown Road, Port Melbourne, VIC 3207, Australia
Ruiz de Alarcón 13, 28014 Madrid, Spain
Dock House, The Waterfront, Cape Town 8001, South Africa

http://www.cambridge.org

First published 2004

Printed in the United Kingdom at the University Press, Cambridge

Typeface Centaur MT 12/14 pt. *System* LaTeX 2ε [TB]

A catalog record for this book is available from the British Library.

Library of Congress Cataloging in Publication Data
Artistic exchange and cultural translation in the Italian renaissance city /
edited by Stephen J. Campbell, Stephen J. Milner.
p. cm.
Includes bibliographical references and index.
ISBN 0-521-82688-8 (hb)
1. Art, Italian. 2. Art, Renaissance – Italy. 3. Art and society – Italy.
4. Culture diffusion – Italy. 5. Regionalism – Italy.
I. Campbell, Stephen J. (Stephen John), 1963– II. Milner, Stephen J., 1963–
N6915.A743 2004
709′.45′09024 – dc22 2003062976

ISBN 0 521 82688 8 hardback

Contents

Illustrations and Table

FIGURES

TABLE

Acknowledgements

The initial catalyst for commissioning this series of essays on the subject of cultural translation in the Italian Renaissance was provided by the conference held at The National Gallery in London on 12–13 November 1999 which accompanied the exhibition 'Florence and the 1470s: Contexts and Contrasts' curated by Pat Rubin and Alison Wright. During a number of the roundtable discussions that followed the conference sessions, I was struck by the regularity with which the question of Florentine cultural relations with other centers within the Italian peninsula arose, and specifically the manner in which such artistic exchange assumed the character of a continuing dialogue in which both imitation and differentiation played equally important roles. Luckily there was ample opportunity to dwell further on these issues as a number of the conference participants happened to be co-fellows that year at the Harvard Center for Italian Renaissance Studies at Villa I Tatti in Florence, including Stephen Campbell with whom I had the pleasure of sharing an office. It was only a short time before I suggested we co-edit a volume on the subject.

We would like to thank, therefore, both the staff and fellows of Villa I Tatti (VIT) for enabling such a collaborative enterprise, Pat Rubin for her encouragement in getting the project underway, the contributors for their patience and industry, and finally Beatrice Rehl and the rest of the editorial team at Cambridge University Press.

Stephen J. Milner

Contributors

Stephen J. Campbell The Johns Hopkins University. Author of *Cosmè Tura of Ferrara: Style, Politics and the Renaissance City 1450–1495* (New Haven and London, 1997) and the forthcoming *Painting, Humanism and the Studiolo of Isabella d'Este.*

Christopher S. Celenza Michigan State University. Author of *Renaissance Humanism and the Papal Curia* (Ann Arbor, 1999), *Piety and Pythagoras and late Quattrocento Florence: The 'Symbolum nesianum'* (Leiden, 2001), and *The Lost Italian Renaissance: Humanists, Historians, and Latin's Legacy* (Baltimore, 2004).

Georgia Clarke Courtauld Institute of Art, London. Author of *Roman House-Renaissance Palaces: Inventing Antiquity in Fifteenth-Century Italy* (Cambridge, 2003) and co-editor of *Architecture and Language: Constructing Identity in European Architecture 1000–1650* (Cambridge, 2000).

Brian A. Curran Pennsylvania State University. Associate Professor in the History of Art and author of *The Egyptian Renaissance: The Afterlife of Ancient Egypt in Early Modern Italy* (Chicago, University of Chicago Press, forthcoming 2005).

Bruce L. Edelstein New York University in Florence. Author of an article on the influence of Eleonora d' Aragona, Duchess of Ferrara, on the public self-fashioning of Eleonora da Toledo (*Quaderni storici*, 2000). Also developing a larger study on Eleonora's patronage of Bronzino.

Morten Steen Hansen The Walters Art Museum, Baltimore. Currently working on studies of Parmigianino and of Pellegrino Tibaldi.

Megan Holmes University of Michigan. Author of *Fra Filippo Lippi the Carmelite Painter* (New Haven and London, 1999) and presently working on popular devotion and art production in Renaissance Tuscany.

Deborah Krohn Bard Graduate Center, New York. Publications include studies of Renaissance decorative arts, patronage, and the history of collecting. She is currently working on a history of the period room.

Stephen J. Milner University of Bristol. Editor and translator of *Machiavelli's Prince and Other Political Writings* (London, 1996) and editor of the forthcoming *At the Margins: Minority Groups in Premodern Italy* (Minnesota, 2005).

Michelle O'Malley University of Sussex. Author of the forthcoming *The Business of Art: The Commissioning Process in Italy 1300–1530* (New Haven and London, 2004) and collaborator on the 'Mapping the Market in Paintings, 1450–1850' project organised by Duke University.

Luke Syson The National Gallery, London. Curator, Italian Paintings 1460–1500. Co-author (with Dora Thornton) of *Objects of Virtue: Art in Renaissance Italy* (London, 2001) and (with Dillian Gordon) of *Pisanello* (London, 2001); co-editor (with Nicholas Mann) of *The Image of the Individual: Portraits of the Renaissance* (London, 1998).

Shelley Zuraw Lamar Dodd School of Art, Georgia. Editor of *Masterpieces of the Renaissance and Baroque Sculpture from the Palazzo Venezia, Rome* (Athens, Georgia, 1996), she is currently working on a study of the sculptural works of Mino da Fiesole.

INTRODUCTION

Art, Identity, and Cultural Translation in Renaissance Italy

Stephen J. Campbell and Stephen J. Milner

THIS BOOK IS DESIGNED TO ENLIVEN THE SCHOLARSHIP AND TEACHING OF Italian Renaissance art and culture by offering a range of methodological perspectives, a re-examination and critique of some of art history's key analytical terms, and a sense of the variety of artistic practice by exploring the dynamics of interaction and resistance in the urban cultures of the Italian peninsula in the period 1400–1550. In subject and method, the essays collected here aim to take stock of what often appears to be a highly specialized and hence disunified field. They also, in different ways, address the very historical principle which has made the isolated case study more typical than the synthetic overview in recent scholarship on the Italian Renaissance: the impulse towards competitive differentiation and individualization among Italian states and social groups.

The essays commissioned for this volume are all variously concerned with ideas of 'cultural translation' in the artistic and intellectual life of Italian cities. Rather than subscribing to the notion of discrete urban cultures and organic regional identities, we are interested in how these interpenetrate and inform each other. In this sense the volume seeks to extend the notion of the Renaissance itself as a product of cultural translation, or as a dialogue with an alien classical past, by examining the processes of cultural exchange between places or groups, and the consequent changes of meaning inherent within such transactions.[1] Such a process is necessarily one of interpretation, which is itself a form of translation; the Latin terms *interpres* and *interpretatio* refer both to an intermediary or go-between as well as to the rendering of a text or object.[2]

Over the past decade, the concept of 'cultural translation' has informed a range of work in history, anthropology, religious studies, musicology, and comparative literature and has principally been used to define the ways in which a self-consciously distinct group (this may be a population, an elite, a profession, an ethnic, or religious enclave) articulates itself in relation to another in an act of self-definition which may involve an assimilation and refashioning of an 'other'.[3] The assimilative dimension to the encounter may be appropriative or imperialistic, but it is not always necessarily so. Jan Assmann, for instance, has examined the elaborate strategies among the civilizations of the ancient Near East to find equivalent names and functions for the gods of neighboring peoples, concluding that 'since the conviction that these foreign peoples worshiped the same gods is far from trivial and self-evident,' the insight, along with the intercultural contact it facilitated "must be reckoned among the major cultural achievements of the ancient world."[4] The work of Assmann and others on the 'translatability of cultures' takes as its starting point the perception of alterity – ethnic, religious, linguistic – between the partners in a cultural exchange. Translation occurs in the laying claim to cultural homologies, or in what Anthony Pagden has fittingly termed the 'misrecognition' of a 'principle of attachment' – which may be visual, ritual, or institutional.[5] In a parallel sense, following the work of Pagden, Edward Said, Homi Bhabha, and Stuart Hall, cultural exchange in the history of art and literature is now frequently discussed within a global and post-colonial perspective, usually between unequal partners and when the perceived exotic or foreign qualities of the other are especially at issue.[6] Such an approach characterizes the important collection recently edited by Clare Farago titled *Reframing the Renaissance,* which locates Italian Renaissance culture in terms of its encounter with the New World, and – as with the collection of essays that we present here – is aimed at a revision of Burckhardtian historiography based on 'the investigation of cultural exchange rather than the taxonomy of national culture.'[7]

Our critique of a national or homogenous Renaissance culture proceeds in a somewhat different direction. In crucial ways the relation of Europe to its 'new worlds' manifestly does not resemble the experience of local differences between Italians in the era of city-states and courts. Although Burckhardt's idea of an emerging 'national consciousness' is an untenable (and possibly ironic) anachronism, 'Italy' was more than a geographical expression to figures such as Brunetto Latini, Dante, Petrarch, Pius II, and Castiglione.[8] By the 1600s 'Italy' was a homogeneous concept in the eyes of the rest of Europe, a perception especially apparent in French, English, and Dutch perceptions, which advocated resistance to the contaminating fashions of the Italians.[9] Italian style in the visual arts became an important signifier of Italian identity among other Europeans; like the Italian language, it was testimony to the existence of what we would now call a culture.[10] Most Italian cities were linked by elements of a common historical memory, a common language (notwithstanding pronounced regional variations), and a common religion (the sense of community was stabilized by, among other things, the migration of the cults of local saints). Yet it is nonetheless the case that by 1400 the Italian peninsula was a conglomerate of diverse political forms which included the kingdom of Naples in the south, the signorial courts of the north, the Papal States of central Italy, and the mercantile republics of Florence, Venice, and Genoa. The new humanist historiography of the fifteenth century was in many respects a genealogy of difference, stressing a diversity of ancient origins and foundational myths.[11] Indeed, the relative tardiness in the evolution of a distinct Italian national identity was in part a consequence of the durability of these regional identities and the variety of cultural milieus they generated. Part of Castiglione's reason for writing *The Book of the Courtier* lay in the imperative to define a series of norms for Italian aristocratic behaviour and customs in the face of pronounced local heterogeneity, because such regional differences could be perceived as a disastrous fragmentation – both cause and symptom of domination by foreign powers: "I do not know by what fate it happens that Italy does not have, as it used to, a distinctively Italian costume: for although the new fashions in use may make earlier ways of dressing appear uncouth, still these were perhaps a sign of our freedom, as the former have proved to be an augury of servitude, in my opinion now clearly fulfilled."[12]

Even while a shared language and geographical proximity generated unprecedented cultural exchange between these centers – one largely facilitated by the itinerant class of humanists and artists who migrated between these centers in the search for patronage – the very intensity of economic and political interdependency precipitated a concern with the *generation* of difference, as Luke Syson and others suggest in this volume. Syson describes the emergence of the court artist as a defining institution of princely states and the special constraints operating in nominally Republican Florence when Bertoldo plays this role for Lorenzo de'Medici. The geographical expansion of many of these centers resulted in the formation of distinct territorial states in which jurisdictional domination and local resistance were not only political but also *cultural*. It is even arguable that the attention to regional difference in language, dress, political organization, and art corresponds to the notion of 'culture' in the modern sense. Like cultures generally, these cultures of Renaissance Italy were unstable and permeable entities. As styles and fashions spread or were imitated from one center to another, they were counterbalanced by assertions or performances of difference; even a common festive and ceremonial mode like chivalry could serve to generate such differences, as Georgia Clarke shows in her essay in this volume. Giovanni della Casa's *Galateo*, written in the 1550s, differs from Castiglione in arguing for regional variation through the principal of decorum:

> the lordly and pompous manners of Naples transferred to Florence would be as oversized and superfluous as the clothes of a large man placed on a midget; and equally the manners of the Florentines would appear meager and inadequate to the noble minds and temperament

> of the Neapolitans. And just because the gentlemen of Venice use an inordinate number of compliments amongst themselves on account of the positions they hold and the votes they cast, it would not be fitting for the magistrates of Rovigo, or the citizens of Asolo to maintain, for no reason at all, that same degree of solemnity in greeting each other.[13]

We might turn here once more to Jan Assmann, who borrows the term 'pseudo-speciation' from biology (where it defines "the formation of artificial subgroups within the same biological species") to describe a movement that counterbalances that of cultural translation because "the formation of cultural specificity and identity necessarily produces difference and otherness vis-à-vis other groups. This can result in the elaboration of absolute strangeness, isolation, avoidance, and even abomination".[14]

Long-standing revisionist tendencies in Renaissance cultural history have emphasized conservatism and normativity in opposition to a Burckhardtian emphasis on novelty and innovation, so the relevance of 'strangeness, isolation, avoidance, and abomination' to our investigation may initially be met with scepticism. Yet it may provide a fitting perspective with which to think about some extreme manifestations of 'cultural specificity' in fifteenth-century Italy, including some which have been explained away as accidental phenomena, such as the personal idiosyncracies of a ruler: consider Sigismondo Malatesta's use of pagan imagery in his refurbishment of S. Francesco in Rimini or his association with neo-pagans such as Gemisthos Plethon, whose bones he interred at S. Francesco in an act of anti-Christian *translatio;* his violent resistance to feudal and papal authority or moral conventions were certainly regarded as abominations by Pius II and the humanist George Trebizond.[15] Yet Sigismondo was engaged in a lifelong struggle to maintain an illegitimate state and to resist the encroachments of the papacy as well as local rivals; his patronage and self-fashioning are extreme manifestations of resistance in the cultural sphere. His deliberately heterodox approach to the adaptation or translation of the pagan past, his production of *romanitas,* is the polar opposite of the Christianized revival of antiquity promoted by his political rivals and adversaries Nicholas V and Pius II.

Considered in these terms, therefore, 'cultural translation' defines not only the process of cultural exchange both between and within centers through an examination of the impact of different sociopolitical contexts on specific artistic practices, but also the role of culture in securing or resisting hegemony. Stephen Milner thus examines the employment of Florentine artists on civic projects in Pistoia in terms of the extremely fraught relations not only between Pistoia and Florence, but also among major corporate groups within Pistoia itself, whilst Deborah Krohn examines the durability and significance of specific cults in San Gimignano as a process whereby subject communities sought to articulate their specificity in the face of centralizing authority.

In a pioneering essay on the politics of artistic exchange in the peninsula from the Middle Ages to the Renaissance, Carlo Ginzburg and Enrico Castelnuovo have studied the deployment of art in the dynamics of 'symbolic domination'.[16] Communes such as Massa Maritima, annexed by Siena in the trecento, received a monumental work of art from a Sienese workshop, which referred in its design, subject matter, and style to a work which had come to embody symbolically the divinely ordained, corporate authority of the Sienese state: the *Maesta* of Duccio. Perhaps nowhere more vividly than in Siena does art operate as a powerful form of cultural self-definition; in fact, long after the heyday of its territorial expansion we find Sienese art operating as an ongoing assertion of autonomy, cultural hegemony, and resistance, reaching its apogee when Sienese artists produced the altarpieces for the cathedral of Pienza, the utopian papal city created by Pius II.[17] The notion of *peripheralization* is employed by Castelnuovo and Ginzburg to define the value of remaining outside the 'cultural center' and to point to minor centers such as fifteenth-century Massa as sites for the production of alternatives, as a resistance to the center.[18] The Sienese painters of the quattrocento looked to the trecento origins of their tradition rather than the 'new' art of Florence not because the conservatism of their patrons constrained them to be provincial, as is so often stated, but because of a resolve to maintain an alternative to the artistic language of Florence. The migrant careers of Vecchietta, Angelo Maccagnino, Francesco di Giorgio, Sodoma, and Beccafumi show the ongoing resilience of the tradition, the successful degree to which this alternative to Florence was maintained. When Giovanni di Paolo painted his version of Gentile da Fabriano's *Adoration of the Magi*, one of the most famous and influential altarpieces to be seen in Florence (albeit properly speaking not by a Florentine artist), he was not 'failing' to produce an accurate copy, but re-rendering the invention of Gentile in terms of the distinctive formal treatments of Sienese art (Figs. 1 and 2). It may be only metaphoric to use the term 'language' or 'translation' here, but it seems more apt to what is taking place than the term 'copy' or 'imitation,' for the graphic elements of Giovanni's adaptation, his 'style', work to recast in a local idiom a 'foreign' original whose semantic units of meaning are preserved along with their paradigmatic structural order.

Such processes are particularly suggested by the term "translation", for in its widest etymological sense it seems to describe aptly a situation in which, although fifteenth-century Italians conceived identity in boundaried terms, that identity was finally actualized, as Ronald Weissmann has suggested, through negotiation across borders, through a projection of the self into the sphere of the other so that difference could be more fully thrown into relief.[19] Florentines such as Petrarch and

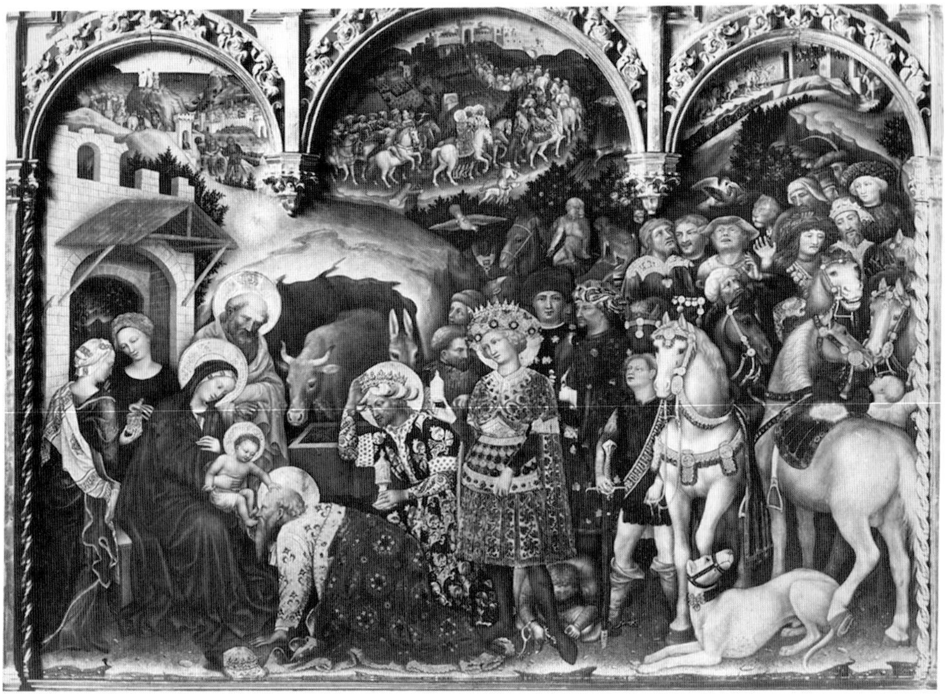

1. Gentile da Fabriano, *The Adoration of the Magi*. On panel. Florence, Uffizi. Photo: Alinari/Art Resource, NY.

Michelangelo were never more Florentine than when in exile; the latter moreover tended to act the part of the courtier or noble to differentiate himself from the normal run of artisans and acted in disdainful solidarity with the role of artisan in his negotiations with courtly and aristocratic patrons.[20] Similarly, the patrician elite of Republican Florence sought to distinguish itself from its social inferiors through the assumption of chivalric practices and rituals associated with the aristocratic court culture of Naples – a practice which, as Bruce Edelstein shows, continues into the sixteenth century with the creation of a Medici court culture. In this sense, the construction of both individual and collective identities drew on a multiplicity of sources of self-invention, the choice of salient element, in keeping with the notion of decorum, being conditioned by the site of performance. For Italy was a place where borders were conceived to exist between urban cultures, yet also within them, and where by the later fifteenth century there was an increasing preoccupation with formal manifestations of difference between and within urban communities.[21] Vecellio's book of regional costumes, the emergence of the Venetian *cittadino* as a class that created a distinct social identity through the forms of its artistic patronage, the proliferation of reactions to Vasari in the form of regional collections of artistic biographies, and the controversies regarding the supposed ascendency of the Tuscan

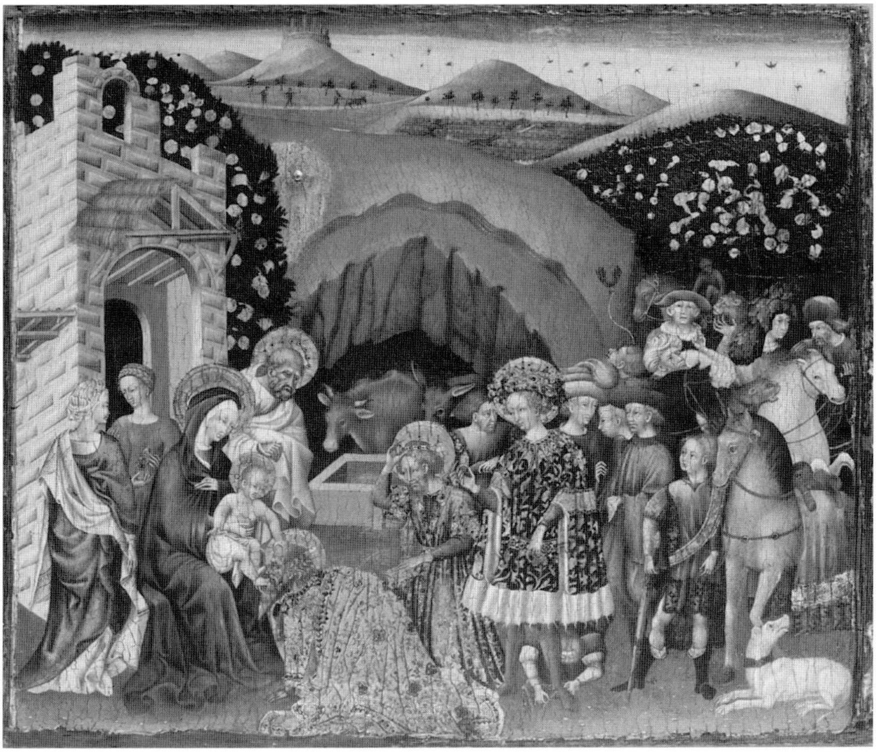

2. Giovanni di Paolo, *The Adoration of the Magi*. On panel. Cleveland, The Cleveland Museum of Art, Delia E. Holden and L. E. Holden Funds, 1942.536. Photo: The Cleveland Museum of Art.

dialect (the *questione della lingua*) are all well-known later manifestations of this tendency, the signs of which are already fully apparent in the quattrocento and even before.[22]

The term 'translation' should finally perhaps be taken as more than a metaphor – its Latin cognate of *translatio* extends beyond the linguistic sphere and defines acts of political and cultural displacement and relocation such as the *translatio imperii* – the transfer of Imperial power which preoccupied medieval political theorists, and *translatio studii*, through which medieval authors represented their relation to the ancient past.[23] The analogy of linguistic translation with cultural enterprise was a palpable one for Renaissance Italians, just as linguistic variation became a symptom or marker of broader cultural differences.[24] In its fullest sense, 'translation' provides a comprehensive and conceptually rich basis for a reconception of what is normally called *influence* in art, *imitation* in literature, *orthodoxy* in religion, and *clientage* in sociopolitical relations. The term 'intertextuality', which appears in the textual criticism of Renaissance humanists to define an allusive intertwining of a literary work with earlier texts,[25] has something of the same range of reference, even more so in its more recent critical elaborations by Julia Kristeva and Roland Barthes.[26]

We have chosen *translation* as opposed to intertextuality because of its implication of specific and local paradigms of historical identity centered on place, on language or dialect, on political institutions and social customs – all of these ways in which fifteenth-century Italians included and excluded themselves from collectivities (or were invited to join or were stigmatized by them).

'Translation', then, is used in the following essays to define a series of relationships across a range of cultural practices. It can define the actual appropriation of a cultural other, such as the papacy's deployment of Egyptian antiquity surveyed by Brian Curran or the experimental and heterodox tendencies of humanism before the Counter-Reformation (some of them fully redolent of 'strangeness, isolation and abomination'), examined here by Christopher Celenza. Because Egypt was increasingly regarded as the origin of all cultures, it could even be perceived as 'untranslatable' – its monuments and hieroglyphs were mystical symbols, the decipherment of which was the revelation of divine essence itself. It therefore provided a prestigious origin within which other cultural meanings could be grounded: papal primacy, primitive Italian culture, the philosophies of Plato and Aristotle, the invention of art and of magic. The appropriation of Egypt thus necessitated a translation of the present into the terms of this imaginary other.

The work of Christian culture in defining alterity through its encounter with and surveillance of marginal and minority identities has elsewhere separately engaged the editors of this volume.[27] In the present collection, it is Morten Steen Hansen who deals with such a situation, where issues of cultural translation were especially urgent: the attempt by immigrant communities to mediate ethnic difference, expressing difference and conformity through the stylistic and iconographic norms of Counter-Reformation religious art. The wealthy Armenian residents of Ancona studied by Hansen use the figures of saints common to Armenian and Roman devotion to mitigate perceptions of their own difference as 'otherness' and to effect their assimilation into Italian mercantile society.

Other essays take up the theme of the self and its translation into authoritative models, whether these are an artistic exemplar, a ritual or religious norm, a canonical literary text, or an imaginary or idealized past. The notion of the cultural norm still exercises a pervasive force in Renaissance studies, above all in the ongoing centrality of Florence as a touchstone – if not as ultimate fount and origin – for a wide range of developments in the culture of the peninsula, especially innovations in politics, scholarly method, art, and technology. The scholarship in this book, although methodologically diverse, seeks a different approach to the transmission of cultural norms, Florentine and otherwise, and is united in the understanding of the *difference* in repetition, where reproductions, imitations, or 'borrowings', by virtue of a transposed market, readership, or scene of beholding, are more productively seen as transformations. This could even operate, as Michelle O'Malley shows, in the negotiations of artists and patrons with regard to the subject matter of works of art; rather than being an attempt to bind legally and delimit an artist's sphere of operation, contracts could sometimes serve merely as a point of departure for ongoing mutations of subject matter. Other authors examine cases in which the implication of a model might be less a reproduction than an alteration or displacement of it, an *appropriation* in accordance with the needs and aspirations of other audiences, patrons, or social elites. For instance, in identifying new strategies for copying works of art in later fifteenth-century Florence, Megan Holmes shows that the works that resulted were far more than reproductions of an original – they were a completely different kind of devotional object, shaped in accordance with the needs of beholders who were far removed from the sphere of the Medici elite. The same could be said of the role of Florentine models for the Roman curial patrons of funerary sculpture; as Shelly Zuraw shows, Florentine sculptural types were transformed in a system of production in which the notion of 'artist' and 'workshop' operate very differently. Similarly, while Florentine types and models circulate widely beyond Florence, they are often adapted by craftsmen and patrons who were invested in a resistance to Florentine cultural hegemony, as Stephen Campbell shows with regard to Ferrara.

A consequence of assuming this perspective is to configure the Renaissance in a 'de-centered' fashion, as "a movement which coexisted and interacted with other movements and indeed with other cultures in a process of permanent cultural exchange across geographical, social and chronological boundaries."[28] Such an approach would ideally address the dynamic cultural dialogue during the Renaissance among Gothic, aristocratic, and popular cultures; between Byzantine scholarly traditions and scholasticism; and between classical and Christian culture, in an extension of Edgar Wind's concept of 'cultural hybridization'.[29] These questions are not dealt with here, nor is the work on translation by scholars in fields such as musicology, but it is hoped that this collection will act as a stimulus to such investigations. We offer instead a methodologically diverse body of work, drawing on intellectual history, political theory, material culture studies, archival scholarship, and the investigation of style. It is our hope that such work will enable the multiple byways of Renaissance scholarship to develop points of translation with each other, resulting in paths of inquiry which are properly situated among disciplines rather than in isolated fields.

NOTES

1. See Leonard Barkan, *Unearthing the Past: Archaeology and Aesthetics in the Making of Renaissance Culture* (New Haven and London: Yale University Press, 1999), xxiv–xxv. A concern with the reuse and transformation of symbols between times and cultures also stands at the heart of Aby Warburg's

analysis of Renaissance culture. See Aby Warburg, *The Renewal of Pagan Antiquity,* trans. D. Britt (Los Angeles: Getty Research Institute, 1999). Warburg's fluid conceptualization of cultural transmission was apparent in his well-known antipathy towards what he termed intellectual 'frontier control'. See Peter Burke, *The Italian Renaissance: Culture and Society in Italy* (Cambridge, UK: Polity Press, 1987), 33.

2. See S. Mailloux, 'Interpretation,' in *Critical Terms for Literary Study,* ed. Frank Lentricchia and Thomas McLaughlin (Chicago: University of Chicago Press, 1995), 121–2.

3. See James Clifford, 'The Translation of Cultures: Maurice Leenhardt's Evangelism, New Caledonia 1902–1926,' in *Contemporary Literary Criticism: Literary and Cultural Studies,* ed. R. Con Davis and R. Schleifer (New York: Longman 1994); S. Budick and W. Iser, eds., *The Translatability of Cultures: Figurations of the Space Between* (Stanford: Stanford University Press, 1996); Jan Assmann, *Moses the Egyptian: The Memory of Egypt in Western Monotheism* (Cambridge: Harvard University Press, 1998); *The Translatability of Cultures. Proceedings of the Fifth Stuttgart Seminar in Cultural Studies,* ed. H. Ziegler (Stuttgart and Weimar: Metzler, 1998).

4. Assmann, 'Translating Gods: Religion as a Factor of Cultural (Un)Translatability,' in *Translatability of Cultures,* ed. Budick and Iser, 25–37.

5. Anthony Pagden, *European Encounters with the New World. From Renaissance to Romanticism* (New Haven and London: Yale University Press, 1993), 48.

6. Pagden, *European Encounters;* Edward W. Said, *Culture and Imperialism* (New York, 1993); Homi K. Bhabha, *The Location of Culture* (New York: Routledge 1994); Stuart Hall, 'The Spectacle of the "Other,"' in *Representation: Cultural Representations and Signifying Practices,* ed. Stuart Hall (London: Sage Books, 1997), 223–79; and Stuart Hall and Paul Du Gay, eds., *Questions of Cultural Identity* (London: Sage Books, 1996).

7. Clare Farago, ed., *Reframing the Renaissance: Visual Culture in Europe and Latin America 1450–1650* (New Haven and London: Yale University Press, 1995); see especially the editor's introduction, 1–20.

8. For a critique of Burckhardt's understanding of these authors as manifesting a national consciousness, see Farago, '"Vision Itself Has Its History": "Race," Nation and Renaissance Art History,' in *Reframing the Renaissance,* ed. Farago; and Farago, 'The Status of the "State as a Work of Art": Re-Viewing Burckhardt's Renaissance from the Borderlines,' in *Cultural Exchange between European Nations during the Renaissance. Acta Universitatis Upsaliensis. Studia Anglista Upsaliensia* 86, ed. Gunnar Sorelius and Michael Srigley (Uppsala: 1994), 17–33. For some general remarks on the 'discrepancy between nation and dynastic realm' that are in some respects applicable to Italy, see Benedict Anderson, *Imagined Communities. Reflections on the Origin and Spread of Nationalism* (London and New York: Verso, 1989), 103. Farago's perspective could be said to neglect the dimension of self-conscious irony in Burckhardt's analogies between Italy and the modern nation state, which were born out of his own anti-modernism and anti-statism and are generally given a strongly dystopian cast. On this dimension see Hayden White, *Metahistory: The Historical Imagination in Nineteenth-Century Europe* (Baltimore and London: Johns Hopkins University Press, 1973), 230–65.

9. On Italian self-consciousness, defined in relation to a cultural 'other' in the late Middle Ages, see Kevin Brownlee, 'The Practice of Cultural Authority: Italian Responses to French Cultural Dominance in *Il Tesoretto, Il Fiore,* and the *Commedia,*' *Forum for Modern Language Studies* xxxiii no. 3 (1997): 258–69. The field of musicology has generated a considerable body of scholarship on Italian reactions to and translations of French musical forms during the fourteenth and fifteenth centuries; see the Introduction by Nino Pirotta in *Il codice Squarcialupi;* ed. F. A. Gallo et al. (Florence: Giunti Barbèra, 1992), 195–211. See also F. A. Gallo, 'Bilinguismo poetico e

bilinguismo musicale nel madrigale trecentesco,' *Ars nova italiana del Trecento* VI (1992): 237–43. On European perceptions of Italy, see, for example, J. L. Lievsay, *The Elizabethan Image of Italy* (Ithaca, NY: Cornell University Press, 1964); Peter Burke, *Fortunes of the Courtier: The European Reception of Castiglione's 'Cortegiano'* (University Park: Penn State University Press, 1996); S. Rossi and D. Savoia, *Italy and the English Renaissance* (Milan: UNICOPLI, 1989), which includes substantial bibliography on this topic. For Dutch and Flemish artists in Rome, see the exhibition catalogue *Fiamminghi a Roma, 1508–1608. Artistes des Pays-Bas et de la principauté de Liège à Rome à la Renaissance* (Ghent: Snoeck-Ducaju & Zoon, 1995). See also Bernard Aikema and Beverly L. Brown, eds., *Renaissance Venice and the North: Crosscurrents in the Time of Bellini, Dürer and Titian* (New York: Rizzoli, 2000).

10. See, for example, Rebecca Zorach, 'The Matter of Italy: Sodomy and the Scandal of Style in Sixteenth-Century France,' *Journal of Medieval and Early Modern Studies* 28, 3 (1998): 581–609, on Mannerism in Europe as an Italian style with strong connotations of perversity and license. For a neo-Burckhardtian view of the role of luxury export goods in creating the notion of Italian culture, see Richard Goldthwaite, *Wealth and the Demand for Art in Italy, 1300–1600* (Baltimore and London: Johns Hopkins University Press, 1993), 243–57. The diffusion of Italian style in Europe has received considerable attention; see most recently, Thomas DaCosta Kaufmann, *Court, Cloister and City: The Art and Culture of Central Europe, 1450–1800* (Chicago: University of Chicago Press, 1995), especially 116–38; see also E. Rosenthal, 'The Diffusion of the Italian Renaissance Style in Western European Art,' *Sixteenth Century Journal* IX, 4 (1978): 33–45.

11. For an example of the role of myths of origin in a city without a Roman foundation, see Patricia Fortini Brown, *Venice and Antiquity. The Venetian Sense of the Past* (New Haven and London: Yale University Press, 1996).

12. Baldesar Castiglione, *The Book of the Courtier,* trans. G. Bull (Baltimore and Harmondsworth: Penguin, 1967), 134.

13. Giovanni della Casa, *Il Galateo,* trans. K. Eisenbichler and K. R. Bartlett (Toronto: Center for Reformation and Renaissance Studies, 1986), 26–7.

14. Assmann, 'Translating Gods,' 25–37.

15. On the image of the pagan gods in S. Francesco, Rimini, see Stanko Kokole, '*Cognitio formarum* and Agostino di Duccio's Reliefs for the Chapel of the Planets in the Tempio Malatestiano,' in *Quattrocento Adriatico. Fifteenth Century Art of the Adriatic Rim,* ed. Charles Dempsey, *Villa Spelman Colloquia,* 5 (Bologna: Nuova Alfa Editoriale 1995), 177–206. On Sigismondo see also Joanna Woods-Marsden, 'How Quattrocento Princes Used Art: Sigismondo Pandolfo Malatesta of Rimini and *cose militari,' Renaissance Studies* 3 (1989): 387–414.

16. Enrico Castelnuovo and Carlo Ginzburg, 'Centre and Periphery,' in *History of Italian Art,* trans. E. Bianchini, ed. E. Bianchini and C. Dorey, 2 vols. (Cambridge: Polity Press, 1994), II, 29–113.

17. For Pienza, see Henk Van Os, 'Painting in a House of Glass: The Altarpieces of Pienza.' *Simiolus* XVII, 1 (1987): 23–38. On quattrocento Siena see, in general, Keith Christiansen, Laurence Kanter, and Carl Brandon Strehlke, *Painting in Renaissance Siena, 1420–1500* (New York: Metropolitan Museum of Art, 1988); on Vecchietta, see additionally Van Os, 'Vecchietta and the Persona of the Renaissance Artist,' in *Studies in Late Medieval and Renaissance Painting in Honor of Millard Meiss,* ed. Irving Lavin and John Plummer (New York: New York University Press, 1977), 445–53. On Sienese art as 'periphery,' see Giovanni Agosti, 'Su Siena nell'Italia artistica del secondo Quattrocento,' in *Francesco di Giorgio e il Rinascimento a Siena,* ed. Luciano Bellosi (Milan: Electa, 1993), 488–509.

18. On this point, see additionally Jan Bialostocki, 'Some Values of Artistic Periphery,' in *Themes of World Art,* 2 vols., ed. Irving Lavin (University Park, Penn.: Penn State University Press, 1992), I, 6–11; Peter Burke, *The European Renaissance: Centers and Peripheries.* (Oxford: Blackwell, 1998); for a consideration of the notion with regard to state formation in Italy, see E. Fasano Guarini, 'Center and Periphery,' in *The Origins of the State in Italy, 1300–1600, The Journal of Modern History* 67, supplement, ed. Julius Kirshner (1995): 74–97.

19. Ronald Weissmann, 'The Importance of Being Ambiguous: Social Relations, Individualism and Identity in Renaissance Florence,' in *Urban Life in the Renaissance,* ed. Susan Zimmerman and Ronald Weissmann (Newark: University of Delaware Press, 1989), 269–80.

20. On exile see Randolph Starn, *Contrary Commonwealth: The Theme of Exile in Medieval and Renaissance Italy* (Berkeley: University of California Press, 1982).

21. On cultural exchange within Italy, see Sergio Bertelli, Nicolai Rubinstein, and Craig Hugh Smyth, eds., *Florence and Venice: Comparisons and Relations,* 2 vols.; vol. I: *Quattrocento;* vol. II: *Cinquecento.* (Florence: La Nuova Italia, 1979–80); Sergio Bertelli and Gian Carlo Garfagnini, eds., *Florence and Milan: Comparisons and Relations,* 2 vols. (Florence: La Nuova Italia, 1989).

22. On reactions to Vasari, see, for example, the case of the Carracci in Bologna who wrote indignant *postille* on the *Lives,* and the production of regional collections of artist's lives conceived to redress Vasari's neglect of other cities by authors such as Carlo Cesare Malvasia in Bologna and Girolamo Baruffaldi in Ferrara. On the Venetian caste of *cittadini,* see A. Zannini, *Burocrazia e burocrati a Venezia in età moderna: I cittadini originari (sec. XVI–XVIII). Memorie, della classe di scienze morali, lettere ed arti,* vol. 47 (Istituto veneto di scienze, lettere ed arti, Venice 1993); on their distinctive activity as patrons and collectors, see Monika Schmitter, *The Display of Distinction. Art Collecting and Social Status in Early Sixteenth Century Venice* (Ph.D diss., University of Michigan, 1997); on the *questione della lingua,* see Giancarlo Mazzacurati, *La questione della lingua dal Bembo all'Accademia Fiorentina* (Naples: Liguori, 1965).

23. See Walther Goez, *Translatio Imperii: Ein Beitrag zur Geschichte des Geschichtsdenkens und der politischen Theorie im Mittelalter und in der frühen Neuzeit* (Tübingen: J. C. B. Mohr, 1958). On *translatio studii* see K. Stierle, '*Translatio studii* and Renaissance: From Vertical to Horizontal Translation,' in *Translatability of Cultures,* Budick and Iser, 55–67.

24. See, for example, Alessandro Nova, 'Folengo and Romanino: The *Questione della Lingua* and Its Eccentric Trends,' *The Art Bulletin* LXXVI/4 (1994): 664–80.

25. For example, Francesco Pucci thus praises the writings Poliziano, 'oratio . . . vario quodam et prope vermiculato intertextu lasciviens, omnesque verborum flosculos captans.' Quoted in Martin McLaughlin, *Literary Imitation in the Italian Renaissance* (Oxford: Clarendon Press, 1995), 201. On the term in Erasmus, see R. J. Schoeck, '"*In loco intertextantur*". Erasmus as Master of Intertextuality,' in *Intertextuality,* ed. Heinrich F. Plett (Berlin and New York: de Gruyter, 1991), 181–92.

26. For an overview see, *Intertextuality: Theories and Practice,* ed. Michael Worten and Judith Still (Manchester: University of Manchester Press, 1990). The English editor of Kristeva's *Desire in Language* makes a distinction between her use of the term, which draws on Bakhtin's theories of linguistic dialogue (and has affinities with the notion of translation), and more conventional notions of influence and textual sources: '[Intertextuality] is defined . . . as the transposition of one or more *systems* of signs into another, accompanied by a new articulation of the enunciative and denotative position.' Julia Kristeva, *Desire in Language. A Semiotic Approach to Literature and Art,* ed. L. S. Roudiez, trans. T. Gora, A. Jardine, and L. S. Roudiez (New York: Columbia University Press, 1980). For a collection of essays which employ the notion of intertextuality

to discuss cultural translation, see *The Italian World of English Renaissance Drama. Cultural Exchange and Intertextuality*, ed. M. Marrapodi and A. J. Hoenselaars (Newark and London: University of Delaware Press, 1998).

27. See the collection edited by Stephen J. Milner, *At the Margins: Minority Groups in Pre modern Italy* (forthcoming Minneapolis: University of Minnesota Press, 2005). For a particularly fraught instance of cultural encounter – the relations of Christians and Jews in late-fifteenth-century Ferrara – see Stephen J. Campbell, *Cosmè Tura of Ferrara. Style, Politics and the Renaissance City, 1450–1495* (New Haven and London: Yale University Press 1997), 64–99.

28. Peter Burke, 'Decentering the Renaissance: The Challenge of Postmodernism,' in *At the Margins.*

29. On hybridization see Edgar Wind, *Pagan Mysteries in the Renaissance*, rev. ed. (Oxford: Oxford University Press, 1980), 24–5. See also Homi K. Bhabha, 'DissemiNation: Time, Narrative and the Margins of the Modern Nation,' in *Nation and Narration*, 314: 'In the restless drive for cultural translation, hybrid sites of meaning open up a cleavage in the language of culture which suggests that the similitude of the *symbol* as it plays across cultural sites must not obscure the fact that repetition of the *sign* is, in each specific social practice, both different and differential.'

PART ONE

HOW TO TRANSLATE

Since the late nineteenth century, art history has drawn on the reproduction and adaptation of *type* as a means of establishing taxonomies or typologies of form, as well as to define historical change in art as an evolutionary progress. The essays in this section explore the theme of types and derivations, models and copies, as well as technologies of transmission. Instead of conceiving such transmission of type as a quasi-biological or genealogical morphology, however, the authors here explore the process as one of negotiation and contestation. The essays are based on archival and technical case studies which point to transmission as a process of selection determined by economic and ideological factors.

The process of translation explored here is also that of the transmission of ideas between artist and client and involves model drawings, contract stipulations, and additional written communications. O'Malley shows that this was very much a two-way process, a dialogue between artists and patrons in which artists were not only relied on for expertise in visualizing subject matter that a patron stipulated, but they also could often modify or transform the subject itself. She concludes that the contracts initially drawn up between artists and patrons were of little binding force with regard to subject matter. In the case of Perugino's 1497 negotiations with the friars of Santa Maria at Vallombrosa, the artist seems to have had some input with regard to the size and number of figures depicted in the altarpiece. In the case of Parmigianino's 1527 Bufalini altarpiece, however, the artist's design process seems to shape the communicative and expressive impact of the finished work in a manner which seems a long way from the subject matter agreed on at an early stage in the process. Subject matter is finally inseparable from considerations of design.

Frequently the communication of intentions from client to artist involves reference to a previous work of art, as with the *modo et forma* clause sometimes included in Italian contracts. All four inquiries in this section explore to some extent the exemplary role of previous works of art. In so doing, they confront questions of value – of what determines a work's exemplary status – and hence of ideology. Holmes shows that the enterprise of the copyist workshop of the 'Lippi and Pesellino Imitator' would have been shaped by a consumer demand for images derived from the work of artists associated with the Medici. Yet more is at stake here than a simple extension of the aura of the original through its copies and derivations, with a consequent enlarging of its hegemonic authority. The copying strategies of the workshop, as reconstructed in Holmes's pioneering research, give rise in her account to a decidedly new kind of artistic product, answering to the specific needs and identities of much larger communities of viewers.

Like Holmes, Zuraw also discusses a situation in which modes of transmission are determined by a large-scale consumer demand. She explores an intriguing situation in which a process of transfer is apparently interrupted: a translated motif – the Florentine 'humanist' tomb – is re-embedded within more local traditions of Roman tomb design. Such a hybridization may be the result of mere expediency – above all the collaborative 'production line' conditions of Roman sculpture workshops in the later fifteenth century – but the coexistence of two sculptural languages is not without an ideological significance. There is a pointed confrontation of two forms of *romanitas*: the Tuscan classicism of Mino and his Florentine predecessors, with its adaptations of the antique triumphal arch, and the modern, gothicising tradition of the Roman Curia, with its evocations of the Christian altar-canopy.

Syson's essay could fittingly be placed in the next section of this book because it is largely concerned with the cultural policies of Florence in dialogue with those of the courts. He presents what he sees as a clear case of Medici emulation of the North Italian princes, in the form of a transposition of the role of the artist-*familiaris.* Lorenzo de'Medici's employment of Bertoldo as an instrument of cultural policy followed the standard practice of the Italian princes whom the Medici now increasingly regarded as their peers. Yet like the other authors in this section, Syson's focus is still on the workshop as the site of creative translation: this is a workshop of a very distinct type, a kind of studio museum devoted to the reproduction, restoration, and emulation of antique sculpture, but within the idiom of a Florentine tradition grounded by Bertoldo in the imitation of Donatello. This systematic manufacturing of Florentine tradition has received considerable attention because among its 'by-products' were the young Michelangelo; Syson reconsiders the relation of Michelangelo and Bertoldo, while closely analyzing some works by other artists connected with the sculpture garden.

I

Subject Matters: Contracts, Designs, and the Exchange of Ideas between Painters and Clients in Renaissance Italy

Michelle O'Malley

The translation of artistic ideas in Italy did not take place only on a global scale, across geographical boundaries. Such transmission also occurred on a local and personal level in the course of the commissioning process, as painters and their clients engaged in an exchange that drew on culturally specific notions of value, quality, and decorous subject matter to define the appearance of a proposed work of art. The word 'appearance' is deliberate. While individual styles and regional qualities of depiction were unquestionably evident in Renaissance painted works, contracts and other documents concerning the commissioning process are devoid of references to style and the disposition of a formal world. Instead, their pictorial terms concern the identity of figures and sometimes their placement and dress.[1] Although it is clear that, after about 1440, people thought of altarpieces as *alla grecha* or *all'antica* in style – that is, in the Greek or the antique style – these terms referred to the shape of the carved frame of an altarpiece, not the approach to its painting.

In terms of appearance, art historians have traditionally considered the exchange between commissioners and painters to have been almost entirely one-sided. The patron has been seen as the party in control, and the primary commissioning document, the contract, as a set of instructions given by a patron to a painter. Revisionist scholarship on the issue of Renaissance painter-patron exchanges about subject matter has argued against such notions of control. It has set out to show that while clients always identified the subject matter to be depicted in a proposed work of art, painters were not passive recipients of learned subjects handed to them by patrons interested in erudite pictures.[2] Both Charles Hope and Creighton Gilbert have argued that artistic programmes were rarely devised, that painters often carried out research on commissioned subjects themselves, and that, in any case, most patrons were primarily interested in obtaining no more than a visually pleasing picture.[3] Further evidence complicates these ideas about the transmission of pictorial information. It suggests not only that both parties may commonly have contributed to deciding appearance, but also that they sometimes collaborated and their interests encompassed basic pictorial concerns. Clients might involve themselves in settling fundamental details of the layout, colour, dress, and placement of the figures in a proposed work, areas traditionally considered by scholars as the preserve of painters,[4] and painters might engage in identifying appropriate subsidiary iconography, and even occasionally in suggesting the type of main figure to be depicted, aspects of a commission long believed to be the purview of clients. Moreover, their exchange was not restricted to the transfer of information about unusual iconography; it also pertained when the content was a common religious subject.

To explore the synergy of exchange between contracting parties, this chapter considers the broad commissioning process. It examines how decisions were made about how a work of art would look, considers the nature of such decisions, and investigates their relationships to the individual parties. This chapter argues that, in the fifteenth and early sixteenth centuries, the dynamic between painters and clients was more complex, and their interests in defining the character of pictures more closely balanced, than has hitherto been assumed. It will also demonstrate that subject clauses in contracts cannot be accepted at face value.

Contracts and the Commissioning Process

Contracts provide formal evidence of the exchange of ideas between commissioning parties. They supply direct information for attribution and date, identify client and place, list details of production, and offer fuel for investigating the content and purpose of a work of art. Studied synthetically, they also offer an insight into the operation of the commissioning process. They do not, however, document that process. Instead, they provide a snapshot of it at a particular moment: the moment when negotiation about the value of materials, delivery deadlines, and usually price had been completed. Negotiation about subject matter, however, was often still in progress. It is probably for this reason that many contracts do not contain much direct information about what was to be painted. Many name only the main figure and note that other figures will be included; some record that information about subjects will be exchanged verbally, after the contract meeting.[5] A typical such phrase appears in the 1487 contract between Filippino Lippi and Filippo Strozzi, concerning the Strozzi Chapel frescoes in Santa Maria Novella, Florence. It notes that Filippo would be 'given' the subjects by his client.[6] A few contracts record indecision about subject matter; they make it clear that subject clauses might record only intermediate decisions about subjects.[7] Thus the detailed clauses that do exist can be deceptive; they convey the impression that painters and clients exchanged pithy agreements that led smoothly and directly to the creation of a work of art. But the evidence, partly embedded in contracts themselves, is that most discussions about subject matter took place outside, and often after, the contract meeting.

Regional differences in contracts are minimal, although artistic practice was varied.[8] Companies of painters were popular in Lombardy and many other northern Italian courts; painters tended to work individually in central Italy and the Veneto. Companies must have settled corporately on a price, but their negotiations with prospective clients were probably similar to those undertaken by single master painters and their clients. Contracts with groups of painters are no different from those with men who worked alone; the parties were listed, materials, procedures and deadlines were recorded, and each painter accepted responsibility for producing his portion of the finished work.[9] The uniformity of contracts is due to the persistence of the classical tradition in Italy and the harmony of notarial training. The formulae of Renaissance contracts were derived from Roman protocols for work contracts.[10] While there were no set structures for the text and no strictures about the inclusion of formulae, the types and range of artists' contract stipulations were uniform throughout the peninsula. Indeed, they were so well known that when painters recorded their own contracts, they used the same stipulations and terminology as those found in notarial documents.[11]

More important variations pertain to differences between the attitudes of courts and republics to the market and to regionally specific concepts of the monetary worth of altarpieces and frescoes. This is a complicated subject, which reflects the values of a culture that, throughout the peninsula, set prices as much by tradition, relationships, and notions of honour and prestige as by more objectively evaluated criteria such as demand, size, or figure-number.[12] Differences in costs, however, had little bearing on the ways people exchanged ideas about the appearance of a proposed work; there is no evidence, for example, that parties spent more time discussing expensive paintings and less time planning cheap ones.

Certainly clients varied in their expertise and experience with commissioning, but in exchange about the subject matter, painters might be as involved in negotiations with individuals who were experienced in ordering works of art, such as Giovanni Tornabuoni, as they were with those who were less knowledgable about the process, such as some convents or civic groups. Contracts, however, only rarely suggest the level of the discussion contracting parties might hold because most are not very detailed about subject matter. Many discussions continued, or were initiated, after the contract meeting, and subject clauses in contracts may therefore disguise nuances and exchanges of ideas that only emerge from other sources.

Only in unusual circumstances, however, were conversations about subjects recorded, and those that survive are drawn from the archives of corporate groups.

They make clear the detailed interest clients might take in every aspect of the pictorial part of a commission and the degree of collaboration in which parties might engage. Private individuals, although often a party to contracts, rarely had occasion to document a discussion about subject matter. Visual documentation indicates, however, that the range and depth of exchange undertaken by confraternities and convents might also characterise transmission about subjects between private clients and painters. Preparatory drawings, for example, convey a sense of how ideas developed and changed as a commission took shape. Works of art whose subjects differ from the outlines of subject matter found in their contracts also testify to continuing exchange between contracting parties. The written and pictorial evidence, taken together, indicates that the commissioning process was often a continuum, with both parties contributing to intermediary discussions about subject matter held between the contract meeting and the moment when brush was put to panel or wall.

Documented Discussions

Scripta, or 'writing,' is the term used for a document that describes subject matter. It is employed today, as it was in the Renaissance, to designate informally recorded notes as well as notarial documents about subjects.[13] *Scripte* suggest how discussions about the iconographic aspects of new works may have been conducted, and the range of information contracting parties might consider when planning a new altarpiece or fresco. The documents make it clear that negotiations on how an altarpiece would look might be protracted and extensive, covering not only iconography, but also details of colour and the manner of representation. *Scripte* were always written by clients and embodied their interests. This makes their references to, and reflections of, collaboration particularly convincing.

The *scripta* drawn up in 1439 in Siena concerning the double-sided San Francesco Altarpiece, for example, is specific about the dynamic between the contracting parties. The contract between Sassetta and the Sansepolcran convent had been signed in 1437, noting that subject matter would be told to the painter after the contract meeting. The friars did not arrive with instructions, however; instead, they went to Siena specifically 'to order and compose the figures and stories of the altarpiece' in consultation with the painter.[14] The document shows that the parties discussed the iconography, the arrangement of the figures, and the broad subjects of the *predelle*. The friars must have arrived with a list of the saints and scenes from the lives of sacred figures whom the convent wished to have depicted. But the discussion of the arrangement and presentation of the figures is likely to have been influenced by the painter, who was the professional in such matters. The painter's expertise is specifically registered in reference to the depiction of the Madonna; her arrangement with angels is left to the discretion of Sassetta. The document also provides evidence that the client had clear ideas about the nature of the depiction of its founder.[15] The image was to follow a prototype in Città di Castello: 'In mezzo San Francescho in un trono como quello di Castello con quelle virtù da capo et i vitii da piei.' The predella scenes of the Passion, a common subject, were to be identified by the painter, but the friars would send information about the scenes for the predella of Beato Raniero, the subject of a local cult with which Sassetta was probably unfamiliar.[16] The *scripta* shows the parties working together to plan the type of the main subjects – the Virgin with angels, St Francis enthroned – and to design the layout of the altarpiece.[17]

The documents connected with the 1497 commission of Perugino by the convent of Sant Maria at Vallombrosa do not mention consultation or collaboration, but they trace a similar interaction between the parties in defining subject matter and its composition.[18] Detailed decisions about the painting of the Assumption were made before the contract was redacted, but the convent continued to consider the altarpiece's figures and their presentation after the contract meeting. Notes were made by one of the friars, probably after a meeting with Don Biagio Milanesi, the general of the Order and the force behind the convent's commission; they expand the description of the subject recorded in the contract.[19] The notes record the size of the main panels and the predella; indicate that the Virgin was to be depicted seated, dressed in a robe painted with ultramarine valued at four florins an ounce, and surrounded by cherubim, seraphim, and eight music-making angels; specify the content of the predella; and list each saint to be painted, observing what each should wear, his attribute, his placement on the panel, and the colour of the friar-saints' habits.[20]

While none of the ideas expressed by the friar is unusual – indeed, a blue-robed, seated Madonna of the Assumption surrounded by cherubim and seraphim was a traditional approach to the subject, and other colour notation refers only to the greyish hue of the robes of the painted friars – the document underscores the level of detail the clients considered. The friar's notes were undoubtedly discussed with Perugino and then used to inform the second, subject-related contract (a formal kind of *scripta*), drawn up with the painter in 1498. This document contains information drawn from the notes. It also records that the figures should be proportional to the size of the panel[21] and makes the number of angels to surround the Virgin less specific – the notes specify eight, the new contract simply stipulates many (*plures*). It notes the use of a fine ultramarine, without a price; probably the parties discussed quality. Taken together, the contract, notes, and subject contract suggest that the painter's input included making recommendations about figure size and probably the number of figures appropriate for the panel, because the painter is likely to have tempered the requirement for a specific number of angels, convincing the convent that he would make a pleasing arrangement of angelic forms.[22] The second contract adds considerable detail to the subject clause of the original agreement, which is itself more detailed than most such contract clauses. It underlines the fact that discussion about subjects did not necessarily end with a contract record of a proposed depiction. Like the *scripta* of Sassetta and the Franciscans, the documentation also makes clear the breadth of the discussion contracting parties might hold on the subject matter of an altarpiece. It records the interest a patron might take in every detail of a work and suggests the painter's role in limiting the specifics about subsidiary figures, which were probably best left to creation during the design process.

The scope of what painters and clients talked about when planning a work is broadened in a *scripta*-like document drawn up for the Madonna of the Rocks altarpiece, commissioned from Leonardo and the de Predis brothers by the Confraternity of the Conception in Milan, in 1483.[23] The document, called simply a *lista*, refers to how the altarpiece would be painted; it was recorded on the same date as the contract but reflects decisions made by the painters and their clients before the meeting with the notary.[24] It was largely copied into the contract.

The *lista* focuses on the decoration of the altarpiece frame, which was already constructed. It outlines the extensive areas to be gilded, details the colours and type of textile decoration to appear on the drapery of the carved figures, and records that incised or *sgraffito* work was to be applied to the seraphim. These ideas may have come from the client or they may have been suggested by the painters[25]; the fact that the *lista* notes pigment names, rather than terms for hues, suggests that the painters were actively involved in its compilation. In contrast to the detail on the painting of the frame, however, information on the work to be done on the panels is summary. The subject matter is briefly outlined, and the parties simply refer to using good-quality colours.[26]

The altarpiece frame represented considerable expense, and no doubt this influenced the confraternity's attention to its decoration.[27] Ordering decoration and composing subject matter are different aspects of the commissioning process, however, and the difference in the amount of attention given to the frame and the panels probably also reflected their stages of execution. While the frame was already carved and constructed, the panels were still to be designed. The parties undoubtedly expected to discuss the details of subject matter and composition further during the design process, and additional exchange, to be discussed later in the chapter, was unquestionably held about the work.

These *scripte* are rare; they are among the few such documents that survive. But contract language makes it clear that conversations about subject matter were commonly held after a contract meeting, noting that information about subjects would be given verbally and specifically recording that the parties would come to an agreement about subject matter. *Scripte* provide a model for these conversations. They show how pictorial matters might have been set by collaboration and negotiation. It seems that commissioners might not only identify figures, but also evolve ideas about how they should be depicted and put forward conceptions of how the whole work should look. These were almost certainly based on their knowledge of existing works of art. Painters might advise on the best arrangement of figures and scenes and on the characters commonly included in particular subjects; they were also relied on to introduce subsidiary figures, such as angels, and background details.[28] Once decisions about subject matter were made, the painter would design the proposed work, usually on paper, for the approval of the client. Drawings that survive for commissions whose contracts record subject matter show that the process of design could take initial subject ideas through several stages and that early conceptions of a work's appearance might change as a design was composed. There are, however, few commissions for which a contract noting subject matter in any detail survives with both a finished work that differs from the contract notations and drawings that record its conceptual development. Two examples are Ghirlandaio's 1485 commission to fresco the Tornabuoni chapel in Santa Maria Novella, Florence, and Parmigianino's 1526 commission to paint the altarpiece for the Caccialupi chapel in San Salvatore in Lauro, Rome. Drawings for these commissions show initial ideas in the process of development and alteration. While the number of such well-documented commissions is limited, the scope of the changes that they show occurring in the design process can also be traced in finished works of art whose subjects deviate from their contract's subject clauses. These also testify to the practise of ongoing exchange between contracting parties. Moreover, the graphic and visual evidence, studied in conjunction with the circumstances of particular commissions, suggests that the input of painters and clients to subject discussions, and the changes they proposed during the design process, were made in different arenas.

The Client and Subject Development

Before turning to drawings and paintings, it is useful to consider the documentation about *disegni* that survives for Signorelli's frescoes in the Cappella Nova of the Cathedral of Orvieto. This augments research on how ideas about subject matter might develop; it particularly throws light on how commissioners might respond to drawings and use them to explain their own evolving ideas about how a work should look. Signorelli's *disegni* for the Orvieto project no longer exist, but at their meeting on 27 April 1500, the Fabbrica (the group responsible for commissioning and overseeing the fresco) used his drawings to argue for certain alterations to the overall decoration of the chapel.[29] First, Signorelli was asked to shift the whole plan to ensure that the figures came to the level of the window. Next, the Fabbrica suggested that, in each arched area, Signorelli might make more figures than those in his *disegno*, 'as appeared best to him', but no fewer than he had already indicated on the sheet.[30]

These discussions did not require another set of drawings to be made for approval. Probably Signorelli, like his clients, used the existing drawings to explain how he might alter matters to suit their needs.[31] The document shows the painter and his clients working together with the drawings to develop their initial ideas about the frescoes. The iconography remained unchanged, but how it was presented – what the frescoes would look like – was a live issue for both parties during the design process.

This was also the case between Domenico Ghirlandaio and Giovanni Tornabuoni in regard to the frescoes of the chapel of the high altar of Santa Maria Novella. After recording a detailed subject clause, the parties clearly continued to exchange ideas. During the design process the layout of the decorations was altered, substitutions were made for some of the scenes originally requested, and the number of figures to be depicted was increased. The working procedure, described in the contract, provided for continued discussion: Ghirlandaio was to show all his designs to Tornabuoni before he began to paint, so that any additions desired by the client could be incorporated into the plans.[32]

There is no record of the parties' meetings and conversations, but in this case drawings survive. They show intermediate stages in the development of the subject matter between that recorded in the contract and that depicted in the finished frescoes. The contract subject clause stipulates the saints to appear on the window wall, and records that seven scenes each of the lives of the Virgin and St John should be painted on the chapel's side walls, listing the subject of each scene and noting that the scenes should be painted one over the other. It may be that the subject matter was copied into the contract from a list. It is, however, unlikely that any painter would have divided each wall into seven narrow slots, and Ghirlandaio probably asserted the fundamental layout immediately. In the frescoes, six scenes are paired and the seventh fitted into the arched area of each wall. More significantly, changes were also made early in the process to the subjects of the scenes to be portrayed. Perhaps the original plan was simply to replace the pictures portrayed in the fourteenth century (these are now lost, and there is no trace of their subjects). The substitutions were probably made by Tornabuoni to reflect his own devotions and the concerns introduced by the expanded patronage rights that he was given by the friars in 1486.[33] The incorporation of the Assumption of the Virgin, for example, may reflect the popularity the subject acquired in the late fifteenth century.[34] The Naming of the Baptist may have been devised to commemorate the birth of Tornabuoni's new grandson and namesake.[35] In addition to these changes in iconography, the

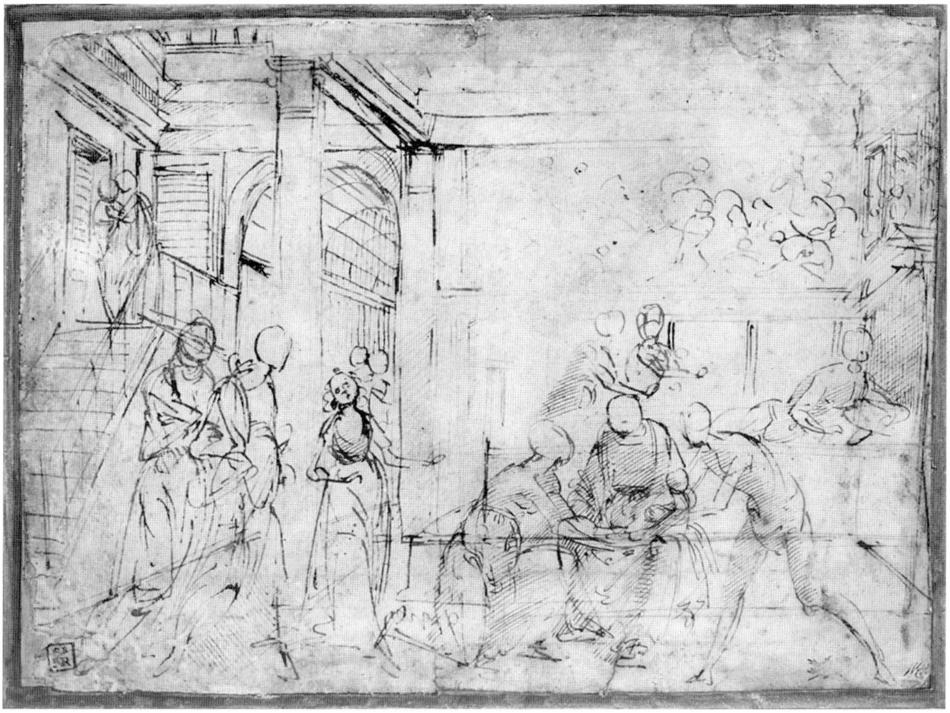

3. Domenico Ghirlandaio, Study for *Birth of the Virgin*. Pen and brown ink. London, The British Museum. Photo: © The British Museum.

number of portrait figures to be depicted in some of the scenes was increased, and Tornabuoni decided that he and his wife would be depicted on the wall behind the altar, replacing the tier of saints originally planned there.

The drawings and the finished frescoes suggest the working method adopted by the painter and his client. In the drawing for the scene of the angel appearing to Zacharias in the temple, for example, names are scrawled over four of the figures depicted outside the architectural space. Ghirlandaio undoubtedly showed the drawing to Tornabuoni, and the sheet suggests that decisions were made about portraits as the parties reviewed the *disegno*.[36] The composition was then subjected to further consideration, and the twelve contemporary figures of the drawing were expanded to nineteen in the finished picture. Each figure is almost certainly a portrait, added as the scene was discussed, probably over subsequent drawings, now lost. In the Visitation fresco, the number of figures was increased after the exploratory drawing was made; two more contemporary figures are depicted than appear on the sheet. In a drawing of the figures and architecture of the Birth of the Virgin, three contemporary women appear (Fig. 3). But two more figures were later required and, probably in response to these additions, Ghirlandaio rotated the room to the left, deepened it, reduced the number of holy figures, and moved them back (Fig. 4).

This gave the Tornabuoni women a wider platform from which to 'observe' Saint Anne, her child, and her serving women.[37]

The character of the drawings and their relationship to the frescoes suggest that Ghirlandaio and Tornabuoni held discussions similar to those recorded between Signorelli and the Orvieto Fabbrica. The drawings – presumably successive drawings – were probably the foundation that Tornabuoni used to discuss additional figures. It was Ghirlandaio, however, who conceived the compositional plans and designed the desired additions to the works, as Signorelli did in Orvieto. The documentation for both commissions shows that negotiations about subject matter could be dynamic and detailed, centring around the visual representations of ideas. This could be the case whether the client was an individual or a corporate group. Furthermore, the commissions suggest that additional figures and changed iconography are likely to reflect the ideas of a client.

This is also evident in the altarpiece painted by Cima da Conegliano for the Coneglianese Scuola dei Battuti, who commissioned him in 1492. At the contract meeting, the Scuola was undecided about the saints to be painted, and the document records this. It stipulates a picture with the Virgin with St John the Evangelist and *either* St Andrew or St Peter.[38] But the completed altarpiece shows that further exchange was held about subjects after the contract was redacted. It depicts the Virgin with six saints: John the Baptist, Nicholas, Catherine, Apollonia, Francis, and Peter. Possibly it was Cima who originally suggested that the members choose two saints to be painted with the main devotional figure; that number may have accorded more decorously with the classical proportions of his *Sacra Conversazione.* But the Scuola must have later completely re-thought the altarpiece and its purpose. Crucially, the *stima* expressly says that the contract was upheld; the subject matter simply remained the subject of debate and negotiation after the contract was signed. Changes made under such circumstances seem not to have been worthy of mention.

Similar discussions about subject matter were held after the contract was signed for Perugino's altarpiece for San Pietro, Perugia. The contract, drawn up in 1495, has a detailed subject clause, requiring 'the Ascension of Christ with the Virgin and the twelve apostles, with angels and other decorations that Perugino knows to be suitable':

> In campo sive quadro ipsius Tabulae Ascentionem D.N.J.C. cum figura et Imagine gloriosissimae Virginis Mariae et XII Apostolorum cum aliquibus angelis et aliis ornamentis, secundum quod in facto cognoverit opportunum.[39]

But the finished panel also includes St Paul and such a figure would not have been among the additions the painter knew to be suitable. Indeed, Paul's place in the

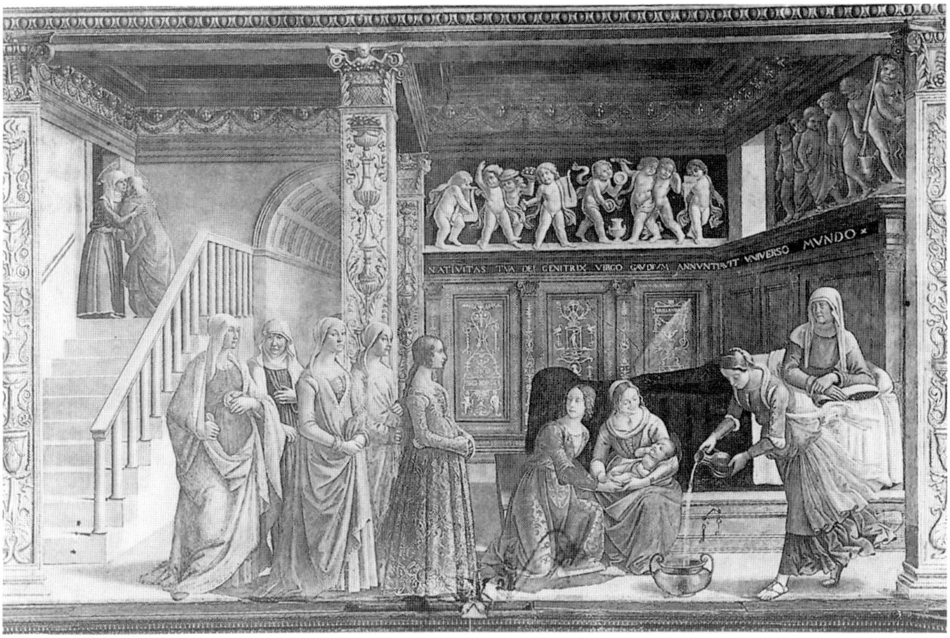

4. Domenico Ghirlandaio, *The Birth of the Virgin*. Fresco. Santa Maria Novella, Florence. Photo: © Alinari.

scene is inappropriate. He was undoubtedly added at the request of the monks since the chapel was dedicated to both Peter and Paul, and St Peter was already included in the apostolic group. St Paul's canonical importance required him to stand next to the Virgin, but since he was not part of the mystery of the Ascension, Perugino placed him psychologically outside the scene. The saint looks pointedly to his left, beyond the circle of apostles who gaze upward. It seems that, like Cima, Perugino worked with the changing requirements of his clients during the design process to produce a picture responsive to their needs. The contract record of the subject did not constrain either party.

The Painter and Subject Development

While figures added after an initial subject decision was recorded probably represent suggestions introduced by clients, changes in the presentation or type of a particular saint and modifications to compositional arrangement are likely to have originated with the ideas of a painter. These represent the creative aspects of formulating the design. Painters' alterations would have been approved in exchange during the design process, probably, as they were in Signorelli and Ghirlandaio's commissions, in discussion over a drawing.

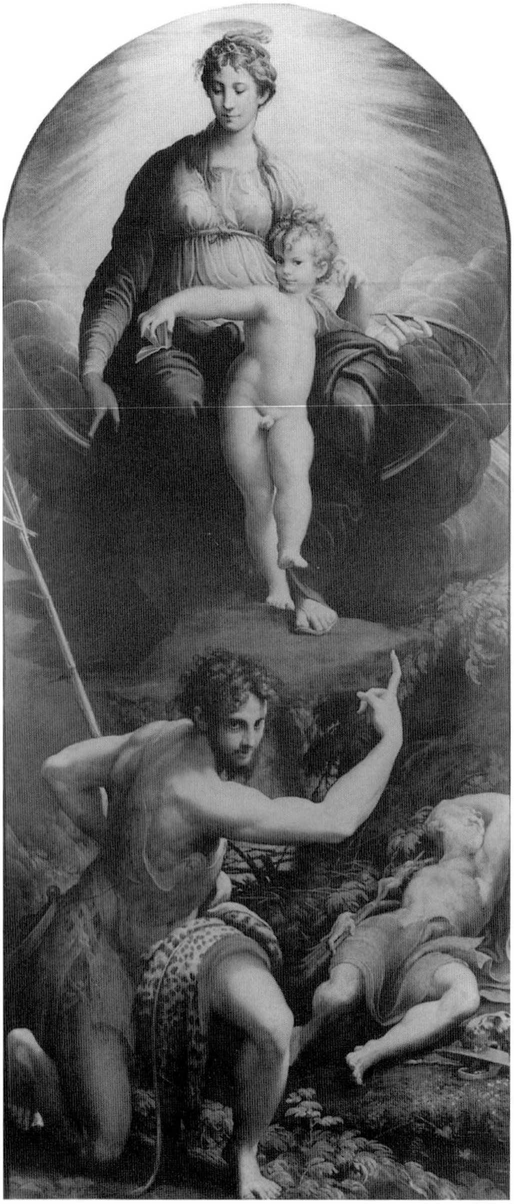

5. Parmigianino, *Virgin and Child with Saints John the Baptist and Jerome.* Oil on Poplar. London, The National Gallery. Photo: © The National Gallery.

An example of changes in the types, not persons, of the figures stipulated in the contract appears in Parmigianino's Vision of St Jerome altarpiece, commissioned in 1526 by Maria Bufalini for the chapel of her deceased husband's family in the Roman church of San Salvatore in Lauro (Fig. 5).[40] The contract has a detailed subject clause: Parmigianino agreed to paint the Virgin, seated with her son in her arms, between St Jerome, a Doctor of the Church, and St John the Baptist, who are to be at her feet.[41]

It was characteristic of Parmigianino to approach new commissions with a wide sense of the artistic possibilities of the work, trying a variety of ideas for compositions and often arriving at an unconventional presentation of the subject matter chosen by his client. For the Bufalini commission, approximately twenty-five studies survive. They are not developmental; instead, they show the painter working through a series of diverse conceptions of the iconography proposed by his client.[42] Among the earliest is a sheet in the British Museum (Fig. 6).[43] It represents the terms of the contract in a dynamic and original composition, which shows the two saints crouching below the Virgin, who hovers over and behind them; the figures look at St John, who seems to be addressing St Jerome. Other studies explore the relationship between the saints: John indicating the Virgin and engaging with the viewer, Jerome psychologically remote from the scene.[44] Eventually, Jerome is shown slumped over, sleeping with his head on his arms (Fig. 7). In later studies, more radical poses are tried, as the concept of the saint becomes divorced from his image as a Doctor of the Church.[45] Other sheets investigate possibilities for the Virgin and Child.[46] In a drawing in Chantilly, the Virgin stands on a large pedestal, filling the composition, and it is difficult to see how saints might have been included.[47] The contract's compositional terms are completely disregarded in a delicate drawing in Parma, which shows the Virgin seated on the far right of the composition, on the same ground line as the saints.[48] It is unclear how this might have related to the tall, thin format of the panel and seems the work of a painter exuberantly exploring the creative possibilities of the figural relationships.

There is no record of how Parmigianino communicated his ideas to his client, or even if Maria Bufalini was aware of the number of unconventional and inventive ideas he was exploring for the work. None of the studies has the character of a contract drawing, which commonly included a whole composition shown within an architectural frame, and no final *disegno* for the altarpiece survives.[49] Nonetheless, because contract drawings were made for most altarpieces commissioned after the mid–fifteenth century, it is likely that the painter submitted to Bufalini a final *disegno* representing the present work, a drawing more finished than most of the surviving studies. The altarpiece was finished before the painter fled Rome for Bologna after the 1527 sack and thus was completed before Maria Bufalini's will was drawn up in Città di Castello in 1528.[50] The will provides for a final payment to the painter and for the altarpiece to be erected in San Salvatore; therefore, it may be assumed that the work was accepted.[51]

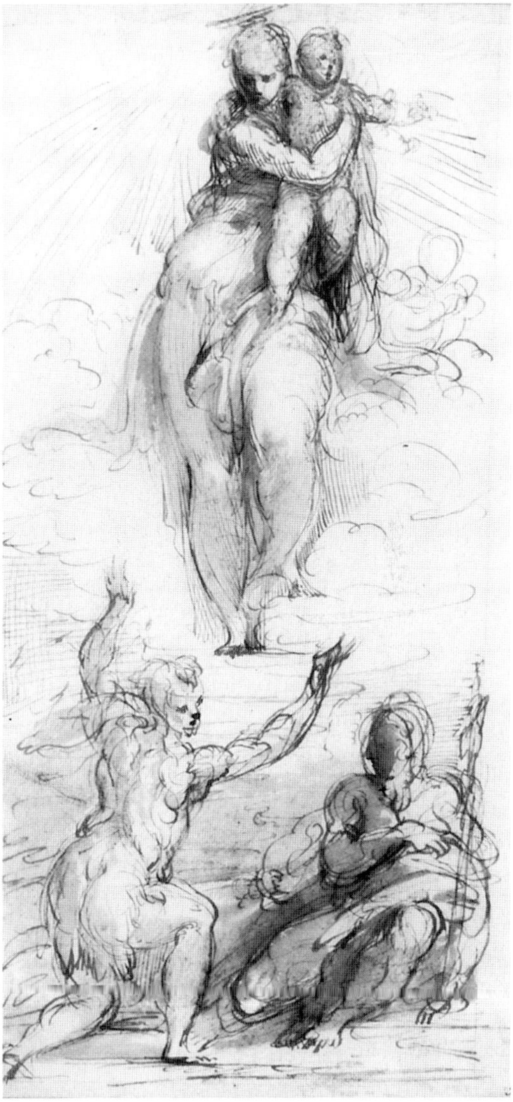

6. Parmigianino, *Study for Virgin and Child with Saints John the Baptist and Jerome*. Pen and brown ink. London: The British Museum. Photo: © The British Museum.

The finished altarpiece has an ambivalent relationship to the subject clause in the contract. While the saints are placed at the Virgin's feet, she is not between them on the picture plane. In addition, Jerome is not depicted as a man of the law, but as a penitent.[52] The body of studies makes it clear that Parmigianino was never constrained by the requirements of the contract. The document's subject description may, in any case, simply have codified an initial idea that he had for arranging the figures named by the client; the description of the Virgin's placement in relation to the saints is unusual. The scope of the ideas considered for the picture strongly suggest that changes were not instigated by Bufalini, but were the artist's own inquiry into how the figures might best be arranged. Nonetheless, Bufalini must have approved the change in St Jerome's persona.

Parmigianino's composition and his approach to its development is original, but the model the commission introduces – that of changes proposed by the painter rather than the client – can be traced in other commissions where the work of art differs from the contract description of the role of a figure or the arrangement of the subjects.

The *Madonna of Rocks* altarpiece, for example, discussed earlier, does not adhere to the type of the Virgin noted in the contract and the *lista,* and there are changes in the figures originally stipulated for the altarpiece. The documents require the Virgin and Child and two prophets,[53] a version of the Immaculate Conception iconography. But Leonardo designed the Virgin with the Child and the young John the Baptist, a completely different type of Marian iconography. This was a particularly Florentine subject, almost certainly proposed by the painter. It is equally certain to have been approved by the client. Because the confraternity was interested in defining all the decorative details of the frame, it is most likely that the members were also interested in discussing – and approving – the design of the panel's subject matter. It seems that the altarpiece already contained a sculpted figure of the *Immaculata,* and it may be that Leonardo argued against repeating the image.[54] Although the contracting parties later became involved in a battle over finances and completion, the changes to the original subject were never a recorded issue.

In the Madonna of the Harpies altarpiece, both parties are likely to have been involved in instituting changes. The work was commissioned from Andrea del Sarto by the Florentine female convent of San Francesco in 1515. The contract has a specific subject clause: it requires the Virgin and Child, crowned with angels, with John the Evangelist on one side and Saint Bonaventura on the other.[55]

After the document was drawn up, however, St Francis, the founder of the Order, was substituted for Bonaventura, its sainted general. This change was certainly introduced by the nuns. They are unlikely to have suggested, however, the alteration to the type of Madonna represented. Instead of the Virgin crowned with angels, as the contract stipulates, Andrea designed an elegant, twisting figure, who balances a book and her child while supported by a pair of putti. Her contraposto is complemented by the turning poses of the saints, and it may be that the painter convinced his clients that a symmetrically crowned Madonna, an older type of subject, would alter the balance of his schema *alla maniera.* The altarpiece is the result of both parties continuing to engage with ideas about subject matter after the initial concept of the subject was recorded in the contract.

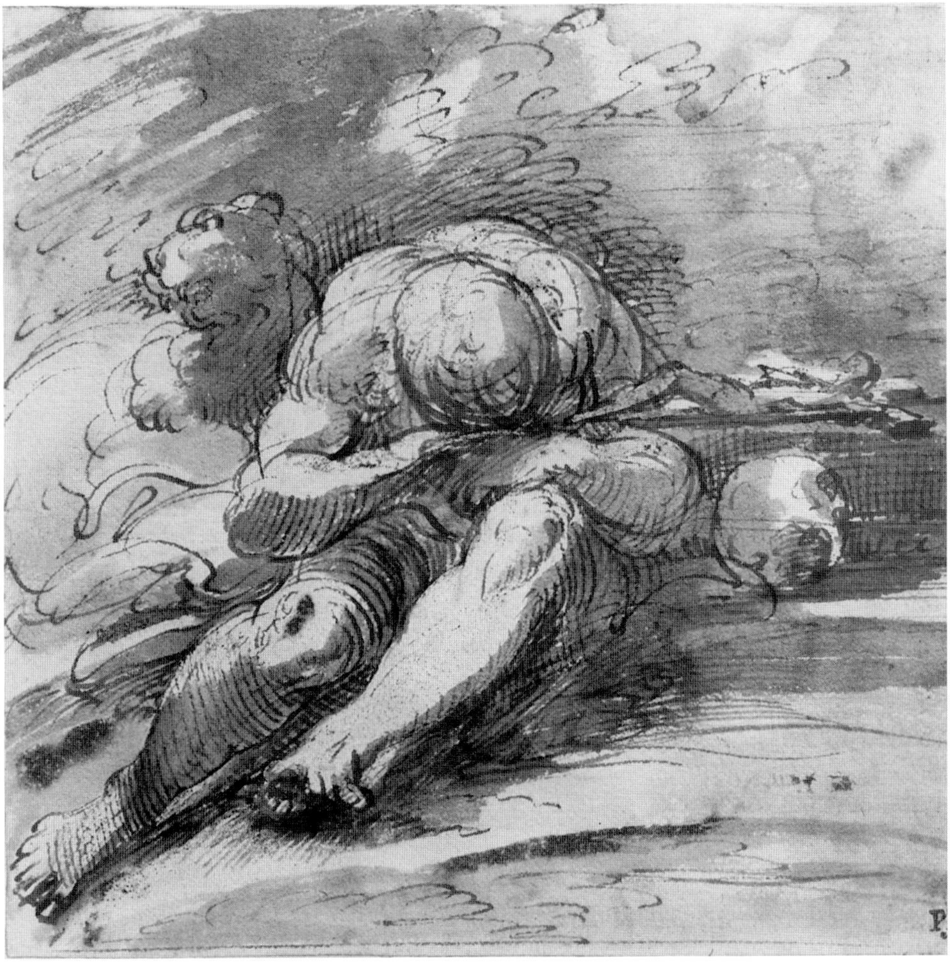

7. Parmigianino. *Study for St Jerome*. Pen and brown wash. London, The British Museum. Photo: © The British Museum.

Conclusion

The written and visual evidence for the development of subject matter indicates that the exchange between Renaissance painters and their clients could be complex and wide-ranging. The number and identity of figures and stories, as well as their placement and colour, were subject to the input of both parties, as painters and clients worked in concert to shape how a new work would look. Both were concerned with the nuts and bolts of defining visual appearance.

The kinds of contributions that painters and their clients made to subject development, however, occurred in different areas. Clients mainly wanted more figures or different scenes.[56] Probably most such alterations, however, could only be made after an initial design had been produced, for this allowed them to reconsider early ideas once a work was in progress. Painters' contributions to subject exchange concerned the details of how figures were composed and pictures arranged. This is not surprising. Their ideas developed during the course of drawing up the design and working through solutions to compositional requirements. In addition, their interests, particularly in the late fifteenth and early sixteenth centuries, were focused on inventing new compositions and designing novel approaches, often to common subject matter.

Most significantly, the evidence demonstrates that neither party considered the subject clause of a contract to be binding. Indeed, the commissions discussed here make it clear that contractual subject stipulations carried little weight. This has wide repercussions for our understanding of the ramifications of contracts. It means, for example, that the subject to be painted, particularly the number of figures to be represented, had little bearing on the fee negotiated for a work, because original fee decisions were not disregarded. Of course, many contracting parties clearly made final decisions about subject matter early in the commissioning process. However, this was not required. Subject references in contracts might merely be notations of an opening round of thoughts on a new work, thoughts that were altered and refined in continuing exchange between the parties as the work of art developed.

NOTES

1. On the concept of composition and the Renaissance, see Thomas Puttfarken, *The Discovery of Pictorial Composition: Theories of Visual Order in Painting 1400–1800* (New Haven and London: Yale University Press, 2000), 52–170; and Charles Hope, '"Composition" from Cennini and Alberti to Vasari,' in *Pictorial Composition from Medieval to Modern Art*, ed. Paul Taylor and François Quiviger (London: Warburg Institute, 2000), 27–44.

2. Here 'subjects' means both figures and the scenes of the lives of Christ, the Virgin, or the saints. Charles Hope ('Altarpieces and the Requirements of Patrons,' in *Christianity in the Renaissance*, ed. Timothy Verdon and John Henderson [Syracuse, NY: Syracuse University, 1990], 538) has shown that the subjects of the main panels of altarpieces are nearly always noted in contracts as particular figures, even when the subject appears to be a narrative, while the narrative subjects of frescoes and predella panels are called *storie.*

3. Charles Hope, 'Artists, Patrons and Advisers in the Italian Renaissance,' in *Patronage in the Renaissance*, ed. Guy F. Lytle and Stephen Orgel (Princeton: Princeton University Press, 1981), 293–343; Creighton E. Gilbert, 'What Did the Renaissance Patron Buy?' *Renaissance Quarterly* 51 (1998): 392–450.

4. On colour, see Timothy McGrath, 'Color and the Exchange of Ideas between Patron and Artist in Renaissance Italy,' *Art Bulletin* 82 (2000): 298–308. McGrath's illuminating article on coloured contract and preparatory drawings argues that some clients participated in decisions about colour. His research supports the idea that clients were concerned with the appearance of their new work, and he arrives at the same broad conclusions about painter-client relationships

to which a study of exchange about subject matter has led me. For bibliography on the role of the client in Renaissance Italy, see McGrath, 'Color and the Exchange,' 306, n. 12. On verbal exchange about subject matter, see Anabel Thomas, *The Painter's Practice in Renaissance Tuscany* (Cambridge: Cambridge University Press, 1995), 106–9; and Lynn F. Jacobs, *Early Netherlandish Carved Altarpieces 1380–1550: Medieval Tastes and Mass Marketing* (Cambridge: Cambridge University Press, 1998), 175.

5. A survey of more than 160 Italian Renaissance contracts for altarpieces and frescoes shows that about 27 percent refer cursorily to subject matter by naming only the main figure or mentioning the submission of a drawing, 16 percent record that there will be verbal exchange, and another 16 percent do not mention subject at all. See the author's *The Business of Art: Contracts and Commissioning Process in Renaissance Italy* (New Haven and London: Yale University Press, forthcoming).

6. Alfred Scharf, *Filippino Lippi* (Vienna: Antol Schroll, 1935), 88: 'E da ogni faccia di essa (la capella) hanno a essere dua Storie, secondo che dal detto Filippo Strozzi li saranno date.'

7. For an example, see the contract for the altarpiece commissioned from Cima da Conegliano in 1492, discussed in n. 38.

8. Regional differences in documents largely concern vocabulary. An altarpiece is referred to as a *tavola* in central Italy, a *pala* or *ancona* in the Veneto. The central Italian and Venetian *predella* is called a *banchetta* in Lombardy. In central Italy and Lombardy the client hires the painter or the painter promises to undertake work for the client; in the Veneto the parties are linked by a verb that refers to their agreement.

9. Compare, for example, the 1448 contracts of the companies of Vivarini and Giovanni d'Alamagna or Mantegna and Niccolò Pizzolo for the Ovetari Chapel with the contract of an individual painter, such as the 1469 contract of Cosimè Tura for painting the chapel of Belriguardo. See, respectively, Vittorio Lazzarini, *Documenti relativi alla pittura padovana del secolo XV* (1908; Venice: Arnaldo Forni, 1974), 191–4; and A. Venturi, 'Cosmè Tura e la capella de Belriguardo,' *Il Buonarroti*, 3rd ser., 3, 2 (1884), 57.

10. The history of contracts, the types of stipulations that appear in artists' contracts, and the other kinds of documents that pertain to commissions have been rigorously studied by Hannelore Glasser, 'Artists' Contracts of the Early Renaissance' (Ph.D. diss., Columbia University, 1965), 21–58; Susan Mary Connell, 'The Employment of Sculptors and Stone-masons in Venice in the Fifteenth Century' (Ph.D. thesis, University of London, 1976), 185–228; and *Giovanni Antonio Amadeo: Documents/I documenti*, ed. Richard V. Schofield, Janice Shell, and Grazioso Sironi (Como: Edizione New Press, 1989), 26–32. See also Evelyn Welch, *Art and Society in Italy 1350–1500* (Oxford: Oxford University Press, 1997), 103–14; and Martin Kemp, *Behind the Picture: Art and Evidence in the Italian Renaissance* (New Haven and London: Yale University Press, 1997), 32–79.

11. See, for example, the documents written by Neri di Bicci, in his *Ricordanze*, ed. Bruno Santi (Pisa: Edizione Marlin, 1976); Andrea Mantegna's 1453 contract with the monastery of Santa Justina, Paul Oskar Kristeller, *Andrea Mantegna* (Berlin: Cosmos Verlag, 1902), 515; Cosmè Tura's 1469 contract for the Este chapel at Belriguardo, Venturi, 'Cosmè Tura,' 57; and Ghirlandaio's 1490 contract with the convent of Palco, in Gaetano Milanesi, *Nuovi documenti per la storia dell'arte toscana dal XII al XVI secolo* (1893; Florence: G. Dotti, 1901), 156.

12. On setting value and regional differences in pay, see Michelle O'Malley, 'Commissioning bodies, allocation decisions and price structures for altarpieces in fifteenth- and early sixteenth-century Italy,' in *The Art Market in Italy, 15th–17th Centuries*, ed. Marcello Fantoni, Louisa C.

Matthew, and Sara F. Matthews Grieco (Modena: Panini Editore, 2003); and idem, *The Business of Art*, forthcoming 2004. Prices set in republics depended on a variety of tangible and intangible factors, negotiated between the parties. Court markets were less open than those in republics and more likely to be controlled by the ruler, at least in regard to the prices he and his household paid. Princes often did not pay their bills or insisted on undercutting a painter's assessment of the value of his work. On pricing issues see Guido Guerzoni; Michelle O'Malley and Evelyn Welch, in *The Material Renaissance*, ed. Michelle O'Malley and Evelyn Welch (forthcoming); on the Sforza, see Evelyn Welch, *Art and Authority in Renaissance Milan* (New Haven and London: Yale University Press, 1995), 254–5; on Mantua, I am indebted to Barbara Furlotti of the Mantuan project Collezionismo Gonzaga 1563–1630, who has generously discussed Gonzaga payment practices with me. I am also grateful for numerous discussions with the members of, and visiting scholars to, The Material Renaissance project of the University of Sussex, funded by the Arts and Humanities Research Board and the Getty Grant Programme.

13. In the agreement between Sassetta and the friars of San Francesco, discussed later, the word *scripta* is used for a report. In Piero della Francesca's 1454 contract with the friars of Sant'Agostino in Sansepolcro, however, the term refers to a notarised document; he was to paint the figures and frames about which the parties were in accord and which would appear in a *scripta* drawn up by the notary and the convent's prior. Milanesi, *Nuovi documenti*, 13, and more fully transcribed in Glasser, 'Artists' Contracts,' 281: 'ad pingendum et ornandum et deaurandum cum illis ymaginibus, figuris, picturis et ornamentis de quibus remanserunt et asseruerunt esse in plena concordia, et apparere inter eos posse et debere quandam scriptam, sive appodissam manu dicti Ser Uguccij et subscriptam manu dicti Prioris ac Nannis alterius operarii.'

14. James R. Banker, 'The Programme for the Sassetta Altarpiece in the Church of San Francesco in Borgo Sansepolcro,' *I Tatti Studies*, 4 (1991): 54–5 'Per commissionem di frati, del Guardiano et deli operieri de'convento del Borgo laquale è data anoi frate Franceschо et frate Michelagnilo de ordinare et componere le figure et l'istorie della taule sì como pare a noi et al maestro insiemi.' Two weeks after the meeting in Siena, the *scripta* and a drawing were presented to the friars and the *operai* of San Francesco, who agreed formally to accept the plan.

15. Ibid., 'la virgine Maria col figliolo in collo et ornata con angeli como al maestro parrà che stia meglio'.

16. Ibid., 'Nella predella del canto dinanze le sto[r]ie della pasione quelle che sono più devote et sono quatro,' and 'nella predella quattro storie de' beato Raniero como noi frate Francescho et frate Michelagnilo ve mandaremo.' It is unclear why the friars did not give Sassetta the exact subjects on the spot; maybe they were themselves unsure of them.

17. In the altarpiece, the figure of St Francis is not enthroned but standing, surrounded by a mandorla and cherubim. Although this is a change in type, which, I argue later, commonly originated with a painter, I think it is unlikely to have been introduced here by Sassetta. The prototype was a model in another Franciscan convent, and such models usually had particular significance for the Orders that chose them. See Michelle O'Malley, 'Memorizing the New: Using Recent Works as Models in Italian Renaissance Commissions,' *Memory and Oblivion: Proceedings of the XXIXth International Congress of the History of Art*, ed. Wessel Reinink and Jeroen Stumpel (Dordrecht: Kluwer, 1999), 803–10. Sassetta's picture probably followed the model. Perhaps the convent misused the word 'enthroned'.

18. Christa Gardner von Teuffel, 'The Contract for Perugino's "Assumption of the Virgin" at Vallombrosa,' *Burlington Magazine*, 137 (1995): 311–12.

19. Ibid., 307.

20. Ibid., 311–12: 'Uno quadro o piano largo br. 4¾ alto br. 5¾ nel quale è una Assumpta a ssedere vestita d'azurro oltramarino fine di fiorin 4 l'oncia, con trono di cherubini et serafini quanti ve ne sia et più agnoli 8 con instrumenti et s[u]oni condecenti.

Et 4 sancti, cioè San Giovanni Gualberto col peviale sopra la cocolla bigia et croce col crocifisso et gruccia colle boche in mano.

Et San Bernardo colla cappa rosata sopra la cocolla bigia, cappello cardinalesco in capo et libro in mano.

Et San Michele arcangelo armato.

Et San Benedecto in cocolla bigia et libro et disciplina in mano et sieno di br. 2 2/3 l'uno al naturale.

Et nell'aria di decto quader non si mettase non azurro oltramarino.

Una predella di vano di 2/3, lunga br. 6 nella quale sia 2 teste col'imbusti tracti al naturale, et 3 historie con più figure di San Giovanni Gualberto, cioè nel mezo quando il crocifixo se l'inchina, da canto quella del f[u]ocho, et dall'altro quella delli spiritati.'

21. Ibid., 312. The placement of God the Father in a circular 'frame' in the lunette, behind which the mandorla seems to slip, may reflect an earlier composition at the convent; see 311.

22. In the painting, the main panel has six angels around the Madonna and another two next to the roundel encircling God the Father. Cherubim appear throughout the heavens.

23. Luca Beltrami, *Documenti e Memorie riguardanti le vita e le opere di Leonardo da Vinci* (Milan: Fratelli Treves, 1919), 19–20.

24. For an extensive discussion of the *lista* see Glasser, 'Artists' Contracts,' 164–9, and 328–30.

25. On clients' involvement in colour decisions, see McGrath, 'Color and the Exchange,' 303. The pigments noted in the *lista* include *lacha fina in cremesi* (crimson lake), *senaprio* (cinnabar), and the commonly cited ultramarine.

26. Beltrami, *Documenti e Memorie,* 19: 'Item. la tavola de mezo facta. depenta in piano. la nostra dona. con lo suo fiollo. eli angolli. facta aolio in tucta. perfetione. con quelli doy. profecti vanno depenti piani. con li colori. fini come edicto de sopra.' Deviation from this subject is discussed later.

27. The price of the frame, including its carving, gilding, and painting, was far greater than the outlay for the pictorial panels. The carved structure alone cost 710 *lire imperiali* (just over 177 ducats). The precise cost of the gilding is unknown, but it may have been as much as 800 *lire imperiali* (200 ducats), the amount for which the painters contracted, which they later claimed was all spent on gilding. Eventually the painters received a further 200 *lire imperiali* (50 ducats), presumably for painting the panels. For the documents, see Beltrami, *Documenti e Memorie,* 12–30, 73–4, 104–7, 121–7; and Glasser, 'Artists' Contracts,' 308–92.

28. Contracts occasionally contain such information. See, for example, Ghirlandaio's 1485 contract for the Tornabuoni chapel (Milanesi, *Nuovi documenti,* 136); Pinturrichio's 1502 contract for the Library frescoes in Siena Cathedral (Gaetano Milanesi, *Documenti per la storia dell'arte senese,* 3 vols. (1854; Utrecht: Davaco, 1969), III, 9–14); and Savoldo's 1524 contract for the altarpiece for San Domenico, Pesaro (*Giovanni Girolamo Savoldo: tra Foppa, Giorgione e Caravaggio,* exh. cat., [Milan: Electa, 1990], 318).

29. For the deliberation documents, see Robert Vischer, *Luca Signorelli und die italienische renaissance* (Leipzig: Veit und Comp, 1879), 350–2. A corpus of drawings survive; Andrew Martindale ('Luca Signorelli and the Drawings Connected to the Orvieto Frescoes,' *Burlington Magazine,* 103 [1961]: 216–20) divided the drawings into three classes, but none are finished drawings for the frescoes, and works in succeeding classes are not developments of those of earlier classes.

30. Vischer, *Luca Signorelli,* 351: 'Johannes Ludovicus Benincasa alter ex civibus existens in dicta Audientia dixit et consuluit quod Mag. Lucas cum figuris veniat usque ad planum fenestrarum, et residuum fiat prout dedit in designo,' and ibid., 352: 'et stuccarla secondo el disegno dato per lo maestro: se come più come parrà allui, ma non con mancho figure che ce habia dato nel disegno per ciascuna archata.'

31. Martindale, 'Luca Signorelli,' argues that there was never a stage of finished studies for the work. There is evidence that individual figures were still being designed when Signorelli began to paint.

32. Milanesi, *Nuovi documenti,* 134–6: 'Cum pacto tamen inter dictum locatorem et dictum conductorem – quod antequam dictus locator – incipiat pingere et ornare aliquam ex hystoriis et pitturis suprascriptis, vel aliquam earum, quod prius et ante amnia teneatur designare et proponere dicto Johanni (Tornabuoni) designum factum ipsius historie et picture fiende: et quod dictus locator possit inde postea talem hystoriam et pitturas inchoare et pingere et ornare cum illis additionibus et eo modo et forma et prout et sicut supra dicto designo declaratum fuerit per dictum Johannem, et in effectu in omnibus et per omnia prout processerit de voluntate ipsius Johannis'.

33. For discussions of the chapel's patronage and analyses of the iconographic ramifications of patronage rights, see Patricia Simons, 'Patronage in the Tornaquinci Chapel, Santa Maria Novella, Florence,' in *Patronage, Art and Society in Renaissance Italy,* ed. F. W. Kent and Patricia Simons with J. C. Eade (Oxford: Oxford University Press, 1987), 221–50, and Rab Hatfield, 'Giovanni Tornabuoni, i fratelli Ghirlandaio e la cappella maggiore di Santa Maria Novella,' in *Domenico Ghirlandaio, 1449–1494,* Atti del convegno internazionale, ed. Wolfram Prinz and Max Seidel (Florence: Centro Di, 1996), 112–17.

34. Hatfield, 'Giovanni Tornabuoni,' 115.

35. Simons, 'Patronage in the Tornaquinci Chapel,' 235.

36. The drawing is in the Albertina, Vienna, Inv. 4860 (L.174).

37. On the position of lay figures in holy spaces, see Charles Hope, 'Altarpieces and the Requirements of Patrons,' 551–4.

38. Peter Humfrey, *Cima da Conegliano* (Cambridge: Cambridge University Press, 1983), 198: 'Quod ipse magister Baptista facere debeat Scole praedicte unam pulchram pallam in ligno cum figuris tribus. S. Virginis marie . . . Sancti Joannis Evengeliste et Sancti Andree sive Sancti Petri'.

39. Fiorenzo Canuti, *Il Perugino* (Siena: Editice d'arte 'La Diana,'1931), 177.

40. See Mary Vaccaro, 'Documents for Parmigianino's "Vision of St Jerome"'; and Sandro Corradini, 'Parmigianino's Contract for the Caccialupi Chapel in S. Salvatore in Lauro,' in *Burlington Magazine* 135 (1993): 22–7 and 27–9, respectively. The contract was drawn up with Parmigianino and his uncle, but it is unclear what the uncle's role in the commission was to have been.

41. Vaccaro, 'Documents,' 26: 'unam tabulam cum imagine beatae Mariae virginis sedente cum Filio in brachiis suis, et imagine beati Hieronimi doctoris Ecclesiae et beati Iohannis baptistae in pede Virginis a medietate dictarum Imaginum sanctorum Hieronimi et Io:Baptistae supradicti'.

42. On the painter's working methods and early work, see A. E. Popham, *Catalogue of the Drawings of Parmigianino* (New Haven and London: Yale University Press, 1971), 1–5; on the Bufalini commission, ibid., 7–9 and plates 95–112.

43. Ibid., plate 95r.

44. Ibid., plates 96v and 97v.

45. Ibid., plates 110 and 111.

46. Ibid., plates 99–103.
47. Ibid., plate 97r.
48. Ibid., plate 98v.
49. Parmigianino was responsible for gilding the carved surround and therefore for presenting a complete altarpiece, not solely a panel; see Corradini, 'Parmigianino's Contract,' 28.
50. Before the artist departed from Rome, it was arranged for the altarpiece to be left in Santa Maria della Pace for safekeeping. For the will, see Corradini, 'Parmigianino's Contract,' 28–9.
51. The work was never placed in San Salvatore. Eventually the family collected it from Santa Maria della Pace and placed it in the family chapel in San Agostino, in Città di Castello; see Vaccaro, 'Documents,' 27.
52. The Marian literature used in the liturgy of the Immaculate Conception was believed in the sixteenth century to have been written by St Jerome, and this may be behind the painter's depiction of the saint. The title *Vision of St Jerome* was only attributed to the painting in the nineteenth century; see Vaccaro, 'Documents,' 23.
53. See Beltrami, *Documenti e Memorie,* 12–20.
54. The *lista* begins with a description of a carved Virgin, probably a representation of the *Immaculata* on the top of the altarpiece; see Beltrami, *Documenti e Memorie,* 19. Item la nostra dona nel mezo. sia la vesta. de sopra. brocato doro azurlo tramarino.' For discussion of the figure and its placement see Glasser, 'Artists' Contracts,' 227–8.
55. John Shearman, *Andrea del Sarto* (Oxford: Clarendon, 1965), 47–9 and 391: 'In qua pingi convenerunt imaginem beatissime Marie semper Virginis cum filio suo in brachio et cum duobus angelis a lateribus capitis qui dictam imaginem Virginis Matris Marie coronant . . . et ab uno latere debeat esse imago beatissimi Iohannis Evangeliste et ab alio Sancti Bonaventure ad usum cardinalis.'
56. Among the few recorded subtractions of figures are Benozzo Gozzoli's seraphs in the Medici Chapel; see David Chambers, *Patrons and Artists in the Italian Renaissance* (Columbia: University of South Carolina, 1971), 96.

2

Copying Practices and Marketing Strategies in a Fifteenth-Century Florentine Painter's Workshop

Megan Holmes

LEONARDO DA VINCI, WRITING IN THE EARLY SIXTEENTH CENTURY, INSISTED that paintings, unlike other artistic and literary forms, could not be copied effectively.

> This [i.e., painting] cannot be copied like letters, where the copy is as significant as the original. This does not imprint itself like sculpture does, where the impression is like the original, relative to the *virtú* of the work. This does not make infinite number of children like printed books; this alone remains noble, this alone honors its authors, and remains precious and unique, and does not ever give birth to children equal to itself.'[1]

The emphasis on the uniqueness, value, and aesthetic and semantic integrity of the original, as well as the privileging of authorial agency found in Leonardo's text, were to become critical positions within the discourse on copying in the visual arts in western Europe from the sixteenth century onward. Leonardo's views, however, were formulated in the wake of revolutionary transformations in reproductive technologies and practices in Italy, across a wide range of artisanal industries and

This article would not have been possible without the generous assistance of Carl Strehlke. I would also like to thank the following individuals and institutions for providing mylar tracings of and technical information about paintings: Keith Christiansen and Charlotte Hale of the Metropolitan Museum of Art in New York; Joanna Webber, Mark Aronson, and Anne O'Connor of the Yale University Art Gallery; Teresa Lignelli and Joe Mikuliak of the Philadelphia Museum of Art; and Alan Chong and Joanne Klaar of the Isabella Stewart Gardner Museum. The material was presented in talks at the National Gallery in London and the University of Michigan, and the insightful comments made by members of the audience have been worked into the final version of the essay. Thanks also to Carmen Bambach, Jonathan Nelson, Beatrice Paolozzi Strozzi, and Virginia Thomas.

cultural fields. During the second half of the fifteenth century, reproduction in the pictorial arts led to a marked increase in the production of Marian images and to new markets and consumers for these commodities. Furthermore, reproduction resulted in modified pictorial renderings – children unlike their parents, to stay with Leonardo's metaphor of biological reproduction – generated within new settings and cultural contexts. In this chapter I focus on a Florentine painting workshop operating during the second half of the fifteenth century that made unprecedented use of mechanical transfer methods. Pictorial reproduction, as practiced by this shop, took on a variety of different forms and seems to have catered to the needs of patrons and consumers from different social ranks and urban communities.

The Workshop of the Lippi and Pesellino Imitator

There is a curious group of Florentine paintings datable to the late 1450s through the mid-1490s that have long fascinated connoisseurs of Italian Renaissance art on account of their substantial number and uniformity. Numbering more than 160, they are composed almost exclusively out of a cast of sixty-four cartoon-generated characters derived, for the most part, from the paintings of Fra Filippo Lippi (c. 1406–69) and Francesco Pesellino (c. 1422–1457) (see Table 1).[2] They are usually attributed to 'the Pseudo Pier Francesco Fiorentino', although Federico Zeri's label 'Lippi and Pesellino Imitators' is more accurate.[3] There is evidence that a number of different painters worked on the individual panels, suggesting that one master employed a variety of assistants, or that a number of different masters worked together in a *compagnia.* It is also possible that the enterprise passed from one workshop to another (via the cartoon stock) during the thirty-five years or so that the panels were produced.[4] I use Zeri's 'Lippi and Pesellino Imitator', but in the singular, to refer to both the master or masters who organized the workshop activity and the painters who worked on the panels over the years.

The only dated work among this group of paintings is a copy of 1459, currently in storage in the Uffizi (Fig. 8), of Pesellino's *Madonna and Child* in Toledo, Ohio (Fig. 9). The reproductive enterprise was in place by this time.[5] While derivative works after Lippi and Pesellino may have constituted the typical products of the workshop, the shop kept apace with artistic developments over the years, adding the tondo to its repertoire, employing painters with more refined tonal modeling, integrating landscapes into the background, and offering a greater *varietà* by adopting a few new figures – young Baptists and angels, some taken from paintings by Filippo Lippi's son, Filippino.[6] Zeri noted how Leonardo da Vinci's *Benois Madonna* and Antonello da Messina's Munich *Virgin Annunciate* made their way into two of the later works.[7] The workshop may also have polychromed relief sculptures of the Madonna and Child, although these are more difficult to identify.[8]

TABLE 1: *Sources for the paintings by the Lippi and Pesellino Imitator*

	Primary figures	Secondary figures	Total
A. Paintings by Filippo Lippi			
**Adoration of the Child* (formerly in the Medici Palace Chapel, now in the Staatliche Museum, Berlin)	44	14	58
Reduced version of the Virgin from the Medici Palace chapel *Adoration of the Child* (above) with Child and angels from the Naples *Adoration of the Child* (below)	10		+10 68
**Virgin and the Child with Angels* for Alfonso of Naples (lost, close copy in The Cleveland Museum of Art)	4	13	17
Adoration of the Child for the Annalena Nunnery, now in the Uffizi, Florence	8		8
**Annunciation*, Galleria Doria Pamphili, Rome	1	7	8
Madonna and Child, Alte Pinakothek, Munich	5	2	7
Madonna and Child with Two Angels (here proposed as a lost work by Lippi, with the closest copy in the Philadelphia Museum of Art)	4	2	6
**Madonna and Child with Angels*, Uffizi, Florence	3	1	4
**St. Jerome in the Wilderness*, Staaliches Lindenau Museum, Altenburg	1		1
Annunciation for the nunnery Le Murate, now in the Alte Pinakothek, Munich		2	2
Madonna and Child, Rau Collection, Switzerland	1		1
Total Number of Paintings:	79		
B. Paintings by Pesellino			
**Madonna and Child*, Isabella Stewart Gardner Museum, Boston	38	5	43
**Madonna and Child with Angels*, Toledo Museum of Art, Ohio	17	19	36
Madonna and Child, ex-Aynard Collection, Lyon (present whereabouts unknown)	24		24
Mystical Marriage of St. Catherine, Strossmayer Gallery, Zagreb	4		4
Total Number of Paintings:	83		
C. Other			
Leonardo da Vinci, *Benois Madonna*, Hermitage Museum, St. Petersburg	1		1
Antonello da Messina, *Virgin Annunciate*, Alte Pinakothek, Munich	1		1

	Primary figures	Secondary figures	Total
Filippino Lippi, Baptist in the *Madonna and Child,* National Gallery, London (possible prototype)		22	22
Filippino Lippi, Baptist in the *Nerli Altarpiece,* Santo Spirito, Florence (probable prototype)		11	11
Filippino Lippi, Angel from the *Vision of St. Bernard,* Badia, Florence		3	3
Total Number of Paintings:	2		
D. Prototypes Unknown			
Young Baptist seen from behind		4	4
Young Baptist (Blumenreich, Berlin, 1931)		1	1
Madonna, Child and Angel (Yale University Art Gallery and Courtauld Institute)	2		2
Madonna, Child and saint (close to Pesellino; Christies' sale, New York (1-11-1991)	1		1
Christ Child (Acton Collection, Florence)		1	1
Very large child with fingertips of joined hands touching		9	9
Angel (Bob Jones University, Greenville)		1	1
Angel (ex-Aubrey House, London)		1	1
Female saint (appears as St. Lucy in a *Mystical Marriage of St. Catherine* (Sotheby's sale, London [4-4-1988])		2	2
Sts. Sebastian and Francis (in a late work based on Pesellino's Gardner Museum *Madonna,* close in style to Ghirlandaio)		1	1
Bishop Saint (Hermitage, St. Petersburg)		1	1
Total Number of Paintings:	3		

Based on 167 paintings by the Lippi and Pesellino Imitator.

* Complete composition considered to have been copied.

The workshop specialized in two categories of production: very close copies of notable paintings by Filippo Lippi and mass-produced Madonna panels based on compositions by Lippi and Pesellino. Key to its success within each of these categories was the effective use of cartoons – pin-pricked drawings used like stencils to replicate the designs. The paintings produced during the 1460s and 1470s in particular, were unusual and entrepreneurial, made possible by what must have been a privileged relationship between the head of the shop and Fra Filippo Lippi and Pesellino.

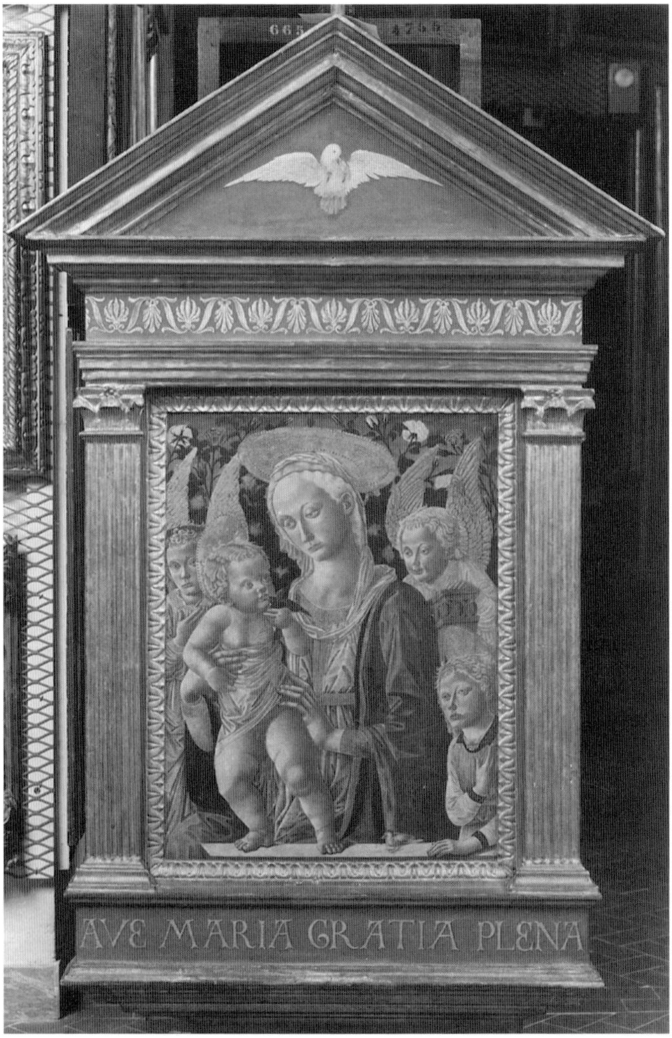

8. Lippi and Pesellino Imitator, *Madonna and Child with Angels,* 1459. On panel. Florence, Uffizi (storage). Photo: Gabinetto Fotografico, Soprintendenza per i Beni Artistici e Storici, Florence.

Copies of Medici Paintings

During the second half of the quattrocento, Lippi's paintings were copied more frequently than those of any other earlier Italian artist, both in drawing studies and in finished compositions – some precise reproductions and others derivative pastiches and free adaptations. At a time when a growing awareness was emerging among artists, patrons, and the public about a painter's particular *maniera* or style, Lippi's style was imitated and reworked in a highly self-conscious way by painters such as Botticelli and Filippino Lippi. Furthermore, Lippi's paintings and the memory of

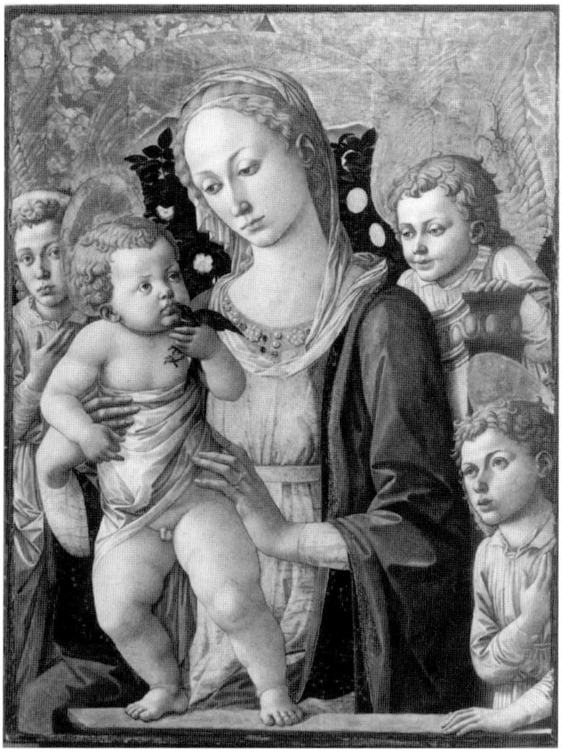

9. Francesco Pesellino, *Madonna and Child with Angels*, c. 1450–55. Tempera on panel. The Toledo Museum of Art, Ohio. Photo: Toledo Museum of Art.

the artist were closely linked to the Medici family. Cosimo "il Vecchio" and his sons Piero and Giovanni had commissioned work from Lippi, as had their political allies. Lorenzo, after failing in his attempt to repatriate the friar's remains, had a tomb built for him in the duomo in Spoleto.

Of the four existing close copies of paintings by Lippi dating from the quattrocento, three are attributed to the Lippi and Pesellino Imitator, suggesting that this bottega, in particular, was approached to carry out this kind of reproduction.[9] Lippi's *Adoration of the Child* (Fig. 10), painted for the Medici Palace chapel in Florence around 1459 (now in the Staatliche Museen in Berlin) and perhaps the single most influential work by the Carmelite painter, was copied (Fig. 11) probably some time in the 1460s or early 1470s.[10] The copy was executed with the aid of at least six separate cartoons: four used to reproduce the principal figures – the Virgin, the Christ Child, the young Baptist, and God the Father – and two for the more detailed features in the landscape, the logs, and tree stump. The placement of the cartoon-generated figures within the copy was approximated, however, as demonstrated by Beatrice Paolozzi Strozzi.[11] A colorful garland was added around the extremities, increasing slightly the dimensions beyond those of the original.

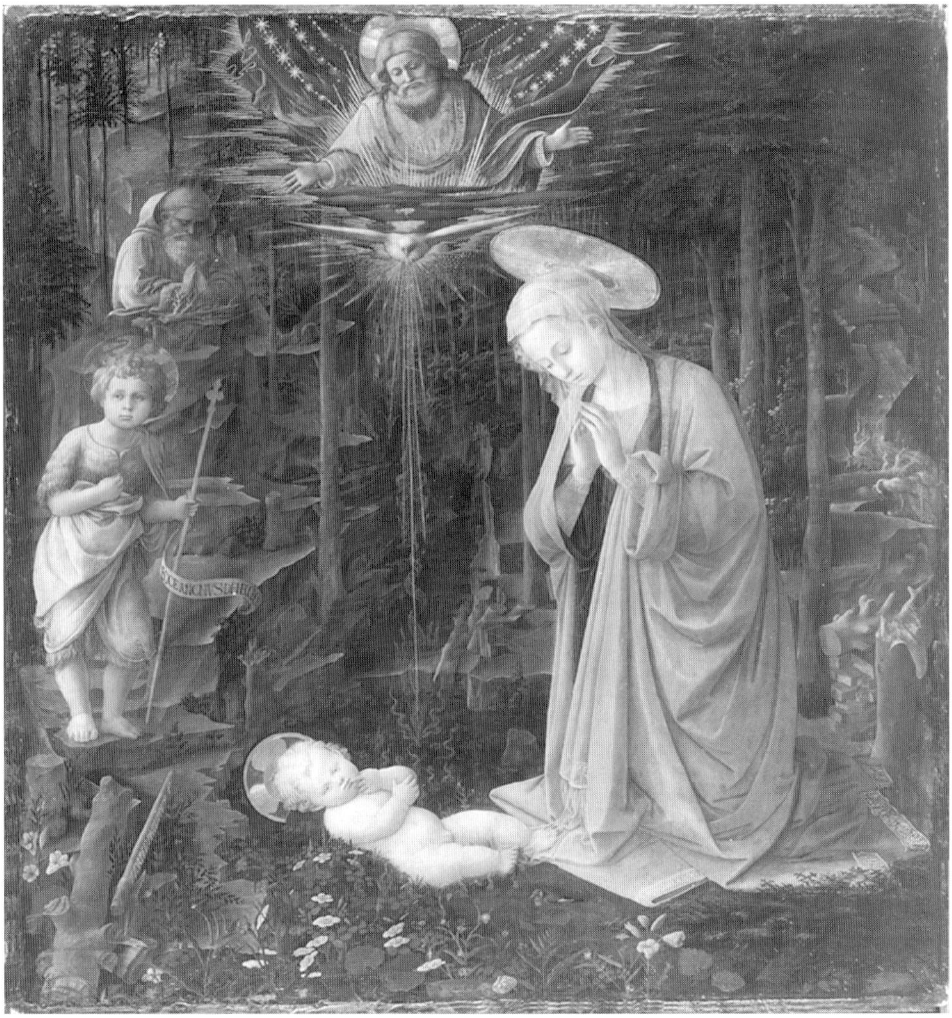

10. Filippo Lippi, *Adoration of the Christ Child with Saint Bernard and the Baptist,* c. 1459. On panel. Berlin, Staatliche Museen Preussischer Kulturbesitz, Gemäldegalerie. Photo: Staatliche Museen.

There is a copy in Bergamo (Fig. 12) by the Lippi and Pesellino Imitator of Lippi's small devotional panel representing *Saint Jerome in the Wilderness* (c. 1455) now in Altenburg (Fig. 13)[12] and a copy in Berlin (Fig. 14) of Lippi's *Annunciation* (c. 1445–50) in the Galleria Doria Pamphilj in Rome (Fig. 15).[13] In all three of these close copies of paintings by Lippi, although the outer dimensions vary somewhat, the central scenes remain on scale with those of the originals. It would appear that cartoons derived from the figures in Lippi's original paintings were used in the reproductive process.[14]

It is also possible that five additional paintings by Lippi were copied in their entirety. A painting of the *Virgin and Child with Angels* in Cleveland (Fig. 16) – a highly

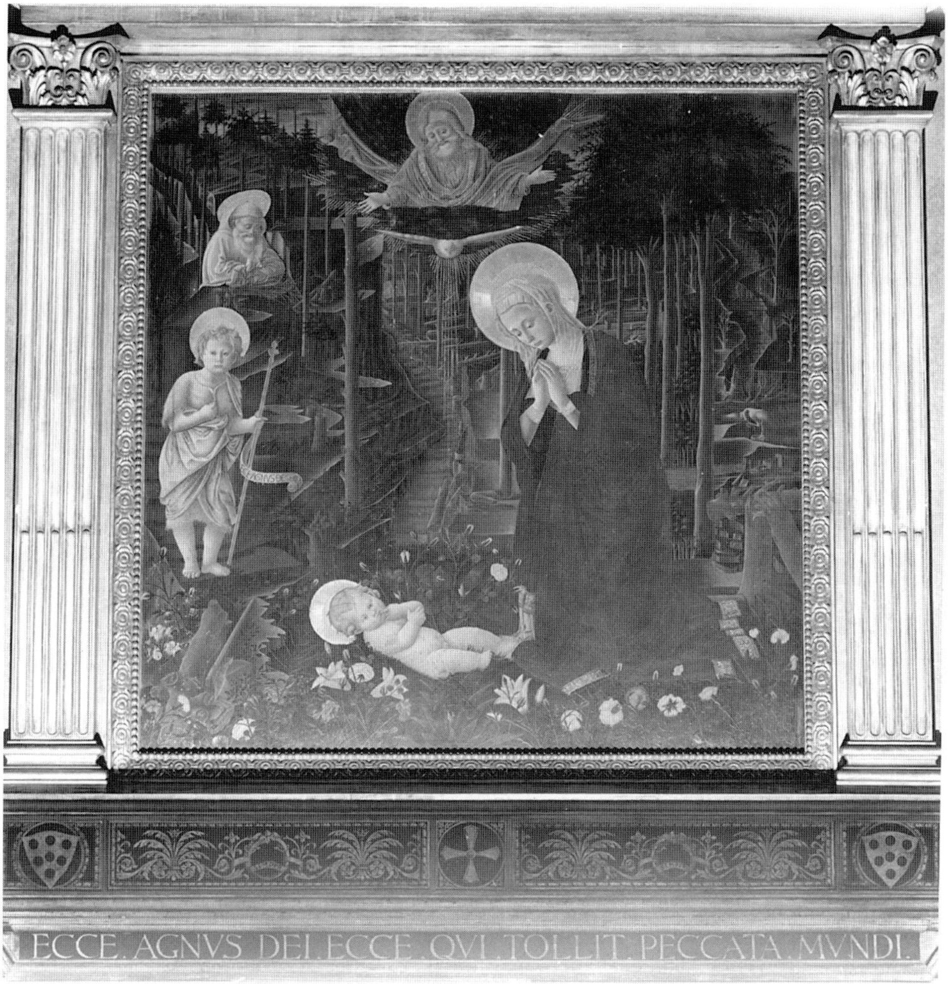

11. Lippi and Pesellino Imitator, *Adoration of the Christ Child*, c. 1460–80. On panel. Florence, Palazzo Medici-Riccardi chapel. Photo: Gabinetto Fotografico, Soprintendenza per i Beni Artistici e Storici, Florence.

finished product by the Lippi and Pesellino Imitator with a very detailed landscape background – has plausibly been related to Lippi's lost central panel for the triptych that the Medici presented to King Alfonso of Naples in 1458, known only in a sketch made by Lippi.[15] The Lippi and Pesellino Imitator clearly had cartoons of the principal figures in Lippi's influential *Madonna and Child with Angels* (c. 1460–65) in the Uffizi, his *Madonna and Child* in Munich (c. 1465), and his *Madonna and Child* (c. 1455) in the Rau Collection in Switzerland and may have executed close copies of these three paintings that included the original backgrounds.[16] Furthermore, a painting of the *Madonna and Child with Two Angels* by the Lippi and Pesellino Imitator in Philadelphia may be a close copy of a lost work by Lippi.[17]

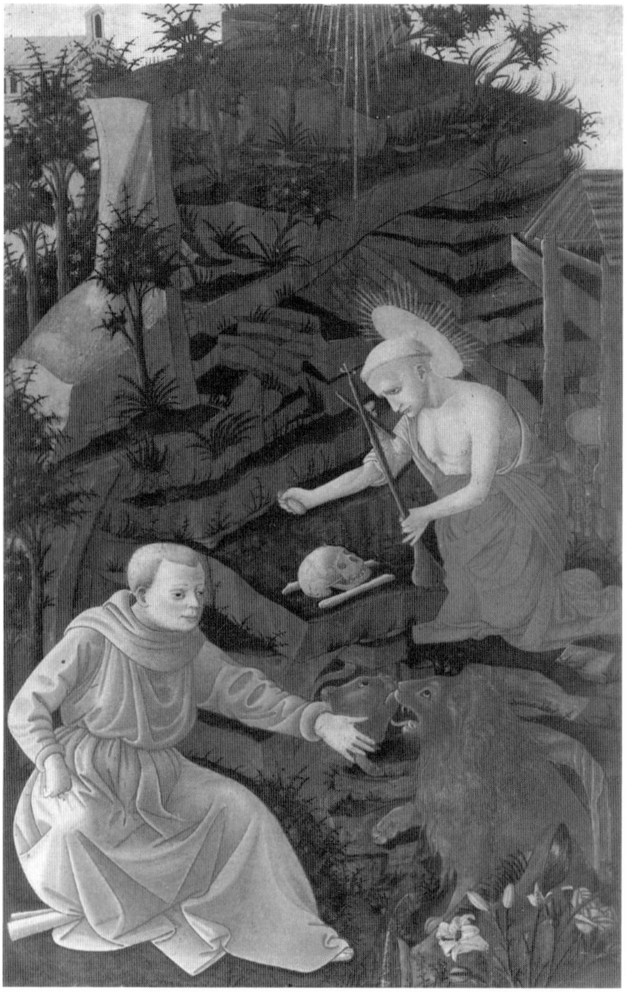

12. Lippi and Pesellino Imitator, *Saint Jerome in the Wilderness*, c. 1460–80. On panel. Bergamo, Accademia Carrara. Photo: Accademia Carrara.

The question of the dating of these precise copies by the Lippi and Pesellino Imitator is a crucial one. It is, however, a problem that may only be resolved tentatively, on the basis of stylistic comparison with the later works by the bottega that reproduce motifs from Filippino Lippi's paintings dating from the 1480s and 1490s. If these copies date from the earlier decades of this bottega's activity – the 1460s and early 1470s, as I believe – then they are of particular interest.[18] The practice of making precise copies of paintings was not standard yet at this time in Tuscany.[19] When it did occur, it was usually in connection with cult images such as the *Annunciation* fresco at SS. Annunziata, with the expectation that the

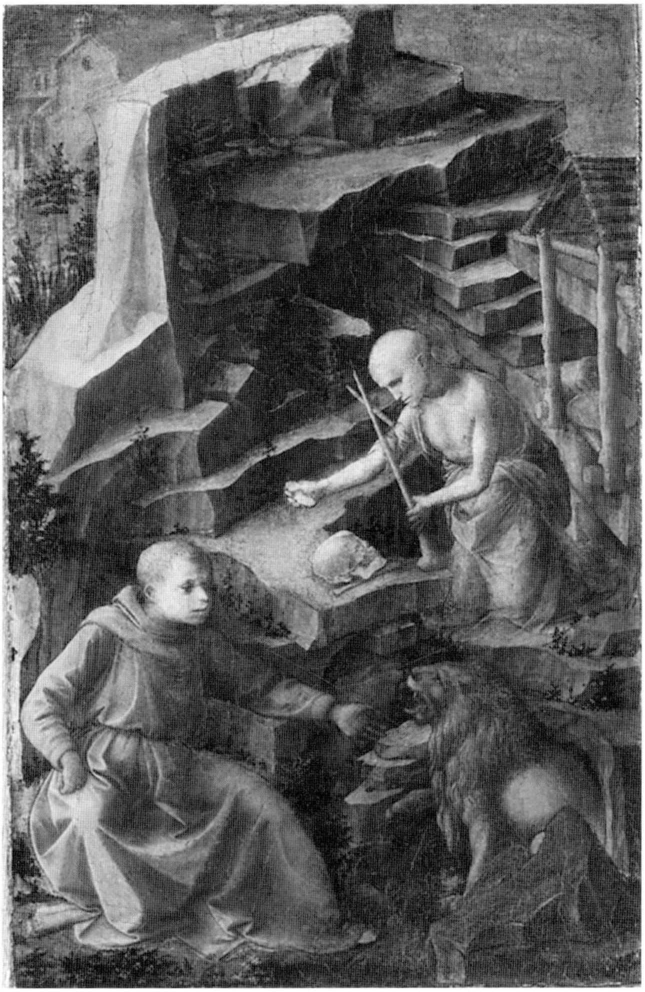

13. Filippo Lippi, *Saint Jerome in the Wilderness*, c. 1455. On panel. Altenburg, Staaliches Lindenau-Museum. Photo: Lindenau-Museum.

copy would tap the extraordinary power of the original.[20] Copies were also made of paintings with important civic associations, such as Giovanni di Paolo's copy of 1449 of Ambrogio Lorenzetti's altarpiece painted 100 years earlier for a side altar in the Siena Cathedral.[21] Copies were also produced when there were ties between the patrons or institutions associated with the related paintings.[22] In all of these cases, however, the degree of fidelity of the copy to the original was far below that found in the Lippi and Pesellino Imitator's copies of Lippi's works. Even when contracts specifically called for paintings to be made in the manner of other works, in what has come to be called the "*modo et forma* clause" in a contract, the clause seems to

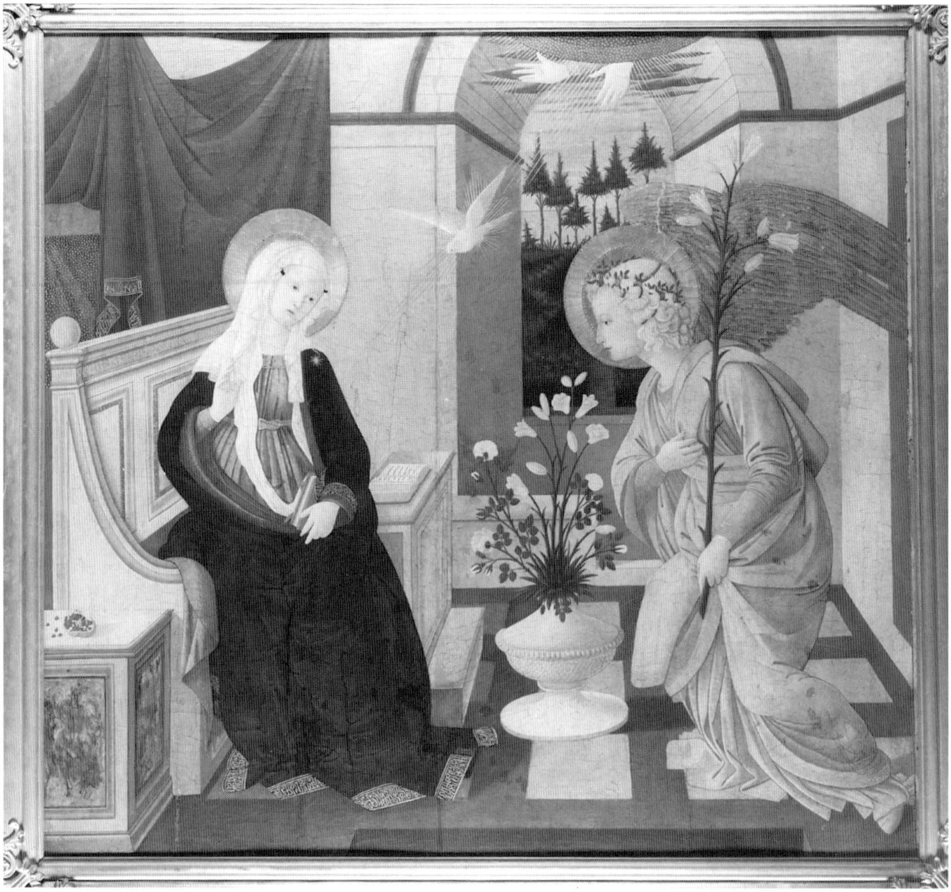

14. Lippi and Pesellino Imitator, *Annunciation*, c. 1460–80. On panel. Berlin, Staatliche Museen Preussischer Kulturbesitz, Gemäldegalerie. Photo: Staatliche Museen.

have referred to material components, such as the framing and the use of gold, that were directly tied to financial considerations, rather than to the pictorial content of the paintings.[23] In those very rare cases when the subject matter or pictorial features are singled out in contracts, the new paintings do not reflect their models with the degree of precision found between the Lippi and Pesellino Imitator's copies and the original paintings by Lippi.[24] Michelle O'Malley, in her work on artists' contracts in the quattrocento, identifies the term for this more standard kind of reproduction as a *similitudine,* made *in modo et forma* or *secondo* a designated prototype.[25] The copying practice followed by the Lippi and Pesellino Imitator, on the other hand, is probably closer to the term *retrahere,* meaning 'to draw again', with its implied manual application. *Retrahere* is the term used by Cennino Cennini in his *Libro dell'arte* (c. 1394–1437) in a section devoted to copying, and it is also found in early-sixteenth-century documents, when this kind of precise replication was more

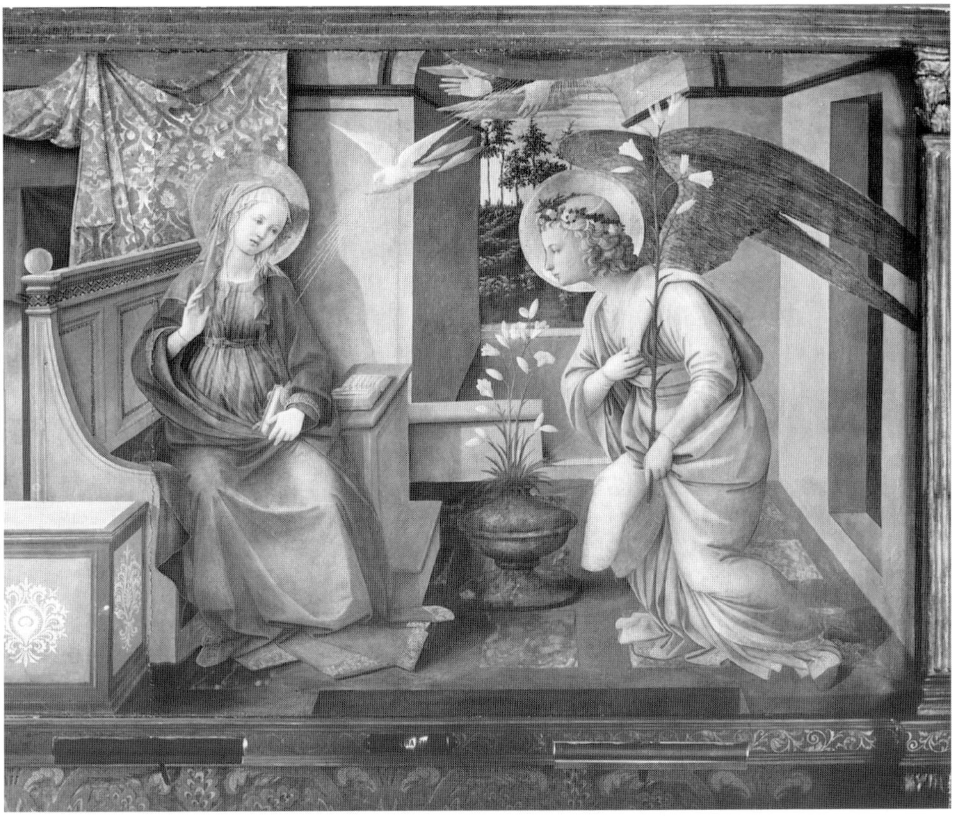

15. Filippo Lippi, *Annunciation*, c. 1445–50. On panel. Rome, Palazzo Doria Pamphili. Photo: Alinari/Art Resource, NY.

common. The most well-known example where the term *retrahere* was used in a contract occurred in 1508 when a second version of Leonardo da Vinci's *Madonna of the Rocks* was commissioned from the artist.[26]

The unusual production of the Lippi and Pesellino Imitator's precise copies after works by Lippi requires some sort of explanation. One causal factor may well have been the Medici family connection with a number of Lippi's original paintings that were copied.[27] Lippi's *Saint Jerome in the Wilderness* (Fig. 13) has been associated with a panel described in the Medici inventory of 1492; nothing, however, is known about the early history of the copy after it (Fig. 12).[28] As mentioned earlier, the *Virgin and Child with Angels* (Fig. 16) by the Lippi and Pesellino Imitator in Cleveland is considered to be a copy of Lippi's lost central panel of the triptych that the Medici sent to Alfonso of Naples in 1458. In the case of the copy (Fig. 11) of Lippi's Medici Palace chapel altarpiece (Fig. 10), the derivative work is documented in the Benedictine nunnery Sant'Apollonia in the late nineteenth century.[29] In speculating that the work may have been commissioned for the nunnery, Beatrice Paolozzi

Strozzi has attempted to tie the iconography to the concerns of the nunnery in the quattrocento.[30] I can add to her study the information that the nunnery, in fact, had a close Medici connection by the early 1470s. Maria, the natural daughter of Piero di Cosimo de' Medici, and, in due time, the mother of Cardinal Luigi de' Rossi, about whom little is known, lived in Sant'Apollonia as a boarder by at least July 1470. She remained there through March 1473 when she moved to the nunnery Le Murate, shortly before her marriage to Lionetto de' Rossi. Her half-brother, Lorenzo de' Medici, paid her annual boarding fee at Sant'Apollonia, as noted in one of the nunnery account books.[31] The attractive hypothesis would be that during Maria's stay at Sant'Apollonia, a copy of the family palace chapel altarpiece was presented to the nunnery. Because evidence confirming that the altarpiece was in Sant'Apollonia in the fifteenth century is still lacking, a more cautious position would be that a Medici family member, friend, or ally requested that these Medici paintings be copied and that this reflects the way that art was increasingly coming to play a role within the complex workings of quattrocento Florentine patronage. We can see this process at work, at the level of interregional cultural politics, in the case of Lippi's triptych that the Medici presented to Alfonso of Naples in 1458. This exchange of a rare and accomplished Florentine artistic performance in the political negotiations between two Italian states was so effective for the Medici that they received a request from a Neapolitan nobleman for a copy. The text of the letter that Giovanni de' Medici sent to his agent in Naples regarding this copy reads as follows: "If the lord Count of Ariano wants another (*un altra*), when you come back [i.e., to Florence from Naples] you can take the drawing (*il disegno*) and see to it. And if he [i.e., the Count of Ariano] is not in a hurry, I think he will get it, especially now that Fra Filippo has gone back to Prato."[32] This reference to a drawing is intriguing. It would appear that a drawing related to the triptych that had been sent off to Naples existed and that the drawing was in the possession of the Medici – assumedly something more detailed and finished than the hasty sketch that Lippi penned in a letter that the Medici preserved among their correspondence. With this request for a copy of Lippi's altarpiece, the drawing was to be used to generate the copy from within Fra Filippo Lippi's own workshop in Prato. If this copy was ever executed by Lippi, there remains no trace of it, although it is compelling to connect the panel in Cleveland by the Lippi and Pesellino Imitator (Fig. 16) with the commission.

These copies of paintings by Lippi owned or commissioned by the Medici would have functioned with reference to their Medici prototypes. They would have generated Medici signifiers within the new settings and cultural sites where they were displayed, inscribing the panels, and the devotion directed toward them, within the spheres of Medici clientage and alliance. The possession and display of a copy of a Medici painting may have functioned as a pointed demonstration of emulation,

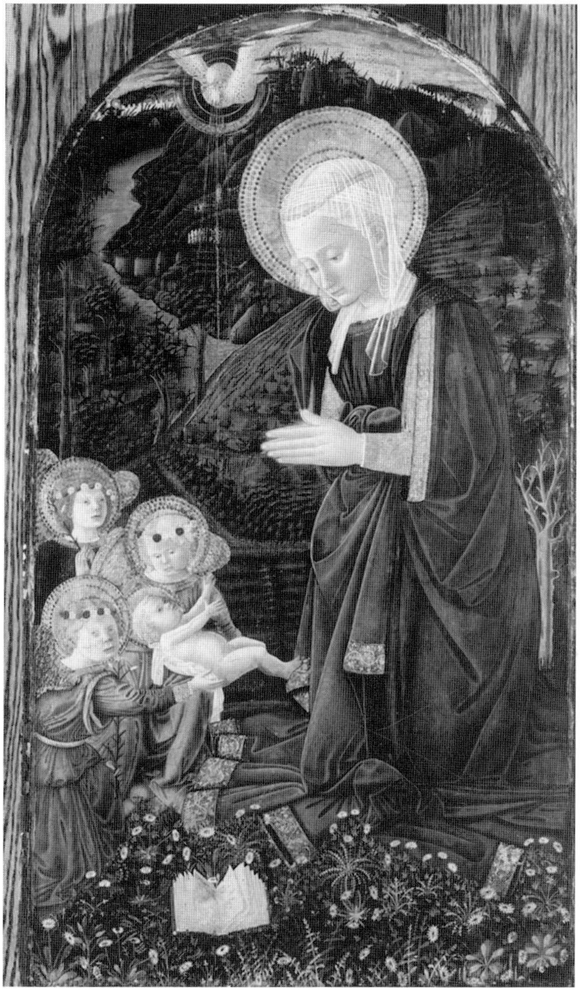

16. Lippi and Pesellino Imitator, *Virgin and Child with Angels*, c. 1406–69. Tempera and gold on panel. Cleveland, The Cleveland Museum of Art, Holden Collection. Photo: © The Cleveland Museum of Art.

allegiance, or friendship (*amicizia*), akin to naming offspring "Cosimo" and "Damiano," the insertion of Medici portraits or patron saints into painted altarpieces, or the celebration of memorial masses for Cosimo de' Medici at a family altar. In turn, the circulation of these reproductions by the Lippi and Pesellino Imitator within patrician society would have reflected back on the originals, endowing them with greater authority as taste-defining, standard-setting, and referential paintings.[33] Another contemporary example of copies being made of paintings that belonged to the Medici, can be seen in the case of Antonio Pollaiuolo's small panels in the Uffizi considered to be reproductions of his lost monumental *Labors of Hercules* (1459) in the Medici Palace.

These copies of Lippi's paintings made for the Medici family by the Lippi and Pesellino Imitator also negotiated prevailing notions about authenticity and mastery in art. They are clearly not in Lippi's own hand – 'in sua proprio mano' – and the possession of Lippi's authorial signature could thus have been perceived as a Medici privilege.[34] But the copies did guarantee their owners the highly valued authentic *invenzioni* of Lippi, translated so faithfully in these cartoon-generated replicas. They mark an increasingly more refined appreciation, on behalf of the patronizing class, for the artist's inspired *invenzioni* as distinct from the devotional function and religious content of the paintings. These copies represent a notable point along a trajectory that begins with the assimilative copying practices of artists like Giovanni di Paolo and Neri di Bicci in the 1440s through the 1470s, where features from earlier and admired paintings were consciously deployed.[35] This trajectory will then lead to the studied *imitazione* and emulation manifest in the art of the early sixteenth century, which was to become one of the characteristic features associated with mannerism. What was being reproduced in these paintings by the Lippi and Pesellino Imitator was the composition in its entirety (*invenzione*) – the subject matter (*materia*) as configured in a particularly compelling way (*forma, istoria*) by a celebrated artist associated with the Medici family. This kind of copy of 'illustrious paintings' was increasingly sought after during the final quarter of the quattrocento and in the following century.[36]

Marian Images: *Colmi da Camera* and Tondi

Alongside these up-market precise copies, the bottega of the Lippi and Pesellino Imitator specialized in devotional images often intended for domestic use, known as *colmi da camera* (or *tabernacoli*) and tondi, representing the Madonna and Child, derived from paintings by Lippi and Pesellino.[37] Lippi's Medici chapel altarpiece was the most frequently utilized model for these devotional images (see Table 1A).[38] It is possible that a set of working cartoons was originally generated in the production of the precise copy and was then used subsequently in the manufacture of a great number of variants designed to accommodate different budgets and tastes. The shop produced an abbreviated version of the Medici Palace chapel Virgin and Child with the original landscape background included (Fig. 17). Alternatively, the Madonna and Child could be displayed against an elaborate rose hedge (Fig. 18). This feature – inspired by Pesellino's *Madonna and Child with Angels* in Toledo – was generated with the aid of cartoons and built up in relief with layers of thick red and green pigment, apparently a specialty of the bottega. There were also versions of Lippi's Medici Palace chapel *Madonna and Child* with a tooled gold background and a blue ground adorned with gilded rays (Fig. 19). The composition also appears in two tondi.[39]

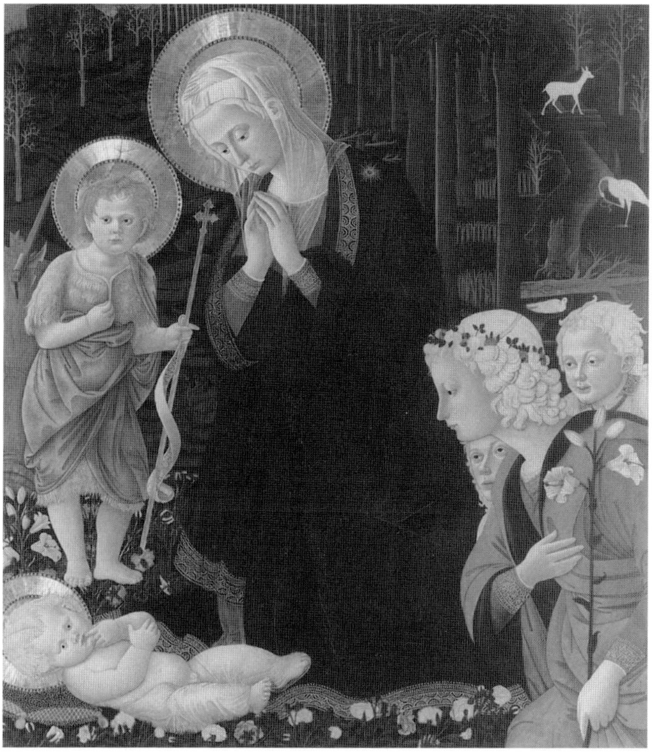

17. Lippi and Pesellino Imitator, *Virgin Adoring the Christ Child with Infant St. John and the Three Angels*, c. 1460–80. Tempera on panel. Bloomington, Indiana, Indiana University Art Museum: Given in Memory of Marguerite Lilly Noyes. Photo: © 2001 Indiana University Art Museum; photographed by Michael Cavanagh and Kevin Montague.

Cartoons derived from Lippi's Medici Palace chapel altarpiece were also mixed and matched with motifs from other works by Lippi and Pesellino. The shop had in its repertory cartoons reproducing figures found in four paintings by Pesellino and at least nine works by Lippi – including both a scale and a reduced version of the Madonna from the Medici Palace chapel altarpiece (see Table 1A and 1B). A panel now in Bloomington, Indiana (Fig. 17) depicting an abbreviated version of the Medici Palace chapel altarpiece, embellishes the core composition with two angels taken from Pesellino's *Madonna and Child with Angels* (Fig. 9) in Toledo and Lippi's *Annunciation* in the Galleria Doria Pamphilj in Rome.[40] The most eclectic assemblage is found in a panel (Fig. 21) that features the Madonna and Child from Pesellino's *Madonna and Child* in the Isabella Stewart Gardner Museum in Boston, attended by three figures from Lippi's Medici Palace chapel altarpiece (God the Father, the Baptist, and St. Bernard), three figures from Pesellino's *Madonna and Child with Angels* in Toledo, and the face of the Angel Gabriel in reverse from Lippi's Doria Pamphilj *Annunciation* in Rome.[41] Some of the Madonna panels composed of simpler

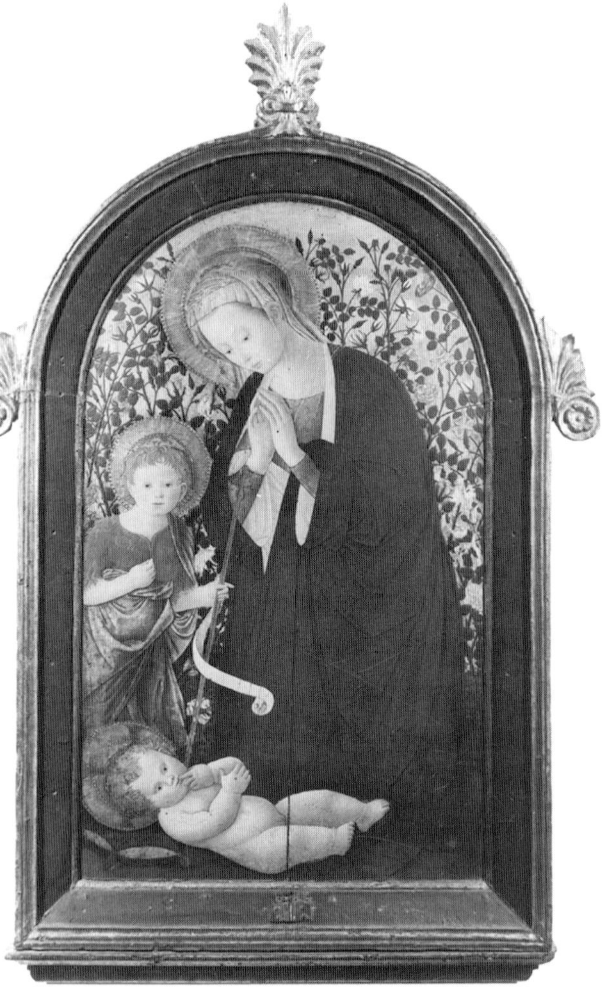

18. Lippi and Pesellino Imitator, *Madonna and Child*, c. 1460–80. On panel. Florence, Museo Bardini. Photo: Gabinetto Fotografico, Soprintendenza per i Beni Artistici e Storici, Florence.

figure groupings were executed in series.[42] In producing for the *colmo* market, this bottega utilized Pesellino's Madonna and Child compositions just as readily as it did those of Lippi (see Table 1A and 1B).

Although no surviving pounced drawings can be associated with the paintings from the bottega of the Lippi and Pesellino Imitator, the examination of a number of these panels with infrared reflectography has revealed traces of *spolvero* beneath the underdrawing in the individual figures.[43] Further evidence in support of this shop's use of cartoons is provided by mylar tracings taken from a number of the panels.[44] When the traced outlines of corresponding figures found in different paintings by the Lippi and Pesellino Imitator are superimposed, they line up with

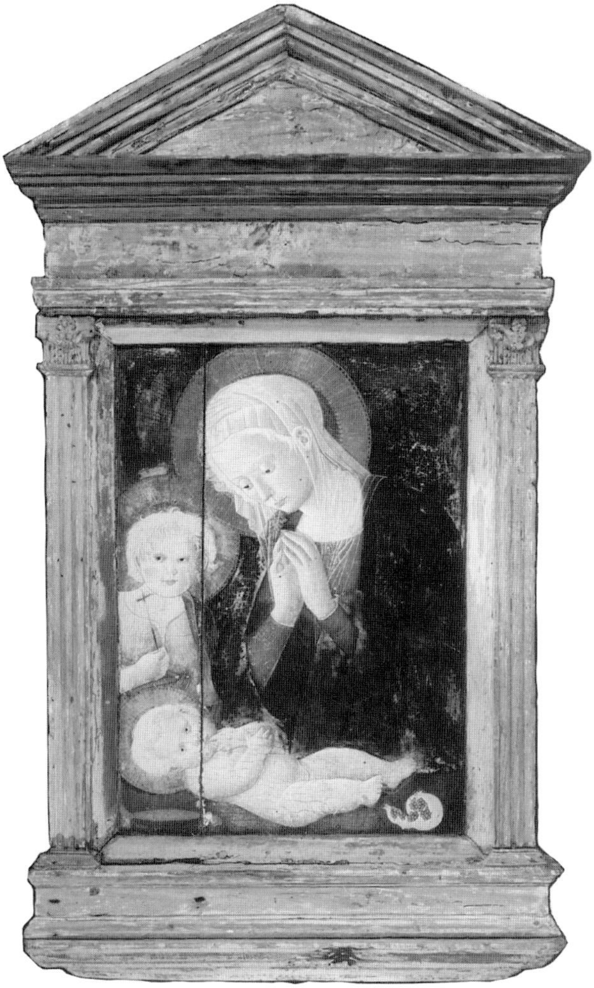

19. Lippi and Pesellino Imitator (Pier Francesco Fiorentino), *Madonna and Child with the Young Saint John*, c. 1455–95. On panel. New Haven, Yale University Art Gallery. Photo: Yale University Art Gallery.

remarkable precision, demonstrating nearly identical contours (Fig. 20).[45] This type of full figure cartoon that the Lippi and Pesellino Imitator relied upon to create these pictorial pastiches came into use only in the 1430s. Prior to this time, since the 1340s, cartoons had been employed primarily to reproduce repetitive ornamental patterns and to execute the more complicated features of the body like heads and hands, and were utilized both in the design process and as a stock of workshop patterns.[46] The cartoons used by the bottega of the Lippi and Pesellino Imitator were probably of the type known as 'substitute cartoons,' generated from a primary cartoon or, as I argue later, from a pounced tracing taken from the actual paintings by Lippi. In this way the valuable sheet preserving the original design would not

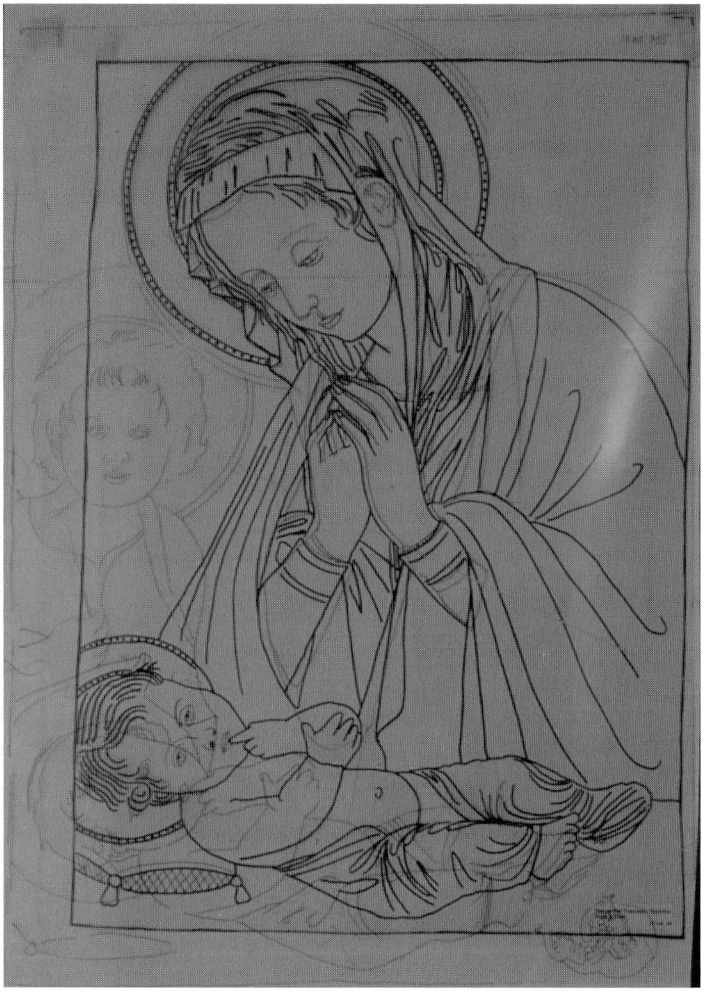

20. Superimposed mylar tracings of two paintings by the Lippi and Pesellino Imitator: *Madonna and Child with the Young Saint John* (Fig. 19) in the Yale University Art Gallery and the *Madonna and Child* in the Philadelphia Museum of Art. Mylar trancings made by Anne O'Connor (Yale University Art Gallery) and Teresa Lignelli (Philadelphia Museum of Art).

suffer from the wear and tear of repeated use (which involved the messy process of rubbing charcoal dust through the perforations when transferring the design onto the panel).[47]

Martin Kemp has used the term 'component pictures' to describe a group of paintings produced in the ambient of Leonardo da Vinci in the first decade of the sixteenth century, where the compositions are pieced together out of features derived from the paintings and drawings of Leonardo (heads, limbs, drapery configurations, poses).[48] He relates this studio practice to Leonardo's own mode of formal composition influenced by Alberti's pictorial grammar of surfaces, members,

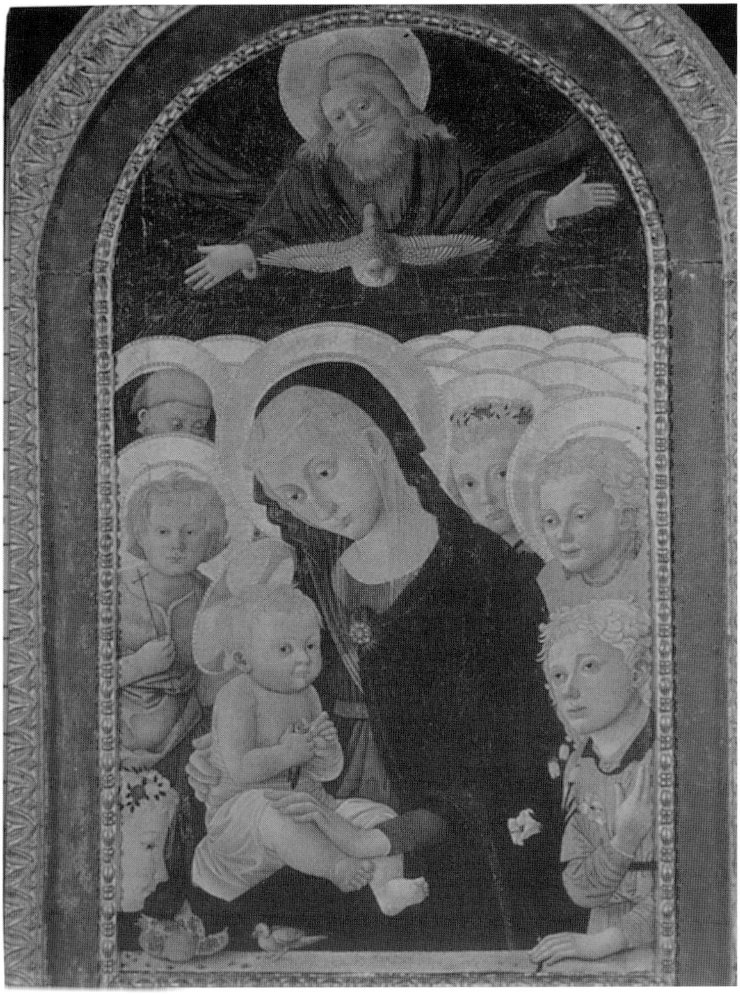

21. Lippi and Pesellino Imitator, *Madonna and Child with Angels and Saints,* c. 1460–80, current location unknown (sold at Sotheby, July 3, 1963, lot. 18). Photo: Author.

bodies, and *istoria.* While the formal syntax of the Lippi and Pesellino Imitator would seem to be of a somewhat different sort, more directly conditioned by market considerations and the reproductive technology utilized, the paintings, too, are composed out of interchangeable component parts.[49] The representational space is conceived in terms of the background (*campo*) and the figures (*figure*), treated as separate units with little attempt to establish a setting through spatial integration. There were four types of backgrounds on offer: landscape, floral, goldleaf, and blue. The elaborately rendered landscapes were probably at the high end of the price list, and the versions with the less expensive blue pigment azurite must have been the cheapest. The works with the rose hedge and with the tooled gold-leaf ground probably represented a middle price range, which accommodated both a taste for the tangible manifestations of the artist's representational skill and the preference for the conspicuous display of expensive materials. The figures in the Lippi and Pesellino Imitator's component pictures are not constructed out of the recombinable body parts that Kemp noted in the Leonardo derivatives, but out of contractible cartoon designs. These cartoon-generated figures could be reproduced in their entirety or truncated down to the essential facial component, according to compositional need. The principal Madonna and Child grouping were available in a range of sizes and poses, with the Madonna shown kneeling or in half length. The Madonna and Child could appear alone, or with attendant figures – the young Baptist, angels, and the rare saint. These secondary figures are cleverly inserted into the interstitial spaces of the paintings and seem to constitute embellishments, added extras, not so much to further elaborate the religious content of the panels as to provide figural ornament around the Madonna and Child.[50] The regularity with which the young Baptist (San Giovannino) appears suggests a particular Florentine devotional protocol associated with these *colmi* and tondi, given the importance of the Baptist in Florentine religious and civic life.

There were standard sizes and framing formats for these Madonna panels produced by the Lippi and Pesellino Imitator, and, one assumes, a corresponding price range.[51] The framing options ranged from the arched molding adorned with scrolls and palmettes with a base below (Fig. 18), to the *alla'antica* variant (Fig. 8) in which a rectangular panel was flanked by fluted pilasters or engaged columns supporting an entablature and gable. There was also the tondo with carved rosettes adorning the frame. There were richly ornamented and simpler versions of each framing format. It is probable that paintings were both made to specification and also purchased from a selection of available stock. The products could be further customized, or personalized, by including the patron's coat of arms on the frame.[52]

The variations in the paintings produced by the Lippi and Pesellino Imitator in size, framing configuration, figure number and pose, background decoration, and the degree of customization constituted what the historian of Chinese art Lothar Ledderose calls a 'system of grades'. These evident grades of distinction in the formal features of similar products, linked to cost variation, patronal rank, and a range of cultural values, would have attracted a larger pool of buyers and ultimately functioned to define and differentiate the social status and tastes of the consumers who displayed these *colmi da camera* and tondi in their homes.[53] The Madonna images would have been prominent features in the relatively sparsely decorated domestic spaces where they were hung – in the bedrooms and antechambers of urban dwellings. The clients of the Lippi and Pesellino Imitator were probably patricians and upwardly mobile artisans.[54] For those who had a vested interest in defining themselves in relation to Florence's dominant family, the Medici, the availability of pictorial stock that reproduced motifs from Medici paintings by Filippo Lippi would have been an attractive feature of the particular 'system of grades' within which the Lippi and Pesellino Imitator's bottega operated. Other features within the framed paintings, however, could have worked toward social differentiation, such as the coat of arms defining specific lineage interests or a dense accumulation of secondary figures denoting the personal spending power of the consumer. For other purchasers of these works, however, the Medici links could well have been irrelevant, with satisfaction derived from the possession and display of the graded product and its use in private devotion.

The *colmi da camera* produced by the Lippi and Pesellino Imitator represented a new version of a product that had been available on the market since the 1430s: the relatively inexpensive mechanically reproduced Madonna and Child image, cast in terra cotta, gesso, and *carta pesta* (papier-mâché), and then polychromed and gilded.[55] The use of cartoons by this bottega facilitated an efficient, mechanical means of producing the painted compositions. The output of the Lippi and Pesellino Imitator is unprecedented in contemporary Italian panel painting. There are forty-four panels by the Lippi and Pesellino Imitator that reproduce the Madonna and Child from Filippo Lippi's Medici Palace chapel altarpiece and another ten that include the Virgin in combination with figures from another Lippi altarpiece (see Table 1A). Pesellino's Gardner *Madonna and Child* appears in thirty-eight copies and variants (Fig. 21; see Table 1B).[56] Both guild regulations, which restricted the number of apprentices in a shop, and the somewhat time-consuming tempera-on-panel technique, kept the volume of production down. The great number of these Madonna panels attests to two contemporary developments. There was a growing demand in Florence among the middle and upper ranks of society for painted and sculpted Marian images during the second half of the fifteenth century, which can be documented in other Italian cities and in northern Europe. The Lippi and Pesellino Imitator's Madonna output can be compared with that of Neri di Bicci in Florence,[57] Sano di Pietro and Matteo di Giovanni in Siena, Giovanni Bellini and Cima da Conegliano in Venice, and Gerard David in Bruges. In the workshops of Bellini, Cima, and David, cartoons were also used.[58] This intense Madonna production, tied to the pivotal role of the Virgin within religious devotion, also conformed with a pattern of increased demand for, and production of, consumer goods during the period, which has been noted by the economic historian Richard Goldthwaite.[59] A second significant development to consider is the greater valuation placed on painting as an art form in Florence over the course of the quattrocento. Painted Madonna panels seem to have been potentially more expensive to produce then painted gesso images, on account of the more costly wooden support and the time involved in the panel preparation and in designing the image.[60] The Lippi and Pesellino Imitator must have been responding to a demand for the flat painted Madonna (*Madonna dipinta in piano,* as distinguished in fifteenth-century documents) as he devised a competitive product at the lower end of the *colmo* market. This is verified by the marked increase in the volume of flat painted Madonna images produced during the final quarter of the century, prior to the adoption of the more economical canvas support in the following century.

The enterprise of the Lippi and Pesellino Imitator should also be considered in relation to other notable advances in the technology (and profitability) of mechanical reproduction at the time, with an increased aesthetic refinement in the products: in the printing of texts, in woodcut and metal plate prints, in metal casting, in della Robbia glazed terracotta series, and in textile manufacture where complex figural scenes could be multiplied on the loom. This cultural phenomenon of replication and component composition presupposed the authority and abstract conceptualization of the prototype being reproduced – whether it be the human body, a drapery study by Leonardo, or an *invenzione* of Filippo Lippi. Replication and component composition also involved an engagement with the formal integrity and structural makeup of the prototype, and a consequent schematization of the original composition. This kind of reproduction was concurrent with what is known as 'eclectic imitation' in literature and should be viewed in relation, rather than in opposition, to the humanist enterprise and to progressive developments within the visual arts.[61]

The more inventive painters of the next generation, like Botticelli and Ghirlandaio, with well-organized shops and acute business acumen, began to produce copies and variants of their own Madonna panels during the 1480s and 1490s. Botticelli's *Madonna of the Magnificat* in the Uffizi is known in five other versions – one of them on a reduced scale, while Ghirlandaio's *Madonna and Child with Angels* in the Louvre exists in at least six close copies associated directly with his shop and over sixteen variants.[62] These copies are considered to have been generated from within Botticelli and Ghirlandaio's own workshops, and, in contrast to the copies and pastiches of Lippi's paintings that had come out of the bottega of the Lippi and Pesellino Imitator a decade earlier, in these the *invenzioni* were rendered closer to the *maniera* of the acclaimed masters – in response to the growing appreciation of the aesthetic and representational qualities of pictorial style.

The Translation of the 'Lippi Effect'

The sophistication of the reproductive technology is impressive, and the technical quality of the paintings by the Lippi and Pesellino Imitator is competent, even if Van Marle lamented over the 'unsuccessful and vulgar imitation of that gutter-snipe type' of Lippi's.[63] Rather than dwell with what has been lost in the translation from the Lippi originals to the copies and pastiches of the Lippi and Pesellino Imitator, as is the usual practice in the assessment of these works, I would like to consider what, in fact, was gained.

The paintings by the Lippi and Pesellino Imitator negotiate a striking characteristic of Lippi's work – what I will call the 'Lippi effect' – also found in the paintings of Pesellino who was considerably influenced by Lippi. This is the tension that Lippi set up between the accessibility of his sacred protagonists, and pictorial devices that function to distance these same figures and resecure them within a sacred hierarchy. Fra Filippo deftly and boldly configured a Virgin who was daringly accessible and intimate, yet endowed with a refined beauty (*bellezza*), grace (*grazia*), and luminosity that placed her beyond the realm of lived experience. The Christ Child and youthful angels may serve as foils to the Virgin, exhibiting greater action within the scene and interaction with the viewer. The devotee is encouraged to imagine the Christ Child in terms of human infancy – with a baby's gestures, sounds, and needs – in the tradition of popular devotional literature and *laude*. In Lippi's paintings, however, there is usually some kind of physical barrier established within the pictorial space to counter the illusion of such extraordinary intimacy and familiarity. This kind of sacred and profane imaging of the Virgin and Child had a precedent in Latin and vernacular poetry and *laude*. It took the friar-painter Lippi, however, with the Carmelites' special relationship to the Virgin and rich experiences within the cloister and the secular world, to stabilize a visual image that gave full form to the human dimensions and qualities of these figures, while preserving their sacred auras.

Like Lippi, the artists in the bottega organized by the Lippi and Pesellino Imitator placed the sacred figures close to the picture plane (Fig. 21), making them intimately accessible to the viewer in the context of private devotion, and provided eye contact between the painted protagonists and the devotee. The distancing mechanisms evident in Lippi's work, however, tend to be eschewed in favor of greater visual and psychological access. The pastiche cut-and-paste mode of composing, the cartoon-medium of transfer, the practice of incising the drapery contours, and the economical application of pigment gave rise to a linear, flat quality in the paintings, with little modeling within broad color fields. As a result, the representational markings in line and color call attention to the surface of the panel, and this in turn contributes to the impression that the sacred figures are at the very threshold of the picture plane. In addition, the assemblage and fragmentation of figures taken from different paintings by Pesellino and Lippi enhance the arbitrary look of the depicted scene, as if the sacred figures had been caught and frozen in an instant of time and presented for the personalized viewing of the individual spectator. This heightened intimacy, particularly in the case of the pastiches derived from Lippi's Medici Palace chapel altarpiece (Figs. 17–19) in which the Virgin is shown in a devotional posture, with her hands together, makes the Virgin an irresistible protagonist for the viewer. She is an active intercessor, the virtual embodiment of the prayer 'Ora pro nobis!' ('Pray for us'), which was sometimes painted on the frames of Madonna images. While the Florentines who owned these *colmi* and tondi may not have had the benefit of the full 'Lippi effect' dependent on the refined aesthetic qualities found in Lippi's Madonna images or the experience of awe and reverence inspired by Lippi's evocation of sacred splendor and beauty, they did have a compelling visualization of their personal investment in Marian intercession.

The Identity of the Lippi and Pesellino Imitator and His Access to the Cartoons

Some have speculated that the Lippi and Pesellino Imitator was a close associate or a member of Pesellino's and Lippi's workshops, who may even have obtained original cartoons from these masters. Piero di Lorenzo di Pratese has plausibly been suggested.[64] He is documented collaborating with Lippi in 1440 and possibly again in 1447 and was a partner of Pesellino's from 1453 until the latter died in 1457. He himself died in 1487, and while this date falls short of the termination of the bottega's activity, it may represent a point at which the direction passed on to another master.[65] The collaborative partnership of Piero di Lorenzo di Pratese with Pesellino makes this artist a particularly compelling candidate, given that Pesellino used full-figure cartoons in his painting production to transfer his drawings onto panel.[66] If this identification is correct, then it may be possible that some of the earlier copies of Pesellino's Madonna and Child paintings were made when Piero di Lorenzo di Pratese was Pesellino's partner.[67]

While some of the cartoons that the Lippi and Pesellino Imitator used could have been inherited from Pesellino, this would seem not to have been the case regarding the cartoons related to Filippo Lippi's paintings.[68] Technical evidence suggests that Lippi did not use cartoons, except in the architectural ornament in his frescoes.[69] In addition, the Baptist figure reproduced by the Lippi and Pesellino Imitator derived from Lippi's Medici Palace chapel altarpiece (Fig. 11) follows the outlines of the figure in Lippi's finished painting (Fig. 10), and not the configuration that Lippi first set down on the panel before he modified the drapery and limbs, visible through the paint film.[70] How, then, could these cartoons related to Lippi's paintings have been obtained? It is possible that tracings were made after the original paintings by Lippi. Cennino Cennini, in his *Libro dell'arte*, provides instructions on how to trace from a panel and it was apparently the means used by Leonardo da Vinci to generate his copy of the *Madonna of the Rocks*.[71] Tracings could have been taken with Lippi's permission, while the paintings were still in his shop, or later, when they were in situ, with the consent of the owners or custodians of the paintings.[72] If this were indeed the case, then interesting issues related to the 'ownership' of Lippi's *invenzioni* and to the 'reproduction rights' – although, of course, these are anachronistic terms.

By Filippo Lippi's death, the bottega of the Lippi and Pesellino Imitator clearly possessed a rich cartoon stock that represented valuable property on which the success of the reproductive enterprise depended.[73] If the cartoons were originally obtained from tracings made when the paintings were still in Lippi's shop with his permission, one wonders whether the early copies and pastiches were executed under the supervision of Lippi or in collaboration, in the form of a short-term *compagnia*. The fact that the bottega cartoon stock was enriched and updated in the 1480s and early 1490s with ancillary figures taken from the paintings of Filippo Lippi's son Filippino suggests that there may indeed have been a close personal relationship between this shop and Fra Filippo and his son.[74] And were Medici family members involved, either directly or indirectly, in having copies made of those works by Lippi that they owned or had commissioned? Their readiness to arrange for the reproduction of Lippi's triptych for Alfonso of Naples suggests that this may indeed have been the case.

Conclusion

Walter Benjamin's essay 'The Work of Art in the Age of Mechanical Reproduction' (1936) described the loss of 'aura' experienced by the work of art through mechanical reproduction in the modern age. Benjamin perceived this process in a positive light as a democratization of visual culture through collective mass consumption and as a product of the technological changes and shifts in perception particular to the nineteenth and twentieth centuries. Even so, scholars working on mechanical forms of reproduction in earlier periods have felt compelled to respond to Benjamin by demonstrating how the copy too could possess aura.[75] Indeed, one can reasonably argue that the paintings by the Lippi and Pesellino Imitator had the potential to inspire the awe and reverence associated with aura – understood both in Benjamin's and in fifteenth-century Florentine terms. These paintings could, in specific contexts, transmit the charismatic power associated with the sacred, with the Medici family, with the acclaimed painter Lippi, with transportative aesthetic experiences, and with luxury consumption.[76] Lippi's original paintings, by virtue of their important role within Medici cultural hegemony, their highly valued aesthetic properties, and the greater distancing of the sacred subjects represented, may have been more privy to this aura than those of the Lippi and Pesellino Imitator – but this may be an elitist position. Aura may have been perceived in a different way within the patrician and artisanal homes where most of the paintings by the Lippi and Pesellino Imitator were displayed than within the Medici Palace, and furthermore, the innovative reproductive technology itself may well have inspired wonder.

By approaching the copying enterprise of the Lippi and Pesellino Imitator as a process of cultural translation, with an emphasis on the recontextualization of the copy and on the hybridity of its formal composition, the terms of the discussion shift. The question of 'aura', while still relevant, is no longer the central concern.[77] In the process of translation, the *invenzioni* and motifs of Filippo Lippi and Francesco Pesellino were commodified for an expanding market, packaged within a variety of products that catered to a range of consumers. The copies and pastiches functioned in complex ways within many different but interrelated cultural registers. They were accessible devotional aids, signifiers of Medicean partisanship, admired artistic *invenzioni,* commodities exchanged in the marketplace, and the material trappings of religious and domestic spaces. They were also implicated in a process of identity formation, functioning as markers of a shared religious culture, but also of subtle grades of social, economic, and cultural differentiation within the heterogeneous urban community.

During the sixteenth century, there was a notable increase in the production of painted replicas – Madonnas for the home, copies of acclaimed paintings by celebrated artists and portraits of high-ranking or 'illustrious' subjects, which were becoming significant terms within the display culture and in the gift-giving economy within European courts. There was also a new delight in utilizing formal quotations from classical and more recent sources within paintings. Visual imagery became more reflexive and interreferential. Praise-worthy *imitazione* and emulation were considered to require inventiveness and imagination in the deployment of the copied motifs that now functioned as 'quotations' or 'references' within a more complex syntactical structure. The kind of copying that had been practiced by the Lippi and Pesellino Imitator was condemned as mechanical and unimaginative by critics such as Anton Francesco Doni 'because it makes the practice of the hand lazy or delays the eye's true judgment (*il vero giudicio dell'occhio*).'[78] The perception of the model-copy relationship became caught up in conflicting notions about the status, value, and utility of the work of art as an aesthetic, performative, and manufactured product and the nature and profitability of the production method.

NOTES

1. 'Questa non si copia come si fa le lettere, che tanto vale la copia quanto l'orrigine. Questa non s'inpronta come si fa la scultura, della quale tal è la impressa qual è la origine, in quanto alla virtù de l'opera. Questa non fa infiniti figlioli come fa li libri stampati; questa sola si resta nobile, questa sola onora il suo autore, e resta preziosa e unica, e non partorisce mai figlioli equali a sé' (c. 1500–5; in Paola Barocchi, ed., *Scritti d'arte del cinquecento,* vol. I (Milan-Naples: Ricciardi, 1971), 74.

2. In the 167 paintings studied, I have been unable to identify the sources of only sixteen of the sixty-eight figure types used (see Table 1).

3. 'The Pseudo Pier Francesco Fiorentino' is a fabricated name usually attributed to Bernard Berenson, but created by F. Mason Perkins in 1928. Berenson, who had actually long resisted the

de-attribution of the group of paintings from the documented painter Pier Francesco Fiorentino (active c. 1474–97) that had been supported by Perkins, Herbert Horne, and Langton Douglas, adopted the name himself in 1932 (F. Mason Perkins, 'Nuovi appunti sulla Galleria Belle Arti di Siena', in *La Balzana* 2 [1928]: 188; Bernard Berenson, 'Quadri senza casa. Il quattrocento fiorentino, II', *Dedalo* 12 [1932]: 693). Federico Zeri proposed the more accurate name for the painter – or painters, as he argued – calling them 'Lippi and Pesellino Imitators.' See his *Italian Paintings in the Walters Art Gallery* (Baltimore: Walters Art Gallery, 1976), 80–1. See also Raimond Van Marle, *The Development of the Italian Schools of Painting*, vol. XIII (The Hague: Martinus Nijhoff, 1931), 428–64.

4. The suggestion that more than one bottega may have been involved in the production of these paintings was made by Lisa Venturini in "Modelli fortunati e produzione di serie," 147–155, *Maestri e Botteghe. Pittura a Firenze alla fine del quattrocento*, eds. Cristina Acidini Luchinat, Mina Gregori, and Antonio Paolucci, (Florence: Silvana Editoriale, 1992), 152.

5. Pesellino's *Madonna and Child with Angels* (44.34) in Toledo measures 72.4 × 54 cm. and is usually dated c. 1450–55. See *Museum News. Toledo Museum of Art*, 110 (Dec. 1945); *The Toledo Museum of Art. European Paintings* (Toledo: Toledo Museum of Art, 1976), 124–5. On the copy by the Lippi and Pesellino Imitator in storage in the Uffizi (156 × 104.5 cm, including the frame), see Luciano Bellosi, ed., *Gli Uffizi. Catalogo generale* (Florence: Centro Di, 1979), 488, n. P1486. There are two other very close copies of the full composition by the Lippi and Pesellino Imitator of Pesellino's Toledo *Madonna and Child with Angels* (Corporation Art Gallery, Glasgow [914]; Christies sale, London, May 24, 1991 [lot 39]).

6. See n. 65.

7. A tondo in the Museo Civico in Arezzo is derived from Leonardo da Vinci's *Benois Madonna*, which is usually dated to the late 1470s (Zeri, 1976, 81), while a small panel set within an *all'antica* frame, once in the Ventura collection in Florence, reproduces Antonello's *Virgin Annunciate* (c. 1472–3) in the Alte Pinakothek in Munich. See Federico Zeri, 'Un riflesso di Antonello da Messina a Firenze', *Paragone* 99 (1958): 16–21.

8. Lisa Venturini in Acidini Luchinat, Gregori and Paolucci, Maestri e Botteghe 153, 156 n. 37.

9. For the one precise copy of a work by Lippi that is not by the Lippi and Pesellino Imitator, see n. 36.

10. For the original painting for the Medici Palace chapel now in Berlin, see Ruda 447–8. On the copy attributed to the Lippi and Pesellino Imitator, see Beatrice Paolozzi Strozzi, 'Originale e copia. *L'Adorazione del Bambino* della bottega di Filippo Lippi', M. Ciatti, 'A proposito di un restauro', and Consorzio Pegasus, 'L'intervento conservativo e restaurativo', all in *I restauri nel Palazzo Medici Riccardi. Rinascimento e Barocco*, ed. Cristina Acidini Lucinat (Milan: Silvana, 1992), 32–49.

11. Strozzi published a montage made with a tracing taken from a reproduction of Lippi's Berlin *Adoration of the Child* placed on top of a reproduction of the copy. The montage demonstrated that while the figure outlines are very close in the copy, the Virgin and God the Father are shifted to the right, while the Baptist and St. Bernard are placed higher (Strozzi, 33 and 35, and fig. 26). There are also considerable differences in the floral ground and sky in the two works (34). For evidence for the use of cartoons, see n. 43.

12. The copy in Bergamo measures 47 × 30 cm. See Francesco Rossi, *Accademia Carrara. Catalogo dei dipinti sec. xv–xvi*. Bergamo: Accademia Carrara and Azienda di Promozione Turistica, 1988), 265, n. 920. The original by Lippi in Altenburg measures 46.8 × 30; I believe it was painted in the mid-1450s, while Ruda dates it to the mid-1430s (Ruda, 382–4).

13. The copy in the Staaliche Museen, Berlin (n.1065) measures 135.5 × 143 (confirmed in correspondence). Lippi's original *Annunciation* (c. 1445–50) in the Palazzo Doria Pamphilj measures 118 × 175 (Ruda, 428–9).

14. Mylar tracings of and the Virgin and Christ Child from paintings by the Lippi and Pesellino Imitator were superimposed on top of Francesco Pesellino's *Madonna and Child* in the Gardner Museum in Boston and the figure contours proved to be precisely aligned. I am still trying to test mylar tracings against Lippi's *Adoration of the Christ Child* in the Staatliche Museen in Berlin.

15. On the sketch, see Ruda 495–6. The panel in Cleveland measures 97.2 × 54.9 cm. See *The Cleveland Museum of Art. European Paintings Before 1500* (Cleveland Museum of Art, 1974), 84. These dimensions would appear to be more or less on scale with those of the lost central panel in Lippi's triptych, to judge by the measurements for the altarpiece provided by Lippi in the sketch (2 $^2/_3$ × 3 braccia, or 154 × 174 cm) – factoring in the size of the surviving original wings of the triptych (also in Cleveland and measuring 81.3 × 29.8 cm each) and the lost predella and framing elements (which could plausibly have added an additional 60 cm to the width and 57 cm to the height). See also Rudolf Hiller von Gaertringen's computations in the new catalogue of the Italian paintings in the Städel collection in Frankfurt (forthcoming).

16. 1. *Madonna and Child with Angels,* Uffizi. There is a photograph in the Berenson Fototeca at I Tatti (Settignano) of a very close copy of the whole composition including the landscape background, set within a tabernacle frame, that seems to be in the style of the Lippi and Pesellino Imitator. I have found no other trace of this painting. There are two works that reproduce the figures from Lippi's Uffizi painting: Museo di Belle Arti in Budapest; a tondo (after 1493) once in the Cook Collection in Richmond (Virginia), auctioned in 1959 in Florence (Salocchi and Faeschi), which also includes the Baptist from Filippino Lippi's Nerli altarpiece that dates from 1494. 2. *Madonna and Child,* Munich. There are four paintings that reproduce the Virgin and Child from Lippi's *Madonna and Child* (Munich, Alte Pinakothek): Venice, Ca d'Oro; Florence, Serristori Collection; Milan, Finarte sale, April 6, 1965, lot 36 (in reverse); San Paolo (Brasil), Museu de Arte (in reverse). The Virgin's head alone is reproduced in several other panels. 3. *Madonna and Child,* Rau Collection, Switzerland. There is just one work that reproduces the Virgin and Child from Lippi's painting: Sotheby sale, Monte Carlo, June 17, 1988, lot 807.

17. Philadelphia Museum of Art, Johnson Collection n. 42 (57.8 × 37.8 cm); see the entry on this painting in Carl Strehlke's catalogue of the early Italian paintings in the John G. Johnson Collection (forthcoming). The panel in Philadelphia reflects Lippi's work of c. 1445–50. See, for example, Lippi's *Madonna and Child* (c. 1445) in the National Gallery of Art in Washington and the Virgin in Lippi's *Annunciation* (c. 1445–50) in the Galleria Doria Pamphili in Rome. There are three other versions of this composition: Brooklyn Museum, New York; ex-Aubrey House, London; Sotheby sale, Nov. 30, 1983, lot 10.

18. The pictorial style evident in these precise copies appears to be consistent. I believe that these copies were made while Lippi was still alive, or shortly after his death, by the principal master responsible for the bottega and his assistants working closely under his direction.

19. On copying practices in the trecento and quattrocento, see Hayden Maginnis, *The World of the Early Sienese Painter* (University Park, Penn.: Pennsylvania State University Press, 2001), 11–18; Michelle O'Malley, 'The Business of Art. Contracts and Payment Documents for Fourteenth and Fifteenth-century Italian Altarpieces and Frescoes' (Ph.D. diss. Warburg Institute, University of London, 1994), 150–64; and 'Memorizing the New: Using Recent Works as Models in Italian Renaissance Commissions', in *Memory and Oblivion. Proceedings of the XXIXth International Congress*

of the History of Art, held in Amsterdam, 1–7 September 1996, ed. Wessel Reinink and Jeroen Stumpel (Dordrecht: Kluwer Academic, 1999), 803–10; Anabel Thomas, *The Painter's Practice in Renaissance Tuscany* (Cambridge and New York: Cambridge University Press, 1995), 213–46 (offering a somewhat different account than the one I present here); Lisa Venturini in Acidini Luchinat, Gregori, and Paolucci, 147–57 and 165–7; Andrew Ladis, 'Sources and Resources: The Lost Sketchbooks of Giovanni di Paolo', in *The Craft of Art: Originality and Industry in the Italian Renaissance and Baroque Workshop,* ed. Andrew Ladis (Athens: University of Georgia Press, 1995), 48–85. On changes in the late quattrocento and cinquecento, see Carmen Bambach, *Drawing and Painting in the Italian Renaissance Workshop* (Cambridge and New York: Cambridge University Press, 1999), 81–136; Rudolf Hiller von Gaertringen, *Raffaels Lernerfahrung in der Werkstatt Peruginos. Kartonverwendung und Motivübernahme im Wandel* (Munich: Deutscher Kunstverlag, 1999); David Landau and Peter Parshall, *The Renaissance Print: 1470–1550* (New Haven and London: Yale University Press, 1994) 103–168.

20. Walter and Elisabeth Paatz, *Die Kirchen von Florenz,* vol. I (Frankfurt am Main: Klostermann, 1955), 158–9; Herbert Kessler, 'Copia', in *Enciclopedia dell'arte medievale* (Istituto della Enciclopedia italiana: Rome, 1994), 264–77.

21. Thomas 227–33. This kind of copying was particularly prevalent in Siena.

22. On the dissemination of the St. Francis cycle in the upper church in San Francesco, Assisi (c. 1300), see Dieter Blume, *Wandmalerei als Ordenspropaganda* (Worms: Werner'sche Verlagsgesellschaft, 1983), chapters 4 and 5; William R. Cook, 'The Cycle of the Life of Francis of Assisi in Rieti: The First "Copy" of the Assisi Frescoes', *Collectanea Francescana* 65 (1995): 115–47. For a later example of a series of four Coronation of the Virgin paintings made for Umbrian Franciscan nunneries by Ghirlandaio, Raphael's bottega and Lo Spagna, see O'Malley, 'The Business of Art', 157–9; and Bambach, 91 and 94.

23. See Hannalore Glasser, 'Artists' Contracts of the Early Renaissance', (Ph.D. diss., Columbia University, 1965; London and New York: Garland, 1977), 65–70; Thomas 111–12; O'Malley, 'The Business of Art', 150–1; and 'Review of *The Painter's Practice* by Anabel Thomas', *Burlington Magazine* 138 (1996): 692.

24. See, for example, Neri di Bicci's *Annunciation* (1458) for Sant'Andrea in Mosciano, which was to be modeled on his earlier *Annunciation* (1455) in the church of San Remigio in Florence, discussed in Megan Holmes, 'Neri di Bicci and the Commodification of Pictorial Values in Florence, 1450–1500,' in *The Art Market in Early Modern Italy,* eds. M. Fantoni, L. Matthew, and S. Matthews-Grieco (Modena: Panini, 2003, 213–23). Another example of this more specific *modo et forma* contract stipulation can be seen in Benozzo Gozzoli's *Madonna and Child with Saints and Angels* (c. 1461; National Gallery, London), commissioned by the Compagnia di Santa Maria della Purificazione e di San Zenobi, based on Fra Angelico's high altar image for San Marco, Florence (c. 1440, Museo di San Marco, Florence), discussed by O'Malley ('The Business of Art', 157) and Thomas (9).

25. O'Malley, 'The Business of Art', 150–1.

26. For Cennini, see n. 71. On the use of the term 'retrahere' in artists contracts, see O'Malley, 'The Business of Art', 151. Martin Kemp cites a reference in 1501 to two apprentices of Leonardo's who were making copies that Leonardo occasionally touched UP: 'dui suoi garzoni fano retrati et lui ale volte i alcuno mette mano' ('The "Madonna of the Yarnwinder" in the Buccleauch Collection Reconsidered in the Context of Leonardo's Studio Practice', in *I leonardeschi a Milano: fortuna e collezionismo,* eds. Maria Teresa Fiorio and Pietro C. Marani [Milan: Electa, 1991] 40).

27. In addition to the three copied Medici works by Lippi described in the text, Lippi's Uffizi *Madonna and Child with Angels,* which may have been copied in its entirety (see n. 16), was in the Villa Medici at Poggio Imperiale prior to being transferred to the Uffizi in 1796, making it possible that it was in the Medici collection early on (although it does not appear in the detailed Medici inventory of 1492).

28. Ruda 383. The inventory of 1492 lists 'Uno quadro chon chornicie messo d'oro, dipintovi uno sancto Girolamo et uno sancto Francesco di mano di Pesello e Fra Filippo, f.10' (E. Muentz, *Les Collectiones des Medicis au xve siécle* [Paris: Librairie de l'art, 1888] 64).

29. A marginal note added beside a description of the painting in a Uffizi inventory of 1881 reads as follows: 'già Cenacolo di S.Apollonia' (Strozzi 33 and 35 n. 6). The altarpiece is not listed in the inventory of paintings taken from Sant'Apollonia (or from any other monastery, for that matter) during the 1808–12 suppression of the monasteries preserved in the Archivio dell'Accademia delle Belle Arti. The panel was in Sant'Apollonia (in the Museo di Andrea del Castagno located in the ex-refectory) from 1891 to around 1915 when it was designated for the refurbished Medici Palace chapel, where it was installed above the altar in 1930. A number of the paintings selected for the new Museo di Andrea del Castagno had been in Sant'Apollonia prior to the final suppression of the nunnery in 1866 (having been returned after the 1808–12 suppression). André Pératé, 'La réorganisation des musées florentins, I. Le Musée de Sant'Apollonia', *Gazette des Beaux-Arts* 34 (1892): 508; Paolozzi Strozzi 33 (where she does not chronicle the passage of the altarpiece from storage in the Uffizi in 1890 to Sant'Apollonia in 1891); Silvia Meloni Trkulja, 'La trasformazione dei Cenacoli in Musei', in *La tradizione florentina dei Cenacoli,* eds. Cristina Acidini Luchinat and Rosanna Caterina Proto Pisani (Florence: Cassa di Risparmio di Firenze, 1997), 108–9.

30. Strozzi, 34.

31. Archivio di Stato, Florence, Corporazioni Religiosi Soppresse dal Governo Francese 82 (Sant'Apollonia), n. 79 (*Libro dei debitori e creditori 1471–1522,* fols. 14v–15r and fols. 28v–29r. The account book begins in 1471, and a payment on July 23 of that year covers Maria di Piero de'Medici's fees for the previous year. The final payment is made on March 11, 1473, when Maria moved to the Benedictine nunnery Le Murate, which Lorenzo had begun to support in 1471. On Maria de'Medici, see Raymond de Roover, *The Rise and Fall of the Medici Bank, 1397–1494,* (Cambridge: Harvard University Press, 1963), 300–2.

32. 'Et se il signor Conte d'Ariano ne vuole un'altra, tornando tu in qua puoi pigliare il disegno et esserne sollicitatore. Et se lui non harà pressa, credo la potrà havere, maxime hora che fra Filippo è ridutto a Prato', Ruda 537–8.

33. Anthony Hughes and Erich Ranfft observe that "reproductive strategies are rarely merely passive but may have a powerful role in providing a frame within which the primary objects are seen" ('Introduction' to *Sculpture and Its Reproductions,* eds. Anthony Hughes and Erich Ranfft (London: Reaktion Books, 1997), 5.

34. See Michelle O'Malley, 'Late fifteenth- and early sixteenth-century painting contracts and the stipulated use of the painter's hand', in *With and Without the Medici: Studies in Tuscan Art and Patronage 1434–1530,* eds. Alison Wright and Eckart Marchand (Aldershot, England: Ashgate, 1998), 155–78.

35. See Ladis, 48–85; Thomas, 236–44; Landau and Parshall, 103–68.

36. Lisa Venturini, in Acidini Luchinat, Gregori, and Paolucci, 165–7. An *Annunciation* in the Accademia dating from the 1470s is a close copy of Lippi's *Annunciation* (c. 1443–45; now in Munich) for the Florentine nunnery church Le Murate, commissioned by Giovanni Benci. The

copy is attributed to the Master of the Johnson Nativity, with the possible intervention of Filippino Lippi (Anna Maria Bernachioni in Acidini Luchinat, Gregori, and Paolucci, 48–9).

37. On Madonna and Child images for the home, see Ronald Kecks, *Madonna und Kind: Das häusliche Andachtsbild im Florenz des 15. Jahrhunderts* (Berlin: Mann, 1988). *Colmi da camera* and *tabernacoli* referred more generically to framed images and objects that were not necessarily of a sacred nature (see, for example, the 1492 inventory of the property of Lorenzo de'Medici in which framed maps and portraits are described as *cholmi* (Muentz 64 ff.). On the Lippi and Pesellino Imitator's tondi, see Roberta Olson, *The Florentine Tondo* (Oxford: Oxford University Press, 2000), 175–6.

38. Lippi's *Madonna Adoring the Christ Child* at the core of so many paintings by the Lippi and Pesellino Imitator was also a standard motif in the shop production of many painters and sculptors during the last quarter of the fifteenth century. One version by the master of the Castello Nativity was displayed in the Medici villa in Castello, suggesting that this subject of the Virgin adoring the Christ Child – which Lippi himself had painted three times for the Medici – had a particular significance for the family.

39. Musee Narbonne in Narbonne; ex-Florence, Galleria Luzetti.

40. Indiana University Art Museum, Bloomington, Indiana (78 × 80); formerly in the collection of Jules Bache in New York. There are three other reduced versions of Lippi's Medici Palace chapel altarpiece that reproduce the landscape background: Altomano collection in Pesaro (ex-Thyssen Collection); Pushkin Museum in Moscow; ex-W. E. Gray Collection in London, current location unknown.

41. This panel is preserved in its original frame; 87 × 49 (panel) and 159 × 79 (frame). It was formerly in the Fitzgerald collection in Heathfield Park (Sussex) and was sold at Sotheby's on July 3, 1963 (lot 18).

42. For example, there are nine paintings known of Pesellino's Gardner Museum *Madonna and Child* in a rectangular format set against a rose-hedge ground.

43. Carl Strehlke and Joe Mikuliak provided me with infrared reflectograms of the paintings in the Philadelphia Museum of Art. The technical examination of the copy of the Medici Palace chapel altarpiece also revealed traces of *spolvero* (Consorzio Pegasus, which conducted the restoration); see 'L'intervento conservativo e restaurativo', in Acidini Luchinat, *I restauri nel Palazzo Medici Ricardi*, 37.

44. Mylar tracings of the following paintings by the Lippi and Pesellino Imitator were made for me by the conservators in the Metropolitan Museum of Art, the Philadelphia Museum of Art, and the Yale University Art Gallery: two works in the Metropolitan Museum of Art (32.100.79 and 65.181.4, by Charlotte Hale); four works in the Philadelphia Museum of Art (Johnson Collection 39–42, by Terry Lignelli); four works in the Yale University Art Gallery (1871.43, 1943.225, 1943.226, 1943.355 by Anne O'Connor). Joanne Klaar at the Isabella Stewart Gardner Museum provided a tracing of the *Madonna and Child* by Pesellino (P16W11) for comparative purposes.

45. The mylar tracings are helpful in verifying the sources of some of the figures around the Virgin and Child. In a panel in the Metropolitan Museum of Art (32.100.79) based on Pesellino's *Madonna and Child with Angels* in Toledo, for instance, the head appearing between the Virgin and Christ is generated with a cartoon derived from the young Baptist in Lippi's Medici Palace chapel altarpiece (already used once in the painting to produce the Baptist figure at the right), while the head just to the right of the Virgin is derived from the Christ Child in Pesellino's Gardner Museum *Madonna and Child*.

46. Carmen Bambach observes that painters such as Paolo Uccello, Domenico Veneziano, and Andrea del Castagno began to use cartoons to reproduce entire figures only in the 1430s and 1440s (197–219). On the early history of the cartoon, see also Hiller von Gaertringen 117–30.

47. On substitute cartoons, see Bambach 283–95. The character of the cartoon stock can be inferred from the disposition of the cartoon-generated figures in the paintings. The cartoons derived from the Medici Palace chapel altarpiece were single-figure sheets. Those related to Lippi's and Pesellino's half-length Madonna images displayed the Madonna and Child together. One cartoon reproduced the group of three angels holding the Christ Child found in the Cleveland *Adoration of the Child* (Fig. 9), while a single, large cartoon existed of the entire composition of Pesellino's *Madonna and Child with Angels* in Toledo (Fig. 2). There may also have been single-figure substitute cartoons of the angels in the Cleveland and Toledo paintings. As has already been mentioned, certain of the background features were also generated with cartoons.

48. Kemp, 'The 'Madonna of the Yarnwinder,' in The Buccleauch Collection Reconsidered in the Context of Leonardo's Studio Practice'.

49. Lothar Ledderose, in his study of modular composition in Chinese art, notes that the phenomenon of component composition in the visual arts occurs in many cultures, particularly during times when there is an increase in production attended by a standardization, rationalization, and mechanization in the process of production. *Ten Thousand Things. Module and Mass Production in Chinese Art* (Princeton: Princeton University Press, 2000), 2–3 and 175.

50. For an example of angels in a painting described as ornament in a fifteenth-century contract, see Michele O'Malley's contribution to this volume.

51. Some of the size variations depended on the prototype used: whereas Lippi's Medici Palace chapel altarpiece was infinitely adaptable within a variety of panel sizes, Pesellino's grand *Madonna and Child with Angels* in Toledo predicated a large format. Only a small percentage of the paintings still have their original frames. The measurements that I have for the panels are not uniform, with some including the frames, and other just the panel. The larger paintings measure 90–100 × 60–70 cm (circa 2 × 1 1/2 braccia), the middle range 60–70 × 40–50 cm (circa 1 1/2 × 1 braccia), and the smaller panels 45 × 30 cm (circa 1 × 1/2 braccia). I have measurements for only nine of the fifteen tondi, with an average of 85 cm in diameter. One can only speculate on the prices, with Neri di Bicci's *Ricordanze* providing a useful guide (see n. 57).

52. See n. 54.

53. Ledderose writes, "Graded products extend the circle of participants in the system. . . . The differences can be subtle and the grading fine-tuned. This permits the owners of these objects to define their respective social position and make it known to their peers, who will recognize the differences. . . . The system of grades has advantages for producers, too. It helps them to organize their production process and allows them to attract customers of different economic means." He also points to a political dimension of component production within a graded system, suggesting that it "contributes to the fostering of social homogeneity and cultural and political coherence" (Ledderose, 5 and 175).

54. A few of the surviving frames display coats of arms that I have not been able to identify, which suggests that the patrons were upwardly mobile artisans. The arms displayed on one *colmo* in the Yale University Art Gallery (1943.226) incorporate the emblem of the Arte dei Vinattieri – one of the lesser guilds involved in the sale of wine. Neri di Bicci's *Ricordanze* contain many examples of artisans requesting that their arms be included on the tabernacle and altarpiece frames. See n. 57 for the social status of the patrons who commissioned *colmi da camera* from Neri di Bicci.

55. On Madonna reliefs, see Anna Jolly, *Madonnas by Donatello and His Circle* (Frankfurt am Main: Peter Lang, 1998); John Pope-Hennessey, 'The Madonna Reliefs of Donatello', *The Study and Criticism of Italian Sculpture* (Princeton: Princeton University Press, 1980), 71–118; Geraldine Johnson, "Art or Artefact? Madonna and Child Reliefs in the Early Renaissance', *The Sculpted Object 1400–1700*, ed. Stuart Currie and Peta Motture (Aldershot, England: Ashgate, 1997), 1–24; Giancarlo Gentilini, *I Della Robbia* (Florence: Cantini, 1992), 32–80; *Il Museo Bardini*, vol. II *Le Sculture*, ed. Enrica Neri Lusanna and Lucia Faedo (Milan: Cassa di Risparmio di Firenze and Electa, 1986).

56. Comparative figures are revealing, even if panel paintings have a higher survival rate than their more fragile sculptural counterparts. There are thirty-one known casts of what seems to have been the most popular sculptural Madonna type associated with Ghiberti, known as the 'Cleveland Madonna' (Jolly, 95). More characteristic numbers for surviving sculptural multiples are between 5 and 15.

57. Given the absence of any documentation for these Madonna panels produced by the Lippi and Pesellino Imitator, a brief look at the 'Madonna sector' of Neri di Bicci's well-documented contemporary painting practice is helpful. While Neri di Bicci's production was considerably more diversified than that of the Lippi and Pesellino Imitator, during the twenty-three years covered by his *Ricordanze* (1453–75), Neri painted at least 125 Madonna images. He averaged a little under four *colmi* per year. Sixty percent of the patrons of these devotional images were artisans and tradesmen (some of whom were middlemen who purchased in bulk), compared with 31 percent who were patricians or members of the seven major guilds. He provided a variety of products in a range of sizes (from roughly 1 to 3 braccia [58 cm to 174 cm] in height), in different materials (panel, gesso, wood, and marble), and with alternative framing configuration very similar to those found in the panels of the Lippi and Pesellino Imitator. Large and ornate *colmi da camera* could cost as much as 40 lire, while a middle-range product sold at around 20 lire, and a small and inexpensive version could cost as little as 5 lire 8 soldi (Neri also had a standardized product that he sold in bulk to dealers at 7 lire). While there is no evidence that he used cartoons to replicate the designs in his painted panels, 99 of the 125 Madonna images mentioned in the *Ricordanze* are identified as sculptural reliefs (compared with only fifteen flat panel paintings). A number of Neri's Madonna and Child *cholmi* were pulled from molds taken from marble reliefs by Desiderio da Settignano. While Neri received the commissions and coordinated the production of these gesso images, the actual casts were usually made by the carpenters who provided the wooden frames into which the gesso casts were set. This mechanical means of reproducing the design, plus the low cost of the principal material used (gesso), made these works inexpensive yet profitable. Neri's least expensive painted gesso reliefs cost around l.5 lire 8 soldi, in contrast to his cheapest painted wooden Madonna panels at about l.8 lire (the prices quoted here and earlier refer to commissions for which Neri was required to supply all of the materials involved in the production). Unfortunately, the low survival rate of cast gesso Madonna images from the period, the poor condition of those that do survive, and the difficulty of attributing the polychroming to a specific painter on the basis of style make it impossible to compare the volume of Neri di Bicci's Madonna production over the fifty years that he painted (c. 1440–92), with that of the Lippi and Pesellino Imitator, on the basis of surviving works. There are, however, around 35 extant painted Madonna panels by Neri, compared with more than 160 by the Lippi and Pesellino Imitator. On Neri's painted gesso reliefs, see Ulrich Middeldorf, review of Neri di Bicci, *Le Ricordanze* (ed. B. Santi), in *Renaissance Quarterly* 31 (1978): 218–221; and 'Some Florentine Painted Madonna Reliefs', in *Collaboration in Italian Renaissance*

Art, ed. Wendy Stedman Sheard and John Paoletti (London and New Haven: Yale University Press, 1978), 77–90; Thomas 286–92; Rita Comanducci, 'Produzione seriale e mercato dell'arte: Firenze 1450–1563', in *The Art Market in Early Modern Italy,* ed. M. Fantoni, L. Matthew, and S. Matthews-Grieco (Modena: Panini, 2003) 105–13.

58. See Kecks; Keith Christiansen, Lawrence Kanter, Carl Strehlke, eds., *Painting in Renaissance Siena 1420–1500* (New York: Metropolitan Museum of Art, 1988), 138–9 and 270–4; Rona Goffen, 'Icon and Vision: Giovanni Bellini's Half-Length Madonnas', *Art Bulletin* 57 (1975): 487–518; Peter Humfrey, *Cima da Conegliano* (Cambridge and New York: Cambridge University Press, 1983); Marilyn W. Ainsworth, *Facsimile in Early Netherlandish Painting: Dieric Bouts's 'Virgin and Child'* (New York: 1993); Jean C. Wilson, *Painting in Bruges at the close of the Middle Ages: Studies in Society and Visual Culture* (University Park, Penn.: Penn State University Press, 1998), Part II. On the use of cartoons in Madonna and Child paintings, see Bambach 101; Wilson 117–31.

59. *Wealth and the Demand for Art in Italy, 1300–1600* (Baltimore and London: Johns Hopkins University Press, 1993).

60. See n. 57 for Neri di Bicci's prices.

61. On eclectic imitation, see John D. Amico, 'The Progress of Renaissance Latin Prose: The Case of Apuleianism', *Renaissance Quarterly* 37 (1984): 351–92.

62. Ronald Lightbown, *Sandro Botticelli* (London: Paul Elek, 1978), vol. II, 42–4; Acidini Luchinat, Gregori, and Paolucci, 150–1 and 163.

63. Van Marle, 461.

64. Anna Maria Bernachioni mentions the names of Piero di Lorenzo di Pratese and Zenobi di Migliore, who both had formed a *compagnia* with Pesellino (Acidini Luchinat, Gregori, and Paolucci 160–1). The documentation for Piero di Lorenzo di Pratese is assembled by Chiara Lacchi (*Il Maestro della Natività di Castello*), where she connects the painter with the 'Master of the Castello Nativity'. I feel, however, that the fit is a better one with the Lippi and Pesellino Imitator.

65. There are forty works that can confidently be attributed to the late production of the bottega (c. 1480–95) because they contain new figure types that date from later in the century. There are new young Baptist and angel figures – eight in all, some of which can securely be related to works by Filippino Lippi, with others bearing a familial likeness to Filippino's figures (see n. 74 and Table 1C). The paintings attributed to the Lippi and Pesellino Imitator that are derived from Antonello da Messina, and Leonardo prototypes are also among this group. These forty late works have many striking characteristics in common. Fourteen of the fifteen tondi associated with this shop are among these late works, as are many of the paintings with landscape backgrounds that are not derived from Lippi's Medici Palace chapel altarpiece. All but two of the paintings in this group that are not tondi – twenty-three panels – are surmounted by arches and are roughly of a similar size, suggesting that there was a greater standardization of the framing format during the final years of the production of these devotional images.

66. On Pesellino's use of cartoons, see Bambach 96–7 and 234–6; figs. 87 and 209. The pictorial style of the Lippi and Pesellino Imitator manifest in the 1459 copy in the Uffizi of Pesellino's *Madonna and Child with Angels* in Toledo and in the precise copies of paintings by Filippo Lippi is closer to the manner of Pesellino than it is to that of Lippi.

67. The *Madonna and Child* attributed to Pesellino in the Isabella Stewart Gardner Museum in Boston is extremely close in composition to a painting in the Christian Museum in Esztergom, Hungary, which is usually given to Pesellino as well. The painting in the Gardner Museum (60 ×

39 cm) is clearly the prototype. It is slightly wider than the panel in Esztergom (60 × 36 cm), is a more accomplished work, and exhibits *pentimenti* that demonstrate changes made during the designing of the panel. While I have not been able to examine the Esztergom panel firsthand, it appears to be closer in style to the early paintings by the Lippi and Pesellino Imitator than to what are considered to be autograph works by Pesellino. There is another version of the subject set in an interior that is also close to the manner of Pesellino (Christies, June, 1970, lot 61).

68. Rudolf Hiller von Gaertringen disagrees with me on this matter, speculating that the Lippi and Pesellino Imitator obtained the actual working cartoons from Lippi (forthcoming catalogue of Italian paintings in the Städel Museum, Frankfurt am Main). On Pesellino's use of cartoons, see n. 66. The pin-pricked drawing of the *Mystical Marriage of Saint Catherine* (Uffizi 1117 E) attributed to Pesellino is close to (but clearly not the source for) a painted version of the subject in the Strossmayer Gallery in Zagreb ascribed to Pesellino that was copied by the Lippi and Pesellino Imitator.

69. Bambach 233; Giordana Benizzi and Paolo Virilli, *Filippo Lippi nel duomo di Spoleto, 1467–1469. Notizie dopo il restauro* (Spoleto: Il Messagero, 1990), 13–17.

70. Ruda 447. Lippi changed the drapery along the Baptist's right upper arm and elbow, and flanking his left thigh.

71. 'è una carta che si chiama carta lucida, la quale ti può essere molto utile per ritrarre una testa o una figura o una mezza figura, secondo che l'uomo trouva, di man di gran maestri. E per avere bene i contorni, o di carta o di tavola o di muro, . . . metti questa carta lucida in su la figura . . . attaccata gentilmente in quattro canti con un poco di cera rossa o verde. Di subito per lo lustro della carta lucida trasparrà la figura, o ver disegno di sotto. . . . Allora togli o penna temperata ben sottile o pennel sottile di vaio sottile, e con inchiostro puoi andare ricercando i contorni e le stremità del disegno di sotto.' Cennino Cennini, *Il libro dell'arte,* ed. Mario Serchi (Florence: Le Monnier, 1991), 34. On Leonardo's copy of the *Madonna of the Rocks,* see O'Malley, 'The Business of Art', 151.

72. The paintings by Lippi that were copied date from the mid-1440s through the mid-1460s, with most dating from the late 1450s and early 1460s (although many of these works are not documented, and the dating is based on stylistic criteria). Among the works where the provenance is known, all were originally displayed in Florence except the triptych sent by the Medici to Alfonso of Aragon in 1458.

73. Carmen Bambach notes that in documented instances cartoons were treated 'like any other form of property – [passed on] as bequests, dowries, or gifts' (92–3). See also Wilson 155–6, where she describes a lawsuit in Bruges in 1519 over a chest of painting supplies that included workshop models, some of which may have been pounced cartoons. In this same court case, there is a reference to an artist's workshop models that had been 'borrowed . . . for a fee' from another painter.

74. An angel from Filippino Lippi's *Vision of Saint Bernard* (c. 1485; now in the Badia in Florence) is clearly the prototype for an angel that appears in three or the later paintings – all tondi (Petit Palais, Avignon; Ex-Hanna Thomson collection, Detroit, Michigan; sold at Sotheby's, New York, January 12, 1979, lot. 147; Collegiata di San Martino, Sinalunga (in reverse). The young Baptist in Filippino's Nerli altarpiece (1494; in Santo Spirito, Florence) may be the prototype for a young Baptist that appears in eleven of the later works. The young Baptist in Filippino's *Madonna and Child* in the National Gallery in London is somewhat similar to a baptist figure that appears in twenty-two of the paintings by the Lippi and Pesellino Imitator, facing in both directions.

75. Walter Benjamin, 'The Work of Art in the Age of Mechanical Reproduction', *Walter Benjamin: Illuminations,* ed. Hannah Arendt (New York: Harcourt, Brace and World, 1968), 219–53. For a recent discussion of the copy that addresses Benjamin's argument, see Anthony Hughes, 'Authority, Authenticity and Aura: Walter Benjamin and the Case of Michelangelo', in Hughes and Ranfft, 29–45. On copying, see also the essays in *Studies in the History of Art* 20 (1989); Hillel Schwartz, *The Culture of the Copy. Striking Likenesses, Unreasonable Facsimiles* (New York: Zone, 1996), 244–57 (on the visual arts in Western culture).

76. In fact, a painting of the *Madonna and Child with the Baptist* by the Lippi and Pesellino Imitator now in Santa Maria del Morbo in Poppi became a venerated votive image in 1530 when the Madonna was said to have intervened to stop the plague.

77. According to Benjamin, aura is a product of the uniqueness of a work of art, its authenticity, distance from the viewer, embeddedness within tradition, and cult value associated with what he perceives negatively as a 'parasitical dependence on ritual' (Benjamin 226; see also Hughes 5). The conception of aura that I present in the text is somewhat different, tied to the various ways in which a representational object could be invested with awe-inspiring power and authority in fifteenth-century Florence.

78. From *Disegno. Partito in più ragionamenti, ne quali si tratta della scoltura et pittura* (1549), quoted in Bambach, 131.

3

Mino da Fiesole's Forteguerri Tomb: A 'Florentine' Monument in Rome

Shelley E. Zuraw

The history of tomb sculpture in fifteenth-century Rome can be characterized, with only slight oversimplification, as one of repetition and replication. So many tombs were erected, for cardinals, bishops, and other important curial figures, that a virtual industry seems to have developed to deal with these commissions. Two or three standard types are easily identified – the single arched form exemplified by the tomb of Cardinal Cristoforo della Rovere in S Maria del Popolo; the box format represented by tombs such as that for Bishop Giovanni de Coca in S. Maria sopra Minerva; and the tombs that seem to be architectural fields for an endless variety of reliefs and details, initiated in part by the Pius II tomb (now in S. Andrea della Valle). Yet it is not possible to assign every tomb produced in Rome as one or the other of these 'types.' Rather, artists and presumably patrons must have designed and ordered sepulchral monuments using bits and pieces borrowed from other examples. The type or types that evolved in this manner are often associated with Andrea Bregno and his workshop. As much as anything else, the generic designation 'style of Andrea Bregno' reflects the lack of solid information about many of these tombs. Often we do not have the documents about particular commissions or about individual sculptors working in Rome that would be needed to clarify issues of attribution and chronology.

As with all artistic developments in quattrocento Rome, the standard approach has been to search for elucidation through the contribution of more well-known

A version of this chapter was presented at the symposium 'Florence and the 1470s: Contexts and Contrasts,' National Gallery of Art, London, November 12–13, 1999. I would like to thank the organizers of the conference – Nicholas Penny, Patricia Rubin, and Alison Wright – for their generous invitation. I would also like to acknowledge the generous advice and assistance provided by Denise Allen, Jack Freiberg, Andrew Ladis, and Debra Pincus in the preparation of both the talk and the essay.

artists. This, simply put, means to track the works produced in Rome by foreign, usually Florentine, artists. The assumption that Roman artists were indebted to Florentine models can be viewed as an academic construct; knowing about the history of Perugino, Botticelli, and the Pollaiuolo brothers, it is easier and more effective to trace their influence on the development of Roman art than to wade through the countless undocumented products of unnamed and unknown artisans. Yet this approach does not seem to have solved any of the real issues associated with Roman tomb design. For the most part, attributions are still uncertain, the relative chronology of the tombs is still based on the death dates of the deceased (a notoriously inaccurate system), and the relationship between major masters and minor carvers can only be presumed. At the heart of these problems associated with design, lies another, the very different means of production employed in the actual creation of tomb monuments in Rome.

The truth about Roman tomb construction in the fifteenth century is that speed was not only a highly prized commodity, but it was also essential. The death of every cardinal and of every pope required a fitting commemoration, and in Rome that meant a monumental marble tomb. It was during the quattrocento that cardinals were summoned to reside under the papacy's watchful eye in Rome; at the same time their ranks were systematically expanded – by deliberately packing the college of cardinals – to reach a number greater than at an other time in the history of the church.[1] Thus, by the end of the century, Roman churches were virtually encrusted with tombs.[2] Accentuating the sheer quantity of such tombs is their similarity; virtually identical forms appear and reappear almost ad infinitum.[3] Roman sculptors and their shops typically worked together for the sake of efficiency.[4] The tradeoff was a formulaic sameness to these tombs, but even this was undoubtably desired by patrons. In Florence demands were different; artistic time could move at a slow and stately pace. The monks at the Badia, for example, first conceived of the new tomb for Count Hugo in 1440, but it was not finished until more than forty years later.[5] In Rome, time was measured in terms of the unpredictable span between one pope and his successor, one cardinal and the next. Speed was of the essence if a tomb was going to be completed while the patron or his heirs still had the money and the appropriate connections.[6]

Both in terms of workshop method and design, Florentine influences did reach Rome, but it was not either as systematic or as overpowering as we tend to think. One example exists in Rome of a tomb for a Tuscan cardinal that was designed and carved by a Florentine sculptor. It allows us to contemplate the introduction of unmistakably Florentine forms into the Roman market. The tomb of Cardinal Niccolò Forteguerri was installed in the Roman church of S. Cecilia in Trastevere probably between 1474 and 1476 (Fig. 22). It represents a remarkably straightforward integration of a Florentine tomb design with other elements already associated with

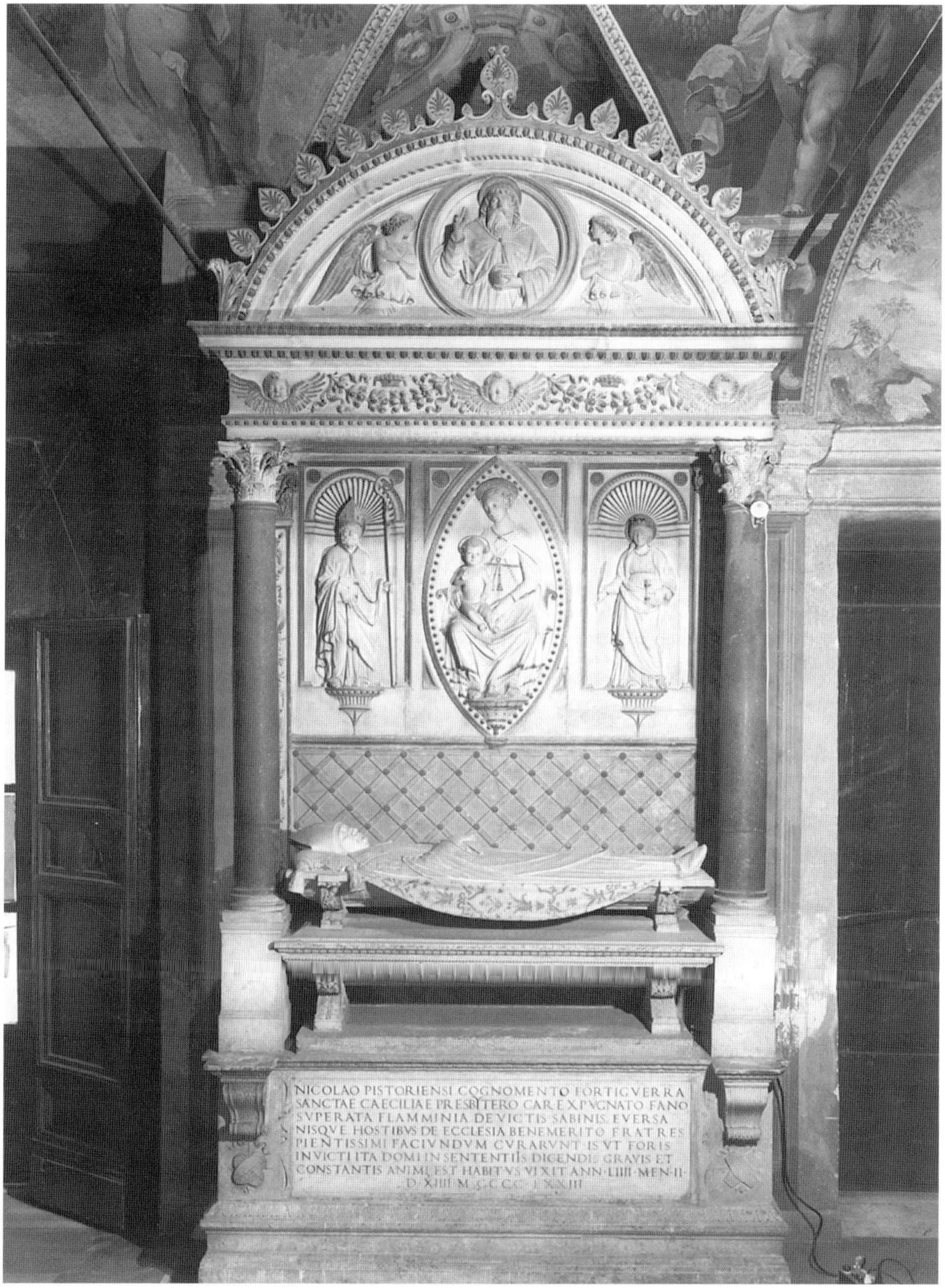

22. Mino da Fiesole, *Tomb of Cardinal Niccolò Forteguerri*, c. 1474–6. Rome, S. Cecilia in Trastevere. Photo: Istituto Centrale per il Catalogo e la Documentazione, Rome, Serie E, 105019.

Roman sepulchral iconography. Through this one example it is possible to consider the transmission of a formal and iconographic program that had been developed in one place and then reapplied in another. The final tomb, however, does not look Florentine. The literal replication of a Florentine tomb type was, apparently, untenable and thus was adjusted to fit local requirements. What was initiated as translation was completed as transformation.

There are no other tombs in Rome that so clearly demonstrate this process of imitation and alteration because there are no other extant tombs that are comparably 'Florentine.' Even other works by Florentine artists cannot be so directly linked to their previous or later production in Tuscany. The Forteguerri tomb can serve as an example of *translatio,* but a unique one. The fact that the Forteguerri tomb is without precedent or progeny does not, however, diminish its importance. Through a careful analysis of the commission, the artist, and the work itself it is possible to isolate what was considered essentially 'Roman' in the development of local tomb iconography. Armed with this information, future considerations of the Roman sepulchral tradition can begin to address issues of more complexity than merely the categorizing of different extant types. While it is not realistic to infer a universal definition of cultural exchange from this solitary example, it can serve to distinguish what artists and patrons considered essential in the construction of an appropriate tomb.

The tomb of Cardinal Forteguerri is perhaps the most telling example of the sculptural interchange between Florence and Rome in the third quarter of the fifteenth century. That exchange is embodied in the career of the artist who produced the work, the Florentine Mino da Fiesole.[7] Although commonly compared, if unfavorably, to his Florentine contemporaries Desiderio da Settigniano and Antonio Rossellino, Mino's progress was quite different from those of his compatriots. Rocketing onto the stage as a sculptor of portrait busts, first for the Medici and then for rich and powerful men across the peninsula, Mino journeyed to Rome in 1454, and it was there that he learned his trade, transforming himself into a sculptor of monumental, public works. Although to Florentine eyes, his reliefs for Cardinal d'Estoutevilles's Altar of St. Jerome from 1464 might seem clumsy, they exemplify the work required of Roman sculptors: large in scale, rapidly produced, and visually evocative of the classical and early Christian heritage of Rome.[8] In Rome marble carving was often less an expression of individual style than it was a response to prevailing forms; it demanded a large workshop, and Mino ran one, efficiently fulfilling his patrons' needs for speed and scale. The Forteguerri tomb, completed during Mino's second period of activity in Rome, reveals a variety of different kinds of workshop intervention. In its unique mixture of Florentine and Roman models, it also strikingly combines imitation and invention.

In 1464, after enjoying almost a decade of continuous employment in Rome, Mino returned to Florence; that same year he joined the Florentine guild of stone carvers. His relatively late matriculation in the guild exposes, as clearly as anything else, his divergence from the normal career path of a Florentine marble carver.[9] In Florence Mino seems to have set about filling the gap left by the death of Desiderio da Settignano. Issuing from Mino's shop in these years came a steady stream of Madonna and Child reliefs, all notable for their exquisite technique.[10] At the same time, Mino took on monumental commissions, combining Florentine expectations with the more eclectic models he had studied in Rome.

The next decade began very well for Mino. Forty-one years old, he was by any contemporary measure a successful artist living an orderly life. He was married to Francesca d'Agnelo di Barone, and they had two living sons. According to Mino's tax returns of 1470, he owned a house near Sant'Ambrogio but was renting it to a cloth worker. The family lived instead on the corner of the via del Proconsulo and his workshop, rented from the monks at the Badia, was just a block from his residence.[11] Work was coming in and going out at a regular, indeed fairly rapid, pace. In 1469 he signed a contract to produce the high altar ciborium for the cathedral in Volterra, a work he finished in 1471. By then he had completed the important tomb for Bernardo Giugni, a work deliberately intended to surpass the prototypes developed by Bernardo Rossellino and Desiderio at S. Croce.[12] His other works for the Badia, including the monumental Madonna and Child relief for the entrance portal, led to negotiations about a new tomb for the monastery's founder Count Hugo of Tuscany, the contract for which was finalized in 1471. Mino was in Florence working on the tomb of Count Hugo for three years when he transferred his base of activity once more to Rome.

Mino began the Count Hugo tomb in the first years of the 1470s (Fig. 23).[13] This work epitomizes his unique fusion of the delicate carving associated with his peers, once known as the little marble masters, and the more hieratic schemes and monumental scale of his earlier Roman projects. The Badia commission also confirmed his reputation in Florence as a carver of public monuments and, thus, along with his prior Roman reputation, presumably brought him to the attention of the Pistoiese cardinal, Niccolò Forteguerri. The Forteguerri tomb, erected on the inner facade wall of S. Cecilia in Trastevere, is an extraordinary amalgamation of Florentine designs and Roman requirements. Begun in all likelihood in early 1474 when Mino set up a workshop in Rome for the second time, the design of the tomb of Niccolò Forteguerri takes off from the point at which Mino suspended work on the Count Hugo tomb. Yet Mino cleverly transformed this Florentine model to fit particular local, that is, Roman, expectations. This tomb exemplifies what made Mino so successful: he was flexible, but not mindlessly so, allowing each work to be redefined by the requirements behind the commission. The Forteguerri tomb opens a window onto a world where Florentine design was desired, but not too much.

Cardinal Niccolò Forteguerri, a member of the impoverished nobility in Pistoia, was born in 1419.[14] A student of canon and civil law in Bologna and Siena, Niccolò

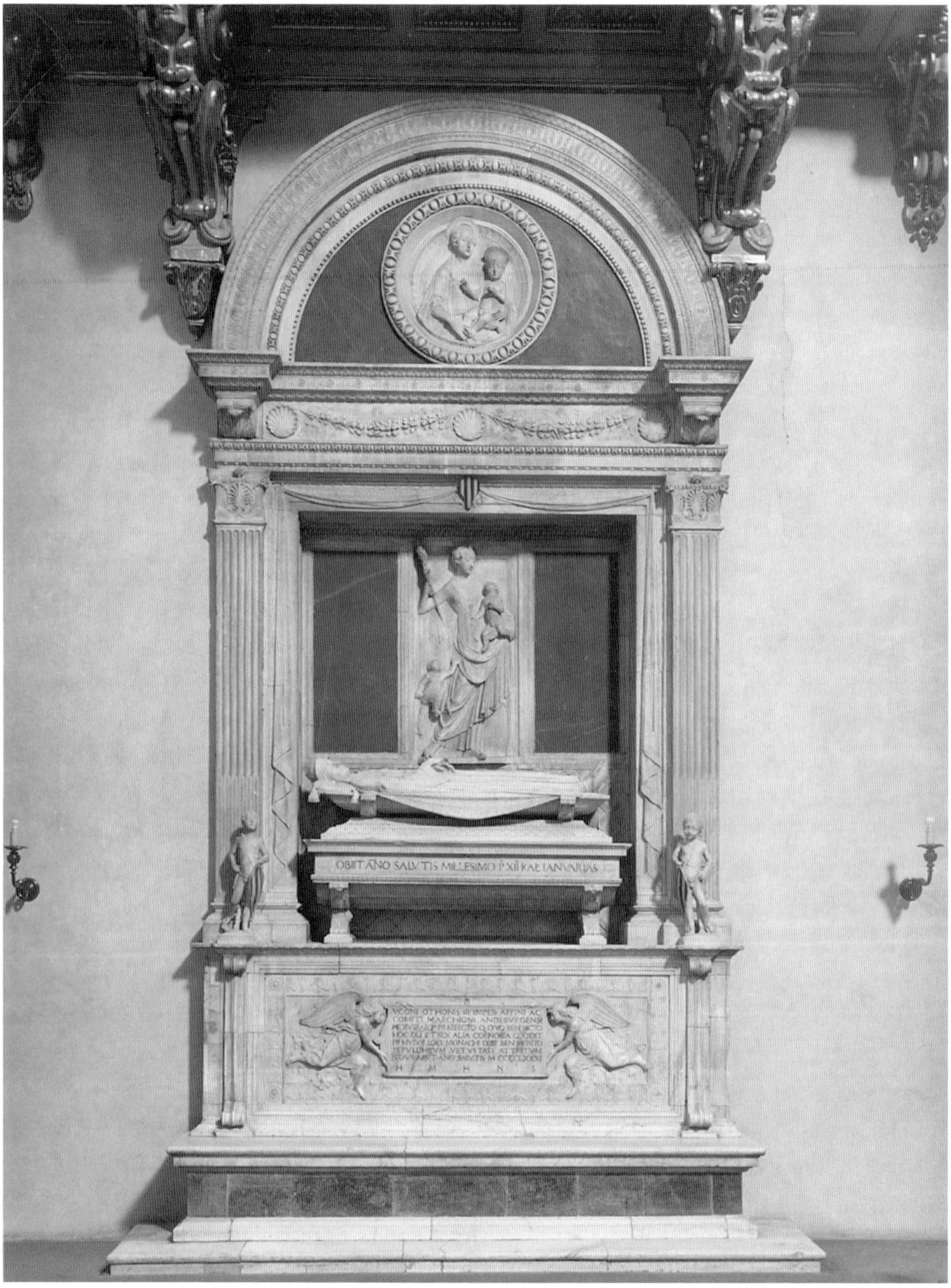

23. Mino da Fiesole, *Tomb of Count Hugo of Tuscany*, 1469–81. Florence, Badia. Photo: The Conway Library, Courtauld Institute of Art, London; negative B 80/2560.

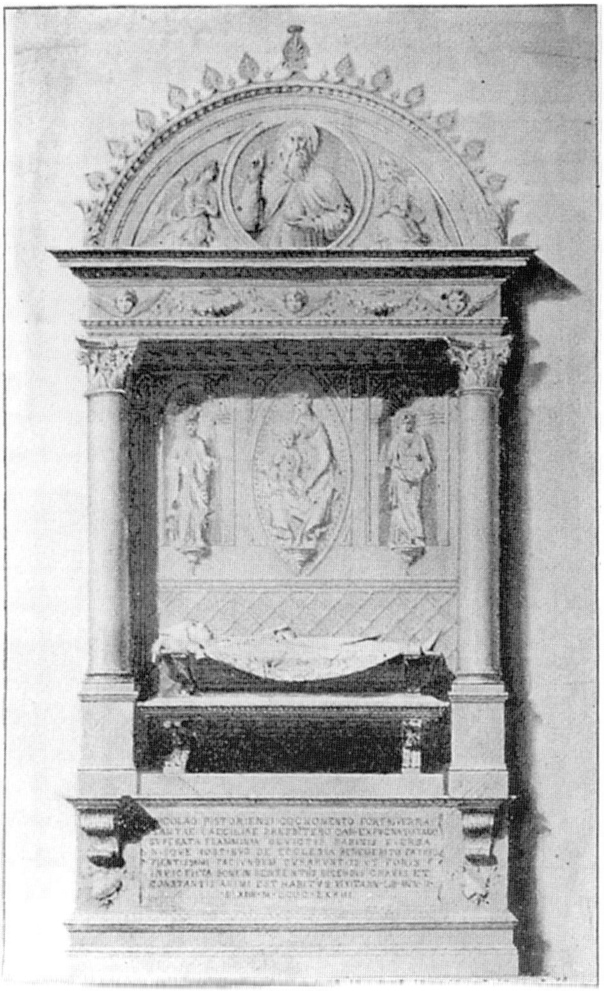

24. Domenico Gnoli, reconstruction drawing of the Tomb of Cardinal Niccolò Forteguerri from *Archivio storico dell'arte* 3 (1890): 269.

became friendly with his distant relative, Aeneas Silvius Piccolomini. The latter, who was elevated to the papacy in 1458 as Pius II, made Niccolò Bishop of Tiano and two years later, in 1460, titular cardinal of S. Cecilia in Trastevere. Active as a military leader and a diplomat for Pius II and then, later, for Paul II, the cardinal spent much of his career traveling and fighting. Upon his death in Viterbo on December 21, 1473, the cardinal's remains were transferred to Rome, where his brothers, as recorded in the inscription, had a tomb erected in his honor.[15]

As it stands today, however, the monument is not the work completed by Mino; it is a modern reconstruction. Fragments of the tomb scattered throughout the grounds of the church were reassembled in 1895 under the direction of Domenico Gnoli (Fig. 24).[16] The original porphyry columns, which had been employed in a

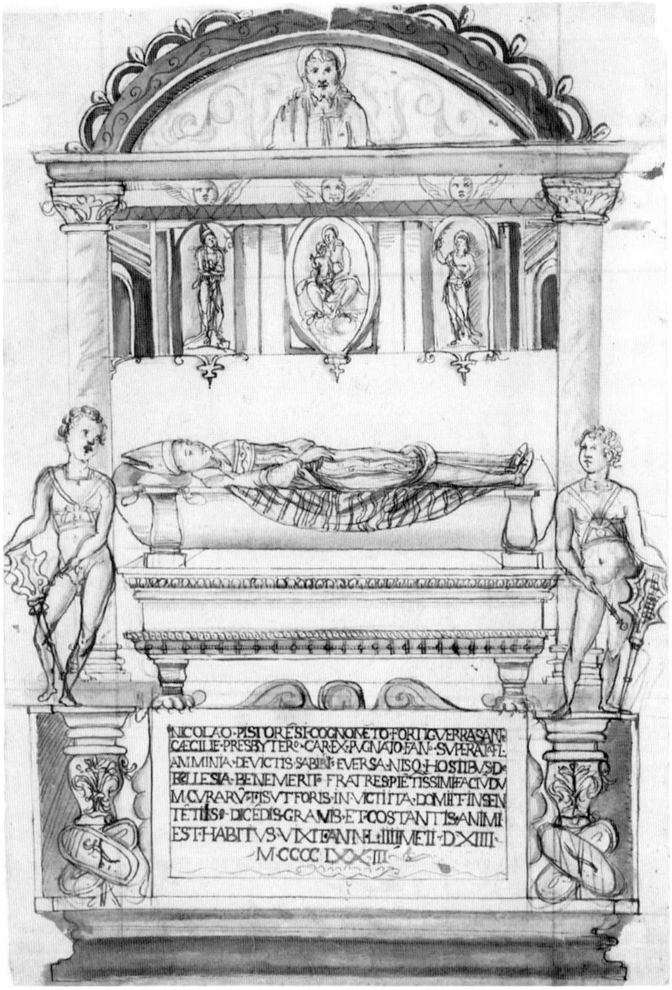

25. *Drawing of the Tomb of Cardinal Niccolò Forteguerri,* Albani Codex, fol. 186. Windsor Castle, Royal Library. Photo: The Royal Collection © 2001, Her Majesty Queen Elizabeth II, Windsor Castle (RL 11900a).

later rebuilding of the crypt, were restored using travertine and paint. From an altar refashioned in the late sixteenth century came the three reliefs with images of the Madonna and Child, Saint Cecilia, and Saint Nicholas along with a monumental lunette enclosing a roundel of God the Father flanked by two angels. To complete the reinstallation, Gnoli added pedestals for the front columns as well as the stucco imitation of carved trellis work on the wall behind the sarcophagus.[17] In Gnoli's reconstruction of the tomb, the corbels before the columns play an essential role: they still bear the marks for the placement of two lost shield-bearing putti.

The original existence of these putti is corroborated by a drawing in the Albani Codex at Windsor Castle. The volume titled 'Tombs of Illustrious Italians at Rome'

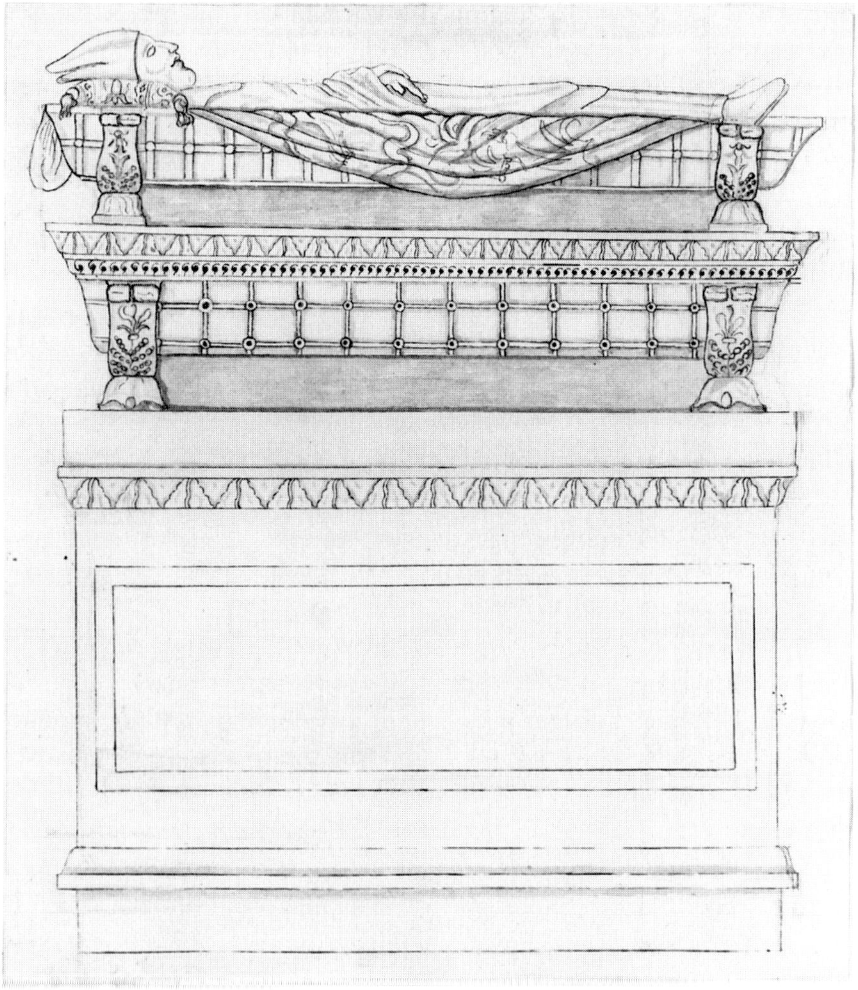

26. *Drawing of the Tomb of Cardinal Niccolò Forteguerri,* Albani Codex, fol. 104. Windsor Castle, Royal Library. Photo: The Royal Collection © 2001, Her Majesty Queen Elizabeth II, Windsor Castle (RL 11819).

is a collection of sketches made in the first half of the seventeenth century for Cassiano del Pozzo's so-called paper museum.[18] Although unknown to Gnoli, two states of the tomb are recorded: one shows the entire tomb (Fig. 25) and the other illustrates just the effigy and sarcophagus (Fig. 26). Unfortunately, little else is known about the tomb's original installation. It is first mentioned in a pastoral visit of 1582 when Cardinal Savello ordered that it be dismantled and that Forteguerri's effigy and sarcophagus be separated from the superstructure of the tomb.[19] It is this detached structure that is recorded in the Albani sketch of the effigy and sarcophagus. The second drawing, of the entire tomb, appears to be a reconstruction of the original, using the fragments still present in the church.[20]

The putti, whose presence is confirmed by the marks on the corbels, are the most obvious visual link to Florence. Two similar figures appear on the Florentine tomb in honor of Count Hugo of Tuscany, the project on which Mino had been working when he came to Rome. The best way to describe the Forteguerri tomb is, in fact, as a Roman adaptation of Mino's tomb for Count Hugo. The chronology bears this out. Within ten days of Cardinal Forteguerri's death, the governors in Pistoia were already contemplating a monument in his honor.[21] That they chose a cenotaph rather than a tomb for their native son implies that they knew a tomb was being planned in Rome.[22] In fact, the Forteguerri tomb already must have been under way by early 1474; and this is corroborated by the tomb's formal relationship to that of Count Hugo. By 1474 Mino had completed at least half of the Badia tomb. Yet he interrupted work on this important Florentine project to go to Rome. When he eventually returned to Florence to finish the Count Hugo tomb, Mino signed a final, revised contract with the monks, yet no hint of rancor about the six-year delay appears in this document. Mino must have abandoned his work in Florence with the compliance of the monks at the Badia.[23] In all likelihood, he had a contract for the Forteguerri tomb project in hand.

Presumably both Mino and the monks in Florence expected the Roman tomb to be completed in a timely fashion.[24] Yet such were the opportunities for a sculptor in Rome that by the end of that same year, 1474, Mino was working on not one, but three tombs in Rome – one for Pope Paul II, another for Cardinal Pietro Riario, as well as that for Cardinal Forteguerri. In January of 1474, just a month after the death of Forteguerri, Pietro Riario, the favorite nephew of the reigning pope, Sixtus IV, unexpectedly died in Rome, and a tomb was ordered from Mino and Andrea Bregno.[25] Then, in October of that same year, Cardinal Marco Barbo returned to Rome and turned his attention to a tomb for his uncle, Pope Paul II.[26] This enormous commission, too, went to Mino, this time in collaboration with Giovanni Dalmata. The latter two tombs were produced as shared workshop projects – with Mino and his assistants working with Bregno and his shop on the Riario tomb, and Giovanni Dalmata and his shop on the papal tomb. The pressure of these commissions must have been overwhelming. Mino's response reflects a modus operandi that he had used earlier. During his first sojourn in the papal city, the sculptor assembled a host of assistants to work with him on the increasingly large commissions he received. This is evident from the range of hands visible on the Santa Maria Maggiore ciborium, completed before 1464.[27] Moreover, the affinities that these assistants display with other artistic traditions indicate that many of them were fully mature stone carvers in their own right, hired on an ad hoc basis to help Mino complete the astonishing number of thirty-six reliefs on the ciborium. Later, during his second sojourn, Mino also employed assistants whose presence can be observed on the Forteguerri tomb. But now there are two distinct groups: resident sculptors without obvious connections to his style and Florentine assistants who came with Mino to Rome in 1474.

From the beginning – because of his obligations to the Florentine Badia on one hand and pressure from the cardinal's heirs in Rome on the other – Mino must have intended to install the Forteguerri tomb in all possible haste.[28] Mino probably began working on the Forteguerri tomb by early 1474, but as the more important papal assignments came up and took precedence, he was forced to use sculptors from Andrea Bregno's shop to help him complete the earlier, but as yet unfinished, Forteguerri tomb. One can only imagine the shuffling of carvers from one task to the next, working on reliefs for the Forteguerri tomb, for the Riario tomb, and for other projects that both sculptors had taken on simultaneously. Mino's Forteguerri tomb involved, like so many other Roman projects, the participation of carvers with widely diverse experiences, all working under the master's guidance.

The means by which Mino sought to expedite the Forteguerri commission was ingeniously simple. He brought not only his Florentine assistants with him to Rome, but even the plans and sketches for the Count Hugo tomb, because the initial work on the Forteguerri tomb seems to be a copy of what he and his workshop had just completed in Florence. Certainly the central section is so close to the earlier work as to be almost a replica. The basic design of the sarcophagus and bier – with the doubled supports below, the fictive roping on the underside, and the elaborate detailing of the bier cloth – is identical to that on the Count Hugo monument. Even more remarkable are the similarities between the two effigies. The cardinal's pose follows exactly that of the count. His clothing has been altered to reflect his different profession, yet unexpectedly and most striking of all, the two effigies share identical physiognomies. Ironically, Mino, so renowned as a portraitist, chose to repress this aspect of public commemoration. In Florence, some logic attaches to this disregard for specificity – Count Hugo had, after all, died almost five hundred years before Mino carved his tomb.[29] In Rome, however, this was certainly not the case. Although the Forteguerri effigy has been cited as a record of the cardinal's actual appearance, Forteguerri, like Count Hugo in Florence, wears the face of Mino's ideal, middle-aged man.[30] There are some reasonable explanations for the formulaic replication of the Florentine effigy and bier on the Roman tomb: there was tremendous pressure placed on Mino to produce this tomb rapidly; he and his assistants worked from drawings already developed for the Count Hugo tomb; and the effigy was carved by members of the Florentine shop based on the model of the Count Hugo effigy, without the master's requiring that the model be altered. Only with the aid of his Florentine assistants was Mino able to reproduce, besides the effigy itself, the bier and its decoration, the sarcophagus, and the putti.

This efficient system breaks down in the upper portions of the tomb, where it becomes increasingly Roman – both in execution and in style. Where the single allegorical figure of Charity appears on the Count Hugo tomb, on the Forteguerri tomb the tripartite division above the effigy contains three reliefs: the Virgin and Child are flanked by Saint Cecilia, the patron saint of the church, and Saint Nicholas, the name saint of the deceased. The enthroned Virgin gazes down at the cardinal, while the Child raises his hand in blessing. These visible assurances of salvation have been shifted from the pediment on the Count Hugo tomb to a place within the aedicula of the Forteguerri so as to reserve the upper lunette for a sterner vision of God the Father. The depiction of the Virgin closely resembles contemporary, half-length reliefs by Mino da Fiesole, although she is now shown full-length.[31] Close parallels exist on contemporary Roman tombs. The Riario tomb includes this same feature, with the Virgin and Child flanked by Saints Peter and Paul accompanied by Cardinal Riario and his brother, who together enact a traditional presentation scene. On the Forteguerri tomb acknowledgment of the cardinal's plea for salvation is made through the gaze and gestures of Christ and his mother.

The carving of the Madonna and Child includes many of the idiosyncrasies associated with Mino. If not entirely autograph, it was certainly completed by a close follower who possessed a full command of Mino's style. In contrast, the flanking saints bear little resemblance to Mino's own work. Among the reliefs associated with Mino's shop in Rome, they most closely approximate those of Saints Agostino and Monica on the tomb of Costanza Ammanati, undertaken by Mino's workshop at the end of the 1470s.[32] By contrast, the entire upper lunette on the Forteguerri tomb has no recognizable affinity with Mino. Rather, the carving style is that of reliefs issuing from Andrea Bregno's workshop. The relief of God the Father blessing is closely related to the comparable subject depicted in the lunettes above the altars in San Gregorio Magno and Santa Maria del Popolo.[33] The flanking angels exhibit analogies with those on the tomb of Cristoforo della Rovere. This tomb in S. Maria del Popolo was a shared commission: Mino da Fiesole and Andrea Bregno's joint responsibility is evident in the lunette where Bregno did the angels and Mino was responsible for the relief of the Madonna and Child in the center.[34]

The sculptures associated with Mino da Fiesole in Rome fall into two general types – there are those that are collaborative projects in the sense that one can identify both the distinctive contributions of Mino and of another documented master; and there are sculptural projects that suggest the presence of other hands, not identifiable by name, working under Mino's direction. The identity of these *scarpellini* is of less concern than is the notion that all of Mino's large-scale Roman sculptures were produced with the help of numerous assistants.[35] Even after Mino's departure from Rome, it is likely that these sculptors continued to work on tombs and other projects that still bear traces of the Florentine master's influence. An example of this continued connection with Mino's style is the unattributed tomb for Maddalena Orsini. It can be compared not only to work on the Forteguerri tomb but also to the tomb of Costanza Ammannati. The similarity between the two female effigies is especially striking, as is the comparable style used for the carving of all three female saints – Cecilia on the Forteguerri tomb, Monica on the Ammannati tomb, and the Magdalen on the Orsini tomb.[36] Increasingly diffuse, this inherited style is mingled with that of Bregno's followers, producing the oddly generic quality shared by a remarkable number of late quattrocento Roman tombs.

The portions of the tomb that recall either the Florentine tomb of Count Hugo or aspects of Mino's generic, Roman style are distinguishable from those elements that are easily related to neither. As one's eyes ascend, less and less of the Forteguerri tomb seems to reflect its Florentine precedent. The distinctions in carving highlight an even more essential difference between the two tombs – their enframing structures. The crowning canopy and crocketed lunette on the Forteguerri tomb are unlike anything planned or produced for the Count Hugo tomb. Instead of an aedicula set into the wall, the Forteguerri tomb projects outward into the space of the church. In Florence, the shape of the Count Hugo tomb evoked, although it did not replicate, a triumphal arch. In Rome, the superstructure recalled an equally suggestive architectural form – the altar canopy. By the middle of the fifteenth century, canopied tombs were common in Rome; the type followed a convention developed centuries earlier for curial commemoration. On the tomb of Cardinal Guglielmo Fieschi (d. 1256), for example, the deceased's sacred role in the church is invoked by the crowning canopy, a motif adapted from altar decoration.[37] The canopied freestanding monument of Cardinal Adam Easton (d. 1398), whose fragmentary tomb now resides on the other side of the entrance portal at S. Cecilia, might have served as a conceptual model for Mino's final design for the Forteguerri tomb.[38] To the Florentine effigy and sarcophagus he appended a canopied frame in compliance with local conventions. Mino's canopy dramatically enhances the connection with altar canopies through its form. Visually as well as symbolically, this association can be demonstrated by comparison first, with Arnolfo di Cambio's ciborium for the high altar of S. Cecilia, and then with Mino's own ciborium for the high altar of Santa Maria Maggiore.[39] The half-dome canopied form on the Forteguerri tomb protects not only the tomb effigy, but also the three interior reliefs that are themselves suggestive of altar decoration.[40] These motifs, so different from the design of the Florentine tomb of Count Hugo, obey Roman specifications. Although unsuitable for a secular ruler in Florence, Roman tradition deemed such references to sacred structures appropriate for the commemoration of a cardinal. The explicitly altar and chapel format of the Forteguerri tomb was evident to those who dismantled it, for it was precisely this portion that was preserved in S. Cecilia as an independent altar.[41]

The Forteguerri tomb, which at first glance seemed so essentially Florentine, is thus revealed to be radically different from its Tuscan prototype. Its canopied structure had no precedent in Florence: it is essentially an amalgamation of Roman formulas. Upon his arrival in Rome in 1474, Mino initially might have intended to construct another version of the Count Hugo tomb, but the final result reflects the formal and thematic requirements of Roman tomb design. Beginning with models developed in a Florentine context, Mino altered the tomb structure to reflect local requirements. Thus, in answer to the question of whether the tomb is Florentine or Roman, one is ultimately forced to acknowledge that it is neither and both.

The final hybrid appearance of the Forteguerri tomb reflects the process by which it was produced. In Florence, the designs of a particular master and his shop were unified by means of a single, harmonious style regardless of the varied media employed, but from the great marble carving shops of the last quarter of the fifteenth century in Rome came works that are, in contrast to those in Florence, extraordinarily eclectic. Yet these distinctions too are the result of the workshop structure.[42] With so few masters and so many monumental marble projects being commissioned in Rome, no master and his shop was able to work in isolation. Sculptors shared projects and they shared assistants. The demand for countless marble tombs, altars, tabernacles, ciboria, portals, statues, and reliefs, most on a monumental scale and all to be done rapidly and efficiently, led inevitably to a system of marble production vastly different from that in Florence.

Whether in Rome or in Florence, Mino da Fiesole's knowledge of two systems of production and his awareness of two distinct traditions, allowed him to construct monuments that were both of and separate from local custom. The giant Roman projects he erected in the 1460s were organized like architectural commissions. Indeed, it might be better to compare the Roman sculptural workshops to stone-carving shops employed on buildings; it is the organization of diverse skills and techniques associated with such shops that most resembles what was required of a sculptor in Rome. In the single decade of the 1470s Mino was involved in the execution of some of the most important marble tombs produced in either Florence or Rome. The Forteguerri tomb is just one example – a particularly conspicuous one because of its relationship to the Count Hugo tomb – of the methods he employed in the construction of a monumental tomb in Rome. Initially conceived in emulation of a Florentine prototype and then altered in adherence to specific Roman traditions, the carving was done by a variety of hands, some local and some foreign. The resulting tomb exposes a surprising diversity of style and content.

The Forteguerri tomb has been treated here as a work designed by a single Florentine sculptor in response to a unique set of circumstances: the artist was asked to produce to a tomb for a Tuscan cardinal who was to be memorialized not in his native city, but in Rome. Mediating between two distinct traditions, the resulting sepulchral monument might best be described as a hybrid. This biological term refers literally the offspring of genetically dissimilar parents, but it might also be used to describe the tomb for Cardinal Forteguerri which, after all, is the result of two distinct tomb traditions. The fact of artistic exchange and cultural translation addressed in this chapter deals first with the flexibility, both physical and conceptual, of the artist involved and then with the broader symbolic purpose of such a refashioning. Ultimately, the amalgamation of external and local ideas revealed in this tomb epitomizes the true nature of the Renaissance.

NOTES

1. The literature on the relationship between popes and cardinals in the Renaissance is vast: see, among others, John A. F. Thomson, *Popes and Princes, 1417–1517; Politics and Polity in the Late Medieval Church* (London: George Allen & Unwin, 1980), 58–74; Charles L. Stinger, *The Renaissance in Rome* (Bloomington: Indiana University Press, 1985), 27–31; Peter Partner, *The Pope's Men. The Papal Civil Service in the Renaissance* (Oxford: Clarendon Press, 1990), esp. 205–6; Franco Cardini, *Alla corte dei papi: Vita, arte e cultura da San Pietro ai giorni nostri* (Milan: Arnoldo Mondadori, 1995), 70–1.

2. Although the effect has been enhanced by later importations of tombs from St. Peter's as well as by sixteenth- and seventeenth-century alterations, the interior of Santa Maria del Popolo is today perhaps the most evocative representative of the incrustration of curial and family tombs.

3. Again, Santa Maria del Popolo can serve as an example of this impression. Besides the tomb of Cristoforo della Rovere (d. 1478), other tombs in the church that replicate aspects of the so-called triumphal arch design include those for Cardinal Giovanni Costa (d. 1508) and Pietro Rocca (d. 1482), as well as the two cinquecento monuments in the choir by Andrea and Jacopo Sansovino for Cardinals Asciano Sforza and Girolamo Basso della Rovere. For the quattrocento tombs in Santa Maria del Popolo, see Anna Cavallaro, 'Introduzione alle cappelle maggiore,' in *Umanesimo e primo rinascimento in S. Maria del Popolo*, ed. Roberto Cannatà, Anna Cavallaro, and Claudio Strinati (Rome: De Luca, 1981), 75–83. Such repetitiousness in design, if not in carving style, can be found not only in Roman tombs but also other monumental works of stone, including church facades (S. Maria del Popolo and Sant'Agostino) and altars (a significant, if often overlooked example, being the now fragmentary altars designed by Andrea Bregno and Luigi Capponi's workshops at the end of the century: see James Von Schmidt, *Die Altäre des Guillaume des Perriers und verwandte Werke. Ein Beitrag zur Geschichte der römischen Quattrocentoplastik* (St. Petersburg: Rudolphe Jassé Internationale, 1899); and Francesco Negri Arnoldi, 'Luigi di Pietro Capponi da Milano,' *Arte lombarda* 6 (1961): 195–201.

4. Although few documents remain that attest to this expectation, the commission for the tomb of Giovan Francesco Brusati in San Clemente may serve as an example: it was awarded jointly to Luigi Capponi and Giovanni di Domenico della Pietra. The commission is discussed and the document transcribed by Domenico Gnoli, 'Luigi Capponi da Milano-scultore,' *Archivio storico dell'arte* 6 (1891): 85–101; and ibid., 'Nuovi documenti: contratti per opere di scultura di Luigi Capponi, milanesi,' 127–8.

5. The first indication of the monks' interest in a new tomb for their founder is a payment to Luca della Robbia for a model in 1440. See John Pope-Hennessy, *Luca della Robbia* (Ithaca and New York: Cornell University Press, 1980), 234, cat. no. 4.

6. Some well-documented examples from the sixteenth century underscore this reality: the lack of a tomb monument for Alexander VI, the speed with which Julius II had the paired tombs in the choir of S. Maria del Popolo erected, and, of course, the tragic story of the Julius tomb itself.

7. The literature on Mino da Fiesole has grown steadily since Giancarlo Sciolla, *La scultura di Mino da Fiesole* (Turin: G. Giappichelli, 1970); for a review of his early career, see Francesco Caglioti, 'Mino da Fiesole, Mino del Reame, Mino da Montemignanaio: un caso chiarito di sdoppiamento d'identità artistica,' *Bolletino d'arte* 74, no. 67 (1991): 19–86; and Shelley E. Zuraw, 'The Sculpture of Mino da Fiesole (1429–1484)' (Ph.D. diss., New York University, 1993), 292–4, and cat. no. 52, pp. 855–60, for a monographic treatment of his entire oeuvre.

8. For a discussion by the author of these reliefs and for illustrations of them after their 1996 cleaning, see *Masterpieces of Renaissance and Baroque Sculpture from the Palazzo Venezia, Rome,* ed. Shelley E. Zuraw, exh. cat. (Athens: Georgia Museum of Art, 1996), cat. nos. 1–4, pp. 40–7.

9. Born in 1429, Mino was already thirty-five years old when he matriculated. Compare this to Desiderio, for example, who although born within a year of Mino, matriculated twelve years earlier in 1453. The documents associated with Mino's guild payments were published by Cornelius de Fabriczy, 'Appunti d'Archivio: Alcuni documenti su Mino da Fiesole,' *Rivista d'arte* 2 (1904): 40–5.

10. The numerous Madonna and Child reliefs attributed to Mino are notoriously difficult to date but have been admired for their Desiderio-like beauty since the nineteenth century. For a review of these reliefs, see Zuraw, 'Mino da Fiesole,' 194–227.

11. Mino's *catasto* from 1470 is transcribed in Cornelius de Fabriczy, 'Portate al Catasto di Mino da Fiesole,' *Rivista d'arte* 3 (1905): 265–6.

12. Shelley E. Zuraw, 'The Public Commemorative Monument: Mino da Fiesole's Tombs in the Florentine Badia,' *Art Bulletin* 80 (1998): 452–77.

13. The precise chronology of the Count Hugo tomb can only be inferred: see Zuraw, 'Public Commemorative Monument,' 452, and idem, 'Mino da Fiesole,' 292–4, and cat. no. 52, pp. 855–60.

14. For a recent brief biography (and bibliography) of Cardinal Forteguerri, see Anna Esposito's entry in *Dizionario biografico degli italiani* 49 (1997), 156–9, s.v. 'Forteguerri, Niccolò'; the author dates the completion of the tomb to 1480 following the suggestion of Arnoldi (see n. 24).

15. The carved inscription on the tomb reads as follows:

> NICOLAO PISTORIENSI COGNOMENTO FORTIGVERRA / SANCTAE CAECILIA E PRESBYTERO CAR. EXPVGNATO FANO / SVPERATA FLAMMINIA DE VICTIS SABINIS EVERSA / NISQUE HOSTIBVS DE ECCLESIA BENEMERITO FRATRES / PIENTISSIMI FACIVNDVM CVRARVNT. IS VT FORIS / INVICTI ITA DOMIIN SENTENTIIS DICENDIS GRAVIS ET / CONSTANTIS ANIMI EST HABITVS VIXIT ANN. LIII. MEN. II. / D. XIIII. M. CCCC. LXXIII

The inscription literally provides a list of the cardinal's military triumphs. Unusual for the time, there are few abbreviations. The lettering and phrasing suggest the most refined Latin. A comparison with the inscription on the Count Hugo tomb (Zuraw, 'Public Commemorative Monuments,' fig. 27) is instructive. The incised lines, abbreviations, and uneven spacing of the Florentine inscription have been replaced here by a far surer technique. As noted by Francesco

Niutti ('Temi e personaggi nell'epigrafia sistina,' in *Un pontificato ed una città. Sisto IV (1471–1484)*, Atti del convegno, 3–7 dicembre, 1984, Roma, ed. Massimo Miglio et al. [Rome: Associazione Roma nel rinascimento, 1986], 406), the Forteguerri inscription is the only cardinal's tomb inscription from the pontificate of Sixtus IV that does not include a formulaic reference to the reigning pope.

16. Gnoli describes the reconstruction done by Camillo Ciavarri in two publications: Domenico Gnoli, 'L'opere di Mino da Fiesole in Roma, Parte IV,' *Archivio storico dell'arte* 3 (1890): 266–71; and idem, 'Miscellanea; Riconstruzione del monumento del cardinal Forteguerri, di Mino da Fiesole,' *Archivio storico dell'arte* 4 (1891): 209.

17. Photographs taken before the reconstruction exist in the Istituto Centrale per il Catalogo e la Documentazione, Rome: they include a single column and capital (Ser. F, n. 89), the relief of St. Cecilia (Ser. F, n. 91), the effigy and inscription (Ser. D, n. 4414), and pilaster capital (Ser. F, n. 87), a single capital (Ser. F, n. 88), and the mandorla-shaped relief of the Madonna and Child (Ser. F, n. 90).

18. In the sketchbook, known as Albani Codex, no. 201, a drawing, fol. 186 (inv. n. 11.900), records the entire tomb including the inscription and the shield-bearing putti; a second drawing, fol. 104 (inv. n. 11.819), depicts the effigy and bier over a pedestal with a blank field for the inscription. This sketch records the same state as the old photograph of the effigy and inscription noted earlier (Ser. D., n. 4414). For a description of this particular volume in the *Museo Cartaceo*, see Henrietta McBurney, 'History and Contents of the Dal Pozzo Collection in the Royal Library, Windsor Castle,' in *Cassiano dal Pozzo*, Atti del seminario internazionale di studi, ed. Francesco Solinas (Rome: De Luca, 1989), 74–94. Among the numerous volumes associated with the paper museum, that dedicated to 'The Tombs of Illustrious Italians' seems the hardest to explain. It fits into none of the main categories of the collection – antiques, architecture, or science. To date it has also not been the subject on an independent evaluation.

19. Archivio di Stato, Rome, Congregazione Religiose Femminili, Benedettine, Santa Cecilia in Trastevere, Busta 4424, Reg. 2. fols. 20r–21v; I wish to thank Jack Freiberg, who generously provided me with transcriptions of these documents. The document referring to the replacement of the stones and tomb slabs that were threatened with ruin was cited by Bertolotti in his discussion of the dismantling of the marble incrustation on the apse wall (Antonino Bertolotti, 'Curiosità storiche ed artistiche, raccolte negli archivi romani,' *Archivio storico, artistico, archeologico e letterario della città e provincia di Roma* 4 [1880]: 11–25). What little is known about the Forteguerri tomb's initial installation comes from the pastoral visit Cardinal Savello made. He apparently decided that three altars in the church were too small, so, in 1584, under the direction of the Abbess Cherubina Cardelli, the body of Cardinal Forteguerri along with his sarcophagus were separated from the superstructure of the tomb. The dismantled tomb is described as having been 'al paro' of the chapel of the Holy Sacrament; the cardinal's body and the sarcophagus were moved to a site where previously there had been an altar dedicated to the Virgin. The remaining portions of the tomb – 'l'adornamento delle colonne et architravi et marmi intagliati con dio Pade, la madonna, S. Zenone et S. Iustina overo Agata [*sic*]' – were preserved as an altar aedicula for a new altar consecrated to the honor of the Madonna, S. Andrea, and all the other apostles, S. Zenone and S. Benedetto Abbate.

20. The dating of the various albums of the paper museum roughly falls into the second quarter of the seventeenth century, at least twenty-five years after the dismantling of the tomb (see n. 18). That the artist(s) of the partial tomb drawing was aware of the complete sketch is suggested by the fact that he/they did not feel required to copy the entire inscription.

21. The cardinal died on December 21, 1473; on January 4, 1474, the Consiglio of Pistoia first considered an 'archa honorabilis seu monumentum cum epitaphio in litteris.' For the cenotaph of Cardinal Forteguerri in the Duomo, Pistoia, see Andrew Butterfield, *The Sculptures of Andrea del Verrocchio* (New Haven and London: Yale University Press, 1997), 137–53 and cat. nos. 21 and 22, pp. 223–8. The most recent consideration of the cenotaph and, in particular, the terra cotta model now in the Victoria and Albert Museum, London is found in Patricia Lee Rubin and Alison Wright, *Renaissance Florence. The Art of the 1470s,* exh. cat. (London: National Gallery of Art, 1999), 150. The complex exchanges between the Pistoiese and the Florentines is discussed by Stephen Milner in this volume.

22. The Roman tomb was the responsibility of the cardinal's two brothers. The funding for the tomb presumably came from the monies left to them in Tuscany because the cardinal's Roman funds were confiscated by Sixtus IV. See n. 28. Giovanni Forteguerri, one of the cardinal's brothers was also buried in the tomb. It is worth noting that this brother was closely associated with the humanist theories of Carlo Marsuppini. It may be that the decision to erect a 'Florentine' tomb reflects his standards. For both Giovanni and the third brother, Pietro; see Paolo Franzese in *Dizionario biografico degli italiani* 49 (1997), 150–1, s.v. 'Forteguerri, Giovanni.' Finally, two other Forteguerri were buried in S. Cecilia in 1473, Cincio and his nephew Giuliano. Their tomb slab now rests in the portico. See Laura Gigli, *Rione XIII. Trastevere, Parte III (S. Cecilia),* Guide Rionali di Roma, 30 (Rome: Fratelli Palombi, 1982), 220. For a photograph, see (Istituto Centrale peril Catalogo e la Documentazione, Rome) E 104741.

23. This exchange may only be surmised. The only document relating to the late phase of Mino's work on the Count Hugo tomb is the 1480 published by Giovanni Poggi, 'Mino da Fiesole e la Badia Fiorentina,' *Miscellanea d'arte* 1 (1903): 98–103.

24. To date the most extensive modern discussion of the tomb remains Francesco Negri Arnoldi ('Il monumento sepolcrale del card. Niccolò Forteugerri in Santa Cecilia a Roma e il suo cenotafio nella cattedrale di Pistoia,' in *Egemonia fiorentina ed autonomie locali nella Toscnana nord-occodentale del primo rinascimento: vita, arte, cultura,* Convegno internazionale, 18–25 settembre, 1975, Pistoia [Pistoia: Centro di studi, 1978], 211–33, esp. 212–16), who suggests a date at the end of Mino's second Roman sojourn, in contrast to Sciolla's comments (*La scultura,* 91–2), who, based on comparisons with the Santa Maria Maggiore ciborium, argues for an earlier date. It should be noted that the Albani Codex sketches that confirm the close association with the Count Hugo tomb were not known to these authors. I was able to study photographs of the Albani Codex at the Biblioteca Hertziana, Rome, and I attempted a revised reconstruction of the tomb in my dissertation (Zuraw, 'Mino da Fiesole,' 861–75, cat. no. 53).

25. For the life of Cardinal Riario, see Paola Farenga, "Monumenta Memoriae;' Pietro Riario fra Mito e Storia,' in *Un pontificato ed una città. Sisto IV (1471–1484),* Atti del convegno, 3–7 dicembre, 1984, Roma, ed. Massimo Miglio et al. (Rome: Associazione Roma nel rinascimento, 1986), 179–216, esp. 208–12. His tomb, in the choir of SS. Apostoli, Rome, is often attributed solely to the sculptor Andrea Bregno; see, for example, Isabelle Frank, 'Cardinal Giuliano della Rovere and Melozzo da Forlì at SS. Apostoli,' *Zeitschrift für Kunstgeschichte* 59 (1996): 97–121, esp. ill. 12. Frank notes correctly that it was the cardinal's uncle, Pope Sixtus IV who erected the tomb in honor of his nephew (p. 114). Riario's apparent lack of interest in his own funerary monument may reflect simply the brevity of the period when he wore a red hat – only fourteen months. That the monument was moved from its original location within the apse of SS. Apostoli is evident from the ground plan and elevations produced of the area by Francesco Fontana in 1708; see Lorenzo Finocchi Ghersi, 'La basilica dei SS. Apostoli a Roma. Le modifiche dell'impianto

medievale nel Quattrocento,' in *Quaderni dell'Istituto di storia dell'architettura. Saggi in onore di Renato Bonelli,* ed. Corrado Bozzoni, n.s. 15–20 (1990–2): 355–66, esp. fig. 13.

26. The date for both the commission and the construction of the tomb of Paul II cannot be confirmed. The most recent discussion of the problem is found in Johannes Röll, *Giovanni Dalmata,* Römische Studien der Bibliotheca Hertziana, 10 (Worms am Rhein: Wernersche Verlagsgesellschaft, 1994), 60–84, esp. 83–4. The pope died in 1471, but it seems unlikely that the tomb was begun immediately. The work, as recorded in an inscription, was the responsibility of Cardinal Marco Barbo and was completed in 1477. According to Vasari, a source of limited value in this case, the work on the tomb took two years (G. Vasari, *Le vite de' più eccellenti pittori, scultori, ed architettori,* ed. G. Milanesi, 2nd ed. (Florence, G. C. Sansoni, 1906), 3: 118. It has been assumed that Mino's arrival in Rome in 1474 was the result of his receiving the commission for this important papal tomb; however, it seems more likely that it was the Forteguerri tomb that brought him to the papal city.

27. Shelley Zuraw, 'Mino da Fiesole's First Roman Sojourn: The Works in Santa Maria Maggiore,' in *Verrocchio and Late Quattrocento Italian Sculpture,* ed. Steven Bule, Alan Phipps Darr, and Fiorella Superbi Gioffredi (Florence, Le Lettere, 1992), 303–19; and Francesco Caglioti, 'Per il recupero della giovinezza di Mino da Fiesole: il 'Ciborio della neve',' *Prospettiva* 47 (1987): 15–32.

28. It is worth noting here that in July 1474 Sixtus IV took over the Roman funds of the cardinal. See Piero de Angelis, 'Tre cardinali benefattori involontari,' in *L'architetto e gli affreschi di Santo Spirito in Saxia* (Rome: 1961), 67–73.

29. The count died on December 21, 1001.

30. This can be demonstrated in a comparison between the cardinal's effigy and the figure of St. Louis of Toulouse from the Riario tomb; see Zuraw, 'Public Commemorative Monuments,' 468 and fig. 28. Butterfield ('Verrocchio,' 156), rejects the identification of the figure of Nicodemus on a relief of the *Entombment* as Cardinal Forteguerri because of its lack of resemblance to the effigy in Rome. Unfortunately, the Roman effigy cannot be used to make any statement about the cardinal's appearance.

31. The full-length Virgin on the Forteguerri tomb is proceeded by Mino's relief of the *Assumption of the Virgin* for the Santa Maria Maggiore ciborium. Stylistically, the relief is comparable not only to the half-length relief of the Madonna and Child in the Metropolitan Museum of Art, New York (inv. no. 42.38.2), but also to the seated Madonna carved for the Riario tomb.

32. The tombs of Costanza Ammannati and of her son, Cardinal Jacopo, stand today in the courtyard of the Palazzo dell'Avvocatura, once part of Sant'Agostino, Rome; see Benedetta Montevecchi, *Sant'Agostino, Le chiese di Roma illustrate,* n.s. 17 (Rome: Fratelli Palombi, 1985), 192–97. Costanza died in 1477, two years before her son. Although problematic for numerous reasons, the tombs seem to have been conceived as a pair, and because the cardinal's tomb indubitably issued from Mino's shop (the relief of the *Last Judgment* on the cardinal's tomb is probably a work by the sculptor's own hand), the production of both must surely be linked to him. It should be noted that both the cardinal and his mother are depicted imploring Christ's mercy at the base of the *Last Judgment.*

33. The altar in S. Gregorio Magno, although earlier than the tomb by ca. five years (1469), was done for Abbot Gregorio VI Amatisco; see Anna Maria Pedrocchi, *San Gregorio al Celio. Storia di una abbazia* (Rome: Istituto Poligrafico e Zecca dello Stato, 1993), 33–4; Francesco Caglioti ('Paolo Romano, Mino da Fiesole e il tabernacolo di San Lorenzo in Dàmaso,' *Prospettiva: Scritti in onore di Giovanni Previtali, vol. 1,* 53–6 [1988–1989]: 245–55), who attributes the work to the 'Maestro di Pio II.' For a comparison of this altar with the high altar from 1473 for S. Maria del Popolo,

see Joachim Poeschke, *Die Skulptur der Renaissance in Italien, Band 1 : Donatello un seine Zeit* (Munich: Hirmer, 1990), 159–60, cat. no. 230. A recent discussion of both these altars and of Bregno's early work in Rome is found in Francesco Caglioti, 'Sui primi tempi romani d'Andrea Bregno: Un progetto per il cardinale camerlengo Alvise Trevisna e un San Michele Arcangelo per il cardinale Juan de Carvajal,' *Mitteilungen des Kunsthistorischen Institutes in Florenze* 41 (1997): 213–52. For a brief overview of Bregno's career, see Gianni Carlo Sciolla, 'Profilo di Andrea Bregno,' *Arte lombarda* 15 (1970): 52–8.

34. For the tomb, see n. 3 to this chapter. Claudio Strinati ('La scultura,' in *Umanesimo e primo rinascimento in S. Maria del Popolo*, exh. cat., ed. Roberto Cannatà, Anna Cavallaro, and Claudio Strinati [Rome: De Luca, 1981], 34) argues that the design of tomb should be assigned to Mino.

35. Some hint of the numbers involved is provided by Stefano Borsi, Francesco Quinterio, and Corinna Vasic Vatovec, *Maestri fiorentini nei cantieri romani del Quattrocento*, ed. Silvia Danesei Squarzina (Rome: Officina Edizioni, 1989), 137–302, their catalogue of Florentine masters working in Rome under Pius II, Sixtus IV, and Innocent VIII.

36. Today in the refectory of S. Salvatore in Laura, the tomb is illustrated in Vincenzo Golzio and Giuseppe Zander, *L'arte in Roma nel secolo XV*, Storia di Roma 28 (Bologna: Licinio Cappelli, 1968), 346–7, tav. CCXXXII,1.

37. Julian Gardner, *The Tomb and the Tiara. Curial Tomb Sculpture in Rome and Avignon in the Later Middle Ages* (Oxford: Clarendon Press, 1992), 34–5. For a reconstruction of the Fieschi tomb, see also Ingo Herklotz, *'Sepulcra' e 'Monumento' del Medioevo; Studi sull'arte sepolcrale in Italie* (Rome: Rari Nantes, 1985), 161–3. The baldachin or canopy tomb (or *enfeu*) is famously discussed by Erwin Panofsky, *Tomb Sculpture* (1964; reprint New York: Harry N. Abrams, 1992), 60–1, 76–7.

38. Gardner, *Tomb and the Tiara*, 130–2.

39. The unusual decoration on the exterior of the lunette was the source of a heated debate between Mario Salmi and Negri Arnoldi (see n. 24). Negri Arnoldi noted the similarity of the decoration to the crockets on the dome of the Santa Maria Maggiore ciborium. Another possible parallel in Mino's work is the now long lunette over the tomb of Cardinal Jacopo Ammannati. It is recorded in another drawing from the Albani Codex 201, fol 106. (inv. no. 11.821). Finally, another parallel can be found in the extraordinary altar monument for the Miroballi in S. Giovanni a Carbonara, Naples. Dated ca. 1470 and attributed to Pietro da Milano by Francesco Abbate, *La scultura napoletana del cinquecento* (Rome: Donzelli, 1992), 7–8. For the ciborium in S. Cecilia, see Valentino Pace, 'Il ciborio di Arnolfo a Santa Cecilia: Una nota sul suo stato originario e sulla sua committenza,' in *Studi di storia dell'arte sul Medioevo e il Rinascimento nel centenario della nascita di Mario Salmi*, Atti del convegno internazionale, Arezzo-Firenze, 16–19 novembre, 1989, vol. 1 (Florence: Polistampa, 1992), 389–400. For the relationship between the two ciboria or, at least, the two artists, see S. Zuraw's 'Mino da Fiesole's Lost Design for the Facade of S. Maria del Fiore,' in *Santa Maria del Fiore. The Cathedral and Its Sculpture*, ed. Margaret Haines, Acts of the International Symposium for the VII Centenary of the Cathedral of Florence, Villa I Tatti, 5–6 June 1997 (Fiesole: Edizioni Cadmo, 2001), 79–93.

40. The relationship between tomb space and a consecrated altar is made explicit in the influential tomb of Boniface VIII (d. 1308). See, most recently, Gardner, *Tomb and the Tiara*, 107–9. For one comment on the 'rapid effect' of the Boniface tomb, see Francis Ames-Lewis, *Tuscan Marble Carving 1250–1350. Sculpture and Civic Pride* (Cambridge: Ashgate, 1997), 188. The Riario tomb provides an obvious, if more elaborate parallel, but other Roman tombs – including the tomb of Cardinal Auxia di Poggio (1484) in S. Sabina, where the two saints and the center Madonna and Child are all half-length – repeat the motif of the triptych.

41. See n. 19.

42. Florentine examples of large workshops during this period are those of Verrocchio – where work was done in bronze, marble, tempera, terracotta, and wood – and the Pollaiuolo brothers, whose output included not only bronze and tempera, but also embroidery designs, silver, and fresco. For a discussion of Florence in this period, see the exhibition catalogue *Renaissance Florence* cited in n. 21.

4

Bertoldo di Giovanni, Republican Court Artist

Luke Syson

In 1925 Wilhelm von Bode published a book devoted to the still-shadowy figure of Bertoldo di Giovanni, which served effectively to define the oeuvre of the Florentine sculptor for more than fifty years. Its subtitle gives a rather misleading sense of its contents: 'Die Kunstpolitik des Lorenzo il Magnifico im Spiegel der Werke seines Lieblingskünstlers Bertoldo di Giovanni.'[1] Beyond an attempt at the artist's biography, and a (rather overextended) catalogue of his works, Bode does not, in fact, go on to tackle the 'art policy' of Lorenzo de' Medici until the last few pages. Here he posits a link between Bertoldo's 'Kleinplastik' and Lorenzo's 'Studium der antiken Kleinkunst', his passion for the collection of small antiquities, ancient coins, gems, and bronzes, as opposed (Bode thought) to a lack of Laurentian *grands projets.* Although this analysis now appears rather limited, Bode's concept of how an individual artist and his works were used not so much to mirror but to embody a patron's artistic policy might be usefully revisited; and the employment by Lorenzo of Bertoldo does seem to be a particularly good instance of such a patron-artist relationship. To show how this alliance of interests functioned, it is necessary first to define Bertoldo, both by comparison with other artists similarly exploited by patrons – primarily dynastic rulers – elsewhere in Italy and by establishing differences between Lorenzo's sculptor and his court artist peers. Having characterised the artist, it should then be possible to identify Lorenzo's *Kunstpolitik* by the close examination of Bertoldo's works executed for *il Magnifico,* and, in particular, of a single commemorative medal used, this essay argues, as a summation of this strategy. Lastly, it seems useful to explore another area of Bertoldo's activity in Lorenzo's service – his teaching at the Medici sculpture garden at San Marco – apparently intended to ensure that a Medici artistic policy was no longer personified by a single artist but established as a collective endeavour among other, younger artists in the city of Florence.

This essay therefore falls, rather approximately, into two parts and is intended to provoke discussion as much as to arrive at concrete solutions. In the first part, it will be argued that Lorenzo de' Medici, by exploiting Bertoldo as an instrument of his cultural policy, was following, but tactfully transforming, what was by then the standard practice of the Italian princes whom he increasingly regarded as his peers. The way in which Lorenzo adopted but modified his model is shown, in particular, through an examination of Bertoldo's deliberately Florentine translation of that most archetypal category of court art: the portrait medal. The second part of the chapter looks at the realisation of Laurentian artistic policy in the hands of Bertoldo and at the way in which his style (and its recognised historical ingredients – the antique and, in particular, Florentine art of the early quattrocento) was taught to his pupils – including Michelangelo. By organising a school with Bertoldo at its head, Lorenzo, it will be proposed, was attempting to establish a collective look for the artistic product of the city of a kind that other rulers had established in the image of their court artists, and one with the same ingredients of ancient precedent and modern Florentine inventiveness that could be perceived in Bertoldo's works, annexing or translating a particular visual tradition into something that was specifically Laurentian.

Embodying Styles: Court Artists and Ruler Portraits

Baxandall, some thirty years ago, underlined the fact that patrons were discriminatory in their choice of artists, showing that stylistic or aesthetic judgements were 'not only about one artist being simply *better* than another, but also about one artist being *different* in character from one another.'[2] This was never more the case than when an artist of reputation was to enter the employ of a particular patron. It also more true of certain categories of art object than others. Because fifteenth-century portraits, for example, are so often perceived as obeying conventions intrinsic to the genre, it is sometimes forgotten that in addition (and connected) to those considerations, selection might be made on authorial and stylistic grounds. A Renaissance patron might choose a portraitist because of the artist's ability to capture a likeness or to idealise his subject according to established criteria and, most frequently, to achieve a balance between verisimilitude and idealisation. The resulting portrait gained additional meaning and value by the fame of its author, however, and by the particular 'talented' style for which that artist was renowned. The concept was pithily encapsulated by Leonardo Giustiniani writing before 1446: 'Alexander the Great desired to be painted by Apelles, the most excellent painter of his age, above all others. Why was this? It was because he realised that his fame – something of which he was most careful – would receive no small addition through the art of Apelles.'[3] Accounts of the relationship between Alexander and his painter, Apelles, and his sculptor, Lysippus, and their exclusive production of his portraits became well-worn clichés of fifteenth-century writings on art, but their constant reiteration unquestionably conditioned the relationship between quattrocento rulers and their modern court artists; direct parallels were drawn, for example, by the Gonzaga marquises of Mantua in their employment of Andrea Mantegna.[4] It is true that members of the Gonzaga family, including Marquis Lodovico himself, expressed their reservations on his talents in the field of portraiture, a fact which at first appears strange, given that his chief labour for nearly a decade (1465–74) was the execution of the group portraits in the *Camera Picta.* The dedicatory inscription of the Camera, however, makes it clear that the room was to be seen as just such a product of the relationship between a ruler and his enormously talented artist: 'For the illustrious Lodovico, second Marquis of Mantua, best of princes and most unvanquished in faith, and for his illustrious wife Barbara incomparable glory of womankind, his Andrea Mantegna of Padua completed this slight [or fine: *tenue*] work in the year 1474.' Lodovico's doubts about Mantegna's ability as a flatterer or capturer of likenesses may have been real (and were later echoed by Isabella d'Este),[5] but it was also the case that if Mantegna's talents were to be used as an expression of Lodovico's own *ingegno,* this association could be best understood by the application of the artist's renowned, recognisable, and recognised style to the features of his patron. Needs must, the portrait conveyed this message better than any other genre; the patron himself came to personify the style.

In his choice of Mantegna and the shaping of their joint projects, Lodovico Gonzaga almost certainly had taken note of the well-remunerated employment of the painter and portrait specialist, Pisanello, by Alfonso V of Aragon. Even if it turned out to be a somewhat temporary arrangement, Pisanello's employment was of enormous importance for the peers and successors of the king of Naples.[6] Although the artist had long received regular commissions from the ruling families of Ferrara, Mantua, and Milan, none of them attempted to gain exclusive control of his talent. Until 1448–9, Pisanello could be defined as a kind of jobbing virtuoso, the Este, Gonzaga, Visconti, and Malatesta content to share his famous talents between them. Pisanello was celebrated as an artist of extraordinary individual gifts and as the leading exponent of a defined courtly style. Alfonso, by bringing him down to Naples, annexed both aspects of his work. Nevertheless, Alfonso's portraits do not differ substantially from those of his princely contemporaries by Pisanello, all intended as a means of conveying both the individual *virtù* and the generic status of his subjects. This homogeneity was, as we will see, abandoned later in the century.

The patron's choice of medium for his image was significant. Although many of Pisanello's portraits were painted, those that survive are mostly medallic (Fig. 27).[7] As summations of the partnership between artist and ruler, these medals do not differ very much from Mantegna's *Camera Picta,* similarly signalled by their prominent signatures. Medals had further connotations, however. They were a highly portable medium, ensuring that the message of the portrait would be disseminated beyond the local purview of the court. They were also enduring. More than that, however, they could be seen, in some sense, as 'official'. This is not to say that they were a practical tool of the state (unlike coins), but because they were conceptually dependent on coins of Alexander and the Roman emperors (whose example, as we have seen, was studied and revered), the scholarly elite who collected both Greek and Roman and modern Italian coins are likely to have recognised that antique coins were not only the means by which ancient rulers had permanently commemorated themselves, their actions, and their virtues, but also that they had done so officially by placing their names and images on their states' coinage.[8] Because medals were created to be their contemporary equivalents, they rendered official, by this association, not merely the portrait, but also the style enshrined within it. Pisanello's style therefore became the sanctioned visual language in which the ruler wished to promote and preserve his image.

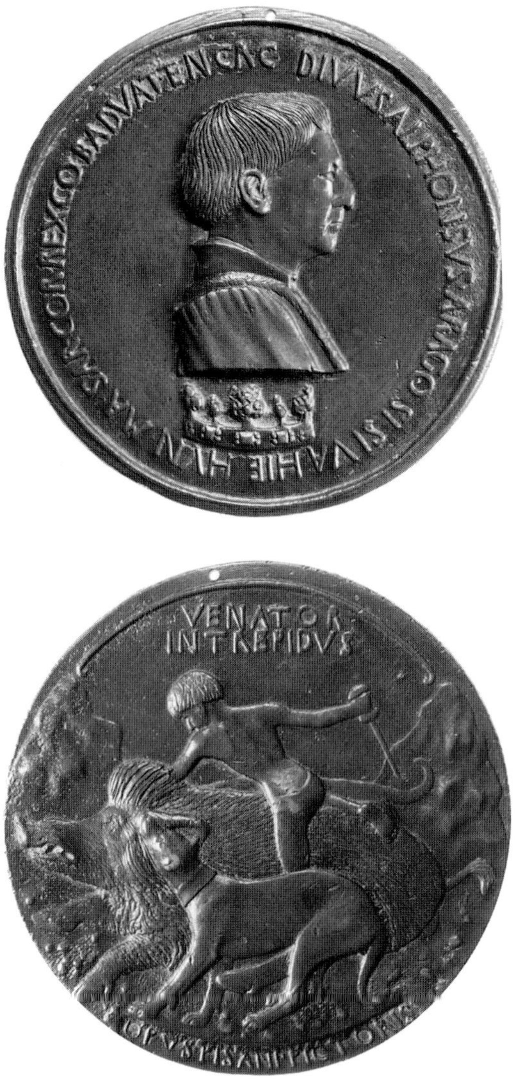

27. Pisanello, *Portrait Medal of Alfonso V of Aragon, King of Naples.* Cast bronze. London, The British Museum. Photo: The Trustees of The British Museum.

It is remarkable to what extent the medals by Pisanello became paradigmatic in medal production of the next two decades. This is not merely a matter of their ingredients: the portrait in strict profile on the obverse, labelled in Latin, and the symbolic or allegorical reverse. Apart from these common features, medals executed for various courts in Italy and France in the 1450s and 1460s by Matteo de' Pasti, Pietro da Milano, and Francesco Laurana, among others, also look stylistically very like Pisanello's.[9] These medals were often executed by artists of no small reputation.

Nevertheless, all but two of Laurana's signed medals, for example, stick rigidly to formulae pioneered by Pisanello, lacking the individual and inventive grace of his portrait busts.[10] Even while his individuality was celebrated in his other works, his medals were therefore evidently expected to continue to transmit the same visual message as those of Pisanello; medallic style and Pisanello's own had become synonymous. His was the normative medallic language of ruler portraiture, and the medallic portrait remained a genre linked with the court.

Thus the creation of a medal in republican Florence in the late 1470s takes on particular significance: Bertoldo di Giovanni's piece marking the failure of the Pazzi conspiracy and with the portraits of two members of the Medici family, Lorenzo and Giuliano (Fig. 28).[11] On 26 April 1478 Lorenzo de' Medici escaped his Pazzi attackers who attempted his murder in Florence Cathedral, and as part of a programme to commemorate his survival – as well as the symbolised martyrdom of his brother Giuliano – he commissioned a medal, the first edition of which, in four specimens, was cast in September of that year. With no court at its centre, Florence was not a city with any sort of medallic tradition. Indeed the making of medals seems to have been deliberately eschewed. Thus, although this was not absolutely the first medal to be made in the city, it was the first of a living member of the Medici family to be cast in such numbers that even a limited circulation could be guaranteed.

If the fact of its manufacture were not in itself remarkable, it becomes doubly so by its complete abandonment of Pisanello's paradigm, by its defiant oddness. In the first place, the medal flouts convention by the representation of real events in an identifiable space,[12] albeit the specific historical circumstances have been rendered symbolic by the representation of the protagonists as classically nude. The three-quarter-view portraits of Lorenzo and Giuliano de'Medici, on either side of the medal, are placed like sculpted busts on top of two scenes of the attack in the choir of Florence Cathedral, so that the brilliantly described architecture and continuous narrative act as plinth, body, and integrated reverse for the two subjects – as if to literally incorporate and internalise these real and crucial moments of political disaster and triumph, symbolic public 'grief', and 'safety'.[13] Moreover by depicting the choir screen in perspective from the south (with the portrait of Lorenzo) and north on either side of the piece, Bertoldo has succeeded in establishing a three-dimensional stage for the drama, a space which can be read only by turning the medal in the hand.

Bertoldo's 'eccentricity' has been read as the extraordinary response to extraordinary events. Fuelled by the established historical custom of putting together ancient texts and more 'truthful' numismatic material, Lorenzo seems to have commissioned this medal as the tangible and enduring equivalent of Angelo Poliziano's Latin narrative, *Pactianae coniurationis commentarium* (*Commentary on the Pazzi Conspiracy*).[14] It seems plausible, given the concordances between his account and Bertoldo's images, that Poliziano, whose numismatic interests are well attested,[15] and whose works often combine ancient literary forms with the use of a modern vernacular, acted as adviser to artist and patron. The deliberately forged link between text and object may have suggested the avoidance of the variously interpretable emblem or allegory in favour of these miniature narratives.

It also seems possible to interpret Bertoldo's stylistic and typological departures in broader, political terms. They might, for example, be explained as devices intended to distance the piece visually from the canonical medal of the dynastic courts – the means by which Lorenzo, who was not, of course, the dynastic ruler of Florence, could issue a medal that was not quite a medal, of making it acceptably republican while it remained recognisably the artistic instrument traditionally associated with the hereditary or princely ruler. Because a similar rejection of Pisanello's model can be traced elsewhere in Italy, this explanation will not entirely do, however. Just such a phenomenon is a feature of medal production in the 1470s, of pieces made by court artists at the behest of the Este, Gonzaga, and Montefeltro rulers, from whom Lorenzo might advisedly have chosen to distance himself.

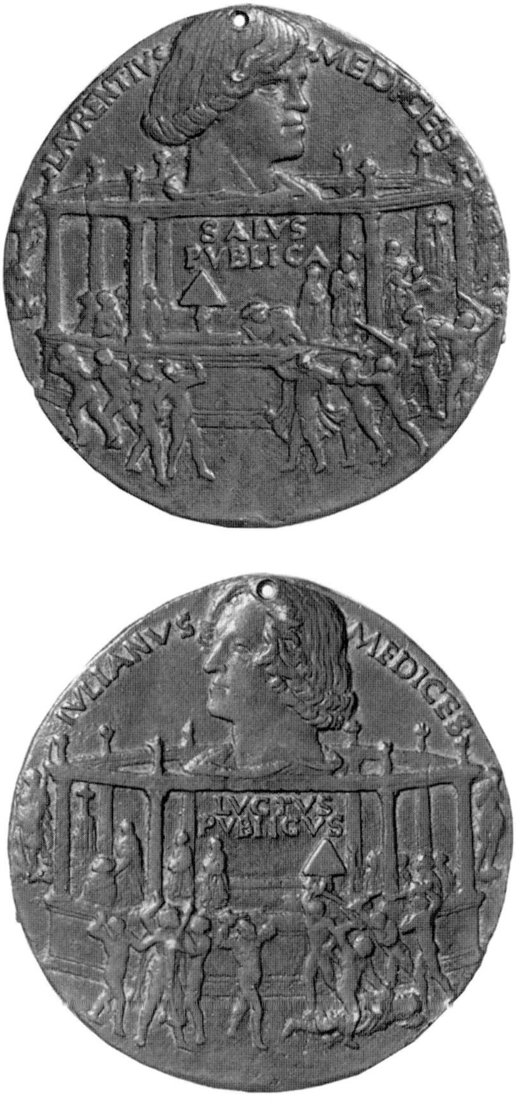

28. Bertoldo di Giovanni, *Pazzi Conspiracy medal.* Cast bronze. London, The British Museum. Photo: © The Trustees of The British Museum.

Alfonso V of Aragon's attempt to assert control over a widely renowned artist had proved a potent example. Other rulers elsewhere in Italy wanted to form mutually rewarding pacts with their own Apelles or Lysippus. Soon after Pisanello's journey south, the rulers of Ferrara and Mantua sought artists who were expected to remain in one place and to devote their primary (if not always exclusive) energies to the artistic projects of their patrons. Ideally, of course, the *ingegnoso* talent of these artists should be real because the patron was to be credited with the recognition and nurturing of their artists' innate skills. Lodovico Gonzaga's efforts to obtain Mantegna were therefore entirely justified. The Este in Ferrara were similarly fortunate in attracting Cosmè Tura back to his native town in 1456.[16] It is also clear, however, that rulers wished to establish such ritualised, symbolic relationships, whether or not the talents of the artist concerned (Angelo da Siena, for example, Cosmè's predecessor or Michele Pannonio, who nearly stepped in for Mantegna) were actually outstanding. The fact of the artist's employment was sometimes as important as the talents of the artist concerned.

Members of rulers' households, these artists are often precisely termed "familiars" – a word which suggests their creative intimacy with their patrons. Or they might be described as 'theirs'. In July 1480 Francesco di Giorgio, for example, was called by his employer Federico da Montefeltro, Duke of Urbino 'mio dilettissimo archietecto' (my most beloved architect).[17] And, in 1472, the presence of Mantegna was requested by Cardinal Francesco Gonzaga to mull over his collection of small antiquities, a private entertainment like that of the musician (another category of employee often treated as an intimate) he asked to come at the same time.[18] Campbell has shown that Cosmè Tura, the son of a cobbler, achieved a sort of nobility as the result of his art, one which legitimised his close working relationship with Duke Ercole.[19] And a familial closeness is well documented between his successor, Ercole de' Roberti, and the ducal family.[20] It is encountered again, at the end of the century, in the informal tone of the correspondence between Isabella d'Este and the sculptor and medallist Gian Cristoforo Romano.[21]

These policies of intimacy, stability and – sometimes – exclusivity were to have dramatic effect on the appearance of what is termed 'court art' – and on court portraiture. No longer was there a single (international) courtly style of the kind which Pisanello's paintings and medals embodied. Instead, as greater political emphasis was placed on the particular virtues of rulers rather than (only) on their dynastic rights, a greater level of identification of individual artist with individual patron was deliberately engendered. In identifying the court artist, and particularly in proposing Bertoldo acted in this way, it is important to think about the multifarious roles that made up their job. The precise configuration of these different jobs varied from court to court, depending on local tradition, on the artist's strengths, and on his patrons' interests. Some, like Mantegna, offered antiquarian expertise, appraising or restoring antiquities offered to their employers. All court artists were expected to produce 'masterpieces' entirely by their own hand.[22] Once employed at court, however, they usually extended their range of activity. They may have been expected to teach, and they were certainly supposed to collaborate. The making of designs for a whole variety of often expensive media – silver and tapestries, for instance, or large-scale painted schemes to be executed by others – was central to the activities of both Tura and Mantegna.[23] Such designing tasks were considered a factor that raised these artists above the herd of journeyman artisans, not least because of the division they enshrined between invention and manufacture. Moreover, through collaboration they were able, crucially, to establish their style as a collective look – a style, unique because it was in their image – for the court.[24]

The desire to create unified styles for court and city found its ultimate expression in another defining area of design in which the court artist was frequently engaged, one which took the division of labour to a still more prestigious level: architecture. Once again Pisanello presents himself as a model, on the evidence of the drawing in Rotterdam of a triumphal arch for Alfonso V.[25] Francesco di Giorgio's enormous flexibility is axiomatic and he needs no introduction as an architect (any more than he does as a painter or sculptor). It is worth noting, however, that, while his painting and engineering skills had earned him considerable respect in Siena, as we have already seen, it was only in Urbino that he was first called an 'architect', a year or so after he had entered the service of Federico da Montefeltro. Indeed the number of painters employed as court artists who added the rôle of architect to their artistic personae is sometimes overlooked. Mantegna and Tura are only known to have made architectural designs for themselves,[26] although this does not exclude the possibility that they may have offered advice to their patrons. Certainly Ercole de' Roberti was often employed as an architect in his last years of service to Duke Ercole I.[27]

The Medal as Manifesto

By the 1470s, therefore, it is not surprising to find that the 'official' medals designed (and sometimes executed) by many of these court artists for their patrons were used to blazon stylistic differences between the courts at which they were employed. Unlike the medals signed by Laurana, those designed by Cosmè Tura, Francesco di Giorgio, and, probably, by Andrea Mantegna look like their other works, and were intended to do so. All of them depart from the norm established by Pisanello, in ways which, if less 'eccentric' than Bertoldo's rejection, can all be described as pronouncedly and innovatively individualistic. Like Pisanello's medals, they were perceived as the product of privileged intimacy between artist and patron, from which both could gain glory.[28] By this date, moreover their highly differentiated design make it even more apparent that they were viewed in addition as officially sanctioned expressions of the visual language in which a particular patron's artistic strategy was to be accomplished.

In most cases there survive only a handful of medals by each of these artists, a single element within their total output. Tura, for instance, is identified as the designer of two medals in very low relief: of the one-year-old Alfonso d'Este with an infant Hercules reverse, dating from 1477, and of his parents, Ercole d'Este and Eleonora of Aragon, made shortly afterwards.[29] The scale of the heads within the medals' circumferences is now significantly larger than those found on Pisanello's medals and there are other departures. Most important, the design element, the mark of the artist's inventiveness in the service of his Este patrons, is stressed by their unusually low relief, which shows off their highly elegant linearity. Before leaving Siena in 1477, Francesco di Giorgio had made only one medal, a

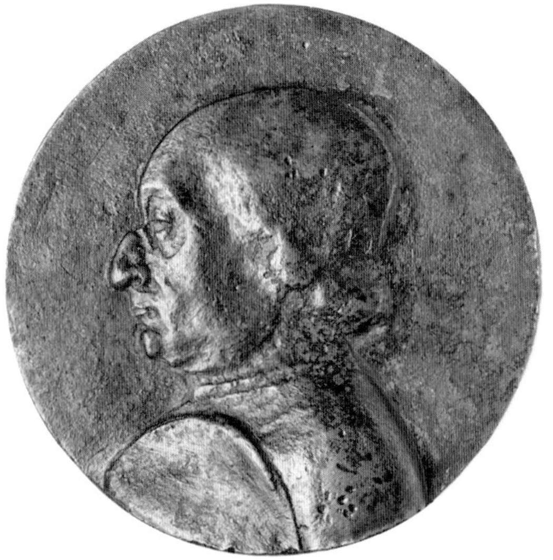

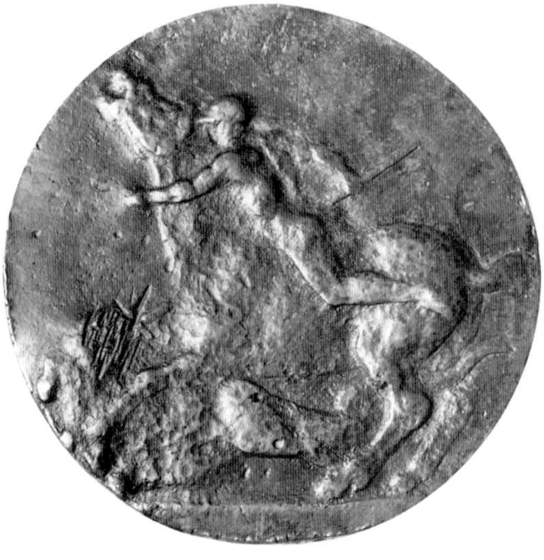

29. Francesco di Giorgio, *Portrait medal of Federico da Montefeltro, duke of Urbino.* Cast bronze. London, The British Museum. Photo: © The Trustees of The British Museum.

conservative and unambitious effort: the portrait of Ambrogio Spannocchi de Piccolomini.[30] Francesco's modelling technique at this stage, especially of the head, depends on Pisanello's. His medal of Duke Federico, dating to the very early years of his time in Urbino and with a reverse which is likely to represent *Bellerophon and the Chimera* (Fig. 29), is markedly different, however. It is notable for a chunky and energetic relief style which is closely related to his sculptural style for works on a larger scale. The British Museum example is the unique cast of an abandoned model, and that it was not finished may be because such individualistic high relief could not be easily or economically reproduced.[31]

The case for Mantegna as a designer of medals is less clear-cut. Five Mantuan medals executed in the 1470s and 1480s are signed by the goldsmith Bartolommeo

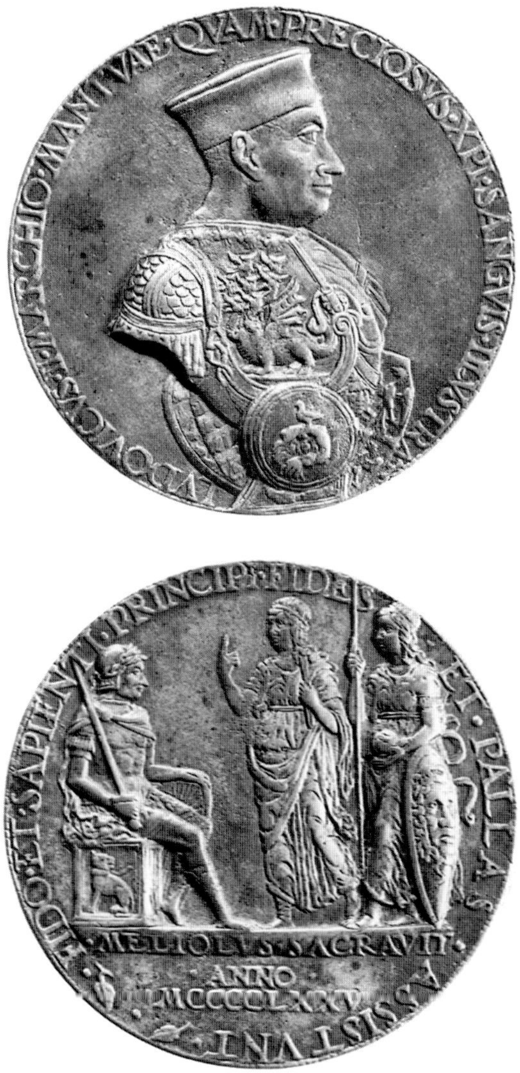

30. Bartolommeo Melioli (perhaps after Andrea Mantegna), *Portrait medal of Lodovico II Gonzaga, marquis of Mantua.* Cast bronze. London, The British Museum. Photo: © The Trustees of The British Museum.

Melioli. These include a 1474 portrait medal of Christian I Oldenburg, king of Denmark, who was portrayed by Mantegna in the Camera Picta. Marquis Lodovico and his son and namesake Protonotary Apostolic Lodovico Gonzaga were also of course depicted in the Camera and their medals signed by Melioli date from the following year. These pieces and that of the future Francesco II are all pronouncedly Mantegnesque in character.[32] The medal of Marquis Lodovico Gonzaga has an obverse portrait which is clearly dependent on his profile image in the *Camera Picta,* while the reverse shows him seated in *all'antica* armour with the Gonzaga emblem of a muzzled dog carved onto the plinth on which he sits, giving a clue to the meaning of the informally posed Gonzaga dog, Rubino, in the Camera (Fig. 30).[33] Melioli's adopted style might be put down to the huge impact of Mantegna's wall paintings. It might also indicate that these medals were designed by Mantegna himself in his rôle as artistic overseer for the court. On the reverse of his medal, Lodovico is counselled by Faith and Pallas, on whose shield is the head of Medusa. This Medusa is clearly not female, however, and instead the little head bears a strong resemblance to Andrea Mantegna's self-portrait bust for his burial chapel at Sant' Andrea. Moreover, it is insinuated (as a kind of signature) into the medal in very much the same way that Mantegna had introduced his image into the painted architectural ornament of the Camera, which it also resembles.[34] Whether or not they were in fact designed by Mantegna, it remains the case that they are Mantegnesque. The stylistic point was made.

Characterising Bertoldo

If these medals from Ferrara, Urbino, and Mantua can be seen as the sanctioned distillations of the visual languages of the regimes they celebrate, are we entitled to interpret Bertoldo's *Pazzi Conspiracy* medal (Fig. 28) in a similar way? Was Bertoldo indeed an artist treated by Lorenzo as an equivalent to Tura or Mantegna? Was, therefore, his medal considered the deliberate result of imitative collaboration between a powerful patron – a quasi-ruler – and a particular kind of inventive artist employed by him and identified with him? Bertoldo's perceived medallic eccentricity is seen to be consistent with medals which employed localised and differentiated styles developed elsewhere in Italy. Was Bertoldo's medal therefore an equivalent summation or manifesto of Laurentian artistic policy and, by implication, of his assumed political status? If so, how can its ingredients be analysed?

Certainly the crushing of the Pazzi conspiracy and institutional changes made to governmental structures in the wake of the Pazzi war did much to consolidate and enhance Lorenzo's personal power in the Florentine republic.[35] Although he may have harboured dynastic ambitions, especially late in life, there is no evidence that he wanted (or needed) to overturn the republic at the time the medal was made. Nevertheless, he evidently felt confident enough of his own position to employ a 'court artist'. Indeed Hauser called Bertoldo 'the ideal court artist', seeing his work as according perfectly with Lorenzo's taste for 'the dainty and the expensive, the trifling and the artistic'.[36] In so saying, he was oversimplifying Bode's view of the artist, and this curious, and curiously influential, assessment requires qualification. Despite his high regard for ancient gems and coins, Lorenzo's activities as a patron were by no means restricted to the small and precious, and he continued to commission works of art from many of the city's leading independent painters and sculptors.[37] Bertoldo self-evidently did not therefore dominate the style and production of art in Florence in the way Mantegna did in Mantua, or Tura in Ferrara. It is clear, however, that Bertoldo was the artist who was to be particularly identified with Lorenzo. Although he rented an apartment near the Duomo in 1478, he is documented as a resident of both the Palazzo Medici (at the end of his life) and, earlier, at the Medici villa at Poggio a Caiano.[38] Residency alone would not be enough to establish his position as a Medici artist-familiar, but we can identify other parallels. We find, for example, that he formed part of the retinue – which included musicians and singers – designed to serve and entertain Lorenzo as he took the waters at Bagni di Morbo in c. 1485, acting as a companion, just as Mantegna had for Cardinal Francesco Gonzaga.[39] Lorenzo called Bertoldo 'nostro',[40] and Giovanni Buoninsegni writing to Lorenzo de' Medici in 1489 referred to the sculptor as 'Bertoldo vostro'. Reports of his death confirm Bertoldo's position as a familiar of Lorenzo. On 29 December 1491 Bartolommeo Zeffi wrote, 'Bertoldo the sculptor, who lived with him [Lorenzo] has died at Poggio of quinsy, much to the said Lorenzo's distress because he loved him as much as any of his familiars [quanto altro suo familiare]'[41] and when Bartolommeo Dei reported the artist's death on 30 December 1491, he stated that 'Bertoldo, most worthy sculptor and the best maker of medals, who always with the magnificent Lorenzo did worthy things, died at Poggio two days ago',[42] a clear indication of how Bertoldo's works were seen as essentially connected to Lorenzo.

What were these worthy things? Like Tura, Mantegna, Francesco di Giorgio, and, later, Ercole de' Roberti, Bertoldo was clearly expected to execute 'masterpieces' expressly intended to reveal his powers of invention. Gombrich, echoing Hauser, called his bronze statuettes and reliefs, dismissively but accurately enough, 'art for art's sake'.[43] Four pieces were recorded in the Medici Palace in 1492. The most important, worth a substantial 30 florins, was the Bargello *Battle* piece, displayed in the 'saletta rimpetto alla sala grande' (little room opposite the Great Hall), the bronze 'restoration' of a marble sarcophagus in the Campo Santo at Pisa (Fig. 31). Two other bronze reliefs, both worth 10 florins, can be identified as the *Crucifixion*, now in the Bargello, and the Louvre *Virgin and Child with Angels* (Fig. 32). A statuette of a centaur, now lost, is also indicated in the inventory as by the hand of Bertoldo (with no valuation).[44] In addition, *The Triumph of Silenus* relief in the Bargello has Piero de' Medici's device of falcon holding a ring in its talons and is usually dated before his death in 1469.[45] It is much worn, a factor which has coloured critical reactions to the piece, but its stylistic kinship with the *Crucifixion*, as well as Bertoldo's known biography, suggest instead that it was made later for Lorenzo, perhaps in the late 1470s. All of these, but especially the *Battle*, were intended as 'masterpieces'. Apart from the *Pazzi Conspiracy* medal, in 1480 Bertoldo signed a piece commemorating Mehmed II, intended by Lorenzo, almost certainly, as a diplomatic gift for the Sultan, and as a demonstration of Florentine artistic prowess.[46] Bertoldo was not the only artist to execute virtuoso pieces for Lorenzo, but the fact that he, rather than, for instance, the equally qualified Antonio del Pollaiuolo or Andrea del Verrocchio, was chosen to execute his medals is surely significant.

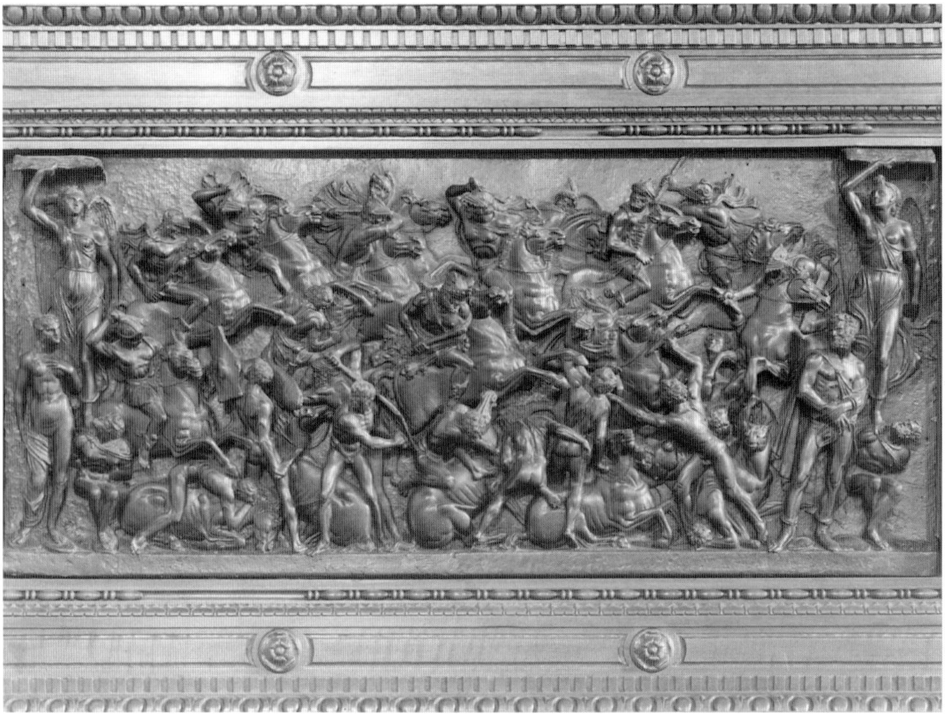

31. Bertoldo di Giovanni, *Battle.* Cast bronze. Florence, Museo Nazionale del Bargello. Photo: Ralph Lieberman.

Bertoldo was not, in fact, restricted to the small scale, and his brief went considerably beyond the reckonings of Bode and Hauser. In 1485 he was paid by the Opera del Duomo to carve two angels with wings and trumpets in wood following models in wax he had presented.[47] More importantly, he designed the glazed terracotta frieze for the façade of Lorenzo's villa at Poggio a Caiano.[48] The specialist technique of the frieze indicates that it must have been executed in the workshop of Andrea della Robbia. Building did not start on the new villa until probably some time in 1485, certainly by 1487,[49] and thus this work must be placed in the last part of his career, some parts perhaps post-dating Bertoldo's death. The workshop must have copied three-dimensional wax models of the type prepared for the angels. Here then we encounter a division of labour – between design and execution – in Bertoldo's practice, of the kind identified in the court activities of Tura and Mantegna. Although no drawings have been identified by his hand (they are thought to have existed),[50] it seems that, on other occasions, he handed over works for others to complete from models. Not all his bronze works, for example, were cast by Bertoldo himself; Adriano Fiorentino was employed as founder for the *Bellerophon and Pegasus,* now in Vienna,[51] and Andrea Guaccialotti in Prato cast the first edition of the Pazzi conspiracy medal from a 'prima impronta' (first cast) supplied by Bertoldo.[52]

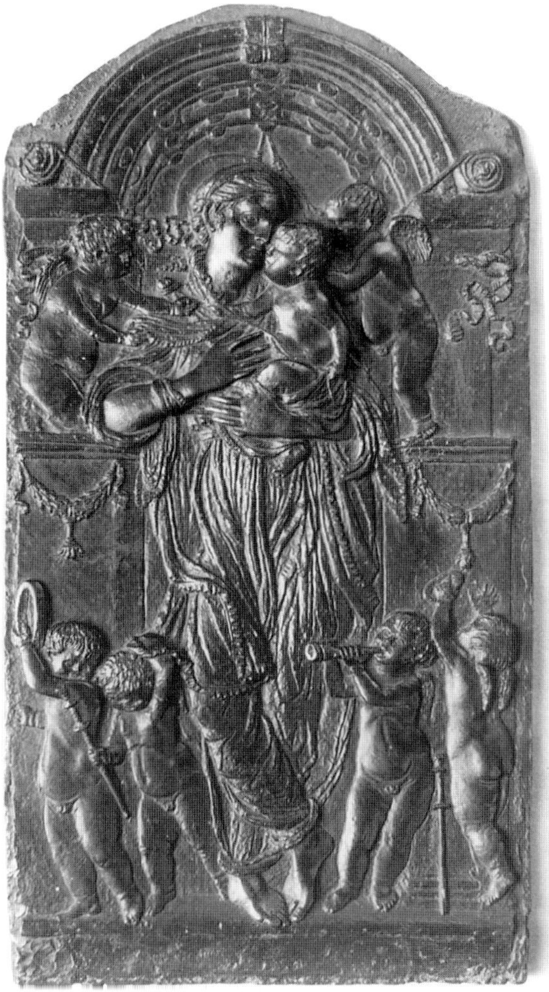

32. Bertoldo di Giovanni, *Virgin and Child with Angels.* Cast bronze. Paris, Musée du Louvre. Photo: Musée du Louvre.

Others of his activities in the service of Lorenzo mirrored those of painters and sculptors who can legitimately be called court artists. Like Mantegna, he clearly possessed some antiquarian expertise, assessing ancient coins and, probably, a bronze head for Lorenzo in 1489.[53] There is also documentary evidence of Bertoldo as an architect or, at least, an architectural expert or adviser. The start of his famous and mightily peculiar 'cookery book' letter of July 1479 to Lorenzo states explicitly, 'I have just this moment thrown away my chisels, drills, compasses, T-square, wax, straw, architecture and perspective'.[54] He assuredly had skills in this area, and was reported to Lorenzo in August 1476 as having made a drawing based on measurements of the façade of, apparently, Florence Cathedral.[55] This episode represents Bertoldo's first documented contact with Lorenzo, and the drawing may have been a design for the façade. It could perhaps be regarded as a proof of design skills and flexibility, both of which would qualify him to work as 'court artist' to Lorenzo.

Bertoldo and Lorenzo's *Kunstpolitik*

Bertoldo's particular relationship with Lorenzo suggests that his Pazzi Conspiracy medal was indeed constructed using the visual style and vocabulary with which Lorenzo wished particularly to associate himself. How then are we to define this style? And was it seen as Bertoldo's alone? Although its production, and its choice of author, can clearly be interpreted as acts of raised political confidence and ambition, Lorenzo nonetheless subtly incorporated other elements in his artistic strategy, which this piece with his portrait might be said to stand for, and were distinctively 'republican'. These were aspects which can be seen to have extended the qualifications of his 'court' artist beyond individual talent alone, to incorporate local tradition with non-courtly associations. Draper has acutely analysed the visual sources of the medal (Fig. 28). First, there is the issue of Bertoldo's individual approach. He shows that the portraits on the medal derived from paintings by Sandro Botticelli, whose portrait of Giuliano was much repeated both by the painter and by his workshop.[56] Even if Bertoldo was following types established by another artist, however, he did not copy them exactly; the heads have three-dimensional solidity alien to Botticelli's prototypes, the features described as heroic and alert rather than melancholy and introspective. In particular, the cubic construction of Lorenzo's head, with its square jaw, prominent lower lip, low, heavy brows rising to an almost perpendicular forehead, combining to create a baleful expression, conforms to Bertoldo's *all'antica* heroic type found elsewhere in his oeuvre: in many of the protagonists of the Poggio frieze and in his bronzes, his *Bellerophon*, and the Frick *Shield-Bearer*.[57] Lorenzo thus epitomises the Bertoldesque.[58]

Draper further demonstrates that, as might be expected in an artist with acknowledged antiquarian interests, Bertoldo benefited from the detailed examination of ancient numismatic material; not only do the flanking allegorical figures relate to statues sometimes placed adjacent to temple architecture on antique coins, but the treatment of the medal's surface also seems intended to invoke their frequently worn appearance. Draper shows this imaginative response to ancient coins to be typical of Bertoldo's approach to both glyptic and numismatic sources in his other works. The antique is therefore one of his ingredients. And the Pazzi medal is stylistically compatible with Bertoldo's transformation of the antique in his most celebrated Medici work, the *all'antica* 'reconstruction' of a *Battle*. Indeed, it can be shown that the composition of groups of battling nudes on the medal was dependent on the poses of the protagonists of this Medici showpiece. Two figures placed next to each other, the attackers of the cloaked Lorenzo, third and fourth from right in the foreground of the Lorenzo side, appear to be miniature renditions of a lunging nude he invented for the *Battle* (third from the right; Fig. 31). In the *Battle* scene the position of the warrior's feet is explained by the fact that he is straddling the body of a fallen soldier, his right foot twisted into the foreground. This peculiarity reappears in the medal, suggesting that Bertoldo's representation of Lorenzo's would-be assassins was based on a pre-existing model. The *Battle* also has allegorical figures standing on either side. If this chronology is accepted, then the medal can be regarded as an official proclamation of Bertoldo's virtuosity in Medici employ, proved in the more limited context of the palace by the *Battle*, the medal, with its portraits introduced, an equivalent piece therefore to Melioli's reduction and transformation of the interior scene of the *Camera Picta*.

Finally, and most importantly, Draper has also shown that Bertoldo's art additionally reveals his citations of styles and motifs found in Florentine painting and sculpture from the first half of the century. In particular, he looked closely and creatively at works by the first heroic generation of Florentine quattrocento artists; Draper identifies Bertoldo's debt, for example, to Masaccio's *Pisa Polyptych* in his description of Christ in the Bargello *Crucifixion*.[59] Above all, however, he formulated his works in the image of Donatello. This is not to say that his emulation was literal; Bertoldo only rarely lifted a figure or motif directly from a piece by the older sculptor. More typically he would explore and re-envisage a method or approach employed by Donatello, always situating these reworkings by their recognisable relationship with particular works by his predecessor. Thus Bertoldo's work might sometimes seem tame in comparison with the feral emotionalism frequently displayed in Donatello's sculpture. Donatello's interest in capturing energy of movement is still apparent in Bertoldo's sculptures, but the sometimes deliberately, awkwardly human poses of Donatello's figures, whose unbalanced stances frequently have the sense of arrested motion now associated with newspaper photographs, have usually been converted by Bertoldo into more classically stable, more self-consciously graceful positions. The Pazzi Conspiracy medal is, one suspects quite deliberately, a case in point. Draper demonstrated that Bertoldo's 'radical' experiment with the representation, in relief, of small, animated figures in a clearly defined space has its roots in Donatello's coloured stucco roundels in the Old Sacristy at San Lorenzo, in particular his *Raising of Drusiana*.[60] The jutting, jerking limbs of Donatello's participants, the brilliantly calculated randomness of the composition, however, are replaced by a more rhythmic arrangement of grounded figures in a progression of set planes, much more akin to an ancient sarcophagus relief.

It might be said that Bertoldo's responses to Donatello's *exempla* were inevitable if Bertoldo, as is reasonably supposed, was his pupil. The documentation of Bertoldo's career is minimal, and there is no record of any apprenticeship. Moreover, Vasari omitted a biography of Bertoldo from his *Vite*. Nevertheless, whenever Bertoldo's name comes up in his biographies of other artists, he is immediately denoted the 'disciple' or 'creature' of Donatello.[61] It was a claim made by Bertoldo himself; in his 1479 'cookery book' letter, Bertoldo quite explicitly termed himself the 'dicepol di donato' [pupil/disciple of Donato], implying both a master-pupil or master-assistant relationship and a sense of his artistic reverence.[62] Vasari wrote that Bertoldo finished the San Lorenzo pulpit reliefs after Donatello's death, a claim that some modern critics have been unwilling to accept and that others have overplayed.[63] To this author, his participation seems plausible, although it was almost certainly restricted to the technical processes of casting and chasing. The attribution to Bertoldo of any one of the narratives, or even the frieze figures, is probably misguided; however, there seems no good reason to question Vasari's categorical statement that Donatello 'left his practice to his disciples', heading his list with 'Bertoldo, a Florentine sculptor who rather imitated him, as can be seen in a very beautiful battle of men on horseback in bronze [the Medici *Battle* piece]'.

But Bertoldo's 'imitation' of Donatello is only partly explained by his training. This insistence on his discipleship can be read as an indication of how he was viewed and exploited by Lorenzo de' Medici. By the 1470s, Donatello's sculpture was regarded as one of the chief glories of the city of Florence, his individual *ingegno* converted to civic genius. Collareta has analysed the literary, primarily humanist view of Donatello.[64] The praises of Donatello were sung by Leon Battista Alberti and many of his scholarly successors: Flavio Biondo, Matteo Palmieri, Giannozzo Manetti. And his legend grew; Alamanno Rinuccini, for example, stated baldly that he was the greatest of all sculptors. His works feature heavily in Francesco Albertini's guide to the 'inclyta ciptà di Florentia' [famous city of Florence] and were especially important, as Baxandall has demonstrated, for Cristoforo Landino in 1481 as he expounded his concept of the cultural heritage of Florence transformed into an instrument of propaganda, to defend the city against its detractors.[65] How his sculptures were regarded may be deduced from popular, probably metaphorical, accounts of his simplicity, his humane liberality, his sharp humour. He featured notably in the civic imagination of Florence; anecdotes and *facetiae* concerning him were repeated long after his death.[66] In this way his Florentine virtues were linked to his identification as the father of the revival of the art of sculpture, the equivalent of his fellow Florentine, Giotto, for painting. Indeed there is some indication that this was interpreted as a specifically Tuscan renaissance. In Ugolino Verino's *De illustratione urbis Florentiae* of 1483 he talks of the 'breathing statues of the Etruscan Donato' in a context in which he is clearly referring to a revival of ancient, Etruscan art.[67] Thus the visual parallels between Bertoldo's *Bellerophon* and the Etruscan bronze group of an athlete holding the harness of a rearing horse, included by Weil-Garris Brandt in the 1999 exhibition, *Giovinezza di Michelangelo,* may be no coincidence, supporting Chastel's earlier hint that Bertoldo had studied such works.[68]

Moreover, it cannot be interpreted as coincidental that so much of Donatello's sculpture, including, of course, the Sacristy roundels, was associated with Medici commissions and sites, or that the sculptor himself was buried at San Lorenzo. (Bertoldo, too, later had masses said for his soul there, partially funded by the Medici bank.[69]) The recognition of Donatello's talent by Lorenzo's grandfather, Cosimo il Vecchio, is likely to have been of immense importance in the construction of his posthumous reputation. For all these many reasons, Donatello (posthumously) and Bertoldo, his pupil, were valued for more than their own innate creative powers. By employing Bertoldo, Lorenzo not only had his image expressed inventively by an *ingegnoso* artist, but he could also annex the style and inheritance of the sculptor, Donatello, of whom Florentines were most proud, an artist moreover already personified as Medicean. By the combination in Bertoldo's works of references to his master's work with the introduction of more accurately cited ancient visual sources, a civic, republican Florentine idiom was transformed into a specifically Laurentian style.

Bertoldo Multiplied: Establishing the 'Workshop' of Lorenzo

If it now seems clear that Lorenzo established Bertoldo as his court artist, albeit one with distinctly Florentine and republican accent, it now remains to be asked whether he fulfilled the last function, identified in the previous section, of such a role. One of the central activities of the court artist was, as we have seen, to establish and promote a collective visual style for a dynastic regime. Was Bertoldo supposed to operate in the same way? Here we arrive at the most contentious aspect of Bertoldo's employment by Lorenzo, as teacher in the Medici sculpture garden at San Marco.[70] In the absence of primary evidence, we are forced to rely on Giorgio Vasari's account in the second-edition *Vite* of Michelangelo, Giuliano Bugiardini, and Pietro Torrigiano. Vasari states that in charge of the garden was Bertoldo, admirably fitted for his rôle as its 'keeper or guardian' as an expert on antiquities. He further writes that in about 1490 Lorenzo, lamenting the lack of good Florentine sculptors, invited the best pupils of Domenico Ghirlandaio to the Garden 'where he wished that they should practice and create a style that would do honour both to himself, the artist, and to his city'.[71] Lorenzo ordered that these young men – tellingly, in the light of how court artists were considered, those deemed 'noble' – should be placed in Bertoldo's care to pursue 'the study of design' and 'the learning of art'.[72] In his biography of Michelangelo, Vasari claims, misleadingly, that although Bertoldo was so old that he could no longer work, he was 'nevertheless a very skilled and well reputed master'.[73] He turns Lorenzo into a model patron: 'May that truly magnificent example of Lorenzo always be imitated by princes and other esteemed men, bringing them honour and perpetual praise; because whoever aids and favours fine soaring geniuses in their lofty designs, from which the world receives so much beauty, honour, ease and usefulness, deserves to live eternally by his fame in the intellects of men.'[74] Certainly this was a nudge to Cosimo I de' Medici, but it was not just a sixteenth-century notion; the recognition and promotion of artistic *ingegno* ascribed to Lorenzo was a well recognised signal of greatness in a ruler.

In recent years the text of Vasari's *Vite* has been subjected to intense scrutiny, his rôle in the creation of a Medicean mythology explored. No one would ever laud his writings as the model of detached historical positivism. But it has proved unwise to claim, as Chastel, Gombrich, and others have done, that the garden, let alone Bertoldo's connection with it, was a part of the Medicean legend. Elam has established that the Medici sculpture garden was not a figment of Vasari's propagandist imagination, but a plot of land in Medici possession, which can be documented from 1475.[75] She has shown that this was a site with a variety of functions. It not only contained a much-visited display of antiquities, but it was also used for the storage of stone.[76] Only the proof that Bertoldo taught there is still missing. Nevertheless, there is considerable supporting evidence that such a school existed and that Bertoldo was its teacher, evidence to be found both in the contemporary literary image of Lorenzo and in the surviving works of many of its ostensible pupils.

It should also be asked that if Bertoldo's court artist role also incorporated his training by Donatello (and his deliberate debt to other earlier Florentine artists), whether any collectivisation of his style was similarly less individualistic. Did Bertoldo's teaching combine his own style with those of the ingredients allied to it? Not the least startling aspect of Lorenzo's initiative is the way in which it sought to supplement the traditional guilds-approved method of training painters and sculptors in workshops. Lorenzo seems to have set up an independent workshop of his own. Clearly he was aware that he was regarded as in some degree accountable for the quality of the visual arts of Florence. In the report by Lorenzo di Filippo Strozzi of his father's canny manipulation of il Magnifico in his rôle as aesthetic arbiter to ensure the grandeur of the Strozzi palace, he uses a telling phrase; Strozzi was told 'that he who ruled desired the city to be adorned and exalted in every way, for just as the good and the bad depended on him, so the beautiful and the ugly would also be attributed to him.'[77] This acknowledged stewardship finds an intriguing echo in a current political metaphor used of Lorenzo. In c. 1470 Benedetto Dei called him the 'maestro della bottega' (master of the workshop), a phrase used in connection with Lorenzo and with the dynastic rulers of other cities, such as Galeazzo Maria Sforza, by Dei and members of his circle in the 1470s and 1480s, and which reappears in the works of Machiavelli.[78] The bottega was, of course, Florence and the image refers to Lorenzo's political position in relation to the governance of the city. However, Dei, a merchant from a family of goldsmiths, was more alert than most to the fact that botteghe have products – not just ideological or systematic, but tangible. It was he, after all, who linked Florentine pride to both its artists and its consumer goods. Might then the Giardino di San Marco have been seen by Lorenzo, responding, as it were, to the metaphor, as a place where he could exercise more formal and

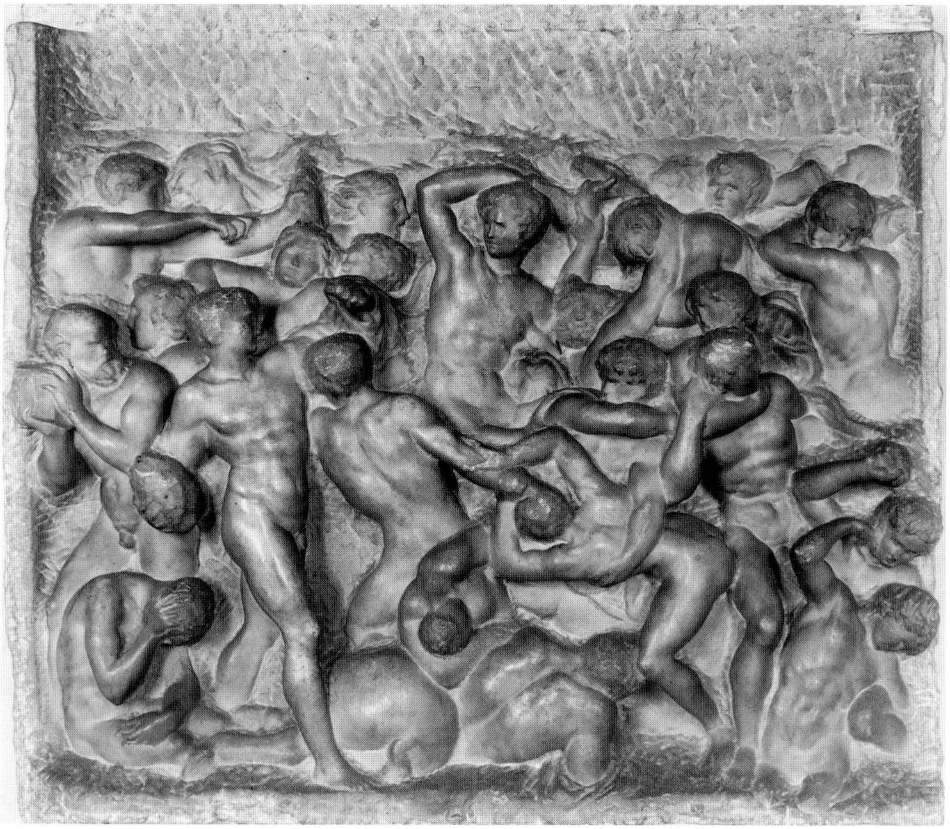

33. Michelangelo, *Battle of the Centaurs*. Marble. Florence, Casa Buonarroti. Photo: Ralph Lieberman.

institutionalised control over one of the most prestigious products of the city, its painting and sculpture?

To argue this case more fully one has to assess the possible aims and the results of Bertoldo's teaching in the Laurentian bottega. It is now accepted that Michelangelo was one of Bertoldo's students. He is even documented as connected with the Garden after Bertoldo's death in 1491, recorded as fleeing it in 1494. Vasari listed his companions. The presence of Michelangelo's friend Francesco Granacci, a fellow student of Ghirlandaio, and of his rival Pietro Torrigiano is not disputed. The 1992 exhibition devoted to the Garden demonstrated in addition close stylistic connections between these artists and Giuliano Bugiardini (another friend of Michelangelo, also from the Ghirlandaio shop), Giovan Francesco Rustici, and Baccio da Montelupo, all three named by Vasari.[79]

What then did Bertoldo teach these young artists at Lorenzo's behest? In particular, how was he supposed to fashion Michelangelo, who was selected early to be his successor as artist-in-residence at the Medici palace? It is already evident that he was

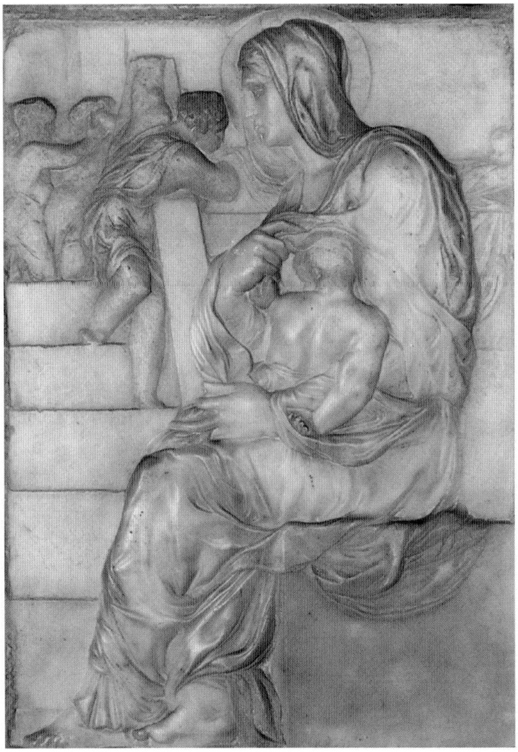

34. Michelangelo, *Madonna of the Steps*. Marble. Casa Buonarroti, Florence. Photo: Ralph Lieberman.

not operating in the same way as the heads of workshops such as those of Verrocchio or Ghirlandaio. The aim was not merely to produce a series of duplicate Bertoldos. What is most striking, on the evidence of works which can be connected with his pupils, is that the productions of the students of the sculpture garden were conceived as essays in imitation of the two key elements in Bertoldo's work, rather than of Bertoldo's style alone. They, too, manifest a retrospective approach both to the antique and to the art of the Florentine (recent) past. On a practical level, Bertoldo – like the head of an ordinary sculpture workshop – was equipped to teach his pupils (some of them already trained as painters) how to model and cast. To judge from the subsequent careers of Rustici and Torrigiano (whom Vasari mentions modelling figures in clay under Bertoldo's instruction), he must have passed on just such skills. Yet although we know him to have executed works in bronze at the beginning of his career, the earliest identifiable works by Michelangelo are both carved in marble: his *Battle of the Centaurs* (Fig. 33) and the *Madonna of the Steps* (Fig. 34), both now in the Casa Buonarroti.[80] Michelangelo's biographers, Vasari and Ascanio Condivi, Michelangelo's pupil and chief apologist, both state that he learned how to sculpt marble in the Garden, through the imitation of 'a head that was there of an old faun, ancient and wrinkled, that was damaged at the nose and smiled at the mouth', a model which he duly surpassed 'through his fantasy'.[81] This story has often been dismissed as a fiction, designed to present the artist as autodidact, and even believers have raised the question as to whether Michelangelo could have learned to carve stone with a bronze worker for his teacher. There is no doubt, however, that Michelangelo learned how to carve marble somewhere, that (as with Verrocchio before him) there is no record of any kind of formal apprenticeship to a stone carver, and even though various solutions to this thorny problem have been posited, they fail to satisfy on grounds of style, chronology, and logic.[82]

And there are good reasons for thinking that Bertoldo was capable of teaching stone carving. It is known that he could carve wood and that he had chisels in his possession. Moreover two surviving reliefs make his supervision, at the very least, of carving by students or collaborators a stronger possibility. An enlarged marble

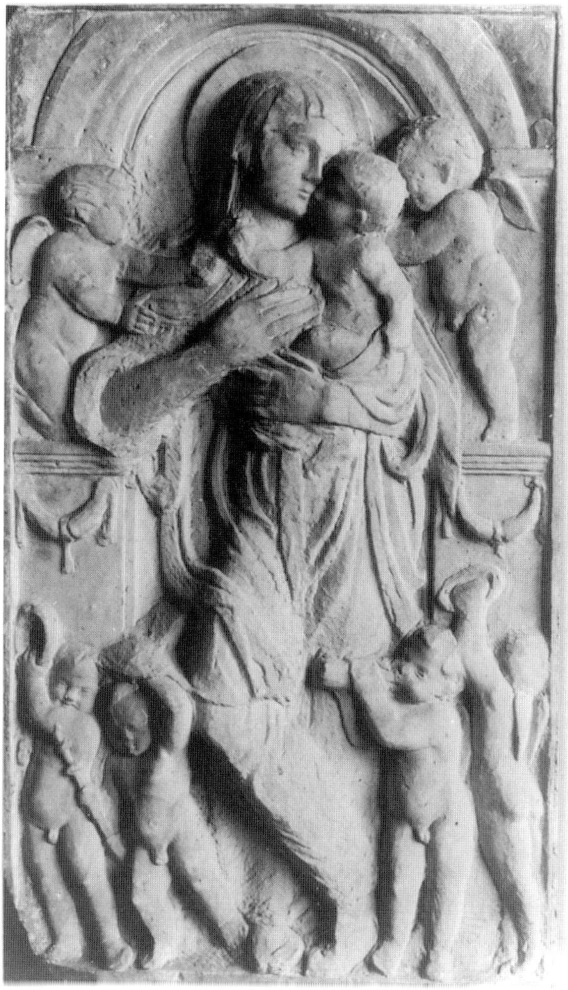

35. After (or pupil of) Bertoldo di Giovanni. *Virgin and Child with Angels.* Marble. Formerly Lanz Collection, Amsterdam (present whereabouts unknown). Photo: Author.

variation, roughly carved after Bertoldo's *Virgin and Child* bronze relief in the Louvre, was last recorded in the Lanz Collection in Amsterdam, whence it had come from the Casa Martelli in Florence (Fig. 35).[83] Draper judged it probably spurious but, if so, one wonders why it is so clearly unfinished; some parts, such as the Virgin's hands and arms are barely blocked out, the marks of the chisels are everywhere apparent. Moreover, many of the forms have been simplified, perhaps for ease of carving – garlands, ribbons, and mouldings eliminated in favour of simpler architectural forms, the Virgin's hair covered with a veil, the heads of the putti at the Virgin's feet raised out of their more challenging positions. Some of these modifications, as well as the increased roundness of the heads, are in tune with the kinds of shifts seen in the early works of Michelangelo, and perhaps this piece may be reinterpreted as a set exercise in carving by an inexperienced hand, one of his fellows in the Garden. Until it reappears, it will difficult to assess the piece properly. However, another artist in his Bertoldo's circle is thought to have carved a now damaged marble relief in the Ashmolean Museum of, significantly, a battling centaur and lapith, whose dramatic poses, although ill-integrated, are interestingly reminiscent of those of some of the figures in Michelangelo's famous relief.[84]

The combination of antique statuary and a stone supply in the Garden suggests in addition that it may well have been the Medici site for the restoration of ancient sculpture. In 1490 a 'full-length marble statue, with carved draperies and no head', excavated during the building of the Palazzo Gondi, was 'carried to the garden of the magnificent Lorenzo de' Medici'.[85] It is likely that Lorenzo sent it there to be restored, although admittedly this is a function of the Garden mentioned neither by contemporaries nor by Vasari. Nevertheless there is a clue in Vasari's account of Michelangelo's 'discovery' by Lorenzo. By stressing the damage to the ancient faun's head, he suggests that an element in Michelangelo's success was his 'finishing' of the work. Although there is no direct evidence that Bertoldo was himself engaged in restoration, and although it might be objected that, because his securely identified works are all modelled, it would be peculiar to find Bertoldo sculpting replacement heads for marbles, the slightly later example of the *bronzista* Antico, frequently called on to restore ancient marble sculptures,[86] indicates that artists of Bertoldo's type, employed as all-rounders by powerful patrons, were not restricted to the exercise of a single technical specialism. It therefore becomes possible that Michelangelo was taught to carve through some involvement in the completion of damaged antiquities in the Garden, rather than through a traditional training in a stone sculptor's shop.

Whether or not such restorations took place in the Garden, it is worth stressing the obvious, that Michelangelo's *Battle of the Centaurs* (Fig. 33) looks more like the work of Bertoldo, his Medici *Battle* relief in particular, than like pieces by any of his contemporaries. Here, at least, Bertoldo was forming the younger artist in his stylistic image, even if the medium was different. The direct influence of Bertoldo on the young Michelangelo has recently been the subject of much scholarly debate. It should be noted, in addition, that, although none of Michelangelo's nudes is copied literally from Bertoldo's *Battle,* two figures, the man wielding a rock in the top right corner and the open-chested youth stepping forward on his right leg, can be found in Bertoldo's sculpture – the former copying a *curete* from the second section of the Poggio frieze, the latter derived from the assassin in the centre of the Giuliano side of Bertoldo's Pazzi Conspiracy medal (Fig. 28). As a precocious demonstration of virtuosity in Medici service, these quotations had meaning, all three sources closely linked to Lorenzo. The medal now looks more than ever as if it was considered a statement of Laurentian style, of which Michelangelo was sensible.

Michelangelo, Donatello, and the Antique: Combining Pasts

Bertoldo's direct impact on the other Garden students is less easily traced. Draper has noted Rustici's debt to Bertoldo in the Villa Salviati reliefs and, to some extent, in his terracottas of fighting horsemen. But he also rightly points out that Bertoldo could hardly be said to have stamped his style discernibly on any of the other participants in his academy.[87] The primary aim was less, however, to reproduce the 'house' style of a master, but to form styles of their own, using Laurentian ingredients. The Garden was surely the place where Michelangelo and his peers learned the vocabulary of antique art, and the siting of ancient sculpture there may have suggested its appropriateness as a school (artists had been studying such objects, informally, for years). But, as we have seen, Bertoldo's inventive powers were often directed at processes of transformation, to the imaginative reworking of antique models. He was therefore peculiarly equipped to teach a similar modernising approach to the antique. The *Battle of the Centaurs* is a case in point, deliberately setting out to recreate an antique sarcophagus relief, but this time, unlike Bertoldo's own similar effort, properly in marble. Its iconography has recently been shown to be a recreation of Plutarch's textual description of the shield of Phidias's *Athena Parthenos,* which included the bald and bearded self-portrait of the sculptor wielding a rock.[88] Moreover although as already stated it bears more resemblance to Bertoldo's sculpture than to work by anyone else, it is also distinctively Michelangelo's own.

Can similar transformations of early quattrocento Florentine art be traced in works be Bertoldo's pupils? The Donatello revival at the end of the quattrocento, and in the first decade of the cinquecento, is long noted, but it has been only tangentially associated with Bertoldo or Lorenzo de' Medici, probably because it manifested itself most clearly only after their deaths.[89] But it is especially apparent in the works of those associated with the Garden. One can cite Rustici's *St George and the Dragon* in Budapest, for instance, as a particularly faithful exercise in Donatellesque *schiacciato* relief, and the references in his Florence Baptistry group of *St John the Baptist preaching* to Donatello's Siena *St John the Baptist* and to his stone prophets from the Duomo are explicit.[90] Michelangelo, too, constantly referred to Donatello throughout his early career. One of the sources for the terrified Christ child, menaced by a symbol of the Passion, in the tondo now in the Royal Academy in London, carved for Taddeo Taddei in 1504,[91] has been identified – a gambolling boy in a famous *Medea* sarcophagus.[92] Equally important, however, was the little boy cowering from the head of the Baptist at the bottom left of Donatello's Siena font relief of the *Feast of Herod.* Michelangelo's infant St John takes his pose from the winged putto standing to the left of Donatello's *Chellini Madonna* (now in the Victoria and Albert Museum), while the Virgin in profile copies both her headdress and the angle of her head and neck from Donatello's bronze relief in Vienna.[93]

Bertoldo, it seems, was therefore expected not only to perform, but also to teach as Donatello's pupil. Here we return to another key aspect of Lorenzo's aims, the establishment of an especially Florentine language. Vasari stated that, beyond antique sculptures, the Giardino di San Marco contained 'many drawings, cartoons, and models from the hands of Donato, Pippo, Masaccio, Paolo Uccello, Fra Giovanni, Fra Filippo and of other masters'.[94] Even if the existence of such drawings and models cannot yet be proved, the story of the presence of works in the Garden by this generation of artists might reflect the fact that Michelangelo drew copies of figures and compositions by Giotto and, especially, Masaccio.[95] (Torrigiano, reported by Cellini, claimed to have broken his rival's nose in the Brancacci Chapel enraged by his constant twitting of 'all those who were drawing there.'[96]) These were not unconsidered choices. Because it was Lorenzo who set up the monument to Giotto in the duomo, he was evidently very aware of the symbolic importance of the style the painter.[97] Like Donatello's sculpture, and like the early works of Michelangelo or Granacci, the paintings of Giotto and Masaccio have little of the detailed prettiness so often encountered in works by both painters and sculptors working in the 1470s and 1480s. This is only one of the ways in which these two generations are artist are linked. If young artists in the 1490s chose to copy their works, it was a question of directed choice rather than because of unconscious 'influence'.[98]

Although the combination of antiquities and works by modern masters is akin to the contents of Squarcione's Paduan 'studio' in the mid-quattrocento, also used for teaching purposes,[99] this part of Vasari's story has been regularly discounted. Because Vasari has been shown to be correct on other counts, one needs to be less sceptical. The modern parts of the Garden teaching collection might then be interpreted as tools for the deliberate cultivation of a return to the values of trecento and early quattrocento art. Moreover, it is likely that Bertoldo possessed relief and fully three-dimensional models by Donatello, paraphernalia that would have formed an essential part of the practice he is said to have inherited from his master (and such bequests of drawings and models were not unusual).[100] Models by Donatello are certainly known to have existed; a 1467 inventory mentions models for the doors of Siena Cathedral which Donatello was to have made in 1457–8: 'Two panels, the designs of the doors of the Cathedral made by Donatello with wax figures upon them'.[101] There is also evidence in Bertoldo's own work that he had access to such models, evidence divined in the relationship between the putti on Donatello's Prato Pulpit reliefs and his *cantoria* for the Florentine duomo[102] and the little boys prancing about in Bertoldo's *Triumph of Silenus.* In this later piece, Bertoldo reuses stock figures by Donatello, depicting them from different angles – most often, revealingly, by turning them around on an axis.[103] More supporting evidence might be adduced in the closeness of the pose of Bertoldo's Louvre bronze of the Baptist to Donatello's Adam on the throne of the Santo *Virgin and Child.*[104] If this

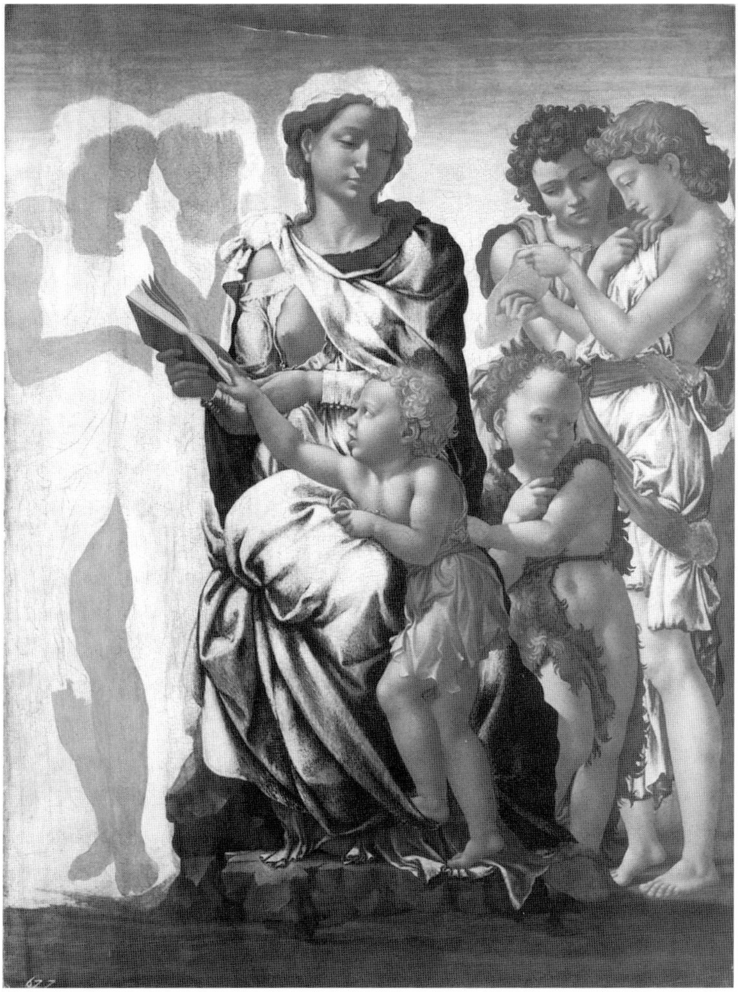

36. Michelangelo, *Manchester Madonna.* On panel. London, The National Gallery. Photo: The National Gallery.

piece does not post-date Bertoldo's brief sojourn in Padua in 1483–4,[105] which it may, the fact that Bertoldo's source was not a Florentine work lends weight to the theory of Bertoldo's inheritance of models.

Donatello's models were thus to be re-envisaged according to a Laurentian programme to promote individual greatness in a new generation of artists. For no one was this more the case than in the work of Lorenzo's special protégé, Michelangelo. The connections between Michelangelo and Donatello have been frequently proclaimed. Borghini famously celebrated the connection between the two artists and was not the only sixteenth-century commentator so to do.[106] Modern critics have cited many examples of the 'influence' of Donatello on Michelangelo.[107] It now looks as if his reverence for Donatello was strategically fostered, however. Indeed

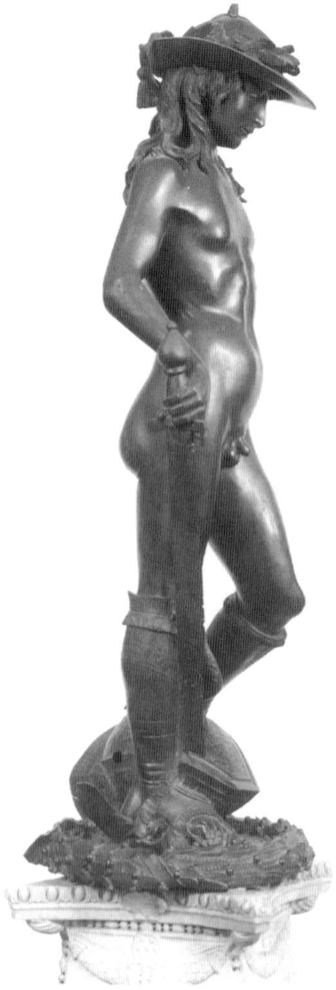

37. Donatello. *David.* Cast bronze. Florence, Museo Nazionale del Bargello. Photo: Conway Library, Courtauld Institute of Art.

it is possible to observe how Michelangelo assimilated the example of his great predecessor to arrive at artistic solutions of his own (such as that demonstrated in the Taddei tondo). If, for example, the *Battle of the Centaurs* was intended primarily as a demonstration of the mastery of the language of the antique, it may be no coincidence that centaurs bear Donatello's signature on the North pulpit in San Lorenzo[108] and that Bertoldo took one as the subject for his lost Medici bronze, the three pieces making perhaps a statement of continuity and revival. Michelangelo's *Madonna of the Steps* (Fig. 34) makes just such a statement. It has the air of an exercise in Donatellism and was defined as such by Vasari.[109] The relief is a not entirely happy patchwork of motifs from the Boston *Madonna of the Clouds* and the Lille *Feast of Herod;* the head of the youth, for instance, leaning over the baluster, collides uncomfortably with the Virgin's halo. Nor is the carving technique consistent or unified.

Two or three years on, it can be seen that Michelangelo had learned to translate Donatello's motifs into something more coherent. The *Manchester Madonna,* which must have been started before Michelangelo escaped Florence for Bologna (and was perhaps interrupted by his flight), has a Masacciesque quality, with its monumental figures and deliberately reduced background (Fig. 36). Even more, as Penny has observed, it is a painting that looks like a sculpture.[110] It does not seem, however, to have been noticed that many of the ingredients of the 'sculpture' are derived from Donatello's works, albeit Donatello's figures have been centred and stabilised (as they often are in Bertoldo's works). Nonetheless, the abstracted melancholy and splendidly regular features of the Virgin are informed by the examination of prototypes by Donatello. She is close, for example, to Donatello's Judith (whose head and veil were to become the Bruges *Madonna*'s), to the *Madonna* and *Saint Justina* in Padua, and to the Orsanmichele *Saint Louis of Toulouse.*[111] Although he is more solidly placed, the adolescent angel on the far right is a clothed and reversed depiction of Donatello's bronze *David* seen in profile (Fig. 37). The Christ Child, leaning forward, must have been based on a piece which closely resembled one of the dancing putti that Donatello executed for the Siena font. With his raised left leg he also resembles a putto at far left of the scene of the *Grape Harvest* on the triangular base of Donatello's *Judith and Holofernes.*[112] Michelangelo has even introduced a strange fold in the Virgin's drapery to explain and justify the pose. St John's serpentine pose is also markedly Donatellesque and may derive from another putto made for the Siena font, the little boy with the tambourine, now in Berlin.[113]

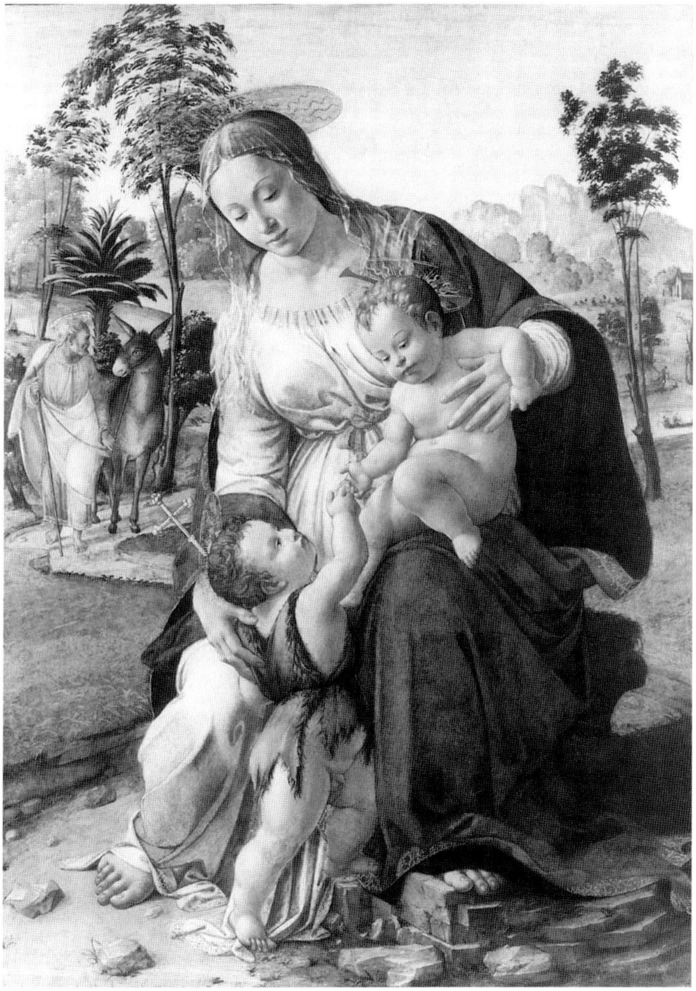

38. Francesco Granacci. *Virgin and Child with St. John the Baptist.* Dublin, The National Gallery of Ireland. Photo: National Gallery of Ireland.

This, in fact, seems to have been something of a stock figure for Michelangelo. Hirst emphasised the link between St John's contrapposto stance and that of the Christ Child in the *Bruges Madonna.*[114] It does not, however, seem to have been remarked that Michelangelo had employed it before, in one of the two little boys, partly obscured, who dance in the background of the *Madonna of the Steps,* where the incompleteness with which it is described may suggest that he had inherited it from elsewhere.

Indeed it is precisely in these figures that we are provided with corroborative evidence that the source of Michelangelo's Donatellism came in the form of three-dimensional models, perhaps those inherited and apparently already employed by Bertoldo, as well as from looking at Donatello's works displayed so prominently in the city. The pose of the Christ Child may well have been used by Bertoldo himself, close to one of the putti at the feet of Bertoldo's Louvre *Virgin and Child* relief, though here he is seen from the back (Fig. 32). When Francesco Granacci used it for his *Virgin and Child with the Infant St John* (now in Dublin) and in its many variations, the figure is not reversed but actually seen from the other side (Fig. 38). Granacci also used the Manchester St John for two of his own, in the pictures of the *Virgin and Child with St John* in Toulon and in San Firenze in Florence.[115] By employing Donatello's models, Bertoldo had succeeded in part of his remit – the instruction of Michelangelo and his companions in a Florentine visual vernacular.

The importance of Bertoldo as a cultural tool for Lorenzo de' Medici cannot therefore be doubted. His employment of Donatello's pupil and his consequent annexation and conversion of a Florentine vernacular language for sculpture (and the visual arts more broadly), is entirely in line with other initiatives undertaken by Lorenzo, especially in the last decade of his life. Bertoldo was evidently expected to perform like a court artist, following models developed in other Italian centres. Unlike Mantegna, Tura, or Francesco di Giorgio, however, he stood for more than his own talent. Through him Lorenzo could transform an aspect of civic, even popular culture (given how available Donatello's works were on the streets and piazze of Florence), and, by emphasising the Medicean elements within that culture and adding new elements to it, turn it into something that was specifically Laurentian. His programme of Donatellism, using the mediating skills of Bertoldo, was intended both to link his patronage with Florentine civic pride and, through its promulgation by the Garden students, to assert visually his authority over the city.[116]

Ultimately and ironically, it was just this dynastic ambition on behalf of his less politically adept son Piero that has caused his efforts to remain largely unrecognised. After Lorenzo's death in 1492, Michelangelo continued to work for Piero, returning to become resident at the Palazzo Medici. The fall and exile of Piero two years later, however, ensured that Michelangelo, moulded into an ideal amalgam of Donatello and the sculptors of antiquity, was not to become the Medici court artist fashioned so deliberately by Lorenzo – or, at least, not in the way that he seems to have envisaged. No medal by Michelangelo of Piero di Lorenzo de' Medici was, or ever could, have been made.

NOTES

1. Wilhem von Bode, *Bertoldo und Lorenzo dei Medici: Die Kunstpolitik des Lorenzo il Magnifico im Spiegel der Werke seines Lieblingskünstlers Bertoldo di Giovanni* (Freiburg im Breisgau: Pontos-Verlag, 1925), 121–9.
2. Michael Baxandall, *Painting and Experience in Fifteenth-Century Italy*, 2nd ed. (Oxford: Clarendon Press, 1988), 26.

3. Michael Baxandall, *Giotto and the Orators: Humanist Observers of Painting in Italy and the Discovery of Pictorial Composition, 1350–1450* (Oxford: Clarendon Press, 1971), 98.

4. Although Mantegna seems to have worked as a portraitist from early in his career, it is likely that his primary reputation for artistic *ingegno* depended on his large-scale religious commissions in Padua and Verona. The best overview and analysis of Mantegna's activities for the Gonzaga court remains Caroline Elam ('Mantegna at Mantua', in *Splendours of the Gonzaga*, exh. cat., London: Victoria and Albert Museum, 1981, ed. by David Chambers and Jean Martineau [Milan: Pizzi, 1981], 14–25), who gives a very clear sense of how and why Mantegna was employed.

5. He said, 'it is true that Andrea is a good master in other things, but in portrait painting he could have more grace, and doesn't do so well'. Rodolfo Signorini, 'Federico III e Cristiano I nella Camera degli Sposi di Mantegna', *Mitteilungen des Kunsthistorischen Instituts in Florenz* (henceforth *MKIF*) 18 (1974), 227–50 (p. 232); Keith Christiansen, 'Portraits', in *Andrea Mantegna*, exh. cat., London: Royal Academy of Arts; New York: Metropolitan Museum of Art, 1992, ed. Jane Martineau (London: Thames and Hudson, 1992), 324–8 (p. 324).

6. 'Documenti e fonti su Pisanello (1395–1581 circa)', ed. Dominique Cordellier, in *Verona Illustrata* 8 (1995): 151–3, doc. 68.

7. The literature on Pisanello's medals is vast, but for, specifically, the question of how the status of the patron was raised by having an artist of Pisanello's heroic stature make his medal, see Luke Syson, 'Opus pisani pictoris: les médailles de Pisanello et son atelier', in *Pisanello: Louvre conférences et colloques*, 2 vols., ed. Dominique Cordellier and Bernadette Py (Paris: La Documentation Française, 1998), I, 377–426; idem, 'Classical Learning and Court Art', in Luke Syson and Dillian Gordon, *Pisanello, Painter to the Renaissance Court* (London: National Gallery, 2001), 86–137.

8. Robert Weiss, *The Renaissance Discovery of Classical Antiquity* (Oxford: Blackwell, 1969), 167–79.

9. George Francis Hill, *A Corpus of Italian Medals of the Renaissance before Cellini*, 2 vols. (London: British Museum, 1930), I, 13–9, 37–43, and II, nn. 45–67, 158–89; Pier Giorgio Pasini, 'Matteo de' Pasti: Problems of Style and Chronology', in *Italian Medals*, ed. J. Graham Pollard, *Studies in the History of Art* 21 (1987): 143–59; Luke Syson, 'Artistic Individuality and the Workshop Tradition', in Syson and Gordon, *Pisanello*, 226–34.

10. Hanno-Walter Kruft, *Francesco Laurana: Ein Bildhauer der Frührenaissance* (Munich: Beck, 1995), 67–77.

11. Wilhelm von Bode, 'Bertoldo di Giovanni und seine Bronzbildwerke', *Jahrbuch der königlich preussichen Kunstsammlungen* 161 (1895): 43–159 (pp. 153–5); Bode, *Bertoldo*, 26–8; Hill, *A Corpus*, I, pp. 240–1, and II, n. 915; James David Draper, *Bertoldo di Giovanni: Sculptor of the Medici Household* (Columbia: University of Missouri Press, 1992), pp. 27, 86–95, cat. 3; idem, catalogue entry, in *The Currency of Fame: Portrait Medals of the Renaissance*, exh. cat., Washington, D.C.: National Gallery of Art, and New York: Frick Collection, 1994, ed. Stephen K. Scher (London: Thames and Hudson, 1994), 129–32; Alison Wright, catalogue entry, in *Renaissance Florence: The Art of the 1470s*, exh. cat., London: National Gallery 1999, ed. Patricia Lee Rubin and Alison Wright (London: National Gallery, 1999), 128–9 (which gives the fullest account of the iconography of the flanking figures).

12. Bertoldo's 1469 medal of Frederick III, with a reverse showing the emperor creating knights on the Ponte Sant'Angelo in the presence of Pope Paul II and his retinue provides the only known precedent for the representation of a real event. See Bode, *Bertoldo*, pp. 35–8; Hill, *A Corpus*, I, 239–40, and II, n. 912; Draper, *Bertoldo*, 23–4, 79–82, cat. 1.

13. SALVS PVBLICA on the Lorenzo side, LVCTVS PVBLICVS on the side with the portrait of the murdered Giuliano. Although Draper correctly transcribes the inscription in his description of

the object (p. 86), elsewhere he writes it as LVCTVS PVBLICA – an error followed by Wright (see n. 11 to the present chapter).

14. Angelo Poliziano, *Della congiura dei Pazzi (Coniurationis Commentarium)*, ed. Alessandro Perosa (Padua: Antenore, 1958).

15. Weiss, *Renaissance Discovery*, 167–79; S. De Maria, 'Fra corte e studio: la cultura antiquaria a Bologna nell'età dei Bentivoglio', in *Il contributo dell' Università di Bologna alla storia della città: l'Evo Antico: Atti del primo convegno, Bologna, 11–12 March 1988*, ed. Guido A. Mansuelli and Giancarlo Susini (Bologna: Comune di Bologna, 1989), 151–216 (p. 153).

16. Stephen J. Campbell, *Cosmè Tura of Ferrara: Style, Politics and the Renaissance City, 1450–1495* (New Haven and London: Yale University Press, 1997), 9, 12; Joseph Manca, *Cosmè Tura: The Life and Art of a Painter in Estense Ferrara* (Oxford: Oxford University Press, 2000), pp. 43, 183. For a recent account of the relationship between Tura, his Este employers, and other Ferrarese patrons, see Stephen J. Campbell, 'Cosmè Tura and Court Culture', in *Cosmè Tura: Painting and Design in Renaissance Ferrara*, exh. cat., Boston: Isabella Stewart Gardner Museum, 2002, ed. Stephen J. Campbell (Milan: Electa, 2002), 1–30.

17. Scipione Borghesi and Luciano Banchi, *Nuovi documenti per la storia dell' arte senese* (Siena: E. Torrini, 1898), 256–7, doc. 160; Gustina Scaglia, *Francesco di Giorgio: Checklist and History of Manuscripts and Drawings in Autographs and Copies from ca. 1470 to 1687 and Renewed Copies (1764–1839)* (Bethlehem: Lehigh University Press, 1992), 14.

18. Paul Kristeller, *Andrea Mantegna* (Berlin and Leipzig: Cosmos Verlag für Kunst und Wissenschaft, 1902), 527, doc. 45.

19. Campbell, *Cosmè Tura of Ferrara*, p. 12, where he notes that the portraitist Baldassare d'Este was also called 'nobil pittore e famigliare' by his Ferrarese employers.

20. Werner L. Gundersheimer, 'The Patronage of Ercole I d'Este', *Journal of Medieval and Renaissance Studies* 6 (1976): 1–18; Joseph Manca, *The Art of Ercole de' Roberti* (Cambridge and New York: Cambridge University Press, 1992), 221, doc. 72; Luke Syson, 'Ercole de Roberti: The Making of a Court Artist', in Denise Allen, Luke Syson, Jennifer Helvey, and David Jaffé, *Ercole de' Roberti: The Renaissance in Ferrara*, exh. cat., Los Angeles: J. Paul Getty Museum, 1999 (London: Burlington Magazine Publications, 1999), v–xiv (p. xi) (published as a supplement to *Burlington Magazine* 141 (1999).

21. Andrea S. Norris, 'Gian Cristoforo Romano: The Courtier as Medalist', in Pollard, *Italian Medals*, 131–41 (p. 133).

22. Kristeller, *Mantegna*, 546, doc. 103.

23. Ibid., 522–3, 526, and 541, docs 31, 32, 42, 85; Eberhard Ruhmer, *Tura: Paintings and Drawings* (New York: Phaidon, 1958), 79–84.

24. See the arguments in Luke Syson, 'Tura and the "Minor Arts": The School of Ferrara', in Campbell, *Cosmè Tura: Painting and Design*, 31–70.

25. Dominique Cordellier in *Pisanello: le peintre aux sept vertus*, exh. cat., Paris: Musée du Louvre, 1996 (Paris: Réunion des musées nationaux, 1996), 415, 418–19, cat. 290. The drawing is often related to building of the Castelnuovo and the drawing is sometimes attributed to Pisanello's shop. George L. Hersey (*The Aragonese Arch at Naples, 1443–1475* [New Haven and London: Yale University Press, 1973], 22–3) argues that the drawing has nothing to do with the Castelnuovo, but this opinion has been questioned more recently by Kruft, *Francesco Laurana*, pp. 35–66, 393.

26. R. W. Lightbown, *Mantegna* (Oxford: Phaidon Christie's, 1986), 120–1; Adriano Franceschini, *Artisti a Ferrara in età umanistica e rinascimentale: testimonianze archivistiche*, vol. 1 (Ferrara and Rome: Corbo, 1993), p. 797, doc. 1235.

27. Manca, *Art of Ercole de' Roberti*, 223–30, docs 77–9.

28. That the medal was perceived in this way in this period is demonstrated by the medallic portrait of Mehmet II by Gentile Bellini, his only such effort, which this self-aggrandising artist signed very probably as the proof and signal of his relationship with the subject of the medal, and, consequently, as a statement of what nature of artist he was. By the 1470s Gentile had become the de facto official artist of Venice, with his position at the Scuola Grande di San Marco and especially after his appointment in 1474 to supervise the decoration of the Sala di Maggior Consiglio. As such he performed as a designer, providing, for example, drawings for reliefs to be executed by Antonio Rizzo for the Scuola. He was also no mean portraitist. These skills made him the ideal artistic representative of the republic in Istanbul, whither he departed on 3 September 1479. His tasks for Mehmet were as various as we have come to expect and certainly included a rôle as artistic overseer. His medal of Mehmet almost certainly was not commissioned by the Sultan himself. It is much more about Bellini himself and, dull and lifeless though it may be, it can be read as an expression of the particular skills and virtues that led him to such an intimate relationship with such a powerful ruler. It does not matter that it was probably not modelled or cast by Bellini, who had no documented skills as a sculptor. Indeed a division of labour may be seen as part of the point. See Hill, *A Corpus*, I, 113–14, and II, no. 432; Julian Raby, 'Pride and Prejudice: Mehmed the Conqueror and the Italian Portrait Medal', in Pollard, *Italian Medals*, 171–94 (pp. 180–2).

29. Hill, *A Corpus*, p. 31, nn. 117–18; Luke Syson, 'Medals and Other Portraits Attributed to Cosmè Tura', *Burlington Magazine* 141 (1999): 226–9. The attribution of the design, although not the execution, is accepted by Monica Molteni, *Cosmè Tura* (Milan: F. Motta, 1999), 190–1; also Campbell, *Cosmè Tura: Painting and Design*, 247–9.

30. See Hill, *A Corpus*, I, 77, and II, n. 306, and Roberto Bartalini, catalogue entry, in *Francesco di Giorgio e il Rinascimento a Siena, 1450–1500*, exh. cat., Siena: Chiesa di Sant' Agostino, 1993, ed. Luciano Bellosi (Milan: Electa, 1993), 160–61, cat. 18.

31. See Hill, *A Corpus*, I, 77, and II, n. 307, and Bartalini, catalogue entry, in *Francesco di Giorgio*, 354–5, cat. 69a.

32. Ibid., I, 47–9, and II, nn. 193–200.

33. Ibid, I, 47–8, and II, n. 194; Rodolfo Signorini, '*Opus hoc tenue*': *la camera dipinta di Andrea Mantegna* (Parma: Artegrafica Silva, 1985), 189–94, 196. It might, given the self-conscious identification of so many court artists as modern Apelles, be worth pursuing the evident stylistic and compositional connection between this medal reverse and Mantegna's drawing of the Calumny of Apelles in the British Museum, generally dated much later.

34. Rodolfo Signorini, 'L'autoritratto del Mantegna nella Camera degli Sposi', *MKIF* 20 (1976); 205–12; Joanna Woods-Marsden, *Renaissance Self-Portraiture: The Visual Construction of Identity and the Social Status of the Artist* (New Haven and London: Yale University Press, 1998), 85–8.

35. Nicolai Rubinstein, *The Government of Florence under the Medici (1434 to 1494)*, 2nd ed. (Oxford: Clarendon Press, 1997), 223–30; Richard C. Trexler, *Public Life in Renaissance Florence* (Ithaca and London: Cornell University Press), 443–4.

36. Arnold Hauser, *The Social History of Art*, 3rd ed., 4 vols. (London and New York: Routledge, 1999), II, 39.

37. For a good recent summary, see Patricia Lee Rubin, 'Patrons and Projects', in Rubin and Wright, *Renaissance Florence*, 34–43.

38. Gaetano Milanesi and Carlo Pini, *La scrittura di artisti italiani (sec. XIV–XVII)*, 3 vols. (Florence: Le Monnier, 1890), I, n.p., doc. 60; Karl Frey, *Michelagniolo Buonarroti: Quellen und Forschungen*

zu seiner Geschichte und Kunst (Berlin: K. Curtius, 1907), p. 44; Draper, *Bertoldo*, 12, 271, 273, 278, docs. 5, 7, 13.

39. Isidore del Lungo, *Un viaggio di Clarice Orsini de' Medici nel 1485, descritto da Ser Matteo Franco* (Bologna: Forni, 1868); Draper, *Bertoldo*, 15, 276–7, doc. 10.

40. In the protocolli of 21 October 1490. See *Protocolli del Carteggio di Lorenzo il Magnifico per gli anni 1473–74, 1477–92*, ed. Marcello del Piazzo (Florence: Olschki, 1956), 426; Draper, *Bertoldo*, 17.

41. F. W. Kent, 'Bertoldo "sculptore" and Lorenzo de' Medici', *Burlington Magazine* 134 (1992): 248–9.

42. Milanesi and Pini, *La scrittura*, I, n.p., doc. 60; Draper, *Bertoldo*, pp. 277–8, doc. 12: Kent, 'Bertoldo "sculptore"', 249, n. 9. The letter continues: "Che n'è danno assai e a llui è molto doluto chè non se ne trovava un altro in Toscana nè forse in Italia di sì nobile ingegno e arte in tali cose". The iteration of nobility and the pairing of innate talent and art – the intellectual and the manual – recalls the terms used of court artists such as the 'noble' Cosmè Tura and Pisanello's 'ingenium atque arte'. See nn. 7 and 16 to this chapter.

43. E. H. Gombrich, 'The Early Medici as Patrons of Art', in *Norm and Form: Studies in the Art of the Renaissance*, 3rd ed. (London and New York: Phaidon, 1978), 35–57 (p. 56). For a balanced and contextualized account of Bertoldo's bronzes and the Pazzi conspiracy medal, see John T. Paoletti, 'Familiar Objects: Sculptural Types in the Collections of the Early Medici', in *Looking at Italian Renaissance Sculpture*, ed. Sarah Blake McHam (Cambridge: Cambridge University Press, 1998), 79–110 (pp. 96–7, and 100–2).

44. Eugéne Müntz, *Les Collections des Médicis au quinzième siecle: le musée – la bibliothèque – le mobilier* (Paris: Rouam, 1888), pp. 61, 84–5; Draper, *Bertoldo*, 113–18, 122–45, 278, and cat. 8, 10, 11, doc. 14.

45. Bode, *Bertoldo*, 70–2; Draper, *Bertoldo*, 107–11, cat. 7.

46. Bode, *Bertoldo*, 18–20; Hill, *A Corpus*, 239, n. 911; Draper, *Bertoldo*, 95–104, cat. 4. The piece is signed OPVS BERTOLDI FLORENTIN SCVLTORIS, a form which echoes the signature of 'Pisano, painter'.

47. Giovanni Poggi, *Il Duomo di Firenze: Documenti sulla decorazione della chiesa e del campanile tratti dall' Archivio dell' Opera* (Berlin; Cassirer, 1909), 284–7; Draper, *Bertoldo*, 275–6, doc. 9.

48. First attributed by John Pope-Hennessy, *Italian Renaissance Sculpture*, 2nd ed. (London and New York: Phaidon, 1971), 303; Draper, *Bertoldo*, 197–220, cat. 20.

49. Giorgio Galletti and Litta Medri, 'La Villa di poggio a Caiano', in *L'architettura di Lorenzo il Magnifico*, exh. cat., Florence: Spedale degli Innocenti, 1992, ed. Gabriele Morolli et al. (Florence, Amilcare Pizzi, Silvana, 1992), 89–100.

50. Alessandro Parronchi, 'The Language of Humanism and the Language of Sculpture: Bertoldo as Illustrator of the Apologi of Bartolomeo Scala', *Journal of the Warburg and Courtauld Institutes* 27 (1964): 108–36 (pp. 134–6).

51. Bode, *Bertoldo*, 88–91; Draper, *Bertoldo*, 176–85, cat. 18. Signed EXPRESSIT. ME. BERTHOLDVS. CONFLAVIT.HADRIANVS.

52. Draper, *Bertoldo*, 271, doc. 4.

53. Ibid., pp. 15, 277, doc. 11.

54. Milanesi and Pini, *La scrittura*, I, n.p, doc. 60; Draper, *Bertoldo*, 7–12, 272–3, doc. 7.

55. Philip Ellis Foster, 'Lorenzo de' Medici and the Florentine Cathedral Façade', *Art Bulletin* 63 (1981): 495–500; Draper, *Bertoldo*, 269–70, doc. 2.

56. R. W. Lightbown, *Sandro Botticelli*, 2 vols. (London: P. Elek, 1978), II, pp. 29–32, cat. B16–20, and Rubin and Wright, *Renaissance Florence*, pp. 126–7, cat. 1.

57. Bode, *Bertoldo*, pp. 94–7; Draper, *Bertoldo*, pp. 146–52, cat. 12.

58. One can trace a similar fleshing out process, designed to put Bertoldo's distinctive stamp on his features, in his rendition of the portrait of Mehmed II, based on the earlier medal signed by Bellini. See n. 28.

59. Draper, *Bertoldo*, p. 126.

60. Ibid., p. 91.

61. Giorgio Vasari, *Le vite de' più eccellenti pittori, sculptori ed architettori*, 9 vols. ed. Gaetano Milanesi (Florence: Sansoni, 1878–82), II, pp. 416, 423; IV, p. 257; VII, p. 141.

62. 'Disipolo' is the term used of two of Donatello's assistants in Padua, Giacomo da Prato and Giovanni da Padova. See H. W. Janson, *The Sculpture of Donatello*, 2 vols. (Princeton: Princeton University Press, 1957), II, 165. At much the same time Bono da Ferrara signed himself similarly as 'Bonus Ferariensis Pisani dis[c]ipulus' on his London panel of St Jerome. See Annegrit Schmitt, 'Bono da Ferrara' in *Pisanello und Bono da Ferrara*, ed. Bernhard Degenhart and Annegrit Schmitt (Munich: Hirmer, 1995), 229–76 (pp. 229–30).

63. Vasari, *Vite*, II, p. 416; on which account are based the following analyses. See, for example, Max Semrau, *Donatellos Kanzeln in S. Lorenzo, Italienische Forschungen zur Kunstgeschichte* (Breslau: S. Schottlaender, 1891), II: Bode, *Bertoldo*, 117–19; Volker Herzner, 'Die Kanzeln Donatellos in San Lorenzo', *Münchner Jahrbuch der bildenden Kunst* 23 (1972): 101–53 (pp. 135–6); Francesco Negri Arnoldi, 'Bellano e Bertoldo nella bottega di Donatello', *Prospettiva* (Studi in onore di Luigi Grassi), 33–6 (1983–4), 93–101; Draper, *Bertoldo*, pp. 18–23; John Pope-Hennessy, *Donatello Sculptor* (New York: Abbeville Press, 1993), 302–4.

64. Marco Collareta, 'Testimonianze letterarie su Donatello, 1450–1600', in *Omaggio a Donatello, 1386–1986. Donatello e la storia del Museo*, exh. cat., Florence: Museo nazionale del Bargello 1985–6, ed. by Paola Barocchi (Florence: Museo nazionale del Bargello, 1985), 7–47.

65. Baxandall, *Painting and Experience*, 118, 136–7.

66. See, for example, Lauro Martines, *An Italian Renaissance Sextet: Six Tales in Historical Context* (New York: Marsilio, 1994), 198–207 (Manetti).

67. Piera Bocci Pacini, 'La riscoperta dell'antico', in *Giovinezza di Michelangelo*, exh. cat., Florence: Palazzo Vecchio, Casa Buonarroti, ed. Kathleen Weil-Garris Brandt and others (Florence and Milan: ArtificioSkira, 1999), 31–48 (p. 41), who cites Mario Martelli, 'Un passo di Ugolino Verino, una collezione, un "castellum" etrusco', *Prospettiva* 15 (1978): 12–18.

68. André Chastel, *Art et Humanisme a Florence au temps de Laurent le Magnifique* (Paris: Presses universitaires de France, 1959), 63–71, 76–82, pl. 14; James David Draper, catalogue entry, in Brandt et al., *Giovinezza di Michelangelo*, 266, cat. 29 (who, however, denies the connection).

69. F. W. Kent, 'Bertoldo "sculptore" again', *Burlington Magazine* 135 (1993): 629–30.

70. André Chastel, 'Vasari et la légende medicéene: l'"Ecole du Jardin de Saint Marc"', *Studi Vasariani*, Atti del convegno internazionale per il VI centenario della prima edizione delle 'Vite' del Vasari (Florence: Istituto Nazionale di Studi sul Rinascimento, 1952), 159–67.

71. Vasari, *Vite*, VII, p. 142: 'dove egli desiderava di essercitargli e creargli in una maniera che onorasse sè e lui e la città sua'.

72. Ibid., IV, pp. 256–7, and VI, p. 201.

73. Ibid., VII, p. 141: 'niendimanco maestro molto pratico e molto reputato'. This is the one element in Vasari's account that can be challenged. Bertoldo's funerary masses were paid for by his mother, making it unlikely that the sculptor had arrived at a grand old age (see Kent, 'Bertoldo "sculptore" again', pp. 629–30). Moreover, if it is assumed that Bertoldo was in his late teens or early twenties when working with Donatello on the San Lorenzo pulpits as his assistant-apprentice, his birth date is more likely to be c. 1443–8 than the c. 1420 usually

proposed, a date which fits in well with his first mention in documents (1463, money deposited by the potter Andrea di Ciaino given to him by Bertoldo di Giovanni di Bertoldo: see James David Draper, 'Bertoldo di Giovanni di Bertoldo', *Burlington Magazine* 136 [1994]: 834) and dated work (the 1469 medal of Frederick III). It is possible Vasari's account was coloured by some folk memory of Bertoldo's ill health – necessitating Michelangelo's position in the household – or, more likely, it is a rationalisation of an otherwise extremely unusual artistic rôle. For further information on his biography, see Louis Alexander Waldman, 'Bertoldo di Giovanni di Bertoldo (again)', *Burlington Magazine* 143 (2001): 758.

74. Vasari, *Vite*, VII, p. 141.

75. Caroline Elam, 'Lorenzo de' Medici's sculpture garden', *MKIF* 36 (1992): 41–84. In this article she corrected some errors of documentation which led to the identification of the wrong Medici garden in the otherwise useful article by Lodovico Borgo and Ann H. Sievers, 'The Medici Gardens at San Marco', *MKIF* 33 (1989): 237–56. Melissa M. Bullard ('Heroes and Their Workshops: Medici Patronage and the Problem of Shared Agency', *Journal of Medieval and Renaissance Studies* 24 [1994]: 179–98) nevertheless wrote (p. 179) that, although Elam had discovered the location of the garden, 'it is altogether another thing to assert, as Vasari does, that Lorenzo had a special school there for young artists.'

76. Michael Hirst, 'Michelangelo in Florence: "David" in 1503 and "Hercules" in 1506', *Burlington Magazine* 142 (2000): 487–92 (p. 488, n. 10).

77. Giovanni Gaye, *Carteggio inedito d'artisti*, 3 vols. (Florence: Molini, 1839–40), I, 354–57, esp. 354–55; trans. Gombrich, 'The Early Medici', 54–5.

78. F. W. Kent, 'Patron-Client Networks in Renaissance Florence and the Emergence of Lorenzo as "Maestro della Bottega"', in *Lorenzo de' Medici: New Perspectives*, ed. Bernard Toscani (New York: P. Lang, 1993), pp. 279–313, esp. pp. 280, 303, and n. 4.

79. *Il Giardino di San Marco: maestri e compagni del giovane Michelangelo*, exh. cat., Casa Buonarroti, Florence, ed. Paola Barocchi (Cinisello Balsamo: Silvana, 1992), passim.

80. The literature on these pieces is vast. For a bibliography, see Kathleen Weil-Garris Brandt, 'I primordi di Michelangelo', in Brandt et al., *Giovinezza di Michelangelo*, 69–84; Eike D. Schmidt, catalogue entry, in ibid., pp. 170–3, cat. 1; K. Weil-Garris Brandt, catalogue entry, in ibid., pp. 188–98, cat. 5, whose theory that Michelangelo continued to work on the *Centaurs* relief over a period of years after the early 1490s is an unnecessary elaboration.

81. Ascanio Condivi, *Vita di Michelagnolo Buonarroti*, ed. Giovanni Nencioni (Florence: S.P.E.S., 1998), p. 11.

82. Margrit Lisner, 'Zu Benedetto da Maiano und Michelangelo', *Zeitschrift für Kunstgeschichte* 12 (1958): 141–218; Idem., 'Das Quattrocento und Michelangelo', in *Stil und Überlieferung in der Kunst des Abendlandes. Akten des 21. Internationalen Kongresses für Kunstgeschictes in Bonn*, 3 vols. (Berlin: Gebr. Mann, 1967), II, Michelangelo, 78–89; William E. Wallace, 'Comment Michel-Ange devint-il sculpteur?', in *Le génie du sculpteur dans l'oeuvre de Michel-Ange*, exh. cat., Montreal: Musée des beaux-arts, 1992, ed. Denise L. Bissonnette (Montreal: Musée des beaux-arts, 1992), 151–69; the catalogue entries by Doris Carl, in Brandt and others, *Giovinezza di Michelangelo*, 276–85, cat. 33–5.

83. Adriaan Pit, 'Quattrocento-Plastik der Sammlung Lanz-Amsterdam', *Münchner Jahrbuch der bildenden Kunst* 7 (1912): 39–57 (pp. 55–6); Raimond van Marle, 'An Unknown Marble Relief by Donatello', *Apollo* 16 (1932): 51–2; Draper, *Bertoldo*, 118. The old attribution to Donatello is clearly misguided.

84. James David Draper, 'Bertoldo e Michelangelo' in Brandt et al., *Giovinezza di Michelangelo*, 57–63 (p. 62).

85. Elam, 'Lorenzo de' Medici's sculpture garden', 41–84 (p. 56); Georg Satzinger, 'Der "konsul" am Palazzo Gondi in Florenz', *Römisches Jahrbuch für Kunstgeschichte,* 30 (1995), 151–89. I am grateful to Georgia Clarke for this latter reference.

86. Ann Hersey Allison, 'The Bronzes of Pier Jacopo Alari-Bonacolsi, called Antico', *Jahrbuch der kunsthistorischen Sammlungen in Wien,* 89–90 (1993–4), 35–310. See, for example, 287, docs 54–5.

87. Draper, *Bertoldo,* 42.

88. Paul Barolsky, *The Faun in the Garden: Michelangelo and the Poetic Origins of Italian Renaissance Art* (University Park, PA: Pennsylvania State University Press, 1994), pp. 66–7.

89. Barocchi (ed.), *Il Giardino di San Marco,* pp. 67–8, who notes that this was a particular interest of Middeldorf and cites, in relation to Michelangelo and Rustici, John Pope-Hennessy, 'The Madonna Reliefs of Donatello', *Apollo* 103 (1976): 172–91 (pp. 189–90).

90. Maria Grazia Ciardi Duprè, 'Giovan Francesco Rustici', *Paragone,* 157 (1963), 29–50; the catalogue entry by Michele Maccherini catalogue entry, in Barrocchi (ed.), *Il Giardino di San Marco,* pp. 145–7, cat. 35; Charles Avery, 'Rustici, Giovanni Francesco', in *The Dictionary of Art,* 34 vols. ed. Jane Turner (London: Macmillan, 1996), XXXI, 447–9.

91. R. W. Lightbown, 'Michelangelo's Great Tondo: Its Origins and Setting', *Apollo* 89 (1969): 22–31.

92. Erwin Panofsky, *Studies in Iconology* (New York: Harper and Row, 1967), 172.

93. It is not coincidental that two other Virgin and Child tondi executed at much the same time by artists associated with the garden are just as clearly dependent on models by Donatello. Rustici's Virgin and Child and St John, made in 1505 for the 'prima sala del magistrato de' consoli dell' arte di Por Santa Maria', now in the Bargello, reverses the Madonna of the Clouds as its starting point and cites, in addition, the Pazzi Madonna. See Joachim Poeschke, *Die Skulptur der Renaissance in Italien,* 2 vols. (Munich: Hirmer, 1992), II, 129–32 (esp. p. 131, pl. 120). An anonymous work in Lisbon has been thought to have been executed by an imitator of Michelangelo, although the scale of the figures and their rather less sturdy forms show that the sculptor's starting point was in the reliefs of Donatello. It combines the Vienna relief with the carved Virgin and Child with three Angels from the Museo dell'Opera del Duomo in Siena. See Giancarlo Gentilini, in Barocchi (ed.), *Il Giardino di San Marco,* p. 90, cat. 18, who dates this piece to 1505–10, regarding it as dependent on the Bruges Madonna. It may in fact be very slightly earlier, imitating not Michelangelo, but common sources in Donatello. Early Virgin and Child paintings by both Granacci and Bugiardini also depend on Donatello models. See, for example, Laura Pagnotta, *Giuliano Bugiardini* (Turin: Allemandi, 1987), 196, cat. 12 (Virgin and Child, Museo Bardini, Florence); Christian von Holst, *Francesco Granacci* (Munich: Bruckmann, 1974), 57, cat. 47, 48 (Virgin and Child, ex-Hardy, London; Virgin and Child with the infant St John, Musée d'Art et d'Archéologie, Toulon). The early sculptures of Torrigiano and Baccio da Montelupo have a pared-down emotional and spiritual simplicity which self-consciously rejects the ornate possibilities of works by the generation of Florentine sculptors before them; Torrigiano's San Gimignano heads of Santa Fina and San Gregorio and Baccio's crucifixes at San Marco and Santa Maria Novella in Florence and Sante Flora e Lucilla in Arezzo are particularly clear examples of this way of sculpting. See Cornelius von Fabriczy, 'Scultura in legno di Baccio da Montelupo', *Rivista d'arte* 1 (1903): 67–8; Alessandro del Vita, 'Un crucifisso di Baccio da Montelupo ritrovato nella chiesa si SS. Flora e Lucilla in Arezzo', *Rivista d'arte* 7 (1910): 90–2; the catalogue entry by Fabio Benedettucci, in Barocchi (ed.), *Il Giardino di San Marco,* pp. 116–18, cat. 23–4; Alan Phipps Darr, 'Torrigiani, Pietro' in Turner (ed.), *Dictionary of Art,* XXXI, 188–92, and Till R. Verellen, 'Baccio da Montelupo', in

ibid., XXII, 15. The same is true of the terracottas by the Maestro di San Giovannino, the artist or artists whom the organisers of the 1992 exhibition sensibly placed in the ambit of the Garden, works that can be stylistically linked to the earliest identifiable mature pieces by the identified Giardino artists. See John Pope-Hennessy, *A Catalogue of Sculpture in the Victoria and Albert Museum,* 3 vols. (London: H. M. Stationery Office, 1964), I, 194–6; Bruce Boucher, *The Sculpture of Jacopo Sansovino,* 2 vols. (New Haven and London: Yale University Press, 1991), I, 6–7, and II, 313–14, cat. 1, 2.

94. Vasari, *Vite,* IV, 256–7.

95. The drawings are Louvre inv. 706, Munich inv. 2191, and Albertina inv. 116, R129. See *Michelangelo e i maestri del quattrocento,* exh. cat., Florence: Casa Buonarroti, 1985, ed. Carlo Sisi (Florence: Cantini edizioni d'arte, 1985), 15, 18–19, cat. 1, 8–9; Michael Hirst, *Michelangelo Draftsman,* exh. cat., Washington, D.C.: National Gallery of Art (Milan: Olivetti, 1988), 6–11, cat. 1–2; Idem., *Michelangelo and His Drawings* (New Haven and London: Yale University Press, 1988), 59–60; Antonio Natali, catalogue entries, in *Il disegno fiorentino del tempo di Lorenzo il Magnifico,* exh. cat., Florence, Gallerie degli Uffizi, ed. Annamaria Petrioli Tofani (Cinisello Balsamo: Silvana, 1992), 32–8, cats 1.7, 1.9, 1.10. It is worth noting that from about this same period there survives a pen and ink study after two of the Apostles sculpted by Donatello for the door of the Old Sacristy at San Lorenzo: Uffizi inv. 260F (see ibid., 39–40, cat. 1.11). It is attributed to Giuliano da Sangallo, and the artist represented the figures with a grace and decorum which diminishes substantially Donatello's original frenetic movements. The paired apostles find an echo in Rustici's Henry VII tomb in Westminster Abbey.

96. Benvenuto Cellini, *Opere,* ed. Enrico Carrara (Turin: U.T.E.T., 1971), 83; *The Autobiography of Benvenuto Cellini,* ed. Charles Hope and Alessandro Nova (Oxford: Phaidon, 1983), 21.

97. Marco Collareta, 'Le "luci della fiorentina gloria"', *Artista* (1991): 136–43.

98. Antonio Manetti's translation of Filippo Villani's trecento biographies of famous Florentines may also be taken as indicative of the pride Florentines took in their artists. He appended short accounts of 'fourteen notable men from 1400 on', an astonishing eight of them artists from the first half of the century, including the six whose works are listed by Vasari as present in the sculpture garden. This acclamation is linked by Gilbert to the reworking and revising of compositions by these artists by others in the 1490s. See Peter Murray, 'Art Historians and Art Critics – IV', *Burlington Magazine* 99 (1957): 330–6; Creighton E. Gilbert, *Italian Art, 1400–1500: Sources and Documents,* 2nd ed. (Evanston, Ill.: Northwestern University Press, 1980), 195–7.

99. Lightbown, *Mantegna,* 15–25; Hugo Chapman, *Padua in the 1450s: Marco Zoppo and His Contemporaries,* exh. cat., London: British Museum, 1998 (London: British Museum, 1998), 30.

100. This suggestion was sensibly made by Borgo and Sievers, 'The Medici Gardens', 248.

101. Volker Herzner, 'Donatello in Siena', *MKIF* 15 (1971): 161–86 (pp. 172–7, 180–3): 'Duo quadri per disemgno delle porti del Duomo fecie Donatello con ficure suvi di ciero'.

102. Janson, *The Sculpture of Donatello,* II, 108–29; John Pope-Hennessy, *Donatello Sculptor,* 92–112; Giorgio Bonsanti, 'Il pulpito di Donatello', in *Donatello restaurato; i marmi del pulpito di Prato,* exh. cat., Prato: Museo dell' Opera del Duomo, 2000, ed. Annamaria Giusti (Pistoia: Artout, 2000), 11–30.

103. In both the Prato pulpit and in Bertoldo's relief, a little boy leaning backwards, with a raised arm standing on the leg on the same side and giving a chorus-girl kick with the other, appears twice in each work. A running figure from the cantoria, his back twisted towards the spectator, creating an energetic diagonal of raised arm and leg also appears twice in the Bargello relief, once seen from behind.

104. Janson, *The Sculpture of Donatello*, I, pl. 295b, II, p. 185, Pope-Hennessy, *Donatello Sculptor*, 214–16, fig. 217.

105. Cornelius von Fabriczy, 'Bertoldo di Giovanni e il suo lavoro pel Santo di Padova', *Rassegna d'arte* 8 (1908): 26; Antonio Sartori, *Documenti per la storia dell'arte a Padova* (Vicenza: N. Pozza, 1976), pp. 19–26; Draper, *Bertoldo*, 273–5, doc. 8.

106. David Summers, *Michelangelo and the Language of Art* (Princeton: Princeton University Press, 1981), 144–5.

107. Although connections between Donatello and Michelangelo have frequently been mentioned, they have not, to my knowledge, been discussed in any systematic way. For Donatello motifs in the drawings of Michelangelo, however, see Charles de Tolnay, 'Donatello e Michelangelo', in *Donatello e il suo tempo*, Atti dell'VIII convegno internazionale di studi sul Rinascimento: Firenze-Padova, 25 Settembre–1 Ottobre 1966 (Florence: Istituto Nazionale di Studi sul Rinascimento, 1968), 259–75.

108. Margrit Lisner, 'Form und Sinngehalt von Michelangelo's Kentaurenschlacht mit Notizien zu Bertoldo di Giovanni', *MKIF* 29 (1980): 299–344 (p. 319, fig. 12).

109. Vasari, *Vite*, VII, 144.

110. Nicholas Penny, 'La Madonna di Manchester', in Brandt et al., *Giovinezza di Michelangelo*, 115–25.

111. Janson, *The Sculpture of Donatello*, II, 165, 183–5.

112. Pope-Hennessy, *Donatello Sculptor*, 286–7 (attributing two of the reliefs, surely erroneously, to Bertoldo, working as Donatello's assistant).

113. Janson, *The Sculpture of Donatello*, II, 66, 73–5.

114. Hirst, *The Young Michelangelo*, 44.

115. Holst, *Francesco Granacci*, 129, 156–7, cat. 3, 43–8. The St John figure turns up again as Christ in a picture rediscovered in St Mary's, Nottingham in the 1950s, attributed by Pouncey to Granacci, and in Bugiardini's Virgin and Child and Saint John in the Galleria Sabauda in Turin. See Witt Library Mount; Pagnota, 1987, pp. 195–6, cat. 10.

116. He played much the same game with sacred music – rebuilding in the 1480s the choirs of the Cathedral, the Baptistry, and SS. Annunziata which had been instituted by his grandfather Cosimo. See Allan W. Atlas, 'Aragonese Naples and Medicean Florence: Musical Interrelationships and Influence in the Late Fifteenth Century', in *La musica a Firenze al tempo di Lorenzo il Magnifico*, Congresso internazionale di studi, Firenze 15–17 Giugno, 1992, ed. Piero Gargiulo (Florence: Olschki, 1993), 15–45 (p. 21). His involvement in the production of popular music and the staging of festivals have been interpreted by Burke and Trexler as his deliberate participation in an artisan culture. See Peter Burke, *Popular Culture in Early Modern Europe* (New York: Harper and Row, 1978), 104, Trexler, *Public Life*, 412–18: Lorenzo himself wrote both laude and *canti carnascialeschi*. The example of the revival of the festivals for the birth of St John the Baptist in 1488 shows, however, that, once again, while he was participating in it, he was also remodelling it in his own image. The description by Tribaldo de' Rossi of the 1491 festa makes it evident that the celebration had been hijacked as a vehicle for Medicean dynastic propaganda. See, for example, Claudio Gallico, 'Dopo una rilettura dei canti carnascialeschi', in Gargiulo (ed.), *La musica*, pp. 143–66; William F. Prizer, 'Laude di popolo, laude di corte: Some Thoughts on the Style and Function of the Renaissance Lauda', in ibid., 167–94; Nerida Newbigin, 'Piety and Politics in the "Feste" of Lorenzo's Florence', in *Lorenzo il Magnifico e il suo mondo*, ed. Gian Carlo Garfagnini (Florence: Olschki, 1994), 19–41.

PART TWO

REGIONAL IDENTITIES AND THE ENCOUNTER WITH FLORENCE

FOLLOWING THE ARTISTIC GENEALOGY FURNISHED BY VASARI'S *LIVES*, THE centrality of Florence in accounts of the evolution of artistic styles has been accepted as axiomatic. Yet in acknowledging the importance of Florence-based artists on stylistic changes elsewhere during this period, few secondary studies have attempted to examine the external circumstances that conditioned the reception of Florentine models beyond Florence. In configuring Florence as source, other artistic centres have been evaluated in terms of their susceptibility to Florentine influence, with the most receptive being seen as the more culturally enlightened. Yet such a model configures cultural influence as a one-way process in which causal agency lies exclusively with the dominant centre. In this context, the concept of 'translation', understood as both formal reinterpretation and spatial displacement, provides a far subtler critical tool than the concept of influence by questioning the assumed passivity of the recipient as subject. By reversing the direction of causal analysis, focus is shifted from the influence of Florentine artists on other centres of artistic activity to the selective process whereby the recipient exercises a certain discernment in the selective assimilation and modification of both artistic practices and forms in line with local considerations. Given the itinerant careers of many artists, translation understood in this sense facilitates the analysis of artistic exchange as a form of cultural dialogue in which artists as interlocutors were required to alter their artistic language in order to align it with local idioms and differing regional practices.

The essays in this section seek to examine the dynamics of these forms of exchange with particular reference to the role of art production in the generation of regional identities. Whilst the first three look to the cultural dialogue between Florence and states beyond the borders of Tuscany – namely, Ferrara, Bologna, and Naples – the remaining two focus on the attempts of subject cities within the Florentine territorial state to maintain a degree of local autonomy in the face of Florentine domination by controlling their city's symbolic economy. What Campbell foregrounds in his examination of the artistic and cultural interchange between Florence and Ferrara is what he terms a 'critical strategy of assimilation' on the part of Ferrarese patrons, which saw Florentines employed in conjunction with other artists drawn from a variety of artistic centres both within Italy and beyond. In charting the various forms of diplomatic, literary, sculptural, and pictorial exchange between the two cities, Campbell not only reveals the means whereby the Ferrarese differentiated themselves from the Florentines in constructing a specific form of courtly identity, but also the manner in which the Florentine republic, and the Medici in particular, appropriated aspects of courtly symbolism in a process that testified to the ambiguity which lay at the heart of both Florentine republican, and Medicean, self-representation. Hence the ambivalence of the myth of Hercules, which was variously interpreted in both a classical and chivalric mode, permitted its simultaneous deployment in Florence in both public and private settings with quite different cultural resonances.

Similar processes of what Clarke terms 'transformative imitation' are evident in Giovanni Bentivoglio's self-imagining in Bologna as witnessed through his programme of urban regeneration, use of chivalric ritual, and commissioning of artworks. In turning simultaneously to Florence and Ferrara in particular, Bentivoglio was able to construct an identity of studied ambiguity that hovered between the cult of the single ruler on the one hand and the pre-eminent citizen within a republican form on the other. In the process the modification of the models chosen helped develop an recognizable local style as witnessed by Giovanni Sabadino degli Arienti's 1490s palimpsest of Boccaccio's *Decameron* which saw the *brigata* transposed from the Arno valley to the spa town of Bagni di Porretana as part of an attempt to fashion a specifically Bolognese vernacular. Such ambiguous self-representation was alien, however, to the kingdom of Naples, which alone amongst the political forms of the Italian peninsula furnished a model for absolutist rule. As Edelstein demonstrates, it is ironic that Neapolitan art in the quattrocento is generally considered 'extraneous to the main development of what is considered the "Italian Renaissance"', given that Neapolitan models were considered 'paragons of Italian style' by monarchical powers beyond the Alps. By way of example Edelstein focuses on the case of the Italian garden constructed at Poggioreale, which provided a model for Charles VIII's garden complexes in France subsequent to his invasion of the peninsula in 1494–5. Far from being an example of the exportation of Florentine architectural style beyond Tuscany, he demonstrates the extent to which the gardens understood as products of the Neapolitan cultural milieu found a receptive audience in ducal Florence through the patronage of Grand Duke Cosimo de' Medici and his consort Eleonora of Toledo in their own complexes at Castello and the Boboli gardens of the Pitti Palace. The belated aristocratization of Florence in line with the wider European movement towards monarchical forms saw the Medici turn to Naples for models which would enhance their pre-eminence and association with kingly powers as part of the family's symbolic redescription after the demise of the republic.

Both Milner and Krohn's essays examine the way in which subject cities within the Florentine territorial state sought to maintain a clearly articulated communal identity despite submission to Florentine jurisdiction. Whilst subject cities provided an undoubted source of patronage for Florence-based artists, Milner demonstrates how the attempts of the Medici to exploit the city's patrimony in service of their own patronage networks periodically saw the production of works of art caught in the wider sociopolitical tensions and patterns of local resistance to a centralising power. In seeking to clarify the circumstances surrounding the contested commission for the Forteguerri cenotaph in Pistoia between Verrocchio and Piero Pollaiuolo, Milner shows how the successful completion of an artistic commission could be sabotaged by well-established practices of obstructionism on the part of resentful parties within subjugated communes. In contrast, Krohn's examination of the construction and decoration of the Santa Fina chapel in San Gimignano illustrates how the exploitation of local cults as subject matter for major decorative commissions furnished a means of resisting Florentine cultural hegemony through the employment of Florentine masters to tell local stories. In both cases an artistic exchange takes place, but not without compromise on the part of the dominant centre. Whilst subject communes may well have lost their political autonomy, they demonstrated a keen consciousness of the role art production played in differentiating them from their rulers and perpetuating the memory of their separateness.

5

'Our eagles always held fast to your lilies': The Este, the Medici, and the Negotiation of Cultural Identity

Stephen J. Campbell

By the fifteenth century Florence had developed a powerful ideology of cultural supremacy that conceived political and artistic authority as inextricably linked. Florentine painting, sculpture, architecture, literature, and the Tuscan dialect itself served as a kind of symbolic capital, for the consumption and imitation of client states from Naples to Burgundy to Hungary.[1] By the end of the century, the myth of the Florentineness of Florentine art – even of Renaissance art – was fully established, and it has proved difficult to resist ever since. Florence is still seen as the kind of urban culture from which things emanate; the traffic in exemplarary styles or models goes only one way. Ferrara, on the other hand, is accorded the status of a minor center, one of the supposed characteristics of which is a derivative and heterogeneous culture, constituted of influences from elsewhere. The fifteenth-century Ferrarese school of painting is still described as a hybrid of Florentine, Paduan, and Netherlandish influences, with lingering vestiges of a provincial archaizing or 'Gothic' aesthetic.[2]

The permeability of quattrocento Ferrarese culture, as opposed to the assumed impermeability of that of Florence, is taken as a sign of its secondary and provincial status. The Ferrarese themselves may even have reinforced such a perception – if we take literally, for instance, diplomatic pronouncements such as that by the orator Ludovico Carbone on a mission to Florence in 1473. Florence, for Carbone on this occasion, is the "splendor and ornament of all Italy," a preeminence manifested especially in the artistic and literary sphere: "If indeed we turn our minds to men of letters, from here [in Florence] have sprung the most prudent doctors, the most respected lawyers, the most famous poets and orators, the most noble painters. The sweetest and most charming of languages is uniquely characteristic of this city, so that with truth I wrote once in a poem of mine: 'If God descended to earth, he would speak no other language than that of the Florentines.' "[3]

In what follows I do not want to necessarily dispute the claim that Florentine art 'influenced' Ferrarese art; I want rather to put the notion of 'influence' under scrutiny, especially the ways in which it suggests a relation between an active and a passive principle. It is a reasonable observation that quattrocento Ferrara was an assimilative culture, but not in any sense that could be considered derivative or impoverished; the instances of appropriation to be considered presently point to something like a critical strategy of assimilation. The second concern is to suggest that such a strategy of self-conscious assimilation also enables us to think about Florence – specifically, about the degree to which Florentine artists and patrons also were mindful of developments elsewhere and devised artistic undertakings in response to these.

The heterogeneity of Ferrarese artistic culture can be seen as manifested in the preferences of patrons. The brothers of Duke Ercole d'Este, who ruled Ferrara before his succession in 1471, commissioned works from a cosmopolitan roster of artists: Mantegna, Jacopo Bellini, Pisanello, Rogier Van Der Weyden, and the tapestry maker Rubinetto da Francia.[4] In Ferrara there was a second major nexus of such cosmopolitan patronage, and one which had long had a decidedly Florentine orientation: this was the household of the bishop, which at least from the 1440s had dominated patronage at the cathedral. The bishops of Ferrara represented the feudal overlordship of the papacy, from whom the Este traditionally held power as papal vicars of Ferrara. The bishops thus technically embodied a superior, and sometimes competitive, locus of authority within the city. For much of the fifteenth century, the Este sought to dominate or curtail the authority of the bishop, which led to frequent jurisdictional clashes, or they were compelled to cultivate favorable relations with the powerful Roverella and della Rovere families, who monopolized ecclesiastical appointments in the Ferrarese state from the 1460s onward.[5] Only in 1493, with the elevation of Ercole's fourteen-year-old son Ippolito to the rank of cardinal, did the Este succeed in having a family advocate within the Roman curia, an advantage long enjoyed by the Gonzaga and Sforza families. Time would ultimately prove how politically urgent this curial connection was. In the 1500s, Cardinal Ippolito would maintain a crucial moral, diplomatic, and military resistance to the hostile Pope Julius II who sought to repossess Ferrara for direct papal rule – but it was just as important that a long era of local jurisdictional tension between sacred and secular authority within the city could come to an end.

Like a rival court, the household of the bishop commissioned Florentine sculptors to produce monumental works for the cathedral. Michele da Firenze produced a statue of the Virgin for the facade in 1443, and in 1451 Donatello undertook some

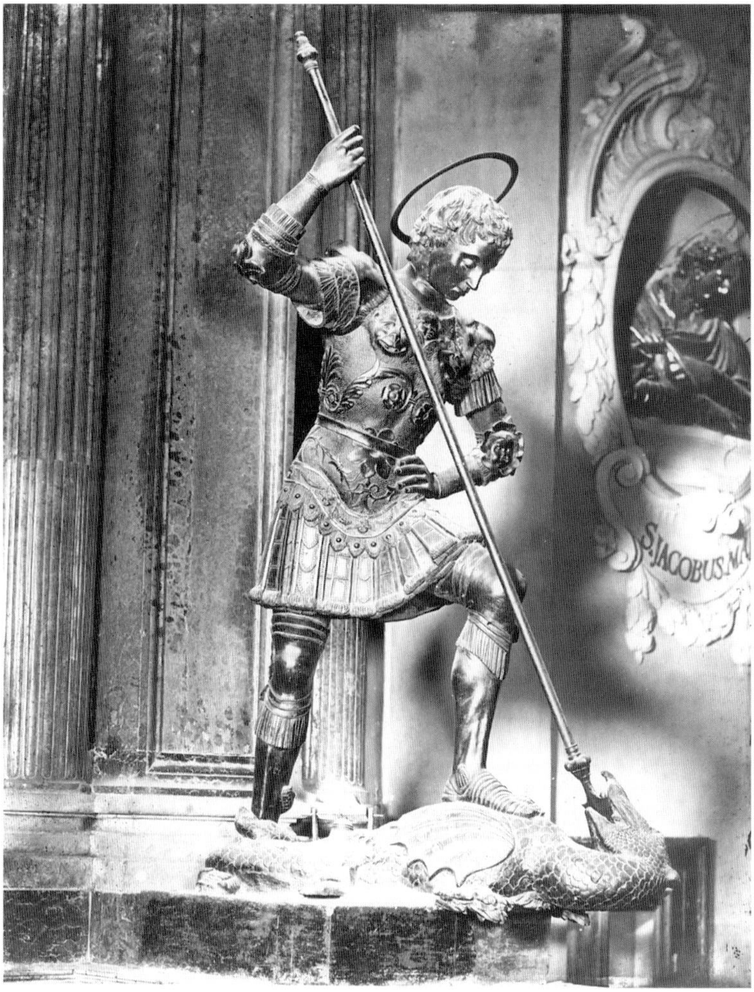

39. Niccolo Baroncelli, *St. George*. Ferrara cathedral. Bronze. Photo: Alinari/Art Resource, NY.

work (the nature of which is not recorded) for Bishop Francesco dal Legname.[6] The Florentine Niccolo Baroncelli, already called to Ferrara by the *commune* to produce an equestrian statue of the late marchese Niccolò III, also received the commission for a rood screen with five life-size bronze figures, for the cathedral.[7] This work, one of the largest monumental bronze groups of the century, has been treated dismissively as a provincial manifestation of the school of Donatello. The *St. George* was deplored for its "mannerism" by Pope-Hennessy and for its failure to "penetrate the surface" of the great Florentine master.[8] Yet this alleged deviation from Donatello might in itself suggest something important about the priorities of Ferrarese patrons – the possibility that Florentine sculptors were sought for their skill as bronze technicians rather than their style. The work is much more easily aligned with the art of Venice

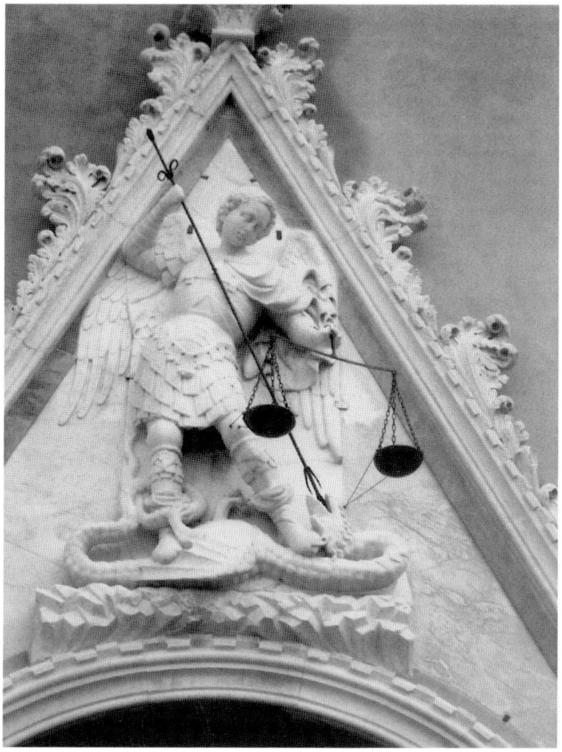

40. Venetian sculptor, *St. Michael.* Marble. Venice, San Michele in Isola, cloister portal. Photo: Author.

or Padua, where Baroncelli had spent a number of years (Figs. 39 and 40).[9] Likewise, the Virgin on the cathedral facade by Michele da Firenze seems to have more to do with Venetian Gothic sculpture than with any contemporary developments in Florence.

The early years of the reign of Ercole d'Este were marked by a shortfall in court employment for other than the humblest painter-decorators; artists like Francesco del Cossa and Ercole de' Roberti worked for patrons in Bologna. Ercole would begin to act as a patron in true princely style only in the ensuing decades, and the scale of his undertakings in the field of architecture and urbanism would be truly dramatic, unmatched by any other Italian patron of the late quattrocento.[10] In the 1470s, however, the church had the competitive edge; the most important works of painting, sculpture, and book illumination in this decade were produced for the household and the relatives of the bishop, Lorenzo Roverella.[11] The Roverella family rivaled the Este in local and international importance, largely because of the strength of their position at the courts of the emperor, the pope, and the king of Naples and through their domination of the major benefices within and adjoining Este territory: Lorenzo, moreover, was papal datary and had been personal physician to

Pius II, while his brother Bartolomeo was cardinal of San Clemente. From 1469 to 1480 the Roverella family were involved in the commissioning of at least three religious works from Cosmè Tura, all for the city's most important churches, when it is far from apparent that the Este were commissioning anything comparable. These were a set of organ-shutters still preserved in the cathedral, and two altarpieces for the Olivetan monastery and ancient episcopal seat of San Giorgio, where a third Roverella brother served as prior during the 1470s.

When Bishop Lorenzo Roverella died in 1474, his tomb was produced in Florence by Antonio Rossellino and shipped to Ferrara where it was assembled in San Giorgio by a local sculptor, Ambrogio da Milano (Fig. 41).[12] The tomb departs from the standard design of Rossellino's Florentine tombs and, in keeping with the curial orientation of the Roverella, follows the Roman type of wall-tomb produced for members of the Papal court – such as Lorenzo's brother Bartolomeo – by Andrea Bregno and Giorgio Dalmata in the later quattrocento.[13] This, and the fact that Rossellino himself did not travel to Ferrara, facilitated an extraordinary act of appropriation by this local artist, who added some crude decorative sculpture (a figure of St. George, two outrageously ithyphallic nude angels), and then signed the entire work as his own: MCCCCLXXV AMBROSII MEDIOLANENSIS OPUS. In fact, until the present century, when payments to Rossellino were discovered, the tomb had been regarded for several centuries as an indigenous Ferrarese product.[14] For the Roverella family, it appears, the prestige value of the work may have lain in its resemblance to Roman models (such as those considered by Shelley Zuraw in this volume), to the extent that they were evidently prepared to countenance an effacement of its Florentine authorship. The situation here contrasts markedly with other 'provincial' outposts of Florentine sculpture, where the work is carefully signed by their author who adds the word 'florentinus' to his name (one example is Agostino di Duccio at Modena[15]). This is all the more remarkable considering that the Roverella tomb is probably the second work made for Ferrara by Rossellino; Richard Stemp has recently made a strong case for the attribution of an earlier tomb, that of Francesco Sacrati in San Domenico, to Rossellino.[16] In this project, from 1461, the tomb was part of a chapel decorated with frescoes by Cosmè Tura, which have now been lost.[17]

Cosmè Tura, on the other hand, manifests a different kind of reaction to the presence of Florentine art in Ferrara. Tura's awareness of Rossellino is signalled by the fragmentary *Virgin and Child* now in the Accademia Carrara, Bergamo, a work which should be seen as a reaction to the work of Rossellino (Fig. 42).[18] Tura responds to Rossellino's *Virgin and Child* on the Roverella tomb, but seems also to be aware of its prototype; the Roverella Madonna relief is itself a copy of the more refined example on Rossellino's tomb of the Cardinal of Portugal from the previous decade, which Tura could also have known as it was one of the most frequently copied of

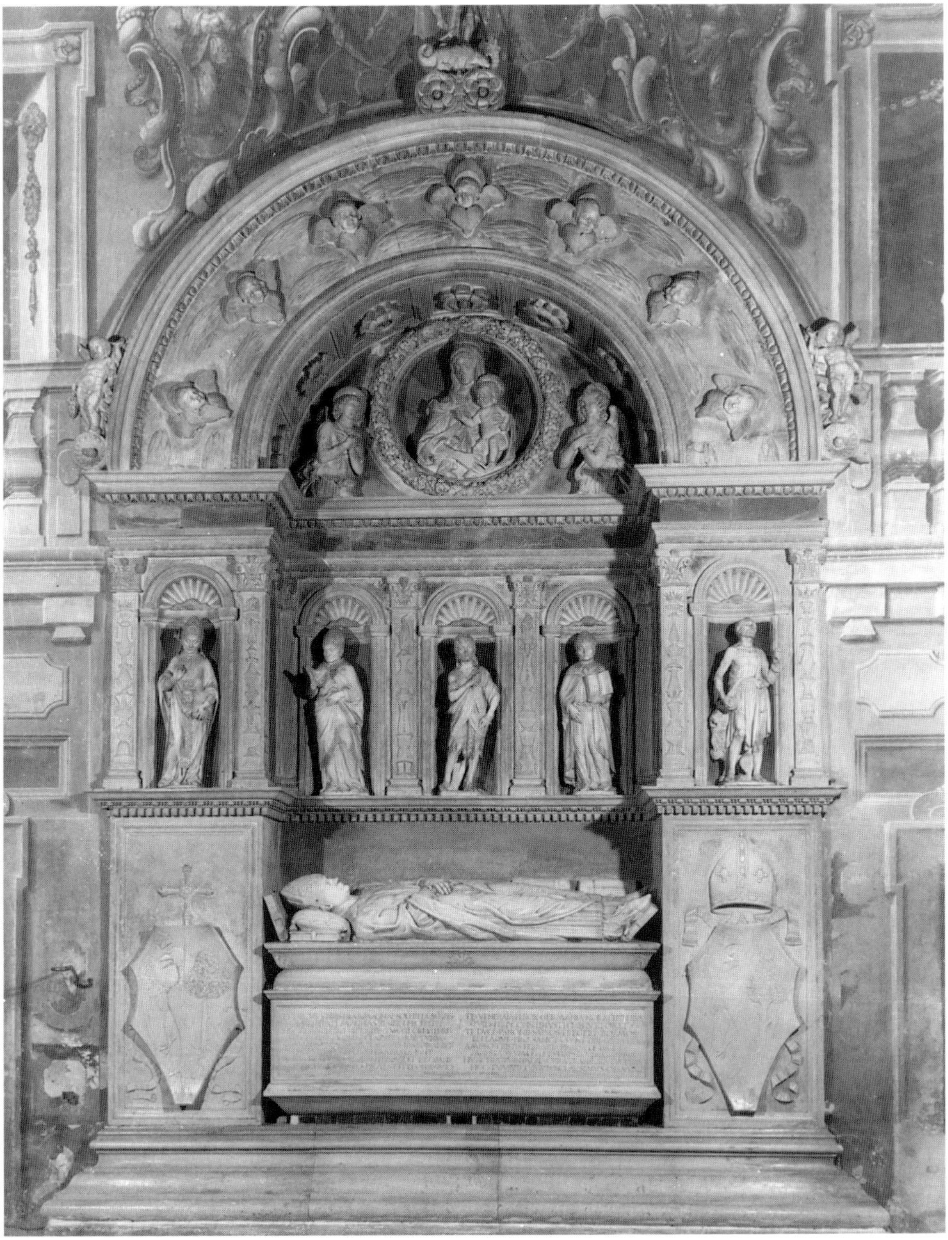

41. Antonio Rossellino and workshop; Ambrogio da Milano, *Tomb of Bishop Lorenzo Roverella*. Marble. Ferrara, San Giorgio. Photo: Archivio fotografico Soprintendenza PSAD, Bologna. Use authorized by the Ministero per i bene e la attività culturali.

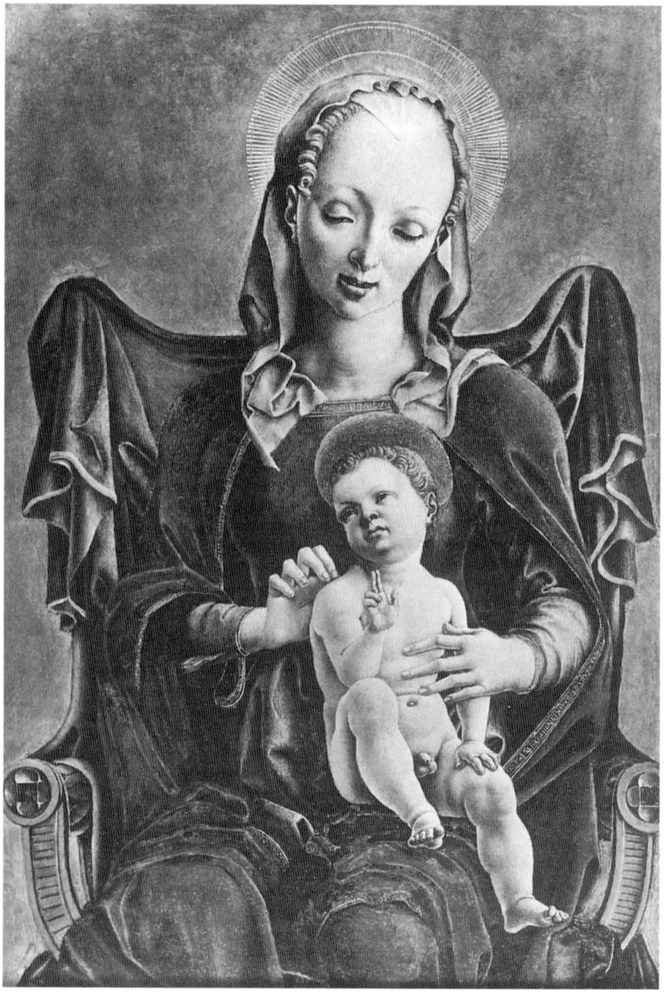

42. Cosmè Tura, *Virgin and Child*. On panel. Bergamo, Accademia Carrara. Photo: Alinari/Art Resource, NY.

Rossellino's Marian reliefs (Fig. 43). There is nothing in previous Ferrarese art that provides a precedent for Tura's Virgin; this is not how this artist normally paints Madonnas (compare it with the Roverella Madonna in London, the *Virgin and Child in a Garden* in Washington, the *Virgin and Child* in the Venice Accademia). Several features of Tura's Virgin uniquely correspond with aspects of Rossellino's two Marian tomb reliefs, which he emphasizes and exaggerates: the presentation of the Virgin in full face, rather than in the far more common three-quarter profile; the hair swept back from the high domelike forehead, the finely arched eyebrows with the downward glancing eyes and parted lips; both works feature the spiraling play of folds in the fall of the veil. Tura varies the pose of the blessing child, who is now nude, but

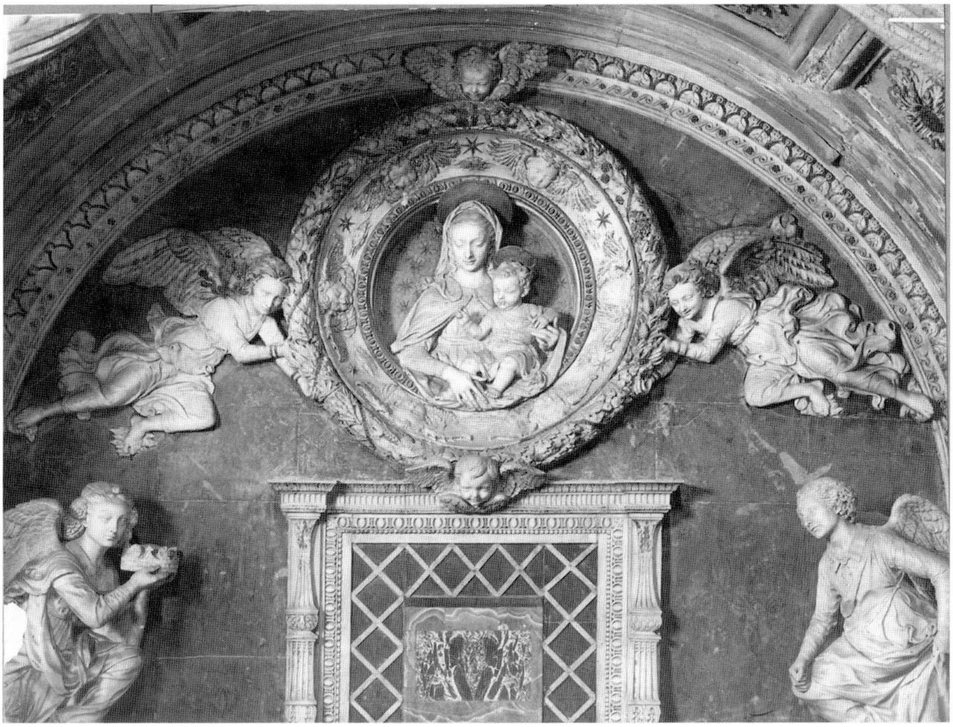

43. Antonio Rossellino, *Virgin and Child* from the Chapel of the Cardinal of Portugal. Marble. Florence, San Miniato. Photo: Alinari/Art Resource, NY.

there is nonetheless the sense that he has studied the child from a different angle – again suggesting a sculptural model – rotating him on the Virgin's knee (the same sculptural model, viewed from a different angle, was used for the infant Hercules in Tura's design for the medal of Alfonso d'Este in 1477[19]). The statement that 'Rossellino influenced Tura' hardly seems to do justice to what is taking place here; this is a reworking of Rossellino's model through an entirely different repertory of artistic forms. Without sacrificing a strong sense of sculptural volume, Tura remakes Rossellino through the unrelentingly reductive idiom of line. The rather daunting severity of Tura's version results from the way in which line rearticulates proportions, emphasizing edges and boundaries and making internal forms more pointed and attenuated. This is a *rifacimento* that asserts a far-from-passive relation to the model, a forceful reworking that goes beyond mere imitation.[20]

That Tura in the 1470s considered himself to be working in a distinctive local idiom, and one that he sought to articulate in relation to an imported model, cannot be proven or documented in any conventional sense; overt statements of a resistance to Florence in the visual arts are made somewhat later, when Tura's style was long out of fashion. Pomponius Gauricus dedicated his treatise on sculpture to Ercole d'Este in 1504, part of which is indeed concerned with a critique of the 'Tuscanici' (chiefly Verrocchio but probably also Pollaiuolo) who exaggerate the musculature of figures in action:

> In Hercules [the veins, nerves and creases of the flesh] should appear differently on the shoulders, muscles, chest and throughout his body – and different again in the figure of Hylas; they should also be different depending on whether Hercules is killing the Hydra, or fighting Antaeus, or tearing the horn from the bull, or engaged in other labors. He should be represented in any case with a certain delicacy, and not like he who made the statue of Colleoni recently erected at SS. Giovanni e Paolo; the common opinion is that he made the horse in such a crudely realistic fashion that the animal appears to be flayed.[21]

Yet for the late quattrocento, inferences regarding resistance might be drawn from parallel evidence. For instance, in the dispatches of Ferrarese agents in Florence, an ambassador will occasionally depart from the routine reportage of events to mention matters of cultural significance, such as the availability of books which the prince might like to acquire. Writing to Ercole d'Este in August 1475, the orator Niccolò Bendidio announced that Cristoforo Landino had just completed his vernacular translation of Pliny's *Natural History* at the behest of the king of Naples. Bendidio is aware of Ercole's interest in acquiring vernacular versions of classical texts for his library, but he has reservations about this particular translation:

> The work is varied and diffuse like nature itself. Because it is full of names of animals and birds and plants and every kind of thing, and these are translated with a Tuscan vocabulary, which in many cases is different from the Lombard, it will appear to a Lombard reader who doesn't have this language to be inconvenient in the case of certain names. The translator might better have used a mixture of Lombard and Tuscan, which even though it might have disrupted the elegance of this language, on the whole this would not have been a bad thing in making the work more commonly readable.[22]

The *questione della lingua* is normally regarded as a later phenomenon, but, as Riccardo Fubini has pointed out, here we have an early assertion of the desire to resist the equation of the Italian *volgare* with Tuscan.[23] Humanists elsewhere took a more extreme view, as in the case of the Neapolitan Giovanni Brancati, writing in 1476: "the Tuscan dialect is completely inelegant, no less difficult to read than to pronounce."[24] This self-consciousness regarding the authority of various Italian dialects is stimulated by the vernacularization of humanist culture, a phenomenon in which the court of Ferrara played a leading role; an astonishing number of translated classical texts were available in the Este library by the 1470s.[25] One of the chief occupations of Ferrarese humanists was to make the classics available in vernacular editions, with the occasional flattering avowal in the prefaces that princes and warriors did not have time to learn Latin and Greek. Polismagna had written to Borso of his version of a work by Pier Candido Decembrio: "I know that you are Ferrarese, and that Ferrara, the glory of Italy, has produced, bred and raised you, and so what language should I use other than the Ferrarese idiom, since it seems to me not to lack elegance any more than any other form of Italian."[26] The 1470s also saw the beginnings of the literary career of Matteo Maria Boiardo, whose early output consisted of translations of Cornelius Nepos, Apuleius, and other authors. Although he incorporated elements of Tuscan, his most famous work, the *Orlando Innamorato,* is composed in the *lingua cortigiana.*[27] Its classic status by the 1520s meant that it would itself be subjected to a Tuscanizing *rifacimento* at the hands of Francesco Berni.

In place of a notion of influence based on passive absorption of an exemplary model, I propose a model of selective and deliberate cultural appropriation for which the term 'translation' seems most suitable. We can think about so-called Tuscan influence in Ferrara in just these terms from the earlier decades of the quattrocento. In 1433 the poet Giovanni Marrasio wrote from Siena to Niccolò III marchese of Ferrara, soliciting an invitation to his court. Marrasio wrote of the Fonte Gaia in Siena, which he and his humanist colleagues commonly referred to as the fountain of the Muses; it so happens that there are nine female figures on the Fonte Gaia. "If you so wish it," he wrote, "I shall *translate* (traducam) the Muses from the Fonte Gaia to the long arm of the shining Po, and I shall sing the praises and titles and deeds of yourself and your ancestors."[28] As I have observed elsewhere, this is indeed what seems to have happened in the next decade, when Leonello d'Este entrusted Angelo da Siena and Cosmè Tura with the decoration of the court *studiolo* of Belfiore with a cycle of the Nine Muses.[29] In several cases the Belfiore Muses appear to be modeled on the pseudo-Muses of the Fonte Gaia, but they have been entirely refashioned, converted into vernacular Venuses of the contemporary courtly world.

During the parallel regimes of Lorenzo de'Medici (1469–94) and Ercole d'Este (1471–1505), various episodes in the interaction of Florence and Ferrara show cultural exchange to be driven by rivalry and mutual emulation, as well as by deep-seated concerns with cultural difference. Florence, in the late 1460s, regarded Ferrara as a small but crucial element in its foreign policy – as a consolidating element in the league of north Italian powers – and intervened as a matter of course in Ferrarese domestic politics.[30] For instance, Florence seems to have initially supported a conspiracy against Duke Borso d'Este, which might have replaced him with a relative more compliant with the interests of the Italian League. After contemplating support for a rival candidate, the *signoria* backed the succession of Ercole d'Este following Borso's death in 1471.[31] Thereafter, the Medici regime cultivated the good disposition of the Este more assiduously than ever before; with increasing strains on their relationship with Venice, the Ferrarese rulers probably could not have afforded to do otherwise. Lorenzo stood as godfather to the second child of Ercole and his consort Eleonora, born in Naples in 1477; the following year, after the Pazzi conspiracy, Ercole received the baton of command of the Florentine alliance, along with the palace of the banished Pazzi family.[32]

This diplomatic rapprochement coincides with a ritualized intimacy – rather characteristic of the exchanges of princes – in the familiar letters of Lorenzo and Ercole. When not dealing with urgent affairs of state, the letters deal with family matters, the loan or donation of horses, falcons, salami, the obtaining of books.[33] Ercole had the kind of status in Ferrara which Lorenzo in Florence possessed in effect, but not in theory. By addressing Ercole on matters of aristocratic prerogative ("per il nostro commune amore et dilectione," as Ercole termed them), Lorenzo could present himself, at least to the eyes of Ercole, as one prince addressing another. It was actually a Ferrarese orator, Antonio Montecatino, who shrewdly observed that Lorenzo's prestige in the city of Florence was enabled by such high-level connections with real princes in neighboring Italian states.[34] The correspondence about dogs, falcons, and courtly favors was given an ennobled character by the same Ferrarese orator, who proclaimed it as a sign of the civilized leisure that was made possible by the peace of Italy: "Leisure multiplies in Italy to such an extent that if nothing else arises there will be more to write about battles of dogs and birds than of armies or deeds of arms. And certainly no less glory falls to those who govern Italy in a pacific state than to those who keep it bellicose, given that the end of war is nothing other than peace."[35] Finally, the Ferrarese perception of Lorenzo as a rich and powerful *parvenu* is summed up in the remarks of Ugo Caleffini, a diarist close to the Este court, when he records the death of Il Magnifico, "first man of Florence, and first man of Italy through a private fortune said to be worth more than one million ducats."[36]

Carbone's visit to Florence, on a journey to Naples in the company of Sigismondo d'Este, Matteo Maria Boiardo, and a magnificent retinue, took place during the first years of Lorenzo's rule, a period when the splendor of Florence's princely allies was put on display in the city as never before. Another occasion was the state visit of Duke Galeazzo Maria Sforza of Milan in 1471, and yet another in June 1473, with the reception of Eleonora of Aragon, princess of Naples, escorted to Ferrara by Sigismondo and his entourage to marry Ercole d'Este. It was Carbone's task on the outward journey to praise Florence, and to acknowledge its supremacy in many respects, but not to do so at the expense of his own native city. His oration rehearses many of the standard themes of Florentine self-praise – the beauty of the city and its physical setting, its antiquity, and its long struggle against tyrants – and insists on the historically intertwined destinies of the Florentines and the Ferrarese. The ancient city of Adria in Ferrarese territory was a Tuscan colony, he says, "and what other prince and people was ever as much united with your republic as the prince and people of Ferrara?" Here he manages to remind the Florentines of their past military dependency on the princes of Ferrara. "However far back you look, you never find any alliance of the Ferrarese without the Florentines. Everywhere in our public spaces are to be seen painted memorials of the ancient covenants between us. Our Eagles always held fast to your Lilies, and our princes were always your faithful leaders and generals (*ductores atque imperatores*)."[37] Although ostensibly alluding to past *condotte* of the Este princes, Carbone touches here on a well-known circumstance of Florentine lack: the absence of a real princely leader and a real court, and all that goes with these.[38] He does this yet more directly, and facetiously, in a Latin account of the 1473 mission to Florence and Naples which he sent to Federico da Montefeltro:

> What can I tell you of the modesty, industry and frugality of such a city, and of how the Florentines place a bridle on the untamed beast? They impose sumptuary laws. What this untamed beast is exactly I don't dare to say, lest I turn women against me. I believe you've heard about how earnestly they maintain the new University at Pisa, so that they lure the most famous masters of learning from all over Italy with huge sums of money. What more can I say? If my lord Ercole ruled over Florence, there is no other place I would live.[39]

The remark about the University of Pisa conceals a point of real tension between Florence and Ferrara, a struggle about human cultural property which would become more acute in the following decade. It was already manifest in the plundering by Florence of personnel from the Este court (such as the humanists Bartolomeo della Fonte and Giovanni Testa Cillenio[40]) and soon also from the prestigious University of Ferrara. The more illustrious names in the faculty of law and medicine were all solicited by the newly reorganized university at Pisa from 1473 onward; Lorenzo was able to bring diplomatic pressure to bear in requesting that Ercole authorize the departure of some of these professors, beginning with the lawyer Bartolomeo Sozzini in April 1473 – two months before Carbone's oration. In at least one later case, that of the physician Francesco Benzi in 1483, Ercole refused to allow the departure.[41]

Does this relationship of the Este and the Medici have any correlative in the visual arts? Both the Republic of Florence, and the princes of Ferrara from about 1430, had used the figure of Hercules as an image of militant sovereignty (so, of course, did many other states). Yet in the case of Florence and Ferrara this is more than the parallel development of a commonplace idea; the image of Hercules circulates between the two regimes during the 1470s, the period of the closest political *rapprochement*. His modern namesake Ercole d'Este, as Carbone reminded the Florentines, was no less than the godson of the republic, whose representative had held him at the baptismal font in 1431. One instance of this circulation is a manuscript frontispiece of Giovanni Camfora's *De immortalitate animae* from the Este library, presented to Ercole in 1472, where the figure of Hercules fighting the Hydra is modeled on one Pollaiuolo's paintings of the Labors of Hercules for the Palazzo Medici, completed a few years before (Fig. 44).[42] Yet the Medici's use of the image of the figure of Hercules, while it certainly relates to a long-standing association of Hercules with Florence, may also be a response to a tradition of Este self-imagery. In her discussion of the Pollaiuolo series, Alison Wright has pointed to the fact that there was considerable precedent for Hercules imagery at the princely courts in Italy and beyond the Alps; Hercules provides a commonplace mythological exemplar of the virtue of fortitude, a predictable component of the self-representation of sovereigns or of those with princely ambitions.[43] Yet nowhere was the image of Hercules cultivated so intensely as at the court of Ferrara. When Piero de' Medici, who commissioned the Hercules cycle from Pollaiuolo, visited Ferrara in 1438, he could have seen the frescoes in the Sala di Ercole in the Palazzo di Paradiso, executed a few years before.[44] The ruling prince, Niccolò III, had also been the dedicatee of what could only be described as a humanist romance, a long narrative by Pier Andrea de' Bassi titled *Le fatiche di Ercole*. In writing this work the author drew heavily on the conventions of chivalric romance, yet he also acknowledges his debt to various Latin and Greek humanists at the Este court, who provided him with material for lengthy philological digressions on the origins of various mythological names and with translations of parts of the *Iliad* that were incorporated in his text.[45] The work is a hybrid of classical and chivalric traditions highly characteristic of Ferrarese court culture, and its most obvious visual counterpart would be the 'gothic' Hercules who appears in a celebrated series of Ferrarese court tapestries, or in the Paradiso frescoes. But Hercules, it appears, was also portrayed *all'antica* in Ferrara by midcentury. Angelo Decembrio's *De supplicationis maiis* includes a description of a painting of Hercules from Leonello's apartment, wearing a lionskin and fighting the Hydra. Most important, Decembrio compares the figure with one from an ancient relief which he had seen at S. Ambrogio in Milan. And Decembrio elsewhere remarks on the ancient portrayal of Hercules as "a gigantic figure like our St. Christopher, partly nude and partly covered by a lionskin."[46] Pollaiuolo's Medici series, in other words, would have made its political argument – that is, its insinuations of Medici primacy – even more effectively to a cosmopolitan audience familiar with the milieu of the Este court.

By placing the image of Hercules in their private residence, yet in a space often devoted to the reception of visiting foreign dignitaries, the Medici were emulating

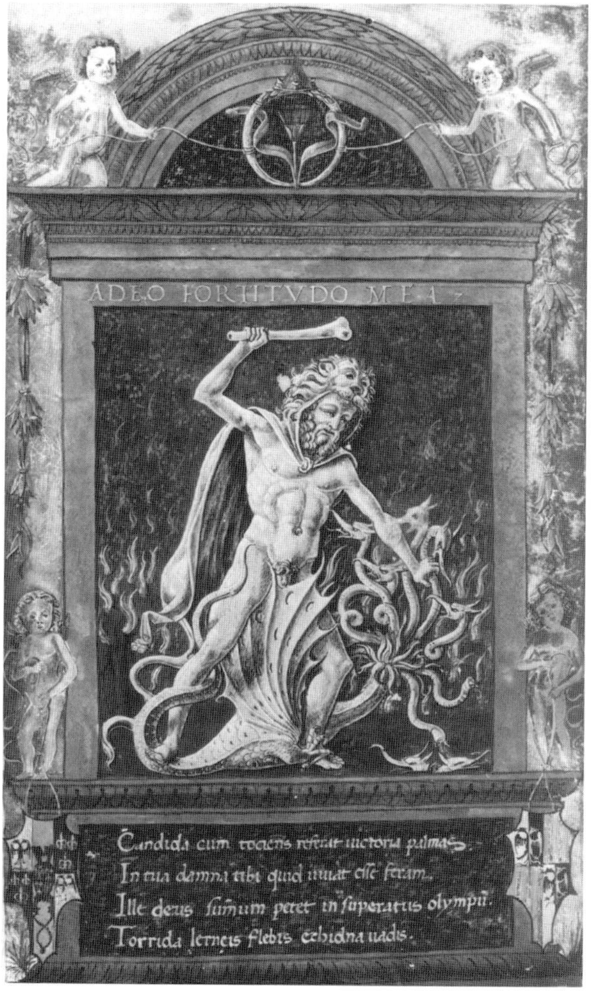

44. Giovanni Vendramin, frontispiece to Giovanni Camfora, *De immortalitate animae*. On parchment. London, The British Library, Add. MS 22325. Photo: by permission of The British Library.

a mode of self-representation specially characteristic of princes. Hercules begins to appear in the ritual exchanges of Florence and its princely allies; a usefully ambiguous symbol, Hercules could signify both the communal sovereignty of Florence, as well as the honoring of an individual ruler. Could the inevitable identification of Hercules with Duke Ercole after 1470 have affected this dual significance of Hercules in Florence itself?[47] Federico da Montefeltro received the gift of a helmet adorned with a silver statue of Hercules in 1474; Ercole d'Este acquired a bronze equestrian statue of Hercules by Bertoldo di Giovanni, probably as a gift from the Medici or the *signoria* in 1478. In that year, in the tumultuous aftermath of the Pazzi conspiracy, Ercole received the baton of command of the Florentine alliance, along with the palace of the Pazzi family itself as an additional reward. Bertoldo's statuette, in any case, reflects a Ferrarese, rather than a Florentine conception of Hercules. Margret Lisner and James Draper have both seen a reflection of Ercole's self-fashioning as a knight, 'el cavaliero estense senza timore,' as he was known in Naples.[48] The chivalric conception of Hercules, still flourishing at Ferrara, also presented him as a mounted knight.[49] Furthermore, the massive proportions of the rider in relation to the horse might be seen as a deliberate evocation of the Baroncelli equestrian monument to Ercole's father, who had himself been hailed as a Hercules. Like the romance of Boiardo, which combines Virgil and Homer with chivalric material, the work is a another instance of a cultural hybrid – both ancient and modern, both Ferrarese and Florentine.

It has often been pointed out that Florence reserved a particular respect for those among its citizens who had distinguished themselves in the service of princes. This was particularly the case with the Florentine *fuorusciti* in Ferrara, the most prominent of whom were two expatriate branches of the Strozzi family, and part-time residents such as the Lanfredini, who by the 1460s, maintained a banking company in Ferrara and Lendinara.[50] In 1469, the first of three letters patent was issued by Borso d'Este, which conferred extraordinary honors on the two brothers, including the rank of ducal *familiares,* the right to maintain a military escort, the privilege of wearing Este devices, and exemption from sumptuary laws prohibiting the use of gold and silver in dress or at table.[51] By 1471, they had become business and political associates of Lorenzo de' Medici, who employed them as diplomatic agents in Ferrara and in Rome. In letters to Ercole d'Este, Lorenzo refers to Giovanni Lanfredini as 'tutto devoto servitore di vostra Excellentia.'[52] Giovanni, in the 1480s, was signing his letters *Johannes Lanfredinus Estensis.*[53]

The Lanfredini, then, were Este courtiers as well as Florentine citizens. Could we see this in any way determining their activity as patrons, above all their famous association with Antonio Pollaiuolo? The most noteworthy artistic commission of the Lanfredini in Florence is the famous fresco decoration by Antonio Pollaiuolo in their villa at Arcetri, a 'bacchic' scene of dancing nude men and one nude woman, with garlands, putti, and an arcade rendered in perspective (Fig. 45). The most thorough recent investigation of these frescoes, that by Alison Wright, has dated them to the early 1470s, the early years of their advancement under Lorenzo de' Medici and under the Este. As a secular, domestic decoration with an *all'antica* flavor, these extraordinary frescoes are without precedent in Florence, although this could reflect the poor rate of survival of such decorations. Yet bearing in mind the strong Ferrarese orientation of the Lanfredini brothers, it is possible to see the La Gallina frescoes as Pollaiuolo's response to the taste of a patron which had been formed among the Ferrarese nobility. Only a tiny fraction remains of the sumptuous palace decorations of quattrocento Ferrara, but what does survive is suggestive for

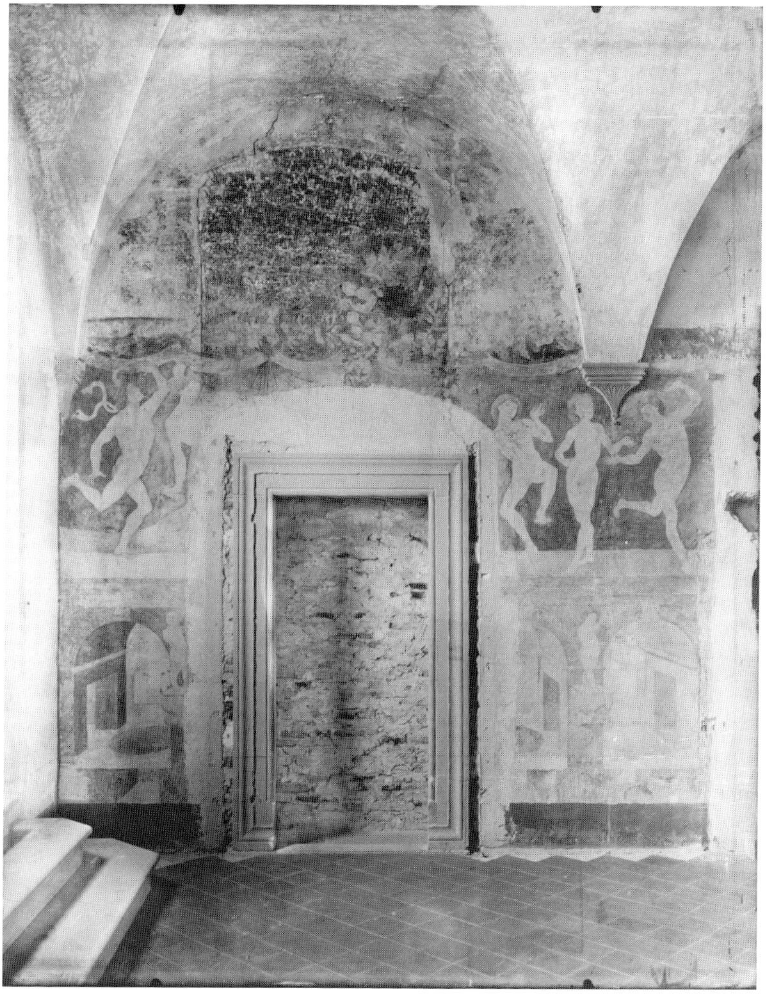

45. Antonio Pollaiuolo, *Dancing Nudes*. Fresco. Arcetri (Florence) Villa Gallina. Photo: Florence, Soprintendenza per i beni artistici e storici, gabinetto fotografico.

thinking about the Arcetri frescoes as a decoration *alla ferrarese*. The lower zone of the Arcetri fresco, an arcade rendered in perspective, occurs in a simpler form in the frescos of the Hall of the Falcons in the Palazzo di Paradiso in Ferrara. Wright has pointed to the parallel of the putti and garlands with similar motifs found in Mantegna's *camera picta* in Mantua, but the prominent Ferrarese examples of this theme are probably of greater significance for the Lanfredini (Sala dei Mesi, Sala degli Stucchi, etc.).[54]

Finally, what of the dancing figures themselves? Surely these epitomize all that is most forward-looking about Pollaiuolo's art, that specially Florentine pictorial science of rendering the body with regard to anatomical structure and the mechanics

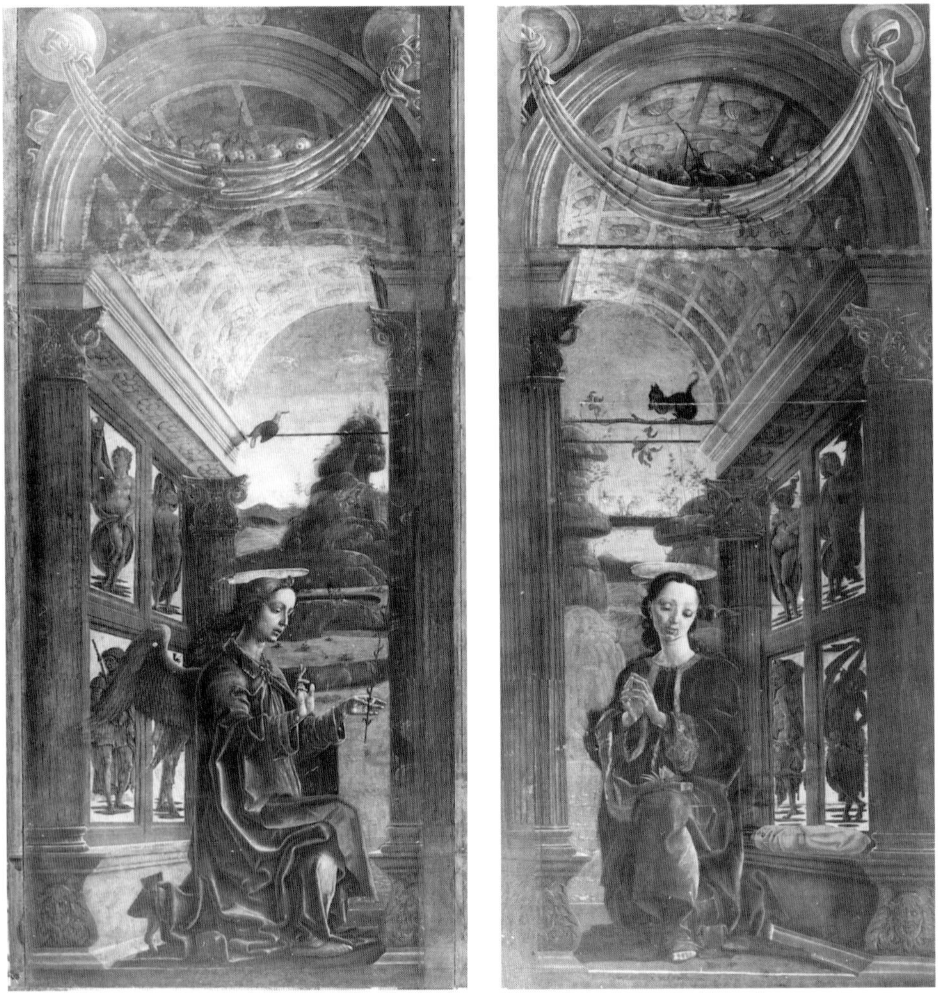

46. Cosmè Tura, *Annunciation*. On canvas. Ferrara, Museo dell'Opera del Duomo. Photo: Archivio fotografico Soprintendenza PSAD, Bologna. Photo: Archivio fotografico Soprintendenza PSAD, Bologna. Photo: Archivio fotografico Soprintendenza PSAD, Bologna.

of movement. Yet Cosmè Tura produced a rather comparable series of animated, sinuous nudes in 1468–9, in his organ-shutters for the cathedral of Ferrara (Fig. 46). Here, in a kind of artistic parenthesis, a work of art within a work of art, Tura demonstrated his mastery of the new canons of human movement as laid down in the second book of Alberti's *De pictura* and as they were being rendered by Andrea Mantegna. Here, however, Tura appears very much as the contemporary, not merely the imitator, of both Mantegna and Pollaiuolo. These figures are also notable as a classicizing rendering of the pagan gods, yet this fact has apparently been consigned to scholarly oblivion by a historiography that, since Warburg, may have foreclosed the possibility of such a rendering in Ferrara around 1470. Warburg's

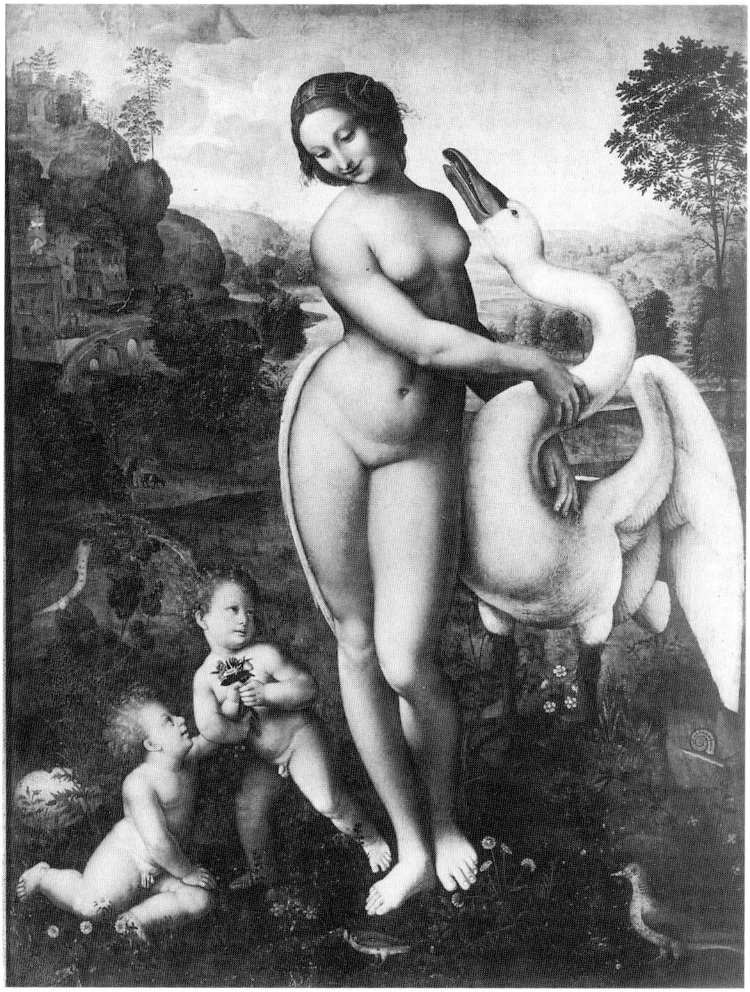

47. After Leonardo da Vinci, *Leda and the Swan*. Rome, Galleria Borghese. Photo: Alinari/Art Resource, NY.

famous essay saw the exactly contemporary gods of the Palazzo Schifanoia frescoes as still struggling to break free from centuries of medieval and oriental 'mistranslation,' and this view of the Ferrarese experience as a kind of 'proto-Renaissance' still casts a long shadow.[55]

The possibility of reverse influence – of a Ferrarese on a Florentine artist, has never been considered. Yet much of Cosmè Tura's professional activity consisted in the production of pattern drawings and designs which circulated widely, in one case at least as far as Milan, and a corpus of drawings was left to one of his *garzoni* in the artist's will made in 1471.[56] Did one of these drawings, or a derivative, ever find its way into the hands of Leonardo da Vinci, who would move to Milan in the following decade (Figs. 47)? Did Tura, in his figure of Venus for the organ-shutters (see the female figure in the upper right of Fig. 46), anticipate the so-called *figura serpentinata* that Leonardo was supposedly to invent in his Leda, about thirty years later? Perhaps Leonardo's *Leda* is a Tuscan translation of a North Italian model, produced after years of experience of the Este and Sforza cultural ambit. Thus when Dosso Dossi modeled his *Enchantress* (Washington, National Gallery) on this figure type, he could have referred to Tura and did not need the mediation of Leonardo's figure, which he is unlikely to have seen.[57] The point is not who did what first, but that we might want to be careful about the basis on which we distinguish between Florentine art and the art of other centers, or, we might say, between the influence of so-called center on so-called periphery. On one hand, we have a conscious attempt at differentiation on the level of language and of visual culture, between the Ferrarese and the Florentines; yet beyond the patriotic compulsion to insist on regional differences, we might find a great deal more in common between the art of the two cities than the *campanilismo* of their ruling elites has conditioned us to expect.

NOTES

1. See Martin Warnke, *The Court Artist: On the Ancestry of the Modern Artist,* trans. D. Mc Lintock (Cambridge and New York: Cambridge University Press: Cambridge University Press, 1993).

2. For a recent example, which still relies on the Paduan workshop of Squarcione as a fountainhead for all 'progressive' or quasi-Florentine developments in North Italian art of the late quattrocento, see Joseph Manca, *Cosmè Tura: The Life and Art of a Painter in Estense Ferrara* (Oxford: Oxford University Press, 1999), 42–3.

3. 'Si vero ad literatos homines animum referamus, hinc medici prudentissimi, hinc jurisconsulti gravissimi, hinc poetae oratoresque insignes, hinc pictores nobilissimi exorti sunt. Linguae dulcedo sermonisque lepiditas huic urbi propria et peculiaris est, ut verissime in carmine illo meo cecinerim: 'Si Deus in terras descendat, non alio quam Florentinorum culto sermone loquatur." Full text of the *Oratio ad Florentinos* in Alfonso Lazzari, 'Un orazione di Lodovico Carbone a Firenze', *Atti e memorie della Reale Deputazione di Storia Patria per le Provincie Modenesi,* ser. V. vol. xii (1919), 187–205. Carbone's oration was praised by Bartolomeo Scala and the Ferrarese humanist wrote to Duke Ercole d'Este, underlining the significance of the fact that a Ferrarese should be praised for his eloquence by the Florentines, 'padri di ogni eloquentia.' For the letter, see Giulio Bertoni, *La biblioteca Estense e la coltura ferrarese ai tempi del Duca Ercole I, 1471–1505* (Turin: Loescher, 1903), 126–7. For a recent translation of the letter, see *Images of Quattrocento Florence. Selected Writings in Literature, History and Art,* ed. Stefano Ugo Baldassari and Arielle Saiber (New Haven and London: Yale University Press, 1999), 307–8.

4. On the presence of these and other foreign artists artists in Ferrara, see Mauro Natale, 'Lo studiolo di Belfiore: un cantiere ancora aperto,' in *Le Muse e il Principe. Arte di Corte nel Rinascimento Padano,* 2 vols., ed. M. Natale and A. Mottola-Molfino (Modena: Panini, 1992), vol. I, 17–44. On the international dimensions of Este patronage see also Lorne Campbell, 'Cosmè Tura and Netherlandish Art' in Stephen J. Campbell et al., *Cosmè Tura: Painting and*

Design in Renaissance Ferrara (Boston: Isabella Stewart Gardner Museum; Milan: Electa, 2002), 71–107.

5. For a survey of relations between the Este and the bishops of Ferrara, see Stephen J. Campbell, *Cosmè Tura of Ferrara. Style, Politics and the Renaissance City, 1450–1495* (New Haven and London: Yale University Press, 1997), 102–7; see also Adriano Prosperi, 'Le istituzioni ecclesiastiche e le idee religiose,' in *Il Rinascimento nelle corti padane: Società e Cultura* (Bari: Laterza, 1977), 125–63, and Peter Partner, 'Francesco dal Legname: A Curial Bishop in Disgrace,' in *Florence and Italy: Renaissance Studies in Honour of Nicolai Rubinstein*, ed. Peter Denley and Caroline Elam (London: Committee for Medieval Studies, Westfield College, University of London 1988), 395–404.

6. For a survey of fifteenth-century sculptural projects, including those connected with the cathedral, see Richard Stemp, *Sculpture in Ferrara in the Fifteenth Century: Problems and Studies* (Ph.D. diss., University of Cambridge, 1992).

7. On Baroncelli, see Wolfgang Wolters, *La Scultura Veneziana Gotica* (Venice: Alfieri, 1976), 94–5; on his presence in Ferrara, Stemp, *Sculpture in Ferrara*, 19f.; on the equestrian monument of marchese Niccolò III d'Este, Charles Rosenberg, *The Este Monuments and Urban Development in Renaissance Ferrara* (Cambridge and New York: Cambridge University Press, 1997).

8. John Pope-Hennessy, *Italian Renaissance Sculpture* (London: Phaidon, 1971), 74.

9. On the San Michele in Isola cloister portal of c. 1430–40, see Wolters, *La Scultura Veneziana*, cat. 176.

10. Ercole's building and urbanistic projects are amply documented and analyzed by Rosenberg, *Este Monuments*, and Thomas Tuohy, *Herculean Ferrara: Ercole d'Este (1471–1505) and the Invention of a Ducal Capital* (Cambridge and New York: Cambridge University Press, 1996).

11. For an account of the Roverella family and their politically charged relations with the Este, see Campbell, *Cosmè Tura of Ferrara*, 100–7.

12. On the tomb, see Eric Apfelstadt, *The Later Sculpture of Antonio Rossellino* (Ph.D. diss., Princeton University, 1987), 188–240.

13. On the 'romanizing' adaptations of Tuscan sculptors working for curial patrons, see the essay by Shelley Zuraw in this volume.

14. Published initially in C. Von Fabriczy, 'Documenti su due opere di Antonio Rossellino,' *Rivista dell'arte* 5 (1907): 165–6. For complete documentation, see Apfelstadt, *Antonio Rossellino*.

15. Agostino's reliefs for the duomo in Modena are signed AUGUSTINUS DE FLORENTIA. See Pope-Hennessy, *Italian Renaissance Sculpture*, 309.

16. Stemp, *Sculpture in Ferrara*, 134.

17. Stemp, 'Cosimo Tura and the Sacrati Chapels in Ferrara,' *Musei Ferraresi* 17 (1990–1): 61–70.

18. On the *Virgin and Child* in the Accademia Carrara, a fragment of a polyptych that may have also included other surviving panels showing St. Francis, St. Dominic, and St. James, see Campbell, *Cosmè Tura of Ferrara*, 93, and Manca, *Cosmè Tura*, 91–3.

19. Luke Syson, 'Medals and other portraits attributed to Cosmè Tura,' *The Burlington Magazine* 141 (1999): 226–9; Campbell, *Cosmè Tura: Painting and Design*, 246–9.

20. On literary imitation in the Renaissance, see George Pigman III, 'Versions of Imitation in the Renaissance,' *Renaissance Quarterly* 33 (1980): 1–32; Thomas Greene, *The Light in Troy. Imitation and Discovery in Renaissance Poetry* (New Haven and London: Yale University Press, 1982): 1–80. For a precocious, early quattrocento account of artistic imitation drawing on the terms of literary imitation, see the *Libro dell'Arte* of Cennino Cennini, as discussed by Andrea Bolland, 'Art and

Humanism in Early Renaissance Padua: Cennini, Vergerio and Petrarch on Imitation,' *Renaissance Quarterly* 49 (1996): 469–88.

21. Pomponius Gauricus, *De sculptura,* ed. P. Cutolo (Naples: 1999), 222–4: 'Alia quidem apparent in Herculis – quoniam Hylae non licet – tergo, lacertis, pectore, cruribus ac toto denique corpore hydram conficientis, alia cum Anthaeo luctantis, alia tauro cornua dissipantis, alia aliter agentis. Dulciter tamen ac non uti ab eo factum est, qui Coleonum ad Pauli nuper posuit: ille enim, ita ut aiunt, cruditer equum imitatus est, ut non aliud quam denudati equi facies videatur.'

22. 'La opera è diffusa e vari come ipsa natura; et perché lo e piena de nomi de animali et ocelli et de herbe et d'ogni cossa, essendo tuti traducti per vocabuli toscani, che pur molti sono differenti da' lombardi, parerà a uno lombardo, che non habii questa lingua, in alcuni nomi fastidioso; che havesse mo mescolato alcuna volta il lombardo col toscano, qui haveria parso deturpata la elegantia de questa lingua, se ben forsi in tutonon fusse stato male, per farla più commune. Intendo che l'prefato signor Re l'ha facto tradure per donare al Illustrissimo duca di Borgogna, quale molto si dilecta di legere.' The letter dated Florence, 20 agosto 1475, is in Modena, Archivio di Stato, Archivio Estense, Ambasciatori esteri, Firenze, I (N. Bendidio); it is published in R. Fubini, 'Cristoforo Landino. Le *Disputationes Camaldulenses* e il volgarizzamento di Plinio: questione di cronologia e di interpretazione,' in *Quattrocento fiorentino politica diplomazia cultura* (Pisa: Pacini, 1996): 330–32.

23. On the controversy see Giancarlo Mazzcurati, *La questione della lingua dal Bembo all'Accademia Fiorentina* (Naples: Liguori: 1965).

24. See Mirko Tavoni, *Il Quattrocento* (Milan: Mulino, 1992), 72.

25. See Bertoni, *La Biblioteca Estense*; Antonia Tissoni Benvenuti, 'L'antico a corte: da Guarino a Boiardo', *Alla corte degli estensi. Filosofia, arte e cultura a Ferrara nei secoli xv e xvi,* ed. M. Bertozzi (Ferrara: Università degli Studi, 1994), 389–404.

26. 'Io scio che tu sei ferrarese et Ferrara, inclita cità de Italia, ne ha producti, alevati et acresciuti et però non saperia io adriciare la lingua se non al ferrarese idioma, il quale, secondo il mio parere, non ha mancho elegantia che alcuno altro italiano parlare.' Quoted in Bertoni, *La Biblioteca Estense,* 123.

27. Tina Matarrese, 'Il volgare a Ferrara all'epoca del Boiardo: Dall'emiliano 'illustre' all'italiano 'cortigiano'.' In *Il Boiardo e il mondo estense nel quattrocento. Atti del convegno internazionale di studi 13–17 settembre 1994,* 2 vols., ed. Giuseppe Anceschi and Tina Matarrese (Padua: Antenore, 1998), vol. II, 611–47.

28. 'Haec si praecipas, ex Gaio fonte Camenas, Traducam ad clari brachi longa Padi.'

29. Campbell, '*Sic in amore furens*: Painting as Poetic Theory in the Early Renaissance,' *I Tatti Studies* 6 (1995): 145–69; and *Cosmè Tura of Ferrara,* 47–51.

30. As the Florentine orator Jacopo Lanfredini was charged to inform Ercole in 1471, 'per conservatione della pace et bene di Italia, noi stimiamo che [Ferrara] sia conservato.' See Lorenzo de'Medici, *Lettere,* 8 vols., ed. N. Rubinstein et al. (Florence: Giunti, 1977), vol. I, 354.

31. Jacopo Trotti, orator in Rome, wrote to Borso warning him to beware of 'the poison of the Florentines.' On Piero de' Medici's implication in the conspiracy of the Pio in 1469, see Edmund Gardner, *Dukes and Poets in Ferrara* (London: Constable, 1904), 103–7; on Lorenzo's refusal to participate in a Gonzaga-backed coup d'état to replace Borso with Niccolò di Leonello d'Este, see Lorenzo de'Medici, *Lettere,* vol. I, 63–4. For additional and later material on the relations of Ferrara and Florence and of the Este with the Medici, see A. Cappelli, 'Lettere di Lorenzo de' Medici detto il Magnifico conservate nell'Archivio Palatino di Modena con notizie tratte dei

carteggi diplomatici degli oratori estensi a Firenze,' *Atti e memorie della Deputazione di Storia Patria per le Provincie Modenesi e Parmensi,* vol. I (1863), 231–320. See also Michael Mallet, 'Lorenzo de Medici and the War of Ferrara,' in *Lorenzo de'Medici: New Perspectives,* ed. B. Toscani (New York: Peter Lang, 1993), 249–61.

32. On Ercole's acquisition of the Palazzo Pazzi, see Tuohy, *Herculean Ferrara,* 152.

33. Some of these letters are published in Cappelli, 'Lettere di Lorenzo de Medici': see 12 Feb. 1480 on falcons, 25 Feb. on salame, 5 Feb. 1485 for Lorenzo's request of a loan of Dio's *Roman History,* 16 Nov. 1490 for a request that Ercole intervene in a dispute involving Jewish bankers in Prato.

34. Quoted in Mallet, 'Lorenzo de' Medici,' 249.

35. Cappelli, 'Lettere di Lorenzo de Medici,' 251, 22 Jan. 1474: 'E non si meravigli V. Ecc.a che gli dia cotal avviso, perchè ancora qui altri assai tengono conto di tali cose. L'ozio moltiplica per modo in Italia che, se non altro sorge, più gli sarà che scrivere di battaglie di uccelli e cani, che di eserciti o fatti d'arme. E certo credo non consequiranno minor gloria quelli che governanno Italia pacifica, che si facessero coloro che le tenevano bellicosa, essendo il fine della guerra non altro che la pace; sicchè l'è da sapersela godere lungamente.'

36. 'primo homo de Fiorenza, et primo homo de Italia per uno homo privato et richo de uno milione de ducati in suso ut dicebat.' Caleffini, *Cronica della Casa d'Este,* April 1492, quoted in Tuohy, *Herculean Ferrara,* n. 122.

37. *Oratio ad Florentinos,* 19: 'Nam qui alii principes aut populi reipublicae vestrae coniunctores unquam fuerunt, quam Ferrarienses? Quantumlibet vetera repetatis, nullam Ferrariensibus societatem sine Florentinis fuisse invenietis; ubique in foro caeterisque publicis locis nostris, extant picta monumenta antiquorum inter nos foederum: semper liliis vestris aquilae nostrae adhaeserunt, principes nostros fidissimos ductores atque imperatores vestros experti estis.'

38. As is famously demonstrated in Richard C. Trexler, *Public Life in Renaissance Florence* (Ithaca: Cornell University Press, 1980).

39. *De neapolitana profectione,* cited in Lazzari, 'Un'orazione di Lodovico carbone a Firenze,' n. 19 'Quid tibi civium modestiam, industriam, frugalitatem enarrem, et nunc fraenum imposuerunt Florentini indomito animali; ornamentorum sumptus coercentes. Quod autem sit indomitum istud animal non audeo dicere ne fortasse mihi succenserent mulieres. Audisti credo quam ardenter ad novum Pisarum Gymnasium intendant, quamque ingenti mercede conducant ex tota Italia clarissimos doctrinarum magistros – Quid multa? Si Hercules meus Florentiae teneret imperium, nusquam libentius habitarem.'

40. On della Fonte, who left Ferrara for Florence at the death of Borso d'Este, see the entry by R. Zaccaria in *Dizionario Biografico degli Italiani,* vol. 36 (1988), 898–902. For Cillenio's sojourn in Ferrara see Stefano Carrai, 'La lirica toscana nell'età di Lorenzo,' in Marco Santagata and Stefano Carrai, *La lirica di corte nell'Italia del Quattrocento* (Milan: Francoangeli, 1993), 100–2.

41. Armando Verde, 'Studenti e professori fra l'Università di Ferrara e l'Università di Firenze: Fine del Quattrocento – inizio del Cinquecento' in '*In supreme dignitatis . . .' Per la storia dell'l'Università di Ferrara, 1391–1991,* ed. Patrizia Castelli. (Florence: Olschki, 1995), 75–105.

42. For a recent discussion of the miniature and its possible authorship by the Paduan Giovanni Vendramin, which does not note the connection with Pollaiuolo, see Jonathan J. G. Alexander et al., *The Painted Page: Italian Renaissance Book Illumination 1450–1550* (London and New York: Prestel, 1994), 76. Pollaiuolo's invention may have been known through an engraving attributed to the Finiguerra workshop; see Arthur M. Hind, *Early Italian Engraving,* 7 vols. (London and New York: Knoedler, 1938), vol. I, 194 and pl. 266.

43. Alison Wright, 'Piero de'Medici and the Pollaiuolo,' in *Piero de'Medici 'il Gottoso' (1416–1469). Kunst im Dienste der Mediceer/Art in the Service of the Medici*, ed. Andreas Beyer and Bruce Boucher (Berlin: Akademie Verlag, 1993), 140–3. Francis Ames Lewis has also speculated that one of Piero de' Medici's devices, the *diamante*, may have been granted to him by the Este on the occasion of the 1438 visit: 'Early Medicean Devices,' *Journal of the Warburg and Courtauld Institutes* 42 (1979): 141.

44. On the Sala di Ercole, see the entry by Ranieri Varese in *Palazzo Paradiso e la Biblioteca Ariostea*, ed. Alessandra Chiappini and Loredana Olivato (Ferrara and Rome: Editalia, 1993), 92–5.

45. See Antonia Tissoni Benvenuti, 'Il mito di Ercole. Aspetto della ricezione dell'antico alla corte estense nel primo quattrocento,' in *Omaggio a Gianfranco Folena* (Padua: Programma, 1993), 773–92; Tina Matarrese, 'Il *materno eloquio* del ferrarese Pier Andrea de'Bassi,' ibid., 793–812; and Mattarese, 'Il mito di Ercole a Ferrara nel quattrocento tra letteratura e arti figurative,' *L'ideale classico a Ferrara e in Italia nel Rinascimento*, ed. Patrizia Castelli (Ferrara: Olschki, 1998), 191–202.

46. Tissoni Benvenuti, 'Il mito di Ercole,' 791–2.

47. By the 1470s, the ancient hero was widely associated throughout Italy with the duke of Ferrara. In Rome and Naples in 1473, the impending marriage of Ercole with Eleonora of Aragon was celebrated with images and theatrical tableaux of Hercules and his labors. Sabadino degli Arienti's famous account of the Este palaces in his *De triumphis religionis* refers to a fresco of 'ancient Hercules' and a gilded statue of Hercules in the gardens at Belriguardo. See Werner L. Gundersheimer, *Art and Life at the Court of Ercole I d'Este: The 'De Triumphis Religionis' of Giovanni Sabadino degli Arienti* (Geneva: Droz, 1972), 52 (for the statue), 59 (for the 'ancient Hercules'), and 67 (for a gold coin issued by Ercole with the device of Hercules and the Hydra).

48. The first reference to the Hercules statuette (attributed to Bertoldo by Wilhelm Bode in 1895) is an Este inventory of the palace of Sassuolo of 11 August 1684. See Margret Lisner, 'Form und sinngehalt von Michelangelos kentaurenschlacht mit notizen zu Bertoldo di Giovanni,' *Mitteilungen des Kunsthistorischen Institutes in Florenz* XXIV/3 (1980), 299–344; James Draper, *Bertoldo di Giovanni, Sculptor of the Medici Household* (Columbia: University of Missouri Press, 1992), 153 ff.

49. Draper, *Bertoldo*, 155: 'A Hercules riding on horseback is not to be found except in lost Ferrarese tapestries, this statuette, and the central figure in the [Bertoldo] *Battle*. It is a thoroughly anticlassical usage, whose rationale results from a courtly, festive overlay upon the ancient horseless species.'

50. L. Fabbri, 'Da Firenze a Ferrara. Gli Strozzi tra casa d'Este e antichi legami di sangue,' in *Alla corte degli estensi*, 91–108; Mildred Mansfield, *A Family of Decent Folk, 1200–1741. A Study in the Centuries Growth of the Lanfredini, Merchant Bankers, Art-Patrons and House-Builders of Florence* (London: T. Fisher Unwin, 1922).

51. For the letters patent on behalf of Jacopo and Giovanni, see Mansfield, *A Family*, 264–7. Borso's letter of 20 February 1469 appoints the brothers *familiares*, with exemption from dues and rights of free transit for their persons, household members, and property; Ercole on 18 February 1475 grants them the right to wear his devices and on 27 February he permitted Giovanni to extend his armed escort from four to ten men.

52. Cappelli, 'Lettere di Lorenzo de'Medici,' 241.

53. Gustave Gruyer, *L'art ferrarais à l'époque des princes d'Este*, 2 vols. (Paris: Plon, 1897), vol. I, 637.

54. Alison Wright, 'Dancing Nudes in the Lanfredini Villa at Arcetri,' in *With and Without the Medici. Studies in Tuscan Art and Patronage 1434–1530*, eds. Eckard Marchand and Alison Wright (Aldershot and Hants: Ashgate, 1998), 47–79. For an illustration of the Palazzo Paradiso murals, see Varese, in *Palazzo Paradiso e la Biblioteca Ariostea*, 92–5.

55. Aby Warburg, 'Italian Art and International Astrology in the Palazzo Schifanoia, Ferrara (1912).' In Warburg, *The Renewal of Pagan Antiquity,* ed. K. W. Forster and D. Britt (Los Angeles: Getty Research Press, 1999), 563–96.

56. For the will of 14 January 1471, see Manca, *Cosmè Tura,* 204–6, doc. 68.

57. As I have proposed in *Cosmè Tura,* 150; Peter Humfrey has maintained the notion of influence from Leonardo on Dossi; see Humfrey with Mauro Lucco, *Dosso Dossi, Court Painter in Renaissance Ferrara* (New York: Abrams, 1998), 90.

6

Giovanni II Bentivoglio and the Uses of Chivalry. Towards the Creation of a 'Republican Court' in Fifteenth-Century Bologna

Georgia Clarke

The image of the ruler of Bologna in the second half of the fifteenth century presented in modern literature is often either of a Maecenas or a tyrant. But the case for either view of Giovanni II Bentivoglio (1443–1508, head of the Bolognese state, 1463–1506) has yet to be fully proven. In recent years Bologna has become the focus of a number of scholars' work, including studies of individual sites of patronage and the work of single artists, and this is welcome attention to a neglected subject. Much, however, is still to be done, not only in the archives but also in visual and other studies of works of art and architecture. The patronage not only of the Bentivoglio but also of patrician families and the interventions of others such as papal legates and governors remain to be explored. This chapter cannot and does not give a full account of Giovanni II Bentivoglio, his patronage, his influence, or his control of Bologna; instead it aims to look at a number of diverse ways in which Bentivoglio presence was made manifest and how this might begin to be considered in relation to the idea of 'cultural translation.'

Chivalric Display

In Bologna on 4 October 1470 the annual celebrations 'to honour the feast of such a saint as our San Petronio' – the city's patron saint – took place in the Piazza Maggiore with a splendid tournament between two *brigate* – the *bianchi* [whites] and the *rossi* [reds].[1] The commander of the whites was the twenty-seven-year-old

This is an expansion of the paper given at the conference 'Florence in the 1470s: Contexts and Contrasts', held at the National Gallery, London, 12–13 November 1999. My thanks to Luke Syson and Stephen Campbell for editorial comments and suggestions.

Giovanni II Bentivoglio, who was 'first citizen' of Bologna, and the reds were led by Antonio Trotti of Alessandria, who had been captain of the Bolognese militia since January 1468.[2] The duke of Milan, Galeazzo Maria Sforza, sent eight horses for Bentivoglio, which arrived in Bologna about three weeks beforehand.[3] Giovanni, after consultation with the duke, decided to ride a steed called Superbo (proud).[4] On the day of the tournament the squads arrived one by one in the piazza, with Giovanni, leading the sixth and final squad of *bianchi*, making a noticeably more splendid entrance than the rest. After much parading, a long, pitched battle took place, which was won by the *bianchi*, and the cry went up of '*sega, sega*' (referring to the *sega*, or 'saw', of the Bentivoglio arms), and a triumphal parade went from the piazza to Bentivoglio's 'royal palace.'[5]

An account of the event is found in a contemporary poem that appears to have been written within a few months by an itinerant Florentine poet, Francesco Cieco, and was then printed in Bologna.[6] The book is undated but may have been printed in 1471, making it one of the earliest works published in the city, although if it was published later, it would demonstrate the continued importance of the tournament.[7] Whilst Giovanni's prominence in the poem could be read as reflecting Cieco's desire for patronage, it could also be seen as evidence of Bentivoglio's support for both the poet and the publication.[8] Another account, in prose, by the Bolognese Giovanni Sabadino degli Arienti, does not seem to have been so well received and remained in manuscript.[9] One reason for its relative lack of success may lie in the fact that Giovanni's position and role in the event were not as emphasized as in Cieco's version; in addition, it was a more chronicle-like narrative that was not as clearly related to the popular, chivalric tradition of tournament descriptions as Cieco's poem.[10] It thus shared little with the type of chivalric literature that was enjoyed by the middle classes and aristocracy in Italy during this period.[11] This formed a notable aspect of court culture in Ferrara, Milan, Mantua, and Naples, but also found an audience in a republican city like Florence.[12] The taste for such literature certainly influenced the staging of tournaments and jousts, and Cieco's presentation added further to chivalric perceptions of the Bolognese event.[13]

While the 1470 celebration was not extraordinary in the history of Renaissance festivities, it does seem to have been thought of as notable by Bolognese commentators. It is mentioned or described in contemporary Bolognese chronicles, while more routine races or contests for the *palio* of S. Petronio in other years were not.[14] It also seems to have been significant to Giovanni; by the time Cieco's poem was published the tournament had already been depicted in Giovanni's palace: 'if you do not believe it you can see it painted/ In the great palace of messer Giovanni.'[15] The recording of the tournament in separate accounts and in print and painting also gives it a significance beyond the norm. It was thus treated not as an ephemeral festivity, but as an historical event that required heroic commemoration.

The 1470 tournament in many ways encapsulates the complexities of Bologna and its 'ruler', Giovanni II Bentivoglio, at this time. First, the setting – the central piazza around which were based various institutions of the state: the Communal Palace that housed not only the oligarchical councils but also the official residence of the papal representative (as Bologna was part of the Papal States), the Palazzo del Podestà, the headquarters of the important notaries' guild, and the huge, incomplete civic basilica of S. Petronio – begun in 1388 as a proud affirmation of Bolognese independence during a period of rejection of papal rule and dedicated to their patron saint, in opposition to the cathedral of S. Pietro. Second, there is the figure of the princely ruler – not represented through his residence or site of power, but as the magnificent provider of courtly entertainment. For, although Bolognese republican/communal authorities continued to function (under papal authority) during the second half of the fifteenth century, from 1466 Giovanni Bentivoglio sat throughout the year on the most powerful government body – the *Sedici* – rather than the alternate six months on and six months off of all other members.[16] Yet his position as virtual head of state was one that required the continuing agreement of the city's leading families as well as papal confirmation, and Giovanni was by no means *signore* of Bologna at this date.

In the Bolognese tournament, however, and in the site of the event, a long-standing civic celebration was transformed into a princely manifestation in the heart of the city. Or, at least, that is the image that Giovanni wanted to be projected and remembered, as the recording of the event in printed and graphic form sought to ensure. Although Giovanni himself did not win the standard, the honour was his – the cry that went up at the end referred to his arms, and the victorious procession proceeded to his palace. The choice of this kind of tournament as the context for such a display can also be seen as deliberately courtly and chivalric, and, as Franco Cardini has defined it, part of the 'theatre of power.'[17] Tournaments and jousts were not just places of display for elite families, 'but also a way to exercise control over the elites and, at the same time, to do diplomacy.'[18] The presence of foreigners and reportage beyond the boundaries of a city were essential components of the event's construction, and ones that Giovanni Bentivoglio sought to ensure.

The Bentivoglio – Rulers of the City?

The Bentivoglio family had come to prominence and power over the course of the century during a series of bloody internecine struggles.[19] On the murder of Annibale Bentivoglio in 1445 the supporters of the Bentivoglio sought a close relative to act as head of their faction and safeguard the interests of Annibale's infant son, Giovanni. Therefore in 1446 Sante Bentivoglio, who had been raised in Florence – where he also had connections to the Medici, was persuaded to come to Bologna to act as their leader and assume the position of 'first citizen.'[20] In 1454 he married Ginevra

Sforza, illegitimate daughter of Alessandro Sforza, lord of Pesaro, and niece of Francesco Sforza, duke of Milan.[21] Sante thus had connections to two of the most powerful families and states in mid-fifteenth-century Italy – the Medici in Florence and the Sforza in Milan. This helped to create a pattern for a policy of political relationships and social rise that Giovanni, successor on Sante's death in November 1463, was to follow and develop.[22] In 1463 Francesco Sforza had intervened to aid the reinforcement of oligarchical and Bentivoglio power in Bologna through renegotiation of papal accords and sought to help bring about Giovanni's marriage to Sante's widow.[23] Giovanni, too, had ties of blood to Milan; he was the son of Donnina Visconti, niece of Filippo Maria Visconti. Giovanni also ensured that he provided strong support for the Medici over the ensuing decades.[24]

The Bentivoglio were not, however, the only leading family in Bologna during this period to seek to enhance their social position through marriages to non-Bolognese nobility and the staging of rich displays. For example, the Malvezzi, on 21 May 1464, seem to have deliberately sought to overshadow Giovanni's marriage to Ginevra Sforza, earlier that same month, with great festivities and many foreign guests for the wedding of Giulio, son of Virgilio Malvezzi, to Camilla Sforza, daughter of Count Marco Attendolo da Cotignola and niece of Francesco Sforza.[25] There was a magnificent entry into the city, along the streets of which were displayed the arms of the duke of Milan, the Malvezzi and the Bentivoglio, and a joust was held in front of Virgilio's palace (next to the Bentivoglio residence).[26] During the years 1454–63 the Malvezzi had also attempted to counter the power of the Bentivoglio by contacts with exiles and other factions.[27] Virgilio, who was of Annibale's and Sante's generation, was, in fact, second only to Giovanni in Bologna and almost as important on the national scene.[28] He and his family were close relations and supporters of Giovanni, and yet were also to some extent his rivals for power.[29] This can perhaps be seen at play in Cieco's presentation of the 1470 tournament, at a period when Giovanni and Virgilio were in conflict to some degree.[30] Two of Virgilio's sons – Giulio and Carlo – were heavily praised in the poem. It was noted that they had not spared money on their apparel 'to honour the whole city' – for example, their 'surcoats made of such beautiful work/ that they seemed lords and not subjects'; but grandiloquent comparison with rulers may perhaps have been an implicit criticism.[31] In contrast, Giovanni – through the prominence given to him by Cieco in the poem as both devisor of and participant in the tournament, including praise of the house of Bentivoglio of which Giovanni represented 'so clear a light' – was presented as de facto leader and a rightfully noble figure.[32]

The identification of Giovanni as ruler of the city was not just a piece of flattery on the part of Cieco. It was reflected in the duke of Milan's lending to him of eight horses for the tournament. Giovanni was an important military and political ally with a role to play in the politics of equilibrium in the shifting alliances and disputes of the Italian states.[33] The centrality of Bologna is suggested by the fact that there was a permanent Milanese agent based in Bologna from 1470 onwards and through the awarding of military *condotte* from 1471.[34] Galeazzo Maria himself noted in the *condotta* of 1 March 1471 that Giovanni was related to him.[35] Yet, despite the ties of blood and marriage, the relationship during the 1470s–90s became a more complicated interplay of assistance and antagonism than it may have been under Francesco Sforza (died 1466). For example, Antonio Trotti, captain of the Bolognese militia in 1470, was from Alessandria in the Milanese Duchy and, in effect, recommended by Milan.[36] Galeazzo Maria had himself been against the S. Petronio tournament – perhaps objecting to its spotlighting of Giovanni; when it could not be prevented, he sent him the eight horses. Cieco downplayed this, merely stating that 'The cloths [of Giovanni's eight horses] . . . / were of white and purple silk [i.e., Sforza colours]/ . . . with the ducal arms.'[37] He also mentioned only in passing that Borso d'Este had sent Giovanni eight horses for his pages, and Cieco ignored the fact that Giovanni's pipers had been sent by Borso and his trumpeters by Lodovico Gonzaga, as noted by Sabadino degli Arienti.[38] It could be argued that these gifts were both a mark of respect and an attempt at control, especially as the horses for Giovanni were clothed in Sforza emblems and colours and those for his pages in Este colours. The rulers in Milan, Ferrara, and Mantua wished to support Giovanni but to keep his ambitions and aspirations to greater status and power in check. Giovanni had different ideas. Indeed, Diana Webb argued that he used 'ever more elaborate *feste* . . . as one of the means by which [he] sought to make his mark on both Italian and European opinion as a prince to be reckoned with.'[39] The "official" account of the 1470 tournament thus raised Giovanni's status and de-emphasized his dependence on other rulers' kindness for the appropriately princely accompaniment of fine horses and personal, as opposed to civic, musicians.

Comparison with the Medici

The celebration of the Bologna tournament in print might also bring to mind the famous Carnival joust won by the twenty-one-year-old Lorenzo de' Medici in Piazza S. Croce in Florence in 1469, which was also recorded in a printed poem – Luigi Pulci's *La giostra di Lorenzo de Medici,* as was Lorenzo's brother Giuliano's victory in a 1475 joust.[40] In the 1469 joust in Florence, the 1470 tournament in Bologna, and the 1475 Florentine joust, the most important figure and family in each city was presented and celebrated in chivalric mode in both the event itself and printed literary form.[41] As Paolo Orvieto pointed out, in the actual events in Florence neither Lorenzo nor Giuliano were the only winners. Other participants and their entourages equalled the Medici for the splendour of their costumes.[42] There were other public events, too, that rivalled these, but they were not as effectively lauded and promoted in literary and printed form as the ones in which the Medici were so prominently involved.[43]

Although Lorenzo and Giovanni were citizens whose families had, during the earlier part of the fifteenth century, come to occupy positions of clear power, that status was not unambiguous. In Lorenzo's case he was *primus inter pares,* but he was not a *signore*. He did not even have the official status of head of government that Giovanni possessed, and his image was wrapped up in the fiction of being a 'private' citizen of the Florentine republic. Yet Lorenzo had more standing on the wider stage because of Florence's greater economic and political importance and independence. That some parity with Giovanni Bentivoglio was seen in Medicean circles, however, is indicated in a report in 1471 from Rome by Gentile Becchi, Lorenzo's tutor. Becchi had asked someone in the papal Curia how he thought Lorenzo and Giovanni compared 'being of the same age,' 'he replied that it was expected that you [Lorenzo] would surpass not messer Giovanni but Cosimo [Lorenzo's grandfather].'[44] They were not the same age, but this was, I think, more of a political comparison. In addition, the Medici and Lorenzo's status in Florence, in combination with their behind the scenes methods of influence and control, may have provided part of the model for Giovanni's rule in Bologna, especially during the 1460s and 1470s.

Lorenzo de' Medici was lauded in chivalric manner in Pulci's poem and the Medici, before and after, made use of chivalric imagery, but this was only an occasional foray into the realm of the knight and the court.[45] In this the Medici were acting within conventions that were recognized in Florence as belonging to the world of chivalry and courts but also seen as local traditions, because the chivalric mode had been used by the Florentines since the end of the fourteenth century.[46] Paolo Orvieto suggests, however, that from 1475 the military and chivalric began to be 'officially marginalized, at least as public exhibitions of the wealth and political power of powerful Florentine families' including by the Medici.[47] For Lorenzo, instead, the dominant image was of the humanist, the poet, the musician, and the civic leader, and the modes and language for those were increasingly classical.[48] The combination of the classical and chivalric modes appeared in Angelo Poliziano's very classical account of Giuliano de' Medici's chivalric victory in Florence in 1475. It is notable that Poliziano's poem – *Stanze . . . cominciate per la giostra del magnifico Giuliano di Piero de Medici* – although written in 1475 was first printed in 1494, and in Bologna not Florence. In addition, this edition of the *Stanze* was dedicated to Giovanni Bentivoglio's son Anton Galeazzo.[49] There may well have been a political aspect to its publication, for in 1494 the Medici's position in Florence was vulnerable. The Bentivoglio, despite some tensions over the years, continued to be their supporters, and in November 1494 Bologna provided a temporary haven for Piero di Lorenzo and Cardinal Giovanni de' Medici on their expulsion from Florence, despite the Florentine *signoria*'s disapproval.[50] The publication of the *Stanze* in Bologna can also be seen within the context of a contemporary interest in the publication of traditional chivalric literature in the 1480s and 1490s.[51] For Giovanni and the Bentivoglio the chivalric remained an important component of their presentation, even if it might also be adapted to the changing tastes of the time. Thus in 1490 he staged another large tournament for the feast of S. Petronio, this time, as contemporaries noted, with identifiably classical aspects to what was still, however, a chivalric contest.[52]

Giovanni II's Military, Chivalric, and Courtly Models

The chivalric interests of Giovanni were also strongly connected to his desire, from at least the 1470s and perhaps earlier, for recognition not just as first citizen but as 'signore' of Bologna. His model for this was not so much Lorenzo but the rulers of the north Italian courts – especially Milan and Ferrara. In 1470, despite Giovanni's appearance in princely guise, this was an aspiration and not a fact. Not only did he have to seek approval from the rest of the ruling council to hold the tournament, but he was not a free agent externally either. His first *condotta* had been awarded by Naples, Milan and Florence, and from 1471 till 1498 he acted as a *condottiere* for Milan, and occasionally other states, and thus was, literally, at the beck and call of others.[53] It should be noted, however, that the Gonzaga and the Este, with more claim to noble status and with greater freedom of action and resources, were often in a similar position.

The profession of military commander was one that Giovanni was proud to proclaim, following in the steps of his father, Annibale, and grandfather, Antongaleazzo.[54] Annibale's tomb in the family chapel in S. Giacomo, perhaps of c. 1445–58, depicted him on horseback carrying the baton of command.[55] Giovanni was portrayed in similar mode on the reverses of two medals by Sperandio, and his bust appeared in mail and sometimes armour on the obverses of three of the four Sperandio portrait medals of him, which were made at points between c. 1463 and the mid-1480s (Fig. 48).[56] One of Giovanni's medals referred to him as 'notable leader of soldiers.'[57] It is possible that this may have been made in relation to the 1470 tournament, or was connected with his receiving a military *condotta* (such as that from Milan in 1471) or a more specific title, rather than just a reference to military prowess. The link to 1470 is perhaps strengthened by the kind of armour represented – probably for a tournament.[58] It could be argued that the depiction with a baton of command would emphasize Giovanni's position as a leader (as he was in the tournament and in reality) rather than his personal fighting abilities; but I think that the personal, chivalric, and military are all implicit in the combination of obverse and reverse images and text.[59]

The medallic image of Giovanni on horseback not only recalled Annibale but also, as Luke Syson has shown, was a specific echo of other rulers' medals, in particular those by Pisanello of Gianfrancesco Gonzaga and Filippo Maria Visconti, as well as Sperandio's own subsequent representation of Federico da Montefeltro.[60] The construction of Giovanni's image in the medals was thus closely bound up with the chivalric mode of the knight, and he is even attended on the obverse of one medal by a page. It also recalled the equestrian statues of military leaders that had been employed not only for *condottiere,* such as Paolo Uccello's fresco of John Hawkwood in Florence cathedral (1436), but also for rulers, like the statue of Nicolò III d'Este that was placed on the main piazza in Ferrara in 1451.[61] The visual language of the *condottiere* was thus translated and associated with that of the ruler.[62]

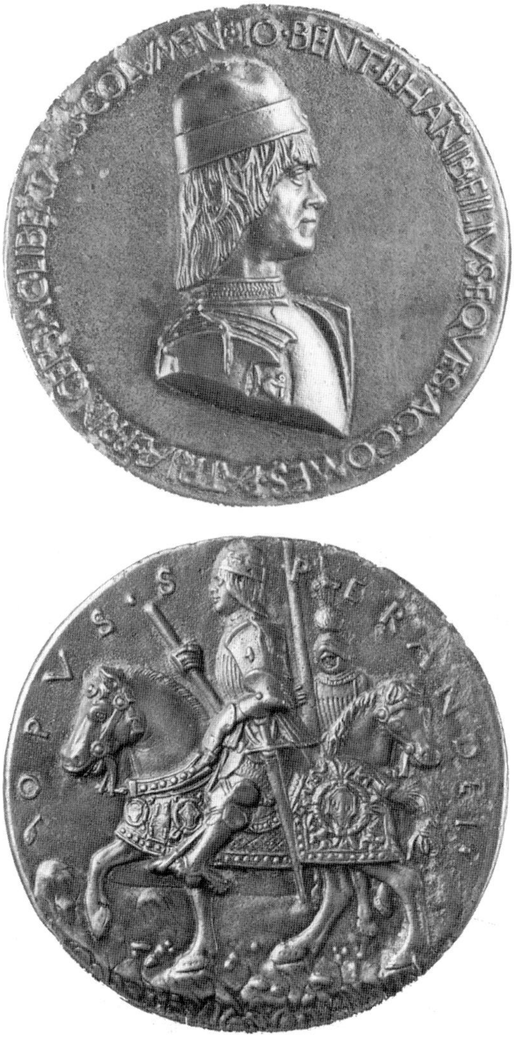

48. Sperandio, *Portrait medal of Giovanni II Bentivoglio.* Cast bronze. Oxford, Ashmolean Museum. Photo: Ashmolean Museum.

Giovanni had been made a knight by the Holy Roman Emperor Frederick III in 1452 and a Palatine count in 1461.[63] Giovanni's own creation of knights was one of the functions that he exercised on a considerable number of occasions, perhaps for the first time on his accession to power on 1 November 1463.[64] He received a further license to do so from Sixtus IV in May 1473.[65] Although those created knights by Giovanni were almost all Bolognese, it can be argued that such actions were within the sphere of the princely ruler rather than the leader of a republic. As Wendy Wegener argued, Giovanni emphasized military and chivalric imagery in the medals and other artworks, as well as in the use of his chapel as 'the setting for creating knights.'[66] Here, in 1490 Giovanni had himself and his sons depicted in armor by Lorenzo Costa in the *Triumph of Fame,* one of a set of canvases made for the chapel c. 1488–90.[67]

Giovanni's image was not exclusively military, but his artistic patronage seems to have been generally directed towards those who had worked for courtly patrons where the chivalric mode was strong. Significantly, he does not seem to have used Florentine artists to depict him or adorn his palace and chapels; instead he looked principally to the court of Ferrara.[68] The medallist Sperandio is an example of such courtly orientation. Sperandio grew up in Ferrara and had worked for Leonello d'Este in the mid-1440s, Borso throughout the 1460s, and for Ercole in 1476, while also producing work for other court rulers and maintaining contact over the years with the Gonzaga.[69] He moved to Bologna in 1478, where he was still living in 1488.[70]

Among the painters that Giovanni employed were the Ferrarese Francesco del Cossa (who may have been working in Bologna from as early as 1462, although he worked at Schifanoia for Borso d'Este c. 1469–70 and died in Bologna in 1476/7), Ercole de' Roberti (working in Bologna by 1473 and again c. 1482–6, before returning to Ferrara), and Lorenzo Costa (in Bologna by 1483 and until 1506).[71] Since all three painters also worked for the Este, their employment could be seen as a deliberate attempt by Giovanni to emulate the rulers of Ferrara. In the case of Roberti, however, his earliest identified paintings appear to have been produced in Francesco del Cossa's workshop in Bologna, although those for Giovanni may have postdated work for the Este in Ferrara.

But why did Giovanni look to Ferrara? The two neighbouring states of Bologna and Ferrara both had important roles to play within the political geography of fifteenth-century Italy and its rival power blocks. Although the papacy had a legal claim on Ferrara, the Este family had established signorial rule – perhaps an obvious model for another aspiring ruler within the papal states.[72] Giovanni Bentivoglio was keen to affirm dynastic succession in Bologna and managed to acquire confirmation of his eldest son Annibale's right to this from Sixtus IV in 1474.[73] In 1478 Annibale was betrothed to Ercole d'Este's illegitimate daughter Lucrezia, whom he married in 1487.[74] This Bentivoglio-Este marriage affirmed the Bentivoglio's social and political standing, but also built on the friendly relationship between Giovanni and Ercole in the 1470s and 1480s.[75] Perhaps, therefore, Giovanni's artistic choices were personal as well as reflecting the prestige of Ferrara.

Bentivoglio Urban and Architectural Interventions

It would be simplistic to view Giovanni Bentivoglio as merely attempting to create a signoria from a republic. The relationship between Giovanni and the Bolognese was complex, and there were perceived benefits for many in his status and attempts to reinforce the independent power and prestige of Bologna.[76]

One of the areas in which both the interests of Bentivoglio and of the city as a whole were advanced was that of urban improvement.[77] In 1470, for example, it is recorded that in August 'the magnificent messer Giovanni [Bentivoglio] with the *reggimento* ordered the paving with brick of the piazza of Porta Ravegnana,' and on 30 August the Bolognese treasury agreed to pay for it, although the drapers – one of the leading guilds whose headquarters were on the piazza – were obliged to maintain the space in perpetuity.[78] This piazza was one of the most important in the city and had six principal roads radiating from it, two of which (Strà Maggiore and Strà S. Stefano) were regularly used for ceremonial entries into the city, one (Strà S. Donato, now Via Zamboni) led to the Bentivoglio palace and one (the Mercato di Mezzo) towards the civic and religious centres, while on the south it joins with the piazza in front of the Loggia della Mercanzia (the Carrobbio). Although the paving of the piazza can be seen as part of a longer-term programme of street improvement, the decision to pave at this particular date is likely to have been connected with the forthcoming October tournament.[79] Given its location, the enhancement of this piazza was both to the advantage of the city and Giovanni: it was seen and passed through by many, if not most, visitors to the city, and certainly those who proceeded on to the Palazzo Bentivoglio down Strà S. Donato.

From the 1470s onwards there was a gradual increase in Giovanni's presence and involvement in architectural and urbanistic projects. At the beginning, though, the most important project for him was the construction of the Palazzo Bentivoglio. In November 1463, on the death of Sante, Giovanni took over the great palace which Sante had started to construct in March 1460 and which was already described by a contemporary chronicler as a 'palace royally begun.'[80] Little is known of work on the palace in the 1460s and 1470s, but the fact that Giovanni took it over, just as he also acquired Sante's wife, is significant. Not only was the palace in the area traditionally inhabited by the Bentivoglio family, but Giovanni ensured that it became his residence – that of the Bentivoglio in power – rather than part of Sante's estate.[81] Giovanni's claim to it was based on the assertion that Sante had come to Bologna from Florence in 1446 owning no property in Bologna and had occupied the house of their ancestors, and more specifically that belonging to Giovanni's father Annibale.[82] The acquisition of a considerable site for the new palace, partly in Giovanni's name, had begun by 1448.[83] In February 1475 Giovanni stated that by Sante's death in November 1463 only the walls of the new palace had been built and had been worth less than 15,000 lire bolognesi but that work under Giovanni meant that it was now worth more than 30,000 lire.[84] Whether this amount was entirely accurate or not, it shows that in the eleven and a half years since he had come to occupy and develop his preeminent position in the city Giovanni had invested considerably in the palace and that it was central to his self-image, just as it had been for Sante.[85]

Sante's architect in 1460 was Pagno di Lapo Portigiani from Fiesole, who had worked at the Palazzo Medici from 1448–51.[86] A number of the stonemasons working in Bologna were from Florence and its environs, but the choice by Sante, a Medici partisan, of one who had worked on the Medici palace may well have been deliberate.[87] The Bentivoglio palace was destroyed in 1507, so it is not possible to make specific or stylistic comparisons of the two buildings. From some rough sketches of the façade in chronicles and other information, it is known that the exterior of the Bentivoglio palace was constructed mostly of brick and a portico ran the length of the ground floor of the main façade – common features of Bolognese architecture.[88] Crenellations topped the façade, which were a feature of prestigious fourteenth-century Bolognese palaces as well as the architecture of power – like the

Palazzo Comunale. Yet the portico gave a more open and apparently less defensive aspect than, for example, the sheer façade of the Palazzo Pepoli – the palace of a family that had ruled Bologna for a period in the mid–fourteenth century.

The architectural language adopted by the Bentivoglio in their palace presented them as citizens rather than princes, in contrast to the castle architecture of the main residences of the Sforza, Este, or Gonzaga, although the size of the Palazzo Bentivoglio showed quite clearly that the family was *primus inter pares*.[89] While there may perhaps have been "Florentine" aspects to the palace – possibly in some *all'antica* details or in the regular, porticoed courtyards – it was clearly Bolognese in materials and idiom. There is a parallel here with Medici creation of parity and difference. The palace that Cosimo built in Florence was notable for its size, expense, and prominence; the materials and architectural language drew on trecento Florentine traditions, and yet there were also subtle shifts, new *all'antica* 'accents' and the use of architectural forms with political implications.[90] The Medici palace was also used for enacting "official" business by Cosimo, Piero, and Lorenzo and, like the Bentivoglio palace, was thus a destination for ceremonial processions through the city.[91] Both the Medici and the Bentivoglio in the mix of conformity to local models with innovation and outside influences in their palace architecture were following a similar pattern to their adoption and transformation of the traditions and forms of public celebrations, such as the jousts and tournament.

If the Bentivoglio palace is lost, a very specific relationship to a Medicean architectural model is evident in the family chapel. This had been acquired by Giovanni's father Annibale in S. Giacomo, diagonally opposite the Palazzo Bentivoglio, just before his murder in 1445. The chapel was rebuilt by either Sante or Giovanni but, while the date and attribution of the design are uncertain, its basic form is that of the Old Sacristy in S. Lorenzo, Florence.[92] This was, therefore, the design that had been used for the Medici family chapel, and its adoption by the Bentivoglio may well have been a deliberate reflection of that choice.[93] Marvin Trachtenberg has argued that in the Medici's own transformation of earlier architectural models for the Old Sacristy they were seeking to 'veil the blunt reference to the princely monument of the north Italian autocracy' and 'disguised the spatial scheme of [the Padua Baptistery] in the stylistic garb of Florence . . . (a harbinger of the shift toward the north-Italian style of political autocracy well-exemplified in Padua that the Medici would impose within a few years).'[94] So perhaps similar arguments can be adduced for the Bentivoglio chapel, with the added layer of specific reference to the Medici as their political allies, models, and even rivals.

If the association of some of the basic architectural forms of the Bentivoglio chapel was with the Old Sacristy, and as Trachtenberg suggests with the private magnificence that the Medici chapel represented, its placement within the church and its decoration were very different.[95] The Bentivoglio chapel is neither an almost independent, closed, architectural structure entered from one corner through a small door, nor was it a sacristy, nor is an architectural order and detailing used as the primary means of articulation and decoration – all features of the Old Sacristy. Instead it is an ambulatory chapel with one wall open to the church so that the interior and altar are visible from outside. In addition, it is placed so that the chapel is conspicuous, as it can be seen immediately on entering S. Giacomo. Its internal architectural organization relates as much to the Paduan Baptistery, with the altar space taking up one side of the chapel separated from the main space by two columns supporting round arches with a higher central arch all within the lower zone of the wall, rather than the Old Sacristy's high serliana supported by pilasters cutting into the upper zone of the wall, and closed side rooms. Like the Baptistery, the walls and vault of the Bentivoglio chapel are filled with figurative decoration, although they work within and with the architecture and space rather than denying these as in the Baptistery – for example, the scenes on the side walls of the chapel are set within fictive architectural arcades. It is thus not a straightforward imitation of the Old Sacristy nor of the Paduan Baptistery, yet elements of both are present and recognizable. In this the Bentivoglio chapel is comparable to the Portinari chapel built at S. Eustorgio in Milan c. 1464–8.[96] Here Pigello Portinari, the Florentine resident branch manager of the Medici Bank, paid homage to Florence and the Medici, but transformed the Old Sacristy by a re-visioning of the chapel in a more local, Lombard architectural guise. In addition, he opened up one wall and made the chapel part of a complex, as well as commissioning a radically different decorative treatment of the interior.

In S. Giacomo, as in the Portinari chapel, a fundamental difference from the Old Sacristy lies in the use of a rich, decorative programme that also changes the viewer's perception and recognition of the architectural space. In the Bentivoglio chapel, alongside religious iconography on the altar wall and in the upper zones, Costa's canvases on the side walls depict dynastic and courtly aspirations, with Giovanni, Ginevra, and their children before the Virgin and Child enthroned, Giovanni and his sons in armour, as well as Ginevra and at least some of their daughters, in the *Triumph of Fame*. Such decoration perhaps recalls a ducal chapel, like Ercole d'Este's Cappella della Corte in the Este castle in Ferrara that included a portrait of duchess Eleonora and her daughter Isabella.[97] Perhaps, too, there was a connection with the decoration of ducal chapels in Pavia or Milan, but too little evidence for these survives.

The Bentivoglio chapel's decoration in the 1480s should perhaps be seen as part of a larger project on the part of Giovanni connected with the construction of a portico alongside S. Giacomo (1477–81), work on the adjoining Bentivoglio chapel

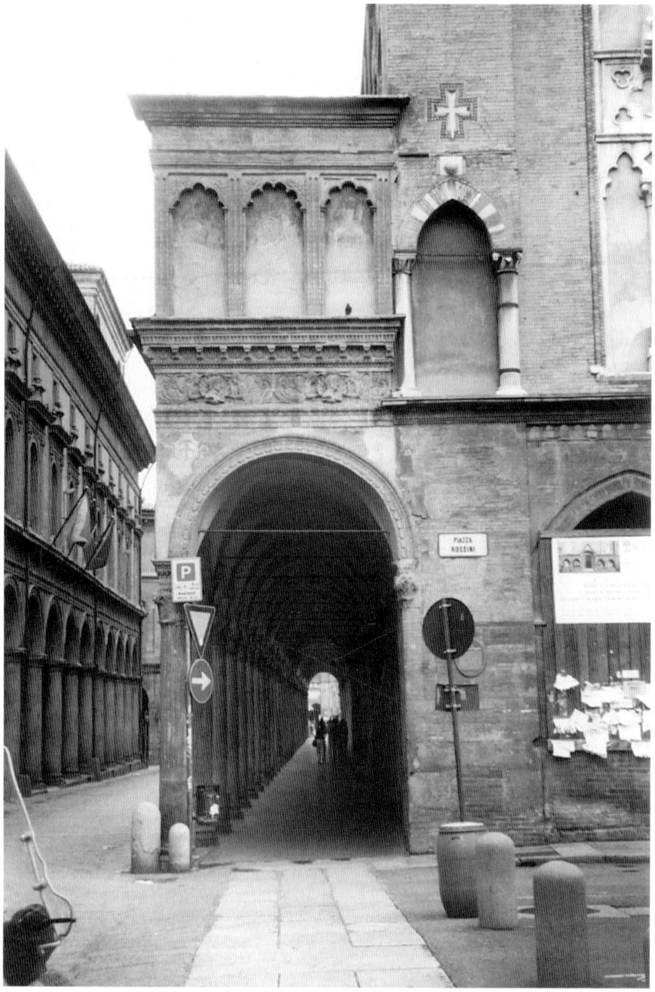

49. Portico of S. Giacomo, Bologna. Photo: Author.

of S. Cecilia in the 1480s and 1490s, and the improvement of Strà S. Donato, also in the 1480s and 1490s (Fig. 49).[98] So, too, the Medici had taken a prominent role in the enlargement of their parish church – S. Lorenzo – and enhancement of the surrounding area, and had achieved this through direct action and pressure on and involvement of other prominent families.[99]

Yet, in public terms, Giovanni was careful at first to operate within boundaries of consensus and cooperation on the architectural and political fronts. The proposal to build the new, up-to-date *all'antica* portico at S. Giacomo (1477–81) appears in the documents as a decision of the ruling council, but the 1478 inscription states that action to restore the portico at public expense was taken and overseen by Giovanni Bentivoglio and Virgilio Malvezzi.[100] Virgilio Malvezzi's involvement was

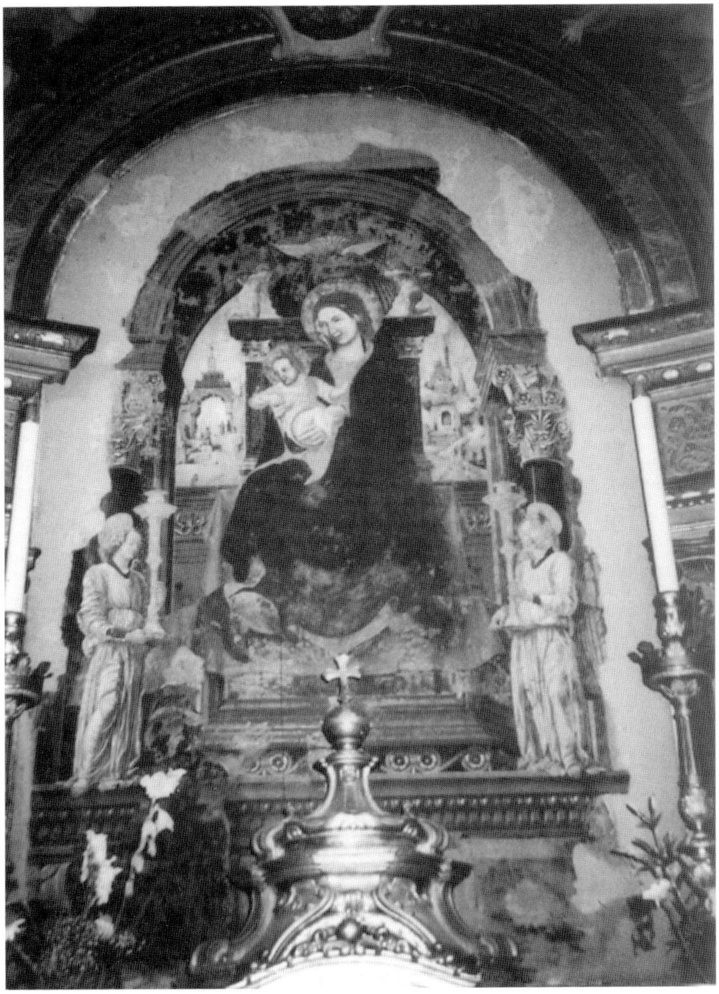

50. Lippo di Dalmasia(presumed) and Francesco del Cossa, *Madonna del Baraccano*. Fresco. Bologna, S. Maria del Baraccano. Photo: Author.

important – not only was his palace directly opposite the portico, but his standing both in the city and outside it was extremely high. In 1479 Sperandio made a portrait medal of Virgilio on which he was referred to as 'glory of the Bolognese fatherland and guardian of liberty' and on the reverse was depicted an allegory of vigilance.[101] This matched the terms in which Giovanni wished to be seen in relation to the city. Indeed, Giovanni was dependent on Virgilio's goodwill for his continued rule, but the relationship was not always one of agreement.[102] The unity that the portico project suggested was, therefore, as expressive as the act of neighbourhood piety and city enhancement that it also represented. At the same time, Giovanni was presented in the inscription, which faced those coming from the city centre, as the most important of the two: 'Giovanni Bentivoglio the Younger, notable knight and leader of the Bolognese Senate,' whereas Virgilio was referred to only by name.[103]

A reminder of the importance and visibility of projects like the portico can be found in Cieco's poem. Both before and after the tournament he notes how the *bianchi* gathered at Giovanni's palace, and how, accompanied by musicians and with wonderfully arrayed pages on horseback, they processed from it through the streets to the Piazza Maggiore. This reference to processional movement through the city emphasizes the importance of streets as places of display – here enhanced by the rich attire of humans and horses, as often also with temporary adornment of hangings and canopies. Permanent enhancement of the city with the construction of new stone or brick porticoes, replacing old wooden ones, would become a particular feature of palace building, renewal, and urban improvement campaigns in the 1480s and 1490s – especially along important ceremonial routes. One of these routes was that from the civic centre to Giovanni's palace that passed the S. Giacomo portico. In addition, at the time of the 1470 tournament and on many other ceremonial occasions, the temporary and permanent articulation of the city's streets highlighted the Bentivoglio palace as a point of destination and departure that equalled the civic centre of the Piazza Maggiore.

The connection, though, was one of mutual dependence, for the Bentivoglio also connected their image and fortunes with those of the city, as in the 1470s or early 1480s diptych portrait of Giovanni and Ginevra set against views of Bologna.[104] The presentation of the Bentivoglio as Bolognese and as defenders of Bologna's traditions and of the city itself was reinforced by Giovanni's 1472 commission of Francesco del Cossa to "repair" the earlier fresco of the Madonna del Baraccano (Fig. 50).[105] This was a miracle-working Virgin to whom the Bentivoglio had been attached since it manifested its miraculous powers in 1402 in relation to Giovanni II's great-grandfather, Giovanni I.[106] It was also at this site that Giovanni II's father, Annibale, had secretly entered the city in 1443 to return Bologna to the rule of the Bolognese – and in the process establish Bentivoglio prominence. In addition, wax or silver votive figures, especially, it seems, of the Bentivoglio, were placed at the shrine.[107] Cossa added the kneeling figures on each side as well as the angels – the man on the left may be Giovanni I – an inscription underneath proclaimed 'Giovanni Bentivoglio lord of Bologna' – a reference to Giovanni I and implicitly to Giovanni II.[108] The Baraccano Madonna was thus literally reframed and appropriated by Giovanni II.

Giovanni II and the City of Bologna

That Giovanni wished to identify himself with the protection of the city is also evident in beneficial clauses in the military *condotte* that Giovanni agreed with Milan.[109] In 1471 it was specified that the troops he would provide could also be used for the defense of Bologna. Subsequently it was stated that any Bolognese territories he recaptured should be returned to Bologna and not go to the duke. In the renewal of 1481, it was agreed that the archers amongst the troops could be used as Giovanni's personal guard. This marked not only a shift towards a more princely demeanour but also an astute financial move, because it meant that the Milanese rather than Giovanni or the Commune paid for these troops.[110] Giovanni's status, and perceptions of him, was most markedly changed with the gift to him in Milan on 1 January 1480 of several feudal Lombard titles – the lordships of Covo, Antignano, and Pizzighettone.[111] On his return to Bologna 'our lord [Giovanni] now began to be called lord, both for the lands he had acquired and even for the dominion that he had over this city and all the government he had in his hands.'[112]

Giovanni's self-presentation was thus a skilful blend of ostentatious and discrete, present and absent – sometimes perhaps acting through others, or having supporters in control of important projects (just as Lorenzo de' Medici often proceeded).[113] Giovanni seems to have concentrated in the 1470s on private, family, and neighbourhood interventions, gradually extending his presence outwards from Bentivoglio domains into other parts of the city from the late 1470s onwards – via artistic, architectural, and political means. He made use of the tools of the prince in his encouragement and staging of events like the 1470 and 1490 tournaments, but he also had to maintain the traditions and customs of the republic.

Situating Bologna

The cultural enterprises of Giovanni and his family reflect a complicated blending and balancing of Bolognese traditions with courtly, Ferrarese, Florentine, Medicean and *all'antica* elements. These references and tastes do not seem to have totally dominated Bolognese culture, for the Bentivoglio court represented one significant aspect of Bologna, but there were other important constituents (such as the university).

It can be argued that Giovanni's sophisticated adoption and adaptation of traditions, styles, and cultural references was part of a broader, cultural balancing act undertaken in many parts of Italy in the late fifteenth and early sixteenth centuries. One, small, example stands as a suggestive illustration of this larger enterprise. In Bologna in 1497 was published a version of the anonymous *Il libro chiamato Buovo di Antona*.[114] This was a tale that had originated in France but which had taken on independent lives in Italy from the fourteenth century onwards – in Veneto-Padano verse, Tuscan prose, Tuscan verse, and Emilian verse.[115] This 1497 edition marked a change from the Padano verse of the edition published in Bologna in 1480, for it looked back not only to the earlier French and courtly models but also to the Florentine Luigi Pulci's almost contemporary *Morgante* (written and being read by August 1478).[116] Daniela Delcorno Branca argued that this version of the *Buovo d'Antona* was consciously written so as to appear to be by a Tuscan author, at least to the eyes of a northern Italian audience. Yet, would every member of a northern Italian or Bolognese audience have been unaware of the non-Tuscan aspects? Was the rewriting and publication of *Buovo di Antona* an attempt at being Tuscan or Florentine, and thus an only partly successful attempt to take on another's guise? Or was it a more subtle and knowing masquerade that was part of the creation and manifestation of a recognizably different artistic and cultural voice? So, too, the Bolognese Giovanni Sabadino degli Arienti in *Le Porretane* of the 1490s translated Boccaccio's *Decameron* from the Arno valley to the Bolognese spa of the Bagni di Porretana as part of a broader contemporary literary enterprise to forge a Bolognese vernacular.[117] So, too, in the 1480s and 1490s, with the works of Costa and the Bolognese Francesco Francia (c. 1447–1517), it might be argued that here was the beginning of a distinctive local painting style that was not dependent on Ferrarese examples, and this was one perhaps promoted by the Bentivoglio.

Sabadino's work, like the work of painters in Bologna, and Giovanni Bentivoglio's artistic and architectural commissions and interventions, as well as his political modus operandi, were not acts of copying, but ones of transformative imitation. The ability to read, translate, and combine diverse models to create new, local, coherent, and identifiable styles and forms represents an act of emulation rather than submission to a cultural norm imposed from without.

NOTES

1. For example, Giacomo di Marco, *Chronicle (1445–71)*, Biblioteca dell'Archiginnasio: Bologna (hereafter AGB), B.1648, cc. 20v–1r, 23r; Francesco Cieco, *Descrizione del gran torneamento di M. Giovanni Bentivoglio di Bologna* (Bologna: s.a) [the text is unnumbered and has no printing marks – my numbering for stanzas]; Giovanni Sabadino degli Arienti, *Il torneo fatto in Bologna il IV ottobre* MCCCCLXX, ed. Antonio Zambiagi (Parma: 1888); Giacomo di Antonio Poggi, *Cronaca (1442–93)*, Biblioteca Universitaria di Bologna (hereafter BUB), ms. 1491, cc. 18r–19r; Fileno della Tuate (or Tua), *Historia*, BUB: ms. 1439, c. 337r; Fileno della Tuate (or Tua), *Sustanziosa narrativa*, BUB: ms. 1438, c. 195v; Giovanni Gozzadini, *Memoria per la vita di Giovanni II Bentivoglio* (Bologna: 1839), 12–17; Lodovico Frati, *La vita privata di Bologna dal secolo xiii al xviii* (Bologna: 1900), 156–7; Albano Sorbelli, *I primordi della stampa in Bologna. Baldassare Azzoguidi* (Bologna: 1908), 139–49; Giacomo Borselli, *Cronica gestorum ac factorum memorabilium civitatis Bononiae*, ed. Albano Sorbelli, *Rerum Italicarum Scriptores*, 2nd ser. (henceforth *RIS*^{2}), XXIII, 2 (Città di Castello: Scipione Lapi, 1911–29), 101; Cherubino Ghirardacci, *Della historia di Bologna parte terza*, ed. Albano Sorbelli, *RIS*^{2}, XXXIII, 1 (Città di Castello: Scipione Lapi, 1915–32), 203–6; Cecilia Ady, *The Bentivoglio of Bologna* (Oxford: Oxford University Press, 1937), 170; Marina Calore, *Bologna a teatro. Vita di una città attraverso i suoi spettacoli 1400–1500* (Bologna: Guidicini e Rosa, 1977), 14; Fulvio Pezzarossa, '"Ad honore et laude del nome Bentivoglio": La letteratura della festa nel secondo quattrocento', in *'Bentivolorum magnificentia'. Principe e cultura a Bologna nel rinascimento*, ed. Bruno Basile (Rome: Bulzoni, 1984), 45–55, 108. Cieco, *Descrizione*, 5: 'Per honorar la fasta di tal sancto/ Petronio nostro.'

2. On Trotti, see Umberto Dallari, 'Carteggio tra i Bentivoglio e gli Estensi dal 1401 al 1542 esistente nell'Archivio di Stato in Modena', *Atti e memorie della R. Deputazione di Storia Patria per le Provincie di Romagna*, 3, 18 (1900), 21, n. 4; Lorenzo de' Medici, *Lettere*, 7 vols., ed. Nicolai Rubinstein and others (Florence: Giunti, 1977–), vol. III, 400 n. 16; *Dispacci sforzeschi da Napoli*, 4 vols. (1 gennaio—26 dicembre 1461), ed. Francesco Storti (Naples: Carlone Editore, 1999), vol. IV, 21, n. 5.

3. Ady, *The Bentivoglio*, 170. For the horses, Cieco, *Descrizione*, 140–5; Sabadino degli Arienti, *Il torneo*, 23–5, 27–35. It was not unusual for horses to be lent for tournaments, jousts, and palii, often as a political or diplomatic gift, Michael Mallett, 'Horse-Racing and Politics in Lorenzo's Florence', in *Lorenzo the Magnificent. Culture and Politics*, ed. Michael Mallet and Nicholas Mann (London: Warburg Institute, 1996), 253–62; Thomas Tuohy, *Herculean Ferrara. Ercole d'Este (1471–1505) and the Invention of a Ducal Capital* (Cambridge: Cambridge University Press, 1996), 241, 254.

4. Cieco, *Descrizione*, 143, 160–1; Ady, *The Bentivoglio*, 170.

5. Cieco, *Descrizione*, 23: 'palazo reale.'

6. In the penultimate stanza (408) the author identifies himself as Francesco, born blind in Florence and now living in Cento. See Giuseppe Frasso, 'Un poeta improvisatore nella "familia" del cardinale Francesco Gonzaga: Francesco Cieco da Firenze', *Italia medievale e umanistica* 20 (1977): 395–400; Pezzarossa, '"Ad honore"', 49.

7. Sorbelli, *I primordi*, 43–5, 139–49; Pezzarossa, '"Ad honore"', 49; Mario Fanti and Anna Maria Scardovi, 'Moduli a stampa del quattrocento bolognese nella Biblioteca dell'Archiginnasio', *L'Archiginnasio* 82 (1987): 49.

8. A manuscript copy, BUB: ms. 604, is illuminated with the Bentivoglio arms, Frati, *La vita*, 156, n. 2; Sorbelli (*I primordi*, 148–9) identifies it as BUB: App. ms. 876; Pezzarossa, '"Ad honore"', 49, n. 33; Carolyn James, *Giovanni Sabadino degli Arienti: A Literary Career* (Florence: Olschki, 1996), 39, 41, 43.

9. James, *Giovanni Sabadino*, 37–44.

10. Ibid., 44, 50.

11. For example, Francesco Foffano, *Il poema cavalleresco dal xv al xviii secolo* (Milan: F. Vallardi, 1904); Amadeo Quondam, 'La letteratura in tipografia', in *Letteratura italiana. Le opere*, 4 vols., ed. Alberto Asor Rosa (Turin: Einaudi, 1993), vol. II, 599–601.

12. For example, Giulio Bertoni, *La biblioteca estense e la cultura ferrarese ai tempi del duca Ercole I d'Este (1471–1505)* (Turin: Loescher, 1903), 69–93; Foffano, 'Il poema', 4–5; Giulio Bertoni, 'La biblioteca di Borso d'Este', *Atti della reale Accademia delle Scienze di Torino* 61 (1925–26): 400–2 – inventory of 1467–8; Elisabeth Pellegrin, *La Bibliothèque des Visconti et des Sforza, Ducs de Milan, au XVe siècle* (Paris: C.N.R.S., 1955), passim, 1426 inventory; Joanna Woods-Marsden, 'French Chivalric Myth and Mantuan Political Reality in the *Sala del Pisanello*', *Art History* 8 (1985): 397–412; Cecil H. Clough, 'Chivalry and Magnificence in the Golden Age of the Italian Renaissance', in *Chivalry in the Renaissance*, ed. Sydney Anglo (Rochester, N.Y.: Boydell Press, 1990), 33–5, 39–40, 41, 44, 45; F. W. Kent, 'An Early Reference to Luigi Pulci's Morgante (August 1478)', *Rinascimento*, 2nd ser., 33 (1993), 209–11; Tuohy, *Herculean Ferrara*, 246–57.

13. Roger S. Loomis, 'Arthurian Influence on Sport and Spectacle', in *Arthurian Literature in the Middle Ages. A Collaborative History*, ed. Loomis (Oxford: Clarendon Press, 1959), 553–9; Tuohy, *Herculean Ferrara*, 248–51.

14. On festivities in Bologna, Frati, *La vita*; Calore, *Bologna*; Pezzarossa, '"Ad honore"', 35–113.

15. Cieco, *Descrizione,* 387–8: 'Se non lo credi tu lo vedrai depinto/ Nel gran palazo di messer giova[n]ni.' Reference seems to have been made in the mid-1490s (although evidence for this date is uncertain) to this painted depiction of the 'first' of Giovanni's tournaments, Ghirardacci, *Della historia,* 371–2; Giovanni Gozzadini, *Delle torri gentilizie di Bologna e delle famiglie alle quali prima appartennero* (Bologna: 1875), 155.

16. On Bolognese government, Paolo Colliva, 'Bologna dal XIV al XVIII secolo: "governo misto" o signoria senatoria?', in *Storia dell'Emilia Romagna,* ed. Aldo Berselli, 3 vols. (Bologna: 1977), vol. II, 13–34; Angela De Benedictis, 'Quale "corte" per quale "signoria"? A proposito di organizzazione e immagine del potere durante la preminenza di Giovanni II Bentivoglio', in *Bentivolorum magnificentia,* 13–33; Angela De Benedictis, *Repubblica per contratto. Bologna: una città europea nello Stato della Chiesa* (Bologna: Il Mulino, 1995); Angela De Benedictis, 'Tra "affratellamento comunitario" e "commensualità rituale". La "condotta di vita" dei cittadini di governo tra '400 e '500', in *L'architettura a Bologna nel Rinascimento (1460–1550): centro o periferia?,* ed. Maurizio Ricci (San Giorgio di Piano: Minerva, 2001), 17–27. On oligarchic and aristocratic government within the papal states, Bandino G. Zenobi, *Le 'ben regolate città.' Modelli politici nel governo delle periferie pontificie in età moderna* (Rome: Bulzoni, 1994), 41–2.

17. 'Il teatro delle armi e delle insegne è prima di tutto teatro del potere', see Franco Cardini, 'Il torneo nelle feste ceremoniali di corte', *Quaderni di teatro,* 7.25 (1984), 9–19 (p. 15); Elena Povoledo, 'Le Théatre de Tournoi en Italie pendant la Renaissance', in *Le Lieu théatral à la Renaissance,* 2nd ed., ed. Jean Jacquot (Paris: Centre National de la Recherche Scientifique, 1968^2), 95–104; Clough, 'Chivalry', 30–5.

18. Cardini, 'Il torneo', 15.

19. Ady, *The Bentivoglio,* 1–30.

20. Ibid., 31–7; Ottavio Banti, 'Bentivoglio, Sante', in *Dizionario biografico degli Italiani* (henceforth DBI), 58 vols. (Rome: Istituto della Enciclopedia italiana, 1960–), vol. VIII, 641–2.

21. Banti, 'Bentivoglio', 643; Pezzarossa, '"Ad honore"', 110.

22. Banti, 'Bentivoglio', 642, 643; Gaspare De Caro, 'Bentivoglio, Giovanni II', in *DBI,* VIII, 623–4; De Benedictis, 'Quale "corte"', 14.

23. Ady, *The Bentivoglio,* 60–2, 137–9; Filippo de Bosdari, 'I primordi della Signoria di Giovanni II Bentivoglio a Bologna (1463–1477)', *Atti e memorie della Deputazione di Storia Patria per le Provincie di Romagna,* n.s. 3 (1951–3), 187–9; De Caro, 'Bentivoglio, Giovanni II', 623–4; Raffaele Belvederi, 'I Bentivoglio e i Malvezzi a Bologna negli anni 1463–1506', *Annali della Facoltà di Magistero dell'Università di Bari* 6 (1967): 42.

24. Ady, *The Bentivoglio,* 63, 68–70, 112, 117, 119.

25. For example, Tuate, BUB: ms. 1438: 191r–v; Borselli, *Cronica,* 97; *Corpus chronicorum bononiensium,* ed. Albano Sorbelli, *RIS*[2] 18.1.4. (Bologna: Scipione Lapi, 1924–30), 322; Lodovico Frati, *Costumanze e pompe nuziali bolognesi nel Medio Evo* (Nozze Cian-Sappa-Flandinet. Bergamo: 1894), 5–6; Calore, *Bologna,* 10; Lorenzo de' Medici, *Lettere,* vol. II, 254.

26. Frati, *Costumanze,* 5.

27. Belvederi, 'I Bentivoglio', 46.

28. For example, Ghirardacci, *Della historia,* 170, 174; Fubini, *Lorenzo,* 254.

29. Virgilio's mother was Giovanna, daughter of Giovanni I Bentivoglio, Giovanni II's great-grandfather. See De Caro, 'Bentivoglio, Giovanni II', 623; Belvederi, 'I Bentivoglio', 61–2; De Benedictis, 'Quale "corte"', 14, 23, and 26. According to Banti, 'Bentivoglio', 643, Virgilio favoured Giovanni over Sante.

30. On Virgilio's opposition to Giovanni in 1470–1, Belvederi, 'I Bentivoglio', 62.

31. Cieco, *Descrizione,* 125–35, 271–2, 298, 369, 127: 'sopraveste facte a si bellopre/ che parean signore e non vasalli,' 130: 'per far honor a tutta la cita.'

32. Cieco, *Descrizione,* 4, 23–7, 137–8, 155–63, 169–93, 196–201, 409, and passim, 138: 'si chiaro lume.'

33. Ady, *The Bentivoglio,* 2, 64–88; De Caro, 'Bentivoglio, Giovanni II', 624–5; Wendy J. Wegener, 'Mortuary Chapels of Renaissance *Condottieri*' (unpublished Ph.D. diss., Princeton University, 1989), 181; De Benedictis, *Repubblica,* 137–56.

34. Ady, *The Bentivoglio,* 66, 75.

35. Pier Luigi Perazzini, 'La cappella Bentivoglio in S. Giacomo Maggiore alla luce di nuovi documenti', *Strenna storica bolognese,* 49 (1999), 371, n. 39, citing Archivio di Stato di Ferrara: Arch. Bentivoglio: lib. 9: n. 36: 'dichiarandolo suo affine, e congionto di sangue'; Ady, *The Bentivoglio,* 74–7; Francesca Bocchi, 'Un fonte di reddito dei Bentivoglio: le condotte militari', *Atti e memorie della Deputazione di Storia Patria per le Provincie di Romagna,* n.s. 20 (1969): 430–1. Giovanni's mother was Donnina Visconti, niece of Filippo Maria Visconti, and his wife, Ginevra Sforza, was a first cousin of Galeazzo Maria Sforza.

36. A letter to the Bolognese government from Milan, 29 January 1468, thanking them for the *condotta* awarded to Trotti and that previously awarded to Giacomo Rossi (leader of one of the squads in the 1470 tournament), Maria N. Covini, *L'esercito del duca: organizazzione militare e istituzioni al tempo degli Sforza (1450–1480)* (Rome: Istituto storico italiano per il Medioevo, 1998), 297, n. 70.

37. Cieco, *Descrizione,* 144: 'Le sopraveste . . . / eran di seta biancha e di morella/ . . . all'arme ducal.'

38. Sabadino degli Arienti, *Il torneo,* 32–3; Cieco, *Descrizione,* 147.

39. Diana Webb, *Patrons and Defenders. The Saints in the Italian City-States* (London and New York: Tauris Academic Studies, 1996), 216.

40. Luigi Pulci, *La giostra di Lorenzo de Medici messa in rima da Luigi de Pulci anno MCCCCLXVIIII,* s. l., s. a.; Clough, 'Chivalry', 30–2; Paolo Orvieto, 'Carnevale e feste fiorentine del tempo di Lorenzo de' Medici', in *Lorenzo il Magnifico e il suo tempo,* ed. Gian Carlo Garfagnini (Florence: Olschki, 1992), 113–14; Paola Ventrone, 'Feste e spettacoli nella Firenze di Lorenzo il Magnifico', in *Le tems revient. 'l tempo si rinuova. Feste e spettacoli nella Firenze di Lorenzo il Magnifico,* ed. Paola Ventrone (Cinisello Balsamo: Silvana, 1992), 21, 22, 28–9; Nerida Newbigin, 'Piety and Politics in the *Feste* of Lorenzo's Florence', in *Lorenzo il Magnifico e il suo mondo* ed. Garfagnini, 32–3.

41. Pulci, *La giostra*; Cieco, *Descrizione*; Ventrone, 'Feste', 28–9; Paola Ventrone, 'Lorenzo's *Politica festiva*', in *Lorenzo the Magnificent,* ed. Mallett and Mann, 110; Newbigin, 'Piety', 34.

42. Orvieto, 'Carnevale', 113–15; Newbigin, 'Piety', 32–5, Lorenzo's *ricordi,* written in 1472, note his own success, 33 and n. 49.

43. André Rochon, *La Jeunesse de Laurent de Médicis (1449–1478)* (Paris: Société d'édition "Les Belles Lettres", 1963), 258; Orvieto, 'Carnevale', 115–16; Newbigin, 'Piety', 33–5.

44. Letter, 14 February 1471, Rochon, *La Jeunesse,* 128, n. 346: 'chome intendeva voi somigliassi il suo messer [Giovanni] Bentivogli, essendo d'una età. Rispuse non che messer Giovanni ma s'aspectava che voi superassi Cosimo'; Richard C. Trexler, *Public Life in Renaissance Florence* (Ithaca, N.Y., and London: Cornell University Press, 1980), 439.

45. For example, in the armed equestrian display in front of the Palazzo Medici in 1459 and the joust of 1469, Ventrone, 'Feste', 28; Paola Ventrone, 'I caratteri della cerimonialità cortese', in *Le tems revient,* 147–8; Paola Ventrone, 'La giostra 'romanza' di Lorenzo del 1469', in *Le tems revient,* 167–8; Ventrone, 'Lorenzo's *Politica festiva*', 109–11. Orvieto, 'Carnevale', 111–13, argues that chivalric

and courtly elements began to disappear, 'o Lorenzo vuole che scompaiono', in festivities and ceremonies from around 1476.

46. Ventrone, 'Feste', 26–9, including on the Festa dei Magi and 'la presenza immanente della cultura cavallaresca nella sensibilità dei fiorentini.'

47. Orvieto, 'Carnevale', 117–18, 117: 'ufficialmente emarginate, almeno come pubbliche esibizioni delle ricchezze e del potere politico delle potenti famiglie fiorentine'; see also Newbigin, 'Piety', 27–8 (and further bibliographic citations) on changes in the Festa de' Magi, 30–1, on the association of military displays more with Lorenzo's grandfather Cosimo (and Lorenzo as a boy) than with Lorenzo's own policies.

48. For example, Ventrone, 'Feste', 29, 33, 37, 44–6; Newbigin, 'Piety', 35–7.

49. Angelo Poliziano, *Stanze . . . cominciate per la giostra del magnifico Giuliano di Piero de' Medici* (Bologna: 1494).

50. Gaspare Nadi, *Diario bolognese,* ed. Corrado Ricci and Alberto Bacchi della Lega (Bologna: 1886), 185.

51. Paola Vecchi Galli, 'Per la stampa a Bologna nel Rinascimento: a proposito di un recente seminario di studi', *Schede umanistiche* 2 (1988): 33–40; Daniele Delcorno Branca, 'Note sull'editoria bolognese nell'età dei Bentivoglio', *Schede umanistiche* 2 (1988): 26.

52. Poggi, BUB: ms. 1491: 47v–53r; Borselli, *Cronica,* 111; Ady, *The Bentivoglio,* 171; Calore, *Bologna,* 15; Pezzarossa, '"Ad honore"', 80–8, 109.

53. De Caro, 'Bentivoglio, Giovanni II', 624 ff.; Bocchi, 'Un fonte', 430–9; Wegener, 'Mortuary Chapels', 180–1; Perazzini, 'La cappella', 371, n. 39.

54. Bocchi, 'Un fonte', 430 – both acting as mercenary captains by 1426; Francesca Bocchi, *Il patrimonio bentivolesco alla metà del '400* (Bologna: Istituto per la storia di Bologna, 1970), 91; Wegener, 'Mortuary Chapels', 178–85.

55. Perazzini, 'La cappella', 356, 357 – a 1675 description of the Annibale relief states that he 'impugna il segno di commando' rather than the sword he now holds. It is not known when it was placed in its present position.

56. George Francis Hill, *A Corpus of Italian Medals of the Renaissance before Cellini,* 2 vols. (London: British Museum, 1930), I, 91, 97, 100, and 104, and II, no. 355, 380, 391, and 404; Wegener, 'Mortuary Chapels', 184; Luke Syson, 'Sperandio of Mantua', in *The Currency of Fame: Portrait Medals of the Renaissance,* exh. cat., Washington, D.C.: National Gallery of Art; New York: Frick Collection, 1994, ed. Stephen K. Scher (London: Thames and Hudson, 1994), 96–7, nos 24, 24a. My thanks to Luke Syson for helpful discussion of these medals and related issues.

57. Hill, *A Corpus,* 97, n. 380: 'IOANNES BENTIVOLUS ARMORUM DUCTOR ILLUSTRIS.' *Armorum ductor* was the usual term for a *condottiere.*

58. For discussion of armour on Pisanello's military medals, Francesco Rossi, 'Pisanello et la représentation des armes: réalité visuelle et valeur symbolique', in *Pisanello: Louvre conférences et colloques,* 2 vols., ed. Dominique Cordellier and Bernadette Py (Paris: La Documentation Française, 1998), I, 297–334. My thanks to Luke Syson for this reference.

59. Rossi, 'Pisanello', 314–15, draws a distinction between military virtues represented by battle armour versus chivalric or noble dynasty represented by tournament or parade armour, but I think that here the imagery implies both aspects. See Syson, 'Sperandio', 97.

60. Syson, 'Sperandio', 96, 101, nos 25, 25a – Hill, *A Corpus,* 7–8, no. 20; 9–10, no. 30; and 100, no. 389.

61. Wegener, 'Mortuary Chapels', 208; Charles M. Rosenberg, *The Este Monuments and Urban Development in Renaissance Ferrara* (Cambridge: Cambridge University Press, 1997), 54–82.

62. Comment by Luke Syson.

63. 1452 – Lando Bottrigari, BUB: ms. 1994: 167r; Borselli, *Cronica,* 90; Sorbelli, *Corpus,* 180; De Caro, 'Bentivoglio, Giovanni II', 623. Palatine count – De Caro, 'Bentivoglio, Giovanni II', 623, giving a date of 1460; Perazzini, 'La cappella', 371, n. 40, citing Archivio di Stato Ferrara: *Arch. Bentivoglio,* lib. 6, n. 20, giving a date of 1461, Sante was made a Palatine count at the same time.

64. Poggi, BUB: ms. 1491: 66v; Andrea Bacchi, *Francesco del Cossa* (Soncino: Edizioni dei Soncino, 1991), 98; Paul Nieuwenhuizen, 'Worldly Ritual and Dynastic Iconography in the Bentivoglio Chapel in Bologna 1483–1499', *Mededelingen van het Nederlands Instituut te Rome* 36 (1996): 201.

65. Poggi, BUB: ms. 1491: 21r; Borselli, *Cronica,* 103.

66. Wegener, 'Mortuary Chapels', 185–6.

67. On the chapel and the paintings, Anna Ottani Cavina, 'La Capella Bentivoglio', in *Il Tempio di San Giacomo Maggiore in Bologna, 1267–1967,* ed. Carlo Volpe (Bologna: Resto del Carlino, 1967), 117–31; Clifford M. Brown, 'The Church of S. Cecilia and the Bentivoglio Chapel in Bologna', *Mitteilungen des Kunsthistorischen Instituts in Florenz* (henceforth *MKIF*), 13 (1967–8), 301–24; Wegener, 'Mortuary Chapels', 191–205; Thorsten Marr, 'Die Erlösungsgallerie von Lorenzo Costa in S. Giacomo Maggiore in Bologna', *Zeitschrift für Kunstgeschichte* 54 (1991): 520–40; Nieuwenhuizen, 'Worldly Ritual', 187–212. Wegener, 'Mortuary Chapels', 202, identified the image as a triumph of Fame and Fortune.

68. On links to Ferrara, Andrea Emiliani, in *Tre artisti nella Bologna dei Bentivoglio,* ed. Franca Varignana (Bologna: Nuova Alfa, 1986), ix–x; Andrea Bacchi, 'Vicende della pittura nell'età di Giovanni II Bentivoglio', in *Bentivolorum magnificentia,* 291–2, 296–8, 300–1, 305–7, 309–11, 314–15.

69. Syson, 'Sperandio', 91, 94.

70. Ibid., 94.

71. Bacchi, 'Vicende', 284–335; Joseph Manca, *The Art of Ercole de' Roberti* (Cambridge: Cambridge University Press, 1992); Kristen Lippincott, 'Cossa, Francesco del', in *The Dictionary of Art,* 34 vols., ed. Jane Turner (London: Macmillan, 1996), vol. VII, 924–7; Kristen Lippincott, 'Roberti, Ercole (d'Antonio) de'', ibid., XXVI, 455–60, and Maria Christian Chiusa, 'Lorenzo Costa (1)', ibid., vol. VIII, 4–5.

72. On Ferrarese history, Werner L. Gundersheimer, *Ferrara: The Style of a Renaissance Despotism* (Princeton: Princeton University Press, 1973), 13–65, 151–3, 156–8, 177–83, 203; Stephen J. Campbell, *Cosmè Tura of Ferrara. Style, Politics and the Renaissance City, 1450–1495* (New Haven and London: Yale University Press, 1997), 5.

73. 1474 – Poggi, BUB: ms. 1491: 21r; Ady, *The Bentivoglio,* 98; Gaspare De Caro, 'Bentivoglio, Annibale', in *DBI,* vol. VIII, 595.

74. For the betrothal, Dallari, 'Carteggio', 23; Bernardino Zambotti, *Diario ferrarese dall'anno 1476 sino al 1504. Appendice al Diario Ferrarese di autori incerti,* ed. Giuseppe Pardi, *RIS*[2], 24.7 (Bologna: Scipione Lapi, 1934–7), 57. For the wedding see, for example, Gabriele Cazzola, '"Bentivoli machinatores". Aspetti politici e momenti teatrali di un festa quattrocentesca bolognese', *Biblioteca teatrale,* 23–4 (1979): 14–38; Pezzarossa, ' "Ad honore" ', 110.

75. Dallari, 'Carteggio', 3, 23.

76. Eric Cochrane, *Historians and Historiography in the Italian Renaissance* (Chicago and London: University of Chicago Press, 1981), 104; De Benedictis, 'Quale "corte" ', 23–5, 29, 30–2.

77. Cochrane, *Historians,* 107; Mark Pritchard, 'The Urban Development of Bologna, 1300–1500' (unpublished Ph.D. diss., University of London, 1994), 350, 360–1.

78. Poggi, BUB: ms. 1491: 18r: 'Il magnifico m.o. Ioane co li regimente del mese d'agosto fece xalegare la piaza de porta Ravignana de prede cotte'; Archivio di Stato Bologna (hereafter ASB), *Comune – Governo, Libri Partitorum*: reg. 6: allegato P: 56r; ibid., allegato Q: 139v–40r/268v–9r; Nadi, *Diario*, 69; Giovanni Battista Comelli, 'Di Girolamo Ranuzzi secondo Conte di Poretta', *Atti e memorie della R. Deputazione di Storia Patria per le Provincie di Romagna*, 3rd ser., 17 (1898–9), 362; Borselli, *Cronica*, 100. See Frati, *La vita*, 205–6; Rosa Tamborrino, 'Bologna: XV–XVI secolo. Società d'arte, potere e significati dello spazio urbano', in *Fabbriche, piazza, mercati. La città italiana nel Rinascimento*, ed. Donatella Calabi (Rome: Officina, 1997), 419, 432, 435.

79. On urban improvement programmes, for example, Pritchard, 'The Urban Development'; Tamborrino, 'Bologna'; Georgia Clarke, 'Magnificence and the City: Giovanni II Bentivoglio and Architecture in Fifteenth-Century Bologna', *Renaissance Studies* 13 (1999): 397–411.

80. Borselli, *Cronica*, 95: 'palatium regale incepit.'

81. The Bentivoglio were recorded as living in this area from at least 1296, Francesca Bocchi, 'I Bentivoglio da cittadini a signori', *Atti e memorie della Deputazione di Storia Patria per le Provincie di Romagna* 22 (1971): 50. In 1475 Giovanni made an agreement with Sante's son Ercole concerning Sante's estate including the Bentivoglio palace. See Bocchi, *Il patrimonio*.

82. Bocchi, *Il patrimonio*, 20, 29; Annibale's house was also on the Strà S. Donato, one house away from the Bentivoglio palace, Ibid., 33, 67.

83. Ibid., 59.

84. Ibid., 29.

85. Ibid., 111 on the palace and Sante's status.

86. Aldo Foratti, 'L'attività di Pagno di Lapo Portigiani in Bologna', in *Miscellanea di storia dell'arte, in onore di Igino Benvenuto Supino* (Florence: Olschki, 1933), 354, 358–60; Isabelle Hyman, 'Notes and Speculations on S. Lorenzo, Palazzo Medici, and an Urban Project by Brunelleschi', *Journal of the Society of Architectural Historian* 34 (1975): 103–4, 111.

87. On those working in the building trade, Guido Zucchini, 'Artigiani a Bologna nei secoli XIV, XV e XVI', *Atti e memorie della R. Deputazione di Storia Patria per l'Emilia e la Romagna* 8 (1942–3): 37–159; 9 (1943–5), 113–59.

88. On the palace, Gozzadini, *Memoria*, 233–8; Bocchi, *Il patrimonio*, 64–5, pl. 3; William E. Wallace, 'The Bentivoglio Palace Lost and Reconstructed', *Sixteenth Century Journal* 10.3 (1979): 97–114; Simonetta Valtieri, *Il palazzo del principe, il palazzo del cardinale, il palazzo del mercante nel Rinascimento* (Roma: Gangemi, 1988), 3–30; Carolyn James, 'The Palazzo Bentivoglio in 1487', *MKIF* 41 (1997): 187–96; Clarke, 'Magnificence', 402–3.

89. Clarke, 'Magnificence', 402. On castles and princes, Joanna Woods-Marsden, 'Images of Castles in the Renaissance: Symbols of 'Signoria'/Symbols of Tyranny', *Art Journal* 48 (1989): 130–7.

90. On Palazzo Medici, see, for example, Georgia Clarke, *Roman House – Renaissance Palaces: Inventing Antiquity in Fifteenth-Century Italy* (Cambridge: Cambridge University Press, 2003), with bibliography.

91. On the Palazzo Medici, its site and use, Caroline Elam, 'Il palazzo nel contesto della città: strategie urbanistiche dei Medici nel gonfalone del Leon d'Oro, 1415–1530', in *Il Palazzo Medici Riccardi di Firenze*, ed. Giovanni Cherubini and Giovanni Fanelli (Florence: Giunti, 1990), 44–7; Giovanni Cipriani, 'Il palazzo nella vita pubblica fiorentina', in *Il Palazzo Medici*, 188–91; Elvira Garbero Zorzi, 'Lo spettacolo nel segno dei Medici', in *Il Palazzo Medici*, 200–6; Newbigin, 'Piety', 30.

92. Giordano Conti, 'Cappelle di derivazione brunelleschiana a Bologna nel secolo XV', in *Filippo Brunelleschi: la sua opera e il suo tempo,* 2 vols., ed. Giovanni Spadolini (Florence: Centro Di, 1980), vol. I, 553–5.

93. Wegener, 'Mortuary Chapels', 190.

94. On the Old Sacristy and Medicean politics, Marvin Trachtenberg, 'On Brunelleschi's Old Sacristy as Model for Early Renaissance Church Architecture', in *L'Èglise dans l'architecture de la Renaissance,* ed. Jean Guillaume (Paris: Picard, 1995), 17, 21–2, and 22–7 on imitations of the Old Sacristy within and outside Florence.

95. Trachtenberg, 'On Brunelleschi's Old Sacristy', 23, on Medicean magnificence.

96. On the chapel, see JoAnne G. Bernstein, 'A Florentine Patron in Milan: Pigello Portinari the Portinari Chapel', in *Florence and Milan: Comparisons and Relations,* 2 vols., ed. Craig Hugh Smyth and Gian Carlo Garfagnini (Florence: Olschki, 1989), vol. I, 171–200.

97. Tuohy, *Herculean Ferrara,* 93.

98. Brown, 'The Church', 313–14; Clarke, 'Magnificence', 406.

99. Hyman, 'Notes', 98–100, 107–8; Caroline Elam, 'Cosimo de' Medici and S. Lorenzo', in *Cosimo 'il Vecchio' de' Medici 1389–1464,* ed. Francis Ames-Lewis (Oxford: Clarendon Press, 1992), 157–80; Trachtenberg, 'On Brunelleschi's Old Sacristy', 25.

100. Gozzadini, *Memoria,* 27; Giuseppe Guidicini, *Cose notabili della città di Bologna ossia storia cronologica de' suoi stabili sacri, pubblici e privati,* 5 vols. (Bologna: 1868–73), vol. II, 65; Nadi (*Diario,* 85) ascribed the rebuilding to Giovanni; Ghirardacci, *Della historia,* 233; Zucchini, 'Artigiani' (1943–5), 152; Deanna Lenzi, 'Regesto', in *Il Tempio di S. Giacomo Maggiore,* 235–6; Rolando Dondarini, 'Gasparo Nadi. Capomaestro bolognese (1418–1504)', in *I portici di Bologna e l'edilizia civile medievale,* ed. Francesca Bocchi (Bologna: Grafis, 1990), 142.

101. Hill, *A Corpus,* vol. I, 98, and vol. II, no. 383: 'BONON[ENSIS] PATRIAE DECUS ET LIBERTATIS CUSTOS.'

102. Bosdari, 'I primordi', 191 n. 17.

103. 'IOANNES BENTIVOLUS IUNIOR EQUES ILLUSTRIS AC SENATUS BONONIENSIS PRINCEPS VIRGILIUSQUE MALVETIUS.'

104. Now in the National Gallery of Art, Washington, D.C. See Clarke, 'Magnificence', 403–5. Usually attributed to Ercole de' Roberti, a view now disputed, although a Ferrarese artist is suggested, Luke Syson, 'Ercole de Roberti: The Making of a Court Artist', in *Ercole de' Roberti: The Renaissance in Ferrara,* exh. cat., Los Angeles: J. Paul Getty Museum, 1999, ed. Denise Allen, Luke Syson, Jennifer Helvey, and David Jaffé (London: Burlington Magazine Publications, 1999), ix, n. 45.

105. Bacchi, 'Vicende', 298; Lippincott, 'Cossa', 925–6.

106. Ady, *The Bentivoglio,* 25; Paul Nieuwenhuizen, 'Kunst, Religie en Politiek in het Bologna van de Bentivoglio's: het Heiligdom van de Madonna del Baraccano tussen 1401 en 1512', *Incontri* ns. 9 (1994): 129–60.

107. Nieuwenhuizen, 'Kunst, Religie en Politiek', 139–40.

108. Bacchi, 'Vicende', 298: 'IOHAN[NES] BENT[IVOLUS] BONONIAE DO[MINUS] OPERA DI FRANCESCHO DEL COSSA DA FERRARA MCCCCL[XXII(?)], it was transcribed in 1880 but is now unreadable; Nieuwenhuizen, 'Kunst, Religie en Politiek',141–2.

109. Bocchi, 'Un fonte', 430–1, 433, and 435.

110. Ibid., 440.

111. Poggi, BUB: ms. 1491: 25v; Dallari, 'Carteggio', 38, n. 62; Borselli, *Cronica,* 104; Ady, *The Bentivoglio,* 72; De Caro, 'Bentivoglio, Giovanni II', 625; Syson, 'Sperandio', 97.

112. Poggi, BUB: ms. 1491: 25v: 'el signore nostro ora el comengarono achiamo signore si per le aguistate tere e si etian per el dominio che avea di guesta citade et tuto el governo avea nele mane.'

113. For example, Caroline Elam, 'Lorenzo the Magnificent and the Urban Development of Renaissance Florence', *Art History* 1 (1978): 43–66; Philip E. Foster, 'Lorenzo de' Medici and the Florence Cathedral Façade', *Art Bulletin* 63 (1981): 495–500; Caroline Elam, 'Lorenzo's Architectural and Urban Policies', in *Lorenzo il Magnifico e il suo mondo,* ed. Garfagnini, 357–82.

114. Daniele Delcorno Branca, 'Fortuna e trasformazioni del *Buovo d'Antona*', in *Testi, cotesti e contesti del franco-italiano. Atti del I° simposio franco-italiano (Bad Homburg, 13–16 aprile 1987),* ed. Günter Holtus, Henning Krauss, and Peter Wunderli (Tübingen: M. Niemeyer, 1991), 285–306.

115. Delcorno Branca, 'Fortuna', 289–90.

116. Delcorno Branca, 'Note', 25–6; Delcorno Branca, 'Fortuna', 290, 293. For *Morgante*'s date, Kent, 'An Early Reference', 209–11.

117. James, *Giovanni Sabadino,* 3.

7

'Acqua viva e corrente': Private Display and Public Distribution of Fresh Water at the Neapolitan Villa of Poggioreale as a Hydraulic Model for Sixteenth-Century Medici Gardens

Bruce L. Edelstein

Of the many forms of government practiced by Italian states during the Renaissance, only one provided a royal model for absolutist rule: the kingdom of Naples. For this reason alone, Naples should be considered exceptional, but the kingdom was also an innovative center for humanist thought and cultural patronage of all types. The wealth and royal status of Naples' Aragonese rulers drew scholars, musicians, and artists to the city throughout the fifteenth century. The literature, music, art, architecture, and other cultural products created in Naples at this time were widely employed by contemporaries outside of the kingdom as paradigms to be emulated, perhaps as much for their perceived excellence as for the royal imprimatur of their patronage. Largely because of Naples' unique political nature, Neapolitan art is generally considered today as extraneous to the main development of what is considered the 'Italian Renaissance.' But in the fifteenth century, Neapolitan models were considered paragons of Italian style outside of the Italian peninsula.

One of the clearest cases of this phenomenon is provided by the introduction of Italian Renaissance garden style into France, which occurred as a direct consequence of the invasion of Italy by Charles VIII in 1494–5; the French king's enthusiastic experience of the gardens he visited in Italy at this time was in no small part responsible for the rapid diffusion of Italian models in gardens created for members of the royal court upon his return home.[1] The most influential Italian garden complex he encountered was the Neapolitan one at Poggioreale (Fig. 51).[2] The villa created for Alfonso II of Aragon at Poggioreale had been completed very shortly before Charles's arrival. It was here that the French king spent the night before making his triumphal entry into Naples and where he would later return to convalesce during an illness. It should be emphasized that the principal goal of the French armies'

Italian campaign was to reclaim Naples from the Aragonese as part of the king's Angevin heritage. It is therefore especially remarkable that Charles encouraged the employment of an Aragonese model in French royal gardens. It may be deduced from this that the complex was perceived as being superior to any other seen by Charles in Italy and that, while he considered the Aragonese to have usurped his Neapolitan throne, their royalty was nonetheless recognizable and could therefore provide a viable model for French royal patronage.

Poggioreale's royal associations, through its patronage and guests, made it an essential stop on the routes of illustrious visitors to Naples. Although the complex was already in a ruined state by 1535, the Holy Roman Emperor Charles V was received there by his viceroy, Pedro de Toledo, prior to the emperor's triumphal entry into the city.[3] Charles's claim to Naples was derived from his maternal Aragonese ancestry, and his reception at Poggioreale forty years after the French king's sojourn there can only have been orchestrated for its political significance.[4] The event is significant for the subsequent history of landscape architecture in Florence, because two great patrons of important Florentine garden complexes were present in Naples at the time: the future grand duke, Cosimo I de' Medici, as a page in his cousin Alessandro's entourage, and Cosimo's future consort, Eleonora di Toledo, daughter of the Spanish viceroy. Thus, both patrons are likely to have known something of the site's historical significance and may well have heard descriptions of its former magnificence from older members of the Neapolitan court. Some idea of the impression Poggioreale might have left on Cosimo and Eleonora in 1535 may be derived from the virtually contemporary Italian travel journal of Johann Fichard, an enthusiastic German visitor to the site in 1536: 'Were [Poggioreale] to be returned to its original splendor, I do not believe that there could be in all of Italy so grand, magnificent or pleasant a bath as this.'[5]

Both Cosimo and Eleonora would subsequently employ the model of Poggioreale in two equally paradigmatic gardens: the duke's villa at Castello and the duchess's Pitti Palace and Boboli Gardens complex.[6] In each case, the imitation of the Neapolitan model may be connected to a desire on the part of the patron to reinforce his or her association with the Hispano-Imperial court. The waterworks at Castello convey a message highlighting the benefits of Medici rule for the city of Florence; the choice of the model of Poggioreale for this project may therefore be seen as an attempt by the young duke to reinforce his associations with the imperial milieu, as his right to rule depended on the aegis of his and his father-in-law's mutual patron, Charles V. The project may also be viewed in the context of other artistic and political projects executed by Cosimo in imitation of contemporary Neapolitan urban renewal under the patronage of Pedro de Toledo. Of these, the most explicit analogy may be made between his foundation of the Uffizi to centralize the bureaucracy in Florence and the viceroy's renovation of the Castel Capuano as the seat of a revised court system

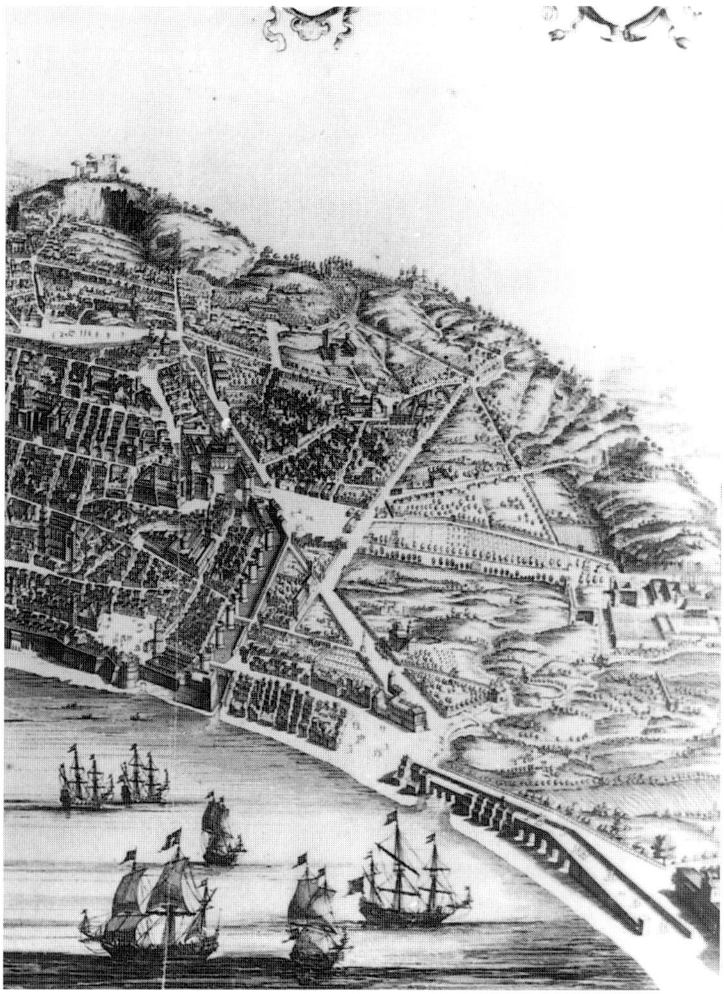

51. Bastien Stoopendael (or Stopendaal), *View of Poggioreale and Porta Capuana* (Detail from: Map of Naples, engraving on copper, Amsterdam: J. Blaeu, dated 1653 but published 1663). Naples, Museo Nazionale di S. Martino. Photo: Soprintendenza per i Beni Artistici e Culturali della Provincia di Napoli.

in Naples.[7] Significantly, Pedro's new tribunal project appears to have taken up a proposal made by Alfonso of Aragon as part of his earlier urban renewal plan, of which the villa at Poggioreale and its waterworks were an integral part. In attempting to create virtually *ex novo* his own princely court, it was natural that Cosimo should turn to Naples for the models of behavior and patronage that could be found both in the actions of its current representative of imperial power and its old royal Aragonese traditions.

Given its enormous influence well beyond the confines of Italy, the decay and ultimate destruction of Alfonso II of Aragon's villa of Poggioreale may be considered one of the greatest losses among those many works of Renaissance art and architecture known to us solely by description and a few odd drawings and views. The villa was commissioned while Alfonso was still duke of Calabria but was not completed until after his succession to the throne as king of Naples in 1494. Alfonso purchased the property at Dogliolo, just to the east of Naples' city walls, in 1485 and the intent to construct a villa and garden complex may be presumed to date from the same time, as Colombo, the author of a seminal article reconstructing the history of the property, demonstrates.[8] Unfortunately, political unrest kept the duke from undertaking the project and Joanpiero Leostello does not record the beginning of work on Poggioreale in his contemporary chronicle, the *Effemeridi,* until February 1487.[9] The design of the palace and its gardens is attributed to Giuliano da Maiano, named specifically by Leostello in connection with the beginning of construction in February 1487; Giuliano was called to Naples at that time to work on Poggioreale and Alfonso's other great commission of residential architecture, the Palazzo della Duchesca.[10] Giuliano died in Naples in December 1490 prior to the completion of the project, however, and the contribution of other architects is generally presumed.[11] In any event, Alfonso himself was frequently present during the construction and is documented as having taken an active interest in its progress[12]; a significant role in the final appearance of the project may therefore be reasonably attributed to the patron.

While the design of Poggioreale was revolutionary in many ways, its most innovative feature was its elaborate waterworks. Like Pius II's Piccolomini Palace in Pienza, where the man-made, ordered landscape of the palace's hanging garden was juxtaposed with the view over the natural, 'wild' Sienese landscape leading towards Monte Amiata, Poggioreale placed regularly planned canals and man-made waterworks against the backdrop of the Bay of Naples.[13] One of the most remarkable features of these waterworks was its use as a reservoir for freshwater that then passed on to the city of Naples to serve the needs of its citizens. Part of the inspiration for this employment of the villa and garden complex must have come from its site, 'the confluence of the Bolla water system, which in antiquity carried the waters of the Sebeto and other streams into Naples.'[14] Thus, the creation at Poggioreale of a new reservoir for freshwater to be transported into the city for the use of the populace was surely planned in emulation of the ancients, a conscious revival of antiquity typical of the sophisticated humanist spirit of the Neapolitan court.[15]

In 1489, only two years after construction was begun on the villa, the duke had a new poplar-lined road constructed linking the area of Naples known as Formello, where the church of S. Caterina is located, to Poggioreale.[16] Here, Giuliano da Maiano was also commissioned to design a new city gate, the Porta Capuana.[17] The project may therefore be seen as a crucial element in the program of Neapolitan urban renewal undertaken by Alfonso.[18] The new road, marked at each end by monumental works of architecture by Giuliano,[19] would have mirrored the water passage between the villa and the city, where copiously flowing fountains would also have marked the ends of a different transportation system. In both cases, these public works would have been interpreted by contemporaries as the benevolent acts of a good prince.

The provision of new freshwater sources to the populace was a common trope in Renaissance descriptions of the ideal prince. In a 1566 description lauding the merits of Naples, and particularly the urban improvement projects executed during the viceregency of Pedro de Toledo, Giovanni Tarcagnota commented, 'But above all, that which a city most requires are fountains of fresh, flowing water [*acqua viva e corrente*] because, beyond the practical benefits that these offer (which is huge and incomparable), they render beautiful, pleasant and lively that city in which they are found.'[20] As Conforti has observed, 'well into the sixteenth century, even in the most populous cities, the principal water supply was provided by wells.'[21] Thus, the continuous flow of springwater, transported by aqueducts and dramatically displayed in fountains, would have been especially remarkable and appreciated in the urban setting. What appears for the first time at Poggioreale, however, is the decision to collect and employ water for spectacular effects and entertainments in a ruler's garden prior to its passage to the city.

The exclusive use of the water from the Bolla system at Alfonso's villa before distribution to the public was apparently quite conscious. In addition to confiscating properties adjacent to Poggioreale to increase the extent of his estate, the duke also redirected the waters from the Bolla canal, thus effectively prohibiting their use by local water mills or for the irrigation of neighboring farms.[22] This allowed Alfonso greater control over the water level and pressure both at his pleasure villa and in the urban outlets in Naples. We may be certain that Eleonora di Toledo's Neapolitan contemporaries were conscious that their urban freshwater supply had previously arrived via the gardens at Poggioreale because the Bolla system aqueduct was partially destroyed in 1528, during the French siege of Naples, a mere four years prior to the arrival of Pedro de Toledo in Naples as viceroy with his family in tow.[23] Furthermore, a plan for the renovation of the system was drawn up during her father's tenure as viceroy, although this appears never to have been executed.[24] Fichard, in his brief description of 1536, specificies that the aqueduct transporting the city's water departed from the gardens.[25] Later in the sixteenth century, the principal reason that the villa was not sold appears to have been its recognized importance as a reservoir for the city.[26]

Of the various water features contained within the gardens of Poggioreale, one structure stands out as especially significant: the *vivaio*.[27] This great fishpond is recorded in documents as the 'sguazzatorio grande'[28] and was central to the entertainments held by Alfonso at his villa: it was probably here, for example, that on the occasion of a banquet held in her honor in 1489, Queen Giovanna entered into a boat and rowed it 'manibus propriis.'[29] The *vivaio* would have served two important functions. The structure was first and foremost a reservoir that would have guaranteed the flow of water to the public fountains in Naples even when the water supply at the source itself was low.[30] In addition, the *vivaio* served as a container for the maintenance of fresh fish. That the 'squazzatorio' must have been stocked with fish may be deduced from the fact that waterfowl were a documented natural presence on this artificial lake.[31] Furthermore, Leostello refers to the presence of a 'peschera a lo poggio' in 1490, and Peruzzi, in his much-discussed Uffizi sketches of the complex, specifically labeled this pool as a 'peschiera,' or fishpond.[32] Because the villa was frequently used for banqueting and entertaining,[33] the possibility to keep fresh fish there would have provided an important addition to the ducal table.[34] More important was the presence of the living creatures darting about in the pool, which would have provided strong visible evidence for the freshness and potability of the water itself. This symbolic aspect of the *vivaio* would have underscored the duke's benevolence in providing such high-quality water to his subjects through its subsequent outlets in the city center.

Poggioreale is often considered one of the supreme examples of the exportation of Florentine architectural style outside of Tuscany.[35] Various studies, however, have helped to highlight the villa and garden complex's debt to ancient typologies maintained in Islamic Spain and Sicily.[36] As such, Poggioreale may be considered one of the most characteristic products of the Neapolitan cultural milieu. In the case of the Florentine translations of Poggioreale, the villa's own Florentine quattrocento architectural language may well have facilitated its adaptation as a hydraulic model, even though Poggioreale's hydraulic system itself owes a greater debt to Islamic garden traditions.[37] In addition, the interest of Lorenzo *il Magnifico* in the project gave it the imprimatur of an important Medici ancestor, a factor that may have been even more important for subsequent employment of the complex as a model at the Medici ducal court.[38] If Poggioreale was conceived of as too overtly 'Spanish' in Florence, where the memory of the sack of Prato in 1512 was still quite vivid and even the duchess herself was conscious of anti-Spanish feeling,[39] the essential roles played by Florentine architects and Lorenzo in the Neapolitan villa complex's development may have helped to make its importation as a model more palatable.

The hydraulic system invented for Alfonso's villa at Poggioreale may be seen as the inspiration for those at both Cosimo I's villa at Castello, just outside of Florence, and Eleonora di Toledo's Boboli Gardens, occupying a significant portion of land just inside the city walls. Each of these gardens was intended to serve as a collection point for various water sources to be richly displayed in the duke's or duchess's private sphere and then passed on to an outlet in the heart of the city's political center. While both projects are known to have been designed with the purpose of

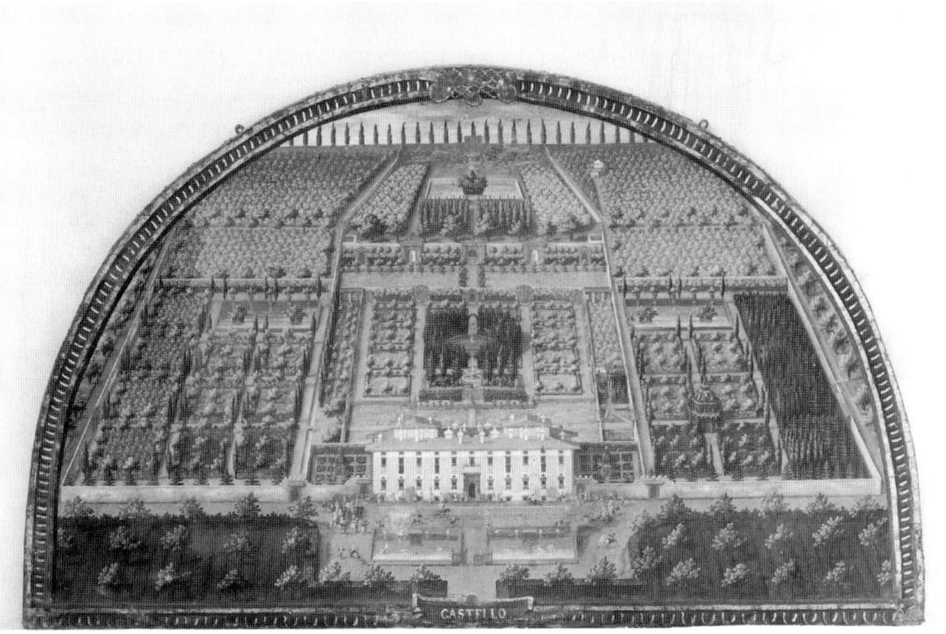

52. Justus Utens, *Castello*, c. 1599. Tempera on canvas. Florence, Museo di Firenze Com'era. Photo: Musei Comunali di Firenze.

benevolently providing a new freshwater source for the citizens of Florence in mind, the connecting aqueducts were never constructed between Castello and Florence; instead, this goal would not be achieved until Bartolomeo Ammannati's Neptune Fountain received its abundant water supply from the Boboli Gardens.

The project to improve the Medici villa at Castello by the addition of new decorative schemes and an elaborate garden complex is especially distinguished (Fig. 52). Among the many grand works of art created for Cosimo I de' Medici, it was the first commission of his reign as duke of Florence, indeed his first major work of patronage, and it was the first Italian garden designed with a unified iconography.[40] Cosimo acceded to the ducal throne following the assassination of his cousin, Duke Alessandro de' Medici, in January 1537. By the following year, little over two years after his journey to Naples in Alessandro's entourage, work was already underway at Castello. The early date for this commission and its proximity to Cosimo's Neapolitan experience suggest both the primacy of the project for the young duke and the likelihood that Poggioreale served as a conscious model for it.

The earliest commissions given by Cosimo for Castello were intended to facilitate the creation of the garden. In 1538, the hydraulic engineer Piero da San Casciano was hard at work on a hydraulic system.[41] Whether or not Tribolo was already capomaestro at Castello at this time is a much-vexed question, and indeed the very nature of this earliest project is unknown.[42] It is likely, however, that it was not nearly so elaborate as the design eventually imposed. In 1542, Tribolo began linking new water sources to the property; as Conforti has suggested, the desire for an increased water supply presumably reflected a project for its increased display in the garden.[43] It was this very abundant supply of water and its highly original employment at Castello that most frequently inspired fascination and comment by visitors to its gardens in the sixteenth and seventeenth centuries.[44]

Tribolo's project strongly conditioned what was eventually created on the site. With the exception of the intended decoration of the grotto at Castello, a complex problem and one that will not be examined here, the main conceit of Tribolo's program was followed rather faithfully in Vasari's subsequent evolution of the garden, although important features initially intended were never executed.[45] Along the main axis, and at significant but subsidiary points flanking it, iconographically charged sculpture proclaimed the message of the generation of water in nature and its benevolent supply to the city of Florence. The water would have appeared to depart from two parallel niches bearing representations of the two mountain sources for Florence's rivers in the Appennine range.[46] From here, the water would have passed underground to representations of the Arno and Mugnone rivers.[47] The water from these fountains would then have passed onto a representation of Florence herself, abundantly served by the two rivers at whose confluence the city lies.[48] The final, and most potent, sculptural expression in the garden was the fountain of Hercules, depicting the ancient hero's labor in which he defeats the giant Antaeus. Lazzaro has convincingly suggested that this group allegorized Cosimo's own wresting of new water sources from the ground, which would in turn have served the city of Florence had Tribolo's original project been completed[49]: like Poggioreale, the freshwater collected and displayed in the duke's gardens at Castello was intended to then be transported onto the city for use by the public.[50]

At Castello we also find a highly charged use of the fishpond in the garden's design. Twin *vivai* were located, not within the private confines of the duke's garden, but in front of the villa's façade, available for public inspection. As at Poggioreale, these would have been employed to guarantee the flow of water to urban outlets.[51] Their location suggests even more strongly Cosimo's pride in the project, however, and his desire to offer visible confirmation of the water's potability.[52] Again, as we have seen at Poggioreale, the presence of living creatures in these open basins would have attested to the freshness of the water source.[53] This function was apparently considered so significant that not only was the pair of *vivai* to have been stocked with fish, but the canals planned by Tribolo to begin the transportation of the water onto the city were also intended to contain fish and crustaceans.[54]

The Castello hydraulic project would have had important humanist overtones, as the site had originally served in antiquity as the main reservoir for the Roman aqueduct that supplied freshwater to the city of Florence; the very name of the place is believed to derive from the Latin word 'castellum,' meaning cistern or reservoir.[55] Indeed, ancient conduits reputedly still supplied the site with water prior to the

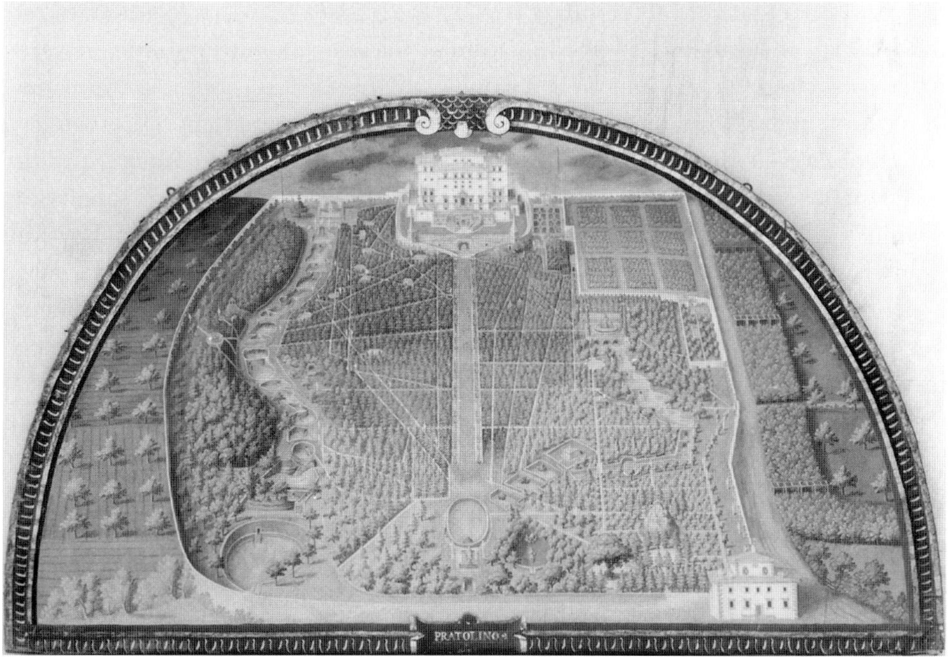

53. Justus Utens, *Pratolino*, c. 1599. Tempera on canvas. Florence, Museo di Firenze Com'era. Photo: Musei Comunali di Firenze.

additions to the hydraulic system commissioned by Cosimo.[56] The ancient aqueduct was, in the words of Lazzaro, 'one of the three principal monuments erected by the Romans at the time of the founding of Florence' and it provided 'proof of the Roman origins of the city and its former splendor.'[57] Had the freshwater at Castello been transported onto Florence, the duke would have been seen as the restorer of this ancient glory.[58] However, a strong public message at the site identifying the patron with his ancient predecessors may have been conveyed precisely by the paired fishponds visible in the Utens lunette.[59] Because an open basin in front of the villa existed prior to the works commissioned by Cosimo at the site,[60] the enlargement of this pool and its revitalization through the arrival of water from new sources provided just such an iconographic opportunity. In any event, the concept at Castello closely adheres to the paradigm established by Alfonso d'Aragona at Poggioreale: a new garden complex at a site just outside an urban capital, with fountains abundantly supplied by a new hydraulic system that revived an ancient one previously associated with the site, and whose waters would then be transported onto the city center for benevolent distribution to the ruler's subjects.

The Castello program, with its intended completion in the provision of water to the duke's Florentine subjects at a public outlet, was subsequently given humorous treatment in the garden of his son, Francesco I, at Pratolino (Fig. 53). Here, the features of the central axis repeated both the general theme of the generation of water and the specific theme of its manifestations in the Florentine *contado* that characterize the program at Castello.[61] The culmination of the main axis at Pratolino, however, was an oval basin with a fountain of a laundress wringing out washing accompanied by a pissing putto. This pair of genre figures would have been humorous in its own right, even for visitors unfamiliar with the Castello garden or the intended outlet of its waters: the washerwoman's son is soiling the water in which she is supposedly cleaning the clothes.[62] Guests who had already been received at Castello, however, would have been able to recognize the witty play on Giambologna's elegant Florence figure for the central fountain there: instead of a nude Venus Anadyomene wringing out her hair as she emerges from her bath, Valerio Cioli's less lofty laundress twisted her washing into the basin.[63] The laundress fountain, however, may also have been intended as a representation of the idea of the benevolent provision of water to the Grand Duke's subjects for their mundane needs, that is, a complement to the intended completion of the water passage at Castello.[64]

At Boboli, the hydraulic works were also considered essential and must have constituted a significant portion of the contribution made by Tribolo in his original design for the garden (Fig. 54).[65] Tribolo's project and the earliest works in the Boboli Gardens have been the object of much study over the past decade.[66] In April 1551, little over a year after Eleonora's purchase of the property, the hydraulic works were well under way[67]; by 1553, this system was already being served by the Fonte della Ginevra, just outside the city walls near Arcetri.[68] As early as 1555, water had not only been provided to the Boboli Gardens, but also transported across the river to the Palazzo Vecchio; documents confirm that the fountain in the first courtyard of the palace was already supplied with water by this date and that it had been brought up to the palace's main floor, where its intended outlet was to have been Ammannati's Juno fountain.[69] The crowning achievement of this vast hydraulic undertaking, however, was to have been the public fountain in the piazza below.

From the outset, then, the creation of the Boboli Gardens may be linked to Cosimo's desire to furnish a new water source to the city of Florence.[70] As we have seen, this project would have had rich symbolic overtones through its connections to the antique, specifically the Florentia of the Augustan era, had it been completed at Castello.[71] While Boboli did not provide this opportunity to highlight the duke's role as a new Augustus, it instead offered a more practical site for the completion of this plan; both the garden's greater proximity to the city center and its steep gradient facilitated its employment as a reservoir for the new public outlet for freshwater.[72]

The iconographically significant features of the garden's waterworks may also be linked to this project.[73] The three principal displays included in Tribolo's original plan were a fountain for the area directly behind the Pitti Palace, a grotto, and a

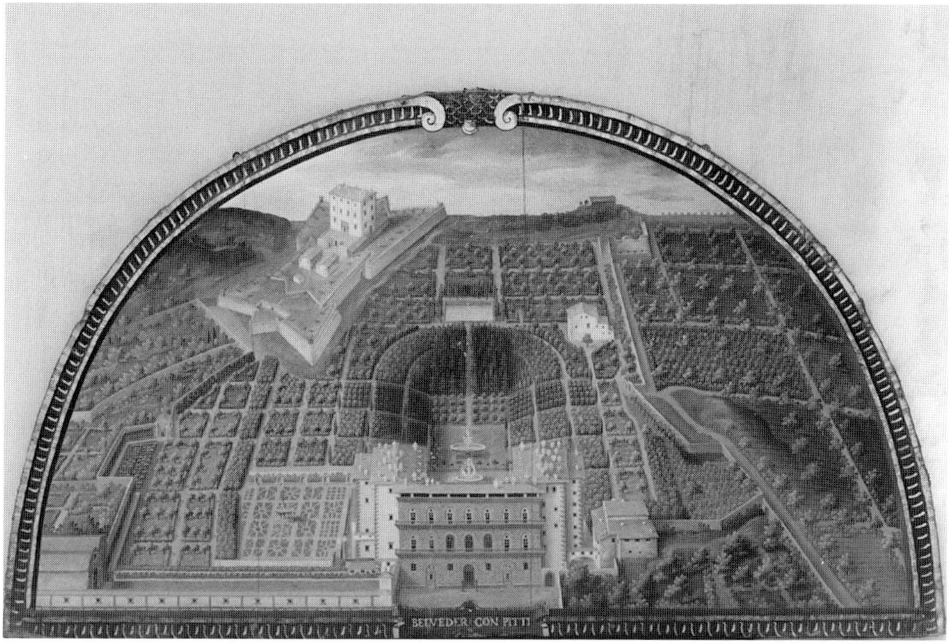

54. Justus Utens, *Belvedere con Pitti*, c. 1599. Tempera on canvas. Florence, Museo di Firenze Com'era. Photo: Musei Comunali di Firenze.

vivaio. Of these, only the grotto, the so-called Grotticina di Madama, survives in something remotely resembling its original form (Fig. 55).[74] The grotto's decoration celebrates fertility themes: at the center of the main niche, is Bandinelli's *She-Goat,* whose swollen udders may refer to the patron's renowned fertility[75] or more generally to the fertility of the gardens, abundantly supplied by freshwater.[76] As Petrucci has recently observed, the iconography of the grotto is also visually linked to at least one of the outlets for the gardens' waters on the opposite side of the river: the fountain in the first courtyard of the Palazzo Vecchio, executed after a design by Vasari.[77] Both the sculptural decoration of the grotto's main niche and Bachiacca's fresco decoration on the vault of the grotto contain references to Verrocchio's *Putto with a Fish,* originally commissioned by Lorenzo the Magnificent for the Medici Villa at Careggi but transferred to the Palazzo Vecchio to serve as the crowning element of Vasari's fountain in these same years.[78]

We can be certain that a major fountain was intended for the area converted in the seventeenth century into the present amphitheater because Tribolo himself oversaw the excavation of the enormous monolithic granite basin on Elba, where he contracted the malarial fever from which he died in September 1550.[79] We cannot, however, be certain of what the subject of that fountain was intended to be; either a Neptune or Oceanus was planned from the outset, or Giambologna's design reflects

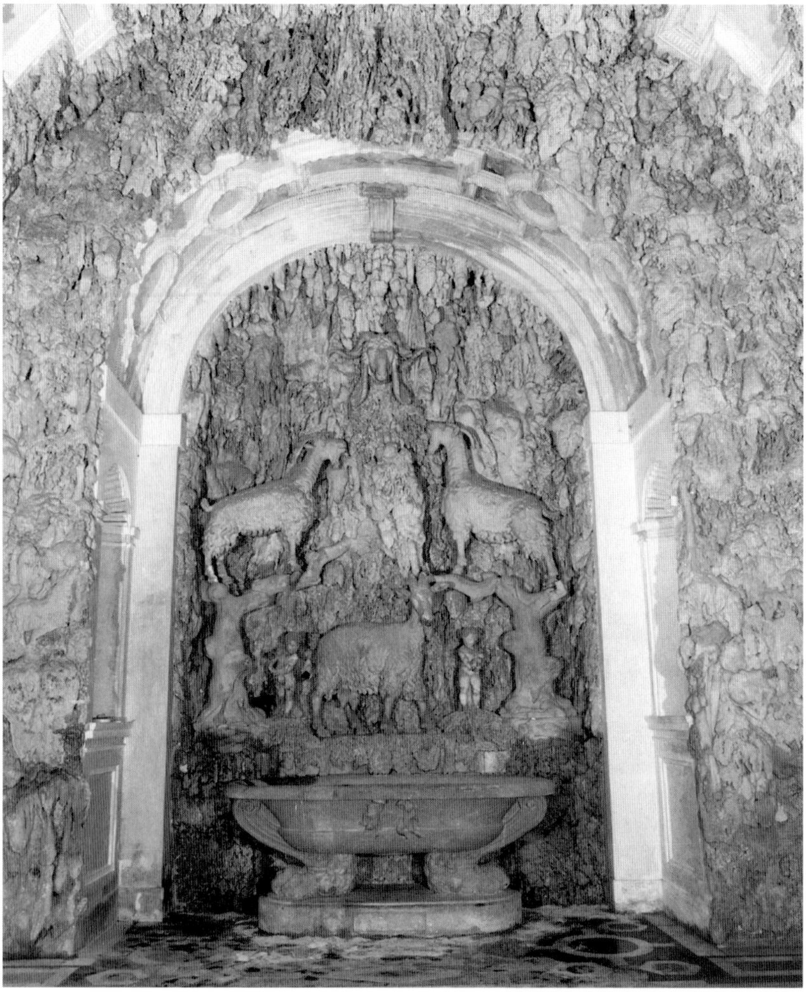

55. David Fortini, Baccio Bandinelli et al. after Niccolò Tribolo, *Grotticina di Madama* (main niche), 1553–5. Florence, Boboli Gardens. Photo: Soprintendenza per i Beni Architettonici ed Ambientali delle Provincie di Firenze e Pistoia.

a change in program after he was awarded the commission in 1567 (Fig. 56).[80] Between Tribolo's death and Giambologna's completion of a sculptural complement to the granite basin, the project was consigned to Bandinelli, whose pupil Giovanni Fancelli executed a fountain for this site, possibly as early as 1556.[81] The subject matter of this fountain is also unknown; in any case, because it is described in documents as a marble 'pilo,' we may presume that it had a candelabrum form similar to Tribolo's Castello fountain basins.

For our purposes, however, it is Vasari's *vivaio,* or fishpond, that is most significant. As Galletti has observed, the position of the pool at the lowest gradient of the garden,

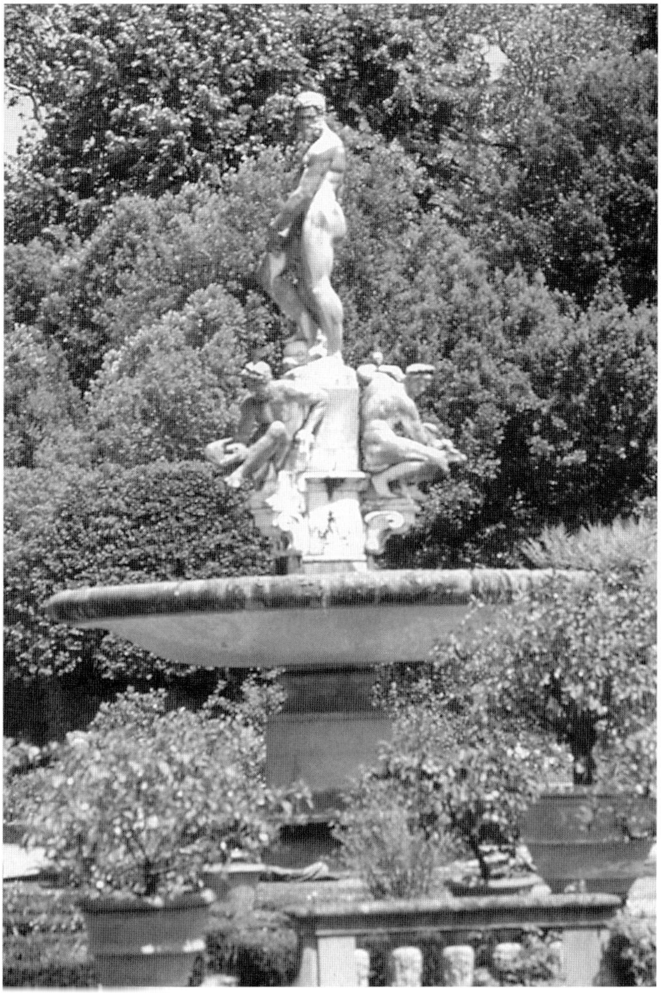

56. Giambologna, *Oceanus Fountain*, 1567–75. Florence, Boboli Gardens. Photo: Author.

'must have served as a collecting basin, guaranteeing the supply of water to the Palazzo Vecchio even when the source itself was low.'[82] While Vasari's frontispiece for the fishpond was not executed until 1557–9, with work continuing through to 1564, the *vivaio* itself was apparently constructed earlier and may even have simply been an adaptation of a basin constructed prior to the purchase of the property by Eleonora in February 1550.[83] Thus the fishpond, with its essential purpose related to the provision of freshwater to the main piazza and the seat of the Florentine government on the opposite side of the river, must have been central to Tribolo's original hydraulic plan for the garden. If the *vivaio,* like those at Castello, was in fact only an adaptation of an already extant pool, it would also have been the central point from which the rest of the project would have been elaborated.

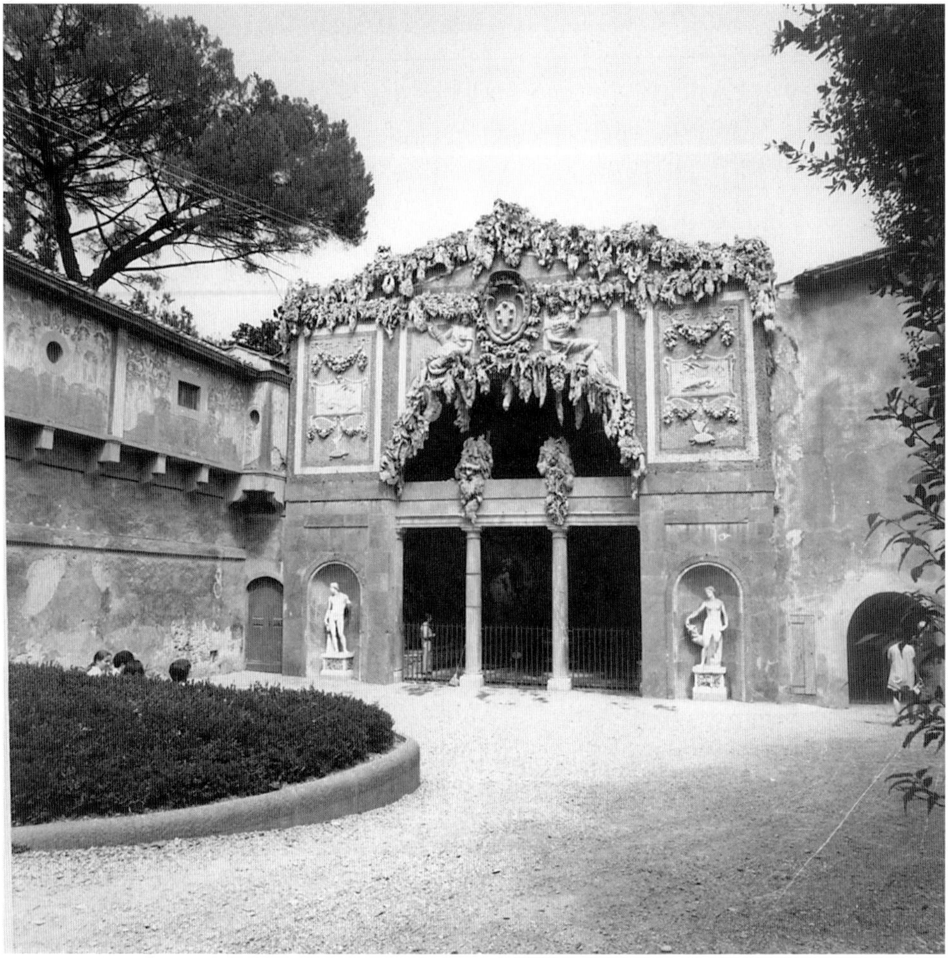

57. Giorgio Vasari, *Frontispiece for Fishpond*, 1556–8 (now: Bernardo Buontalenti, Grotta Grande, Façade, 1583–9). Florence, Boboli Gardens. Photo: Soprintendenza per i Beni Architettonici ed Ambientali delle Provincie di Firenze e Pistoia.

The *vivaio* itself was destroyed with the creation of Buontalenti's Grotta Grande, begun in 1583 (Fig. 57). Fortunately, Buontalenti simply incorporated Vasari's preexisting façade into the grotto's new one. We can, then, reconstruct the appearance of the *vivaio:* an open pool, presumably rectangular, preceded by the severe architecture in pietra forte and white and red marble of the lower story of the Grotto's façade. In the lateral niches of this frontispiece, were placed Bandinelli's *Apollo* and *Ceres,* gifts from the sculptor to his patron, Eleonora di Toledo, where they remain today.[84] The composition also included Giovanni Fancelli's *Peasant Emptying a Cask,* executed after a design by Bandinelli (Fig. 58).[85] Fancelli's *Peasant* would have been a fountain element, either at the edge or the center of the basin, whose wine cask would have

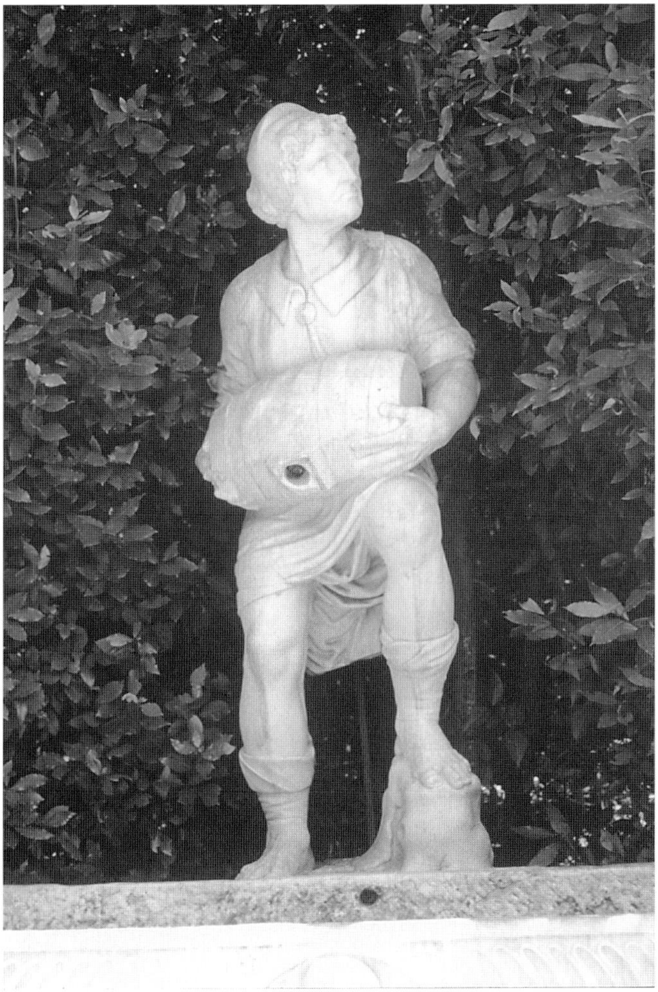

58. Giovanni Fancelli, called Nanni di Stocco, after Baccio Bandinelli, *Peasant Emptying a Cask,* c. 1556. Florence, Boboli Gardens. Photograph: Author.

flowed with water. The *Peasant Emptying a Cask,* while artistically modest, is a seminal work; it is the first known example of the type of rustic genre sculpture that would become so popular in subsequent gardens throughout Europe.[86]

The composition of the *vivaio,* then, would have combined practical and ornamental features while displaying an iconography that was an unusual mix of high and low culture.[87] *Apollo* and *Ceres,* the sun god and the harvest goddess, would have been linked to the *Peasant* as the deities responsible for the bountiful harvest represented by the never-ending flow of 'wine' from the peasant's cask.[88] Thus, the benevolence of the gods renders possible the prosperity of the peasant, an obvious parallel to the ducal couple's benevolent provision of freshwater to their subjects

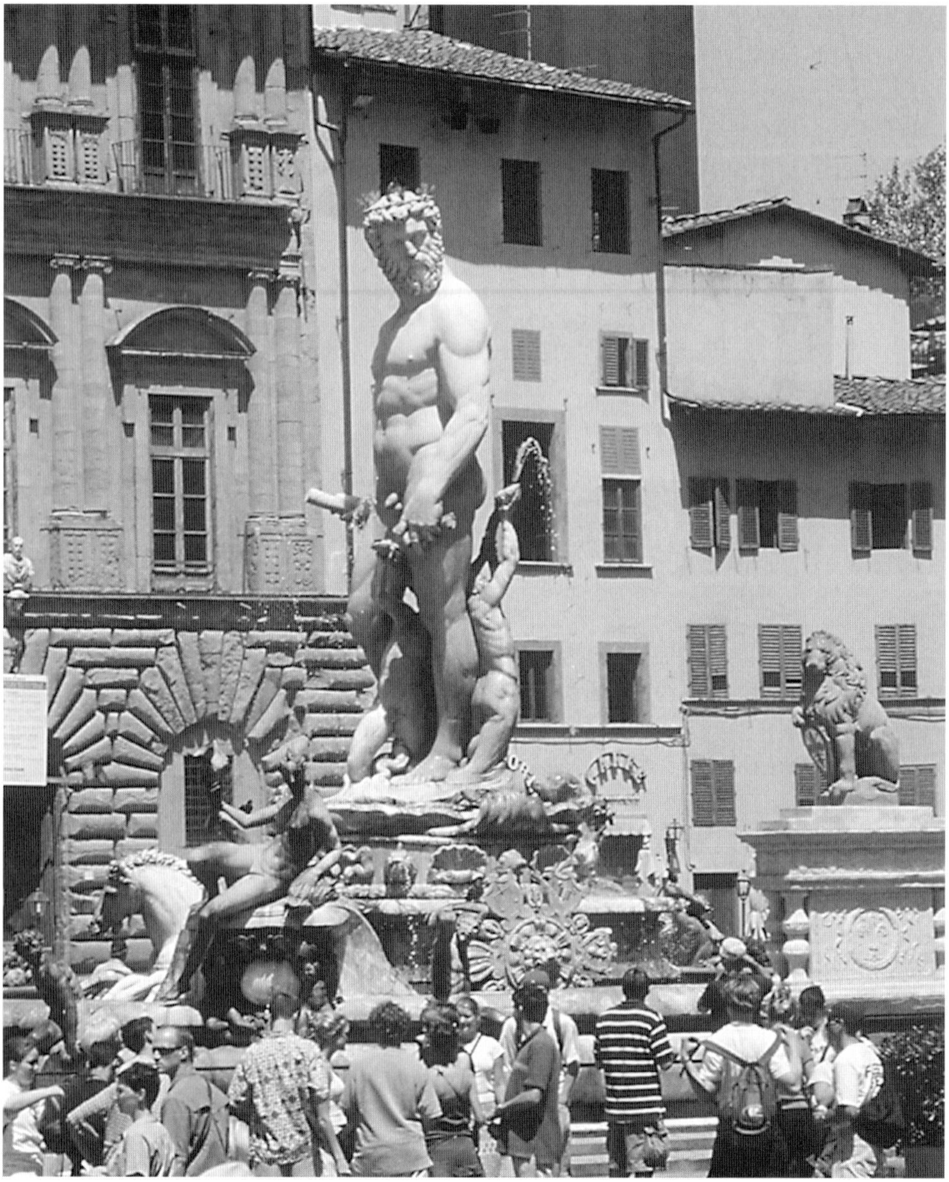

59. Bartolomeo Ammannati, *Neptune Fountain,* 1560–5 and 1571–5. Florence, Piazza della Signoria. Photo: Author.

in the square on the opposite side of the river. As Galletti has aptly observed, the *vivaio*'s significance as the nexus of the two water systems, public and private, would have been evident, as it was the point at which the water emerged from its invisible underground conduits.[89] Presuming that the *vivaio* continued to be supplied with fish meant to be consumed at the ducal table, the presence of the living creatures

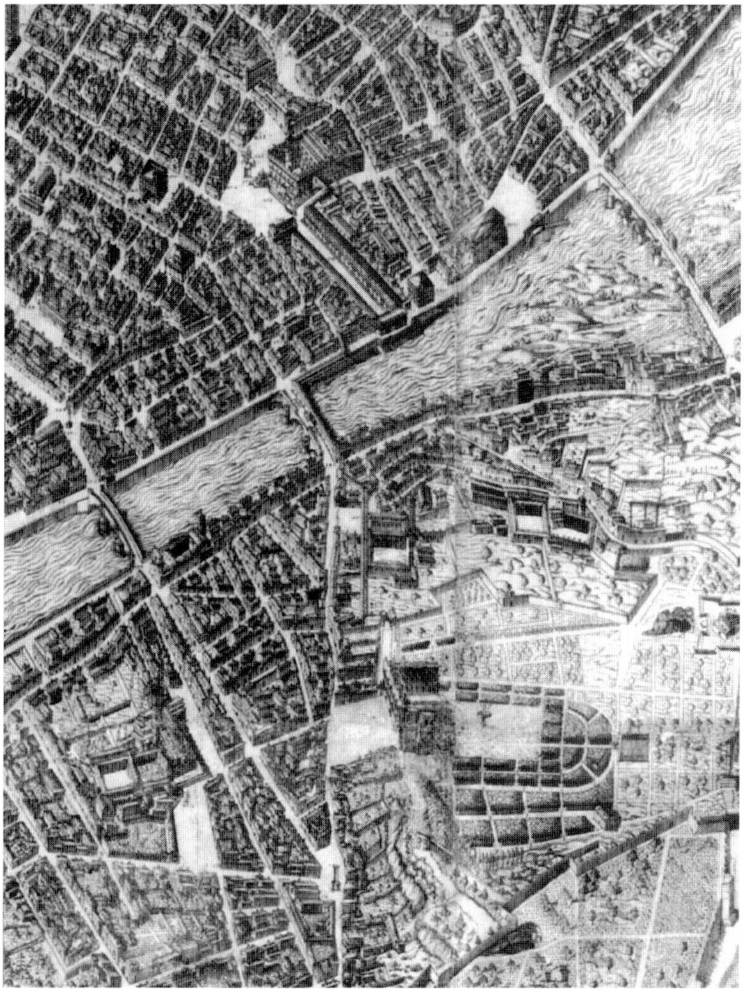

60. Stefano Buonsignori, *Map of Florence*, 1584, detail. Photo: Musei Comunali di Firenze.

darting about in the pool would again have provided strong visible evidence for the freshness and potability of the water itself.[90] As at Castello, the adherence to the model established at Poggioreale is striking.

Obviously, the final, public outlet of the water was of even greater importance. Ultimately, the work that would occupy this privileged position in urban Florence was Ammannati's Neptune Fountain (Fig. 59). It is worth considering, however, that the project was originally to have been executed by Bandinelli, who as early as 1550 had commissioned the extraction of the marble block from the quarries at Carrara and by 1551–2 was hard at work on the fountain's design.[91] The date is obviously significant and highlights once again that the program to bring water through the duchess's new garden and then on to serve the public in the piazza was essential to Tribolo's original project for the Boboli Gardens.[92] Had Bandinelli lived to complete the work, each important iconographic feature along the water passage through the Boboli Gardens and then out into the public sphere would have been marked by a sculpture either executed by Bandinelli or by one of his assistants according to his designs. Bandinelli had not been part of Tribolo's team at Castello[93]; indeed, Tribolo is reputed to have been one of Bandinelli's hated rivals.[94] The extraordinary importance accorded to Bandinelli, then, in the context of the Boboli Gardens should be attributed to Eleonora's patronage, because the duchess was renowned for protecting the sculptor's interests at court.[95]

The fountain eventually created by Bandinelli's former pupil, Ammannati, and his assistants nonetheless reveals the fundamental importance of the new water source in the composition.[96] By 1565, the supply of water arriving at the piazza was already deemed insufficient for the dramatic display that Cosimo desired for the work. A new aqueduct linking the same Fonte della Ginevra to the piazza and the palace fountains was begun that year.[97] This aqueduct was celebrated in a 1567 portrait medal of Cosimo, whose reverse displays Neptune on his chariot drawn by sea-horses and in the background the Roman-style arcades of the aqueduct[98]; the imagery of the medal thus highlights Cosimo's rule not just as fountain patron but as transporter of freshwater to the city center.[99] As Campbell has demonstrated, the fountain's basin was originally intended to continuously overflow.[100] This manner of displaying the new water source emphasizes the abundance of the water's flow, suggesting the copiousness, fertility, richness, and well-being that would have been considered the benefits of the duke's benevolence in providing the new water source to the heart of Florence.[101] Here, as at Castello, the project recalls the urban renewal context of the Poggioreale paradigm. In the Neapolitan model, the completion of the aqueduct bearing the freshwater from the villa to the city center was complemented by the creation of a new road linking the two; in Florence, the construction of the Vasari corridor in 1565 would have offered a similar visual parallel for the conveyance of water between the two zones, although this route would have been reserved for the exclusive use of the ducal family (Fig. 60).[102]

Eleonora's imitation of Poggioreale at the Pitti-Boboli complex may be linked to other works of her patronage that emphasize her Hispano-Neapolitan heritage and the important ties to the Habsburg line that she brought with her to Cosimo as his consort.[103] It is worth considering that Eleonora's preference for Bandinelli may well be attributable to similar considerations, because Bandinelli had been accorded the extraordinary favor of a knighthood by the emperor himself.[104] As for the confirmation of the duchess's knowledge of Poggioreale, a gift made by Eleonora to her brother apparently recalled a specific aspect of the decoration there. In 1542, Eleonora sent ten glazed terracotta roundels executed by Santi Buglioni, the heir to the della Robbia workshop, and his assistant, Lorenzo Marignolli, to García de

Toledo for the garden of his villa at Chiaia in Naples.[105] These were almost certainly commissioned in emulation of the della Robbian glazed terracotta busts depicting heroes of the Aragonese line that adorned the grand garden loggia overlooking the *vivaio* at Poggioreale, offering important evidence that Alfonso d'Aragona's villa was well known to the patron of the Pitti-Boboli complex.[106]

Subsequently, the continued employment of the Pitti Palace and Boboli Gardens as the locus of spectacular court festivities maintained well into the seventeenth century the tradition of classically inspired entertainments established at Poggioreale.[107] In 1589, during the celebrations held for the marriage of Grand Duke Ferdinando I to Cristina di Lorena, the courtyard of the Pitti Palace was temporarily flooded for the performance of a naumachia.[108] The practice itself recalls the main villa structure at Poggioreale, whose courtyard could be flooded at will.[109] Although there is no evidence that mock naval battles were ever held at Poggioreale,[110] Alfonso's employment of this feature as a water jest to douse guests while dining in the courtyard was well known through Serlio's description and was almost certainly recalled in the planning of the 1589 event.

The villa and garden complex at Poggioreale was distinguished from its outset as a work of royal patronage and established a new standard for the design and decoration of suburban pleasure villas throughout Italy and beyond. The hydraulic system developed for this project was one of its most sophisticated features and may be considered as especially avant-garde for its time. The translation of this model from one court to another at a temporal distance of a half-century or more suggests both the importance of Poggioreale as a hydraulic precedent and its princely associations, which surely accounted in no small part for its subsequent emulation. The employment of this system as a model in the sixteenth-century projects for the Medici examined here means that two distinct, extant Florentine garden complexes preserve for us an idea of that paradigmatic lost original created for the Aragonese in fifteenth-century Naples.

NOTES

1. See A. V. Antonovics, '"Il semble que ce soit là un vrai Paradis terreste": Charles VIII's conquest of Naples and the French Renaissance', in *The French Descent into Renaissance Italy 1494–95: Antecedents and Effects*, ed. David Abulafia (Aldershot: Ashgate, 1995), 316.

2. On Charles's experience of Poggioreale, see Antonovics, 'Charles VIII's conquest', 318–19, 321–4; Antonio Colombo, 'Il palazzo e il giardino di Poggioreale', *Archivio storico per le province napoletane* 10 (1885): 203–6; Christoph Luitpold Frommel, *Die Farnesina und Peruzzis Architektonisches Frühwerk* (Berlin: De Grutyer, 1961), 90–2; Kenneth Woodbridge, *Princely Gardens: The Origins and Development of the French Formal Style* (New York: Rizzoli, 1986), 35, 39–41, 61, 68. Fra Giocondo and the gardener Pacello da Mercogliano would accompany Charles upon his return to France from Naples; for their influence on subsequent French architecture, see also Roberto Pane, *Il Rinascimento nell'Italia meridionale*, 2 vols. (Milan: Edizioni di Comunità, 1977), vol. II, 47; Franco

Strazzullo, 'Documenti per il palazzo e giardini di Poggioreale', *Asprenas* 10 (1963): 49; Summonte to Michiel, in Fausto Nicolini, *L'arte napoletana del rinascimento e la lettera di Pietro Summonte a Marcantonio Michiel* (Naples: Ricciardi, 1925), 172. I thank Anna Bisceglia for her kind assistance in obtaining a photograph of the Stoopendael view of Naples.

3. Strazzullo, 'Documenti', 49.

4. Indeed, as Colombo, 'Il palazzo', 315, observes, Poggioreale's condition was so poor that Charles chose to reside elsewhere, at the Villa del Martirano. The banquets held at Poggioreale during Charles's 1535 residence in Naples, thus, assume symbolic connotations as occasions emphasizing the emperor's Aragonese heritage and the legitimacy of his claims to the Neapolitan throne. The royal associations with this site were so strong that in 1703, when the villa's state was even more ruinous, king of Spain Felipe V had a temporary baldachin constructed on the public road nearby to make his triumphal entry into Naples from here; Colombo, 'Il Palazzo', 338.

5. August Schmarsow, 'Excerpte aus Joh. Fichard's "Italia" von 1536', *Repertorium für Kunstwissenschaft* 14 (1891): 374: 'Quod si ad pristinum suum nitorem reduceretur aliquando, non puto in tota Italia et amplius et magnificentius et amoenius lavacrum esse posse.' Fichard's use of the word 'lavacrum' appears especially noteworthy for the following discussion of the villa and garden complex; see also Ulrika Kiby, 'Poggioreale: Das erste Nymphäum der Renaissance', *Die Gartenkunst* 7 (1995): 72–3, who both cites and discusses the importance of Fichard's text. For Poggioreale as a bath complex, see George L. Hersey, 'Water-Works and Water-Play in Renaissance Naples', in *Fons Sapientiae: Renaissance Garden Fountains,* ed. Elisabeth B. MacDougall (Washington, D.C.: Dumbarton Oaks, 1978), 70–1; Fritz-Eugen Keller, 'Die Zeichnung Uff. 363A von Baldassare Peruzzi und das Bad von Poggio Reale', *Architectura* 1 (1973): 32–5.

6. The specific relevance of Poggioreale as a model for the design of the apartments in the Pitti Palace was noted by Leon Satkowski, 'The Palazzo Pitti: Planning and Use in the Grand-Ducal Era', *Journal of the Society of Architectural Historians* 42 (1983): 346, 349.

7. See Claudia Conforti, *Giorgio Vasari architetto* (Milan: Electa, 1993), 160; Satkowski, *Giorgio Vasari: Architect and Courtier* (Princeton: Princeton University Press, 1993), 39.

8. Colombo, 'Il Palazzo', 190.

9. Joampiero Leostello da Volterra, *Effemeridi delle cose fatte per il Duca di Calabria (1484–1491),* ed. Gaetano Filangieri (Naples: Accademia reale delle scienze, 1883), 132. See also Colombo, 'Il Palazzo', 190–1; Cornelius von Fabriczy, 'Toscanische und obertialienische Künstler in Diensten der Aragonesen zu Neapel', *Repertorium für Kunstwissenschaft* 20 (1897): 87; George L. Hersey, *Alfonso II and the Artistic Renewal of Naples 1485–1495* (New Haven and London: Yale University Press, 1969), 60.

10. See Colombo, 'Il Palazzo', 193; Fabriczy, 'Toscanische und obertialienische', 91–2; Frommel, *Farnesina,* 90; Hersey, *Alfonso II,* 60; Roberto Pane, 'Le Effemeridi di Joanpiero Leostello', *Napoli nobilissima* 7 (1968): 77; Giorgio Vasari, *Le vite de' più eccellenti pittori scultori ed architettori* (1568), ed. Gaetano Milanesi, 9 vols. (Florence: Sansoni, 1878–85), vol. II, 470.

11. The names subsequently associated with the project are derived from Summonte to Michiel, in Nicolini, *L'arte napoletana,* 72; see Colombo, 'Il Palazzo', 197; Fabriczy, 'Toscanische und obertialienische', 95; Frommel, *Farnesina,* 90, 97; Hersey, *Alfonso II,* 73–5. For the death of Giuliano in Naples, see also Fabriczy, 'Toscanische und obertialienische', 89; Pane, 'Le Effemeridi di Joanpiero Leostello', 81; Vasari, *Vite,* vol. II, 473–4.

12. Colombo, 'Il Palazzo', 194; Hersey, *Alfonso II,* 62. See also the anonymous sixteenth-century chronicle, published as 'Racconti di storia napoletana', *Archivio storico per le province napoletane* 23 (1908): 503, which states of Alfonso, 'molto si dilettò d'architettura.'

13. On the importance of the view from the site, see Giovio's description, cited by Sonia Maffei, 'La Villa di Poggioreale e la Duchessa di Alfonso II d'Aragona in una descrizione di Paolo Giovio: moduli dell'elogio e tradizione antica', *Annali della Scuola Normale Superiore di Pisa,* 4th ser., *Quaderni* 1–2 (1996): 163–4. See also Colombo, 'Il Palazzo', 191; Frommel, *Farnesina,* 90–1, 96; Frommel, 'Poggioreale: problemi di ricostruzione e tipologia', in *Giuliano e la bottega dei da Maiano,* ed. Daniela Lamberini, Marcello Lotti and Roberto Lunari (Florence: Octavo, 1994), 104; Hersey, *Alfonso II,* 64.

14. Woodbridge, *Princely Gardens,* 35. Colombo, 'Il Palazzo', 191, notes that the system is recorded from at least the Middle Ages; similarly, Frommel, *Farnesina,* 90. Hersey, *Alfonso II,* 96–7, notes the Renaissance tradition tracing the origins of the system back to Virgil's day. See also, ibid., 61; idem, 'Water-works', 65; Kiby, 'Poggioreale', 75; Pane, 'Le Effemeridi di Joanpiero Leostello', 78.

15. For other aspects of the design of Poggioreale that revived local ancient types, see Hersey, *Alfonso II,* 58–9; Cesare De Seta, *Le città nella storia d'Italia: Napoli* (Rome: Laterza, 1981), 88; idem, 'La struttura urbana di Napoli tra utopia e realtà', in *Rinascimento da Brunelleschi a Michelangelo: la rappresentazione dell'architettura,* ed. Henry Millon and Vittorio Magnago Lampugnani (Milan: Bompiani, 1994), 360–61. For the Neapolitan hydraulic system, see Hersey, *Alfonso II,* 95–7; Keller, 'Die Zeichnung', 31.

16. Colombo, 'Il Palazzo', 194–5. See also Frommel, *Farnesina,* 90; Hersey, *Alfonso II,* 62.

17. On the Porta Capuana and the restoration of the adjacent city walls, see Hersey, *Alfonso II,* 44–57; see also Isabella Di Resta, 'L'ambiente napoletano da Giuliano da Maiano al Mormando', in *Giuliano,* ed. Lamberini, Lotti and Lunardi, 93; Fabriczy, 'Toscanische und obertialienische', 90; Vasari, *Vite,* vol. II, 470–1. The Porta Capuana was in all likelihood the principal focus of the view towards the west from the villa, Hersey, *Alfonso II,* 64. According to the anonymous sixteenth-century chronicle, Alfonso's interest in reviving this particular area of the city was a result of his first son having been born in the Castel Capuano: 'Racconti', 503.

18. On urban renewal under Alfonso, see Hersey, *Alfonso II,* esp. 58: 'In many ways the most important part of the renewal consisted of Alfonso's new villa, Poggioreale'. See also De Seta, *Napoli,* 85; Di Resta, 'Ambiente napoletano', 92.

19. See Hersey, *Alfonso II,* 70.

20. Giovanni Tarcagnota di Gaeta, *Del sito et lodi della città di Napoli con una breve historia de gli re suoi & delle cose più degne altrove ne' medesimi tempi avenute* (1566; reprint with introduction by Strazzullo, Rome: Benincasa, 1988), 16v: 'Ma sopra tutto quello, di che ha di bisogno per suo maggiore decoro una città, sono le fontane di acqua viva, e corrente; che oltre la commodità, che danno, che è grandissima, & incomparibile, fanno vaga, lieta, & quasi viva quella città dove sono.'

21. Conforti, 'Acque, condotti, fontane e fronde: le provvisioni per la delizia nella villa medicea di Castello', in *Il teatro delle acque,* ed. Dalu Jones (Rome: Elefante, 1992), 79.

22. Colombo, 'Il Palazzo', 192.

23. For the destruction of the Bolla aqueduct, see Colombo, 'Il Palazzo', 311–12. For the arrival of Pedro de Toledo, see the contemporary diarist Gregorio Rosso, *Istoria delle cose di Napoli sotto l'imperio di Carlo V cominciando dall'anno 1526 per insino all'anno 1537* (Naples: Gravier, 1770), 45 (as 4 September 1532); 'Racconti', 715 (as 12 September 1532). The chronicler, ibid., 717, observes that Pedro upon his arrival 'curiosamente ha voluto intendere tutte l'azioni delli Re retropassati', confirming the probability that Poggioreale's history and function would have been well known at his court.

24. Hersey, *Alfonso II*, 95, n. 74. However, in his 1600 biography of Pedro, Scipione Miccio refers to drainage projects executed by the viceroy in the area just outside of Naples around the Sebeto river; these may be a record of the completion of some of this project; 'Vita di Don Pietro di Toledo, Marchese di Villafranca, composta da Scipione Miccio, cittadino napolitano', in Francesco Palermo, 'Narrazioni e documenti sulla storia del regno di Napoli dall'anno 1522 al 1667', *Archivio storico italiano* 9 (1846): 22. Also, a 1574 government engineer's report on the condition of Poggioreale contains a reference to 'lo appartamento facto per don Pietro de Toledo' (Strazzullo, 'Documenti', 52); Pedro presumably therefore either built or restored an apartment on the property.

25. Schmarsow, 'Excerpte', 374: 'Ibi locus, ubi derivatur aquaeductus in urbem.' See also 'Racconti', 503.

26. See Colombo, 'Il Palazzo', 320–1. The reasons adduced by the governmental body, the Camera della Sommaria, in 1571, against selling the property were (ibid., n. 1): 'per serbare memoria dei Re Aragonesi, e perchè attraverso Poggioreale passava l'acquedotto che alimentava il maggior numero dei pozzi e delle fontane nella città.' See also Pane, *Il Rinascimento nell'Italia meridionale*, vol. II, 39–40; Strazzullo, 'Documenti', 50 n. 24. In the seventeenth century, the continual sale of rights to water rerouted away from the villa for use at nearby water mills and for the irrigation of local farms repeatedly caused the wells and fountains of Naples to run dry, Colombo, 'Il Palazzo', 332–3.

27. For the centrality of the fishpond in the design of the garden's hydraulic system, see Kiby, 'Poggioreale', 71.

28. Kiby, 'Poggioreale', 75, interprets the contemporary references to the 'sguazzatorio' as referring exclusively to the bath/nymphaeum portion of the garden that she reconstructs. However, the term appears to have been used more frequently in connection with the fishpond; see Colombo, 'Il Palazzo', 202, esp. n. 2, regarding the meaning of the word 'sguazzatorio', which he clearly demonstrates meant 'vivaio' or nymphaeum. The contemporary references to dining at the 'sguazzatorio' would appear to distinguish this practice from dining in the 'grotta'; I would therefore suggest that the former referred to repasts served under the loggia facing the fishpond while the latter to those served in the bath/nymphaeum.

29. Leostello, *Effemeridi*, 225–6; see also Colombo, 'Il Palazzo', 196; Hersey, *Alfonso II*, 62; Pane, 'Le Effemeridi di Joanpiero Leostello', 78.

30. Giorgio Galletti, 'La genesi della Grotta Grande di Boboli', *Artifici d'acque e giardini: la cultura delle grotte e dei ninfei in Italia e in Europa*, ed. Isabella Lapi Ballerini and Litta Maria Medri (Florence: Centro Di, 1999), 230, has observed this function for the *vivaio* subsequently constructed in the Boboli Gardens, see below, 467, and n. 82. The *vivaio* should be identified with the 'uncovered cistern that supplies the delightful fountains' at Poggioreale mentioned by Summonte (cited in translation by Hersey, *Alfonso II*, 96); similarly, in Fichard's 1536 description, the *vivaio* is identified as a 'lacus', or cistern. See Schmarsow, 'Excerpte', 374, and Kiby, 'Poggioreale', 72.

31. The presence of aquatic birds here is specifically noted by Leostello, *Effemeridi*, 238; see Colombo, 'Il Palazzo', 202; Pane, 'Le Effemeridi di Joanpiero Leostello', 78. In an entry of 15 July 1489, Leostello also recalls that fish were served at a banquet at the villa, although he does not specify how or where they had been kept fresh until they were prepared. Giovio specifically notes both the presence of numerous types of birds and fish; see Maffei, 'La Villa', 163–4.

32. Leostello, *Effemeridi*, 353. Peruzzi's sketches (Uffizi 363A r. and v.) were first published by Heinrich von Geymüller, in idem and Carl von Stegmann, *Die Architektur der Renaissance in Toscana*, 12 vols. (Munich: Bruckmann, 1885–1909), vol. IV, ii, 10–11, figs. 39–40; for a review

of the interpretations of these drawings and relative bibliography, see most recently Frommel, *'Poggioreale',* 104–6; Kiby, 'Poggioreale', 69–72, 74–5. For the employment of the *vivaio* as a fishpond, see also Frommel, *Farnesina,* 95.

33. Indeed, entertainment may well be considered its primary purpose; see Hersey, *Alfonso II,* 63.

34. The desire to offer fresh fish at banquets should in itself be considered avant-garde as fish had been stygmatized as an inferior food source in the Middle Ages; see Allen J. Grieco, 'Fiordiano Malatesta da Rimini e i trattati di ittiologia della metà del cinquecento', in *Scrivere il Medioevo: lo spazio, la sanità, il cibo,* ed. B. Laurioux and L. Moulinier-Brogi (Rome: Viella, 2001), 307. Grieco notes that the medieval classification system that condemned fish consumption survived through the late quattrocento; Poggioreale would thus rank as one of the earliest Italian sites where fish were considered a prized comestible.

35. See, for example, James Ackerman, 'Le regioni dell'architettura italiana rinascimentale', in *Rinascimento da Brunelleschi a Michelangelo,* ed. Millon and Magnago Lampugnani, 322; De Seta, 'Struttura urbana', 360. However, see Frommel, *'Poggioreale',* 109, who convincingly observes that Poggioreale is not derived from 'un prototipo fiorentino... Poggioreale ed il modello per il palazzo Reale sono caratterizzati invece da pregnanti torri angolari, e sono quindi i successori dei castelli e dell'architettura dinastica....' Nonetheless, Neapolitans recognized Florence as the leader in the new architectural style, as is confirmed by Summonte's famous letter to Michiel: 'La architettura, per tanti anni ignorata, cominciò, sì come dixi in principio, in Fiorenza, son circa cento anni, ad recuperarsi' (Nicolini, *L'arte napoletana,* 170).

36. Most recently, Kiby, 'Poggioreale', 71–2, 74–5, 77–8 (with references to the previous literature). See Frank Joseph Alvarez, 'The Renaissance Nymphaeum: Its Origins and Its Development in Rome and Vicinity' (unpublished Ph.D. diss., Columbia University, 1981), 29–40, for the disappearance of the nymphaeum in the West following the fall of the Roman Empire and its preservation in the Islamic world, especially the Islamic-style Norman garden palaces of Palermo: the Zisa and the Cuba. Kiby notes that these same Sicilian garden complexes also supplied essential models for Poggioreale's fishpond.

37. See Alvarez, 'The Renaissance Nymphaeum', 45, 47–8; Frommel, *'Poggioreale',* 111; Pane, 'Le Effemeridi di Joanpiero Leostello', 83.

38. While Lorenzo's direct participation in the design of the villa is not universally accepted, his essential role as an advisor is confirmed by his documented recommendations of architects for the project. See, among others, Ackerman, *The Villa: Form and Ideology of Country Houses* (Princeton: Princeton University Press, 1990), 79, 86; Jacob Burckhardt, *The Architecture of the Italian Renaissance,* ed. Peter Murray, trans. James Palmes (London: Secker & Warburg, 1985), 11, 137; Frommel, *'Poggioreale',* 108; Hersey, *Alfonso II,* 60 n. 12, 69, 73; Ludwig H. Heydenreich, *Architecture in Italy 1400–1500,* ed. Paul Davies (New Haven and London: Yale University Press, 1996), 133; Milanesi, in Vasari, *Vite,* vol. II, 470 n. 2 †, 483; Pane, *Il Rinascimento nell'Italia meridionale,* II, 38, 54–5; Vasari, *Vite,* vol. III, 271–3; Woodbridge, *Princely Gardens,* 35.

39. See Edelstein, review of *Bronzino's Chapel of Eleonora in the Palazzo Vecchio,* by Janet Cox-Rearick, *The Art Bulletin* 76 (1994): 174, esp. n. 18.

40. For the villa and garden complex as Cosimo's first work of patronage and Tribolo's original program, see Vasari, *Vite,* vol. VI, 71–85. On the question of the iconography's author, see Conforti, 'Il giardino di Castello come immagine del territorio', in *La città effimera e l'universo artificiale del giardino: la Firenze dei Medici e l'Italia del '500,* ed. Marcello Fagiolo (Rome: Officina, 1980), 158 n. 1 (as Pierfrancesco Riccio); idem, 'L'invenzione delle allegorie territoriali e dinastiche del

giardino di Castello a Firenze', in *Il giardino come labirinto della storia* (Palermo: Centro Studi di Storia e Arte dei Giardini, 1984), 190–7 (as Luca Martini, subsequently followed by Cristina Acidini Luchinat, in idem and Galletti, *Le ville e i giardini di Castello e Petraia a Firenze* (Ospedaletto: Pacini, 1992), 41); Detlef Heikamp, 'La Villa de Castello', *L'Oeil,* 151–3 (1967), 56 (as Benedetto Varchi); Liliane Châtelet-Lange, 'The Grotto of the Unicorn and the Garden of the Villa di Castello', *Art Bulletin* 50 (1968): 57 (as Tribolo, later revised by Varchi). On the authorship of the program, see now also Lapi Ballerini, 'Niccolò Tribolo e la Grotta degli Animali a Castello', in *Artifici d'acque e giardini,* ed. idem and Medri, 269. On the villa's history and the garden's iconography, see (with references to the previous literature): Acidini and Galletti, *Castello e Petraia,* 13–134; Conforti, 'Immagine del territorio', 152–61; idem, 'Il giardino di Castello e le tematiche spaziali del Manierisimo', in *Il giardino storico italiano: problemi di indagini, fonti letterarie e storiche,* ed. Giovanna Ragionieri (Florence: Olschki, 1981), 147–63; Claudia Lazzaro, *The Italian Renaissance Garden: From the Conventions of Planting, Design, and Ornament to the Grand Gardens of Sixteenth-Century Central Italy* (New Haven and London: Yale University Press, 1990), 167–89. See also the bibliography cited by Conforti, 'Acque, condotti', 76 n. 1.

41. Conforti, 'Acque, condotti', 76; Galletti, *Castello e Petraia,* 19, 22, 67, who assigns responsibility for the entire project in 1537 to Piero da San Casciano (although he notes that the initial focus appears to have been primarily on the transportation of water to the site), followed by Tribolo's arrival and control in 1538; Vasari, *Vite,* vol. VI, 71, 76. For a concise history of the hydraulic works at Castello, see now also Galletti, 'Tribolo maestro delle acque dei giardini', in *Niccolò detto il Tribolo tra arte, architettura e paesaggio,* ed. Elisabetta Pieri and Luigi Zangheri in *Quaderni di Ricerche Storiche* 7 (2001): 151–60; Lapi Ballerini, 'Grotta degli Animali', 270–1.

42. See Lapi Ballerini, 'Grotta degli Animali', 268, esp. n. 4, regarding the attribution problem. See also Acidini, *Castello e Petraia,* 42; Châtelet-Lange, 'Grotto of the Unicorn', 51; Vasari, *Vite,* vol. VI, 71.

43. Conforti, 'Acque, condotti', 76–7. Essential to this interpretation is Vasari's account, Vasari, *Vite,* vol. VI, 71–7 (76): 'Perchè il Tribolo, preso l'assunto di guidare tutta quella muraglia da sè, s'avvedde, ancor che fussero in gran copia l'acque state condotte, che nondimeno erano poche a quello che egli si era messo in animo di fare.' See also Galletti, *Castello e Petraia,* 67, 163; Lapi Ballerini, 'Grotta degli Animali', 270–1; Lazzaro, *Italian Renaissance Garden,* 167, 171, n. 23.

44. Lazzaro, *Italian Renaissance Garden,* 168.

45. Vasari (*Vite,* vol. VI, 99) himself claimed to have continued the project 'secondo il disegno e modello ... del Tribolo.' On the problem of the original grotto project, see (with references to the previous bibliography): Acidini, *Castello e Petraia,* 45–6, 109–20; Conforti, 'La grotta "degli animali" o "del diluvio" nel giardino di Villa Medici a Castello', *Quaderni di Palazzo Te* 6 (1987): 71–80; Lapi Ballerini, 'Grotta degli Animali', 271–9; Lazzaro, *Italian Renaissance Garden,* 178–9; Satkowski, *Giorgio Vasari,* 106. For the portions of the Varchi-Tribolo program that were never executed, see Vasari, *Vite,* vol. VI, 83–4; see also Acidini, *Castello e Petraia,* 50; Galletti, *Castello e Petraia,* 68–70; Lazzaro, *Italian Renaissance Garden,* 177.

46. Vasari, *Vite,* vol. VI, 77–8. These were apparently never executed in permanent form and were substituted in Vasari's completion of the project by Ammannati's single figure (cast in 1563; first installed in the garden in 1565), representing the entire Appennine range in the center of the upper *vivaio,* see Acidini, *Castello e Petraia,* 45–6, 130; Galletti, *Castello e Petraia,* 76; Lazzaro, *Italian Renaissance Garden,* 178, 184, 186; Satkowski, *Giorgio Vasari,* 105–6.

47. Vasari, *Vite,* vol. VI, 77–8. The only portion of these compositions still extant is the figure of *Fiesole,* companion to the Mugnone, now in the Museo Nazionale del Bargello, Florence; for

an image and discussion of these niche fountains, see Acidini, *Castello e Petraia,* 46–7; Lazzaro, *Italian Renaissance Garden,* 177–8.

48. Vasari, *Vite,* vol. VI, 78–9. The conceit of the generation of the Arno and Mugnone rivers and their confluence at a representation of Florence must predate Niccolò Martelli's 1543 description of the garden; the description, written when the garden was only partially complete, demonstrates that at the very least this iconographic program had already been established by that time. See Herbert Keutner, 'La statua del Giambologna', in *Fiorenza in villa,* ed. Cristina Acidini (Florence: Alinari, 1987), 43; see also Acidini, *Castello e Petraia,* 42, 48–9, 191–5; Lazzaro, *Italian Renaissance Garden,* 174–7.

49. Lazzaro, *Italian Renaissance Garden,* 174, 177. The group has also been interpreted as an allegory of Cosimo's victory over the Florentine exiles in the battle of Montemurlo, see (with references to the previous literature): Acidini, *Castello e Petraia,* 49–50; Keutner, 'La statua del Giambologna', 43; Lazzaro, *Italian Renaissance Garden,* 174. Vasari (*Vite,* vol. VI, 81) offers no clues as to his understanding of the group's meaning, although he does devote significant attention to the fact that the spectacular jet produced by the fountain contained the waters united from all the various sources that had been brought to the property, suggesting to me the validity of Lazzaro's reading. On the history and condition of the fountain and the attribution of its various parts, see (with references to the previous literature): Acidini, *Castello e Petraia,* 93–9; Lazzaro, *Italian Renaissance Garden,* 172–4.

50. On the original intent for the garden's water to be transported on to Florence, see Vasari, *Vite,* vol. VI, 84–5; see also Acidini, *Castello e Petraia,* 52; Lazzaro, *Italian Renaissance Garden,* 167. The only public outlets completed were the fountains at the end of the avenue leading away from the villa toward Florence, on the present via Reginaldo Giuliani; however, fountains for public use in this position are already recorded in the fifteenth century, see Acidini, *Castello e Petraia,* 13.

51. The garden's upper *vivaio,* containing water brought from the adjacent property at La Petraia, would also have ensured adequate water pressure, see Galletti, *Castello e Petraia,* 75; according to Vasari, this feature was part of Tribolo's original plan (Vasari, *Vite,* vol. VI, 76). Lazzaro (*Italian Renaissance Garden,* 198) notes that the upper *vivaio* at Boboli, where Stoldo Lorenzi's *Neptune* was subsequently installed, similarly served as 'the reservoir for the aqueduct in the garden'; Malcolm Campbell ('Giambologna's Oceanus Fountain: Identifications and Interpretations', in *Boboli 90: Atti del convegno internazionale di studi per la salvaguardia e la valorizzazione del giardino,* 2 vols. ed. Cristina Acidini and Elvira Garbero Zorzi [Florence: Edifir, 1991], vol. I, 91) states that it 'served as a fishery, as well as a water supply for the irrigation of the garden, the activation of its fountains, and, ultimately via conduits, as a water supply for the city' (see also idem, 'Hard Times in Baroque Florence: The Boboli Garden and the Grand Ducal Public Works Administration', in *The Italian Garden: Art, Design and Culture,* ed. John Dixon Hunt [Cambridge: Cambridge University Press, 1996], 171, 173). Acidini (*Castello e Petraia,* 45) links the two by observing that the trapezoidal basin at Castello served a function 'che sarebbe poi ripreso nel nucleo primevo di Boboli, pure di progettazione tribolesca.' Although these two features are clearly analogous, I have not included discussion of them here as I have not yet been able to determine the precise date for construction of the upper *vivaio* at Boboli nor whether it constituted a feature of Tribolo's original plan.

52. A similar purpose may be attributed to the tours of the underground hydraulic system, which contained walkable corridors for inspection and maintenance, given to various visitors to the garden in the sixteenth and seventeenth centuries. These were certainly intended to show off

the marvelous engineering of the design. However, they would also have provided an opportunity to demonstrate the cleanliness of the conduits and, consequently, the hygienic nature of the water. For the eyewitness reports, see Heikamp, 'Il giardino di Castello: per una ricognizione archeologica', in *Fiorenza in villa,* ed. Acidini, 9.

53. Thus, one may wish to interpret the presence of the unicorn in the Castello grotto as an intended sign of the water's purity, as does Châtelet-Lange, 'Grotto of the Unicorn', esp. 58; see also Lazzaro, *Italian Renaissance Garden,* 182. Similarly, the presence of a statue of Aesculapius in the garden would have attested to the health benefits of its waters, ibid., 177.

54. Vasari, *Vite,* vol. VI, 74; see also Châtelet-Lange, 'Grotto of the Unicorn', 51. At least one of these canals was almost surely executed, because it appears in an eighteenth-century plan of the city, see Mariachiara Pozzana, 'Il Viottolone di Castello', in *Antico e futuro nel territorio mediceo di Castello,* ed. Alessandro Vezzosi (Florence: Giunti, 1989), 56.

55. Milanesi, in Vasari, *Vite,* vol. VI, 71 n. 1; Vasari, *Vite,* vol. VI, 72–3. See also Acidini, *Castello e Petraia,* 13; Frido Chiostri, *L'acquedotto romano di Firenze: considerazioni generali e note tecnologiche sulla morfologia strutturale e sulle fasi operative della costruzione* (Florence: Clusf, 1973), 72–3; Lazzaro, *Italian Renaissance Garden,* 167.

56. Vasari, *Vite,* vol. VI, 73. See also Châtelet-Lange, 'Grotto of the Unicorn', 51; Heikamp, 'Giardino di Castello', 10; Lazzaro, *Italian Renaissance Garden,* 167.

57. Lazzaro, *Italian Renaissance Garden,* 167–8. Portions of the aqueduct were apparently still visible in the second half of the eighteenth century; Heikamp, 'Giardino di Castello', 10; Lazzaro, *Italian Renaissance Garden,* 167.

58. See Lazzaro, *Italian Renaissance Garden,* 168, 187.

59. On the idealization enacted by Utens in his lunette view of the complex, see Lazzaro, *Italian Renaissance Garden,* 169; for a fresh discussion of this problem, see also Galletti, *Castello e Petraia,* 70.

60. Vasari, *Vite,* vol. VI, 73. See also Acidini, *Castello e Petraia,* 13; Châtelet-Lange, 'Grotto of the Unicorn', 51; Chiostri, *Acquedotto romano di Firenze,* 76–8; Heikamp, 'Giardino di Castello', 10, who refers to a Catasto document of 1457 in which the area of the villa is described as 'luogo ditto al vivaio' (however, without archival citation); Pozzana, 'Viottolone di Castello', 56.

61. On the iconography of the garden at Pratolino see Suzanne B. Butters, 'Pressed Labor and Pratolino: Social Imagery and Social Reality at a Medici Garden', in *Villas and Gardens in Early Modern Italy and France,* ed. Mirka Beneš and Dianne Harris (Cambridge: Cambridge University Press, 2001), 61–87 (esp. 78–87); Lazzaro, 'From the Rain to the Wash Water in the Medici Garden at Pratolino', in *Renaissance Studies in Honor of Craig Hugh Smyth,* 2 vols., ed. Andrew Morrogh, Fiorella Superbi Gioffredi, Piero Morselli, and Eve Borsook (Florence: Giunti Barbèra, 1985), vol. II, 319–26; idem, *Italian Renaissance Garden,* 162–6.

62. See Anthea Brook, 'Sixteenth Century "Genre" Statuary in Medici Gardens and Giambologna's Fontana del Villano', in *Boboli 90,* ed. Acidini and Garbero, vol. I, 122; Lazzaro, 'Rain to Wash Water', 321; idem, *Italian Renaissance Garden,* 152, 165. The humor of the group may partly account for its enormous popularity with sixteenth- and seventeenth-century visitors to the garden. For various descriptions, from Montaigne's of 1580 to John Evelyn's of 1645, see Charles Avery, 'The "Garden called Bubley": Foreign Impressions of Florentine Gardens and a New Discovery relating to Pratolino', in *Boboli 90,* ed. Acidini and Garbero, vol. I, 150–1. The admiration expressed by later English visitors to Pratolino may also be partly attributable to the misconception that the Laundress had been executed by Michelangelo; Evelyn thought so,

as had Henry Wotton, stated in his *Elements of Architecture* of 1624 (*The Genius of the Place: The English Landscape Garden 1620–1820,* ed. John Dixon Hunt and Peter Willis [Cambridge, Mass.: MIT Press, 1988], 50, 66).

63. See Lazzaro, 'Rain to Wash Water', 321; idem, *Italian Renaissance Garden,* 151.

64. A similar concept may have laid behind the installation of another pair of genre figures by Valerio Cioli, the Lavacapo group, executed between 1595 and 1597, which depicted a woman washing her son's hair: 'The group was placed (it is not certain when) on the edge of the Neptune Fountain in the Boboli garden, directly behind the sea god, as though ordinary people had come to the fountain to use its water for this everyday function and become fixed in stone' (Lazzaro, *Italian Renaissance Garden,* 151); see also Cristina Acidini, 'La fontana del Nettuno, viaggi e metamorfosi', in *Boboli 90,* ed. Acidini and Garbero, vol. I, 44; Brook, '"Genre" Statuary', 123. For an alternative reading of the Laundress fountain at Pratolino as 'a comic but learned reference to Bianca Cappello as Diana-Luna, patron goddess of the chase', see D. R. Edward Wright, 'Some Medici Gardens of the Florentine Renaissance: An Essay in Post-Aesthetic Interpretation', in *Italian Garden,* ed. Hunt, 56; for the moralizing gloss given to the group by Francesco De' Vieri in his contemporary description of the garden and the alchemical significance it likely held for the project's patron, see Butters, 'Pressed Labor and Pratolino', 79, 83–6.

65. It is perhaps worth noting that between being assigned the two garden projects, Tribolo was also made responsible for overseeing Florence's sewer system, Vasari, *Vite,* vol. VI, 124.

66. Essential contributions for the recognition of Tribolo's authorship of the garden and the reconstruction of his plan (with references to the previous literature) are Gabriele Capecchi, 'Un "anfiteatro di verzura" nel giardino di Boboli', *Antichità viva,* vol. 24, nos. 5–6 (1995), 35–43; Galletti, 'Genesi della Grotta Grande', 228–39; Lazzaro, *Italian Renaissance Garden,* 196. Of particular interest is Alessandro Rinaldi, '"Quattro pitaffi sanza le lettere": i primi anni del Giardino di Boboli e lo "spartimento" del Tribolo', in *Boboli 90,* ed. Acidini and Garbero, vol. I, 19–30. See also Capecchi, 'Il progetto del Tribolo e la formazione dell'*Orto dei Pitti* nel Cinquecento', in *Niccolò detto il Tribolo,* ed. Pieri and Zangheri, 137–49.

67. Capecchi, *Il giardino di Boboli: un anfiteatro per la gioia dei granduchi* (Florence: Medicea, 1993), 23; idem, 'Anfiteatro di verzura', 38. See also Conforti, 'Acque, condotti', 78; Rinaldi, ' "Quattro pitaffi" ', 20–1, 24.

68. Capecchi, *Giardino di Boboli,* 23; idem, 'Anfiteatro di verzura', 38; Conforti, 'Acque, condotti', 78–9; Galletti, 'Genesi della Grotta Grande', 228; Lazzaro, *Italian Renaissance Garden,* 191 n. 2; Rinaldi, ' "Quattro pitaffi" ', 24.

69. For the documents regarding the hydraulic works and analysis of these, see Ettore Allegri and Alessandro Cecchi, *Palazzo Vecchio e i Medici* (Florence: S.P.E.S., 1980), 221–2; Galletti, 'Genesi della Grotta Grande', 230; Heikamp, 'Il Concerto poetico di statue', in *Il Concerto di statue,* ed. Alessandro Vezzosi (Florence: Alinea, 1986), 15. For the fountains (with references to the preceding bibliography), see Allegri and Cecchi, *Palazzo Vecchio,* 223–9; Heikamp, 'Il Concerto poetico di statue', 12–48. The Juno Fountain is of particular interest because, as Campbell ('Observations on the Salone dei Cinquecento in the Time of Duke Cosimo I de' Medici, 1540–1574', in *Firenze e la Toscana dei Medici nell'Europa del' 500,* 3 vols., ed. Giancarlo Garfagnini [Florence: Olschki, 1983], vol. III, 821–84) has convincingly suggested, the group refers to the women of the Medici house, and specifically to Eleonora, through whose garden and benevolence was to have been brought the fountain's water supply; See also Lazzaro, *Italian Renaissance Garden,* 152–4, 198.

70. This connection is made by Lazzaro, *Italian Renaissance Garden,* 191. See also Vasari's Life of Brunelleschi in which the description of the Boboli waterworks and the definition of Cosimo as 'magnanimo principe' appear closely related, Vasari, *Vite,* vol. II, 372–4.

71. Rinaldi ('Quattro pitaffi', 24) notes another connection between the hydraulic works at Castello and Boboli. An entry dated 29 May 1551 in one of Eleonora's accounts for the project describes the measure of piping being supplied for the gardens as 'of the same size as those at Castello.' As Rinaldi aptly observes: 'Il ricalco tecnologico . . . allaccia Boboli e Castello "per li rami" dell'impianto idraulico in uno stretto rapporto di parentela. . . .' On the ties between the two projects, see also Acidini, 'Fontana del Nettuno', 34; Rinaldi, 'Quattro pitaffi', 27–8.

72. It is possible that the concept of tapping new water sources to serve garden features and then the public welfare in Florence was first considered at Boboli rather than Castello. Lazzaro (*Italian Renaissance Garden,* 167) suggests that the project to construct an aqueduct between Castello and Florence postdated the beginning of work at Boboli and was only intended to augment the flow to the Neptune Fountain, already supplied by Boboli's waters. If this were the case, then the Neapolitan paradigm would have been employed for the first time in the duchess's garden, suggesting that this connection might be even stronger than I have presented here. However, Vasari, *Vite,* vol. VI, 84–5, specifically criticizes Tribolo in his account of the Castello project for having failed to execute this aqueduct, so desired by Cosimo, suggesting that the concept was at least considered prior to Tribolo's death and that it was probably first proposed in connection with Castello's waters.

73. See Lazzaro, *Italian Renaissance Garden,* 198, regarding a different group of three features in the Boboli Gardens: 'Each celebrates the water that played over them, from the new aqueducts built by Cosimo.'

74. On the Grotticina's history and present state, see Laura Baldini Giusti, 'Le Mille Stanze del Re. Palazzo Pitti–Grotticina di Madama', *Bollettino d'arte,* 6th ser., vol. 64, (1979): 92–7; Lazzaro, *Italian Renaissance Garden,* 200; Medri, 'I restauri del Novecento nelle grotte artificiali del giardino di Boboli. Due episodi emblematici: la grotticina di Madama (1553–55) e il suo giardino segreto', in *Il giardino storico all'italiana,* ed. Francesco Nuvolari (Milan: Electa, 1992), 171–8. For Bandinelli's and Fancelli's sculptural contributions, see Vasari, *Vite,* vol. VI, 188.

75. Paolo Giovio called her 'a veritable Gaia spat forth' from the earth ('id est un'altra Gaia sputata') and 'la fecundissima Signora Duchessa: Giovio, *Lettere,*' 2 vols., ed. Giuseppe Guido Ferrero (Rome: Istituto Poligrafico dello Stato, 1956–8), vol. I, 306–7. On Eleonora's fertility and its representation in the visual arts, see Edelstein, '"*La fecundissima Signora Duchessa*": The Courtly Persona of Eleonora di Toledo and the Iconography of Abundance', in *The Cultural World of Eleonora di Toledo: Duchess of Florence and Siena,* ed. Konrad Eisenbichler (Aldershot: Ashgate, 2004, forthcoming), 71–97. Human fertility was also associated in Renaissance texts with the water provided by Alfonso d'Aragona's aqueduct to Naples, Hersey, 'Water-Works', 64.

76. Lazzaro (*Italian Renaissance Garden,* 194) gives this interpretation to the Oceanus Fountain's original setting in the amphitheater of evergreens behind the palace; see also Campbell ('Giambologna's Oceanus Fountain', 98) on the fertility imagery of Giambologna's colossal figure. The grotto itself naturally recalls the pumice-encrusted, nymph-inhabited caves described by both Virgil in the *Fourth Georgic* and Sannazzaro in Book XII of the *Arcadia* as the underground sources of celebrated rivers: Virgil, *Eclogues; Georgics; Aeneid I–IV,* trans. H. Rushton Fairclough (Cambridge, Mass.: Harvard University Press, 1999), 244; Iacopo Sannazaro, *Opere volgari,* ed. Alfredo Mauro (Bari: Laterza, 1961), 113 (on both Virgil's and Sannazzaro's texts, see David

Quint, *Origins and Originality in Renaissance Literature: Versions of the Source* [New Haven and London: Yale University Press, 1983], 32–69). However, the presence of Bandinelli's *She-Goat* suggests an equally important reference to Virgil's *Fourth Eclogue,* in which the return of the goats whose udders are swollen with milk is one of the unmistakeable signs of the arrival of the golden age; Virgil, *Eclogues; Georgics; Aeneid I–VI,* 50. If the imagery of Eleonora's grotto was intended to refer to Sannazzaro's *Arcadia,* this would provide further evidence of the employment of the Aragonese court's cultural products as models for sixteenth-century Medici court patronage; on possible allusions to other passages in Sannazzaro's *Arcadia* contained in the grotto, see Francesca Petrucci, 'L'ultimo progetto del Tribolo', *Artista: critica dell'arte in Toscana* (1999), esp. 192–3.

77. On the fountain, see Allegri and Cecchi, *Palazzo Vecchio,* 227–9.

78. Petrucci, 'L'ultimo progetto', 190; on the basis of these iconographic connections, Petrucci offers the interesting hypothesis that Tribolo himself may have been responsible for suggesting this employment of Verrocchio's *Putto* prior to his death. If this were true, it would provide further confirmation of the importance of the transport of water beyond the confines of the Boboli Garden in Tribolo's original project.

79. Vasari, *Vite,* vol. VI, 97–8 (esp. 97): 'Dopo queste cose fu mandato il Tribolo da Sua Eccellenza nell'isola dell'Elba, non solo perchè vedesse la città e porto che vi aveva fatta fare, ma ancora perchè desse ordine di condurre un pezzo di granito tondo di dodici braccia per diametro, del quale si aveva a fare una tazza per lo prato grande de' Pitti, la quale ricevesse l'acque della fonte principale.' See also Acidini, *Castello e Petraia,* 56; Campbell, 'Giambologna's Oceanus Fountain', 90; Lazzaro, *Italian Renaissance Garden,* 192; Rinaldi, 'Quattro pitaffi', 24–5.

80. See Capecchi, 'Anfiteatro di verzura', 38, who refers to the problem of the fountain's design as an 'incertezza progettuale'. See also (especially for Giambologna's stylistic debt to Tribolo in this work), Campbell, 'Giambologna's Oceanus Fountain', 94–5; Lazzaro, *Italian Renaissance Garden,* 192–5. Campbell, 'Giambologna's Oceanus Fountain', esp. 95–100, presents provocative evidence to reidentify Giambologna's figure as a representation of Neptune and the fountain's great basin as Oceanus.

81. Capecchi, *Giardino di Boboli,* 23; the aqueducts to supply this fountain were completed by 1553, ibid., 23–4. See also Rinaldi, 'Quattro pitaffi', 24–5.

82. Galletti, 'Genesi della Grotta Grande', 230. The more general function of *vivai* as reservoirs for the supply of water to fountains, grottoes, and other waterworks within the ducal and grandducal gardens in and around Florence had already been observed by Luigi Zangheri, 'L'acqua a Pratolino, da elemento naturale ad artifizio "maraviglioso" (analisi fondata sulle piante dei condotti conservate a Praga)', in *Gardino storico italiano,* ed. Ragionieri, 355–61 (see esp. 356–7 for his seminal discussion of the importance of collecting pools and fishponds for the smooth functioning of the garden's water features in all seasons), and idem, 'Tra abilità e tecnologia: l'acqua nelle grotte del manierismo', in *Arte delle grotte: per la conoscenza e la conservazione delle grotte artificiali,* ed. Cristina Acidini, Lauro Magnani, and Mariachiara Pozzana (Genoa: Sagep, 1987), 9. On Pratolino's fishponds, see now also Butters, 'Pressed Labor and Pratolino', 72.

83. The basin may already have been in existence by 1551, see Rinaldi, 'Quattro pitaffi', 21; see also Galletti, 'Genesi della Grotta Grande', 230. For the history and reconstruction of Vasari's fishpond, see esp. Zangheri, 'Vasari e la Grotta Grande', in *Boboli 90,* ed. Acidini and Garbero, vol. II, 398–401; see also Galletti, 'Genesi della Grotta Grande', 230–1; Heikamp, 'La Grotta grande del Giardino di Boboli', *Antichità viva* 4 (1965): 30. Interestingly, Vasari's design was executed simultaneously with a veritable boom in the publication of ichthyology treatises; see Grieco, 'Fiordiano Malatesta', 309.

84. However, see Zangheri, 'Vasari e la Grotta Grande', 400–1, for a rather different reconstruction of Vasari's *vivaio.* Zangheri proposes that the fishpond was located within a roofed structure corresponding to the first room of Buontalenti's grotto and that the second room of the later structure was also constructed by Vasari as a grotto appendix to the pool. While the archival evidence gathered by Zangheri and others does provide confirmation for significant construction of walls around the fishpond, support is lacking for the hypothesis that the structure was vaulted; the attribution of the second chamber to Vasari is also not documentary but rather stylistic. Bandinelli's gift of the statues and the attribution of the design to Vasari both appear for the first time in Vasari's *Life* of the sculptor (Vasari, *Vite,* vol. VI, 180).

85. See Vasari, *Vite,* vol. VI, 188, for the attribution of the *Peasant* to Fancelli and Bandinelli. Recently, Galletti ('Genesi della Grotta Grande', 231), appears to express some doubt about the association (first made by Bertha Harris Wiles, *The Fountains of Florentine Sculptors and their followers from Donatello to Bernini* [Cambridge, Mass.: Harvard University Press, 1933], 96) of this sculpture with the subsequent identification of Vasari's fishpond as the 'vivaio del villano'. Apropos, Vasari only states that the 'villano che vota un barile pieno d'acque' was executed 'per un vivaio', without specifying which fishpond. Zangheri, 'Vasari e la Grotta Grande', makes no reference to the *Peasant* and does not include it in his reconstruction of the *vivaio.* However, see Rinaldi, 'Quattro pitaffi', 21, who suggests that the placement of Fancelli's *Peasant* on the fishpond actually preceded Vasari's frontispiece design.

86. See Brook, '"Genre" Statuary', 113–20; Butters, 'Pressed Labor and Pratolino', 68; Heikamp, '"Villani" di marmo in giardino', in *Il giardino d'Europea: Pratolino come modello nella cultura europea,* ed. Alessandro Vezzosi (Milan: Mazzotta, 1986), 63; Lazzaro, *Italian Renaissance Garden,* 200; Medri, 'Le sculture del Giardino di Boboli fra il Cinquecento e il Seicento', in *Palazzo Pitti: L'arte e la storia,* ed. Marco Chiarini (Florence: Nardini, 2000), 260; Rinaldi, 'Quattro pitaffi', 21.

87. However, see Brook, '"Genre" Statuary', esp. 118–20, for the ancient origins of the *Peasant* typology and its dissociation from the low-life themes inherent in contemporary Flemish genre painting.

88. The idea of the celebration of fertility through the conjunction of earth and water would similarly have been present in Tribolo's original grotto design for the duke's garden at Castello, with its niche fountains representing Neptune and Pan, see Lazzaro, *Italian Renaissance Garden,* 179; Petrucci, 'L'ultimo progetto', 193, assumes Tribolo's rejection of this project and associates this with the transference of these iconographic themes to various parts of the new Boboli project. Regarding the play between flowing water and flowing wine in Fancelli's *Peasant,* see also ibid., 192. For De Vieri's moralizing reading of the statue in its subsequent employment at Pratolino, see Butters, 'Pressed Labor and Pratolino', 79.

89. Galletti, 'Genesi della Grotta Grande', 231. It is possible that Vasari intended a reference to this transition from private to public usage of the water marked by the *vivaio* in his design for the frontispiece. The façade conforms to a public typology, that of the ancient Roman 'façade nymphaea', water outlets that 'functioned mainly as utilitarian and decorative elements of Roman town planning'. See Alvarez, 'The Renaissance Nymphaeum', 15.

90. Filippo Baldinucci, *Notizie dei professori del disegno da Cimabue in qua,* 5 vols., ed. F. Ranalli (Florence: Batelli, 1845–7), vol. II, 499, reports that the central oculus of the vault in the main chamber of Buontalenti's grotto originally featured a fishbowl, through which light filtered as fish darted about, creating extraordinary effects in the grotto below. The presence of the fishbowl suggests to me that the original symbolism of the *vivaio* may have been so potent for the Medici that they wished to preserve it even after the conversion of the fishpond into the grotto. See also

Heikamp, 'Grotta grande', 37; Lazzaro, *Italian Renaissance Garden,* 201; Francesco Maria Soldini, *Il Reale Giardino di Boboli nella sua pianta e nelle sue statue* (1789; reprint, Rome: Multigrafica, 1976), 31 n.** [*sic*].

91. On the early date for Bandinelli's commission and the original design for the Neptune Fountain, see Acidini, 'Fontana del Nettuno', 39–41; Campbell, 'Observations on Ammannati's *Neptune Fountain:* 1565 and 1575', in *Renaissance Studies in Honor of Craig Hugh Smyth,* ed. Morrogh, Superbi, Morselli, and Borsook, vol. II, 119–21, 124–6; Keutner, 'Un modello del Bandinelli per il Nettuno della fontana di Piazza della Signoria a Firenze', in *Scritti di storia dell'arte in onore di Roberto Salvini,* ed. Cristina De Benedictis (Florence: Sansoni, 1984), 417 (esp. n. 2, for the possibility that the block itself had been quarried significantly earlier); Lazzaro, *Italian Renaissance Garden,* 191 n. 1.

92. Indeed, Bandinelli was also eager to contribute to the success of the hydraulic aspect of the project; in a letter of c. 1551–2, the sculptor asks Luca Martini to refer the discovery of a new water source on his property in Fiesole to the duchess and suggest its potential utility in supplying the new fountain, *Raccolta di lettere sulla pittura, scultura ed architettura scritte da' più celebri personaggi dei secoli XV, XVI e XVII,* 8 vols. ed. Giovanni Bottari and Stefano Ticozzi (Milan: Silvestri, 1822–25), vol. I, 97 (letter XL, also cited by Allegri and Cecchi, *Palazzo Vecchio,* 222).

93. Eleonora had, by and large, reformed the same équipe from Castello for the execution of the Boboli Gardens; see Rinaldi, 'Quattro pitaffi', 27. Bandinelli's preeminence is therefore all the more striking.

94. The sculptors' rivalry is suggested by various incidents recounted by Vasari in the *Lives,* such as Bandinelli stealing the commission for the tomb of Giovanni delle Bande Nere away from Tribolo (Vasari, *Vite,* vol. VI, 86, 168); or Pierino da Vinci's father, dissatisfied with Bandinelli's instruction, removing the boy from Baccio's workshop and placing him with Tribolo (ibid., 121).

95. Vasari, *Vite,* vol. VI, 188, specifically attributed Bandinelli's commissions at Boboli to Eleonora's patronage: 'Servivasi ancora la duchessa assai di Baccio nel giardino de' Pitti.' For the duchess's protection of Bandinelli, see also ibid., 184, 186–8. Similarly, Lazzaro, *Italian Renaissance Garden,* 200: 'Until her death in 1562, Eleonora of Toledo seems to have exerted considerable influence on the development of the garden, particularly in the choice of her favorite sculptor, Baccio Bandinelli, for a number of projects.' Campbell ('Giambologna's Oceanus Fountain', 91) observes that, with the assignment of the fountain project for Tribolo's granite basin to the artist, 'briefly, Bandinelli was in overwhelming command of artistic projects in Florence.' In a letter of 11 February 1552 to Jacopo Guidi, Bandinelli acknowledged that he received this commission directly from Eleonora; *Raccolta di lettere,* ed. Bottari and Ticozzi, vol. I, 93: 'diligentemente ho osservato lo spazio del prato, dove vuol far la fonte, faronne qualch'invenzione, come m'ha comandato la nostra ill. signora duchessa.' Immediately following this statement, the sculptor also promised to make 'qualche disegno della fontana di Piazza, come mi comandò l'ill. duca', revealing once again how closely related the two projects were. The letter is also cited by Campbell, 'Giambologna's Oceanus Fountain', 91 n. 7.

96. For the history of the Neptune fountain and references to the preceding literature, see Heikamp, 'La fontana del Nettuno in Piazza della Signoria e le sue acque', in *Bartolomeo Ammannati: scultore e architetto, 1511–1592,* ed. Niccolò Rosselli Del Turco and Federica Salvi (Florence: Alinea, 1995), 19–25. For the Bandinellian heritage of the work as executed, see Campbell, 'Observations on Ammannati's *Neptune Fountain*', 119–21; Keutner, 'Modello del Bandinelli', 417–26.

97. The beginning of construction on the aqueduct is recorded by Lapini, *Diario fiorentino di Agostino Lapini dal 252 al 1596,* ed. Giuseppe Odoardo Corazzini (Florence: Sansoni, 1900), 145.

On the hydraulic system linking the fountain to the Fonte della Ginevra, see Heikamp, 'Fontana del Nettuno', 21, who observes that Cosimo had even considered creating a third aqueduct to supply the fountain with water (presumably the one executed under Ferdinando II in 1635, which supplies the Moses grotto and Susini's Artichoke Fountain at the rear of the Pitti courtyard; see Campbell, 'Giambologna's Oceanus Fountain', 103–4; idem, 'Hard Times in Baroque Florence', 170–3; Lazzaro, *Italian Renaissance Garden,* 210). See also Allegri and Cecchi, *Palazzo Vecchio,* 222; Massimo De Vico Fallani, 'Naturalismo e agraria nell'architettura di Boboli', in *Boboli 90,* ed. Acidini and Garbero, vol. II, 571–5; Lazzaro, *Italian Renaissance Garden,* 191.

98. Allegri and Cecchi, *Palazzo Vecchio,* 222; Galletti, 'Genesi della Grotta Grande', 233; Lazzaro, *Italian Renaissance Garden,* 191. See also Campbell ('Observations on Ammannati's *Neptune Fountain*', 116–7) who highlights the importance of the medal as a source for understanding Ammannati's first project for the fountain.

99. On the imagery of the medal, see Maria Ann Conelli, 'Boboli Gardens: Fountains and Propaganda in Sixteenth-Century Florence', *Studies in the History of Gardens & Designed Landscapes* 18 (1998): 304–6, who aptly observes, 'Cosimo attached such importance to the building of the aqueduct and his role as "water-giver" to the city that, on his death in 1574, this aqueduct was given primary importance in Cosimo's funerary apparatus.' Conelli, following Lazzaro and Campbell, justly highlights the importance of the passage of water through the Boboli Gardens to the Neptune Fountain and the iconographic kinship between Ammannati's Neptune and Giambologna's Oceanus (see esp. Campbell, 'Giambologna's Oceanus Fountain', 96–101; and Lazzaro, *Italian Renaissance Garden,* 195–6; but also Acidini, 'Fontana del Nettuno', 36). She appears, however, to have been unaware of the new aqueduct constructed in 1565 (that is, the one celebrated in both the medal and the ephemera for Cosimo's funeral) and presumes that the Neptune and Oceanus fountains would have belonged exclusively to the same hydraulic system.

100. Campbell, 'Observations on Ammannati's *Neptune Fountain*', 123–5, who posits that this would already have been an important feature of the fountain designed by Bandinelli; see also Heikamp, 'Fontana del Nettuno', 22. Campbell ('Giambologna's Oceanus Fountain', 106) notes that in Giambologna's original design for the Oceanus fountain, Tribolo's monolithic granite basin would similarly have overflowed.

101. This iconography would have been partially compromised when the height of the Neptune Fountain's basin was lowered, following an order given by Francesco I in 1572; thereafter, the fountain's overflow would have been less dramatic. However, the changed height would have offered the advantage of improving the visibility of the fresh spring water contained within it, apparently the principal motivating factor behind this change; see Campbell, 'Observations on Ammannati's *Neptune Fountain*', 124–5.

102. Vasari, *Vite,* VII, 703–4. On the Corridoio Vasariano, see (with references to the previous literature), Conforti, *Giorgio Vasari architetto,* 184; Lazzaro, *Italian Renaissance Garden,* 196; Satkowski, *Giorgio Vasari,* 56–9. Significantly, the corridor originally terminated at Vasari's fishpond and, as Satkowski, 57, observes, 'there is no way of ascertaining if Vasari wanted to bring the passageway directly into the Palazzo Pitti.'

103. See, for example, the distinctive employment of the impaled Medici-Toledo coat of arms embraced by the Habsburg eagle in works executed for Eleonora, such as the the vault decorations of the Camera Verde, Eleonora's audience hall in the Palazzo Vecchio, and originally in the vault fresco of her adjacent chapel as well: Edelstein, review of Cox-Rearick, 174; idem, 'Observations on the Genesis & Function of Bronzino's Frankfurt *Modello* for the Vault Decoration in the

Chapel of Eleonora', in *Coming About . . . A Festschrift for John Shearman*, ed. Lars R. Jones and Louisa C. Matthew (Cambridge: Harvard University Art Museums, 2001), 157–63; idem, 'The *Camera Verde:* A Public Center for the Duchess of Florence in the Palazzo Vecchio', *Mélanges de l'École Française de Rome: Italie et Méditeranée,* 115, 1 (Oct. 2003). See this latter as well for a discussion of the grotesques in the Camera Verde, which may similarly allude to Eleonora's Neapolitan roots. On Eleonora's Hispano-Neapolitan heritage in general, see idem, 'Nobildonne napoletane e committenza: Eleonora d'Aragona ed Eleonora di Toledo a confronto', *Quaderni storici* 104 (2000): 295–329.

104. Vasari, *Vite,* vol. VI, 154.

105. Archivio di Stato di Firenze, Mediceo del Principato 600 ('Ricordi' of majordomo Pierfrancesco Riccio), 10r (15 April 1542): 'Et addì detto che pagasse al Marignolle scudi III per conto delle teste di terra. Fa per mandare al Vicerè di Napoli;' 13v (27 July 1542): 'Feci una poliza a Michel Ruberti che pagasse al Marignolle et a Santi Buglione scudi VIII sopra le teste di terra per mandare a Napoli;' 17r (28 Sept. 1542): 'Feci sottoscriptione a uno conto del Marignolle e di Sancti Buglioni di scudi 35 per le X teste di terra vetriate per la duchessa per mandar a Napoli, saldo per m.o Tribolo, a Michel Ruberti.' See also Gaetano Guasti, *Di Cafaggiolo e d'altre fabbriche di ceramiche in Toscana secondo studi e documenti in parte raccolti dal comm. Gaetano Milanesi* (1902; reprint, Bologna: Forni, 1980), 168; Cecchi, 'Il maggiordomo ducale Pierfrancesco Riccio e gli artisti della corte medicea', *Mitteilungen des Kunsthistorischen Institutes in Florenz* 42 (1998): 133. These were not the only works donated by the duchess to her brother for the decoration of his garden. Eleonora also gave García two sculptures, one by Pierino da Vinci and one by Stoldo Lorenzi, that were themselves originally gifts to the duchess from Luca Martini, see (with references to the previous literature): Alessandro Conti 'Pierino da Vinci, Napoli e la figura di giovinetto del Louvre', in *Pierino da Vinci,* ed. Marco Cianchi (Florence: Becocci, 1995), 29–30, in which serious doubts are expressed about the identification of the Louvre sculpture with the figure described by Vasari as having been given by Eleonora to García; Heikamp, 'Luca Martini, i suoi amici artisti e Pierino da Vinci', in ibid., 68, in which the identification of the Louvre sculpture as the work donated by the duchess to her brother is accepted.

106. For the busts and their attribution, see Colombo, 'Il Palazzo', 198–9; Hersey, *Alfonso II,* 65 (in both cases, as ornaments to the main villa rather than the loggia; however, the busts are clearly depicted in a 1641 view of the loggia, see David Marshall, 'A View of Poggioreale by Viviano Codazzi and Domenico Gargiulo', *Journal of the Society of Architectural Historians* 45 [1986]: 32–46; idem, *Viviano and Niccolò Codazzi and the Baroque Architectural Fantasy,* [Milan: Jandi Sapi, 1993], 104). For their destruction during the seventeenth century, see Colombo, 'Il Palazzo', 336.

107. On the spectacles held in the Boboli Gardens and the evolution of the gardens' central element from a 'natural' to a formally constructed amphitheater, see Capecchi, 'La costruzione del "Gran Teatro di Boboli" e l'intervento di Pietro da Cortona, *Antichità viva* 25 (1996): 31–42 (with references to the previous literature).

108. On the entertainments offered in the Pitti Palace courtyard for the marriage of Ferdinando I de' Medici to Cristina di Lorena in 1589, see Anna Maria Petrioli Tofani, 'Uno spettacolo a Pitti nel 1589', in *Scritti di storia dell'arte in onore di Ugo Procacci,* 2 vols., ed. Maria Grazia Ciardi Dupré Dal Poggetto and Paolo Dal Poggetto (Milan: Electa, 1977), vol. II, 476–85; James M. Saslow, *The Medici Wedding of 1589: Florentine Festival as 'Theatrum Mundi'* (New Haven and London: Yale University Press, 1996), esp. 96–7 (regarding the technological problem presented by the flooding of the Pitti courtyard), 168–9 (for the performance of the naumachia), 260 (cat.

87, for the Orazio Scarabelli engraving depicting the event, with previous bibliography). See also Francesco Gurrieri and Judith Chatfield, *Boboli Gardens* (Florence: Edam, 1972), 22.

109. This feature was recorded by Serlio (cited by Colombo, 'Il Palazzo', 200; Hersey, *Alfonso II*, 65; idem 'Water-Works', 72–3; Pane, 'Le Effemeridi di Joanpiero Leostello', 78) and later by F. Leandro Alberti, *Descrittione di tutta Italia* (Bologna: Anselmo Giaccarelli, 1550), 167v.

110. Hersey (*Alfonso II*, 65), specifies: 'It may also have been possible of course to stage mock naval battles, though I have found no documents for such events.'

8

The Politics of Patronage: Verrocchio, Pollaiuolo, and the Forteguerri Monument

Stephen J. Milner

THE TERRITORIAL STATE HAS LONG BEEN RECOGNISED AS AN IMPORTANT source of major commissions for artists based in Florence with the vast majority undertaking work in subject communes such as Arezzo, Pisa, Cortona, San Miniato, and Volterra. Pistoia was no exception in this regard, and the role of Florentine artists in enriching the artistic patrimony of Renaissance Pistoia has long been recognised, from Brunelleschi's work on the silver altar of San Jacopo and the completion of a reliquary for the same saint by Ghiberti's workshop in the early years of the quattrocento to the work of Pesellino, Filippo Lippi, the Pollaiuolo, Verrocchio, the Rossellini, Piero di Cosimo, and Benozzo Gozzoli, amongst others, in the second half of the century.[1] Yet although the importance of representational practices as a means of exercising symbolic, as opposed to economic or political, power has become a central concern of much cultural criticism,[2] relatively little attention has been paid by Renaissance art historians to the politics involved in commissioning artists from Florence as dominant centre, to produce works of art for consumption in subject communes at the periphery.[3] The intention of this study, therefore, is to examine one particular commission from this particular perspective. The commission in question was that for the Cenotaph of Cardinal Niccolò Forteguerri (1419–73) in the Cathedral of San Zeno in Pistoia.

The decision by the city's Consiglio Generale to erect a cenotaph in honour of the cardinal was taken in January 1474, just two weeks after his death. A competition was organised which was won by Verrocchio in May 1476. From the surviving terracotta bozzetto (Fig. 61), it is clear that the monument was intended to figure nine almost life-size figures with Christ enthroned, framed by a mandorla borne by four angels,

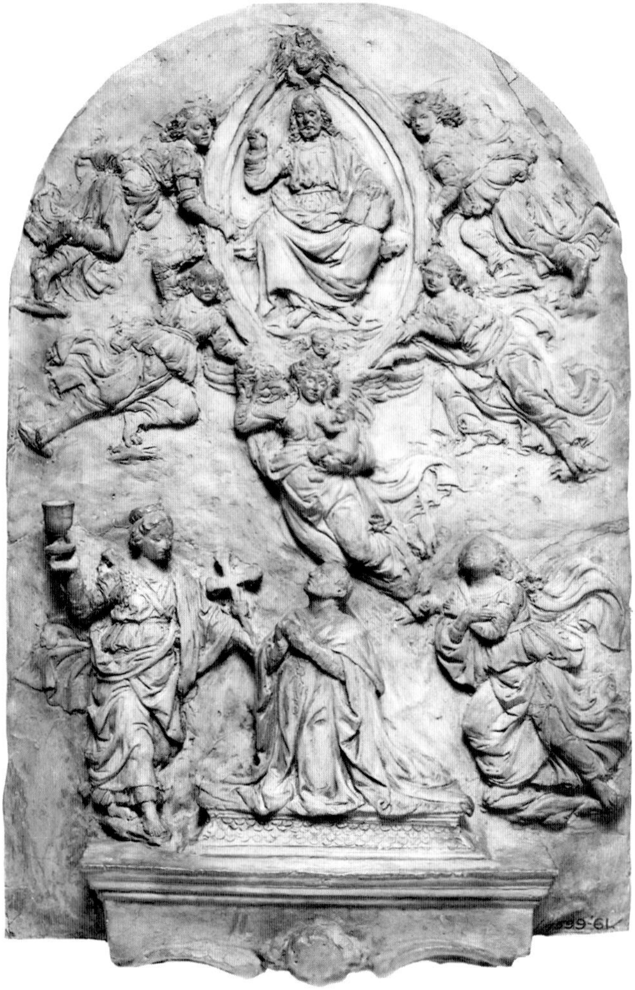

61. Attributed to Andrea Verrocchio, *Bozzetto for the Cenotaph of Cardinal Niccolò Forteguerri*. Terracotta. London, Victoria and Albert Museum. Photo: © V&A Picture Library, London.

occupying the upper half of the piece. At the lower level, the kneeling cardinal, his eyes turned upwards towards Christ, was to be surrounded by the three theological virtues of Faith, Hope, and Charity. As a design it was without precedent, both in terms of its dynamic and pictorial narrative style – which stood in marked contrast to the static form of most funerary monuments of the time – and in terms of its size and high-relief sculpture. According to Pope-Hennessy, 'had it been completed, it would have been the most richly figured monument of the whole century.'[4] As it now stands, however, it is more a monument to changing tastes, an eclectic mix of period styles reflecting the work of four artists carried out over two hundred and seventy-six years (Fig. 62).

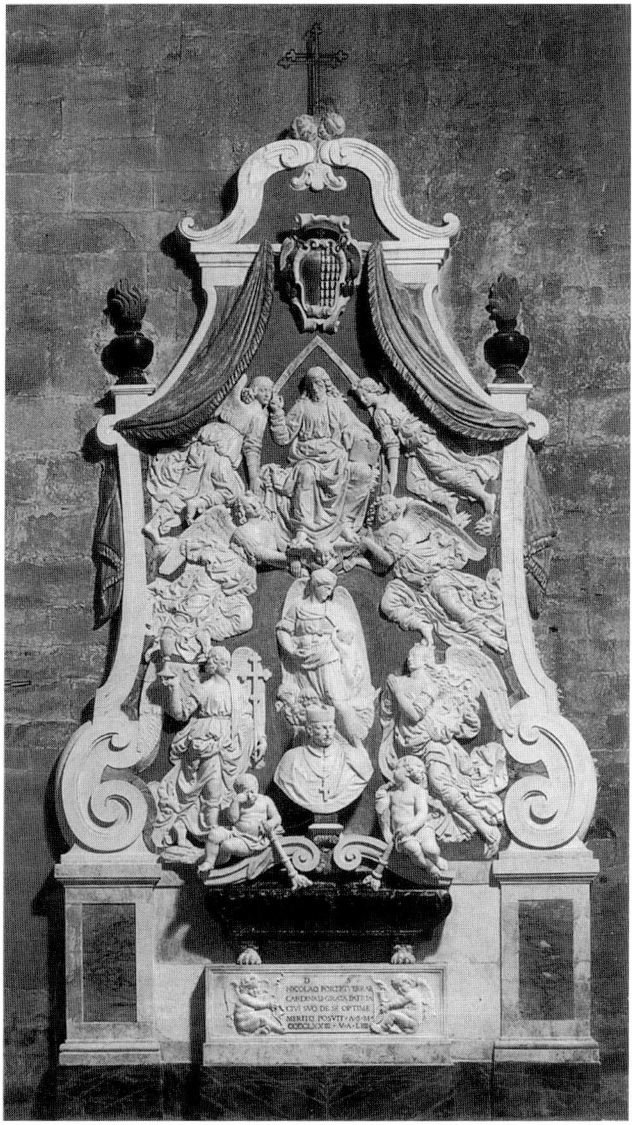

62. Andrea Verrocchio and others, *Cenotaph of Cardinal Niccolò Forteguerri*. Marble. Pistoia, cathedral. Photo: Soprintendenza per i Beni Architettonici ed Ambientali delle Provincie di Firenze e Pistoia, cat. no. 212301.

Yet the fame of the commission rests less on the stylistic originality of the intended final product than on the contested gestation of the commissioning process. As Butterfield has stated, 'No sculpture by Verrocchio has proved more difficult to understand than the Forteguerri monument in the cathedral of Pistoia', whilst Wilder, some sixty years earlier, noted how 'its history has been confused and unfortunate'.[5] For although Verrocchio won the commission by a straight majority vote in the city's Consiglio, attempts were subsequently made to reassign the work to Piero Pollaiuolo – who is known to have been involved with another Pistoiese commission for a sacramental tabernacle of the *Corpus Domini* at roughly the same time – by the committee established to oversee the project. As part of the campaign to displace Verrocchio, the committee wrote a famous letter to Lorenzo de' Medici in March 1477 seeking his support. Given the supine tone of their subsequent letter to Lorenzo, it is clear they received an abrupt repost to their request, Verrocchio being confirmed in the commission. Despite the relative abundance of published documentation relating to the affair, confusion still surrounds much of the commission.[6]

In seeking to explain exactly what was going in on in this case, the intention is to examine the affair as an example of how an artwork could become what de Certeau has termed a 'practiced place', a space where larger social, political, and ideological tensions were played out between different groups.[7] Much of the confusion relating to the monument's history is a direct result of the multiplicity of interests seeking accommodation within the cenotaph, for as a major addition to the city's symbolic economy, it was instrumental in the fashioning of familial, communal, ecclesiastical, and, given Pistoia's position as subject city, patrimonial identities. In providing an anatomy these constituencies, the aim is to explain both their investment in the commission and their role in the contention arising from the often contradictory desires which motivated the project from the beginning. The difficulty in understanding the commission, therefore, is best read as a function of its assimilation into the contested field of sociopolitical patronage.

In this context an explanation is required of the numerous changes in the personnel elected by the commune to oversee the work; of the reasons behind the invitation to Pollaiuolo to submit a model design; of the exact role assumed by both the Florentine Commissioners on Pistoiese affairs and Lorenzo de' Medici in the commission's development; of the role of the recently appointed Bishop of Pistoia Niccolò Pandolfini; and finally of the source of opposition to Verrocchio's candidature. To date, the summaries in the secondary literature are largely based on literal readings of the published documents without widening the scope of investigation to consider the personnel involved or place the contested commission within the broader field of events within the Pistoia of the 1470s. Rather, the celebrity of the commission is almost wholly based on its status as a noteworthy and unique example of the intervention of Lorenzo *il magnifico* in matters artistic.[8] The reality, however, was somewhat different, and the key to understanding the contention surrounding the commission lies in the nature of the prevailing political culture at the time of the monument's commissioning.

Patronal Tensions

Although a subject town within the larger Florentine territorial state, Pistoia's relation as 'subject' and 'client' to Florence was far more complex than these terms might suggest. In fact the relation of Pistoia as periphery to Florence as centre, or Pistoia as city to Florence as state, was characterised by negotiation rather than benign submission to imposed authority. It is within this broader political context that control of the city's symbolic economy became an ideological and highly politicised concern.

Infamous for its factions since the duecento, Pistoia had been under Florentine jurisdiction since 1401. Traditionally civic peace had been secured through the long-established tradition of dividing communal offices between the rival Societies of San Paolo and San Giovanni. In 1457, however, Cosimo *il vecchio* sanctioned a wholesale revision of the city's electoral procedures, radically altering the political landscape and rendering civic peace dependant upon the arbitration of the Medici, who sought pre-eminence through the effective management of the city's patronage. Nobody exploited this development as much as Lorenzo, who not only shunned the Pistoiese associates preferred by Giuliano de' Medici prior to 1468, but actively sponsored his own agents, mostly drawn from lesser families of the Pistoiese *popolo.*

The 1470s witnessed unparalleled innovation in the city's affairs, with Lorenzo's interventions assuming an almost princely character. Through the combined agency of Florentine-elected *podestà* and captains, Florentine commissioners sent to address specific issues, and local agents, Lorenzo undertook a root and branch overhaul of the city's institutions, electoral procedures, and statutes.[9] Major civic reforms in 1474 and 1477 served to realign the constitution of the city's elite,[10] whilst the years 1473–4 and 1477–8, which spanned the period of the Forteguerri controversy, accounted for 341 of the 600 letters sent to Lorenzo by the Pistoiese, the decade as a whole seeing a threefold increase in the volume of correspondence between Pistoia and Lorenzo in Florence.[11] In 1473–4 the city floated its own Monte della Pietà with the aid of Medicean intervention,[12] and the strategically important post of *spedalingo* to the largest charitable institution and landowner the 'Ospedale di Santa Maria dei poveri', known locally as the *Ceppo,* was fiercely contested on no less than three occasions between 1474 and 1479. In December 1474, through the sponsorship of Giuliano della Rovere and the assent of Lorenzo, the aggressive Niccolò Pandolfini, a champion of ecclesiastical rights in the face of secular encroachments, was appointed the city's bishop.[13] As if to confirm Lorenzo's princely status, the commune actually gave itself over to him personally *in balìa* in December 1476. Resistance to these changes came in a variety of forms, the most extreme being a Pistoiese-based plot to assassinate Lorenzo in 1478.[14]

Given that the form of patrimonialism exercised by the Medici over Pistoia was premised on the mutual exchange of favours within the market place of symbolic capital, many deals involved elaborate and protracted periods of negotiation. Significantly, artistic patronage was also implicated within these forms of negotiation, both as a site of trade and as a possible site of resistance. Yet the Medici were not the only Florentines interested in the city's patrimony, as the Pistoiese also had to contend with Pandolfini's ambitious plans for the jurisdictional and symbolic aggrandisement of his diocese. Far from being a quaint instance of Lorenzo's interest in the visual arts, this commission clearly illustrates how the politics of patronage extended into every realm of civic and religious life. Even in Pistoiese terms, the extent of conflict on the issue suggests that something more than artistic preference for one particular model over another was at stake.

Cardinal Niccolò Forteguerri (1419–73) was well aware of his native city's propensity for contesting patronage and the Medici's ambiguous position as arbiters and exploiters of such disputes. As bishop of Tiano and titular cardinal of Santa Cecilia in Rome, he was one of Pistoia's most eminent citizens, and he was alone amongst Pistoiese in addressing the Medici as equals, clearly conscious of the utility of his own patronage network to the Medici.[15] During his lifetime Forteguerri was a regular correspondent of both Giovanni and Piero di Cosimo de' Medici, and later of Lorenzo, on a range of issues from straightforward requests relating to Pistoiese affairs to trading matters and wider patronage concerns, more than fifty of his letters surviving in the *Medici avanti il principato* archive.[16] It is clear from this correspondence that he was well aware of the significance of the innovations taking place within Pistoia, and in April 1471 he sent a candid letter reminding Lorenzo of the danger of partiality in the management of the city's affairs and asking him to intervene in the dispute over the administration of the *Ceppo* hospital.[17] Not surprisingly when he established the *Pia Casa della Sapienza* by an act of donation in August 1473, the terms of the donation and the rubrics of the Sapienza's constitution sought to consolidate the family's controlling interest in its management whilst limiting the potential for its appropriation by other interested parties.[18] As it was, the family invested great effort in protecting their patrimony and enforcing the terms of their illustrious predecessor's legacy in the face of Medicean encroachment.

The problems faced by the Forteguerri in relation to their governance of the Sapienza were replicated in the patterns of behaviour which can be observed regarding the disputed commission for the cardinal's cenotaph. Whilst the family secured permanent representation on the commissioning panel, the personnel elected and nominated by the commune changed dramatically as a consequence of the larger changes in the balance of power within the city's councils. When the Pistoiese Consiglio del Popolo passed a provision on 2 January 1474 to permit the spending of 300 gold florins to erect a cenotaph in the cardinal's honour, it was undertaken

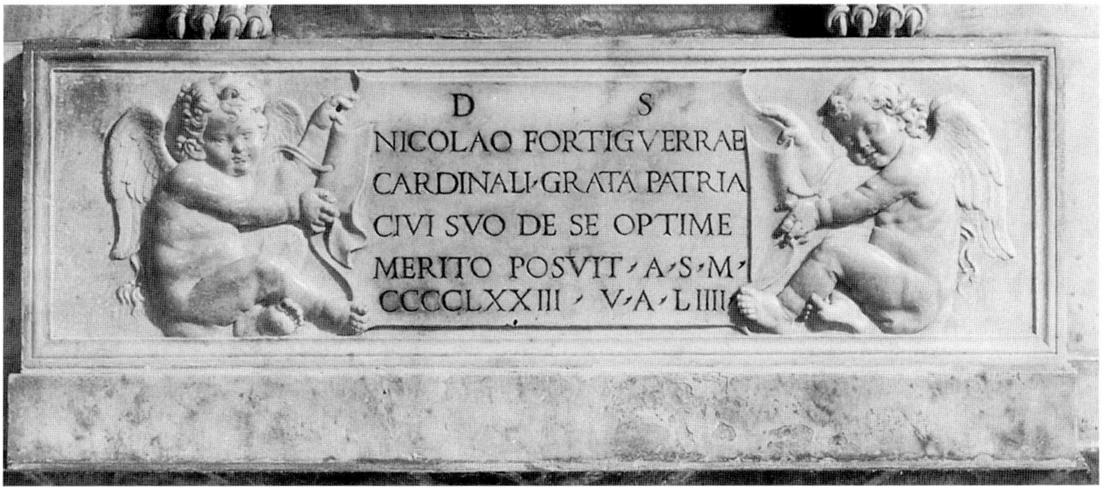

63. Andrea Verrocchio and others, *Epitaph of the Cenotaph of Cardinal Niccolò Forteguerri*. Photo: Soprintendenza per i Beni Architettonici ed Ambientali delle Provincie di Firenze e Pistoia, cat. no. 212299.

as a token of gratitude and pride on the part of both the commune and the family for his contribution to the city and his achievements: 'in perpetual honour of the city of Pistoia and gratitude for the gifts bestowed upon the city by the most reverend cardinal', the epitaph eventually reading, 'Nicolao Fortiguerrae Cardinali Grata Patria Civi Suo De Se Optime Merito Posuit' (Fig. 63).[19] Whilst both parties envisaged benefiting from such an act of memorialisation, however, any initial unity of purpose was problematised by the divisive issue of awarding the commission as the politics of patronage were played out between family, ecclesiastical, communal, and external (Florentine and Medicean) interests.

In this context the jurisdictional powers and role of the Florentine Commissioners on Pistoiese affairs and their relation to Medicean agents within Pistoia in general, and Lorenzo in particular, is key to understanding the origins of the dispute. For it was through the agency of these ad hoc committees of so-called *Commissarii* that Lorenzo secured his hegemony over the territorial state in the 1470s.[20] Elected from amongst the Florentine patrician elite and normally staffed by known clients of the Medici, they directly intervened in electoral reforms, and oversaw the effective exploitation of territorial patrimonies, artistic or otherwise, and the granting of privileges to selected clients.

Traditionally, discussions of the role of Florentine Commissioners in the Forteguerri affair have concentrated on the four officials elected to oversee the wider pacification of the city by the Tre Maggiori, Otto di Guardia, and Consiglio del Cento in Florence in June 1476.[21] Yet the influence of commissioners on the project's gestation actually dates back to August 1474. For between the formation of the initial committee charged with overseeing the commission in January 1474 and the formation of a revised committee on 14 June 1475 the intervention of two commissioners elected to oversee the civic reforms of August 1474 had resulted in a strategic attempt to realign the city's patrician elite. Indeed, the commissioners in question, Jacopo Guicciardini and Donato Accaiuoli, not only added selected names (*arroti*) to the lists of those eligible for certain major civic offices (*squittini*), but also excluded others in a practice well rehearsed by pro-Medicean officials who composed the electoral bags in Florence (the *accopiatori*). Despite considerable local opposition to these changes, they were formally ratified by the Florentine councils and had a definite impact on the personnel of the revised Forteguerri committee of June 1475.[22] Both the original and the revised committees were made up of fourteen individuals: the four operai of the Opera di San Jacopo, the four Ufficiali della Sapienza, and the six citizens elected by the Consiglio del Popolo.[23] All these bodies were effected by the revised civic reforms. In addition to the election of six new communal representatives, both the Ufficiali della Sapienza and the Operai of San Jacopo, positions traditionally held by the leading patrician families, had changed.[24]

Although some members of the original committee remained, the alterations were significant. In particular, both Cherubino Tonti and Carlo di Giovanni Cantansanti were replaced. In December 1465, at the time of the Pitti crisis in Florence, Tonti was one of the prime movers in an attempt to grant *balìa* over Pistoia to the eminent patrician Baldinotto Baldinotti, and he clearly had an extensive patronage network of his own within the city, one correspondent with the Medici referring specifically to the 'Cherubino faction' as late as 1477. His marginalisation, aided and abetted by the Florentine officials resident within the city, saw his eventual disqualification from holding any form of civic office.[25] Whilst Tonti was consistently hostile to Medici interventions, the Cantansanti had been longtime associates of the Medici, Francesco acting as private notary to Giovanni di Cosimo in the period prior to his death.[26] Lorenzo's decision to switch allegiances away from such established clients in favour of the more mercantile families and *gente nuova* of Pistoia effected a large-scale alteration in the balance of power within the city.

This is clearly reflected in the addition of the son of a Pistoiese shoemaker, one Mariano Panichi, to the revised committee in a move which had a significant impact on the future gestation of the Forteguerri commission. Not only did he replace Tonti on the revised committee, but he also replaced Cantansanti as Pistoian notary to the Medici.[27] Ser Mariano di Giovanni di Ser Giunta Panichi, to give him his full name, was a key figure in Laurentian Pistoia as a whole and in the Forteguerri affair in particular. In fact he is known to have visited one of Lorenzo's preferred notaries, Niccolò Michelozzi, at Careggi to learn more details concerning the cardinal's death in late 1473.[28] Yet to date nobody has drawn attention to his appearance on more than three occasions in the documentation published by Kennedy and Covi.[29] This is no doubt because he appears under four name variants, Ser Marianus Iohannes, Ser Mariano di Nanni, domino Mariano Nannis Panico, and Mariano Panichi.

As a childhood friend and Lorenzo's notary, Panichi became one of his most trusted allies, accompanying him on trips round Tuscany in 1463 and later in 1465 and 1466 to both Milan and Naples. Chancellor of Fucecchio in 1465, he renounced his office to take up service in the Medici household, securing the position of Capitano de' fanti of the Palazzo della Signoria in Florence in the aftermath of the Pazzi conspiracy, a post ironically sought by Cardinal Forteguerri for one of his own clients in November 1464.[30] Given Panichi's proximity to Lorenzo, he became the major beneficiary of the political realignment within Pistoia, successfully securing key appointments for friends and relations. It is no surprise, therefore, to find him closely allied with the work of the Florentine commissioners delegated to oversee Pistoiese affairs in the 1470s. It was through the intervention of Donato Acciaiuoli and Jacopo Guicciardini in the 1474 revised reforms that Panichi was taken out of the bag for the position of Gonfaloniere di Giustizia and placed in the strategically more important bag for the Operai di San Jacopo.[31] That sections of the Pistoiese elite resented his pre-eminence and, in his absence, sought to circumvent his authority is apparent in the kind of strategy deployed in the case of the Forteguerri commission.

Contesting the Commission

The implementation of the communal decision to invite tenders for the Forteguerri monument contract taken in January 1474 finally took place under the authority of the newly composed committee in June 1475. Nearly a year later, on 15 May 1476, five models were presented to the city's councils for consideration. Both the timing and the closeness of the vote are noteworthy. The models were presented when the balance of power within the city was being hotly contested and resentment in some quarters at Florentine intervention was at its height, and just four weeks prior to the appointment of the four Florentine Commissioners on Pistoiese affairs responsible for the pacification of the city. Although Verrocchio's model based on the figure of God the Father and the cardinal virtues secured a narrow victory by a vote of 43–35, the majority was seven votes short of the fifty-vote total required for the awarding of the commission according to the terms of the original provision of January 1474.[32] As far as can be ascertained, no vote was as close during the whole decade. Set within the context of communal division, a split vote of these dimensions automatically assumes a political hue.

Sadly the names of the other contestants are unknown, yet as regards the election procedures, the original stipulation that the winning model had to secure at least fifty votes suggests this case conformed with standard practice within Pistoia in relation to competition for artistic commissions – namely, a straight head-to-head contest between the two most popular models, the others having been eliminated in earlier votes. It is highly unlikely that the Pollaiuolo were involved at this stage; the most probable rival to Verrocchio with the requisite skills to execute such a prestigious commission and with a proven record in Pistoia is Antonio Rossellino.[33]

The exact chronology of developments in the months following the vote is unclear, but it is possible to reconstruct in some detail the context within which the dispute over the allocation of the contract took place and the extent to which the commission continued to animate the Pistoiese. Despite drawing up Headings of Peace between the respective factions on 13 September 1476, it was still deemed necessary to extend the authority of the four commissioners appointed to oversee the pacification and administration of all matters pertinent to the peace and tranquillity of the city until November 1477.[34] The further centralisation of power within Florentine and Medicean hands in this period was enhanced by Mariano Panichi's appointment on 15 September 1476, only two days after the ratification of the Headings of Peace, as Pistoiese ambassador to the Florentine Commissioners, a post which came with a salary of 50 lire per annum and was, as far as can be established, without precedent in Florentine diplomatic practice.[35] Strategically the appointment was crucial as a stage in the transition of the city to Lorenzo's overall control. Under the guise of saving the Pistoiese money, it reduced the numerous orators and ambassadors the Pistoiese were accustomed to send to Florentine magistracies and influential citizens, Panichi's becoming the sole official representative voice when addressing the four Commissioners on Pistoiese affairs based in Florence. Significantly, the extension of the commissioners' authority also extended to matters relating to the Forteguerri commission which was clearly perceived as a continuing source of tension.

When, at the prompting of Bishop Pandolfini, Pistoia eventually gave itself over to Lorenzo *in balìa* on 9 December 1476, the hope was that the acrimonious differences that had characterised the preceding months would finally be settled.[36] Such a move was not only a result of divisions within the patriciate as a consequence of Medicean intervention in communal affairs, but was also a consequence of the total collapse of relations between the communal and ecclesiastical authorities in the city which had a commensurate impact on the gestation of the Forteguerri commission and saw previously excluded members of the commissioning panel seeking to regain influence through the agency of another communal committee.

On 3 October 1476, the priors and the Dodici di Collegio, acting on the authority previously granted them by the Consiglio del Popolo, had elected six citizens 'to draw up headings regarding the administration of funerals and the building of sepulcres' (Appendix I). Amongst their number were both Piero Cellesi and the previously excluded Cherubino Tonti.[37] Not surprisingly given the unprecedented encroachment on the Bishop's jurisdiction, these moves sparked an unholy row, with Pandolfini taking his complaint directly to Florence. The response was almost immediate. Reacting to the Pistoiese provision on the same day, the Florentine Commissioners on Pistoiese affairs, acting on the authority granted them by the Florentine Tre Maggiori and Consiglio del Cento, passed a lengthy and detailed provision 'Concerning the defence of the Bishop's honour and the reparation of the Cathedral', which was not only registered in the deliberations of the Florentine Signori and Collegi, but also transcribed into the records of the Pistoiese Consiglio on 8 October 1476.[38] The terminology used not only testifies to how seriously the Florentines perceived the Pistoiese provision of 3 October to be, but also lists the issues over which the six, together with the Florentine Capitano di Custodia, had been granted authority, including their ability to send ambassadors to Florence, Rome, and even the pope to complain about the perceived maladministration of the cathedral. In ordering the original provision to be destroyed and threatening those responsible with massive fines and possible excommunication, the Florentines hoped to have quashed any further acts of brazen opposition.[39]

Notwithstanding the provision, however, the Pistoiese sent two ambassadors to the commissioners on 7 October to discuss the matter, prompting Pandolfini to send a letter to Lorenzo notifying him of their election whilst complaining of the Pistoiese's 'iniquity', adding 'and yet they are already beginning to disobey the commissioners' orders and fall foul of the penalties listed in their judgement.'[40] The same day the Otto di Guardia summoned Cherubino Tonti and his relations to Florence, the commissioners subsequently banning Cherubino from Pistoia.[41] Despite these reverses, the communal ambassadors must have secured concessions from the Florentines, as on 12 November an eight-man committee was elected by the priors and the Dodici di Collegio with authority to enter negotiations with Pandolfini concerning the decoration and refurbishment of the cathedral, and included in the eight were both Cherubino Tonti and Piero Cellesi.[42] As it transpires, this particular committee seemed more involved in the commissioning of Piero Pollaiuolo for the cathedral's *Corpus Domini* sacramental tabernacle than with the cenotaph, but given Pollaiuolo's involvement in the contested Forteguerri commission, it sheds new light on the interrelation of the two major commissions and explains in part how Pollaiuolo came to be involved in the dispute. Equally significant, as will become apparent, is the fact that three communal officials served on both committees, including Piero Cellesi.[43]

It was during these months that the revised Forteguerri committee began negotiations with Verrocchio concerning the price to be paid for the work, in keeping with the authority granted them on 15 May 1476. At some stage towards the end of that year, in all likelihood prior to mid-November, Verrocchio demanded 350 gold florins from the committee, yet with only 300 florins at their disposal they dismissed him and returned to the Consiglio on 23 January 1477 to secure an increased allowance to secure a work worthy of the cardinal's memory. To this end the Consiglio passed a motion to increase the allowance to 380 gold florins, at the same time granting the committee powers to levy a tax of one quattrino per lira on goods passing through the city's gates for the following two years, a privilege they enforced in March 1477.[44] The logical course of action at this stage would have been to reopen negotiations with Verrocchio as the elected artist. That certain members of the committee had alternative plans is suggested by the intervention in the same January meeting of the Consiglio of a key player in the dispute, namely, Piero Cellesi.

In seeking permission to spend up to 380 florins on the commission, Cellesi demanded that the money be spent on either the model passed by the Consiglio or 'another more beautiful model.' In a typically adroit move, the passing of the provision effectively transferred authority to award the contract from the communal councils to the committee, which was then able to 'award it to the said Andrea or to any other person considered worthy by us.'[45] In voting the monies, Piero Cellesi addressed the Consiglio, recommending they write to Ser Mariano in Florence to notify him of their decision, one Rainaldo Benedetti being paid 20 soldi on 11 October for carrying letters to Panichi in Florence.[46] The dispute over costs, therefore, provided the necessary pretext for approaching Piero Pollaiuolo, and Cellesi was central to this approach as the citizen who enabled the possible reassignment of the commission.

His record as obdurate Pistoiese and arch-competitor in the dispersal of Pistoiese patronage in the face of Florentine authority was without parallel. In the same month of January 1477, one of Lorenzo's agents in the city, Canon Antonio Marchetti, wrote that Cellesi was seeking to countermand a letter written by the Florentine commissioners ordering the city council to pay monies owed the city's organist, despite the fact the letter 'was of such a tone that I did not imagine anyone would presume to speak against it.'[47] Later, in December of the same year, not being eligible himself, he sought to block Lorenzo's preferred appointment for the position of *spedalingo* of the Ceppo and install his own candidate.[48]

The pretext for approaching Pollaiuolo was provided, as noted earlier, by the artist's involvement at precisely this time in negotiations for the completion of a *Corpus domini* tabernacle for the cathedral in Pistoia. Chronologically the *Corpus domini* negotiations came shortly after the breakdown of negotiations with Verrocchio over the price of the Forteguerri commission but coincided exactly with the granting of the commission to Verrocchio back in Florence by the four Commissioners on Pistoiese affairs. The committee's invitation to Pollaiuolo to submit a model must have been issued within a matter of days prior to the commissioners' decision, the committee agreeing to defer further proceedings until such time as the drawings were submitted. It is impossible to know whether Pollaiuolo had submitted his model prior to the council meeting of 23 January 1477 when Cellesi sought permission for the original committee to award the contract to either Verrocchio or another more worthy artist. From the account of the confusion presented in the committee's letter to Lorenzo and dated 11 March 1477, it appears that upon learning of the Florentine commissioners' decision the committee wrote to acknowledge Verrocchio's winning of the contract, submitting to the commissioners' authority in their guise as 'obedient sons.' Unfortunately, this letter seems lost, and the exact date they received news of the commissioners' decision in Verrocchio's favour remains a mystery. It is noteworthy, however, that they clearly failed to notify Pollaiuolo that the contract had been granted by a higher authority and was no longer theirs to dispense. The fact that they continued meeting in January and early March 1477 suggests they still felt they had legitimate jurisdiction over the commission.

Competing Jurisdictions

The committee was not the sole body at this time with legitimate authority to oversee the commission. New documents which shed important light on the chronology of events also permit the confusion concerning the commission to be read as part of a deliberate ploy by the committee in Pistoia to challenge the authority of the four Commissioners on Pistoiese affairs based in Florence. We know from the 1483 document published by Covi that on 15 November 1476 the four commissioners awarded the contract, underwritten by the Florentine notary Ser Anastasio Vespucci, to Verrocchio over the heads of the Pistoiese committee.[49] The Pistoiese committee's decision potentially to reassign the commission, as discussed earlier, was therefore taken some ten weeks after the commissioners' ruling. To date, the account of the confusion presented by the Pistoiese committee in their letter of March 1477 to Lorenzo has been taken at face value – namely, that they were unaware of the decision taken in Florence when making their deliberations. It is now clear that commissioners in Florence not only awarded the contract to Verrocchio, but at the same time appointed three Operai to oversee the commission: Piero Forteguerri, Mariano Panichi, and Giovanni d'Abram Gatteschi.[50] Whilst it is known that the Pistoiese committee of fourteen was rationalised to just three sometime prior to 1483, the date of the change has remained a mystery. That it actually took place simultaneous to the awarding of the contract to Verrocchio in November 1476 in Florence is key. Previously it was plausible that a lack of communication meant the Pistoiese were unaware of a Florentine deliberation involving Florentine officials and a Florentine artist. It is highly implausible, if not impossible, however, that the commissioners could appoint three Pistoiese operai, including both the cardinal's brother and Mariano Panichi, to the project without news reaching Pistoia or without the operai in question being consulted, especially as Cellesi's brother Filippo is known to have visited Lorenzo in January 1477. Between mid-November 1476 and the correspondence with Lorenzo in March 1477, therefore, there were two bodies with jurisdiction over the commission and a third committee meeting with the city's

Bishop to co-ordinate the decoration of the cathedral, including Pollaiuolo's *Corpus Domini* sacramental tabernacle. Whilst the authority of one was derived directly from Pistoia's own civic councils, the authority of the other was derived indirectly from the civic councils in Florence through the agency of the Florentine Commissioners on Pistoiese affairs. The third committee was a consultative body that was in all likelihood imposed by either Lorenzo or the commissioners on an unwilling bishop. Both of the bodies concerned solely with the Forteguerri commission were composed exclusively of Pistoiese citizens, however.

From mid-November 1476, therefore, Mariano Panichi was serving on both committees seeking to award the same contract to two different artists. A possible explanation of this bizarre scenario is that Panichi was resident in Florence during these months. In fact Panichi's role as go-between, mediating between the commune, the Florentine commissioners, and Lorenzo, was often complicated by his own absences from Pistoia as Capitano de' fanti in Florence.

Matters came to a head when Pollaiuolo actually submitted his model. Having failed on procedural and political grounds, the original committee was seeking to deny Verrocchio the commission on aesthetic grounds. In their own words, Pollaiuolo's model 'seems to us more beautiful and more worthy of art and is more pleasing to Piero, brother of the said Monsignore, and to all his family, and similarly to us and to all the citizens of our city who have seen it.'[51] This famous letter to Lorenzo is a fine example of the manner in which Pistoiese individuals and institutions sought to renegotiate decisions taken by the authorities in Florence. Sadly, only the letter to Lorenzo remains, although the committee refers to the fact that they had also petitioned (*preghato*) the commissioners in Florence asking whether they would be so kind as to 'have a few words' with Verrocchio and select Pollaiuolo's model instead.[52] That the committee sought to proceed through both formal and informal channels is typical of the sort of parallel correspondence the Medicean patrimonial form of government generated. It is significant that they make no mention at all of the three operai appointed by the Florentine commissioners to oversee the project. The rhetorical force of their letter to Lorenzo was premised on the extent of consensus within Pistoia concerning the preference for Pollaiuolo's model, as rarely was such consensus between so many constituencies secured. The final sentence is masterly in treading a fine line between deference to Lorenzo's authority and flattery of his knowledge of the arts on the one hand, and, on the other, itemising the interested parties who would be offended by his refusal to comply with their request:

> We are now forwarding to you, in your role as our patron, the aforementioned models since in such matters, as in all others, you are most well informed. And we are certain you seek the honour of the said

> Monsignore and his family and the whole of our city, to the extent that, if our opinion is right, you would lend your help and favour to our desire, which pertains to nothing but the honour of our city and the memory of the said Monsignore.[53]

Lorenzo's reply to the committee's letter of 11 March is seemingly lost, yet from the tenor of the committee's response on 17 March, it is clear Lorenzo was not best amused. Any chance of negotiating a deal were clearly scuppered by Lorenzo's reply, the submissive and self-deprecating tone of the committee's letter placing full authority in Lorenzo's hands concerning both the granting of the commission and the price whilst acknowledging their own shortcomings in seeking to pass judgement on matters about which they had little knowledge. Nothing further is heard of the original committee subsequent to this letter. Lorenzo's inevitable vexation with the original committee over the commission was undoubtedly a result of their obdurate refusal to submit to the commissioners' authority over a four-month period and the extensive lengths to which they went in attempting to reattribute the contract to their favoured candidate. This was no doubt compounded by his having to reconcile the tensions between the Florentine bishop and the commune concerning the administration of the city's ecclesiastical patrimony, including the issue of the reparation and decoration of the cathedral as a whole. Contrary to what some critics have inferred, however, it is clear Lorenzo did not confirm the awarding of the contract to Verrocchio in his reply.

Two new documents show that some six months later a decision had yet to be made, final confirmation of Verrocchio's victory only coming in late December 1477. The first reference comes in a section of a letter written to Lorenzo by the Ufficiali della Sapienza on 14 September 1477 (Appendix 2). Towards the end of their petition to Lorenzo to intervene in their appeal against the levy of a tax by the Pistoiese Monte della Pietà, the ufficiali refer to the commission. Noting the decision of their predecessors to grant Lorenzo full authority over the matter, the present incumbents ask Lorenzo, when time permits, to come to some decision so that work could go ahead.[54] The second reference is contained within the 1477 Pistoiese reforms drawn up by the four commissioners and nine elected Pistoiese reformers. Dated 22 December 1477, the forty-seventh rubric confirms the validity of the original contract of November 1476 with all its terms and conditions as underwritten by the commissioners' notary Ser Anastasio Vespucci (Appendix 3).[55] In a clear reflection of the tensions caused by the issue the rubric begins 'in order to avoid arguments and scandals' ['per litibus et scandalis evitandis']. Significantly, the same incipit is also found in the following rubric through which the Florentine commissioners granted extensive privileges to none other than Ser Mariano Panichi. By enshrining such decisions within legislation, the commissioners finally overruled any local opposition, thereby foreclosing any resistance and leaving no room for further negotiation.

Local Associations

The previous account requires some explanation as to why the revised committee introduced Pollaiuolo as a complicating factor and what exactly they had against Verrocchio. In addition to being part of the resistance politics pursued by opponents of persistant Medicean interference, I believe the answer also lies in the extent to which the relative artists were considered Pistoiese. Verrocchio's seeming distaste for provincial commissions of this kind is testified by the incomplete state of both the Madonna della Piazza altarpiece and the Forteguerri monument, both of which passed to his former pupil Lorenzo di Credi, whilst an attempt to identify possible allies in securing the Forteguerri commission reveals only Giovanni Morelli, one of the four Florentine Commissioners on Pistoiese affairs in 1476 who, earlier in 1466, was an operaio on the commissioning panel for Verrocchio's *Christ and St. Thomas* for the Or' San Michele.[56]

The Pollaiuolo family, by contrast, had extensive Pistoiese connections dating back to the early part of the century and, most important, close connections with both the influential Panciatichi family and the city's Bishop Niccolò Pandolfini. As major landholders in the commune of Quarrata, their land purchasing during the 1470s and 1480s involved business dealings with major Pistoiese institutions and on several occasions they nominated specific Pistoiese to act as their legal procurators.[57] Significantly, Quarrata was also one of the areas where the Panciatichi had major landholdings including their palace 'La Magia'.[58] In addition to the links in the *contado,* the Pollaiuolo were also neighbors of a branch of the Panciatichi in Florence, whilst their links with the city's cathedral date back to the 1450s when they were involved in a commission issued by the Opera di San Jacopo for two silver candlesticks. Antonio Pollaiuolo is also known to have accompanied Piero di Cosimo to the baths near Pistoia some time between December 1461 and late 1469.[59] Tradition also maintains that Bishop Pandolfini commissioned a silver belt inlaid with gold from the Pollaiuolo some time between 1475 and 1480, although there is no verifiable documentary evidence to support the claim.[60]

Another possible Pollaiuolo ally was the city's chancellor, Antonio Ivani, who was appointed in the autumn of 1476 just weeks prior to the height of the controversy. As former chancellor of rebellious Volterra and known Medicean client, he was deeply involved in the pacification of Pistoia in this period. Evidence of his support is found in a letter to Marsilio Ficino datable circa 1477, in which he wrote describing Pollaiuolo as the new Praxiteles, the Athenian sculptor thought most successful in marble. According to Chastel, the letter may well have been a reply to a letter of recommendation written by Ficino himself in relation to the monument commission.[61]

The definitive establishment of the three operai's authority to oversee the commission in December 1477 did not, however, bring the wrangling to an end. Although their preference for Pollaiuolo had been overlooked, the Forteguerri family still sought to exercise influence over the gestation of the commission through the agency of successive family members who served as operai in the years prior to Verrocchio's death. Like his brother Niccolò, Piero Forteguerri proved himself a resolute defender of the family's interests in the face of Medicean encroachments on their patrimony. In the weeks either side of the famous letter of March 1477 discussed earlier, Piero wrote to Lorenzo lamenting how 'communal business is conducted contrary to the city's needs', and later complaining about the new culture of clientage and its impact on the election of teaching staff to the Sapienza, pointedly asking Lorenzo to 'make that election which will be most useful and most fitting for such an institution as I'm sure is your intention.'[62] Piero's status as one of the three operai nominated by the Florentine commissioners to bring the work to fruition saw him serving alongside Lorenzo's chief agent, Mariano Panichi.

When Piero Forteguerri died in 1483, however, he was replaced by communal election by his cousin Domenico di Jacopo Forteguerri. Piero's demise saw the removal of the closest relative of the deceased Cardinal Niccolò, and, given the rest of the Forteguerri family's more frosty relation with Panichi, the latter's resumption of total control over the project. The addition of a proviso to Domenico's election that a majority of 2:1 was sufficient to carry any proposal concerning the monument signalled the marginalisation of the Forteguerri family's input during Panichi's lifetime. Subsequent payments to Verrocchio in 1483 were made through Panichi's agency, and when a contract for the completion of the monument was negotiated on October 3 1488, Lorenzo di Credi was made accountable to Mariano in person.[63] Domenico Forteguerri's frustration became apparent in January 1483, however, when he successfully prevented Mariano's son from securing a scholarship to the Sapienza, despite the personal intervention of both Panichi and two letters of recommendation sent by Lorenzo de' Medici.[64]

When Panichi was murdered in a factionally inspired attack just days after the signing of the contract with Credi and just four months after Verrocchio's own death, the Forteguerri's influence once again resumed as they secured two of the three positions of operai for the first time. Whilst various scholars have commented on Michele di Domenico's replacement of his father, the replacement of Panichi by one Antonio di Marco has been less noted. He was in fact Michele's cousin and also a Forteguerri.[65] In the following months the operai tracked down more of the missing funds, making a first payment to Lorenzo di Credi just five months after his signing the contract to finish the monument and once again providing the impetus for the long overdue completion of the work.

Conclusion

This chapter reading has sought to highlight the complex of competing agendas which animated the commission of the funerary monument of Cardinal Niccolò Forteguerri. As a cenotaph, its principal function was the commemoration of the deceased cardinal, an instance of art being deployed to overcome the transience of the subject through the creation of a permanent object of recollection.[66] Yet beyond the immortalisation of the cardinal's life and character, the monument constituted part of the larger process of civic storytelling, recalling the role of family, church, and commune in the cardinal's life, all three constituencies basking in his reflected glory. Establishing consensus between the interests of these three entities alone was problematic, as all three had legitimate grounds for intervening in the commissioning procedure. Yet in this particular case, Pistoia's position as subject town and Medicean attempts to exploit the city's patrimony in service of their own patronage networks saw the commission caught within the nexus of sociopolitical tensions which characterised civic life in Pistoia. In this context, it is fitting that a commission which struggled to accommodate such a multiplicity of readings should have itself been fashioned by a multiplicity of hands, its fractured state serving as a metaphor for its fractious past.

APPENDICES

1} **ASPistoia: Provvisione e riforme, 44 (1476), c.16r.** 3 October 1476. Election of six citizens by the priors and Dodici di Collegio, on the basis of authority granted them by the Consiglio del Popolo, to look into funerals and sepulchers.

Margin = capitulatores funerarum

Anno, indictione, mense, die, e loco soprascriptis. Magnifici Domines Priores, Vexilifer Iustitie, et laudabili offitium Duodecem de Collegio Popoli et Comunis civitatis Pistorii in numeris sufficentibus collegialiter congregati (in su). Attempta autoritate eis data per Consilium Populi civitatis Pistorii de eligendo sex cives ad capitulandi circa funus exequias et sepulturas fiendas, misso dato facto inter eos partito et secreto scruptineo ad fabas nigras et albas e obtempto partito secundum formam ordinamentorum (civis) comunis Pistorii, elegerunt infrascriptos auctoritatem et commissionem eis concessus predictum Consilium circa predicta videlicet: Petrus Iacobi Cellensis, Cherubinus Desiderii de Tontis, Bartholomeus Filippi de Fabronis, Lucas Antonii Ser Clementis, Jacobus Antonii Matei, Antonius Jacobi domini Lotti.

2} **ASF, Medici Avanti il Principato, XXXV, 719.** Letter of the Ufficiali della Sapienza of 14 September 1477 to Lorenzo de' Medici.

Magnifice ac Generose vir ecc. La fede che sempre a auta la nostra comunita im publicho et im privato nella Vostra Magnificenza ci fa pigliare sicurta a pregare quella che essendosi posta certa imposta sopra i beni della Sapientia e beni a quelli vinta per li Uffitiali del Monte di costi e avendo noi privilegi et exemptione per tali beni vi piaccia prestarci l'usato favore che tali privilegi e exemptione ci sia observata come piú apieno sara exposto alla Vostra Magnificenza per messer Lodovicho taviani di qui nostro doctore e lectore. Al quale vi piaccia dare piena fede in quello che circa a questo per lui vi sara exposto. E perche per li nostri predecessori si die a Vostra Magnificenza piena commissione della Sepoltura del Reverendissimo Kardinale di Tiano preghiamo quella quando vede il tempo oportuno ci pigli qualche determinatione perche tale opera abbiamo effecto come piú apieno vi sara exposto per detto Messer Lodovicho. Rachomandiamo questo luogo a Vostra Magnificenza offerendoci sempre a vostri commandamenti paratissimi.

Ex pistorio die xiiii Settembris mccccLxxvii
Vostri Magnifici Servitores
Offitiales Sapientie Reverendissimi Kardinalis [de] Theano

3} **Pistoia, Biblioteca Forteguerriana, MS.B 169, fol. 28r.** Forty-seventh rubric of the 1477 reforms of the city of Pistoia, drawn up and issued by the four Florentine Commissioners on Pistoiese affairs together with the nine nominated Pistoiese Reformatori – 22 December 1477.

[In margin] Andree verochii locatio.

xlvii Item per litibus et scandalis evitandis, deliberaverunt et deliberando confirmaverunt locationem per ipsos commissarios factam sub die xv novembris 1476 andree del verrochio de novo sepulcro conficiendo in memoriam reverendissimi Domini Cardinalis de Tiano modis, formis, temporibus, et de pretio in omnibus et per omnia et pro ut et fient latius et apertius constat in ipsa locatione et conducta rogata per Ser Anastasium de Vespucciis civem et notarium florentinum anno mense et die predictis.

NOTES

1. For recent surveys see Enrica Neri Lusanna and Chiara d'Afflitto, 'Le Arti figurative' in *Storia di Pistoia*, 4 vols, vol. III, *Dentro lo stato fiorentino: dalla metà del XIV alla fine del XVIII secolo*, ed. Giuliano Pinto (Florence: Le Monnier, 1999), 379–400; Anna Padoa Rizzo, 'Arte a Pistoia nel Quattrocento. Presenze fiorentine, risposte locali: un mosaico da ricomporre', in *L'Età di Savonarola: Fra' Paolino e la pittura a Pistoia nel primo '500*, ed. Chiara d'Afflitto, Franca Falletti, and Andrea Muzzi (Venice: Marsilio, 1996), 37–49.

2. See, for example, *Representation: Cultural Representations and Signifying Practices,* ed. Stuart Hall (London: Sage, 1997) and *Production of Culture/Cultures of Production,* ed. Paul Du Gay (London: Sage, 1997).

3. The classic treatment of this theme in the visual arts remains Enrico Castelnuovo and Carlo Ginzburg, 'Centre and Periphery' in *History of Italian Art,* 2 vols., ed. Peter Burke, trans. Claire Dorey (Cambridge: Polity Press, 1994), vol. II, 31–112. See also Gilles Deleuze and Félix Guattari, 'City/State', *Zone* 2 (1986): 195–9. The term 'symbolic economy' derives from Pierre Bourdieu, *Outline of a Theory of Practice,* trans. Richard Nice (Cambridge: Cambridge University Press, 1977), 159–97.

4. John Pope-Hennessey, *An Introduction to Italian Renaissance Sculpture,* 4th ed., 3 vols. (London: Phaidon, 1996), vol. II, 165.

5. Andrew Butterfield, *The Sculptures of Andrea del Verrocchio* (New Haven and London: Yale University Press, 1997), 137; Clarence Kennedy, Elizabeth Wilder, and Péleo Bacci, *The Unfinished Monument by Andrea del Verrocchio to the Cardinal Niccolò Forteguerri at Pistoia* (Northampton, Mass.: Smith College, 1932), 8. On the monument's restoration and history, see *I Medici, Il Verrocchio e Pistoia. Storia e restauro di due capolavori nella Cattedrale di S. Zeno,* ed. Franca Falletti (Livorno: Sillabe, 1996), especially the essays by Butterfield, 18–26, and Falletti 27–37.

6. Forty-five documents were published in Kennedy et al., *The Unfinished Monument,* and more recently Dario A. Covi, 'Four New Documents Concerning Andrea del Verrocchio', *The Art Bulletin* 48 (1966): 97–104. For a summary of the affair, see Andrew Butterfield, *The Sculptures,* 137–8 and 223–8. Butterfield's analysis is based wholly on the published documents cited earlier, as is the resumé of Francesco Negri Arnoldi, 'Il monumento sepolcrale del Card. Niccolò Forteguerri in Santa Cecilia a Roma e il suo cenotafio nella cattedrale di Pistoia', in *Egemonia fiorentina ed autonomie locali nella Toscana nord-occidentale del primo rinascimento: vita, arte, cultura,* Settimo convegno internazionale, Pistoia, 1975 (Pistoia: Centro di studi, 1978), 211–21. Other similar summaries can be found in Piero Adorno, *Il Verrocchio: Nuove proposte nella civiltà artistica del tempo di Lorenzo Il Magnifico* (Florence: Casa editrice Edam, 1991), 195–6; Maud Crutwell, *Verrocchio* (London: Duckworth, 1904), 125–31; Charles Seymour Jr., *The Sculpture of Verrocchio* (Greenwich, Conn.: New York Graphic Society, 1971), 60; and Günter Passavant, *Verrocchio: Sculptures, Paintings and Drawings* (London: Phaidon, 1969), 177–8.

7. Michel de Certeau, *The Practice of Everyday Life,* trans. Steven Rendall (Berkeley: University of California Press, 1984), 117.

8. In his 1991 study of Verrocchio, for example, Adorno characterised Lorenzo's intervention in the Forteguerri commission as the work of a man of leisure with time to indulge in letters, philosophy, and art 'which even extended to the settlement of provincial disputes like the one surrounding the Forteguerri cenotaph.' See Adorno, *Il Verrocchio,* 196.

9. See Stephen J. Milner, 'Lorenzo and Pistoia: Peacemaker or Partisan?', in *Lorenzo the Magnificent: Culture and Politics,* ed. Michael Mallett and Nicholas Mann (London: The Warburg Institute, 1996), 235–52.

10. For the 1474 reforms see Archivio di Stato di Firenze (henceforth ASF), *Tratte,* 1494, cc. 157r–83r, and cc. 144r–56r for the subsequent addition of *arroti* by the Florentine commissioners. For the 1477 reforms, see Pistoia, Biblioteca Forteguerriana, MS B.169.

11. See Stephen J. Milner, 'Rubrics and Requests: Statutory Division and Supra-Communal Clientage in Fifteenth-Century Pistoia', in *Florentine Tuscany: Practices and Structures of Power,* ed. William J. Connell and Andrea Zorzi (Cambridge: Cambridge University Press, 2000), 312–32. Archivio di Stato di Pistoia (henceforth ASPt), *Provvisioni e riforme* (henceforth *PR*), 44, cc.

43v–4r, 9 December 1476; 'quod omnes auctoritas potestas atque iurisditio qua habet civitas pistorii et consilium predictum sit et esse intelligatur translata et concessa in dictum Magnificum Laurentium.' The provision passed by 72 votes to 5.

12. On the Ceppo see AA.VV., *Spedali Riuniti Pistoia 1277–1977 Centenario. Contributi per la storia dello spedale del Ceppo di Pistoia* (Pistoia: Società pistoiese di storia patria, 1977), which was also published as a volume of *Bullettino Storico Pistoiese* 79 (1977). On the Monte in Pistoia see Ilvo Capecchi and Lucia Gai, *Il Monte della Pietà a Pistoia e le sue origini* (Florence: Olschki, 1975).

13. For Pandolfini's letter requesting he be considered for the post, see ASF, *Archivio Mediceo avanti il principato* (henceforth *MAP*), XXX, 926: 1 October 1474; and for della Rovere's letter of thanks to Lorenzo subsequent to Pandolfini's appointment ASF, *MAP*, XLVI, 379: 4 January 1475.

14. See Lorenzo de' Medici, *Lettere*, 7 vols., ed. Nicolai Rubinstein et al. (Florence: Giunti, 1977–), vol. III, 291–2, n. 18.

15. For accounts of Forteguerri's life, see J. B. Fortiguerra, 'Nicolai Fortiguerrae Cardinalis Vita', in F. A. Zaccharia, *Biblioteca pistoriensis* (Bologna: Forni: 1752), 239–40; Giovanni Forteguerri, *Cenni storici intorno alla donazione del Cardinale Niccolò Forteguerri ed alla fondazione della Pia Casa di Sapienza in Pistoia* (Florence: 1857); and Lucia Gai, 'Niccolò Forteguerri nei suoi rapporti con l'ambiente culturale pistoiese del Quattrocento', *Studi Storici Pistoiese* 1 (1976): 57–72.

16. Several of these letters have been published. See Medardo Morici, 'Il Cardinale Niccolò Forteguerri e Giovanni di Cosimo de' Medici', *BSP*, II (1900), 110–14; and Alfredo Chiti, 'Un mazzetto di lettere del Cardinale Niccolò Forteguerri', *BSP*, III (1901): 69–75. For Forteguerri's correspondence with Pius II, see Gaetano Beani, *Niccolò Forteguerri*, 137–66.

17. ASF, *MAP*, XLVI, 98: 12 April 1471.

18. A copy of both the donation of 23 August 1473 and subsequent Papal bull of 24 May 1474 can be found in Luigi Bargiacchi, *Storia degli istituti di beneficenza, d'istruzione ed educazione in Pistoia e suo circondario dalle respettive origini a tutto l'anno 1880*, 4 vols. (Florence: 1883–84), vol. IV, 7–17. Manuscript copies of the donation include ASF, *Statuti delle Comunita 'Autonome' e 'Soggette'*, 605, cc. 1r–19r and ASF, *Catasto*, 897, cc. 148v–9r.

19. Kennedy et al., *Unfinished Monument*, doc. 1, p. 75: 'pro honore perpetuo civitatis Pistorii et gratitudine benefitiorum per ipsum reverendissimum dominum Cardinalem collatorum in civitate Pistorii'.

20. On the office of commissioner see William J. Connell, 'Il Commissario e lo Stato Territoriale Fiorentino', *Ricerche storiche*, 18 (1988), 591–617.

21. The four commissioners – Girolamo Morelli, Loysius Guicciardini, Piero Minerbetti and Tommaso Ridolfi – were mandated on 17 June 1476. See ASF, *Signori: Legazioni e commissarie: Elezione, istruzione, lettere*, 19, c. 34r–v.

22. ASF, *Tratte*, 1494, c. 156r.: 'A dì xxvi d'agosto 1474: Pe signori collegi et octo fu confermato la correctione e supplimento facto sopra la nuova riforma di pistoia del 1474. Ancora approvorono la Borsa degl'operai di San Jacopo'. The initial 1474 imborsazione for the post of Vexilifier di Iustitia, for example, included thirty-seven names, whilst the revised list numbered forty, six of whom were added by the commissioners. Although both the initial and revised bags for the Operai di San Jacopo included twenty-four names, the revised list included five names added by the commissioners.

23. The committee was initially consituted by the following: the six communal representatives elected on 2 January 1474 were Antonio di Jacopo Lotti, Lorenzo Taddei, Simone Cellesi, Bartolomeo Ammannati, Jacopo Bonfanti, and Niccolò Bracciolini: the four Ufficiali della

Sapienza until 30 June 1475 were Ser Niccolò di Bartolomeo di Polito, Carlo di Giovanni Cantansancti, Marco di Jacopo Forteguerri, and Cherubino di Desiderio Tonti: the three Operai di San Jacopo were Francesco de' Rossi, Antonio di Marco Jacobi, and Matteo di Antonio Mattei. See Kennedy et al., *Unfinished Monument,* doc. 1, 75–76; ASPt, *PCS,* 390, c. 1r, and ASPt, *Opera di San Jacopo,* 8, c. 160v. On the Opera di San Jacopo's role as communal banker and commissioning body see Lucia Gai and Giancarlo Savino, *L'Opera di S. Jacopo in Pistoia e il suo primo statuto in volgare (1313)* (Pisa: Pacini, 1994), 139–54.

24. The newly elected communal representatives were Domenico Forteguerri, Ser Niccolò di Bartolomeo di Polito, Ser Mariano Panichi, Lodovico di ser Niccolò di Ser Guglielmo, Antonio Jacobi domini Lotti, and Piero Cellesi. The four Ufficiali della Sapienza from 1 July 1475 were Giuliano di Simone Fioravanti, Ser Clemente di Tarato Grifoni, Niccolò Bracciolini, and Giovanni d'Andrea di Giovanni. The Operai of San Jacopo as of 19 July 1475 were Ser Bono Francesco Allegri, Lotto di Giovanni de Amannatis, Jacopo Benedetto Consolini, and Lorenzo Taddei di Giovanni, the latter being replaced by Antonio Tarati Grifoni sometime prior to May 1476. See Kennedy et al., *The Unfinished Monument,* doc. II, p. 76; ASPt, *PCS,* 390, c. 18v, and ASPt, *PR,* 43, c. 470r and 524v.

25. See ASF, *MAP,* LXXXII, 89: 19 December 1465 for a copy of the provision granting *balìa* to Baldinotti and signed by Tonti. For the comments of Canon Antonio Marchetti to Lorenzo concerning the extensive influence of Tonti see ASF, *MAP,* XXXV, 977: 23 December 1477. Another high-profile casualty in this marginalisation of previously eminent families was Neri Fioravanti, who was jailed in Florence between November 1474 and January 1475. See ASF, *MAP,* LXXXV, 107: 10 November 1474.

26. There are more than twenty letters to Francesco Cantansanti in the MAP archive in the years prior to 1463, including six written by Cherubino Tonti. See for example ASF, *MAP,* LXXXVIII, 53: 20 August 1461; and *MAP,* XCVIII, 516, undated.

27. Tensions between Panichi and the partnership of Tonti and Francesco Cantansanti date back to at least 1466 when Mariano wrote to Lorenzo concerning a long-running land dispute which originated in 1454. See ASF, *MAP,* XXII, 69: 2 July 1466.

28. See Mario E. Cosenza, *Biographical and Bibliographical Dictionary of the Italian Humanists,* 6 vols. (Boston MA: G. K. Hall, 1962–7), vol. III, 2176.

29. Since the completion of this piece, a brief account of Mariano's activities has appeared in William J. Connell, *La città dei crucci: fazioni e clientele in uno stato repubblicano del '400* (Florence: Nuova Toscana Editrice, 2000), 105–22.

30. For these early years, see the comments of Riccardo Fubini in Id., Lorenzo de' Medici, *Lettere,* I, xxv–vi, and 7, 14–16, 18–20, and 309. For Forteguerri's letter see ASF, *MAP,* XLVI, 44: 18 November 1464.

31. See ASF, *Tratte,* 1494, c. 145v. Mariano's name was crossed out of the list of Gonfalonieri, a marginal note stating 'Die 26 Augusti 1474 per commissarios fuit positur in Borsa operariorum', and added as the sixth name to the list entitled 'Operai arroti pe comissarii sono cinque cioe.'

32. See Kennedy et al., *Unfinished Monument,* doc. I, p. 75: 'et dictum modellum et locum referant Consilio approbandum per dictum Consilium per plures fabas non pautiores quinquaginta' and doc. III, p. 76: 'Modellum factum per Andream del Varocchio de Florentia [..] habuit fabas nigras xliii quatenus fuit maior aliis repertis in dicto scruptinio modellorum, et sic fuit approbatum per dictum Consilium per plures fabas nigras pro sic non obstantibus 35 fabas albas in contrarium'. The margin was also ten votes short of the two-thirds plus one majority required in most Pistoiese councils for a provision to pass. Given the total number of eligible

voters was one hundred and one, the total of seventy-eight votes cast shows an attendance level of just over three-quarters at this particular meeting.

33. See Luca Caburlotto, 'Giovanni Rossellino e il monumento a Filippo Lazzàri in San Domenico a Pistoia', *Paragone: Arte* 15–16 (1997): 3–23; and Eric Apfelstadt, 'The Later Sculpture of Antonio Rossellino' (unpublished Ph.D. diss., Princeton University, 1987) 2 vols., vol. I, 7.

34. For copies of the Headings of Peace of 13 September 1476 see ASF, *Tratte,* 44, fol. 249r–78v; and BNCF, *Fondo Gino Capponi,* Cass. 10, 9, cc. 1v–7v. For the initial extension of the commissioner's authority see ASF, *Provvisione e registri,* 167, cc. 144r–5r, 28 September 1476; and the further extension in ASF, *Deliberazione in forza di speciale autorità,* 34, cc. 180r–2v, 3 October 1476.

35. See the transcribed letter of the commissioners to the Pistoian Consiglio del Popolo concerning arrangements for the meeting of his salary in ASPt, *PR,* 45, c. 38v: 22 July 1477. On 11 October 1476 the Consiglio voted 20 soldi in payment to Rainaldo Benedecti for the transport of letters from Ser Mariano Capitano in Florence. See ASPt, *PR,* 44, c. 20r.

36. See above note 11. In the autumn of 1476, the Otto di Guardia also called specific individuals to Florence as part of the pacification process, Cherubino and Bartolomeo Tonti being summoned on 7 October. See ASF, *Otto di Guardia,* 43, c. 35r–v: 7 October 1476.

37. The other members of the six were Bartolomeo Fabbroni, Luca d'Antonio Buonvassali, Jacopo Mattei, and Antonio di Jacopo domini Lotti. See ASPt, *PR,* 44, c. 16r: 3 October 1476.

38. ASF, *Signori e collegi: deliberazioni in forza di speciale autorità,* 34, cc. 180r–2v: 'Contra honorem Episcopi et circa reparatione cathedralis'. See the transcription in ASPt, *PR,* 44, fols 17v–19r: 8 October 1476.

39. The volume containing the original deliberation of 25 August 1476 was ordered to be destroyed, accounting for the two-month gap in the records of civic deliberations. The volume ASPt, *PR,* 43 finishes in June 1476, whilst ASPt, *PR,* 44 starts on 1 September. Volume ASPt, 45, the first volume penned by the newly appointed chancellor, Antonio Ivani, begins on 26 December 1476.

40. ASPt, *PR,* 44, c. 16r. The two elected were Niccolò Taviani and Jacopo Mattei. For Pandolfini's lament see ASF, *MAP,* XXXIII, 823, 7 October 1476: 'e già cominciano a contrafare alle ordine de' Comissarii e cadere nelle pene di detto ordine'. See ASF, *MAP,* XXXIII, 824, for a letter written by Antonio Marchetti and Antonio Ippolito to Lorenzo thanking him for his intervention in securing the honour of both Pandolfini and the cathedral chapter in the face of the actions of 'questi sfienti di qua'.

41. For the Tonti clan's summons to appear in Florence see ASF, *Otto di guardia* 43, cc. 35r–v; and *MAP,* 33, 1068: 30 December 1476. They were subsequently relegated by the Florentine commissioners. See *MAP,* XXXV, 106: 24 January 1477.

42. The eight elected on 12 November to meet with Pandolfini were Ser Clemente Tarati Pauli, Cherubino Tonti, Piero Cellesi, Francesco Sozofanti, Jacopo Antonii Matei (one of ambassadors), Antonius Jacobi Bartolomei de Lotti, Paulum Magistri Michaelis, and Francesco Lodovico Dondoli. See ASPt, *PR,* 44 cc. 37v–8r.

43. See Stephen J. Milner, 'Piero Pollaiuolo's Lost Sacramental Tabernacle of the *Corpus Domini*', forthcoming in the *Journal of the Warburg and Courtauld Institutes,* 67 (2004).

44. See Kennedy et al., *Unfinished Monument,* doc. IV, 76–7, and doc. V, 77–8.

45. The two phrases used were 'aliud modellum pulchrius' and 'allogarla a decto Andrea et a ogni altro che ci paresse'. See Kennedy et al., *Unfinished Monument,* doc. IV, p. 77, l. 9, and doc. VI, p. 78, l. 16.

46. ASPt, *PR,* 44, cc. 19r–v and c. 20r.

47. ASF, *MAP,* XXXV, 98, 22 January 1477: 'Et era di tale tenore che non pensavo alcuno presumesse contradirla. Nientedimeno Piero Cellesi . . . '. See a full transcription of the letter in Stephen J. Milner, 'Organ Culture and Organ Contracts in Renaissance Pistoia', *Recercare* 12 (2000): 77–94.

48. ASF, *MAP,* XXXV, 979: 15 December 1477.

49. There is no trace of the contract in the two volumes of Vespucci's protocolli for the relevant years. See ASF, *Notarile antecosimiano,* 21063 and 21064. The commissioners wrote to the Pistoian Consiglio on 11 October 1476 requesting the Opera di San Jacopo meet the expenses of 'Ser Anastagius' for the costs incurred in horses, messengers, and supplies whilst employed in the process of pacification, amounting to the not inconsiderable sum of 6 florins, 74 lire, and 19 soldi. Piero Cellesi, in addressing the motion, recommended the Consiglio write to Mariano Panichi in Florence advising him of their decision. See ASPt, *PR,* 44, c. 19r–v.

50. The account of the commission furnished by Butterfield, *Sculptures,* 224–8 is confusing due to his use of the term "Operai" to refer to both the original committee members and the three nominated by the Florentine commissioners. Although the original committee included the Operai of the Opera di San Jacopo, its members were never referred to as Operai. Pollaiuolo submitted his model to the committee, therefore, *not* to the three Operai.

51. See Kennedy et al., *Unfinished Monument,* doc. VI, p. 78: 'il quale ci pare più bello et più dengnio d'arte et più piace a contento di messer Piero, fratello di decto Monsignore, et di tucta la sua famiglia, et simil di noi et di tucti e' ciptadini della nostra ciptà, che l'ànno veduto'.

52. Ibid: 'et per questo abbiamo preghato decti Commissari che se pare loro usare alchuna cortesia a decto Andrea'.

53. Ibid: 'Ora a voi, come a nostro protectore, mandiamo e' decti modelli, perchè di simile cose et d'ogni altra n'avete pienissima intelligentia, et siamo certi desiderate l'honore di decto Monsignore et sua famiglia et di tucta la nostra ciptà, ché, essendo vero quello ci pare, ci prestiate il vostro aiuto et favore al nostro disiderio, che non intende ad altro che allo honore della ciptà, et alla memoria di decto Monsignore'.

54. See Appendix 2.

55. See Appendix 3.

56. See Andrew Butterfield, 'Verrocchio's Christ and St Thomas: chronology, iconography and political context', *Burlington Magazine* 134 (1992): 288.

57. See Maud Crutwell, *Antonio Pollaiuolo* (London, Duckworth, 1907), 233–46, for the *catasti* of the Pollaiuolo family and Alberto Chiapelli, 'I beni di Antonio del Pollaiuolo nel contado di Pistoia', *BSP* (1901): p. 110.

58. See Renato Stopani, 'Profilo storico del territorio di Quarrata', in *Quarrata: Storia e territorio* (Florence: Studio Immagini, 1991), ed. Fiora Bellini, 13–76; and Chetti Barni, *Villa La Magia: una dimora signorile nel contado Pistoiese (secc. xiv–xix)* (Florence: Edam, 1999), 19–42.

59. Eve Borsook, 'Two letters concerning Antonio Pollaiuolo', *Burlington Magazine* 115 (1973): 464–8.

60. See Kennedy et al., *Unfinished Monument,* 15; and Sergio Ortolani, *Il Pollaiuolo* (Milan: Ulrico Hoepli Editore, 1948), 154: '1475–80 (?) Una cintura d'argento a incrostazione d'oro, in collaborazione con Piero, per Niccolò Pandolfini vescovo di Pistoia'.

61. See André Chastel, *Marsile Ficin et l'art* (Geneva: Droz, 1996) 2nd ed., 36.

62. ASF, *MAP,* XXXV, 190: 18 February 1477; and ASF, *MAP,* XXXV, 282: 13 March 1477.

63. Kennedy et al., *Unfinished Monument,* doc. XVI, 82; and Covi, 'Four New Documents', 101–2.

64. See ASPt, *Sapienza* 391, c. 10v; and the letters in del Piazzo, *Protocolli,* p. 272–3. For related documentation see Armando F. Verde, *Lo Studio fiorentino, 1473–1503: ricerche e documenti,* 5 vols. (Florence: Istituto nazionale di studi sul Rinascimento, 1973–94), vol. III, i, 170–3. See also Verde, *Lo Studio,* vol. III, ii, 735, where Verde provides further information on Niccolò Panichi but fails to make the connection with these events, which are noted elsewhere in the same work.

65. Kennedy et al., *Unfinished Monument,* doc. XVII, 82. It is worth noting that in the aftermath of Panichi's murder, Giovanni di Piero Forteguerri, a leading member of the other pro-Cancelliere branch of the family, was summoned to Florence by the Otto di Guardia in an attempt to diffuse factional tensions within the city. See BNCF, Rossi Cassigoli, nn. 62–3: Pietro Arferuoli, *Historie delle cose più notabili seguite in Toscana, et altri luoghi, et in particolare in Pistoia manoscritto in due tomi,* 1628, vol. I, p. 191; and Jacopo Maria Fioravanti, *Memorie storiche della città di Pistoia* (Lucca, 1758): 367–9.

66. On memorials, see the observations of Mary Carruthers, *The Craft of Thought: Meditation, Rhetoric, and the Making of Images 400–1200* (Cambridge: Cambridge University Press, 1998), 35–40.

9

Between Legend, History, and Politics: The Santa Fina Chapel in San Gimignano

Deborah L. Krohn

ONLY RECENTLY HAVE HISTORIANS BEGUN TO EXPLORE THE QUESTION OF how Florence made its state. Conspicuously absent is a discussion of the role that works of art – painting, sculpture, and architecture – played in the expression or reflection of Florentine hegemony.[1] Yet no adequate account of this process is possible without some discussion of what was, perhaps, the most enduring, if not necessarily the most immediately potent, of all the instruments at the metropolis's disposal. In what follows, I look at the history of a monument created in commemoration of a local saint in the town of San Gimignano, which became Florentine in 1353. Roughly a century later we find the civic authorities hiring leading Florentine artists to create a monument to one of the city's heroines. The story of its creation opens a window on the process by which free cities were made subject and a region made into a state, ambiguities and all. The Santa Fina chapel demonstrates the dynamic of cultural translation between Florence and San Gimignano. On one hand, Florentine artists were the natural choice for an important commission in this period, but the works they produce are purely local in flavor, resisting a complete cultural subjugation that would mirror the political status of San Gimignano.

In 1457, the general council of the civic government of San Gimignano resolved to build a burial chapel for Fina, a local saint who died in 1253. The monument which took shape in the Collegiata over the next forty years stands as one of the most beautiful chapels created in fifteenth-century Tuscany and demonstrates the predominance of Santa Fina in the civic and religious life of the people of San Gimignano. Among the artists and craftsmen who collaborated on it were Domenico Ghirlandaio, Giuliano da Maiano, and Benedetto da Maiano. The chapel is emblematic of the relationship between Florence and San Gimignano in terms of cultural exchange. But to understand the motivations of those who carried out the chapel project, we need first to examine how the hagiographic tradition shaped the civic identity of the town.[2]

In his first novel, *Where Angels Fear to Tread* (1909), E. M. Forster alludes to the Santa Fina chapel, located in a church that he has disguised by giving it the pseudonym of St. Deodata. The scorn with which the monument is described is meant to satirize the popularity of San Gimignano as a stop on the Grand Tour, encapsulating a critique of mass travel and the tradition of the Grand Tour itself. By the early years of the twentieth century, thanks to massive restorations, the town embodied the tourist's nostalgia for medieval times. Despite rule from Florence that would continue through the Risorgimento, the town succeeded in preserving its identity undiminished. The roots of its strategy of remaining Tuscan without becoming Florentine are visible in this fifteenth-century project that employed metropolitan artists to erect the most fashionable of monuments to a long-dead saint whose localness was the secret of her success.

The creation of a chapel commemorating the life and miracles of a local saint by public authorities is not unique to San Gimignano. André Vauchez, Anna Benvenuti, and others have outlined an entire field of cultural history dedicated to the study of what may be termed 'civic religion.'[3] Indeed, San Gimignano had several patron saints, among whom was Fina.[4] And because the fifteenth-century chapel was by no means the first monument dedicated to her in the town, the role played by cultural policy in the formation of the territorial state can be illuminated by examining the story of Fina and the creation of her chapel in this context. The proliferation of images of local saints in San Gimignano during the fifteenth century suggests that as the commune became less autonomous from Florence in political and economic matters, its government saw fit to assert, as if in *contrapasso*, a more vigorous local identity. The specific history of Santa Fina explains why she in particular became the vehicle for this demonstration.

The circumstances of San Gimignano's subjugation to Florence are a lesson in the subjectivity of history. The simple fact that Florence had increased taxation by a factor of three by the early fifteenth century was likely the cause of what Enrico Fiumi referred to as the 'decadenza' of San Gimignano. This idea has been largely confirmed by Giovanna Casali's recent analysis. Florence's domination certainly did not change art patronage patterns in San Gimignano immediately, however. Many commissions for public projects, such as the monumental fresco cycles lining the nave of the Collegiata, were given to Sienese artists until the early fifteenth century.[5] Although the 100-year hiatus between the so-called voluntary subjugation and the initiation of major decorative projects, inspired by Florentine models and commissioned from Florentine artists, cannot be explained solely in economic terms, the increasing dependence of San Gimignano on Florence resonated at a cultural level. Likewise, because much of San Gimignano's history has been penned by local erudites, the gradual slippage on many fronts that led to what is referred to as a 'definitive subjugation' is recounted almost as a fairytale, with the subjugation clearly marking the end of a golden age of independence and initiating a period of decline. Whether or not San Gimignano, along with many other Tuscan communes, was actually in a state of decline, economically and fiscally, during the second half of the fourteenth century, is disputed by historians and demographers.[6] As Casali has recently confirmed, internal weakness within San Gimignano played an important role in its progressive subordination to Florence.[7] Powerful patronage networks grew throughout the course of the fifteenth century, putting increasing pressure on provincials to secure the support of prominent Florentines and, in particular, at least after 1466, on Lorenzo de' Medici himself.[8] The extent to which we can read the presence of Florentine artists in San Gimignano as a consequence of Florentine hegemony reflects the way in which the story of subjugation is told and the projection of the past that it conjures up. It is my contention that many of the issues in the memorializing of San Gimignano's past as a response to the takeover are crystallized in the fifteenth-century chapel's story.

I

Fina's life story as it has been transmitted to us is concise and purposeful. Fina dei Ciardi was born in San Gimignano, probably in 1238.[9] At the age of ten she came down with an illness that constrained her to lie immobile for the remainder of a short and excruciating life.[10] Her qualifications for sainthood consisted in two things: in her stoic reaction to the grim disease that befell her at a tender age and in the miracles she inspired after death.

Local people began to venerate Fina almost immediately after her death in 1253. A series of fifteen witness reports gathered in the fourteenth century provide valuable information concerning the growth of the cult of Santa Fina and the physical trappings associated with it.[11] Most of the accounts were written between 1310 and 1313 and consist of descriptions of miracles that occurred at the moment of Fina's death. Ex-votos are recorded at her tomb as early as 1310.[12] Witnesses recorded the appearance of ships and hands fashioned of wax and locks of hair.[13] In fact, this miracle-working cult survived through the fifteenth century, as we can glean from documentary sources. In 1482, Onofrio di Pietro, operaio, or head of the board of works of the Collegiata, paid the woodworker Bartolomeo da Colle a small sum 'for three *tavole* which he made around the Santa Fina chapel where the images of wax are.'[14]

Although she was referred to interchangeably as a saint or a *beata* at least from the early fifteenth century, Fina was never canonized.[15] The witness accounts collected in the fifty-year period following her death indicate that an attempt was made to have her formally sanctified in Rome, but repeated attempts into the sixteenth century confirm that this objective was never met. Although popes approved her cult on at least two occasions, this did not lead to a real trial.[16]

We can trace the history of Fina's predominance in the civic pantheon of San Gimignano through the series of monuments preceding the creation of the fifteenth-century chapel. Fina's place of burial was a locus of veneration from the day of her death in 1253, but sources provide conflicting information about various translations of the earthly remains. At first, a raised wooden casket was placed in the cloister of the Collegiata.[17] The town statutes of 1255 report that a baptistry, gates, and a stone pulpit were to be made with revenues from offerings left at her tomb.[18] In the same year, Guido Marabottini, rector of a new hospital established in memory of Fina, expressed the desire to build a chapel in the name of the saint in the hospital.[19] This project was not approved by the ecclesiastical authorities of the commune – perhaps they were worried that another chapel would cut into the income from Fina's tomb. A subsequent rector was able to persuade the authorities, and a chapel was supposedly built in the hospital.[20]

In 1322, the operai of the Collegiata asked permission to move the body of Fina, presumably from the cloister, into an *alavello,* or raised wall-tomb. This was finished in 1326, when the tomb, containing her remains, was placed on the inner façade wall of the Collegiata.[21] A reliquary bust, conserved now in Benedetto da Maiano's tabernacle on the altar of the chapel of Santa Fina in the Collegiata, was created at this time in order to house the saint's skull.[22]

A fresco of Santa Fina, painted on a pilaster near the inner façade wall, probably also dates from the mid-1320s.[23] Fina stands against a blue background in a fictive trefoil niche. In her left hand, she holds a small bouquet of simple flowers, the 'viole di Santa Fina.' Her right hand grazes the white wimple of a woman who seems to kneel at her feet, perhaps a patron.

Fina's tomb, conserving its form of a raised *alavello,* was probably moved sometime before 1374, when a chapel dedicated to Fina was founded on the outer wall of the central nave, across from which is now an anonymous, undated fresco.[24] The fresco depicts Fina lying on her plank as Saint Gregory the Great appears at her side (Fig. 64). She wears a simple reddish gown.

Beldia, her faithful caregiver, wearing a white wimple, supports Fina's head, while a pack of rodents cavort in the foreground.[25] Fina's eyes are open, and her left hand is raised. She lies on her back on the almost corporeal plank, painted carefully to emphasize its role as protagonist in her suffering and tilted to display her even more directly. An inscription to the left of the three-sided fictive structure in which she lies describes the scene: 'Apparet Fine Doctor Gregorius almae/revelans obitum promictens munera palmae [Doctor Gregory appears to kind Fina revealing her death and promising the rewards of the palm].'

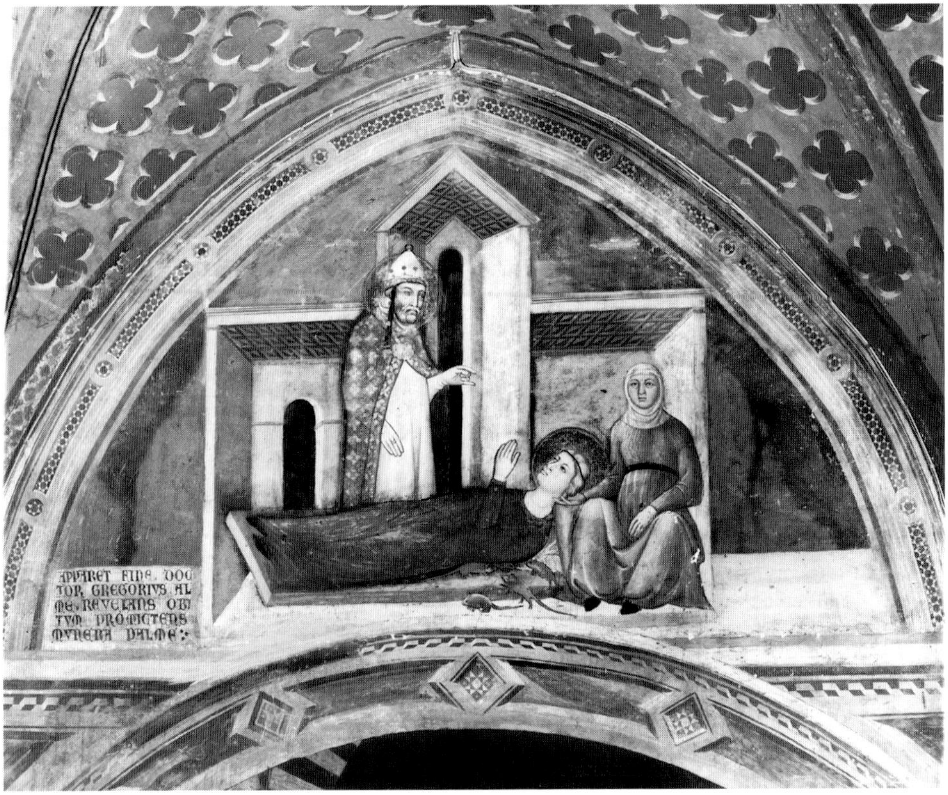

64. Anonymous, *Death of Santa Fina.* San Gimignano, Collegiata. Photo: Soprintendenza per il Patrimonio storico artistico e demoetnoantropologico di Siena e Grosseto. Use authorized by The Italian Ministry for Cultural Heritage and Activities.

Gregory is the grammatical subject of the inscription, reinforcing Fina's relationship to this pope-saint. This early altar of Santa Fina was consecrated to both Fina and Gregory. From the beginning, Fina had been linked to Gregory. Eight days before his feast day, he made an appearance, deeming Fina worthy of receiving the privileged information concerning the date of her death. Perhaps Fina's tie with this saint was intended to function as a further demonstration of her sanctity. Gregory both legitimized her cult and fufilled the role of confessor, which is conspicuously absent in narratives of Fina's life. The legend implies that Fina's holiness attracted Gregory to her. A pope's explicit praise of a local holy woman can only have had positive propagandistic significance for the commune, as well as reinforcing the status of full sainthood which only canonization could guarantee.

In 1402, the bust of Fina made in the 1320s was placed within a tabernacle commissioned by the Operai of the Collegiata, Michele Morgatti and Michele Lapi (Fig. 65).[26] This tabernacle, disassembled, now on display in the Museo Civico in San Gimignano, presents the only narrative depiction of the life of Fina before

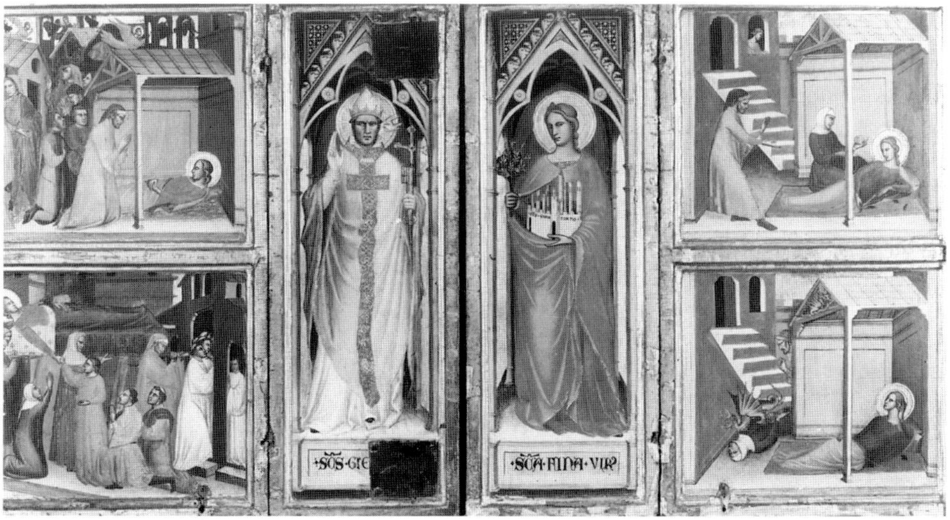

65. Lorenzo di Niccolò Gerini, *Tabernacle of Santa Fina.* San Gimignano, Museo Civico di San Gimignano. Photo: Alinari/Art Resource, NY.

the fifteenth-century chapel and would probably have been the focal point of a reliquary altar, perhaps underneath the raised sarcophagus. Attributed to the Florentine painter Lorenzo di Niccolò Gerini, it is not included in the few discussions of the oeuvre of the painter that exist.[27] Lorenzo di Niccolò was already working in San Gimignano in 1401 when he was commissioned by a private patron to execute an altarpiece with scenes from the life of San Bartolomeo for the Collegiata, which includes an image of Fina.[28] In addition to this, he executed several altarpieces in and around Florence, including one for the high altar of the church of San Marco in 1402.[29]

The tabernacle consists of four double-sided panels with engaged, gilded frames. On what was presumably the front, Saints Fina and Gregory are depicted on two panels that must have served as doors.[30] On the right, Fina cradles a model of the city in her left arm, appropriating Saint Gimignanus's role as patron saint, while in her right hand she holds a bouquet of the ubiquitous 'viole di Santa Fina.' She wears a simple green gown and no head-covering. On the left panel, Saint Gregory holds a cross and raises his right arm in blessing. Each of the other two panels has been divided into two pictorial fields. In the first episode, Fina is depicted lying on her side on the plank in a simple loggia, probably designed to represent the interior of her house. A woman wearing a white wimple – perhaps the veil of a tertiary – holds out food to Fina, while a third figure chases away mice who disport themselves before Fina's plank. Fina wears a simple green gown and has a golden halo.

In another vignette, Fina is depicted lying on her plank in her green dress and halo, recently deceased. The mice have been transformed into flowers, angels can be seen ringing bells in the towers of the buildings, and many citizens crowd around the body of the saint. In the scene below this, townspeople have shouldered Fina, transforming the plank into a bier on which she is carried into the church. Fina's right arm reaches out, depicting the moment in which she miraculously heals the arm of her nurse Beldia. She wears the green gown and halo here as well.

The reverse of the tabernacle is divided into narrative fields that depict additional miracles. On the upper-left-hand panel, Fina lies on a shelf-type support, similar to a raised sarcophagus, in a church in front of which people are gathered to witness an exorcism. This may be a clue to the appearance of Fina's tomb on the inner facade wall of the church as it was set up in 1326 before being moved, as discussed earlier.[31] The remaining scenes on the reverse are more generic, but employment of a common miraculous iconography would have confirmed the citizens' claim to Fina's holiness through articulation in the visual language appropriate to a late-fourteenth-century hagiographic image.

II

In 1457, the civic government resolved to build a new chapel in commemoration of Fina. In 1468, the superintendant of the board-of-works, Onofrio di Pietro, was given explicit power to hire and remunerate craftsmen to work on the chapel, establishing his instrumental role in the creation of the chapel.[32] Also in 1468, Florentine architect Giuliano da Maiano was paid 'for his effort when he came here to make a drawing for the Chapel of Santa Fina'.[33] A new consciousness of space, proportion, and design, which seemed to inform the entire building and decoration of the Collegiata during the second half of the fifteenth century, included the construction of a vaulted crossing and several distinct chapels in addition to that devoted to Fina. Authorities expressed the desire to clear the nave walls of the altars that obscured the monumental fresco cycles depicting the Old and New Testaments completed during the second half of the fourteenth century. A joint decision made in 1458/9 by the canons of the Collegiata and the priors to move these altars was intended to make the church 'civilior et pulchrior'.[34] This was carried out over several years, since we find a reference in 1462 authorizing the operai and the bishop of Volterra to clear away the remaining altars, restoring the church to a 'pristinus situs'.[35]

The use of the word 'civilior' to describe the effects of the removal of private altars suggests that for the commune, manifestations of private devotion in a space that was both highly sacred and highly civic were undesirable. Periodic payments for cleaning of the Old and New Testament frescoes during the period of construction are further evidence that the visibility of these frescoes, which featured repeated communal insignia in their marginal zones, was at issue even when the entire church must have seemed more like a workshop than a decorous and pious place.[36] While the moving of older altars seems to signal a lack of respect for the past, when placed in the context of other gestures it may be considered a form of historicism in which a specific moment in the history of the church and its decoration was being privileged – a moment closer to the time when San Gimignano was a free city, before its subjugation to Florence.

The restoration of Lippo Memmi's *Maesta* in the Palazzo Communale, commissioned by the civic government and carried out by Benozzo Gozzoli during 1460s, testifies further to the importance of conserving that past in San Gimignano. While Gozzoli's intervention is clearly visible to modern eyes, he was attempting to extend the fourteenth-century fresco in a way that blended, in both style and iconography, with the earlier imagery.[37] It was also in the fifteenth century that the local authorities collected and bound a group of twelfth- and thirteenth-century notarial and communal documents. The so-called Libro Bianco was created with the explicit purpose of preserving materials considered essential for the history of the town, perhaps a hedge against the Florentine version of history.[38]

As funding for the chapel project increased, the descriptive language in the communal deliberations evolved. In the founding act of 1457, the communal authorities invoked God and the saints. In 1469, twelve years later, a new element was added to the vocabulary. The word *sacellum*, used by Leon Battista Alberti in *De Re Aedificatoria* to mean a small antique temple, replaced *cappella*, a more conventional choice, which was used in the 1457 act.[39] A 1469 deliberation began with the following assertion:

> Since history clearly demonstrates that the divine cult must be celebrated with the greatest reverence, and even the Romans venerated their gods with so much fervor that domestic cares and comforts were put aside, how much greater need is there for us, to whom has been given true religion, to make the Santa Fina chapel for the honor and beauty of God and the republic.

The chapel must not be neglected due to lack of funds, it continued, so monies were to be made available to Onofrio di Pietro.[40]

Documents show that by 1471 the chapel was under construction, but the process was lamentably slow.[41] 'There is no one who would deny how much dignity and glory belong to the body of a blessed one, and how much commendation go to those who diligently ornament and adorn that blessed figure with external splendor', we read in a 1472 document. It continues, 'And not only was it the custom of the Christian sects, but even of the pagans who never even knew Christ, to whom it was pleasing, and the highest responsibility, to honor their Gods and to build large and worthy temples and to adorn them with profuse ornament'.[42] The priors of San Gimignano, good Christians all, nevertheless saw fit once again to defend the service of Fina by comparison with their pagan ancestors. Not only that. As I discussed previously, an earlier chapel dedicated to Fina had grown up around her tomb, first outside the church and later on the inner façade wall, before being moved to somewhere near its present location, but we do not find the word 'sepulcher' before 1472. The invocation of a Roman past is on one hand an echo of humanist culture in fifteenth-century Italy, but it is also a phenomenon that can be observed throughout the history of Italian cities from the Middle Ages onward. Although the seemingly contradictory coexistence of Christian custom with reverence and emulation of antiquity fascinated Aby Warburg and his followers, recent studies have suggested that this was not, in fact, remarkable.[43] During the high Middle Ages, many Italian cities integrated legendary or real figures from ancient Rome into their civic pantheons, such as Virgil in Mantua.[44] For the priors of San Gimignano, it was no heresy to compare local pious traditions to those of ancient Rome as long as the truth of Christianity triumphed implicitly over the precedent set by antiquity. Identification with an ancient past also allowed San Gimignano to share the glorious heritage being claimed for Florence. Invocation of the Romans in a sacred context was a local and competitive expression of the fashion for antiquity that marked Florentine high culture of the period.

It has been suggested that Sienese efforts to canonize Saint Catherine and seat a bishop during the 1450s inspired the elders of San Gimignano to create the Santa Fina chapel.[45] The deliberation that mentions the 'sepulcher' for the first may indeed reflect events in Siena, but the extent to which the chapel project was connected to the initiative of San Gimignano's ecclesiastical independence from Volterra should not be exaggerated. Fina had been venerated in San Gimignano since the day of her death, and the impulse to rebuild her chapel must be seen in light of the long and powerful tradition of civic piety.

III

It is not surprising that Fina still played a central role in the religious life of the citizens of San Gimignano in the mid–fifteenth century, when the chapel project was initiated. The earlier narrative structure of Fina's life was expanded and elaborated in the chapel's design and execution. The chapel is located off the right aisle of the Collegiata, across from the earlier anonymous fresco (Fig. 66). Scenes painted in fresco by Ghirlandaio and his shop cover two of three walls in the chapel and focus on two episodes in Fina's life (Figs. 67 and 68). In the vaults above the chapel are the four Evangelists; in the three lunettes that rise above a continuous frieze of putti are the church fathers, San Nicolà da Bari and Saint Gimignanus, who holds a model of the city. Old Testament prophets reside in the spandrels beneath the frieze.

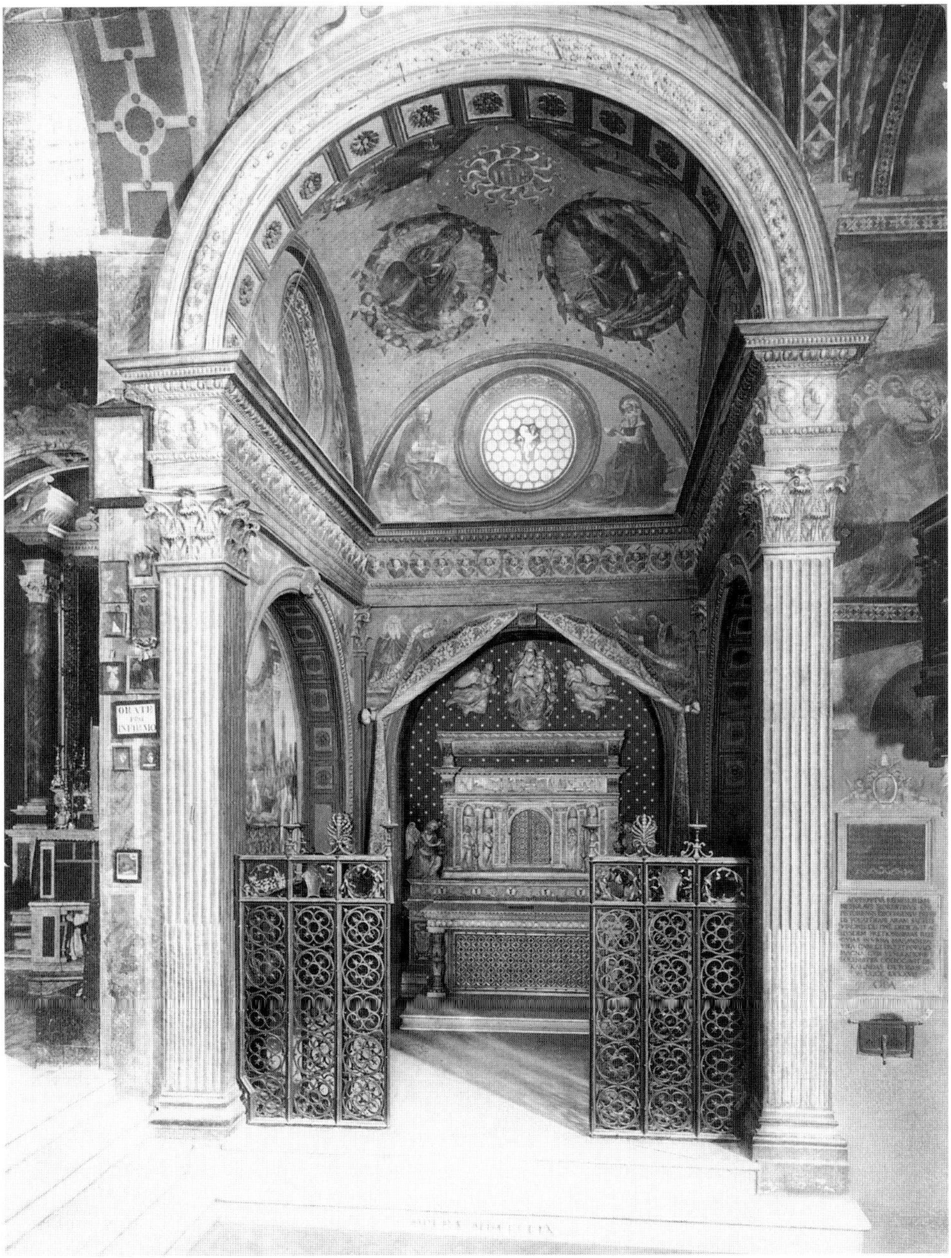

66. *Chapel of Santa Fina.* San Gimignano, Collegiata. Photo: Alinari/Art Resource, NY.

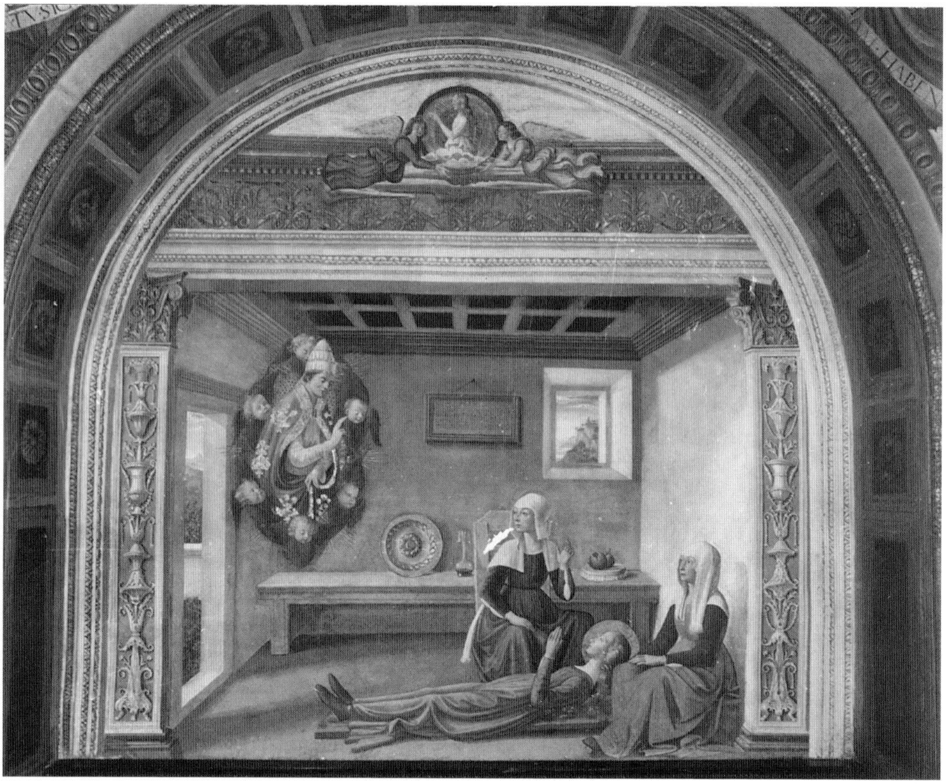

67. Domenico Ghirlandaio, *Death of Santa Fina*. Fresco. San Gimignano, Collegiata. Photo: Soprintendenza per il Patrimonio storico artistico e demoetnoantropologico di Siena e Grosseto. Use authorized by The Italian Ministry for Cultural Heritage and Activities.

The Announcement of St. Gregory, on the right as one enters the chapel (Fig. 67), depicts Santa Fina lying on a plank on the floor of a sparsely furnished room. Three other figures are present: Nurse Beldia supports Fina's haloed head, seated on the floor behind the invalid. A second woman, Bonaventura, daughter of Beldia and an important witness to Fina's miracles, sits on a low chair and gazes in awe, one forearm raised in a gesture of surprise, at St. Gregory. He appears in a mandorla surrounded by putti-heads and holds two fingers up in a gesture of blessing. On a bench along the back wall rest a decorative gold platter, a glass flask half-filled with wine, and a plate holding two bursting pomegranates, symbols of the Eucharist and the Passion. On the right, a rectangular window gives onto a hilly landscape, which can also be seen from an opening on the far left of the composition.

A Latin inscription hangs from a nail in a gilded frame on the back wall of the room. The inscription contains St. Gregory's message to Fina: "Parata esto, filia, quia dies solennitatis meae ad nostrum es ventura consortium cum sponso tuo perenniter permansura [Be prepared, daughter, for on the day of my feast you

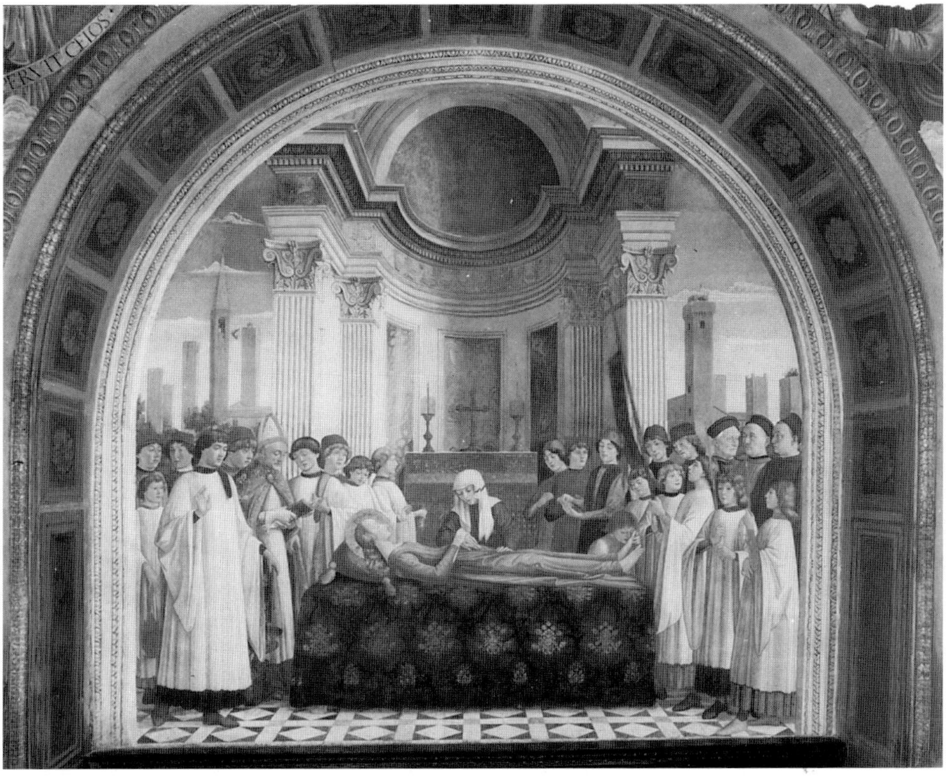

68. Domenico Ghirlandaio, *Funeral of Santa Fina.* Fresco. San Gimignano, Collegiata. Photo: Soprintendenza per il Patrimonio storico artistico e demoetnoantropologico di Siena e Grosseto. Use authorized by The Italian Ministry for Cultural Heritage and Activities.

will be taken up into our company and reamain there with your bridegroom]." This text may be compared with that in the early-fourteenth-century scene of Gregory's appearance to Fina painted on the nave arch facing the chapel. The earlier inscription reads as follows: "Dr. Gregory, appears to kind Fina, revealing her death and promising the rewards of the palm." The earlier text is descriptive, merely explaining the image and the importance of Gregory's message in the third person, using the voice of an omniscient narrator. In Ghirlandaio's fresco, Gregory himself is addressing Fina directly in the second person, using the future tense as opposed to the present. Ghirlandaio's fresco effectively circumvents the need for explicated narration. The use of the third person in the earlier Fina fresco serves to mediate between the image and the viewer. By the time Ghirlandaio painted the chapel, the purpose of the representation had changed from explanation and verification to commemoration.

Another change in the iconography of the fifteenth-century version of the story is the addition of a second woman as witness to the appearance of St. Gregory.

Bonaventura was the daughter of Beldia and also attended Fina at the moment of her death. Her inclusion suggests that elaboration of the basic story had taken place.[46] The immediacy of experience was guaranteed by Gregory's direct address to Fina, recorded in the inscription represented in the rhetorical guise of a framed wall hanging. Versimilitude was increased by inclusion of a second person who stood in for the viewer, signaled on a textual level by the use of direct address. In the earlier fresco, Beldia was the only witness to Fina's calling by Gregory (Fig. 66). In Ghirlandaio's elaboration, spectators are given a role in the holy events, much as they bear witness in Ghirlandaio's later frescoes in the Sassetti and Tornabuoni chapels in Florence.

The story has been condensed and cleaned up. The rodents swarming around Fina's recumbent corpse in the legend and earlier fresco are banished to the margins, where a lone rat cowers in the upper-left corner under the bench. Flowers sprout from the plank, although according to the legend they do not bloom until Fina has died. Here they are in evidence while she is still among the living, because Gregory's visit occurred eight days before her death. Rather than sacrifice the effectiveness of the story through a fragmentary and sequential representation of events, the narrative strategy employed presents all the evidence simultaneously.[47]

Across the chapel space, a second narrative fresco depicts Fina's funeral and several posthumous miracles (Fig. 68). Fina lies in state on a bier draped in gold-embroidered damask, while a group of men and boys, clerics and laymen, gather around her. Some are clearly portraits of prominent citizens, as I have suggested elsewhere.[48] The scene takes place within a hemicyclical apse set against a vertical cityscape representing San Gimignano. The apse is decorated with panels of fictive porphyry and colored marble framed by corinthian pilasters. An altar, on which are candelabra and a cross, stands at the center of this sacred space. Behind this structure, the characteristic towers of San Gimignano rise, lending a strong local flavor to the scene and juxtaposing the classicizing vocabulary of the later fifteenth century with the medieval townscape, a visual counterpart to the allusions to ancient Rome nestled in the official acts. Iconography follows legend in details such as the angel flying to the bell tower on the left to toll the communal carillon, the healing of nurse Beldia's withered hand, and the restoration of a blind boy's sight through the touch of the dead Fina's foot. In both frescoes, Fina wears a simple pomegranate-colored gown with white underclothes peeking out at the neckline and wrists, and a halo.

The painting of the frescoes was substantially complete by May of 1478, when a special assignment of cash was provided so that the Operaio Onofrio di Pietro, could 'satisfy those whom he owes for the painting of the chapel, the construction of the sepulcher, and other expenses'.[49] In October of 1478, a second payment recorded that money was to be used to satisfy Onofrio's creditors who painted the chapel.[50] From the wording of the act, it is clear that the chapel was a collaborative effort

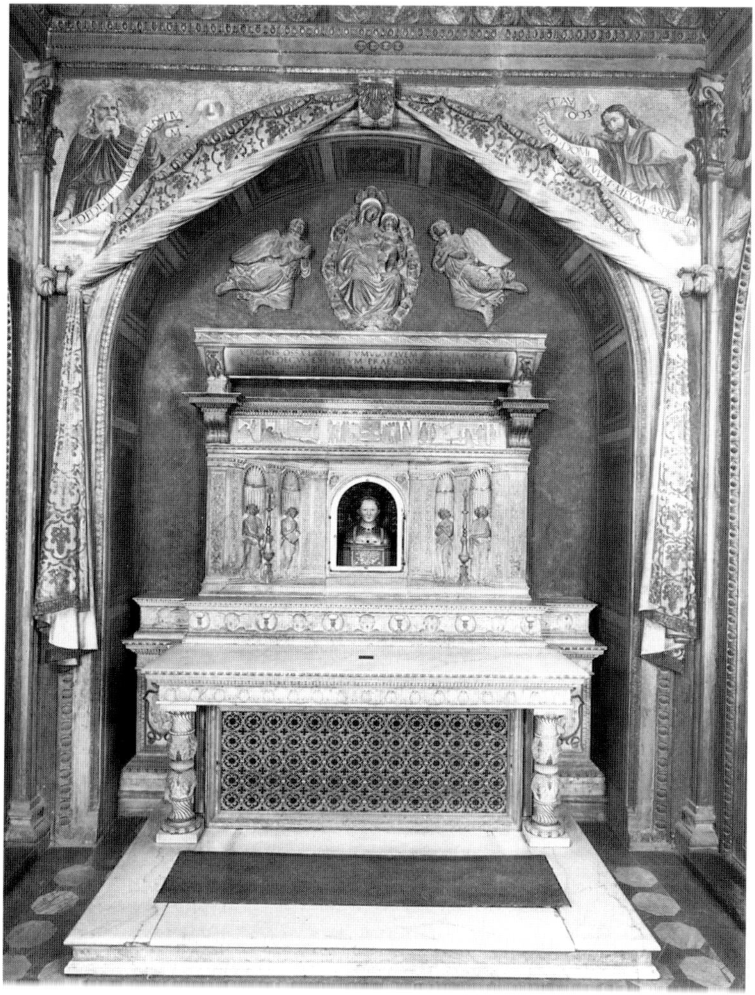

69. Benedetto da Maiano, *Altar of Santa Fina*. San Gimignano, Collegiata. Photo: Soprintendenza per il Patrimonio storico artistico e demoetnoantroplogico di Siena e Grosseto. Use authorized by The Italian Ministry for Cultural Heritage and Activities.

rather than the work of a single artist. The year 1478 may be established as a *terminus ante quem* for the frescoes.

This dating amends previous attempts to date the frescoes to 1475.[51] This earlier dating is based on the inscription on Fina's sarcophagus, which makes specific reference to the frescoes.[52] The combined sarcophagus, altar, and reliquary carved by Benedetto da Maiano is the third major component of the chapel decoration under consideration here (Fig. 69). As in the frescoes, a reliance on textual sources is evident in the monument. A payment for an 'epitaph' of Santa Fina to Benedetto da Maiano from 1490 suggests that Onofrio di Pietro had commissioned the inscription, but does not say when. Fina's body was not moved to the new sarcophagus until the consecration of the chapel in 1488, and Onofrio died in 1489, which explains the wording of the payment: 'In primo a Benedetto da Maiano insino a di 29 di Maggio fiorini due lire 13 per lo epitaffio di Santa Fina el quale aveva allogato Nofri'.[53] Onofrio had commissioned the inscription at some prior point, and there must have been a contractual agreement stipulating that Benedetto was to inscribe the sarcophagus with this text provided by Onofrio.[54] Cadogan and Garzelli date the frescoes to 1475–7 based on stylistic evidence observed in drawings.[55] The completion date of 1478 thus confirms their conclusions.[56]

The inscription on the tomb invites the viewer to learn about the life of Fina by literally reading the images which are on the walls of the chapel, painted in fresco by Ghirlandaio:

> The bones of a virgin lie hidden in the tomb which you, stranger, admire.
> Her honor serves as an example and protects her people.
> Her name was Fina; this is her hometown; You ask what her miracles were?
> Read these walls which teach by means of living signs.
>
> (Virginis ossa latent tumulo quem suspicis, hospes.
> Haec decus, exemplum praesidiumque suis.
> Nomen Fina fuit; patria haec; miracula quaeris?
> Perlege quae paries vivaque signa docent.
> Anno domini MCCCCLXXV)[57]

Three scenes from the life of Santa Fina are illustrated on a sculptural predella placed between the head reliquary and the sarcophagus. The central scene depicts the funeral of the saint, appropriate for a funerary monument. The miracles of the curing of Beldia's arm and the healing of cripples are represented in a kind of shorthand in the low relief of the panels. In the left panel, Fina lies with her shoulders supported by Beldia, while Gregory hovers very close to her. In an adjacent room of the house, a man holding crutches sits waiting for an audience with Fina, documenting her thaumaturgic qualities in life as well as after death. In the right panel Fina appears hovering above the bier of a child whom she has brought back to life. As in the eyewitness testimony of Fina's miracles, women are more closely involved with miraculous events than men. One woman is shown kneeling in prayer above the bier of the child, and two others seem to be rushing to bear witness to the scene.

An elaborate series of classicizing moldings frame the three panels; these extend the interplay between architectural detail, painting, and sculpture that animate the ensemble. Allowing for differences which the varying media dictate, the iconographic vocabulary in these sculptural narratives is very similar to that used in the frescoes. Reduplication of imagery in the chapel suggests that the events of Fina's life from which the creators of the chapel could draw were limited, throwing into relief the two themes that recur in the aspects of the *vita* that artists and patrons emphasized: the miraculous appearance of St. Gregory and the miracles with which Fina was credited.[58]

It is significant that the ideal viewer is projected as an outsider. An important clue to the chapel's message lies in the tomb inscription. The viewer, called 'hospes', approaches the chapel as a 'stranger' or 'guest'. The importance of the chapel for San Gimignano's public image is emphasized by the assumption embedded in this text that Santa Fina is unknown and that the images in the chapel are to serve as a key for a visitor or pilgrim. Florentines were known to frequent San Gimignano, and in August of 1460, Giovanni di Cosimo de' Medici was the first of many Medici to make the trip when he stopped over on his way to the Baths of Morba.

The deliberations of the civic government present a different species of evidence from inscriptions, which were composed for public consumption. The works of art that remain are still the best evidence for concepts of identity and expression that lay at the heart of the public discussion, but these texts are rich with layers of meaning that we can unpack as we read between the lines. Having examined the prominence of Santa Fina in the myth of the city presented in the fabric of her chapel, it makes sense to ask who the men were who commissioned the chapel.

As the communal deliberations confirm, there was a Florentine podestà, six priors, a gonfaloniere of the Guelf party, and three captains also 'della Parte Guelfa'. A small staff served the podestà, and a communal treasurer and notary recorded official business and kept records. A number of small committees were frequently delegated to carry out specific tasks, including the decoration of public places and the supervision of building projects such as walls or fortifications. Other communal officials included a tower-keeper, doctor, criminal lawyer, various tax collectors, trumpeters, grain-weighers and keepers, 100 crossbow archers, guards at the gates, a grammar teacher, and a clock-winder.[59] The priors were elected from the four quarters of the town, as they had been as early as the thirteenth century, for terms of two months. Every two months the entire government changed, except the podestà, who remained in office for six months. Participation in elected office seems to have been transferred through families for several generations, filling the bimonthly rosters with strings of patronymics.

Unlike Florence, where biographical information is readily available for most prominent citizens, information for San Gimignano is fragmentary. An examination of the frequency with which individuals served in the government confirms the notion that a patrician elite predominated within a republican structure, as in Florence. Although the Florentine *Catasto* of 1427, carried out in the *Distretto* in 1429, is a useful instrument for the early years of the fifteenth century, later records of taxation, called *Estimi,* contain almost no demographic or biographical information.

During the course of the fifteenth century, San Gimignano remained on the margins of the political turmoil that beset Florence. Supportive of Florence's military campaigns against the duke of Milan in the late 1420s, San Gimignano nevertheless objected to the levying of the first *Catasto* under Giovanni de' Medici in 1428. Casali discusses some of the background for this resistance. San Gimignano's statutes of 1425 contained new laws articulating its responsibilities in maintaining the fortress which had been built during the second half of the trecento with a great deal of local money. These statutes also describe many dilapidated or ruined buildings which testify to continuing economic hardship.[60] While neighboring Volterra mounted a successful resistance that was severely punished by the Florentines, San Gimignano eventually paid its revenues.[61] Later on, Lorenzo de' Medici took the side of private adventurers mining alum illegally within Volterran territory. Volterra rebelled, precipitating its formal submission to Florence.[62] San Gimignano sided with Lorenzo, reinforcing unconditional support for the dominant city that was only to increase over the years.

IV

Viewed against this backdrop, the creation of the Santa Fina chapel was not just an antiquarian pursuit carried out by the local goverment. The initiation of a second feast day for Fina was occasioned by a new miracle credited to her: that of halting the plague that struck San Gimignano in 1478.[63] In 1480 the Sangimignese Apostolic Secretary Lodovico Ridolfi petitioned Sixtus IV on behalf of the commune to authorize the celebration. Permission was granted, and from this point Fina was honored twice yearly: on the date of her death and on the first Sunday in August.[64] This second feast included a procession and a solemn mass. In 1481, Onofrio di Pietro, operaio, received money from the general council of San Gimignano, as well as from donations that he himself garnered, for decorating a processional baldachin to carry the head of Fina on the occasion of a newly instituted feast for the Saint.[65] In April 1482, a certain Lorenzo di Bartolomeo da Firenze 'bandieraio' was paid for decorating twenty silk flags with the arms of the commune and the head of Santa Fina for a baldachin for carrying the head of Santa Fina,[66] as well as eight painted standards to support the baldachin.[67] Like other objects commissioned by Onofrio di Pietro from Florentine craftsmen, these standards were brought from Florence, two months later.[68]

In 1484 two payments, one for eight glass lamps[69] and the second for a key to the chapel,[70] indicate that the chapel was complete. Once the body of the saint was moved into place, the chapel could be consecrated. Onofrio di Pietro was one of two orators chosen, in 1485, to request a bishop's presence at the transfer of Fina's body to the new tomb.[71] The consecration of the chapel took place three years later, on September 28, 1488. Bishop Niccolò Pandolfini of Pistoia conducted the ceremony, which consisted of moving the bones of Fina into the sarcophagus 'placed above the altar in the chapel of the same Blessed Fina.' The deliberation states that the event took four hours, that everyone in the town was present, and that afterward the bishop celebrated the mass in the chapel.[72]

Of the public works sponsored by the civic government of San Gimignano to honor its patron saints, the chapel of Fina was the most costly, complex, time-consuming, and, ultimately, successful. Santa Fina was a living link back to the glory days of the commune, in which wealth from travellers on the Via Francigena piled up in the towers that characterised the city's skyline. This period, *her* period, was the one canonized by the civic authorities through the act of collecting its documentary records to help preserve historical record of the town. The inscription on Fina's tomb entreats the visitor to *perlegere,* to read thoroughly, the examples depicted. By returning the chapel to its archival and iconographic contexts, we can do so with eyes attuned to the fifteenth century. What we then see is a town whose fathers recognized in a famous daughter a means of affirming an independent identity belied by the brute facts of political subjugation and economic decline. And if there was no alternative to the use of the conqueror's artists – this was, after all, the highest style of the day – they were at least being used to commemorate, for as long as the walls of the Collegiata would stand, a San Gimignano free from Florence.

NOTES

1. See the bibliography and notes in *Florentine Tuscany. Structures and Practices of Power,* ed. William J. Connell and Andrea Zorzi (Cambridge and New York: Cambridge University Press, 2000); and Samuel K. Cohn Jr., *Creating the Florentine State: Peasants and Rebellion, 1348–1434* (Cambridge and New York: Cambridge University Press, 1999). For a discussion of the relationship between Florence and San Gimignano with specific reference to urbanism and the changing shape of the town, see Giovanna Casali, *San Gimignano. L'evoluzione della città tra XIV and XVI secolo* (Florence: Olschki, 1998).

2. Aside from references in the many general studies of San Gimignano and its monuments, the Santa Fina chapel has not been the object of monographic study until recently. A 1978 article by Doris Carl ('Der Fina-Altar von Benedetto da Maiano in der Collegiata zu San Gimignano,' *Mitteilungen des kunsthistorischen Institutes in Florenz,* 22 No. 3, 265–86) supplied a comprehensive discussion of the original composition of the reliquary altar and tomb. In her dissertation, Linda Koch, 'The Santa Fina Chapel in San Gimignano. The Promotion of a Female Saint and the Early Christian Revival in the Renaissance' (Ph.D. diss., Rutgers, The State University of New Jersey, 1991), made use of the some of the same documentary sources as cited here, but, as the title suggests, addresses specific issues and comes to different conclusions. See also two articles by Linda Koch that develop references to Eucharistic symbolism and its theological significance

in various elements of the Santa Fina chapel: 'The Portrayal of Female Sainthood in Renaissance San Gimignano: Ghirlandaio's Frescoes of Santa Fina's Legend,' *Artibus et Historiae* 19, no. 38 (1998): 143–70; 'The altar-shrine of Santa Fina: local sainthood and church authority in Quattrocento San Gimignano,' *Studies in Iconography* 21 (2000): 181–236. Research for my dissertation, 'Civic Patronage of Art in Renaissance San Gimignano,' Harvard University, 1992, on which much of the present article is based was carried out at the same time, but all transcriptions and translations are my own. Some of my earlier conclusions are summarized in the catalogue entry on the chapel in Jean K. Cadogan, *Domenico Ghirlandaio. Artist and Artisan* (New Haven and London: Yale University Press, 2000), 203–7.

3. André Vauchez defines civic religion as 'l'ensemble des phénoménes religieux – cultuels, dévotionnels, ou institutionnels – dans lesquels le pouvoir civil joue un rôle déterminant, principalement à travers l'action des autorités locales et municipales,' in *La Religion Civique à l'Époque Médiévale et Moderne,* Actes du colloque organisé par le Centre de recherche 'Histoire sociale et culturelle de l'Occident. XIIe–XVIIIe siècle' de l'Université de Paris X-Nanterre e l'Institut universitaire de France (Nanterre, 21–23 juin 1993), Collection de l'École Française de Rome 213 (1995), 1. See also Anna Benvenuti Papi, 'Bibliographie sur les formes de l'identité civique à travers les cultes locaux dans l'Italie communale,' in the same volume, 513–15.

4. See the author's Ph.D. dissertation, Harvard University, 1992, Chapter VI: 'The San Bartolo Chapel and the Cult of Patron Saints in San Gimignano.'

5. On the waning of Siena's influence, see Wolfgang Loseries, 'Das Ende der sienesischen Tradition in San Gimignano: Sano di Pietro, Benozzo Gozzoli und die Familie Ridolfi,' *Mitteilungen des Kunsthistorischen Institutes in Florenz,* 37 (1993): 153–85.

6. A good summary of the debate can be found in Patrizia Salvadori, 'Florentines and the Communities of the Territorial State,' in *Florentine Tuscany,* ed. Connell and Zorzi, 207–24.

7. Casali, 1998, p. 91.

8. Salvadori, 'Florentines,' 211. On the extent of Medicean political patronage in the subject town of Pistoia, see Stephen J. Milner's article in this volume.

9. Fina's first *vita* was compiled around 1300 by Fra Giovanni del Coppo, *Historia, vita et morte di Sancta Fina da San Gimignano.* Two later manuscript versions are in the Biblioteca Nazionale Centrale, Florence: 1) BNCF Magliabecchiano II. IV. 105 (old collocation: Cl.XXXVIII P.1 Cod. 4), Anon., *Leggendario delle Sante Vergini e Martiri,* a codex written between November 1473 and May 1474. Fina's story is found on f. 126r.–f.33v. 2) BNCF Magliabecchiano XXXV. 204bis, a codex written by Frater Jacobus Geminianensis in 1538. This was probably the source for the first Italian version by Jacopo Manducci, *La historia, vita e morte di Sancta Fina di San Gimignano* (Florence: Tosi, 1598). This text may also be found in *Acta Sanctorum,* Venice, 1735, vol. II, March 12, 235–42. A transcription is found in Francesco Zambrini, *Leggenda di Santa Fina da San Gimignano scritta nel buon secolo della lingua di Fra Giovanni di Coppo della medesima Terra* (Imola: Galeati, 1879) and is translated by M. Mansfield, *The Legend of the Holy Fina, Virgin of San Gimignano: Now First Translated from the Trecento Italian of Fra Giovanni del Coppo* (London: Chatto and Windus, 1908). Subsequent treatments include Teodoro Ferroni, *Vita della B. Fina da San Gimignano* (Florence: Papini, 1644); relevant sections in Vincenzio Coppi, *Annali, Memorie ed Huomini Illustri di San Gimignano* (Florence: Bindi, 1695; reprint, 1976); Pietro Paolo Maria de Medici, *Ragguaglio istorico della vita, miracoli e culto immemorabile della gloriosa vergine santa Fina di San Gimignano* (Florence: Albizzini, 1750); Ignazio Malenotti, *Vita di Santa Fina* (Colle Val d'Elsa: Pacini, 1836); relevant sections in Luigi Pecori, *Storia della Terra di San Gimignano* (Florence: Galileiana, 1853); Guido Batelli, ed., *Leggenda di S. Fina da San Gimignano* (Florence: 1919). According to Enrico Castaldi, *Santa Fina nelle testimonianze dei*

coetanei e nei ricordi dell'arte (San Gimignano: Unione Tipografica, 1927), his source for accounts of Fina's life and miracles is 'un codicetto, in pergamena, del tempo stesso in cui erano raccolte . . .', but he does not say where this was. See also Paul Clemen-Bonn, 'Die Geschichte der Heiligen Fina von San Gimignano,' *Italienische Studien Paul Schubring zum 60 Geburtstag Gewidmet* (Leipzig, 1929) and a discussion her life and miracles in Chiara Frugoni, 'The City and the 'New' Saints,' in *City States in Classical Antiquity and Medieval Italy,* ed. Anthony Molho, Kurt Raaflaub, and Julia Emlen (Ann Arbor: University of Michigan Press, 1991), 72–91.

10. The exact nature of her illness is still in question. Hypotheses range from a tubercular malady to leprosy. For speculation, see Iole Vichi Imberciadori, *Fina dei Ciardi* (San Gimignano: Graficalito, 1979), 8.

11. Castaldi, *Santa Fina,* 7. Michael Goodich (*Vita Perfecta: The Ideal of Sainthood in the the Thirteenth Century* [Stuttgart: Hiersemann, 1982], 191) gives the example of these accounts of Fina's life, collected originally by Fra Giovanni del Coppo, as evidence of an episcopally initiated trial, but, as he points out, laypersons without ties to the papal curia were not likely to be canonized by the pope. In the sixteenth century, Sixtus V initiated the Congregation of Rites and Ceremonies, which standardized the types of evidence required for canonization in an attempt to take away the right of de facto canonization from the bishops (49).

12. Castaldi, *Santa Fina,* 31ff.

13. Castaldi, *Santa Fina,* 38–40.

14. Archivio Storico Comunale San Gimignano (hereafter ASCSG) 2936 (QQ3) 1482 6 May, fol. 136v. On Onofrio di Pietro, see Deborah L. Krohn, 'Onofrio di Pietro and the Opera della Pieve in San Gimignano,' *Opera: Carattere e ruolo delle fabbriche cittadine fino all'inizio dell'Età Moderna,* I Tatti Series, no. 13 (Florence: Olschki, 1996), 345–70.

15. On the question of the relationship between saints and *beati,* see Goodich in *Vita Perfecta,* 21: 'No clear distinction appears to exist between the terms 'beatus' and 'sanctus' although the latter was apparently used somewhat more frequently to denote saints canonized by the pope himself. The mere establishment of a saint's feast day, made to conform with the supposed date of his death, was in itself a denfinitive act.'

16. Sixtus IV approved her cult and feast of March 12 in 1481; Paul III granted the right to say mass in her name and referred to her as 'licet nondum canonizata.' Gregory XIII (1579) and Clement IX (1669) renewed these privileges. See Medici, *Ragguaglio istorico,* 149–52.

17. Castaldi, *Santa Fina,* 16. See also the discussion of the early history of Fina's burial, largely based on Castaldi's account, Carl, 'Der Fina-Altar,' 275–7.

18. The pulpit, made by Nicoletto da Poggibonsi, was at the fourth column on the left side of the Collegiata. Two marble inscriptions indicate that the pulpit was placed there in 1257.

19. Despite large amounts of source material in the San Gimignano communal archive about the hospital of Santa Fina, no monograph exists dealing with its history. For discussions of the various functions of late medieval hospitals in the area of San Gimignano, see Mario Battistini, *Gli spedali dell'antica diocesi di Volterra* (Pescia: G. Franchi, 1932). See also Henk W. van Os, *Vecchietta and the Sacristy of the Siena hospital Church* ('s-Gravenhage: Staatsuitgeverij, 1974), which concentrates on the fourteenth-century decoration of the hospital in Siena and outlines a similar history in terms of communal involvement and the importance of patron saints; also D. Gallavotti Cavallero, *Lo spedale di Santa Maria della Scala in Siena: Vicenda di una committenza artistica* (Florence: La Casa Usher, 1985); and Lucia Sandri, *L'Ospedale di S. Maria della Scala di S. Gimignano nel quattrocento* (Florence: Società Storica della Valdelsa, 1982), which deals primarily with the care of orphans and abandoned children, an important function of many late medieval hospitals.

20. Castaldi (*Santa Fina,* 19) suggests that this project was carried out and that it is the present entryway to the hospital, decorated with frescoes by Bastiano Mainardi in 1510 and housing the two Torrigiani busts of Fina and Gregory which are still in situ. A modern chapel in the hospital conserves the very wooden plank, supposedly there since 1256, on which Fina spent her last years.

21. Castaldi, *Santa Fina,* 19. This is now the site of the Gozzoli fresco.

22. Dating was confirmed when the bust was cleaned. See Alessandro Bagnoli's discussion in *Mostra di opere d'arte restaurate* (Genoa: Sagep, 1983), 23–7. The skull was reunited with the body only in 1738. See Medici, *Ragguaglio istorico,* 145. Bagnoli tentatively attributes the bust to the Sienese goldsmith Manno di Bandino (24). The presence of a gilded wooden skullcap inside the bust, in which Fina's skull was presumably housed, suggests that this was the earlier of two head reliquaries. Constructed of pieces of leather sewn together and covered by a layer of canvas, the surface of the bust was gilded and painted. The second bust of Fina, attributed to Mariano d'Agnolo Romanelli, is discussed by Bagnoli in *Il Gotico a Siena,* ex. cat., (Florence: Centro Di, 1982), 333. Its original location is unknown.

23. Castaldi, *Santa Fina,* 20; see also Enzo Carli and Jole Vichi Imberciadori, *San Gimignano* (Milan: Electa, 1987), 37. Giovanni Previtali in 'Introduzione ai problemi della bottega di Simone Martini,' *Simone Martini e 'chompagni'* (Florence: Centro Di, 1985), atttibutes this to 'aiuto di Memmo [Filippuccio].'

24. Cited in Bagnoli, *Il Gotico,* 333: ASCSG, Ms. 106, fols. 190–1: the chapel was founded in the testament of Bartoluccio di Berto, 22 August 1374. Presumably, this chapel was supressed in the fifteenth century when the new Santa Fina chapel was being planned. See Castaldi, *Santa Fina,* 20 and 45, n. 8. There is some confusion as to whether Fina's remains were moved from the inner façade wall when this chapel was founded or moved only when the fifteenth-century chapel was consecrated in 1488. It is possible that the remains were moved three times: once before 1374, then a second time back to the inner façade wall, perhaps during an outbreak of plague to concentrate thaumaturgic power in one place, then to their current location in the chapel. This would be supported by an inscription cited by Carl, 'Der Fina-Altar,' 283, n. 54.

25. Attributed in the past to Niccolò di Segna; Marco Torriti (*La Collegiata di San Gimignano e il suo Museo d'Arte Sacra* [Poggibonsi: 1988], 27) argues against this but does not suggest an alternative.

26. The operai 'fecero fare il tabernacolo per conservarvi la sacra testa di Santa Fina,' ASCSG, Ms. 106, fols. 190–1, cited in Bagnoli, *Il Gotico,* 333.

27. See J. A. Crowe and G. B. Cavalcaselle, *A History of Painting in Italy,* 6 vols. (London: John Murray, 1903), vol. II, 269–71; Richard Fremantle, *Florentine Gothic Painters from Giotto to Masaccio* (London: Secker and Warburg, 1975), 391–400. During the nineteenth century, one side of the tabernacle was in the sacristy, and the other remained in the chapel of Santa Fina (see Clemen-Bonn, 'Die Geschichte', 20).

28. This painting is now in the Museo Civico in San Gimignano. St. Bartholomew is enthroned; there are four scenes from his life, with eight saints in the predella, including Fina, Gregory, and so on. An inscription on the hem of St. Bartholomew's clothing reads as follows: LAURENTIUS NICHOLAUIA DE FLORENTIA PINSIT; underneath the saint another reads: S.BARTOLOMEUS APOSTOLUS AN.MCCCCI QUESTA TAVOLA FECE FARE NICHOLAJO DI BINDO KASSUCCI.

29. This altarpiece was given to the church of San Domenico in Cortona, perhaps as a Christmas present by Cosimo and Lorenzo de' Medici when they had it replaced with Fra Angelico's altarpiece. See the Cortona priors' letter of thanks, dated 26 December 1438,

published by Giovanni Gaye, *Carteggio inedito d'artisti,* 3 vols. (Florence: G. Mollini, 1839), vol. I, 140. This is a good example of a Florentine work of art being used by the Medici for explicitly diplomatic purposes in relation to a Florentine subject city.

30. Marks left by hinges and a lock suggest the form which the tabernacle must have originally had.

31. Castaldi, *Santa Fina,* 19 and n. 34 to this chapter.

32. See Krohn, 'Onofrio di Pietro.'

33. ASCSG 2936 (QQ3), 1468, 16 May, fol. 111r. Cited in Enrico Castaldi, 'Artefici che lavorano nella Insigne Collegiata ai tempi dell'Operaio Onofrio di Pietro,' *Scritta per la costruzione della cappella di San Bartolo su disegno di Giuliano da Maiano* (Colle d'Elsa, 1921), 44. An earlier payment (1466) to Giuliano is for a drawing presumed to be the redesign of the entire east end of the Collegiata: published in Pecori, *Storia della terra,* 508; and Castaldi, *Santa Fina,* 42. This is the sole evidence for Giuliano's direct involvement as 'architect' of the chapel. For a discussion of Giuliano's role see Krohn, *Civic Patronage of Art,* 144–8.

34. ASCSG 179 (NN125) 1458/9, 7 February fol. 179v.: 'quod ipsis altaribus depositis restituetur civilior et pulchrior situs plebi'.

35. ASCSG 180 (NN126) 1462, 11 December fol. 348v.: 'et de concordia patronum querant et curent quod illa reliqua altaria que sint in plebe . . . tollantur e medio et restituatur pristinus situs, forma et decor ipsi plebi prefate.'

36. An example of this: ASCSG 2936, (QQ3) 1467 June 26 fol. 109r: 'Item. A di detto a ser Niccolò prete lire due per la sua fatica de nettare le storie del vechio e nuovo testamento della pieve.' The same man, perhaps the official janitor of the Opera, was also paid for cleaning the frescoes on June 30, 1468 (ASCSG 2936, [QQ3] 1468 June 30 fol. 111v) and for 'sua fatica di scomberare calcinacci et pietre erano nella pieve' (ASCSG 2936, [QQ3], 1467 2 October fol. 109r). Payments to Niccolò prete for 'sweeping' the old and new testament cycles are published by P. Bacci, 'Le statue dell'Annunciazione intagliate nel 1421 da Jacopo della Quercia,' *La Balzana,* n.s., vol. I, no. 4, (1927) 165, n. 1. This may be the same Niccolò di Luca, who becomes one of two operai in 1491 and who is credited with providing a design for the bust of Onofrio di Pietro executed by Benedetto da Maiano. Evidently, he worked his way up in the hierarchy of the Opera.

37. On the subject of restoration of other works of art in fifteenth-century San Gimignano, see Cathleen Hoeniger, *The Renovation of Paintings in Tuscany 1250–1500* (Cambridge and New York: Cambridge University Press, 1995), 147–9.

38. See *Il Libro Bianco di San Gimignano,* ed. Donatella Ciampoli (Siena: Cantagalli, 1996), with an introduction summarizing the documents by Daniel Waley. Although there is no definite date for the compilation of the material, it took place sometime during the fifteenth century.

39. See Hans-Karl Lücke, *Leon Battista Alberti De re aedificatoria Florenz 1485: Index verborum,* 4 vols. (Munich: Prestel, 1979), vol. III, 1199.

40. ASCSG 183 (NN129) 1469 15 July fol. 117v.: 'Quod divini cultus honores sint summa cum reverentia celebrandi, veteres historie clare demonstrant et presertim Romanorum qui tanto fervore eorum Deos venerabantur ut domesticis obmissis curis et commodis quicquid poterant in eos conferebant, quanto magis igitur nos quibus vera et immortalis religio concessa est facere debemus.'

41. Ibid., 1470/1, 5 February fol. 233r.

42. ASCSG 184 (NN130) 1472 7 July fol. 34r.: 'Quante dignitatis et glorie sint terre ille, que decorate sunt aliquo corpore beato, et quante commendationis sint illi, qui omnibus eorum viribus, omnique cura et diligentia student corpus illud cum apparatibus exterioribus ornare

atque illustrare, nemo est qui nesciat. Et non solum ad hoc intenta fuit semper religio et septa christianorum, verum etiam et illa paganorum et eorum qui Christum nunquam cognoverunt, quibus, ut legitur, semper cura fuit et summa diligentia deos suos observare, et in eorum decus et honorem templa amplissima construere, atque illa ornatissimis apparatibus illustrare.'

43. Aby Warburg, 'Francesco Sassettis letztwillige Verfügung,' *Kunstwissenschaftliche Beiträge August Schmarsow gewidmet* (Leipzig: Hiersemann, 1907), and the discussion of this theme in E. H. Gombrich, *Aby Warburg: An Intellectual Biography,* 2nd ed. (Chicago: University of Chicago Press, 1986), 168–77.

44. For the use of ancient Roman symbols in medieval Italy, see Paolo Golinelli, 'Quando il santo non basta più: simboli cittadini non religiosi nell' Italia bassomedievale,' in *La religion civique,* ed. Vauchez, 381ff.; and Golinelli, 'Quando il santo non basta più.'

45. Carl, 'Das Fina-Altar,' 266. She also cites the Sangimignesi desire to have a vicar forain, or official delegate of the bishop of Volterra, as an expression of ecclesiastical independence, but this has a long history in San Gimignano. See Pecori, *Storia della terra,* 636.

46. Bonaventura herself submitted a deposition in the early fourteenth century, probably solicited as part of the canonization procedure; Castaldi, *Santa Fina,* 10 and 32.

47. This is consistent with transformations in narrative strategies during the fifteenth century in Italy. This can be seen directly in the many instances of reframing of polyptychs to create unified fields. See Lisa Venturini, 'Restauri quattrocenteschi. Neri di Bicci, Domenico Ghirlandaio,' *Kermes* 7 (1994): 28 and n. 2.

48. Krohn, 'Onofrio di Pietro,' 358.

49. ASCSG 186 (NN132) 1478 23 May fol. 131v. 'Ad hoc ut Honofrius Petri operarius opere sacrestie plebis Sancti Geminiani possit et valeat satisfacere his qui ab eo habere debent pro pictura cappelle Sancte Fine et eius sepulcri constructione, et pro aliis quam fieri fecit ad ornamentum dicte capelle.'

50. ASCSG 186 (NN132) 1478 23 May fol. 131v.

51. The one exception is Milanesi, who, in the notes to the 1568 edition of Vasari's *Lives* assigned the frescoes to 1487, suggesting that, due to Mainardi's assistance, they would have to have been painted while he was at work on the frescoes of the chapel of S. Bartolo in Sant' Agostino, San Gimignano. See Vasari, *Le vite de' più eccellenti pittori, scultori ed architettori,* 9 vols., ed. G. Milanesi (Florence: Sansoni, 1906), vol. III, 275.

52. Artur Rosenauer, 'Zum Stil der frühen Werke Domenico Ghirlandaios,' *Wiener Jahrbuch für Kunstgeschichte* 22 (1969): 80. Rosenauer follows earlier opinion in accepting the date inscribed on the sarcophagus of 1475 as the date of completion of the frescoes, given that Ghirlandaio was in Rome by November 1475 to work on the frescoes of the Vatican library of Sixtus IV. See Jan Lauts, *Domenico Ghirlandaio* (Vienna: Schroll, 1943), 12.

53. Carl, 'Der Fina-Altar,' 1978, 266: ASCSG 2936 (QQ3) 8 May 1490 fol. 153r.

54. Crowe and Cavalcaselle suggested that the payment was for finishing details of the tomb such as the carved curtain rather than for the inscription (Vol. VII, 1896, 200), but they did not have the document itself – only Pecori's opinion that the amount given Benedetto was 'alcune somme di danaro,' *Storia della terra,* 519, n. 1.

55. Jean Cadogan, 'Reconsidering some aspects of Ghirlandaio's Drawings,' *Art Bulletin,* 65 (1983), 281; Annarosa Garzelli, 'Problemi del Ghirlandaio nella cappella di Santa Fina: Il ciclo figurativo nella cupola e i probabili disegni,' *Antichità Viva,* 24, No. 4 (1985), 11–25.

56. See the discussion of the dating summarized in Cadogan, *Domenico Ghirlandaio,* 201.

57. The inscription has been attributed to the humanist Giambattista Cantalicio who was teaching grammar in San Gimignano in 1475 and wrote a series of epigrams about Santa Fina. See G. B. Valentini (Cantalicio), 'Lode della Santa,' in *Opera Poetica,* (Venice: Benalius, 1493), cited in M. Morici, 'Giovan Battista Valentini, detto il Cantaliccio,' *Miscellanea storica della Valdelsa,* 13 (1905), 19.

58. See also the discussion of narrative in Ghirlandaio's frescoes in Koch, 'Portrayal of Female Sainthood,' 147, where the author suggests that the events depicted focus on Fina's physical sufferings to emphasize her symbolic role as the church itself. Koch's argument, while full of interesting observations, assumes a high level of theological sophistication on the part of Ghirlandaio (or his advisors), which has not been borne out in other contexts.

59. A complete list of these offices garnered from the 1428 Catasto can be found in Enrico Fiumi, *Storia economica e sociale di San Gimignano* (Florence: Olschki, 1961), 189–90.

60. Casali, *San Gimignano,* 87–9.

61. Pecori, *Storia dell Terra,* 212–13.

62. On Volterra, see the concise discussion with extensive notes in Lorenzo Fabbri, 'Patronage and its Role in Government: The Florentine Patriciate and Volterra,' in *Florentine Tuscany,* ed. Connell and Zorzi, 225–41.

63. The virulence of the outbreak was such that the government ceased to function in the normal way. Official records ceased between 2 April 1478 and 7 October 1478, creating a lacuna.

64. Medici, *Ragguaglio istorico,* 102; and Pecori, *Storia della terra,* who gives the first year of the new feast as 1481.

65. ASCSG 187 (NN133) 1481, 13 July fol. 90r.

66. Castaldi, *Santa Fina,* 47.

67. ASCSG 2936, (QQ3) 1482, 10 April fol. 136v.

68. Ibid. 12 June fol. 137r.

69. ASCSG 2936, (QQ3) 1484, 16 June fol. 139r.

70. Ibid. 15 September fol. 140r.

71. ASCSG 188 (NN134) 1485, 10 September f. 97r.

72. Ibid. 1488, 28 September f. 260r. Bishop Pandolfini was an important figure in the landscape of Medicean domination in Pistoia, as Stephen J. Milner discusses in his chapter in this volume.

PART THREE

NEGOTIATING THE CULTURAL OTHER

THE QUESTION OF THE RENAISSANCE IN RECENT SCHOLARSHIP, WHEN IT IS raised at all, is often considered as a question of borders. These borders are chronological, raising questions about periodization, as well as spatial: the question of the origins of Renaissance culture, the critique of nationalist accounts in favor of histories centered on cultural exchange. While much recent scholarship has dwelt on the question of the encounter of Western Europeans with the ethnic and religious 'other' presented by Turks, Jews, and Native Americans, the three essays included in this section pursue a somewhat different focus. Instead of presenting the Other as something held at a distance to be objectified and distinguished from the self, these essays in various ways deal with attempts to translate the self *into* the other. Two of the essays deal with the humanist enterprise of *translatio* in this sense of identifying with the historically and culturally remote: the idea of Egypt as embraced by Roman humanists around 1500, and the ancient philosopher mystics as seen by the philosopher and translator Marsilio Ficino. The third essay deals with a more synchronous circumstance of self-translation: Hansen shows how Catholic devotion and imagery are drawn on by an Armenian immigrant merchant in the cosmopolitan city of Ancona who patronized Titian and Pellegrino Tibaldi.

As explored by Celenza the question of orthodoxy is also a question of cultural translation because it involves questions of the uses of a cultural 'other'. Celenza, a scholar of Ficino, brings the perspective of an intellectual historian to bear on the model of center and periphery. His essay is part of a broader critique of a long-standing taxonomical tendency in intellectual history, which tended towards a transhistorical reification of categories of belief or philosophical allegiance: 'in the case of Marsilio Ficino, the question is not whether he was orthodox or heterodox, hermetic or classically Neoplatonic, but in what sort of intellectual field his work was situated and how did the field change over time.' The intellectual field is made not only of ideas but is constituted in addition by institutions, and by patronage. Ficino's increasingly curious intellectual preoccupations, which are pronounced to be 'heterodox' or pagan by later historians, are produced by Ficino's change of position within the intellectual field, a *translatio* of Ficino himself which he does not fully control.

While several scholars have dealt with the Renaissance rediscovery of Egyptian antiquity, Curran relates Renaissance manifestations of 'egyptomania' not simply to a putatively disinterested humanist scholarship but, like Celenza, he explores its potential ideological ramifications, which are signaled by a specially intense deployment of Egyptian themes in the Rome of Leo X. Curran explores how the physical remains of a culture long regarded as redolent of pagan idolatry, and displayed since antiquity as triumphal spoils within the city of Rome, became useful for the implicit identification they allowed between the papacy and the ancient Egyptian institution of sacred monarchy. The hieroglyphs, obelisks, and sphinxes displayed in Roman fountains and piazze allowed the papacy to appear both as autocratic and charismatic, as well as to provide testimony to the imaginary origins of Italian culture and the papacy itself.

Considerable recent scholarship has dealt with the representation of ethnically or socially marginal groups in the early modern period. Such representations assumed a particular urgency in the culture of early capitalism, when the growth of international trade saw the emergence of expatriate mercantile communities in Italian cities. The movement of capital brought about an increased visibility of difference, and a certain anxiety regarding the presence of groups distinguished by religion and ethnic origin. This was above all the case in the Papal States, where since the mid–fifteenth century coercive measures had been taken against the communities of Jewish bankers, pawnbrokers, and physicians. Proponents of unity within the Papal State pushed for repressive measures against the Jews in particular, despite their centrality to the economic life of many subject cities. Hansen's essay on Ancona reflects on manifestations of antijudaism in a maritime trading city of the Papal State but also explores the strategies of assimilation by a member of another group which was classed as distinct by ethnicity and religion. The patronage of an Armenian merchant shows to a striking degree how art could be used as an instrument of translation, and how elements of Armenian Christianity were treated in the language of the Italian altarpiece to suggest harmony and continuity.

10

From Center to Periphery in the Florentine Intellectual Field: Orthodoxy Reconsidered

Christopher S. Celenza

One of the most arresting manifestations of cultural translation occurs when thinkers are compelled to address the foreignness of an admired but historically remote culture. How to decide what should be adapted into the thinker's own environment, and what should be rejected? How should the thinker determine the criteria for judging the usefulness of the imported material or the present need that might be served by its adaptation? In fifteenth-century Italy, these questions could appear in many guises, for, as the editors argue in the introduction to this volume, Italy can be seen as a unity that encompassed plurality. An Italian cultural style, 'Italianness,' was recognized by foreigners, by those in 'exile' like Petrarch, and by certain literati, whereas the different localities on the peninsula all had their own particular styles and traditions of which they were proud and protective. On the peninsular level, centers and peripheries interacted in complex ways: an artist, say, in a 'peripheral' place might engage in his own work with a style engendered in a 'center' in a manner that furthered the center's ideological needs even as it maintained his own independence; in 'translating,' the artist thus simultaneously resists a cultural master narrative while seeming to acquiesce to the needs of a dominant culture. An itinerant literary humanist in search of patronage might engage in a similar project, dedicating to prospective patrons works translated from Greek to Latin, even as the works he dedicated to them carried mixed messages.[1] And even within individual localities, intellectual cultures were far from homogeneous; in the various urban centers, questions of cultural translation were played out daily, as thinkers presented often-conflicting positions in the public arena. As they struggled to gain intellectual capital, thinkers in Renaissance life often oscillated between the constantly shifting coordinates of center and periphery as these were manifested locally. How and why did this oscillation happen? How did characteristically Renaissance practices of cultural translation contribute to the shifting fortune of a thinker's place and reputation within an individual culture? This essay engages these questions by focusing on a problem often left undefined in studies of Renaissance intellectual culture, that of orthodoxy.

'Orthodoxy' is normally thought of as the condition of being 'orthodox.' The Greek etymological roots of these words, as is well known, signify a combination of 'rightness' or 'correctness' with 'opinion.' Someone who is 'orthodox,' in other words, is someone who holds the right opinion. Thus 'orthodoxy,' in the words of the *Oxford English Dictionary*, means 'belief in or agreement with what is, or is currently held to be, right, especially in religious matters.' The word *orthodoxia* in Greek, however, is not a common one, at least in classical Greek; it is in late antiquity that the word comes into its own.[2] Among ancient Latin writers up through the Silver Age, the word is unattested. We find it, however, in some patristic writers. Augustine in his *De vera religione* (5.9) uses the word *orthodoxus* to signify one who is in adherence with the true Catholic faith. We find forms of the word in medieval Latin as well, although in the scholastic lexicon it is not used in connection with heresy.[3]

But etymology can only take us so far. Often passed over when intellectual historians of Renaissance Europe use the word is that orthodoxy as a word and phenomenon is reactive. It is intimately tied to the concept of heresy and appears most clearly when heresies are articulated: orthodoxy *fit, non nascitur*, and here, in the subcelestial realm, there is no ultimate source for orthodoxy, no magic book in which orthodoxy's truths are clearly reposed.[4] Not that this is theoretically a problem in the history of Christianity, for Christianity is a revealed religion in which the process of contestation is essential to revelation. Medieval thinkers in the tradition of Augustine, Aquinas for example, routinely attributed the presence of evil, which includes heresy, to God's providential design, a way to make a larger good come out of a smaller evil. Heretics – and heresies – were put on earth by God as a factor by which faith could be tested, renewed, and then more clearly articulated.[5]

The problem becomes clearer, however, when we consider that what is revealed is God's truth, but the mechanisms of its revelation and articulation are human beings. Who decides when a point of orthodoxy has been reached, who is left out, what doctrines are endorsed, what written texts are essential to revelation – all are questions capable of endless argument. But I think the latter question is most relevant, if we are considering Renaissance intellectuals. For oftentimes when Renaissance intellectuals came close to violating, or indeed violated, the malleable boundaries of religious orthodoxy, it was the final result of an expansion in the canon of acceptable texts. Because the term 'orthodoxy,' as indicated earlier, is a bit slippery, it is useful to consider canon formation in conjunction with orthodoxy, because it helps shift the focus where it really belongs: away from religion in the abstract and onto small communities of intellectuals and the manner in which they receive and generate new ideas. In this study, then, I elaborate a theoretical framework to discuss the problem of orthodoxy and apply the framework to one thinker, Marsilio Ficino (1433–99), the most important Renaissance Platonist, whose wide-ranging influence in his own era can be compared to that of Sigmund Freud in ours.[6]

As mentioned earlier, orthodoxies do not develop except in relation to heresies. Heresies evolve when previously unencountered ideas or transformations of ideas threaten in some way those who believe themselves the keepers of an as yet undefined, taken-for-granted orthodoxy. Max Weber drew a famous distinction in his work on religion when he described two fundamental types, the priest and the prophet.[7] The priest is institutionally enfranchised, officially sanctioned by a recognized religious agency, whereas the prophet is an 'individual bearer of charisma, who by virtue of his mission proclaims a religious doctrine or divine commandment.'[8] Both struggle to influence the laity, and the priests often coopt the innovations of the prophets. Yet what does one do when one encounters priest and prophet in one? How to configure the dual identity of being both part of the established socioreligious order and a challenge to it, such as was, in some respects, Marsilio Ficino? Ficino was one of the leading intellectuals of the fifteenth century, who by the 1480s had won distinction for his translations of the Platonic corpus and for his attempts to adapt the thought of Plato and his later followers to the needs of a modern Christian civic sphere. Yet the more Ficino delved into the later Platonic and esoteric tradition, the more we see him not necessarily advocating, but studying thoughts and practices which suggest a more unconventional and charismatic vocation: ritual practices such as fumigations, recourse to the planetary intelligences and to 'demons' evoked with hymns and under the name of pagan gods. How then do we understand an esoteric intellectual, Marsilio Ficino, against a meaningful social backdrop?

First we must mention that there has been a tendency on the part of scholars to impose, sometimes unwittingly, a post-Tridentine orthodoxy onto pre-Tridentine intellectuals who were unaware of the sorts of rigid boundaries and borders which would later develop within the broad umbrella of early modern Catholicism.[9] One of the greatest students of Marsilio Ficino, Paul Oskar Kristeller (1905–99), tended in this direction, often stressing the religious orthodoxy of Renaissance thinkers of many different intellectual orientations.[10] Thus even when there are textual artifacts, such as Marsilio Ficino's *De triplici vita* and various treatises of Pietro Pomponazzi, that suggest that their authors at least had an interest in thinking in a manner unbounded by a restrictive orthodoxy, Kristeller's tendency was to find a way to fit them into the mold of theologically informed thinkers highly conscious of orthodox boundaries. He usually did this by emphasizing the few lines in which those thinkers officially asserted only so much as the Church allowed them to assert, even as the bulk of their treatises would have served as the vehicle for the transmission of much dangerous or at least novel and destabilizing forms of thought.[11] This strict focus on the stated intention of the author supposedly safeguards the thinker from the agendas of later interpreters but, by the same token, restricts the ability of scholars to pursue plausible readings that might be found in between the lines of Renaissance texts. There are different ways of reading, of course, but if we are dealing with issues of cultural translation as applied to Renaissance intellectuals, the multidimensionality of their texts should be brought into relief, and there is no better way of doing this than by considering the social dimension of the text and situating it as such in the context of intellectual communities.[12]

What constitutes an intellectual community? Presumably, it is a limited group of people who possess a shared set of interests informed by common material for reflection. It is in the process by which that material changes that we can locate the changing structure of intellectual communities. Integral individual thinkers with separately evolving missions, the members of an intellectual community are also social beings, who evolve their ideas and select their reading materials in the context of a rich complex of social, political, economic, and cultural factors. If we are thinking about the history of humanism and philosophy, we must find a way to determine how and why groups of intellectuals choose what to read, and what material comes into circulation among them.

The historiography of science and the recent sociology of intellectuals can help us formulate the questions. Thomas Kuhn, for obvious reasons, comes to mind. His initial view regarding 'paradigm shifts' and their relation to the transition from 'normal' to 'revolutionary' science is well known.[13] 'Normal' science happens when a group of thinkers shares a method of investigation of a certain problem, informed by consensus on the hypotheses used; the consensus reflects the fact that they share a paradigm. As their work proceeds, the data gathered in general confirm their presumptions. The methods used are standardized and the results are more or less what is expected – 'normal' science. But when enough data amass that do not fit the paradigm, 'revolutionary' science occurs. The old paradigm draws attack and under the powerful personality or personalities of one or more leaders a new paradigm, or set of shared assumptions, emerges. The move toward normal science recurs; the paradigm has shifted. For our purposes, Kuhn is important because his ideas can help us formulate questions regarding the formation of literary canons in the Renaissance. When certain set texts are not responding adequately to the needs of small communities of intellectuals, new texts are brought from the margins to the center; but new questions must be asked of these new texts, and so, the general set of assumptions changes. We can further refine this notion by examining the thought of Gaston Bachelard and Pierre Bourdieu.

In developing his theories, Bachelard (1884–1962) was reacting to the profound changes of his day in the history of physics, specifically to Einsteinian relativity and to the development of quantum theory and the disturbing, concomitant notion that in observing an environment, one inevitably changes it.[14] For him, these new developments meant a breakdown in the traditional Cartesian mind-body distinction and suggested the sterility of Kantian universals. Epistemology had to become reflexive and dialectical, reactive to the data nature offered through the continual experimentation of human beings, whose 'science' was an ongoing rectification of past errors and was quite literally a constructed enterprise. Bachelard's view of the development of theories was also important, for although it was dialectical, it was not dialectical in the Marxist sense, where one theory is replaced by another that contradicts it. Rather, new theories were seen to evolve which included former ones. In the words of David Swartz, Bachelard's dialectical reason situates the previous theory in a broader conceptual space that highlights both its strengths and its limitations. This mode of dialectical thought can include several theories, which at a given level of logic contradict each other by virtue of their limits, but, when situated within a broader framework, stand in complementary relationships.[15]

When a theory or set of theories emerges that has the capacity to encompass or interrelate those prior to it, Bachelard's 'epistemological break' happens.[16] The advantage of considering Bachelard in conjunction with Kuhn is apparent: in our quest to understand the changing structure of intellectual communities over time, this consideration allows us to soften the radical breaks which the normal-revolutionary science distinction sometimes implies. By stressing the notion that new ways of approaching problems are often the result of conscious or unconscious attempts to encapsulate and transcend, rather than simply oppose, previous frameworks, we have the advantages of both synchronic and diachronic styles of interpretation, for we can begin to think about a shared moment in time among a group of intellectuals, even as we try to account for change over time.[17] These concerns can be amplified if we consider the work of the sociologist Pierre Bourdieu.

In his work, Bourdieu has evolved certain central theoretical postulates which all attempt to transcend seemingly fixed categorical hermeneutic differences.[18] The most important meta-theoretical aspect of his thought for our purposes is his insistence on thinking relationally and not in terms of ideal categories. This insistence is at the root of most of his key concepts, all of which seek to obviate the traditional and seemingly inescapable divide between subject and object. There are three interconnected concepts that I examine here: *habitus, capital,* and *field.*

The concept of habitus has to do with subconscious structuring dispositions which actors bring with them into their field of activity. In Bourdieu's own words habitus is 'a system of durable, transposable dispositions, . . . principles which generate and organize practices and representations.'[19] Or, again, 'the habitus is the universalizing mediation which causes an individual agent's practices, without either explicit reason or signifying intent.'[20] The habitus, in other words, represents a kind of generative principle that can govern and produce the actor's behavior. For those concerned with medieval and Renaissance studies, it will come as no surprise that the first time Bourdieu used the term habitus was in the *postface* to his translation, published in 1967, of Erwin Panofsky's *Gothic Architecture and Scholasticism*.[21] There Bourdieu highlighted the notion that for Panofsky scholasticism was more than a set of doctrines; it was a set of structuring attitudes – mental habits that could inform an entire approach to the world. Here it is important to note the prereflective nature of the habitus. The assumptions that bind together those who share the habitus are beneath the level of conscious articulation – together they constitute a *doxa*; they are taken for granted and as such form the outer limits of the possible.[22] But when these assumptions are voiced, or when there are attempts to define them, they can produce orthodoxy and heterodoxy, because the formerly undefined limits of the possible are crossed:

> Orthodoxy, straight, or rather *straightened* opinion, which aims, without ever entirely succeeding, at restoring the primal state of innocence of doxa, exists only in the objective relationship which opposes it to heterodoxy, that is, by reference to the choice – *hairesis,* heresy – made possible by the existence of competing possibles and to the explicit critique of the sum total of the alternatives not chosen that the established order implies.[23]

To return to habitus, it is worth mentioning that it is a Latin term with a rich medieval history and is in fact the medieval Latin translation of Aristotle's *hexis,* which for Aristotle was a trained and trainable capacity that one brings from potentiality to actuality by repeated practice; it is a mean between potency and act.[24] Although Aristotle's and Bourdieu's habitus are different in many ways, the focus on practice unites them.[25] For Bourdieu, the notion of practice is closely tied to the ideas of capital and field.

His concept of capital widens the focus of the term 'capital' as normally considered in the Marxist tradition to include 'all forms of power . . . material, cultural, social, or symbolic,' so that in addition to material capital, an actor can amass cultural, social, and symbolic capital.[26] This assumes that much of what actors do is agonistic and that those who find themselves in a given 'field' will be struggling within that field to attain the sorts of capital appropriate to it. But what is a field? Let us take the idea of an intellectual field, which is 'that matrix of institutions, organizations, and markets in which symbolic producers, such as artists, writers, and academics, compete for symbolic capital.'[27] For example, the intellectual field in Florence was not defined by an old, venerated university tradition, as in other cities like Padua or Bologna. This absence of a fixed university presence enabled a certain heterogeneity of thought; nonetheless, intellectual life was largely sustained through private patronage, which imposed constraints of its own, even as it gave rise to a complex system of patron-client and client-client relations. As Bourdieu wrote, 'to think in terms of field is to think *relationally*.'[28] A field, in other words, is a network within which we can situate a thinker and his or her intellectual products. That thinker has conscious aims, but the intellectual product he or she produces is also the result of structuring forces, all of which interact continually and relationally with the thinker. There is thus a subjective element, the thinker, and the objective exterior world, the field, with which that thinker interacts on many levels. The danger of this approach of course is that the 'field' becomes a kind of explanatory deus ex machina, providing all the answers when one asks why an intellectual did what he or she did. Used reasonably, however, the concept can provide a stimulus to thinking relationally and to considering thinkers in relation not only to the established traditions to which they consciously orient themselves, but also in relation to multiple forces, coactors, and economic and social circumstances that might otherwise escape one's purview.

The ramifications of these theoretical considerations for Renaissance intellectual history are important. First, knowledge is social and socially created; no thinker develops positions in a vacuum, or in conscious or subconscious anticipation of a later ideal. Second, thinking generationally and relationally presupposes a certain sort of question. In the case of Marsilio Ficino, the question is not whether he was orthodox or heterodox, hermetic or classically Neoplatonic, but in what sort of intellectual field was his work situated and how did that field change over time?

As in other parts of early modern Europe, the Florentine intellectual field was embedded in a sociopolitical matrix, in which private wealth and powerful patrons helped otherwise unenfranchised intellectuals find a means of practicing their craft.[29] The limitations of this sort of system are obvious: the intellectual casts himself in the mold of subordinate to his patron, even as he attempts to carry out satisfying and challenging work, and in varying degrees the patron has some share in the form of intellectual production. But the possibilities allowed by the patronage network were formidable. The specific form of patronage was personal and took into account the *amicitia* between client and patron. Not only the cultural products of patronage but even the very *forma mentis* of the client were affected by the personal dimension of patronage.[30] Also, because originality had to be cast in an appropriate form, one characteristic of much Renaissance Latin discourse was a kind of hidden textual embedding, not quite subversion, but a mode of thought where subversive readings could be possible, or intellectual independence maintained.[31] Sociologically speaking, on a large scale this was, perhaps, a way for intellectuals to solidify a sphere of possible action, a separateness in which they could maintain freedom of operation, as the political face of Europe was moving ever closer to the development of sovereign states and sovereign styles of rulership in the city-state world.[32] If these are certain general, synchronic features of intellectual fields in early modern Europe, we must also remember the diachronic, generational concerns that shaped the Florentine environment in the 1480s through the mirror of its appreciation for ancient texts.

We often forget the tremendous sense of vitality, excitement, and newness that the Renaissance hunt for new texts generated.[33] Part and parcel of the humanist movement, this hunt led figures like Giovanni Aurispa, Francesco Filelfo, and others to respond to the humanist conviction, as old as Salutati practically and Petrarch theoretically, to include and appropriate the Greek as well as the Latin heritage in their reconstruction of antiquity – an intramental colonial precursor, perhaps, to the voyages of discovery of the sixteenth century. But as the main lines of scholarly inquiry grew clearer – as figures such as Leonardo Bruni established chronologies and histories and solidified the basis of their knowledge of classical antiquity – the nature of scholarship changed. As the fifteenth century wore on, it was no longer avant-garde to write, in either ultra- or moderately Ciceronian fashion, a narrative history, in Latin, of your particular region; rather, it became routine. Those who were doing it had moved from the pulsing forefront of intellectual life – located often extra-institutionally at the social field's periphery – and had joined the hardened, polished, elite, enfranchised center.[34] Consequently, the front lines of classical literary scholarship changed in nature; we see the rise of the philological commentary in the late fifteenth and early sixteenth centuries, well represented by Poliziano, Beroaldo, and others. Now, the focus was not so much synthetic as particular and precise.[35] In the mid- to late fifteenth century, we also see a deepening of interest in Florence in the Platonic tradition, which was related to changing social and political conditions. This interest in the broader form of Platonism fueled the use of texts from late antiquity, which a number of thinkers, especially Marsilio Ficino, wanted to include in the canon of acceptable philosophical and religious works.[36] Debates and controversies, fears and recriminations over orthodoxy eventually ensued.

Marsilio Ficino found himself in this canon-expanding intellectual field in the 1480s, and he was at least partially its architect. He had gained renown in Florence in the early 1460s, when Florence's great patron, Cosimo de' Medici, had entrusted him with the translation of Plato's works. Since then, he had produced a number of his most important works, including his *On the Christian Religion* (*De christiana religione*), his translations and commentaries on Plato, his translations of the *Corpus hermeticum* (The Hermetic Corpus), and his *Platonic Theology* (the *Theologia Platonica*). He had been sensitive to a dual mission of advancing the frontiers of learning by devoting attention to issues and problems outside the realm of contemporary concerns and communicating to an intellectual public and a public at large. He translated into Tuscan some of his own works and wrote some originally in Tuscan. He saw himself as a doctor of souls in Florence, and the initial following that he developed was consequent with that mission. As Arthur Field has shown, after a dramatic and fractious 1450s (among whose many signal events were the peace of Lodi, the ouster of the Medici, and their forceful reascendency in 1458), the time was ripe for an ideology of love, friendship, and harmony, which Marsilio Ficino helped develop.[37] A learned, elite following gathered around Ficino. He advised members of his circle how they might tolerate bad fortune and the snipes of enemies. He stressed that true religion was suffused with love and that the love between friends was religious.[38] After the death of Cosimo, his first patron, he gradually solidified his contacts with the Medici, even if he never established the same sort of relationship he had had with Cosimo. In the early 1470s Ficino established an especially close relationship with Lorenzo de' Medici, only to see time and circumstance change its nature.[39]

By the early 1480s, Ficino had amassed a significant amount of social and cultural capital. His *On the Christian Religion* had established him as a thinker deeply concerned with traditional Christian problems, and his *Platonic Theology* had made an important statement defending Christianity against some of the by then traditionally heterodox positions, especially those associated with Averroism. He had also published his *Platonis Opera Omnia,* thus opening up a new world of Greek philosophy to European intellectuals.[40] But by the 1480s Ficino's dual mission was being tested in a number of ways. He was beginning to realize that the frontiers of his own scholarship were located in understanding Plotinus, the later Platonist often taken as the exemplar of Neoplatonism. Yet for Ficino, understanding Plotinus meant interpreting him, and interpreting him meant using every hermeneutic means at his disposal to integrate Plotinus into the *prisca theologia,* the gradually unfolding but heavily veiled unified wisdom that God had given to mankind and revealed gradually through various interpreters.[41] Ficino had to turn to increasingly esoteric styles of interpretation that did not have the capacity to communicate as directly as before with Florence's civic leaders; nor were they always as firmly in line with traditional orthodoxies. As to Ficino's social field, he kept his Medici patronage, but he gradually grew to seem one of many artists and intellectuals under that wing of culture, rather than the center of intellectual life, even as his relationship with Lorenzo remained solid and once more approached its formerly high affective dimension.[42] Given his hermeneutic concerns and the choices he was making in his scholarship, and given the constitution and evolution of the Florentine sociopolitical field, Ficino lost some cultural capital in the 1480s, as intellectual life began to go in new directions because of the broadened and multifaceted Florentine intellectual field.[43]

What was the Florentine intellectual field? Thinkers found themselves embedded in a social matrix, to be sure, where patronage in all its dimensions was an essential part of their daily lives. But an individual intellectual's social position was shaped and conditioned by the intellectual field, where thinkers advanced competing positions, all of them vying for a specific place in the debate on canonicity and literary legitimacy.

One could find institutionally grounded, university-centered Aristotelianism and professors who engaged actively with Averroist traditions of Aristotelian hermeneutic, even if abjuring Averroist heresies. They were part of the Florentine *Studium generale*, refounded by Lorenzo in 1473. As Armando Verde and James Hankins have shown, these professors were necessary to keep the university in step with the traditional concerns so important to students of philosophy. As such, Lorenzo patronized them and had them brought to the Studio, in which he was so heavily invested.[44] By the late 1480s these philosophers were well established there.

There was also a growing newer style of philosophical inquiry, which embraced traditional areas of philosophy in a philologically sophisticated manner. This philological sophistication is exemplified in Angelo Poliziano's miscellanistic style of scholarship, in which it was becoming clear that philology was a style of thought, so that the highest level of verbal and definitional precision was to be sought by weighing as many textual examples and testimonies as possible.[45] Poliziano's philological style was most evident in his *Miscellanea*, which, he wrote, were inspired by the *Attic Nights* of the second-century C.E. Silver Age Latin author Aulus Gellius, which had contained similarly precise and learned discussions.[46] The philological sensibility pervaded almost all of Poliziano's prose work and formed part of his identity as an intellectual; it was also fundamentally at odds with Ficino's style of interpretation. Poliziano's new philological techniques are strikingly modern, but he evolved them in relation to factors in his intellectual environment, in an agonistic social context in which the resolution of textual questions was an important means toward the end of amassing cultural capital.[47] Natural philosophy was seen in a new way and a certain variety of empiricism began to manifest itself, suggested early on by Lorenzo Buonincontri's approach to Manilius, then refined in Poliziano's own study of Pliny.[48] That Poliziano's approach was opposed to Ficino's must be conceded; when Poliziano in the 1492 *praelectio* to his university course on Aristotle's *Prior Analytics* (Poliziano's *Lamia*) skewered the figure of Pythagoras and sarcastically sent up the mysterious Pythagorean sayings, the *akousmata*, there can be little doubt that he was taking aim at Ficino.[49]

There were also the traditional accouterments of a court society, as the Medici were in step with evolving European trends. Luigi Pulci's scatological persona forced even Lorenzo de' Medici, his professed friend, to distance himself, but his presence on the intellectual landscape reminds us of the level of courtly activity, just as the richly classical vernacularism of Poliziano's *Stanze per la Giostra*, completed in the late 1470s, along with Lorenzo's own *Stanze*, serve to point up the same trend.[50] This, too, was not the place for Ficino's fundamental interiority and was at least part of the reason for Ficino's seeming distance from Lorenzo through much of the 1480s.

There is the presence of the young Pico della Mirandola to round out the picture. He was part of the intellectual field, although thanks to his private wealth his relation to Medici patronage was not conditioned by financial concerns. The experience of 1486–87, his abortive Roman *disputatio,* flight to France, and salvation by Lorenzo – was a central transformative one in his experience, for it solidified and gave direction and vigor to the divergent path he would tread vis-à-vis Ficino. In his 1491 *De ente et uno* (*On Being and the One*), he argued that Plato and Aristotle had agreed on the ontological places of Being and One, Pico averring that the two philosophers had suggested that Being and One were coextensive when most would argue that Plato had placed One above Being. For this latter 'misinterpretation' Pico blamed later Platonists, and, as Michael Allen has pointed out, lurking behind these later Platonists was the figure of Marsilio Ficino. Ficino would go on to change his own commentary on the *Parmenides* to counter Pico's arguments.[51]

Finally, there was in the Florentine intellectual field the rising tide of an antispeculative fideism represented by Savonarola, a stance to which Pico and Poliziano in the few years remaining to them would adhere. Savonarola's emphasis on faith over reason and his condemnation of 'vanities' of all sorts was intimately related to Florentine civic traditions, as was the way in which Savonarola preached and disseminated his message.[52] This fideistic tendency also harmonized with the evolution of the Florentine sociopolitical field, as the elite who had once surrounded Ficino now gathered around Savonarola. Ficino's scholarly work, growing ever more esoteric in these years, was not a part of Savonarola's style of public piety and controlling orthodoxy. Toward the end of the 1490s, differing versions of orthodoxies were developed, and Savonarola fell victim to the strife in 1498; his body, having been hanged, was publicly burned in the Piazza della Signoria, along with two of his confréres. Ficino never permanently reconciled himself to the Savonarolan trend, although he tried to support it early on – certainly, I think, as a result of the pressures the changing intellectual field was exerting, although that need not make his seeming *voltes-face* less-than-sincere changes of opinion.[53] In 1494, Ficino played down his devotion to astrology, that most un-Savonarolan practice; Poliziano perceived Ficino to have recanted his views, praising him and suggesting that there was nothing wrong with a philosopher, who learns more every day, changing his opinions, indeed, nothing wrong with a philosopher accommodating his views to the opinion of the crowd.[54] The deaths of Pico and Poliziano, his fellow agonists in the Florentine intellectual field, took away from Ficino those who would debate with him concerning astrology, and he returned to his former opinion on astrology and its use. In his bitter *Apologia* after Savonarola's death Ficino even suggests that Savonarola himself – the 'prince of hypocrites, led on by a diabolical spirit'– had been under the influence of poor stars and had been subject to *improbis demonibus.*[55]

Ficino found himself a part of what was in effect a court society, though he was not really a court intellectual.[56] This is one of the many reasons why Hankins's recent studies concerning the status of the Platonic academy have been so valuable.[57] Ficino, although actively engaged in various forms of didactic activity from the local to the international level, turned into an essentially separatist philosopher, embracing the study of materials and a mode of investigation which fundamentally preserved and isolated him from the center of Florentine intellectual life. Given the earlier comment on the Florentine intellectual field, we can say that Ficino was extra-institutional.

I add only one caveat here, and this has to do not so much with the intellectual field, in which intellectuals implicitly or explicitly vie to have their competing positions accepted and understood. We must foreground the social field and the rules of acceptable social behavior in a court society, and the paramount place within that culture of restraint, documented later by the courtly *sprezzatura* of Castiglione but manifested as well in late-fifteenth-century Florence, which, although technically still a republic, was well in line with European courtly aristocratic norms.[58] When intellectuals who were part of the just-sketched field differed with one another, the forms of their adversarial techniques were conditioned by restraint, whereby ardent advocacy of anything but the traditional virtues was looked down on. In configuring the Florentine intellectual field and the many different possible antagonistic positions within it, we should keep the subtlety in mind that would compel intellectuals to express their positions in such a way that they would not be seen as violating acceptable boundaries of *amicitia*. Ficino's anger about Savonarola thus says something important about the function Savonarola served. In the 1470s and early 1480s, there had been a doxa of communal *amor*, embodied by the diverse sources and mentalities unified in Botticelli's *Primavera* and conditioned by courtly restraint.[59] Then, in the late 1480s and early 1490s, the unspoken boundaries of that doxa were strained if still unnamed, as competing positions developed and coexisted. Finally, in the mid-1490s Savonarola voiced concerns about the very substance of the doxa – multivalent, unspoken, capable of subsuming manifold approaches to current intellectual problems – and in so doing, to echo Sartre, wreaked havoc by finding a name for what had up until then been lived namelessly.[60] The Savonarolan era created orthodoxy in late quattrocento Florence by defining a field of action as heterodox.

Ficino's treading on the boundaries of orthodoxy comes on the cusp of this transformation in Florentine society and should thus not be seen only as the result of a personal philosophical quest, but also as a social phenomenon, a way to distinguish a position for himself within a complex and changing intellectual field while remaining true to his core convictions. His increasingly esoteric concerns led him to see himself at the frontiers of orthodoxy, even as he was convinced himself of the primarily Christian nature of his mission. In 1489, he published a three-part work, *De triplici vita*.[61] The first book, which had been written almost a decade earlier, is on caring for the health of scholars, the second on prolonging life, and the third is on making one's life agree with the heavens. Ficino's stated goal is that *De triplici vita* serve as a manual of health for the learned.[62] In his general assumption that celestial forces and planetary conjunctions had real effects on the substances of remedies as well as on the healing process itself, Ficino was well in line with medieval and early Renaissance tradition. But in his attempt in the third book not only to use but also to manipulate the heavens, Ficino was treading on ground that had been viewed with suspicion throughout the Middle Ages.[63]

In the first two books one finds a number of medical recipes and recommendations. There is certainly a disjuncture between the first two books and the third, which represents a commentary on a particularly difficult and controversial aspect of Plotinus's oeuvre, his work on the soul. In elaborating Plotinus and attempting to configure the human soul's power, Ficino enters into astral magic and the manipulation of heavenly forces. Despite the seeming differences among the books, there are also commonalities, the most noteworthy of which is Ficino's propensity for inclusiveness. Ficino indicates that human efficacy is the key; remedies of whatever sort that the human operator can employ are part of his purview in all three books.

One of the most arresting sections of the second book comes when Ficino advocates some rather daring treatment for an elderly man in need of medical care. It often happens, Ficino writes, that when one reaches the age of seventy (sometimes sixty-three), the tree of the human body decays, because its moisture has dried up. If this happens, 'this human tree must be moistened by a human, youthful liquid in order that it may revive. Therefore choose a young girl who is healthy, beautiful, cheerful, and temperate, and when you are hungry and the moon is waxing, suck her milk; immediately eat a little powder of sweet fennel properly mixed with sugar.'[64] This latter step will help integrate the milk into the human body. Rhetorically the bounds of orthodoxy are stretched here, elasticizing the border for what follows immediately:

> Careful physicians strive to cure those whom a long bout of hectic fever has consumed, with the liquid of human blood which has distilled in the fire at the practice of sublimation. What then prevents us from sometimes also refreshing by this drink those who have already been in a way consumed by old age? There is a certain common and ancient opinion that certain wise old women who are popularly called 'screech-owls' [*stringes*] suck the blood of infants as a means, in so far as they can, of growing young again. Why shouldn't our old people, namely those who have no [other] recourse, likewise suck the blood of a youth? A youth, I say, who is willing, healthy, happy, and temperate, whose blood is of the best but perhaps too abundant. They will suck, therefore, like leeches, an ounce or two from a scarcely-opened vein of the left arm; they will immediately take an equal amount of sugar and wine;

> they will do this when hungry and thirsty and the moon is waxing. If they have difficulty digesting raw blood, let it first be cooked together with sugar.[65]

A number of things must be taken into consideration here. First, there is the sort of argument Ficino will later employ, in the *Apologia* to the *De triplici vita:* if these things exist in nature (which God has created and given us for our benefit), why not use them?[66] The way Ficino frames this argument, however, is noteworthy and suggestive of his fluid sense of the boundaries of orthodoxy. For he takes care to mention the 'screech-owls or 'stringes' in Latin. In discussing them, Ficino vaguely echoes the language of Pliny, when he uses the words 'a certain common and ancient opinion'; Pliny was uncertain what bird exactly was meant by the name, although aware that it was used in curses.[67] The most detailed description of the conduct of the screech-owls is in Ovid's *Fasti,* where the possibility is raised that the blood-sucking birds are women transformed into birds by enchantment.[68] Beyond this, especially noteworthy is the manner in which Ficino connects this bird lore to 'certain wise women' ('aniculas quasdam sagas'). For all of these terms had inevitably to evoke the specter of witchcraft, whose stereotypical features were stamped indelibly by a work of which Ficino could not have been ignorant, indeed may even here be echoing: the *Malleus Maleficarum* – the 'Hammer of Witches,' published in 1486 by the Dominican inquisitors Heinrich Krämer and Jakob Sprenger, a book prefaced by Innocent VIII's 1484 Bull *Summis desiderantes* (a pope, incidentally, with strong ties to the Medici).[69] Also, the adjective 'saga' used by Ficino connotes, in addition to prophetic ability, one who practices witchcraft,[70] and of course the term 'screech-owls' – 'stringes' would have evoked the Italian 'striga' (or 'strega'), 'witch.'[71] In addition to the fears about the rising tide of witchcraft that the institutional church was expressing, Ficino published *De triplici vita* just two years after Innocent VIII condemned Pico della Mirandola's projected disputation at Rome, for 'renovating the errors of pagan philosophers,' and for endorsing 'certain arts, disguising themselves as natural philosophy, harmful to the Catholic faith and humankind, sharply damned by the canons and doctrines of Catholic doctors.'[72]

Ficino's stance is noteworthy because, despite all the reasons he would have had for rewriting this position, he does not condemn it, or even qualify it; often in book three he will take care to distinguish his reporting the efficacy of a certain practice from his appearing to advocate it.[73] A few short chapters later, Ficino winds up a discussion of the manner in which the elderly can receive benefits from the planets (2.13), saying that one must have inner faith in these things and believe that 'faith is the life of medicines that conduce to life,' and that 'God will favor you when you supplicate him, and that the things created by him, especially the celestial things, have without a doubt a marvelous power to lengthen or preserve life.' The nourishing powers of human milk and blood are perhaps not celestial, but are part of God's created world nonetheless, and hence suitable for medical use.

Ficino's medical suggestion that it is licit to ingest human blood is also part of a folkloric tradition in premodern Italy that condones the uses of products such as human cranial powder, urine, milk, excrement, and blood for the curing of various ailments.[74] This blood-drinking passage in Ficino's oeuvre is helpful to us precisely because it makes explicit a fact that is always implicitly true: the boundaries between 'high' and 'low' culture in premodern Europe were malleable and not always located where we might expect them. Ficino the philosopher-physician is also Ficino the canon-expanding reader magus and teller of tales, and borders that we create between those aspects of his personality impose later assumptions about culture on a time to which they would have been alien.[75]

De triplici vita as a whole is permeated by the notion of an animate cosmos, which divinity has endowed with life. This cosmos is distinct from God (as it would not be later in the thought of Giordano Bruno), but nonetheless divinely alive. In book three these notions are brought to the fore in a more complex way, for Ficino here discusses how human beings can access nature's divine power. The point of departure for book three is Plotinus, Ficino tells us, although he is reading Plotinus through post-Plotinian lenses.[76] I do not enter into discussion of specific problems there because they have been treated elsewhere. Instead I should like to emphasize only that there are fundamental ambiguities in Ficino's work regarding matters pertaining to orthodoxy, especially regarding the animation of statues and the use of demons. He himself in the treatise repeatedly worries that he will be misperceived as advocating certain heterodox practices, and even as he is at pains to deny his advocacy of them, he reveals his belief in their efficacy. Although his conceptions regarding ritual efficacy are chock full of ancient, late ancient, and high medieval antecedents from the philosophical tradition, it is in the complex of intellectual stances that make up the late ancient post-Plotinian tradition, as I have suggested elsewhere, that the true model for his position regarding the efficacy of ritual is found.[77]

Ficino's tendency to stretch the boundaries of orthodoxy is closely tied to his style of discourse in *De triplici vita*. For there, unlike in the *Platonic Theology,* his stance is that of the prophetic revealer of truth and not the scholastic expositor. His confusion has been cited as being unphilosophical, and it must reflect at the very least Ficino's own fears and ambivalences regarding what he was writing about.[78] But perhaps, in an intellectual field such as the Florentine one of the late 1480s and early 1490s, the concept of 'philosopher,' infused as it is with post-Enlightenment implications regarding the necessity of external coherence and consistency in a thinker's work, along with the concomitant notion that the mind and body are fundamentally split, is not useful in analyzing Ficino. His work does not display a remarkable consistency in this regard.[79] But there is an internal coherence in his style of thought and in the relationality in which his thought unfolds. Ficino pushed and pulled at the borders of orthodoxies intellectual and religious, expanding the canon of Platonic-Christian philosophy. In so doing, he staked out his own individual position in the Florentine intellectual field, even as the choices he made in his own enterprise of cultural translation moved him from the center to the periphery of the city's social field.

NOTES

1. Christopher S. Celenza, '"Parallel lives": Plutarch's *Lives,* Lapo da Castiglionchio the Younger (1405–1438) and the Art of Italian Renaissance Translation,' *Illinois Classical Studies* 22 (1997): 121–55.

2. Forms of the word appear in the works of late ancient Greek authors including Damascius, Eusebius, Gregory of Nazianzen, Gregory of Nyssa, Chrysostom, Origen, Porphyry (commentary on Plato's *Timaeus*), and Proclus (commentary on Plato's *Timaeus*), among others; see the *Thesaurus Linguae Graecae,* CD-Rom E, distributed by the University of California, Irvine, Classics' Department.

3. Du Cange, *Glossarium medii aevi latinitatis,* 4:737. More commonly, medieval and Renaissance writers will use the Latin equivalent, 'recta opinio.'

4. John B. Henderson, *The Construction of Orthodoxy and Heresy* (Albany: State University of New York Press, 1998); Walter Bauer, *Orthodoxy and Heresy in Earliest Christianity* (Philadelphia: Fortress Press, 1934); Peter Godman, *The Saint as Censor: Robert Bellarmine between Inquisition and Index, Studies in Medieval and Reformation Thought,* 80 (Leiden, Boston, and Cologne: Brill, 2000), 178.

5. Augustine, *De genesi ad literam contra Manichaeos,* 1.1, *Patrologia Latina* 34.173; Aquinas, *Summa theologiae,* 2a2ae, 11, esp. art. 3; and for evil, 1a, 49, 2, resp. The position went back to Paul, 1 Cor. 11, 19: 'Nam oportet et hereses esse ut et qui probati sunt manifesti fiant in vobis.'

6. For recent literature on Ficino see T. Katinis, 'Bibliografia ficiniana: studi ed edizioni delle opere di Marsilio Ficino dal 1986,' *Accademia* 2 (2000): 101–36; and Paul Oskar Kristeller, *Marsilio Ficino and His Work after Five Hundred Years* (Florence: Olschki, 1987).

7. Max Weber, *Economy and Society: An Outline of Interpretive Sociology,* 2 vols., ed. G. Roth and C. Wittich, various translators (Berkeley, Los Angeles, and London: University of California Press, 1978), vol. 1, 399–640.

8. Ibid., 439.

9. For the term 'early modern Catholicism', see John W. O'Malley, *Trent and All That: Renaming Catholicism in the Early Modern Era* (Cambridge and London: Harvard University Press, 2000).

10. Kristeller's contributions to the study of Ficino are almost innumerable, but a few stand out: for Kristeller's synchronic distillation of Ficino's thought, see his *Il pensiero filosofico di Marsilio Ficino,* 2nd ed. (Florence: Le Lettere, 1988), which contains an overall study of Ficino's philosophy, with 'philosophy' conceived along the lines of the problems posed by classical German idealism; Kristeller's early work gathering materials on Ficino is central to his outlook: see idem, *Supplementum ficinianum,* 2 vols. (Florence, 1937); he maintained a lifelong interest in Ficino studies: see idem, *Marsilio Ficino and His Work after Five Hundred Years.* For a discussion of Kristeller and his oeuvre, see my *The Lost Italian Renaissance: Humanists, Historians and Latin's Legacy* (Baltimore, The Johns Hopkins University Press, 2004), chapter 2.

11. For Ficino, there is the fact that in Kristeller's synthesis of Ficino's thought, *Il pensiero filosofico di Marsilio Ficino,* only pages 334–40 discuss astrology and magic; see also Celenza, 'Late Antiquity and the Florentine Renaissance: Historiographical Parallels,' *Journal of the History of Ideas* 62, no. 1 (2001): 17–35. For Pomponazzi, see Kristeller's 'The Myth of Renaissance Atheism and the French Tradition of Free Thought,' in his *Studies in Renaissance Thought and Letters,* 4 vols. (Rome: Storia e letteratura, 1993) vol. III, 541–54 (orig. English publication 1968); and his portrait of Pomponazzi in *Eight Philosophers of the Italian Renaissance* (Stanford: Stanford University Press, 1964), 72–90 (89–90).

12. For the social logic of the text, see Gabrielle M. Spiegel, *The Past as Text: The Theory and Practice of Medieval Historiography* (Baltimore, The Johns Hopkins University Press, 1999).

13. Thomas Kuhn, *The Structure of Scientific Revolutions,* 3rd ed. (Chicago and London: University of Chicago Press, 1996); the first edition appeared in 1962; Kuhn presented some modifications to his views in *The Essential Tension: Selected Studies in Scientific Tradition and Change* (Chicago and London: University of Chicago Press, 1977).

14. Gaston Bachelard, *The New Scientific Spirit,* trans. A. Goldhammer (Boston: Beacon Press, 1984); cf. Mary Tiles, *Bachelard, Science and Objectivity* (Cambridge and New York: Cambridge University Press, 1984). I have found very useful David Swartz, *Culture and Power: The Sociology of Pierre Bourdieu* (Chicago and London: University of Chicago Press, 1997).

15. Swartz, *Culture and Power,* 32.

16. The notion of a 'coupre epistemologique,' present in Bachelard, was popularized and used systematically by Louis Althusser and thus gained greater currency in French thought than it might have; cf. Louis Althusser, *For Marx*; trans. B. Brewster (New York: Pantheon, 1969), 257; Swartz, *Culture and Power,* 32.

17. For the problems that the opposition between diachronic and synchronic styles of interpretation have presented in accounts of Renaissance intellectual history, and for a fuller discussion of these intellectual concerns, see my *The Lost Italian Renaissance,* Chapters 2 and 3.

18. A good introduction to Bourdieu's thought is in his *Outline of a Theory of Practice,* trans. R. Nice (Cambridge and New York: Cambridge University Press, 1977); and in general in Swartz, *Culture and Power.*

19. Bourdieu, *The Logic of Practice* (Stanford: Stanford University Press, 1990), 53; Swartz, *Culture and Power,* 100.

20. Bourdieu, *Outline,* 79.

21. Erwin Panofsky, *Architecture gothique et pensée scolastique,* trans. Bourdieu (Paris: Editions de Minuit, 1967), postface at 136–67.

22. For doxa, see Bourdieu, *Outline,* 164–71.

23. Ibid., 169.

24. See, e.g., Aristotle, *Nicomachean Ethics,* 1098b33 et seq. For the medieval use compare Aquinas, *Summa contra gentiles,* 1.92: 'habitus potentiae alicuius perfectivus est'.

25. Bourdieu has on occasion claimed some relation to Aristotle's view, though as critics have pointed out, his *habitus* is unlike Aristotle's in many ways. Swartz, *Culture and Power,* 108.

26. The quotation is from Swartz, *Culture and Power,* 74.

27. Ibid., 117.

28. Pierre Bourdieu and Loic J. D. Wacquant, *An Invitation to Reflexive Sociology* (Chicago and London: University of Chicago Press, 1992) 96; Swartz, *Culture and Power,* 119.

29. In general on patronage see the studies in *Patronage, Art, and Society in Renaissance Italy,* ed. F. W. Kent and P. Simons (Oxford: Oxford University Press, 1987).

30. Melissa M. Bullard, 'Marsilio Ficino and the Medici: The Inner Dimensions of Patronage,' in *Christianity and the Renaissance: Image and Religious Imagination in the Quattrocento*, ed. Timothy Verdon and John Henderson (Syracuse: Syracuse University Press, 1990), 467–92.

31. Riccardo Fubini, 'All'uscita dalla Scolastica medievale: Salutati, Bruni, e i "Dialogi ad Petrum Histrum",' *Archivio storico italiano* 150 (1992): 1065–99; Celenza, "Parallel lives."

32. For the later development of this trend and the move on the part of intellectuals toward mathematization to secure an independent sphere of action, see Timothy J. Reiss, *Knowledge, Discovery and Imagination in Early Modern Europe: The Rise of Aesthetic Rationalism* (Cambridge and New York: Cambridge University Press, 1997).

33. Heiko Oberman, in *Itinerarium Italicum: The Profile of the Italian Renaissance in the Mirror of its European Transformations*, ed. H. A. Oberman and T. Brady, *Studies in Medieval and Reformation Thought*, 14 (Leiden, Boston, Cologne: Brill, 1975), xx.

34. See Celenza, 'Late Antiquity and the Florentine Renaissance.'

35. See Anthony Grafton, *Joseph Scaliger: A Study in the History of Classical Scholarship*, 2 vols. (Oxford, 1983–93), vol. 1, 9–100; and Konrad Krautter, *Philologische Methode und humanistische Existenz: Filippo Beroaldo und sein Kommentar zum Goldenen Esel des Apuleius* (Munich: Fink, 1971).

36. See Celenza, 'Late Antiquity and Florentine Platonism,' in *Marsilio Ficino: His Theology, His Philosophy, His Legacy*, ed. M. J. B. Allen and V. R. Rees (Leiden, Boston, and Cologne: Brill, 2002), 71–97; idem, 'Antiquité tardive et platonisme florentin,' in *Penser entre les lignes: philosophie et philologie au Quattrocento*, ed. Fosca Mariani Zini (Lille: Presses Universitaires du Septentrion, 2001), 197–226.

37. See Arthur Field, *The Origins of the Platonic Academy of Florence* (Princeton: Princeton University Press, 1988); and Melissa M. Bullard, *Lorenzo Il Magnifico: Image and Anxiety, Politics and Finance* (Florence: Olschki, 1990), 215–45.

38. See, for example, the letters to Cavalcanti and Filippo Contronio in Marsilio Ficino, *Lettere*, ed. S. Gentile (Florence: Olschki, 1990); also in Ficino, *Opera omnia* (Basel, 1576; repr. Turin: Barrera, 1959), 632–3.

39. See Bullard, 'Marsilio Ficino and the Medici' and the important studies of Riccardo Fubini, 'Ficino e i Medici all'avvento di Lorenzo il Magnifico,' *Rinascimento*, 2nd ser., 24 (1984): 3–52; idem, 'Ancora su Ficino e i Medici,' *Rinascimento*, 2nd ser., 27 (1987): 275–91; both now contained in idem, *Quattrocento fiorentino: Politica diplomazia cultura* (Pisa: Pacini, 1996).

40. For the chronology of Ficino's work, see Kristeller, *Supplementum Ficinianum*, 1: lxxvii–clxvii; idem, 'Marsilio Ficino as a Beginning Student of Plato,' *Scriptorium* 20 (1966): 41–54, reprinted in idem, *Studies in Renaissance Thought and Letters*, vol. III, 93–108; and S. Gentile, 'Sulle prime traduzioni dal greco di Marsilio Ficino,' *Rinascimento*, 2nd ser., 30 (1990): 57–104.

41. See Michael J. B. Allen, *Synoptic Art: Marsilio Ficino on the History of Platonic Interpretation* (Florence: Olschki, 1998).

42. One of many: see James Hankins, 'Lorenzo de' Medici as a Patron of Philosophy,' *Rinascimento*, 2nd ser., 34 (1994): 15–53; high affective dimension: Bullard, 'Marsilio Ficino and the Medici.'

43. For political dimensions and Ficino's relations with the rival Valori family, see Mark Jurdjevic, 'Prophets and Politicians: Marsilio Ficino, Savonarola, and the Valori family'; forthcoming, *Past and Present* (2004).

44. See Armando Verde, *Lo studio fiorentino, 1473–1503: Ricerche e documenti* (Florence: Istituto nazionale di studi sul rinascimento, 1973–), vol. 2; and Hankins, 'Lorenzo de' Medici as a Patron of Philosophy.'

45. On Poliziano, see Vittore Branca, *Poliziano e l'umanesimo della parola* (Turin: Einaudi, 1983); John D'Amico, *Theory and Practice in Renaissance Textual Criticism: Beatus Rhenanus between Conjecture and History* (Berkeley, Los Angeles, and London: University of California Press, 1988), 23–7; Peter Godman, *From Poliziano to Machiavelli: Florentine Humanism in the High Renaissance* (Princeton: Princeton University Press, 1998); Grafton, *Joseph Scaliger*, vol. 1. 9–100; and Ida Maier, *Ange Politien: La formation d'un poète humaniste (1469–1480)* (Geneva: Droz, 1966); for a precise introduction to his style of miscellanistic criticism, see Jill Kraye, 'Cicero, Stoicism, and Textual Criticism: Poliziano on ΚΑΤΟΡΘΩΜΑ,' *Rinascimento*, 2nd ser., 23 (1983): 79–110.

46. Angelo Poliziano, *Miscellaneorum centuria secunda* in idem, *Opera* (Venice: Aldus Manutius, 1498) unpaginated and idem, *Miscellaneorum centuria secunda*, ed. V. Branca and M. Pastore Stocchi (Florence: Olschki, 1978).

47. Godman, *From Poliziano to Machiavelli*, 3–133, is especially lucid on the manner in which Poliziano's agonistic context shaped the evolution of his scholarhip.

48. On Buonincontri, see Arthur Field, 'Lorenzo Buonincontri and the First Public Lectures on Manilius (Florence, ca. 1475–78),' *Rinascimento*, 2nd series 36 (1996): 207–25; on Poliziano and Pliny, Godman, *From Poliziano to Machiavelli*, 98–106.

49. See Poliziano, *Lamia: Praelectio in priora Aristotelis analytica*, ed. A. Wesseling, Studies in Medieval and Reformation Thought, 38 (Leiden, Boston, and Cologne: Brill, 1986); Christopher S. Celenza, *Piety and Pythagoras in Renaissance Florence: The Symbolum Nesianum*, Studies in the History of Christian Thought, 101 (Leiden, Boston, and Cologne: Brill, 2001); and Jill Kraye, 'Ficino in the Firing Line: A Renaissance Neoplatonist and His Critics,' in *Marsilio Ficino: His Theology, His Philosophy, His Legacy*, 377–98.

50. Hankins, 'Lorenzo de' Medici as a Patron of Philosophy.' For Laurentian culture, see Angelo Poliziano, *Stanze cominciate per la Giostra di Giuliano de' Medici*, ed. V. Pernicone (Turin: Loescher, 1954); Lorenzo de' Medici, *Stanze*, ed. R. Castagnola (Florence: Olschki, 1986); Richard C. Trexler, *Public Life in Renaissance Florence* (New York: Academic Press, 1980; reprint, Ithaca: Cornell University Press, 1991), 428–52; Charles Dempsey, *Inventing the Renaissance Putto* (Chapel Hill and London: University of North Carolina Press, 2001).

51. See Michael J. B. Allen, 'The Second Ficino-Pico Controversy: Parmenidean Poetry, Eristic and the One,' in ed. Gian Carlo Garfagnini, *Marsilio Ficino e il ritorno di Platone: Studi e documenti*, 2 vols. (Florence: Olschki, 1986) vol. 2: 417–55, now in Allen, *Plato's Third Eye: Studies in Marsilio Ficino's Metaphysics and Its Sources* (Aldershot and Brookfield: Ashgate, 1995) as study number X; Eugenio Garin, *Giovanni Pico della Mirandola: Vita e dottrina* (Florence: Le Monnier, 1937); and Louis Valcke and Roland Galibois, *Le périple intellectuel de Jean Pic de la Mirandole, suivi du Discours de la dignité de l'homme et du traité L'être et l'un* (Sainte-Foy, Quebec; Presses de l'Université Laval, 1994).

52. See Donald Weinstein, *Savonarola and Florence: Prophecy and Patriotism in the Renaissance* (Princeton: Princeton University Press, 1970); Lorenzo Polizzotto, *The Elect Nation: The Savonarolan Movement in Florence, 1494–1545* (Oxford: Clarendon Press, 1994); and especially Allen, *Synoptic Art*.

53. Excellent material in Carol V. Kaske, 'Ficino's Shifting Attitude Towards Astrology in the *De vita coelitus comparanda*, the letter to Poliziano, and the *Apologia* to the Cardinals,' in Garfagnini, ed., *Marsilio Ficino e il ritorno di Platone*, vol. 2, 371–81. Melissa Bullard, 'The Inward Zodiac: A Development in Ficino's Thought on Astrology,' *Renaissance Quarterly* 43 (1990): 687–708, and Jurdjevic, 'Prophets and Politicians.'

54. Ficino's letter to Poliziano, dated 20 August 1494, is in *Opere* 958. Poliziano's letter is edited in Kristeller, *Supplementum*, vol. 2, 279: 'Nam nec mutare sententiam turpe philosopho, qui cottidie plus videt et ad opinionem vulgi saepe se non inutiliter accomodat.'

55. It is edited in Kristeller, *Supplementum,* vol. 2, 76–9. 'Hypocritarum princeps', 77.

56. On Florence and the transition to a court society, see Roberto Bizzocchi, *Chiesa e potere nella Toscana del Quattrocento* (Bologna: Mulino, 1987), 351–2; Brown, *Medici* in *Florence,* 247–62.

57. James Hankins, 'Cosimo de' Medici and the "Platonic Academy,"' *Journal of the Warburg and Courtauld Institutes* 53 (1990): 144–62; and idem, 'The Myth of the Platonic Academy of Florence,' *Renaissance Quarterly* 44 (1991): 429–75.

58. Celenza, *Piety and Pythagoras,* chapter 3 and, for the lived feel of fifteenth-century Florentine life, Lauro Martines, *April Blood: Florence and the Plot Against the Medici* (Oxford: Oxford University Press, 2003).

59. Charles Dempsey, *The Portrayal of Love: Botticelli's Primavera and Humanist Culture at the Time of Lorenzo the Magnificent* (Princeton: Princeton University Press, 1992).

60. Jean-Paul Sartre, *L'idiot de la famille.* 3 vols. (Paris: Gallimard, 1971), vol. 1, 783.

61. I cite from Marsilio Ficino, *De triplici vita,* ed. and trans. Carol V. Kaske and John Clark (Binghamton, N.Y.: MRTS, 1989).

62. Ficino, proem to *De triplici vita* (102–5).

63. Nancy Siraisi, *Medieval and Early Renaissance Medicine: An Introduction to Knowledge and Practice* (Chicago and London: University of Chicago Press, 1990), 68–9, 149–52.

64. Marsilio Ficino, *De triplici vita,* 2.11.

65. Ibid.

66. Ibid., *Apologia,* ad fin.

67. Pliny, *Historia Naturalis,* 11.39.95.

68. Ovid, *Fasti,* 6.132–68; cf. 141: 'sive igitur nascuntur aves, seu carmine fiunt.' Other ancient testimonies regarding the screech-out, all of which are associated with magic and witchcraft or at least unsavory activities, include Ovid. *Met* 7.269 and Propertius, 4.5.17, Plautus, *Pseudolus* 3.2.21 (820).

69. See the entries in Ludwig Hain, *Repertorium Bibliographicum,* 2 vols. (Stuttgart: J. G. Cotta, 1826–38), vol. 4 (with supplement: Walter Arthur Copinger, Supplement to Hain's Repertorium bibliographicum; or, Collections toward a new edition of that work, 2 pts. in 3 vols. [Milan: Görlich, 1950], 9238–42). For four excellent approaches to the problem of witchcraft, very different but complementary, see Stuart Clark, *Thinking with Demons: The Idea of Witchcraft in Early Modern Europe* (Oxford: Clarendon Press, 1997); Robin Briggs, *Witches and Neighbors: A History of European Witchcraft* (Oxford: Blackwell, 1996); Brian P. Levack, *The Witch-Hunt in Early Modern Europe,* 2nd ed. (London and New York: Longman, 1995); and Walter Stephens, *Demon Lovers* (Chicago: University of Chicago Press, 2002).

70. Apuleius, *Metamorphoses,* 2.21.

71. Present famously in Dante, *Purgatorio,* 19.

72. See the edition of Innocent's 1487 bull in Pico della Mirandola, *De hominis dignitate, Heptaplus, De ente et uno e scritti vari,* ed. Eugenio Garin (Florence: Vallechi, 1942); and Stephen A. Farmer, *Syncretism in the West: Pico's 900 Theses (1486): The Evolution of Traditional Religious and Philosophical Systems,* Medieval and Renaissance Texts and Studies, 167 (Tempe, Arizona, 1998), 15–16, from whom the quotation is drawn.

73. See, for instance, Ficino, *De triplici vita,* 3.15, 3.18, and 3.20.

74. Piero Camporesi, *Bread of Dreams* (Chicago: University of Chicago Press, 1989), 40–55.

75. On the need to think carefully about the categories of 'high' and 'low' when approaching early modern culture, see Guido Ruggiero, *Binding Passions: Tales of Magic, Marriage, and Power at the End of the Renaissance* (Oxford and New York: Oxford University Press, 1993); and for the classic

statement of the reciprocal relationship between 'low' and 'high' culture see Carlo Ginzburg, *The Cheese and the Worms: The Cosmos of a Sixteenth-Century Miller,* tran. A. Tedeschi and J. Tedeschi (Baltimore: The Johns Hopkins University Press, 1980; reprint, New York: Penguin, 1982), xiii–xxvi.

76. See Brian P. Copenhaver, 'Scholastic Philosophy and Renaissance Magic in the *De vita* of Marsilio Ficino,' *Renaissance Quarterly* 37 (1984): 523–54; Celenza, 'Antiquité tardive' and idem, 'Late Antiquity and Florentine Platonism.'

77. Celenza, 'Antiquité tardive' and idem, 'Late Antiquity and Florentine Platonism.'

78. Copenhaver, 'Scholastic Philosophy and Renaissance Magic.'

79. Michael J. B. Allen, *The Platonism of Marsilio Ficino: A Study of his Phaedrus Commentary, its Sources and Genesis* (Berkeley, Los Angeles, and London: University of California Press, 1984), x–xi.

11

The Sphinx in the City: Egyptian Memories and Urban Spaces in Renaissance Rome (and Viterbo)

Brian A. Curran

In his letter on the arts of antiquity, published as a prologue to the second edition of Giorgio Vasari's *Vite* in 1568, Giovanni Battista Adriani, the Florentine scholar, orator, and 'official historian' of Duke Cosimo I de' Medici, devotes a few lines to the artistic accomplishments of the Egyptians[1]:

> Herodotus, that most ancient historian, who had searched many lands and seen, heard and read of many things, writes that the Egyptians had been the most ancient people of which there was memory, and that they were solemn observers of their religion if anyone was, and that they adored and recognized their idolatrous gods under the various figures of strange and diverse animals, and that these were fashioned in gold and silver and other metals, and in precious stones and almost every material that was able to receive form. And some of these images have been preserved up until our own day, having been very much seen as manifest signs of these very powerful and endowed people, and of their very rich kings, and further from a proper desire to prolong the memory of them for infinite centuries, and further than this the memory of their marvelous intelligence and singular industry and profound science of divine things, as well as human. . . . Following these people, I myself can inform you that the art of good drawing and of coloring, and of sculpture and of representation in whatever manner, and in every manner of form, was held in great esteem [by them]. As for architecture, it should not be doubted that they were great masters, as is still seen in the pyramids and other stupendous edifices of their art that survive and will continue to last, as I myself believe, for infinite centuries.[2]

Adriani's evaluation of the skills of the Egyptian artisans, and his reference to monuments that he has evidently seen for himself, might surprise readers who assume that the Western discovery of Egyptian art was a nineteenth-century, post-Napoleonic phenomenon.[3] And, although his only named examples are the pyramids, there can be little doubt that Adriani was referring, in addition to the obelisks, to statues of 'idolatrous gods' and 'strange animals', and other monuments that could be seen in Rome during his time (Fig. 70).[4] As Adriani and his contemporaries understood, these works had been brought from Egypt in antiquity as spoils of conquest and tokens of a civilization whose gods, Isis, Serapis, and the others, had been granted a place among the protectors of the empire.[5] In his effort to explain the ancients' enthusiasm for these works, Adriani draws on the paradoxical thesis, promoted by Herodotus and other ancient historians, that the Egyptians, otherwise characterized as a 'barbarian' and ethnically distinct people, were also the originators of many of the fundamental disciplines of human civilization.[6] As the purported inventors of organized religion, theology, the worship of the divine through images, historical record keeping, 'natural philosophy', and the use of the visual arts for commemorative purposes, a piece of the Egyptian 'legacy' could be claimed by virtually all later peoples, Greeks, Romans, and Renaissance Italians included.[7] In this essay, I consider some of the ways this notion influenced the cultural activities of several generations of artists, scholars, and patrons in Rome during the Renaissance. My attention is directed, for the most part, to responses to, and appropriations of, Egyptian monuments in Rome during the pontificates of Alexander VI (1492–1503) and Leo X (1513–21), two very different pontiffs who found Egyptian monuments and their imagery eminently suitable for the promotion of their respective agendas. In so doing, I hope to illuminate some of the curious ways that notions of cultural inheritance and translation functioned in the context of the broader 'revival of antiquity' in Renaissance culture.[8]

By the end of the Imperial era, after generations of imports (supplemented by the production of imitations) the city of Rome had become a virtual open-air museum of Egyptian antiquities. During the Middle Ages, however, the majority of these monuments had been abandoned and buried in the ruins of the declining capital. Of the nearly fifty obelisks that once stood in the city, only the great obelisk of the Vatican (Fig. 71) remained standing in its original location, rising above the buried *spina* of the Circus of Gaius and Nero on the south flank of St. Peter's Basilica.[9] While the memory of its Egyptian origin had been lost (a circumstance possibly facilitated by its lack of a hieroglyphic inscription), the obelisk became even more famous through its identification as the tomb of Julius Caesar.[10] There were several other less famous obelisks that could also be seen in Rome at this time, like the obelisk of Domitian in the extramural circus of Maxentius at the 'Capo di Bove.'[11] Two smaller

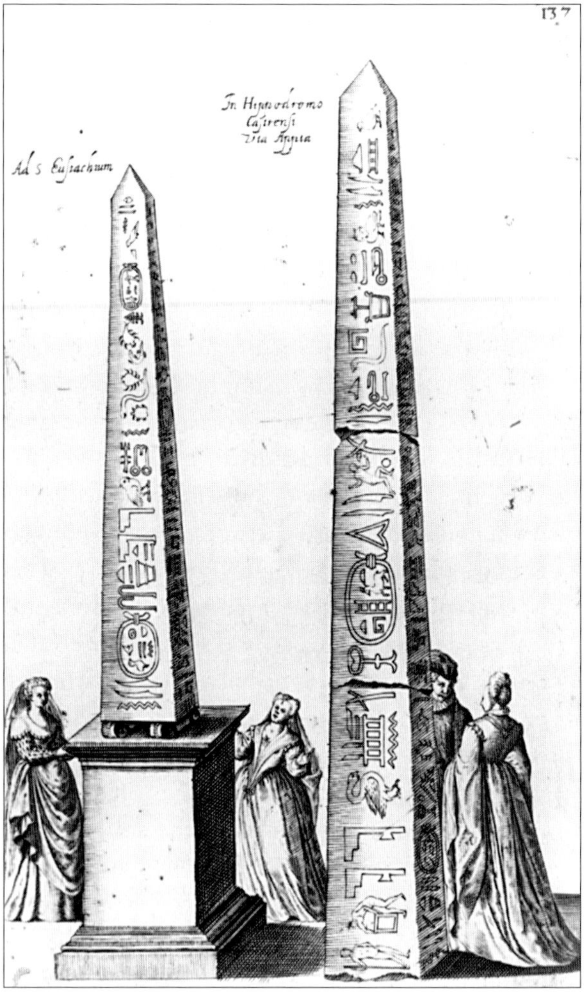

70. Theodore de Bry, *Roman Obelisks.* From Jean-Jacques Boissard, *I–VI Pars Romanae Urbis Topographiae & Antiquitatum* (Frankfurt, 1597–1602), vol. I, pl. 137. Photo: Marquand Library of Art and Archeology, Princeton University Library.

obelisks stood upright in the center of the city: the upper shaft of an obelisk of Rameses II, which had been restored in the later Middle Ages and was located in the northeastern corner of the Piazza del Campidoglio, and the second and more complete obelisk, likewise inscribed for Rameses II, in the Piazza di San Macuto, which was *re*-erected at some time during the early fifteenth century (the piazza was also decorated with fragments of other obelisks, which had been set into the walls of the surrounding buildings).[12] Both of these obelisks probably came from the Iseum Campense, the great sanctuary of Isis that occupied a substantial plot in the Campus Martius in antiquity.[13] The Iseum was also the likely source for the pair

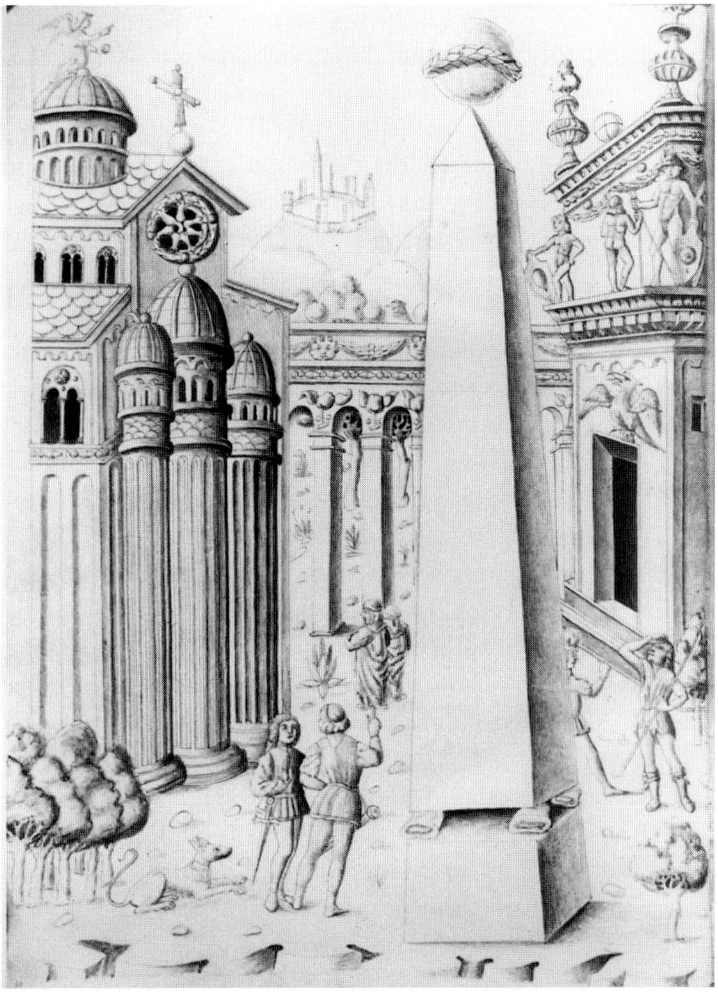

71. *Roman Scene with the Vatican Obelisk.* From Giovanni Marcanova, *Collectio Antiquitatum* (c. 1465). Garrett Collection of Medieval and Renaissance Manuscripts No. 158, Manuscripts Division, Department of Rare Books and Special Collections, Princeton University Library. Photo: Princeton University Library.

of granite lions with hieroglyphic inscriptions of the fourth century B.C. pharaoh Nectanebo I (Fig. 72), which had been installed in the Piazza della Rotunda (in front of the Pantheon) by the end of the twelfth century.[14] Another likely refugee from this complex was the baboon of gray-brown marble, called the *Cacco* or *Macacco,* that was set up on the porch of S. Stefano del Cacco by the fourteenth century.[15] Across town, visitors to the Lateran could see another pair of Egyptian lions, carved from black granite and uninscribed, that crouched before the equestrian statue of Marcus Aurelius.[16] It is clear from their preservation and installation in major urban spaces that both the lions and the obelisks were regarded as valuable antiquities and significant tokens of Rome's ancient power and *imperium*.[17] The Roman Imperial associations of the Vatican and Capitoline obelisks are evident from their association with Caesar and the Capitol, while the lion, in particular, was a leading symbol of Rome and the empire during this period.[18] For evidence of the high status of the lions, we need only consider the numerous adaptations of them produced by the 'Cosmati' sculptors of the thirteenth century.[19] These same sculptors were also responsible for a series of sphinxes with Pharaonic *nemes*-headdresses, unmistakable evidence that at least one pair of Egyptian sphinxes was also visible at this time.[20]

So although it is clear that these monuments were valued as 'manifest signs' of Roman antiquity and magnificence, we have no evidence that their medieval admirers were aware of their Egyptian origins. Indeed, as Karl Giehlow has demonstrated, the recognition of Rome's Egyptian antiquities as Egyptian was the accomplishment of a group of early humanists, including Niccolò Niccoli (1364–1437), Poggio Bracciolini (1380–1459), Flavio Biondo (1392–1463), and Leon Battista Alberti (1404–72), who approached the 'problem of the obelisks' with Pliny's *Natural History* and the newly discovered manuscripts of Ammianus Marcellinus and Horapollo in hand.[21] Pliny provided an account of the obelisks' origins and their transport to Rome, described their manufacture from the distinctive *granito rosso* of Aswan, and identified their inscriptions as the 'sacred letters' of the Egyptians.[22] Ammianus brought the story of the obelisks up to the fourth century and provided a more detailed explanation of the hieroglyphs, and Horapollo provided what appeared to be a sign-for-sign 'dictionary' of these images.[23] With these sources to guide them, it was not long before the humanists began to write and speculate about the hieroglyphs on their terms.[24] The first to identify them in print was Poggio, in this passage from *De varietate fortunae* (begun c. 1432–3 and completed in 1448):

> And there is no need to tell about the obelisks, which were transported, from Egypt with great effort and expense, as Pliny records. One only is conserved upright in the city, that was erected in the Vatican by C. Caesar Caligula in honor of the Divine Augustus and sacred to the Divine Tiberius. I saw another one of them, a little smaller, and with various figures of animals and birds that the ancient Egyptians used in the place of letters, lying in the hippodrome on the Via Appia, broken into four pieces. There are also other erected fragments of obelisks, one on the Campidoglio, and another in the *regione* today called Pigna, and others in smaller pieces, of which all [historical] memory is lost.[25]

Poggio's discussion was seconded and amplified by Flavio Biondo, whose account in the *Roma instaurata* (1443–6) draws at length (and frequently verbatim) from both Ammianus and Pliny.[26] And so the devoted students of ancient Rome suddenly found

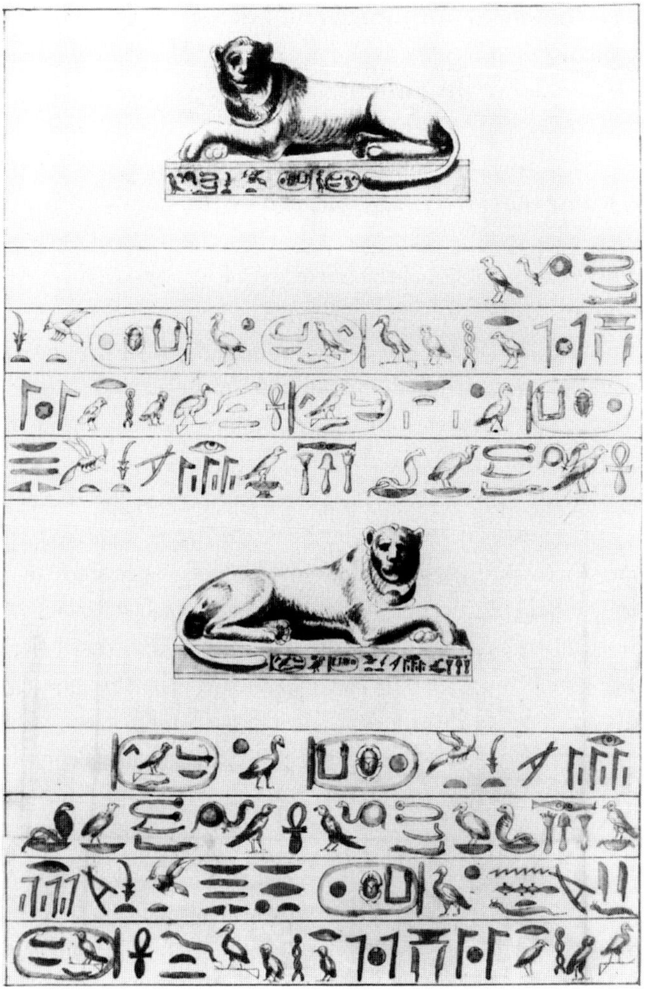

72. *Pantheon/Nectanebo Lions*, c. 1564. Biblioteca Apostolica Vaticana, Vat. lat. 3439, fol. 2r. Photo: Biblioteca Apostolica Vaticana.

themselves in an urban landscape liberally seasoned with Egyptian monuments and hieroglyphs, described by Biondo (paraphrasing Tacitus) as 'the earliest documents of human history . . . visible today, impressed upon stone.'[27] Fired with the excitement of recognition, did they rush to put their sources to the test and attempt to decipher these inscriptions for themselves? If so, their efforts must have met with frustration, because the record is virtually silent on this point.[28] In the earliest semidocumented case, the merchant-archaeologist Cyriacus of Ancona claimed to have copied an inscription in 'Phoenician letters' (his term for the hieroglyphs) that he found near the summit of the Great Pyramid of Giza in September 1436. He reports that he sent a copy of this transcription to Niccoli in Florence, because he was the 'man most interested in these things.'[29] As it turned out, Niccoli would have had little time to study them; he died only a few months later.[30] After that, the trail of the Cyriacan hieroglyphs grows cold. For the earliest surviving copy of an Egyptian hieroglyphic inscription, we have to skip a generation or two, to the 1480s or slightly earlier, to consider the fascinating copies of the inscriptions on the Pantheon-Nectanebo lions that appear in two manuscripts compiled by the Carmelite humanist Michele Fabrizio Ferrarini (d. 1492).[31] Ferrarini, a self-proclaimed follower of Cyriacus of Ancona, apparently made copies of the abridged Horapollo that his predecessor had prepared, possibly in connection to his Egyptian trip.[32] In his first, possibly earlier transcription (now in Paris) the Nectanebo hieroglyphs are precisely copied and arranged according to their original appearance on the statues' bases. They are also glossed with letters and numbers, which suggest the possibility that they were being checked against other monuments and, one presumes, the relevant literary sources.[33] By the time these hieroglyphs were copied out again, on a folio in Ferrarini's Reggio Emilia manuscript, they had been redeployed to form a decorative border in a manner that anticipates Giulio Romano's hieroglyphic decorations in the Loggia of the Muses in the Palazzo del Te, Mantua, datable to c. 1528.[34] In the latter case, the signs in question were copied from the base of the Sphinx of the late Egyptian pharaoh Achoris, which was one of a pair installed on the Campidoglio in the early 1500s, most likely by order of Pope Leo X (discussed later). 'Hieroglyphic' figures of an Egyptian sphinx and a lion of the Pantheon type were also included in Giulio's decoration, which suggests that his hieroglyphic borders could have been informed by Ferrarini's earlier experiments.[35]

As Ferrarini's (apparently abortive) study and subsequent 'creative' application of the Nectanebo hieroglyphs suggests, the idea of the hieroglyphs proved too attractive to be abandoned because of a few philological problems. Indeed, from the middle of the fifteenth century, the hieroglyph emerged as a cultural and artistic phenomenon in its own right. The key passage is Leon Battista Alberti's 'endorsement' of the hieroglyphs in the *De re aedificatoria* (in progress by 1452 and printed in 1485).[36] For Alberti, these 'Egyptian letters' held the promise of a universal language of images (*imagines*) that could transcend the limitations of speech-related script and communicate to learned men of any culture or age.

> The Egyptians . . . maintained that each nation knew only its own alphabet, and that eventually all knowledge of it would be lost – as has happened with our own Etruscan . . . whereas the method of writing they used could be understood easily by expert men all over world, to whom alone noble matters should be communicated. . . . Our own Latin ancestors chose to express the deeds of their most famous men through sculpted histories. This gave rise to columns, triumphal arches, and porticoes, covered with histories in painting, or sculpture.[37]

Alberti's claim that Egyptians anticipated the decline of their culture and devised the hieroglyphs to preserve the memory of their accomplishments represents a neat synthesis of the available sources, including Ammianus and Horapollo.[38] With their ability to communicate to elites across linguistic and cultural barriers (while concealing their meanings from the ignorant masses), the hieroglyphs would appear to provide an ideal system for recording and preserving sacred doctrines and other 'noble matters' for posterity.[39] Alberti also associates the hieroglyphs with the origins of representational art as a whole and proposes that the system passed from the Egyptians to other ancient peoples, including the Greeks and Romans. This thesis harmonizes nicely with Alberti's earlier citation of the 'Egyptian' Hermes (from the Latin *Asclepius*) in *De Pictura* (1435): 'The most ancient writer Trismegistus believes that sculpture and painting originated together with religion. He addresses Asclepius with these words: "Man, mindful of his nature and origin, represented the gods in his own likeness".'[40]

Thus, according to Alberti, the disciplines of art, religion, and historical commemoration were co-joined at their point of (Egyptian) origins, a notion that developed an added resonance for Adriani and his contemporaries in light of the iconoclastic attacks of the Reformation.[41] As eminently successful commemorative monuments that had survived the fall of their own civilization and passed through the preservative efforts of the Romans to the present day, the hieroglyphs would appear to have fulfilled the prophecy of Hermes Trismegistus: 'O Egypt, Egypt, of your religion nothing will remain but fables, which your own children will not believe. Nothing will be left but words engraved on stones to tell of your pious works.'[42]

Indeed, just as the Egyptian monuments had survived the ages to ornament the public spaces of Rome, so the Egyptians' image-writing was proclaimed by Alberti to be both esoteric and universal. It might even be said that despite their expressed confidence in the translatability of the hieroglyphs, their appeal to the humanists was even stronger at the level of their obscurity, especially the idea that these signs were accessible only to an initiated few. As is well known, the hieroglyphs provided a useful model for the emblematic inventions of the Renaissance.[43] Alberti took an early step in this direction with his personal 'hieroglyph' of the winged 'flying eye', which he explained as a symbol of the swift and supreme power of vision.[44] What this also meant, or would come to mean, was the 'revival' or appropriation of Egyptian forms and the appropriation of surviving Egyptian monuments for contemporary purposes. Alberti was possibly involved with, and certainly aware of, one of the earliest and most ambitious of these endeavors, Pope Nicholas V's project to move the Vatican obelisk to the piazza in front of St. Peter's.[45] According to his secretary Gianozzo Manetti, the pope envisioned the obelisk's 'translation' into a Christian triumphal column, held aloft by life-size bronze statues of the Evangelists with a figure of the risen Christ at its summit.[46] Contemporary reports refer to machines devised to lower and move the monument, and drawings of the 1460s (Fig. 71) show that the base of the obelisk was cleared in possible anticipation of the transfer.[47] The project was abandoned after Nicholas' death but was reconsidered and revived by various popes until 1586, when the obelisk was finally moved and re-erected by the unstoppable Sixtus V, who subjected the monument to a ritual exorcism and consecrated it to the Holy Cross.[48]

Although the 'urban life' of Rome's Egyptian antiquities entered a relatively static phase in the second half of the quattrocento, with only scattered discoveries and few, if any, restorations of the monuments, the considerable prestige of the Egyptians continued to expand with the discovery and dissemination of the Greek *Hermetica.*[49] These supposedly Egyptian texts were translated into Latin in 1463 by Marsilio Ficino, whose commentaries proclaimed Hermes Trismegistus as a contemporary of Moses and the founder of a divinely inspired 'ancient theology.'[50] Ficino also promoted a Neoplatonist reading of the hieroglyphs as a mystical and virtually divine system of encoding the 'sacred mysteries', a notion somewhat in conflict with the commemorative-historical function also promoted by the ancient sources.[51] So successful was this Hermetic revival that the Egyptian sage was granted a place of honor on the mosaic pavement of the duomo in Siena in 1488.[52] Perhaps the most spectacular manifestation of the exalted status of the Egyptians at the end of the quattrocento may be seen on the vault of the 'Sala dei Santi' in the Borgia Apartment of the Vatican Palace, frescoed by Pinturicchio for Pope Alexander VI from 1493 to 1495. Here, the story of Osiris and Isis proclaims the Borgia Pope's descent from the mythical priest-king and founder of Egyptian civilization through the family's heraldic device, the Ox of the Borgia, whose lineage is traced to the cult of the Osirian sacred bull, Apis.[53]

The details of Egyptian myth could have been culled from the sources by any well-informed humanist in Alexander's court. But the genealogical and heraldic exploitation of this material points to the influence of the Dominican friar Giovanni Nanni, known to posterity as Annius of Viterbo (c. 1432–1502).[54] In 1498, inspired perhaps by the success of Ficino's edition of the *Hermetica,* Annius published his own collection of 'rediscovered' texts, the *Antiquitates,* which he attributed to Berosus of Chaldea and other ancient authors, but actually forged himself and supported with his own extensive commentaries.[55] These texts, so Annius claimed, presented the 'true' history of Italy and the foundation of Etruscan civilization by Noah (also known as Janus), who established his capital in Annius' hometown of Viterbo in post-Diluvian times.[56] Prominent among Annius' cast of characters is the Egyptian Osiris, who came to Italy with his son, Hercules Libyus (or Aegyptius) in the sixth century after the Flood to liberate Noah's colonies from a race of evil giants.[57] After ruling in Viterbo for ten years, Osiris returned to Egypt, where he was killed by his jealous brother Typhon. In response, Hercules and his possible mother Isis (Annius isn't sure) struck back at Typhon and launched a second 'Egyptian' liberation of the world that brought Hercules, and eventually Isis, to Italy, where they restored the peaceful civilization instituted by Noah.[58]

The frescoes on the vault of the Sala dei Santi follow this narrative fairly closely, with the most significant departure being the Borgian emphasis on Apis and bulls. The scenes from the lives of the saints on the walls below, especially the large fresco of the *Disputation of Saint Catherine in Alexandria,* serve to unite the mythical foundation of Egypt with the sacred history of the Church, a conception in complete harmony with Annius' central theme: the fundamental unity of Italian, Hebrew, and Egyptian culture.[59] This 'diffusionist' model of human and sacred origins was hardly original in its basic assumptions, rooted as it was in classical and patristic traditions that also served Ficino's more intellectual (and genuinely scholarly) project. Annius' principal source, Diodorus Siculus' 'Universal History', was itself the product of a Hellenistic and early Imperial discourse that sought to establish the basic unity of the world that had been united by Alexander and the Caesars.[60] As Ingrid Rowland has shown, Annius' 'new sacred history' provided a useful and ultimately divine sanction for the ideology of papal kingship, themes that were exploited with particular *bravura* by the Augustinian preacher Egidio da Viterbo during the pontificate of Alexander's successor, Julius II.[61]

If this 'historical' justification was not enough to support the legitimacy of the Borgia and others who sat on the throne of St. Peter (and by extension, Janus and Osiris), Annius was prepared to provide further assistance in the form of genealogies that traced the origins of his patrons to his ancient heroes. 'Fantastic genealogies' of this type were common enough in the courtly culture of the period, as the studies of Roberto Bizzocchi and Marie Tanner have shown.[62] But Annius may be considered unique in providing both the 'original' source texts (the forged *Antiquitates*) and the genealogical constructs that he derived from them. For the Farnese, an important family in Viterbo as well as Rome, Annius composed a family tree that traced their origins directly to Osiris.[63] He probably provided one for the Borgia, whose basic elements can be extrapolated from the genealogy of the rulers of Spain that appears in the *Antiquitates.*[64] Following these criteria, the Borgia, as self-proclaimed cousins of the kings of Aragon, could claim direct descent from Hercules the Egyptian, and thus from his father Osiris.[65] The figure of Hercules atop the shrine of Apis in the Borgia frescoes provides compelling visual support for this thesis, which served to establish the Borgia as legitimate rulers of Hercules' two domains, Italy and Spain.[66]

In addition to his 'editorial' and genealogical enterprises, Annius also labored to support his theories with 'archaeological' evidence in the form of inscriptions, statues, and other finds. Some of these finds were authentic antiques, whereas others were apparently manufactured to Annius' orders.[67] His principle 'Egyptian' discovery, the *Columna Osiriana* (Fig. 73), now in the Museo Civico of Viterbo, would appear to fall somewhere between these two poles.[68] As early as 1492–3, Annius identified this assemblage: a twelfth- or thirteenth-century marble lunette set into a frame with profile heads of quattrocento date that he 'discovered' on the pulpit of the Cathedral of S. Lorenzo in Viterbo, as a monument, carved in the 'sacred letters of the Egyptians,' to commemorate Osiris' victory over the giants.[69] In a startling and unprecedented chapter of the *Antiquitates,* Annius goes beyond the generalities of Alberti and presents a word-for-word pseudo-translation of the tablet's imagery.[70] An excerpt captures its supposedly historical and commemorative character:

> Our ancestors, in order to keep always before our eyes the eternal memory of the antiquity of our city, posted a column or tablet of alabaster on the *rostra* of the former temple of Hercules, now the temple of Saint Lawrence. It is the monument of Osiris' triumph, inscribed with sacred Egyptian letters in the form of birds, animals, heads and trees, about which the authors often write. And Pliny, in his *Natural History* says that these images that you see are Egyptian sacred letters (hieroglyphs). Therefore, on this column there is a space, in the middle of which is the trunk of an oak tree, resembling a compounded scepter, the tops of whose branches form the image of an eye. These images are particular to Osiris, as Xenophon affirms. Both he and Macrobius, in the first book of the *Saturnalia,* confirm this, saying that to express Osiris in the sacred letters they carved a scepter, and they [also] represented him with the image of an eye. And by this sign they showed Osiris. Moreover, they placed on this tree trunk not one but many scepters, because he ruled not only one, but every part of the world, as Diodorus writes. . . . Therefore, these . . . effigies are to be read in this fashion: 'I am Osiris the king, who was called against by the Italians and hastened to fight against the oppressors of the Italian dominion. . . . I am Osiris, who taught the Italians to plow, to sow, to prune, to cultivate the vine, gather grapes, and make wine, and I left behind for them my two nephews, as guardians of the realm from land and sea.'[71]

Annius' 'translation' is a masterpiece of pseudo-scholarship. Proceeding from his initial identification of the oak tree and vines as a 'disguised' representation of the scepter and eye hieroglyphs of Osiris' name as described in Macrobius' *Saturnalia,* he proposes a reading of the signs in sentences directly inspired by Diodorus' account of the hieroglyphic epitaphs of Osiris and Isis in Nysa, which begin with the same declamatory 'I am' (*Ego sum*) formula.[72] Here, as elsewhere, Annius relies on Poggio Bracciolini's Latin translation, which had been printed in 1472, rather than the Greek original.[73] He also draws, less directly, on Diodorus' description of the 'hieroglyphic'

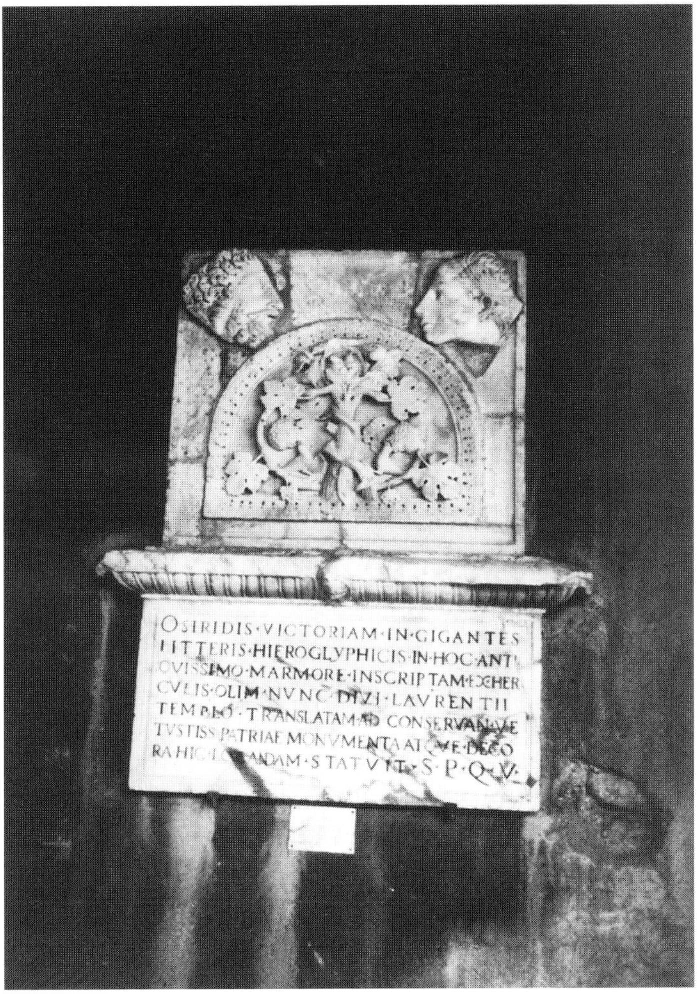

73. The *Columna Osiriana*. Viterbo: Museo Civico. Photo: Author.

columns raised in conquered lands by the Egyptian Pharaoh Sesostris, which Alberti interpreted as ancestors of the triumphal columns of the Romans.[74]

With all this in mind, it is still difficult for a present-day observer to comprehend how this manifestly un-Egyptian object could have been presented to Annius' contemporaries as an 'Egyptian' or hieroglyphic monument. After all, by 1498, the Roman humanists had long since distinguished the obelisks from objects of local, Roman manufacture. Perhaps one explanation for its acceptance, in Viterbo at least, is its presumed manufacture by local artisans in a local material.[75] Because Alberti had promoted the notion that the Romans and other ancient peoples had adopted the hieroglyphs, it was possible for Annius and his contemporaries to conceive of them as a transcultural image-system. It is also possible that Annius' 'discovery' of the *Columna* drew on his familiarity with a second non-Egyptian 'hieroglyphic' ensemble: the collection of antique marble friezes of sacrificial and naval objects that had been installed, in the later Middle Ages, in the choir and pulpits of the Basilica of San Lorenzo fuori le mura in Rome.[76] As is well known, these friezes provided the model for the hieroglyphs in the *Hypnerotomachia Poliphili,* which was published in Venice in 1499, one year after the release of the *Antiquitates.*[77] One does not need to accept the attribution of the *Hypnerotomachia* to the 'Roman' Francesco Colonna of Palestrina to be intrigued by the similarities between these installations in the Roman and Viterbese churches of St. Lawrence.[78] In any event, the Osirian *Columna* was accepted as authentic, in Viterbo at least, for many years, as evidenced by its installation (along with other Annian 'finds') in Viterbo's town hall, the Palazzo dei Priori, where it was provided with a Latin inscription derived from Annius' 'translation.'[79]

Ernst Gombrich has argued that the death of Alexander VI and the election of his successor, Julius II (1503–13), heralded a decline in the fortunes of Egypt in Renaissance Rome, a development motivated in large part by Julius' disdain for anything associated with his predecessor.[80] For Gombrich, Julius' rejection of two Egyptianizing schemes by Bramante – a proposed reorientation of St. Peter's to face the Vatican obelisk and an inscription in rebus-like 'hieroglyphs' for the main portal of the Belvedere – reflected the pope's hostility toward anything that smacked of Egypt, hieroglyphs, and strange theories about either emanating from the general direction of Viterbo.[81] A third incident, not mentioned by Gombrich, would appear to support his thesis. According to the account of Laelius Podager, the discovery, c. 1511–12, of the obelisk originally raised as the *gnomon* of the Augustan sundial in the Campus Martius was greeted with calls for its excavation and restoration. But the pope was 'too distracted by his wars' to be bothered, and the barber who discovered the obelisk 'finally lost his patience and buried this miracle of antiquity all over again.'[82]

But the Egyptological situation in Julius' Rome was more complicated than these incidents suggest. As noted previously, Annius' ideas were received in positive terms, and even developed into a full defense of his policy of papal *imperium,* by Julius' favorite preacher, Egidio da Viterbo.[83] The earliest surviving drawings of obelisks with 'archaeologically correct' hieroglyphic inscriptions date from this period, which suggests, like the account of Podager cited earlier, that interest in these monuments was far from dead in Julian Rome.[84] And there is evidence that Pope Julius himself could be receptive to Egyptianizing themes when they suited his own ends.[85] But however we choose to interpret the attitudes of his predecessor, it is clear that the election of Giovanni de' Medici as Pope Leo X (1513–21) inaugurated a new era of enthusiasm for Egypt and its antiquities in Rome.[86] This Leonine 'Egyptian Revival' can be understood, on one level, as a by-product of the pope's generous patronage of humanist and antiquarian studies.[87] But, as I hope to demonstrate here, Pope Leo's interest in Egypt was marked by a far more systematic and programmatic agenda, in which Rome's Egyptian antiquities come to acquire a much deeper and more specifically papal and Medicean significance.

Leo's interest in Rome's antiquities is exemplified by his appointment of Raphael as director an ambitious project to reconstruct Rome's appearance in antiquity.[88] For this project, Raphael assembled impressive teams of artists and scholars, including Andrea Fulvio, who was the leading Roman topographer of his day and something of an expert on obelisks and hieroglyphs.[89] Several other key figures in Egyptian studies were also associated with Raphael and Pope Leo's circle. These included Pietro Bembo, the proud owner, by the early 1520s, of the *Mensa Isiaca,* an Egyptianizing bronze tablet of Roman date, and the Ferrarese humanist Celio Calcagnini, a sophisticated student of hieroglyphs and Egyptian mythology.[90] But the most notable of these early 'Egyptologists' was Pierio Valeriano (1477–1558), who began his monumental study of the 'sacred letters' of the Egyptians, the *Hieroglyphica,* during Leo's pontificate.[91] Despite his association with these scholars, however, the extent of Leo's personal interest in Egypt remains elusive. In his youth, as the son of Lorenzo *il Magnifico* he had been tutored by such Egyptologically inclined humanists as Ficino, Angelo Poliziano, and Valeriano's uncle, Fra Urbano Bolzanio, who had traveled in Egypt and was considered something of an authority on the hieroglyphs in his adopted home, Venice.[92] His father's collection included at least one Egyptianizing work, the Ptolemaic sardonyx cup (with an elegantly classical Egyptian sphinx) later known as the *Tazza Farnese.*[93] Later, as pope, Leo owned a statue of Isis that provided the model for a golden image carried in the Carnival procession of 1520.[94]

What is clear enough, however, is Leo's willingness to exploit Egyptian imagery in his public and private commissions. Among the ephemeral monuments created for his triumphal *entrata* into Florence in 1515 was a full-scale copy of the Vatican obelisk, erected at the north end of the Ponte S. Trinita.[95] In Rome, Leo was able to work with the 'real thing', as it were, and it is at this point that the restoration of Rome's Egyptian antiquities takes on the appearance of a deliberate program.[96] Toward the end of 1517, for example, Leo ordered the transfer of the colossal statues of the Tigris and the Nile from the Monte Cavallo to the portico of the Palazzo dei Conservatori on the Campidoglio.[97] Leo may also have been responsible for installing the aforementioned sphinxes with hieroglyphic inscriptions of the Neferites I and Achoris on the steps of the Senator's palace in the same piazza.[98] They were recorded here for the first time in Andrea Fulvio's *Antiquaria Urbis,* published in 1513 (the first year of Leo's pontificate).[99] Their prior history is unknown, but they may have been visible above ground (here or at another location), where they could have supplied the model for the Cosmati sphinxes of the thirteenth century.

In any event, their appearance on the Capitol coincides with the renovations undertaken for the ceremonies of September 1513 that bestowed Roman citizenship on the pope's brother Giuliano de' Medici and his nephew Lorenzo.[100] This was not the end of their travels. In about 1547 they were moved to separate locations in the piazza and the conservator's palace, and in the early seventeenth century, went to the Villa Borghese (they are now in the Louvre, Paris).[101] During their time on the Campidoglio, however, they achieved the status of prominent 'civic' antiquities in their own right.[102] They also attracted the attention of artists like Guilio Romano (as noted earlier), Francisco de Hollanda, and the draftsman of the *Codex Ursinianus* (c. 1564, Fig. 74), whose renditions testify to the contemporary fascination with their hieroglyphic inscriptions.[103]

While Leo's connection with the sphinxes is admittedly circumstantial, he was certainly associated with the restoration of the Egyptian lions in the Piazza della Rotunda.[104] Sometime around 1515, the lions were set up on cylindrical bases on either side of a large porphyry basin, which had also been in the piazza for centuries.[105] At about the same time, the lions at the Lateran were similarly restored and set up on columns in front of the statue of Marcus Aurelius.[106] The similarity of the installation marks it as a pendant to the Pantheon restorations.

Taken as a whole, these restorations suggest a host of possible associations. Most obviously, the Pantheon and Lateran statues are literally 'leonine'; that is, they physically represent the name of their papal restorer. This is hardly unexpected. From the time of his election, the king of beasts became a ubiquitous symbol of Leo's papacy. Poets invoked the Florentine *Marzocco* and the Lion of Juda, and lions of every stripe appeared on the pope's coins, medals, tapestries, frescoes – everywhere.[107] Rulership, vigilance, justice, clemency, Rome, *imperium,* and Christ himself were just some of the host of meanings and concepts embodied by the 'hieroglyph' of the lion.[108] And there were myriad associations with Hercules, exploited by Egidio da Viterbo when he praised the pope as a 'second Hercules' and noted that the *signum leonis* had been carried by this Tuscan hero in the form of the lion skin.[109] Thus it seems that, like Alexander and Julius before, Leo could be receptive to Annian associations when they served his public and political purposes. As a Tuscan and a Roman (through his mother, Clarice Orsini), Leo's rise to the throne of Peter pontificate was hailed as fulfilling the Etruscan-Roman destiny. The painted decorations of the Capitoline theater of 1513 presented the most elaborate public expression of this theme, with scenes of the Etruscan Janus greeting Saturn on his arrival in Latium, and others that showed the ancient Etruscans instructing the first Romans in the liberal and sacred arts.[110]

At the Pantheon, the imperial and Roman associations were especially strong, thanks to the monument's association with Agrippa, and by extension, Augustus, the Roman prototype with whom Leo was most often compared. Following the

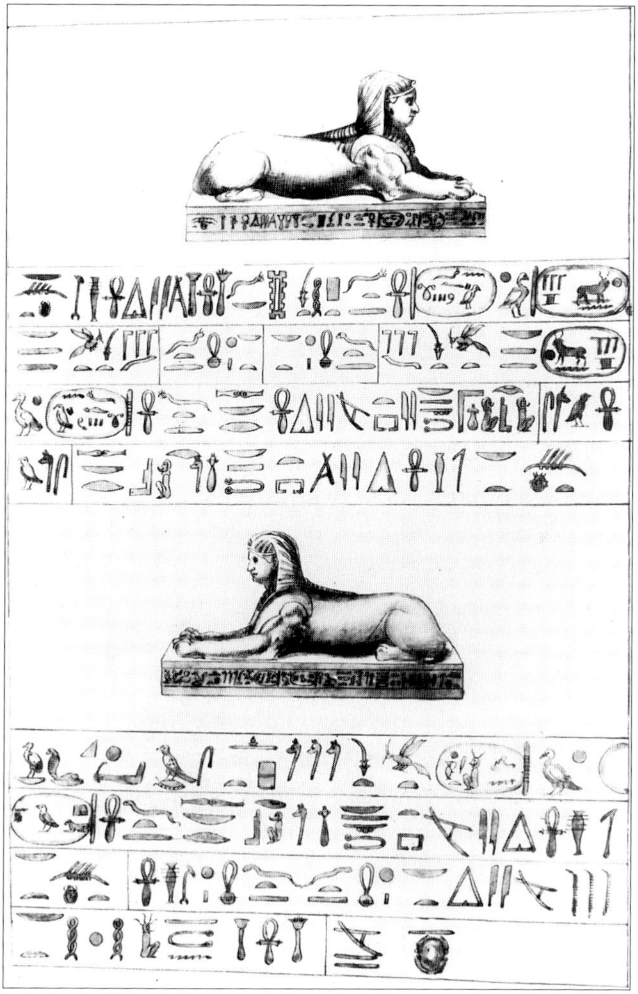

74. *Campidoglio Sphinxes,* c. 1564. Biblioteca Apostolica Vaticana, Vat. lat. 3439, fol. 1v. Photo: Biblioteca Apostolica Vaticana.

war-ravaged pontificates of Alexander VI 'Maximus' and Julius II (the 'second Julius Caesar'), the election of Leo, the 'new Augustus', was hailed as a *Rex pacificus,* whose pontificate would inaugurate a new age of peace.[111] Even after his death, Leo's pontificate was praised in these terms as a 'second golden age.'[112] To an extent, Leo inherited this reputation from his father, Lorenzo *il Magnifico* likewise considered a master of 'peaceful rule' and enlightened patron of the arts.[113] In Florence, Lorenzo and the Medici had taken to promoting associations with Augustus in both art and letters.[114] And antique busts of Agrippa and Augustus, gifts from Pope Sixtus IV to Lorenzo himself, featured prominently in the decoration of the Medici palace in Florence.[115]

Awareness of the Egyptian origins of these monuments was expanding throughout this period, thanks to the efforts of Leo's court archaeologists. In 1527, Andrea Fulvio explained the Pharaonic sphinx attributes of the Roman Nile statues as symbols of Egypt.[116] At the same time, he identified the Pantheon lions as Egyptian by their hieroglyphic inscriptions and reported the then-current opinion that the lions and the basin had been taken from the nearby baths of Agrippa.[117] An alternate theory identified the *vaso* as the sarcophagus of Agrippa himself and held that it had been installed, with the lions, on the pediment of the Pantheon as part of his funerary monument.[118] Given these associations, it is not implausible that Leo sought to associate himself in this way with Agrippa and Augustus, founders of the empire through their victory over Antony and Cleopatra and the conquest of Egypt.[119] At the end of the century, an even greater exploiter of the Egyptian legacy, Sixtus V, renewed the Imperial and sacred-historical aura of Leo's Egyptian lions when he transferred the pair from the Pantheon to his new *Fountain of Moses,* where they were transformed into waterspouts, water rushing forth from their dark stone mouths.[120] In the same vein, Sixtus ordered the installation of Capitoline lions as waterspouts at the foot of the Capitoline *cordonata.*[121]

That the sphinx and the Egyptian lion were adopted by Leo as Egyptianizing variations on his leonine emblem is demonstrated by their proliferation in the decorations that the pope and his nephew, Giulio de' Medici, commissioned for the Vatican Palace, the Villa Madama, and other locations.[122] In all of these instances, these creatures harmonize nicely with Valeriano's explanation of the sphinx as a symbol of human intelligence and dominion over the animals of the world.[123]

A final project would appear to present the climax and synthesis of all these themes. In the summer of 1519, excavators working on the restoration of the Via Leonina (the present Via Ripetta) under the supervision of Raphael and Antonio da Sangallo the Younger, discovered one of the twin obelisks from the Mausoleum of Augustus.[124] That the mausoleum had been decorated with these monuments was known from the sources, and fragments of one of them had been identified in the 1490s and then forgotten.[125] But now, and in stark contrast to Julius' neglect of the Campus Martius obelisk a few years earlier, the broken fragments of the obelisk, along with its base, were quickly extracted and moved into the street near the church of San Rocco, and plans for its restoration were almost immediately discussed.[126] According to the Venetian diarist Marino Sanuto, Raphael proposed to raise it in front of St. Peter's as a kind of surrogate for the Vaticanus.[127]

A second proposal envisioned re-erecting the obelisk in the nearby Piazza del Popolo. A drawing by Antonio da Sangallo the Younger (Fig. 75) reveals one of the more fantastic proposals for its erection in this location.[128] We see the obelisk, supported on its ancient bases by a set of tortoise-shaped astragals, with the whole thing held aloft on a stepped foundation with four elephants, topped by a group of

Egyptianizing sphinxes with Pharaonic headdresses that support the block of the base.

With this improbable monument, Leo's architect (Sangallo, Raphael, or both) seems to have exceeded even the most ambitious schemes of Nicholas V. But it is notable, and perhaps indicative of the ensuing shifts in taste from the mid-quattrocento, that the imagery of this ensemble is far more secular, Imperial, and Egyptianizing than Nicholas's Christianizing scheme. As for specific elements, the tortoise astragals provide a deliberate echo of the bronze ornaments employed by Leo's father Lorenzo on the funerary monument of *his* father and uncle, Piero and Giovanni de' Medici, in S. Lorenzo, Florence. There is at least the possibility of an Augustan reference here as well, because it has been argued that the S. Lorenzo turtles make reference to the Medici's adoption of the Augustan motto *Festina Lente* ('Make Haste Slowly'), a popular maxim that also found expression in the hieroglyphs of the *Hypnerotomachia.*[129] If this thesis is correct, the application of these creatures to a reused ornament from the emperor's mausoleum would seem more than appropriate.

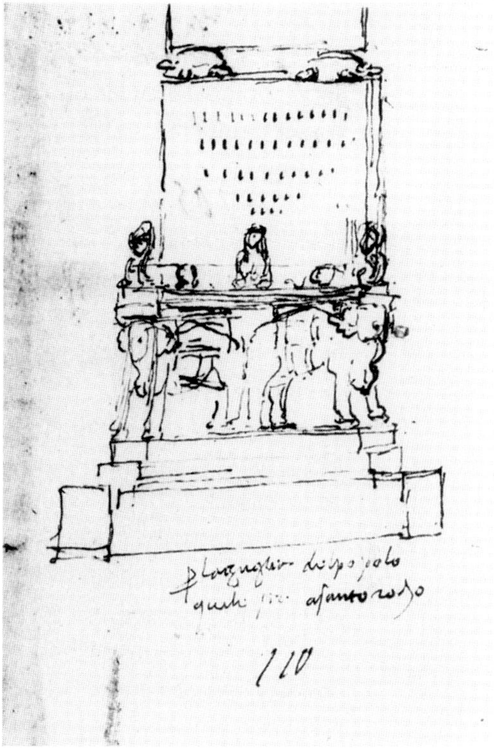

75. Antonio da Sangallo the Younger. *Project for the Augustan/San Rocco Obelisk in Piazza del Popolo* c. 1519. Florence, Uffizi, Gabinetto Disegni e Stampe (UA 1232 r). Photo: Use authorized by The Italian Ministery of Cultural Heritage and Activities.

Both the elephants and the sphinxes suggest the influence of the obelisk-monuments of *Hypnerotomachia,* but the pachyderm also alludes to the memory of Leo's late elephant, Hanno, whose brief but brilliant career established him as a kind of 'living antiquity' and a recurring emblem of the Medici papacy.[130] The pope's elephants had their Augustan overtones as well; they recalled Augustus' dedication of a group of four obsidian elephants to the Temple of Concord.[131] Leo's humanist courtiers would have recognized these creatures as appropriate symbols of the *Pax Augustana* (and *Leonina*) because they were traditionally explained as strong and fearless but inherently peace-loving animals.[132] Finally, the sphinxes, as emblems of the Medici papacy and symbols, as Plutarch and Pico della Mirandola had noted, of the mysterious doctrines of the Egyptians, provided a fitting ornament for the restored memorial of the Roman conqueror of Egypt and the Tuscan pope whose sacred kingship drew from the traditions of Janus, Osiris, Augustus, and Peter.[133] To underline this point, we need only consider an early plan for the tombs of Leo and Clement VII in the choir of the Dominican church of S. Maria sopra Minerva, where a pair of colossal antique basins (of Egyptian granite) were to be supported, like the Popolo obelisk, on the backs of a set of Egyptianizing sphinxes.[134] The tombs would have made an appropriate ornament for this church the apse of which rose over the remains of the Iseum Campense and where the remains of Annius of Viterbo had been laid to rest in 1503.[135]

Unfortunately, as it turned out, both the original tomb project and the Popolo obelisk proposal were eventually abandoned, and we can only speculate, in the latter case, as to the impression this spectacular ensemble might have made on pilgrims entering Rome from this heavily trafficked gate. The pieces of the obelisk remained in the street, an obstacle to all, until they were eventually repaired and the obelisk re-erected at S. Maria Maggiore by Sixtus V in 1587.[136]

So what of the sphinx in the city? How much, in the end, can we realistically infer from Leo X's peculiar and only partly realized program of Egyptianizing restorations and imagery? The archaeological acuity of Leo's restorations, not to mention his evident sensitivity to the plurality of historical and ideological associations these monuments could bear, mark him as a worthy pupil of his tutors Poliziano, Urbano, and Ficino. He surely found his ideal agent in the person of Raphael, who seamlessly fused the talents of courtier, artist, and interpretive archaeologist.[137] Leo's disposition of Egyptian antiquities in Rome's public spaces might signify little more than his identification with Augustus and his claim to inherit the universal dominion of the Roman Emperors. The range, scale, and subtlety of his Egyptianizing projects, however, prompts us to ponder the possibility of a more focused and deliberate attempt to appropriate the primordial sovereignty of the Egyptian god-kings. So far as we know, Leo made no Borgia-like claims to descend from Osiris and his progeny, although as a Tuscan he could have considered himself a qualified successor to Janus, Hercules, and the other heroes of the Annian universe.[138] But his well-known designation as a Medici-*medicus* is rich in associations with the thaumaturgic power of healing associated with an ancient priesthood: Mosaic, Etruscan, and Christological, surely, but also quite logically Egyptian, through the tradition that linked all of these arts and practitioners to the *prisca theologia* and sages such as Hermes Trismegistus.[139] The *Metamorphoses* of Apuleius, widely read and admired in cinquecento Rome, provided an evocative glimpse of the mystical practice of the Egyptian cults in the Imperial city.[140] Filippo Beroaldo had published his learned commentary on the text in 1500, and it was in Leo's Rome that Agnolo Firenzuola commenced work on his popular vernacular adaptation of the *Metamorphoses, L'Asino d'oro* (completed 1525).[141] In the imagery of the Leonine obelisk, the decorations of the Vatican *Logge,* and the pages of Valeriano's *Hieroglyphica,* Egypt seems to resonate as much for its mysterious and ultimately untranslatable connection to the origins of civilization itself as it does to the more evident (and expected) claims of imperial and pharaonic inheritance. This untranslatability lends an ambiguity to the Leonine project that may be frustrating to its present-day interpreters but that is singularly appropriate to Leo's urban image of the sphinx, the enigmatic guardian of mysteries and poser of riddles.

NOTES

1. For Adriani, see G. Miccoli, 'Adriani, Giovanni Battista,' *Dizionario biografico degli Italiani*, vol. I (1960), 309 (Rome: Instituto della Enciclopedia Italiana).

2. Giovanni Battista Adriani, 'Lettera di M. Giovambatista di M. Marcello Adriani a M. Giorgio Vasari nella quale brevemente si racconta i nomi e l'opere de' più eccellenti artefici in pittura, in bronzo ed in marmo . . . ', in Giorgio Vasari, *Le vite de' più eccellenti pittori, scultori ed architettori* (1568), in *Le opere di Giorgio Vasari*, 9 vols., ed. Gaetano Milanesi (Florence: Sansoni, 1906, 2nd ed., 1981), vol. I, 19: 'per quanto scrive Erodoto, antichissimo istorico, il quale cercò molto paese e molte cose vide, e molte ne udì, e molte ne lesse; gli Egizj essere stati antichissimi di chi si abbi memoria, e della religione, qualunche fusse la loro, solenni osservatori; i quali li loro Idii sotto varie figure di nuovi e diversi animali adoravano, e quelli in oro, in argento, ed in altro metallo, ed in pietre preziose, e quasi in ogni materia, che forma ricever potesse, rassembravano; delle quali imagini alcune insino alli nostri giorni si sono conservate, massimamente essendo stati, come ancora se ne vede segnali manifesti, quei popoli potentissimi e copiosi di uomini, ed i loro re ricchissimi ed oltre a modo desiderosi di prolungare la memoria loro per secoli infiniti; ed oltre a questo di meraviglioso ingengo e d'industria singolare e scienza profonda, così nelle divine cose nelle umane. . . . Appresso costoro mi avviso io che fosse in gran pregio l'arte del ben disegnare e del colorire e dello scolpire e del ritrarre in qualunche maniera, ed ogni maniera di forme; perciocchè dell'architettura non si debbe dubitare che essi non fussero gran maestri, vedendosi di loro altre ancora le piramidi ed altri edificij stupendi, che durano e che dureranno, come io mi penso, secoli infiniti.'

3. For Egyptian revivals in Western art, see Nikolaus Pevsner and S. Lang, 'The Egyptian Revival,' in *Studies in Art, Architecture, and Design*, vol. I, ed. Nikolaus Pevsner (New York: Walker, 1968), 212–35, 245–8; James Stevens Curl, *The Egyptian Revival* (London: Allen and Unwin, 1982), revised as *Egyptomania; The Egyptian Revival-A Recurring Theme in the History of Taste* (Manchester and New York: Manchester University Press, 1994); Rudolf Wittkower, *Selected Lectures of Rudolf Wittkower*, ed. D. M. Reynolds (Cambridge and New York: Cambridge University Press, 1989), 36–126; Dirk Syndram, *Ägypten-Faszinationen: Untersuchungen zum Ägyptenbild in europäischen Klassizismus bis 1800* (Frankfurt am Main: Lang, 1990); *Egyptomania: Egypt in Western Art 1730–1930*, ed. Jean-Marcel Humbert, Michael Pantazzi, and Christiane Ziegler (Exh. cat., Paris: Réunion des Musées Nationaux, 1994).

4. For knowledge of the pyramids and other Egyptian monuments in the Renaissance, see Karl Dannenfeldt, 'Egypt and Egyptian Antiquities in the Renaissance,' *Studies in the Renaissance* 6 (1959): 7–27; Leslie Greener, *The Discovery of Egypt* (New York: Viking, 1966), 34–57; Michael Greenhalgh, 'The Monument in the *Hypnerotomachia* and the Pyramids of Egypt,' *Nouvelles de l'estampe* 14 (1974): 13–16; Jeanine Guérin-Dalle Mese, *Égypte: La mémoire et le rêve. Itinéraires d'un voyage, 1320–1601* (Florence: Olschki, 1991); Deborah Howard, *Venice and the East: The Impact of the Islamic World on Venetian Architecture 1100–1500* (New Haven and London: Yale University Press, 2000), 44–6.

5. See Anne Roullet, *The Egyptian and Egyptianizing Monuments of Imperial Rome* (Leiden: Brill, 1972); O. Lollio Barberi, G. Parola, and M. P. Toti, *Le antichità egiziane di Roma imperiale* (Rome: Libreria dello Stato, 1995).

6. For classical and Jewish-Biblical attitudes toward Egypt, see Siegfried Morenz, *Die Bewegung Europas mit Ägypten, mit einem Beitrag von Martin Kaiser über Herodots Begegnung mit Ägypten* (Zürich and Stuttgart: Artemis, 1969); Jan Assmann, *Moses the Egyptian: Mnemohistory and the Construction of Egypt* (Cambridge and London: Harvard University Press, 1997).

7. See James R. Harris, ed. *The Legacy of Egypt,* 2nd ed. (Oxford: Clarendon Press, 1971).

8. For a recent discussion of the 'revival of antiquity' in relation to ancient art, see Leonard Barkan, *Unearthing the Past: Archaeology and Aesthetics in the Making of Renaissance Culture* (New Haven and London: Yale University Press, 1999).

9. For the obelisks, see Erik Iversen, *Obelisks in Exile,* 2 vols. (Copenhagen: Gad, 1968), esp. vol. 1; Cesare D'Onofrio, *Gli obeleschi di Roma: storia e urbanistica di una città dall' età antica al XX secolo,* 3rd. ed. (Rome: Cassa di Risparmio, 1992); Giovanni Cipriani, *Gli obelischi Egizi: Politica e Cultura nella Roma Barocca* (Florence: Olschki, 1993); and Géza Alföldy, *Der Obelisk auf dem Petersplatz in Rom. Ein historisches Monument der Antike* (Heidelberg: Winter, 1990).

10. For a discussion of this interpretation, see Iversen, *Obelisks in Exile,* vol. I, 20–4.

11. For the Capo di Bove obelisk, now in the Piazza Navona, see Iversen, *Obelisks in Exile,* vol. I, 76–92; D'Onofrio, *Obelischi,* 288–301; and Rudolf Preimesberger, 'Obeliscus Pamphilius: Beiträge zu Vorgeschichte und Ikonographie des Vierströmebrunnes auf Piazza Navona,' *Münchner Jahrbuch der Bildenden Kunst,* 25 (1974): 77–162.

12. For this obelisk, now in the Piazza dell Rotunda, see Iversen, *Obelisks in Exile,* vol. I, 101–7; D'Onofrio, *Obelischi,* 29–60. For the fragments, see Katya Lembke, 'Alcune osservazioni sull'obelisco di Urbino,' *Xenia Antiqua* I (1992): 13–20,

13. For the Iseum and the monuments associated with it, see Serena Ensoli Vittozi, *Musei Capitolini: La Collezione Egizia* (Rome, 1990), 30–8 (cat. no. 2–5), 42 (cat. no. 8), 52–3 (cat. no. 11), 59–70; and Katja Lembke, *Das Iseum Campense in Rom: Studie über den Isiskult unter Domitian* (Heidelberg: Winter, 1994).

14. First noted by Magister Gregorius, *De Mirabilibus,* 21; see Roberto Valentini and Giuseppe Zucchetti, *Codice Topografico della Città di Roma,* 4 vols. (Rome: Tipografia del Senato, 1940–53), vol. III, 158–9. For the lions, see Giuseppe Botti and Pietro Romanelli, *Le Sculture del Museo Gregoriano Egizio* (Vatican City: Tipografia poliglotta vaticana, 1951), 14–18 (no. 26–7); Roullet, *Egyptian Monuments,* 131–2 (cat. no. 273–4); and Lembke, *Iseum Campense,* 223–4 (cat. no. 13–14).

15. See Botti and Romanelli, *Sculture,* 114–15 (cat. no. 181); Roullet, *Egyptian Monuments,* 125 (cat. no. 245); and Lembke, *Iseum Campense,* 238 (cat. no. 36).

16. See Roullet, *Egyptian Monuments,* 130–1 (cat. no. 271–2); A. Giuliano, 'La statue equestre di Marco Aurelio prima del suo trasferimento in Campidoglio,' *Xenia* 7 (1984): 67–76; and Lucilla de Lachenal, 'Il monumento nel Medioevo fino al suo trasferimento in Campidoglio,' in *Marco Aurelio: Storia di un monumento e del suo restauro,* ed. A. M. Vaccaro and Anna Mura Sommella (Milan: Silvana, 1989), 129–55.

17. For the symbolic and political associations of Roman antiquities in the Middle Ages, see Richard Krautheimer, *Rome: Profile of a City, 312–1308* (Princeton: Princeton University Press, 1980), 187–202; and Norberto Gramaccini, *Mirabilia: Da Nachleben antiker Statuen vor der Renaissance* (Mainz: von Zabern, 1996).

18. Gramaccini, *Mirabilia,* 145–147, 169–81; Philip Jacks, *The Antiquarian and the Myth of Antiquity: The Origins of Rome in Renaissance Thought* (Cambridge and New York: Cambridge University Press, 1993), 54–67.

19. See K. Noehles, 'Die Kunst des Cosmaten und die Idee der Renovatio Romae,' *Festschrift Werner Hager zum 65 Geburstag* (Recklinghausen: Bongers, 1966), 7–37; Roullet, *Egyptian Monuments,*

7–9; P. Montorsi, 'Su alcuni leoni di Vasalletto che derivano da un modello egiziano,' in *Roma anno 1300: Atti della IV Settimana di studi di storia dell'arte medievale dell'Università di Roma 'La Sapienza,' 19–24 maggio 1980,* ed. Angiola Maria Romanini (Rome: L'Erma di Bretschneider, 1983), 655–74, and Peter C. Claussen, *Magistri doctissimi Romani: Die römischen Marmorkünstler des Mittelalters* (Stuttgart: Franz Steiner Verlag, 1987), 112–15, 122–5.

20. See Roullet, *Egyptian Monuments,* 7–8; Ib Lydholm, 'The Cosmati and the Cathedral at Anagni,' *Analecta Romana Instituti Danici* 10 (1982): 7–22; Claussen, *Magistri Doctissimi,* 121–3, 126–32; Wittkower, *Selected Lectures,* 43–6, figs. 3–9.

21. Karl Giehlow, 'Die Hieroglyphenkunde des Humanismus in der Allegorie der Renaissance,' *Jahrbuch der Kunsthistorisches Sammlungen des Allerhöchsten Kaiserhauses* 32 (1915): 1–229, esp. 12–37. For the discovery of Ammianus, see R. Cappelletto, 'Niccolò Niccoli e il codice di Ammiano Vat. lat. 1873,' *Bollettino del comitato per la preparazione dell'edizione nazionale del classici greci e latini,* n.s. 26 (1976): 57–84.

22. Pliny the Elder, *Natural History,* XXXVI. 14.66–74.

23. Ammianus, XII. 16. 19–20 and XVII. 4.1–23. Niccoli knew Horapollo from the manuscript obtained by Christoforo Buondelmonti in 1419 and brought to Florence c. 1422. It is now in the Biblioteca Laurenziana, Ms. 69. 27. See Giehlow, 'Hieroglyphenkunde,' 12–18. For a translation of Horapollo's text, see George Boas, trans., *The Hieroglyphics of Horapollo* (New York: Pantheon, 1950, reprinted with a forward by Anthony Grafton, Princeton: Princeton University Press, 1993). For editions and translations, see Sandra Sider, 'Horapollo,' in *Catalogus translationum et Commentariorum: Medieval and Renaissance Latin Translations and Commentaries,* vol. VI (Washington, D.C.: Catholic University of America Press, 1986), 15–29, and vol. VII (1992), 325 (Addenda et corrigenda). For the presumed author, see J. Maspero, 'Horapollon et la fin du paganisme égyptien,' *Bulletin de l' Institut Française d'Archéologie Orientale* 11 (1914): 164–95; and Garth Fowden, 'The Pagan Holy Man in Late Antique Society,' *Journal of Hellenic Studies* 102 (1982): 33–59, esp. 46–8.

24. See Giehlow, *Hieroglyphenkunde;* Ludwig Volkmann, *Bilderschriften der Renaissance* (Leipzig: Teubner, 1923); Erik Iversen, *The Myth of Egypt and Its Hieroglyphs in European Tradition* (Copenhagen: Gad, 1961, reprint Princeton: Princeton University Press, 1993); Liselotte Dieckmann, *Hieroglyphics: The History of a Literary Symbol* (St. Louis, Mo.: Washington University Press, 1970); Maurice Pope, *The Story of Archaeological Decipherment* (New York: Scribner, 1975, rev. ed., 1999), 11–42; Rudolf Wittkower, 'Hieroglyphic Studies in the Early Renaissance,' in Wittkower, *Allegory and the Migration of Symbols* (London: Thames and Hudson, 1977), 114–28; Don Cameron Allen, *Mysteriously Meant: The Rediscovery of Pagan Symbolism and Allegorical Interpretation in the Renaissance* (Baltimore and London: The Johns Hopkins University Press, 1979); and Charles Dempsey, 'Renaissance Hieroglyphic Studies and Gentile Bellini's "Saint Mark Preaching in Alexandria",' in *Hermeticism and the Renaissance. Intellectual History and the Occult in Early Modern Europe,* ed. I. Merkel and A. G. Debus (Washington, D.C.: The Folger Shakespeare Library, 1988), 342–65.

25. Text in *Visitiamo Roma nel Quattrocento: La città degli Umanisti,* ed. Cesare D'Onofrio (Rome: Romano società editrice, 1989), 81–2: 'Quid referam obeliscos, quos magno cum labore et sumptu ex Aegypto advectos Plinius meminit? Unum tantum urbs retinet, qui est in Vaticano a C. Caesare Caligula positus Divo Augusto, et Divo Tiberio sacer. Vidi alterum paulo minorem variis animalium, aviumque figuris, quibus prisci Aegyptii pro litteris utebantur, iacentem in hyppodromo, via Appia, quator frustis confractum. Sunt et aliorum particulae quaedam erectae, altera in Capitolio, altera in regione quae hodie Pinea appellatur, reliquis non solum contritis, sed omni memoria delitis.' For Poggio, see Roberto Weiss, *The Renaissance Discovery of Classical Antiquity* (Oxford: Blackwell, 1969, 2nd. ed., 1988), 63–6.

26. Biondo, *Roma instaurata,* XLI–XLVIII, LXI–LXV; in D'Onofrio, *Visitiamo Roma nel Quattrocento,* 121–35, esp. 134–5, citing Tacitus, *Annals,* XI. 15.

27. Biondo, *Roma instaurata,* LXV; in D'Onofrio, *Visitiamo Roma nel quattrocento,* 134–5 (citing Tacitus, *Annals,* XI. 15).

28. Thus Weiss's remark, in *The Renaissance Discovery of Classical Antiquity* (1988), 156, that, 'in the field of epigraphy Egyptian hieroglyphs could scarcely have aroused less interest.'

29. Cyriacus of Ancona, *Kyriaci Anconitani itinerarium nunc primum ex ms. cod. in lucem erutum ex bibl. illus. clarissimique Baronis Philippi Stosch,* ed. Laurentius Mehus (Florence, 1742, reprint Bologna, 1969), 51. For Cyriacus' Egyptian trip, see C. C. Van Essen, 'Cyriaque d'Ancona en Égypte,' *Mededelingen der Koninkijke Nederlandse Akademie van Wetenschappen, Afdelins Letterkunde,* Niewe Reeks, Deel 21, n. 21 (1958): 293–306; and Phyllis W. Lehmann, *Cyriacus of Ancona's Egyptian Visit and its Reflections in Gentile Bellini and Hieronymus Bosch* (Locust Valley, N.Y.: J. J. Augustin, 1977). In Francesco Scalamonti's biography of Cyriacus, the hieroglyphs on the obelisk at Constantinople are called 'Phoenician letters,' see Francesco Scalamonti, *Vita viri clarissimi et famosissimi Kyriaci Anconitani,* ed. Charles Mitchell and Edward W. Bodnar, Society of Jesus (Philadelphia: American Philosophical Society, 1996), 14, 38–40, 111–12 (38–42).

30. For Niccoli's death in February 1437, see Giuseppe Zippel, *Niccolò Niccoli* (Florence: Bocca, 1890), 64, n. 1.

31. I am indebted to the brilliant scholarship of Giancarla Periti, who brought these transcriptions to my attention, and I am presently working with her on a more detailed study of the Ferrarini hieroglyphs. For background, see Claudio Franzoni, 'Gli studi antiquari di Michele Fabrizio Ferrarini,' in *Il 'Portico dei Marmi': Le Prime Collezioni a Reggio Emilia e la Nascita del Museo Civico,* exh. cat. (Reggio Emilia: Commune di Reggio Emilia, 1999), 25–37.

32. See Giehlow, 'Hieroglyphenkunde,' 161–2; Van Essen, 'Cyriaque d'Ancona en Égypte,' 302–3.

33. Michele Fabrizio Ferrarini, in Paris, Bibliotèque Nationale, Ms. Par. Lat. 6128, fol. CXXXv–CXXXIr.

34. M. Ferrarini, *Antiquarium sive Divae Antiquitatis Sacrarium,* Reggio Emilia, Biblioteca A. Panizzi, Ms. C 398, fol. XXVv. For more on this manuscript, see C. Franzoni, 'La sorte del codice reggiano C 398 di Michele Fabrizio Ferrarini,' in *Il 'Portico dei Marmi',* 39–42; Claudio Franzoni, Alessandra Sarchi, 'Entre Peinture, Archéologie et Muséographie: *l'Antiquarium* de Michele Fabrizio Ferrarini,' *Revue de l'Art* 125.3 (1999): 20–31.

35. For the Palazzo del Te hieroglyphs, see Bertrand Jaeger, 'L'Egitto antico alla corte dei Gonzaga: La Loggia delle Muse al Palazzo Te ed altre testimonianze,' in *L'Egitto fuori dell'Egitto, Dalla riscoperta all'Egittologia,* ed. C. Morigi Govi, S. Curto, and S. Pernigotti, (Bologna, 1991), 233–53; and B. Jaeger, 'La Loggia delle Muse nel Palazzo Te e la reviviscenza dell'Egitto Antico nel Rinascimento,' in *Mantova e l'Antico Egitto da Giulio Romano a Giuseppe Acerbi* (Florence: Olschki, 1994), 21–39.

36. The date of 1452 refers to Alberti's reported presentation of the book to Nicholas V. See Cecil Grayson, 'The Composition of L. B. Alberti's "Decem libri *de re aedificatoria*",' *Münchner Jahrbuch der Bildenden Kunst* 11 (1960): 152–61, Cecil Grayson argues that the book was completed c. 1452, when a copy or version was reportedly presented to Pope Nicholas V. But recent opinion tends to see the book as a work in progress until Alberti's death in 1472. See John Onians, *Bearers of Meaning: The Classical Orders in Antiquity, the Middle Ages, and the Renaissance* (Cambridge, 1988), 147; Robert Tavernor, *On Alberti and the Art of Building* (New Haven and London: Yale University Press 1998), 15; and Anthony Grafton,

Leon Battista Alberti: Master Builder of the Italian Renaissance (New York: Hill and Wang, 2000), 266–9.

37. Alberti, *De re aedificatoria,* VIII, 4; translation from J. Rykwert, N. Leach, and R. Tavernor, ed., Leon Battista Alberti, *On the Art of Building in Ten Books* (Cambridge: MIT Press, 1988), 256–7; Latin text in Leon Battista Alberti, *L'Architettura (De re aedificatoria),* ed. and trans. Giovanni Orlandi, 2 vols. (Milan: Edizionni il Polifilo, 1966), vol. II, 697–9.

38. For Alberti and the hieroglyphs, see Giehlow, 29–33; Iversen, *Myth of Egypt,* 65–6; Wittkower, 'Hieroglyphic Studies,' 117–20; Claudio Finzi, 'Leon Battista Alberti: Geroglifiche e gloria,' in *L'Egitto fuori dell'Egitto: Dalla riscoperta all'Egittologia,* ed. C. M. Govi, S. Curto, and S. Pernigotti (Bologna: CLUEB, 1991), 205–8.

39. For the tradition of 'concealed wisdom', see the classic study by E. H. Gombrich, 'Icones Symbolicae: Philosophies of Symbolism and Their Bearing on Art,' in *Symbolic Images: Studies in the Art of the Renaissance II* (New York and London: Phaidon, 1972, 2nd ed., 1978), 123–95.

40. L. B. Alberti, *De Pictura* II, 27; in Leon Battista Alberti, *'On Painting' and 'On Sculpture': The Latin Texts of 'De Pictura and De Statua',* ed. Cecil Grayson (London and New York: Phaidon, 1972), 62–3.

41. For the hieroglyphs in the post-Reformation 'defense' of images, see Gianfranco Cantelli, 'Introduzione', in Michele Mercati, *Gli obelischi di Roma,* ed. G. Cantelli (Bologna: Cappelli, 1981), 9–32.

42. Hermes Trismegistus, *Asclepius,* III, 24; translation adapted from *Hermetica: The Greek 'Corpus Hermeticum' and the Latin 'Asclepius' in a New English translation,* ed. Brian A. Copenhaver (Cambridge and London: Cambridge University Press, 1992), 81; and *Hermetica: The Ancient Greek and Latin Writings Which Contain Religious or Philosophic Teachings Ascribed to Hermes Trismegistus,* 4 vols., ed. Walter Scott (London, 1924–36), I, 343. For Alberti's thinking on commorative monuments, see Jonathan B. Reiss, 'The Civic View of Sculpture in Alberti's "De Re Aedificatoria",' *Renaissance Quarterly* 32 (1979): 1–17.

43. For these developments see Giehlow, 'Hieroglyphenkunde,' 138–59; Volkmann, *Bilderschriften der Renaissance;* Mario Praz, *Studies in Seventeenth-Century Imagery,* 2nd. ed. (Rome: Edizioni di storia e letteratura, 1964); and Daniel Russell, 'Emblems and Hieroglyphics: Some Observations on the Beginnings and Nature of Emblematic Forms,' *Emblematica* 1 (1986): 227–39.

44. See Giehlow, 'Hieroglyphenkunde,' 35–37; Renée Watkins, 'L. B. Alberti's Emblem, the Winged Eye, and His Name, Leo,' *Mitteilungen des Kunsthistorischen Instituts in Florenz,* 9 (1960): 256–8; Laurie Schneider, 'Leon Battista Alberti: Some Biographical Implications of the Winged Eye,' *Art Bulletin* 72 (1990): 261–70; Christine Smith in *The Renaissance from Brunelleschi to Michelangelo: The Representation of Architecture,* ed. Henry A. Millon and Vittorio Magnago Lampugnani (Milan: Bompiani, 1994), 453–5 (cat. no. 40–2); Luke Syson and Giancarlo Gentilini, in *Leon Battista Alberti,* ed. Joseph Rykwert and Anne Engel (Milan: Electa, 1994); 474–5 (cat. no. 72–3); Tavernor, *On Alberti,* 31–6; and Grafton, *Leon Battista Alberti,* 105–7.

45. On this point, see Brian Curran and Anthony Grafton, 'A Fifteenth-Century Site Report on the Vatican Obelisk,' *Journal of the Warburg and Courtauld Institutes* 58 (1995): 234–48.

46. Gianozzo Manetti, *Vita Nicholai summa pontificis* (c. 1455) in *Rerum Italicarum Scriptores,* ed. L. Muratori, vol. III, 2 (Milan, 1734), col. 934; translation in Torgil Magnuson, 'The Project of Nicholas V for Rebuilding the Borgo Leonino in Rome,' *Art Bulletin* 36 (1954): 89–115, esp. 93. For Nicholas V's urban and architectural projects, see Carrol W. Westfall, *In This Most Perfect Paradise: Alberti, Nicholas V, and the Invention of Conscious Urban Planning in Rome, 1447–1455* (University Park: Pennsylvania State University Press, 1974); Charles Burroughs, 'Below the Angel: An Urbanistic

Project in the Rome of Pope Nicholas V,' *Journal of the Warburg and Courtauld Institutes* 45 (1982): 94–124; Manfredo Tafuri, 'Cives esse non licere: The Rome of Nicholas V and Leon Battista Alberti: Elements toward a Historical Revision,' *Harvard Architectural Review* 6 (1987): 61–75; and Charles Burroughs, *From Signs to Design: Environmental Process and Reform in Early Renaissance Rome* (Cambridge: MIT Press, 1990).

47. The drawing is from Giovanni Marcanova's *Quaedam antiquitatum fragmenta* (Padua, 1465), Princeton University Library, Ms. Garrett 158, fol. 6v. For discussion, see Curran and Grafton, 'Fifteenth-Century Site Report,' 237. For obelisk-machines of the fifteenth century, see Giustina Scaglia, 'Drawings for Machines for Architecture from the Early Quattrocento in Italy,' *Journal of the Society of Architectural Historians* 25 (1966): 90–114; and A. Carugo, 'Gli Obelischi e le macchine nel Rinascimeto,' in Domenico Fontana, *Della trasportatione dell' Obelisco Vaticano* (Rome, 1590), ed. A. Carugo (Milan, 1978), xxi–lx, lx–lxxx.

48. See Fontana, *Della trasportazione;* William B. Parsons, *Engineers and Engineering in the Renaissance,* rev. ed. (Cambridge: MIT Press, 1968), 155–73; Iversen, *Obelisks in Exile,* vol. I, 27–44; D'Onofrio, *Obelischi,* 137–85.

49. For example, in 1471 Alberti entertained some Florentine guests by showing them the site of the buried Augustan obelisk in the Circus Maximus, which was abandoned until the pontificate of Sixtus V. See Iversen, *Obelisks in Exile,* vol. I, 67–9.

50. For the most up-to-date translation, see Copenhaver, *Hermetica.* For the character and reception of these texts, see Scott, *Hermetica,* vol. I, 1–111; A.-J. Festugière, *La révélation d'Hermes Trismégiste,* 4 vols. (Paris: Lecoffre, 1950–54); Frances A. Yates, *Giordano Bruno and the Hermetic Tradition* (Chicago and London: University of Chicago Press, 1964), 1–19; Erik Iversen, *Egyptian and Hermetic Doctrine* (Copenhagen: Museum Tusculanum Press, 1984); Garth Fowden, *The Egyptian Hermes: A Historical Approach to the Late Pagan Mind* (Cambridge and New York: Cambridge University Press, 1986); Brian Copenhaver, 'Hermes Trismegistus, Proclus, and the Question of a Philosophy of Magic in the Renaissance,' in *Hermetism and the Renaissance,* 79–110; and Michael J. B. Allen, 'Marsilio Ficino, Hermes Trismegistus and the Corpus Hermeticum,' in *New Perspectives on Renaissance Thought,* ed. John Henry and Sarah Hutton (London: Duckworth, 1990), 38–47.

51. For Ficino and hieroglyphs, see Giehlow, 'Hieroglyphenkunde,' 22–4; Iversen, *Myth of Egypt,* 64; Wittkower, 'Hieroglyphic Studies,' 115–16; Dieckmann, *Hieroglyphics,* 34–8; and Gombrich, 'Icones Symbolicae,' 158–60.

52. See Iversen, *Myth of Egypt,* 42–3; and Bruno Santi, *The Marble Pavement of the Cathedral of Siena* (Florence: 1988), 13–14.

53. For the Sala dei Santi, see Giehlow, 'Hieroglyphenkunde,' 44–6; Fritz Saxl, 'The Appartamento Borgia,' in Saxl, *Lectures,* 2 vols. (London: The Warburg Institute, 1957), vol. I, 174–88; N. Randolph Parks, 'On the Meaning of Pinturicchio's Sala dei Santi,' *Art History* 2 (1979): 291–317; Ingrid D. Rowland, *The Culture of the High Renaissance: Ancients and Moderns in Sixteenth-Century Rome* (Cambridge and New York: Cambridge University Press, 1998), 46–53; and Sabine Poeschel, *Alexander Maximus: Das Bildprogramm des Appartamento Borgia im Vatikan* (Weimar: VDG, 1999), 131–81.

54. Annius' influence on the cycle was proposed by Giehlow and accepted by Saxl, Parks, and Poeschel (see previous note). Paola Mattiangeli ('Annio de Viterbo inspiratore di cicli pittorici', in *Annio da Viterbo: Documenti e ricerche,* vol. I, ed. G. Baffoni and P. Mattiangeli [Rome: Consiglio nazionale delle ricerche, 1981], 257–303) has provided the most convincing argument for Annius' influence, questioned most recently by Rowland, *Culture of the High Renaissance,* 58–9.

For more on Annius and his works, see Roberto Weiss, 'Traccia per una biografia di Annio da Viterbo,' *Italia mediovale e umanistica* 5 (1962): 425–41; F. N. Tigerstedt, 'Ioannes Annius and Graecia Mendax,' in *Classical, Medieval, and Renaissance Studies in Honor of Berthold Louis Ullman*, 2 vols., ed. C. Henderson (Rome: Edizioni di storia e letteratura, 1964), vol. II, 293–310; Walter Stephens, 'Berosus Chaldaeus: Counterfeit and Fictive Editors of the Early Sixteenth Century' (Ph.D. diss., Cornell University, 1979); C. R. Ligota, 'Annius of Viterbo and Historical Method,' *Journal of the Warburg and Courtauld Institutes*, 50 (1987): 44–56; W. Stephens, *Giants in Those Days: Folklore, Ancient History, and Nationalism* (Lincoln and London: University of Nebraska Press, 1989); Anthony Grafton, *Forgers and Critics: Creativity and Duplicity in Western Scholarship* (Princeton: Princeton University Press, 1990), 48–68, 100–18; A. Grafton, 'Invention of Traditions and Traditions of Invention in Renaissance Europe: The Strange Case of Annius of Viterbo,' in Grafton, *Defenders of the Text: The Traditions of Scholarship in an Age of Science, 1450–1800* (Cambridge and London: Harvard University Press 1991), 76–103; and Rowland, *Culture of the High Renaissance*, 53–9.

55. My notes are to the first edition, *Commentaria Fratris Ioannis Annii Viterbensis ordinis praedicator, theologiae professoris super opera diversorum auctorum de Antiquitatibus loquentorum* (Rome, Eucharius Silber, 1498); and the 1552 version, *Berosi sacerdotis chaldaici, antiquitatum Italiae ac totius orbis libri Commentariis Joannis Annii Viterbensis*, 2 vols. (Antwerp: I. Steelsii, 1552).

56. The story is told in the 'Defloratio Berosi Chaldaica,' Annius, *Commentaria* (1498), fol. N viii–Yv; *Berosi sacerdotis* (1552), 35–209. See Stephens, *Giants*, 109–35, for a summary.

57. See Annius, *Commentaria* (1498), fol. Piiir–Pvv (215–20); *Berosi sacerdotis* (1552), 66–75.

58. Annius, *Commentaria* (1498), fol. Rivv–Yi (242–94); *Berosi sacerdotis* (1552), 108–79.

59. See Parks, 'Sala dei Santi', 291–9; Rowland, *Culture of the High Renaissance*, 49–51; and Poeschel, *Alexander Maximus*, 131–62.

60. On this point, see Assmann, *Moses the Egyptian*, 13–14.

61. Rowland, *Culture of the High Renaissance*, 53–9, 149–50.

62. See Marie Tanner, *Last Descendant of Aeneas* (New Haven and London: Yale University Press, 1993); and Roberto Bizzocchi, *Genealogie incredibili: Scritti di storia nell' Europa moderna* (Bologna: Il Mulino, 1995).

63. Annius' Farnese genealogy was included in his *De Viterbii viris et factis illustribis*, written c. 1491 and dedicated to Cardinal Ranuccio Farnese. The original is lost, but fragments survive in the letters of Alessandro Farnese, see A. Frugoni, ed., 'Carteggio umanistico di Alessandro Farnese, dal cod. GL. Kgl. S. 2125, Copenhagen,' in *Nuova collezione di testi umanistici inediti e rari*, vol. VIII (Florence: Olschki, 1950), 61–4; Weiss, *Renaissance Discovery*, 126, n. 2; and Mattiangeli, 'Annio da Viterbo,' 266–8.

64. The thesis of an Annian genealogy of the Borgia was proposed by Giehlow, 'Hieroglyphenkunde,' 44–6; and developed by Saxl, 'Appartamento Borgia', 183–8; Weiss, 'Traccia per una biografia,' 434–5; and Mattiangeli, 'Annio da Viterbo,' 260–9.

65. Annius, *Commentaria* (1498), fol. ki r–kv v (p. 419–28), *Berosi sacerdotis* (1552), 290–307, see Stephens, *Giants*, 134–8.

66. On this point, see Mattiangeli, 'Annio da Viterbo,' 290–5. For Alexander VI and the Borgia in Italy, see Ludwig Frieherr von Pastor, *History of the Popes from the Close of the Middle Ages*, 40 vols. (London: K. Paul, Trench, Trübner & Co., 1923–40), vol. V–VI; Michael Mallet, *The Borgias: Rise and Fall of a Renaissance Dynasty* (London: Bodley Head, 1969).

67. For Annius as 'archaeologist', see Giehlow, 'Hieroglyphenkunde', 42–5; Roberto Weiss, 'An Unknown Epigraphic Tract by Annius of Viterbo,' in C. P. Brand et al., *Italian Studies Presented to E. R. Vincent* (Cambridge: Heffner, 1962), 101–20; Stephens, 'Berosus Chaldaeus,' 155–76; Adriana

Emiliozzi, *Il Museo Civico di Viterbo: Storia delle raccolte archeologiche* (Rome: Consiglio Nazionale delle Ricerche, 1986), 19–36; and Rowland, *Culture of the High Renaissance,* 56–8.

68. Some of the following draws from my prior study, B. Curran, 'De sacrarum litterarum aegyptiorum interpretatione: Reticence and Hubris in Hieroglyphic Studies of the Renaissance: Pierio Valeriano and Annius of Viterbo', *Memoirs of the American Academy in Rome,* 43/44 (1998/1999): 139–82.

69. The tablet was first described by Annius in *De marmoreis Volturrhenis tabulis* (1492–3), ed. Weiss, 'Unknown Epigraphic Tract', 107–20, esp. 114–15. See I. Faldi, *Museo Civico di Viterbo: Dipinti e sculture dal Medioevo al XVII secolo* (Viterbo: Agnesotti, 1955), 60–1 (no. 38); Weiss, 'Unknown Epigraphic Tract,' 119, n. 53; Mattiangeli, 'Annio da Viterbo,' 296–302; and Emiliozzi, *Museo Civico,* 29–31.

70. Annius, *Commentaria* (1498), fol. Aiiiv–Aivr (4–5), fir–fiiiv (371–376); *Berosi sacerdotis* (1552), 380–90.

71. Annius, *Berosi sacerdotis* (1552), 380: 'Maiores nostri, in templo olim Herculis, nunc divi Laurentii, ut semper ante oculos nostros aeterna vetustatis huius urbis memoria teneretur, pro rostris posuit columnam. i. tabulam alabastrinam. Osiriani triumphi monumentum, avibus, & animalibus & capitibus & arboris, id est, sacris Aegyptiis literis excisam, de quibus saepe authores scribunt. Et Plinius in Naturali Historia has inquit quae vides effigies Aegyptiae sacrae literae sunt. In hac itaque columna est spatium, in cuius medio est truncus et arboris quercus instar sceptri multiplicis, in quorum sceptrorum summo duo rami circulum faciunt instar sceptri multiplicis, quae effigies est propria Osiridis, ut ait Xenophon. Quod & Macrobius in primo Saturnalia confirmat, dicens, Osirim exprimentes Aegyptii sacris literis insculpunt sceptrum, inque eo speciem oculi exprimunt, et hos signo monstrant Osirim. Ponuntur autem in hoc trunco arboris non unum, sed plura sceptra, quia non in una, sed omni parte orbis imperavit, ut Diodorus scribit . . . '; and 389: 'Sum Osiris rex, qui evocatus ab Italis contra oppressores Italici imperii festinus occurri, . . . Sum Osiris, qui docui Italos arare, serere, putare, vinitare, vindemiare et vinum conficere et eis duos reliqui custodes imperii mari et terra nepotes meos.'

72. Macrobius, *Saturnalia,* I. 21. 12; Diodorus, I. 27. 3–6. For discussion, see Mattiangeli, 'Annio da Viterbo,' 297–302; Stephens, 'Berosus Chaldaeus,' 167–70; and Curran, 'De sacrarum litterarum,' 172–7.

73. See Poggio, *Diodori Siculi Historiarum priscarum libri VI a Poggio in Latinum Traducti* (Venice: per Andrea Iacobi Katharensem, 1476), fol. P. 12v, for the relevant passages.

74. Alberti, *De re aedificatoria,* VII. 16, citing Diodorus, I. 53–8. This notion was in keeping with the Medieval conflation of obelisks and columns, a tradition, exemplified by the fusion of the Vatican obelisk with the *Columna Julia,* that continued into the Renaissance.

75. At one point, Annius allows that the *Columna* might be a replacement or copy of the original, see Annius, *Berosi sacerdotis* (1552), 390.

76. For the S. Lorenzo fragments, which were moved to the Palazzo dei Conservatori in the mid-sixteenth century, see Phyllis Pray Bober and Ruth Rubinstein, *Renaissance Artists and Antique Sculpture: A Handbook of Sources* (London: Harvey Miller, 1987), 225–6 (no. 194); and L. Leoncini, 'Storia e fortuna di cosidetto fregio di S. Lorenzo,' *Xenia* 14 (1987): 59–110.

77. See Giehlow, 'Hieroglyphenkunde,' 46–79; Iversen, *Myth of Egypt,* 66–70; Wittkower, 'Hieroglyphic Studies,' 118–20; Giovanni Pozzi, 'Les hieroglyphes de l'Hypnerotomachia Poliphili,' in *L'Emblème a la Renaissance,* ed. Y. Giraud, (Paris: Société d'édition d'enseignement supérieur,

1982), 15–27; Jean Céard and Jean-Claude Margolin, *Rébus de la Renaissance: des images que parlent,* 2 vols. (Paris: Maisonneuve et Larose, 1986), vol. I, 68–76; and B. Curran, 'The 'Hypnerotomachia Poliphili' and Renaissance Egyptology,' *Word and Image* 14 (1998): 156–85.

78. The case for the Roman Francesco Colonna has been argued by Maurizio Calvesi and his associates, see Calvesi, *Il sogno di Poliphilo prenestino* (Rome: Officina, 1980); and idem, *La 'pugna di amore in sogno' di Francesco Colonna Romano* (Rome: Lithos, 1996). For the more convincing attribution to the Venetian Friar, see Maria Teresa Casella and Giovanni Pozzi, *Francesco Colonna: Biographia e Opere,* 2 vols. (Padua: Antenore, 1959); and Patricia Fortini Brown, *Venice and Antiquity: The Venetian Sense of the Past* (New Haven and London: Yale University Press, 1997), 287–90. On a recent attribution to Alberti, see B. Curran and A. Grafton, 'Review of *Leon Battista Alberti's Hypnerotomachia Poliphili,* by Liane Lefaivre, Cambridge, Mass., MIT Press, 1997,' *Journal of the Society of Architectural Historians* 59 (2000): 528–30.

79. See Curran, 'De sacrarum litterarum,' 174.

80. E. H. Gombrich, 'Hypnerotomachiana' (1951), in Gombrich, *Symbolic Images,* 102–8.

81. See ibid. For further discussion, see Enzo Bentivoglio, 'Bramante e il geroglifico di Viterbo,' *Mitteilungen des Kunsthistorischen Instituts in Florenz* 16 (1992): 167–74.

82. A. Laelius Podager, in *Epigrammata antiquae urbis,* ed. A. Mazzocchi (Rome: Jacopo Mazzocchi, 1521); Vat. lat. 8492, fol. 21 r. See Iversen, *Obelisks in Exile,* vol. I, 147–8; D'Onofrio, *Obelischi,* 387–8. For an illustration of the page, see Anthony Grafton, et al., *Rome Reborn: The Vatican Library and Renaissance Culture* (New Haven and London: Yale University Press 1993), 119, pl. 94.

83. Rowland, *Culture of the High Renaissance,* 148–50. For further discussion see John W. O'Malley, *Giles of Viterbo on Church and Reform* (Leiden: Brill, 1968); J. W. O'Malley, 'Fulfillment of the Golden Age under Pope Julius II: Text of a Discourse of Giles of Viterbo,' *Traditio* 25 (1969): 265–338.

84. See Curran, 'De sacrarum litterarum', 144–50.

85. See B. Curran, 'Cleopatra and the Second Julius: Egyptology and Imperial Inheritance in High Renaissance Rome,' in *Cleopatra and Egyptomania,* Papers of the Symposium at the University of California, Irvine, ed. Margaret M. Miles (University of California Press, forthcoming, 2005).

86. As noted years ago by Pastor, *History of the Popes,* VIII, 243.

87. For the career and patronage of Leo X, see William Roscoe, *The Life and Pontificate of Leo the Tenth* (London: D. Bogue, 1846); Ferdinand Gregorovius, *History of the City of Rome in the Middle Ages,* trans. A. Hamilton, 8 vols. (London: Bell, 1894–1902), vol. VIII, part 1, 312–58; Pastor, *History of the Popes,* vol. VII–VIII; Domenico Gnoli, *La Roma di Leone X* (Milan, 1938); V. Fanelli, 'Il Ginnasio greco di Leone X a Roma,' *Studi romani* 9 (1961): 379–93; John Shearman, *Raphael's Cartoons in the Collection of Her Majesty the Queen* (London: Phaidon, 1972); Vincenzo De Caprio, 'L'area umanistica romana 1513–1527,' *Studi romani* 29 (1981): 321–35; John F. D'Amico, *Renaissance Humanism in Papal Rome* (Baltimore and London: Johns Hopkins University Press, 1983); Janet Cox-Rearick, *Dynasty and Destiny in Medici Art: Pontormo, Leo X, and the Two Cosimos* (Princeton: Princeton University Press, 1984); and Rowland, *Culture of the High Renaissance,* 211–44.

88. For Raphael's project, described in the famous 'Letter to Leo X', see Weiss, *Renaissance Discovery,* 94–7; Christof Thoenes, 'La "Lettera" a Leone X,' in *Raffaello a Roma: Il Convegno del 1983,* ed. C. Frommel and M. Winner (Rome: Edizioni dell'elefante, 1986), 373–81; Francesco P. Di Teodoro, *Raffaello, Baldassar Castiglione e la 'Lettera' a Leone X* (Bologna: Nuova Alfa, 1994); and Rowland, *Culture of the High Renaissance,* 226–30.

89. See R. Weiss, 'Andrea Fulvio Antiquario Romano (c. 1470–1527),' *Annali della Scuola Normale Superiore di Pisa,* ser. II, vol. 28 (1959): 1–44; and Weiss, *Renaissance Discovery,* 86–9. For Raphael as archaeologist, see Arnold Nesselrath, 'Raphael's Archaeological Method,' in Frommel and Winner, *Raffaello a Roma,* 357–71.

90. For Bembo and the *Mensa Isiaca,* see Giehlow, 'Hieroglyphenkunde,' 111, n. 2; Sabine Eiche, 'On the Dispersal of Cardinal Bembo's Collections,' *Mitteilungen des Kunsthistorisches Institutes in Florenz* 27 (1983): 353–9; and Curran, 'De sacrarum litterarum,' 144–6. For Calcagnini and hieroglyphs, see Giehlow, 'Hieroglyphenkunde,' 80–2; and *La letteratura delle immagini nel Cinquecento,* ed. Gennaro Savarese and Andrea Gareffi (Rome: Bulzoni, 1980), 57–68.

91. Pierio Valeriano, *Hieroglyphica, sive de sacris aegyptiorum aliarumque gentium literis commentarii Ioannes Pierii Valeriani Bolzanii Bellunensis* (Basel: Palma Ising 1556; rev. ed. Lyons: Frelon, 1602, reprint New York: Garland, 1976). For Valeriano's life, works, and hieroglyphic studies, see Giuseppe Cali, *Della vita e delle opere di Giovanni Pierio Valeriano* (Catania: Niccolò Ciannotta, 1901), 25–6; Giehlow, 'Hieroglyphenkunde,' 113–29, Guido Bustico, 'Due umanisti veneti: Urbano Bolzanio e Pierio Valeriano,' *Civiltà moderna* 4 (1932): 86–103, 344–79; Iversen, *Myth of Egypt,* 70–3; Pope, *Story of Archaeological Decipherment,* 24–7; V. Lettere, 'Dalle Fosse, Giovanni Pietro (Pierio Valeriano),' *Dizionario biografico degli Italiani,* vol. 32 (Rome, 1986), 84–8; Margaret Daly Davis, 'I geroglifici in marmo di Pierio Valeriano,' *Labyrinthos* 9 (1990): 47–77; Kenneth Gouwens, *Remembering the Renaissance: Humanist Narratives of the Sack of Rome* (Leiden: Brill, 1998), 143–67; and Julia Haig Gaisser, *Pierio Valeriano on the Ill Fortune of Learned Men: A Renaissance Humanist and His World* (Ann Arbor: University of Michigan Press, 1999).

92. For Fra Urbano, see Giehlow, 102–13; Luigi Beschi, 'L'Anonimo Ambrosiano: un itinerario in Grecia di Urbano Bolzanio,' *Accademia Nazionale dei Lincei, Rendiconti, Classe di scienze morali, storiche e filologiche,* ser. 8, 39 (1984): 3–22; and L. Gualdo Rosa, 'Dalle Fosse (Bolzanio), Urbano,' *Dizionario biografico degli Italiani,* vol. 32 (Rome, 1986), 88–92; and Curran, 'De sacrarum litterarum,' 158–62, 178–9.

93. For the 'Tazza Farnese', see N. Dacos, A. Giuliano, U. Pannuti, and A. Grote, *Il tesoro di Lorenzo il Magnifico: Repertorio delle gemme e dei vasi* (Florence: Sansoni, 1972–3, 2nd ed., 1980), 26–7, 69–73 (no. 43); Bober and Rubinstein, *Renaissance Artists and Antique Sculpture,* 104–5 (no. 68); and Carlo Gasparri, *Le gemme Farnese* (Naples: Electa Napoli, 1994), 74–83.

94. Pastor, *History of the Popes,* vol. VIII, 174–5.

95. Ilaria Ciseri, *L'ingresso trionfale di Leone X in Firenze nel 1515* (Florence: Olschki, 1990), 74–7.

96. I have treated this theme in a paper, 'Raphael's Egyptian Captives: Egyptology and Imperial Triumph in the Rome of Leo X,' presented at the Southeastern College Art Conference, 1999. Some of this material derives from that paper, now being revised as a chapter in my forthcoming book, *The Egyptian Renaissance: The After life of Ancient Egypt in Early Modern Italy* (Chicago: University of Chicago Press, forthcoming, 2005).

97. Rodolfo Lanciani, *Storia degli scavi di Roma e notizie intorno le collezione romane di antichità,* 2nd ed. (Rome: Loescher, 1989–94), vol. I, 241; Bober and Rubinstein, *Renaissance Artists and Antique Sculpture,* 101–2 (no. 65); Serena Ensoli, 'La decorazione scultorea della scalinata del Palazzo Senatorio,' in *La facciate del Palazzo Senatorio in Campidoglio: Monumenti di storia urbana di Roma,* ed. Maria Elias Tittoni (Pisa: Ospedaletto, 1994), 100–32.

98. For the sphinxes, see Roullet, *Egyptian Monuments,* 134–5 (cat. no. 284–5); Ensoli Vittozzi, *Musei Capitolini,* 12–13; Ziegler, in Humbert et al., *Egyptomania,* 87–91 (cat. no. 29–30); and Lollio Barberi, *Antichità egiziane,* 200–2 (cat. no. 47).

99. Andrea Fulvio, *Antiquaria Urbis per Andream Fulvium* (Rome, 1513), fol. Eiir (lines 20–3).

100. See Fabrizio Cruciani, *Il teatro del Campidoglio e le feste romane del 1513, con la ricostruzione architettonica del teatro del Arnaldo Bruschi* (Milan: Il Polifilo, 1969); Arnaldo Bruschi, 'Il teatro capitolino del 1513,' *Bollettino del Centro Internazionale di Studi di Architettura Andrea Palladio* 16 (1974): 189–218; and Charles Stinger, 'The Campidoglio as the Locus of "Renovatio Imperii" in Renaissance Rome,' *Art and Politics in Late Medieval and Early Renaissance Italy: 1250–1500*, ed. Charles M. Rosenberg (Notre Dame and London: University of Notre Dame Press, 1990), 135–56.

101. Ulisse Aldrovandi, 'Delle statue antiche che per tutta Roma in diversi luoghi, e case si veggono,' in Lucio Mauro, *Le antichità della città di Rome breviussima raccolte da chiunque ne ha scritto*, 3rd ed. (Venice: G. Ziletti, 1562), 115–315, esp. 270.

102. See Fritz Saxl, 'The Capitol during the Renaissance: A Symbol of the Imperial Idea,' in *Lectures*, 200–14; Tilmann Buddensieg, 'Zum Statuenprogram in Kapitolsplan Paulus III,' *Zeitschrift für Kunstgeschichte* 32 (1969): 177–229; A. Marino, 'Idoli e colossi: la statuaria antica sulla piazza del Campidoglio da Sisto IV a Leone X,' in *Roma, centro ideale della cultura dell'Antico nei secoli XV e XVI: da Martino V al sacco di Roma 1417–1527*, ed. Silvia Danesi Squarzina (Milan: Electa, 1989), 237–47.

103. For Giulo's interest, see Jaeger, 'La Loggia delle Muse nel Palazzo Te,' 21–39.

104. J. F. Fichard noted the restoration in 1536, see 'Italia autore Joanne Fichard,' *Frankfurtisches Archive für ältere deutsche Litteratur und Geschichte* III (1815): 1–130, esp. 56–7. The drawing by Francisco de Hollanda, Escorial Cod. 28-1-20 fol. 16 v, shows the lions and basin with a section of Leo's dedicatory inscription (now lost), see E. Tormo y Monzó, E., *Os Desenhos das antiqualhas que vio Francisco d'Ollanda, pintor português* (Madrid: Rates, 1940), 79–80. See Suzanne B. Butters, *The Triumph of Vulcan: Sculptor's Tools, Porphyry, and the Prince in Ducal Florence*, 2 vols. (Florence: Olschki, 1996), 116–17, n. 38.

105. For the basin, later employed as the sarcophagus of Pope Clement XII in the Lateran (1740), see C. Pietrangeli, *San Giovanni in Laterano* (Florence: Nardini, 1990), 171–2, 244; and Butters, *Triumph of Vulcan*, 116–17.

106. The installation is recorded in the 'Fossombrone Sketchbook', Biblioteca Civica Passionei, Fossombrone, Inv. n. disegni Vol. Nr. 3 (= Cod. C. 5. Vi), fol. 73r–v; see Arnold Nesselrath, *Das Fossombroner Skizzenbuch* (London: Warburg Institute, 1993) 175–9, and by Maarten van Heemskerck, Berlin, Kupferstichkabinett, I, fol. 71r; C. Hülsen and H. Egger, *Die Römischen Skizzenbuch von Marten van Heemskerck im Königlichen Kupferstichkabinette zu Berlin*, 2 vols. (Berlin, 1913–16, reprinted 1975), vol. I, 36–9.

107. For the lion as the symbol of Leo X, see Marilyn Perry, '"Candor Illaesus": The "Impresa" of Clement VII and other Medici Devices in the Vatican Stanze,' *The Burlington Magazine* 119 (1977): 676–86; Shearman, *Raphael's Cartoons*, 17–20; F. Mancinelli et al., *Raffaello in Vaticano* (Milan: Electa, 1984), 44–5 (no. 27–8): Bernice Davidson, *Raphael's Bible: A Study of the Vatican Logge* (University Park: Pennsylvania State University Press, 1985), 9, 20–5, 63–73; and Claudia Lazzaro, 'Animals as Cultural Signs: A Medici Menagerie in the Grotto at Castello,' in *Reframing the Renaissance: Visual Culture in Europe and Latin America, 1450–1650*, ed. Clare Farago (New Haven and London: Yale University Press 1995), 197–227.

108. Valeriano gives some thirty-eight 'primary' meanings for the lion in the first book of the *Hieroglyphica* (1602), 1–14, dedicated to Duke Cosimo I de' Medici.

109. John Shearman, 'The Vatican Stanze: Functions and Decoration,' (1971) in *Art and Politics in Renaissance Italy*, ed. George Holmes (Oxford: Oxford University Press, 1993), 200–2, 234, n. 234, citing Egidio's *Historia viginti saeculorum* (1513–18, dedicated to Leo X), Biblioteca Angelica, Ms. Lat. 351, fol. 6v, 36r, 316r. See also Cox-Rearick, *Dynasty and Destiny*, 146–52.

110. Stinger, 'Campidoglio,' 143–51.

111. For Leo as Augustus, see Shearman, *Raphael's Cartoons,* 14–17; Cox-Rearick, *Dynasty and Destiny,* 108–13, Charles L. Stinger, *The Renaissance in Rome* (Bloomington: University of Indiana Press, 1985, 2nd ed. 1998), 12, 246–7.

112. Paolo Giovio, *De vita Leonis Decimi Pont. Max. libri IIII* (Florence, 1548, 2nd ed., 1551), 68, translated in T. C. Price Zimmerman, *Paolo Giovio: The Historian and the Crisis of Sixteenth-Century Italy* (Princeton: Princeton University Press, 1995), 23.

113. See *Lorenzo dopo Lorenzo: La fortuna storica di Lorenzo il Magnifico,* ed. P. Pirolo (Milan: Silvana, 1992).

114. Florentine historians in the period of Lorenzo and Leo began promoting the idea that the city had been founded by Augustus. See Giovanni Cipriani, *Il mito etrusco nel rinascimento fiorentino* (Florence: Olschki, 1980), 31–2, citing Angelo Poliziano's *De civitatis Florentinae origine.*

115. Shigetoshi Osano, 'Due "Marsia" nel giardino di Via Larga: La ricezione del decor dell'antichità romana nella collezione medicea di sculture antiche,' *Artibus et Historiae* 34 (1996): 95–120.

116. Andrea Fulvio, *Antiquitates Urbis Romae* (Rome: Silber, 1527), Eiiir (Regiones fol. XXI); Ruth O. Rubinstein, 'The Renaissance Discovery of Antique River-God Personifications,' in *Scritti di storia dell'arte in onore di Roberto Salvini* (Florence: Sansoni, 1984), 257–63.

117. Fulvio, *Antiquitates Urbis Romae,* 94: 'Eminent hodie ante templi aditum ex priscis ornamentis duo pari forma leonis ex Marmaridu[m] lapide sub nigro suis basis collocati cu[m] hieroglyphicis notis inter porphiritica labrae proximis M. Agrippa & Neronis (ut creditur) thermis post ruinas ibi collocata.'

118. The basin is described in these terms by Flamminio Vacca ('Memorie di varie antichità trovate in diversi luoghi della città di Roma (1594)', in *Roma antica di Famiano Nardini,* 4 vols., ed. A. Nibby [Rome: Stamperia de Romanis, 1820], vol. IV, 17–18) and finds visual expression in a sixteenth-century drawing from Cassiano dal Pozzo's Museum Chartaceum; see Mirka Benes in 'The Paper Museum of Cassiano dal Pozzo', *Quaderni Puteani* 4 (1993): 126 (no. 79).

119. See the discussion in Butters, *Triumph of Vulcan,* 113–17.

120. For the lions at the Moses Fountain, see Cesare D'Onofrio, *Le fontane di Roma,* 3rd ed. (Rome: Romana società, 1986), 107–9, 210–3; Simona Benedetti, 'L'acquedotto Felice da Porta Furba alla Mostra del Mosè,' in Sandro Benedetti et al., *Sisto V: Architettura per la città* (Rome: Multigrafica, 1992) 91–129; and Tod Marder, 'Sisto V e la Fontana del Mosè,' in M. Fagiolo and M. L. Madonna, *Sisto V: vol. I: Roma e il Lazio* (Rome: Libreria dello Stato, 1992), 521–43.

121. See Carlo Pietrangeli, 'Le fontanelle dei Leoni sulla rampa Capitolino,' *Capitolium* 29 (1954): 267–70; Ensoli Vittozzi, *Musei Capitolini,* 71–85, 88–89.

122. See Curran, Raphael's Egyptian Captives.

123. Valeriano, *Hieroglyphica* (1602), 14. For more on sphinxes, see Heinz Demisch, *Die Sphinx: Geschichte ihrer Darstellung von den Anfängen bis zur Gegenwart* (Stuttgart: Urachhaus, 1977), 167–75; and John F. Moffitt, 'A Hidden Sphinx by Agnolo Bronzino "*ex tabula Cebetis Thebani*",' *Renaissance Quarterly* 46 (summer 1993): 277–307.

124. See A. Mercati, 'Raffaello d'Urbino e Antonio da Sangallo Maestri delle Strade di Rome sotto Leone X,' *Rendiconti della Pontificia Accademia Romana di Archeologia* 1 (1923): 121–9; Jones and Penny, *Raphael,* 226, 253, n. 69; M. Tafuri, in *Raffaello architetto* ed. C. L. Frommel, S. Ray, and M. Tafuri (Milan: Electa, 1984), 84–7; C. L. Frommel, 'Papal Policy: The Planning of Rome During the Renaissance,' *Journal of Interdisciplinary History* 17 (1986): 39–65.

125. For the Mausoleum obelisks, noted by Ammianus and the fourth-century Regionary catalogues, see Iversen, *Obelisks in Exile,* vol. I, 47–54, 115–27; and D'Onofrio, *Obelischi,* 85–94. The 1490s 'discovery' is noted by Bernardo Rucellai, *Commentarium in Publ. Victorem de regionibus urbis (c. 1497) in J. Tartinius, Rerum Italicarum scriptores,* vol. II (Florence, 1748), col. 1004; see Iversen, *Obelisks in Exile,* vol. I, 48, n. 3.

126. For contemporary plans and drawings, see Iversen, *Obelisks in Exile,* I, 48–51; D'Onofrio, *Obelischi,* 88–94; and Anna Maria Riccomini, *La ruina di sì bela Cosa: Vicende e trasformazioni del Mausoleo di Augusto* (Milan: Electa, 1996), 30–69.

127. Vincenzo Golzio, *Raffaello nei documenti, nelle testimonianze dei contemporanei e nella letteratura del suo secolo* (Vatican City and Spoleto: Panetto and Petrelli, 1936), 101.

128. Uffizi UA 1232r, inscribed 'per la guglia dil popolo quali si è a santo rocho,' see Tafuri, in *Raffaello architetto,* 229–30 (cat. no. 212); and D'Onofrio, *Obelischi,* 93, fig. 45.

129. Thesis proposed by Wendy Stedman Sheard, 'Verrocchio's Medici Tomb and the Language of Materials: With a Postscript on His Legacy in Venice', in *Verrocchio and Late Quattrocento Italian Sculpture,* ed. Steven Bule and Alan P. Darr (Florence: Le Lettere, 1992), 63–90; and questioned by Andrew Butterfield, *The Sculptures of Andrea del Verrocchio* (New Haven and London: Yale University Press 1997), 207–9. For 'Festina Lente' in the *Hypnerotomachia,* see Godwin, *Hypnerotomachia,* 69, 74–5, 153–4 (with tortoise). Tortoise astragals provide support for two later Medici obelisk projects. The first was discovered at the Iseum Campense and erected c. 1574–88 in the Villa Medici, Rome (since 1790 in the Boboli gardens, Florence). See D'Onofrio, *Obelischi,* 236–7; Lembke, *Iseum Campense,* 204 (no. 50). The second is the pair of modern obelisks in the Piazza di S. Maria Novella, Florence (1608–9).

130. See Tafuri, *Raffaello architetto,* 230 (for *Hypnerotomachia* influence); and D'Onofrio, *Obelischi,* 93–4 (on the resemblance to Nicholas V's scheme). For Leo's pet pachyderm Hanno, see Matthias Winner, 'Raffael malt einen Elefanten,' *Mitteilungen des Kunsthistorischen Institutes in Florenz* 11 (1964): 71–109; and Silvio A. Bedini, *The Pope's Elephant* (Manchester: Carcanet, 1997).

131. Pliny the Elder, *Natural History,* XXXVI. 67.196–7.

132. See Donald F. Lach, *Asia in the Making of Europe, vol. II: A Century of Wonder: The Visual Arts* (Chicago: University of Chicago Press, 1970), 124–58.

133. Plutarch, *De Iside et Osiride* 9 (354c); and *De hominis dignitate,* in *De hominis dignitate, Heptaplus, De ente et uno, e scritti vari,* ed. Eugenio Garin (Florence: Vallecchi, 1942), 156.

134. The designs are preserved in drawings by Antonio and Giovanni Battista da Sangallo. See G. Giovannoni, *Antonio da Sangallo il Giovane,* 2 vols. (Rome: Tipografia Regionale, 1959), vol. I, 245–6, 381–4; Detlef Heikamp, 'Die Entwurfziechnungen für die Grabmäler der Mediceer-Päpste Leo X und Clemens VII,' *Albertina Studien* 4 (1966): 134–54; Simonetta Valtieri, 'Sistemazioni absidali di chiese in funzione di 'Mausoleo' in progetti di Antonio da Sangallo il Giovane,' in *Antonio da Sangallo il Giovane: La vita e l'opera,* ed. G. Spagnesi (Rome: Centro Studi per la Storial dell' Architettura, 1986), 109–18; *The Architectural Drawings of Antonio da Sangallo the Younger,* 2 vols., ed. C. L. Frommel and N. Adams (Cambridge and London, 1994–2000), vol. I, 45–6 (fig. 39, 40), vol. II, 117–18, 210–12.

135. Weiss, 'Traccia', 436.

136. For the later history of the obelisk, see Iversen, *Obelisks in Exile,* vol. I, 48–54; and D'Onofrio, *Obelischi,* 235–41.

137. Philipp Fehl, 'Raphael as a Historian: Poetry and Historical Accuracy in the Sala di Costantino, Vatican Palace,' *Artibus et Historiae* 14 (1993): 9–76.

138. Cipriani, *Il mito etrusco,* 28; O'Malley, *Giles of Viterbo,* 30–1, 123, 190; Cruciani, *Il teatro del Campidoglio,* 31–3; Davidson, *Raphael's Bible,* 22–3.

139. For Leo X as *medicus,* see Shearman, *Raphael's Cartoons,* 15, 77–80; Davidson, *Raphael's Bible,* 23; Cox-Rearick, *Dynasty and Destiny,* 30, 34, 39–40, 141.

140. See J. Gwyn Griffiths, ed., Apuleius of Madauros, *The Isis-Book: Metamorphoses, Book X* (Leiden: Brill, 1975).

141. Filippo Beroaldo, *Commentarij a Philippo Beroaldo conditi in Asinum aureum Lucii Apulei* (Bologna, 1500); see Giehlow, 'Hieroglyphenkunde,' 132–43; Denys Drysdall, 'The Hieroglyphs at Bologna,' *Emblematica* 2 (1987): 225–47. For Firenzuola's translation, see Aldo Scaglione, 'L' "Asino d'oro" e il Firenzuola,' *Giornale storico della letteratura italiana* 126 (1949): 225–49; John Shearman, *Mannerism* (New York: Penguin, 1967), 38–9; Agnolo Firenzuola, *On the Beauty of Women,* ed. Jacqueline Murray (Philadelphia: University of Pennsylvania Press, 1992), xiii–xvii.

12

Immigrants and Church Patronage in Sixteenth-Century Ancona

Morten Steen Hansen

During the first part of the sixteenth century, Ancona emerged as one of the most affluent centers of international trade in the Adriatic. To stimulate development the city encouraged the settlement of foreign merchants, so that by the 1520s Ancona had acquired the cosmopolitan character for which it was known throughout the century.[1] Among the manifestations of increased wealth were commissions for painted and sculpted altarpieces in prominent locations from the most sought-after artists of the day. Because Ancona had no school of painters of its own of any importance, artists from other parts of Italy were employed. A considerable number of the patrons came from the immigrant communities. This study addresses works of art commissioned by immigrants with regard to their particular status in the city. Emphasis is placed on the Armenian Giorgio Morato, who on three occasions commissioned major altarpieces for the churches of Ancona.

While the foreigners could belong to the wealthiest part of society, they had no direct access to political influence. The Consiglio Generale, which since 1532 had been subordinate to the papacy, only had local nobility among its members.[2] The city's economic progress was to a large extent a result of the presence of foreigners, but Anconitan noblemen apparently preferred to regard these immigrants as peripheral entities. That impression is conveyed by the dialogue titled *Diporti notturni,* published in Ancona in 1580 (but dated the year previously) by Francesco Ferretti, a member of the Anconitan nobility and knight of the naval Order of Santo Stefano.[3] When describing the public festivities of his city, Ferretti included the 'rich, extravagant' costumes of the foreign groups in Ancona as part of the spectacles: 'Greek, Arab,

I would like to thank Gino Corti, Elizabeth Cropper, Roberto Dominichini, and Gunver Skytte.

Turkish, Moorish, Armenian, Hungarian, Polish, Bohemian and many other sorts of the most beautiful, fantastic things from overseas.'[4]

Ferretti's fascination with the foreigners as a strange and beautiful ornament hardly takes account of the actual role they played in the economic life of his city. Seen in the light of the *Diporti notturni*, and considering the immigrants' exclusion from political influence, the foreigners' acquisition of spectacular works of art became a way of displaying social status. The altarpieces included elements that called attention to the patrons' geographical, ethnic, and religious backgrounds, but only to inscribe these within notions of civic piety. By that term I mean to designate an act of public devotion, that reflected on and thereby benefited the community as a whole, either through dedications to Ancona's patron saints or by the sheer fame which a particular work of art brought to the city.

Our earliest example is the Croatian merchant and patrician Alvise Gozzi, the patron of the high altar in the destroyed church of San Francesco in Alto, for which Titian painted the altarpiece dated 1520 (Fig. 76).[5] When it was installed, it was the most splendid painting in the *maniera moderna* in Ancona. Through his donation Gozzi glorified the cult of the Franciscans and added to the fame of the city. He is depicted kneeling in prayer recommended to the Virgin and Child by St. Blaise, the patron saint of Gozzi's native city Ragusa (Dubrovnik). Because the cult of St. Blaise was common on the Italian peninsula, his presence also alludes to familiar religious practices in the Marches. The altarpiece could be said to foreground the patron's ethnicity only to resituate it in a context of local piety.

A different approach to self-representation was taken by the Venetian merchant Tomaso Cornovi della Vecchia. In April 1555 he acquired the patronage rights of the high altar in the church of San Domenico (Appendix 1).[6] Pellegrino Tibaldi originally received the commission for the altarpiece, but according to Vasari it was given to Titian instead because of disagreements between the patron and Tibaldi. The latter provided a stucco ornament 'grandissimo e bellissimo' for the high altar, which is now lost.[7] Upon Tomaso's death his brother Pietro took over the patronage of the high altar, where Titian's *Crucifixion* was installed on 22 July 1558 (Fig. 77). Through archival research I have discovered that Tomaso was still alive toward the end of May that year. He, and not his brother Pietro as otherwise presumed, must have been the disaffected patron mentioned by Vasari.[8] Tomaso's now lost sarcophagus in red porphyry was positioned in front of the high altar, on which an inscription in the same material was placed.[9] The coat of arms, known from a seventeenth-century manuscript copy, was placed on both sides of the altar (Fig. 78). Above, it pictures a figure holding a horn or cornucopia in reference to the family name, with a lily in the lower field. The Cornovi della Vecchia brothers thus identified themselves as Venetians through the most famous artist of their city.

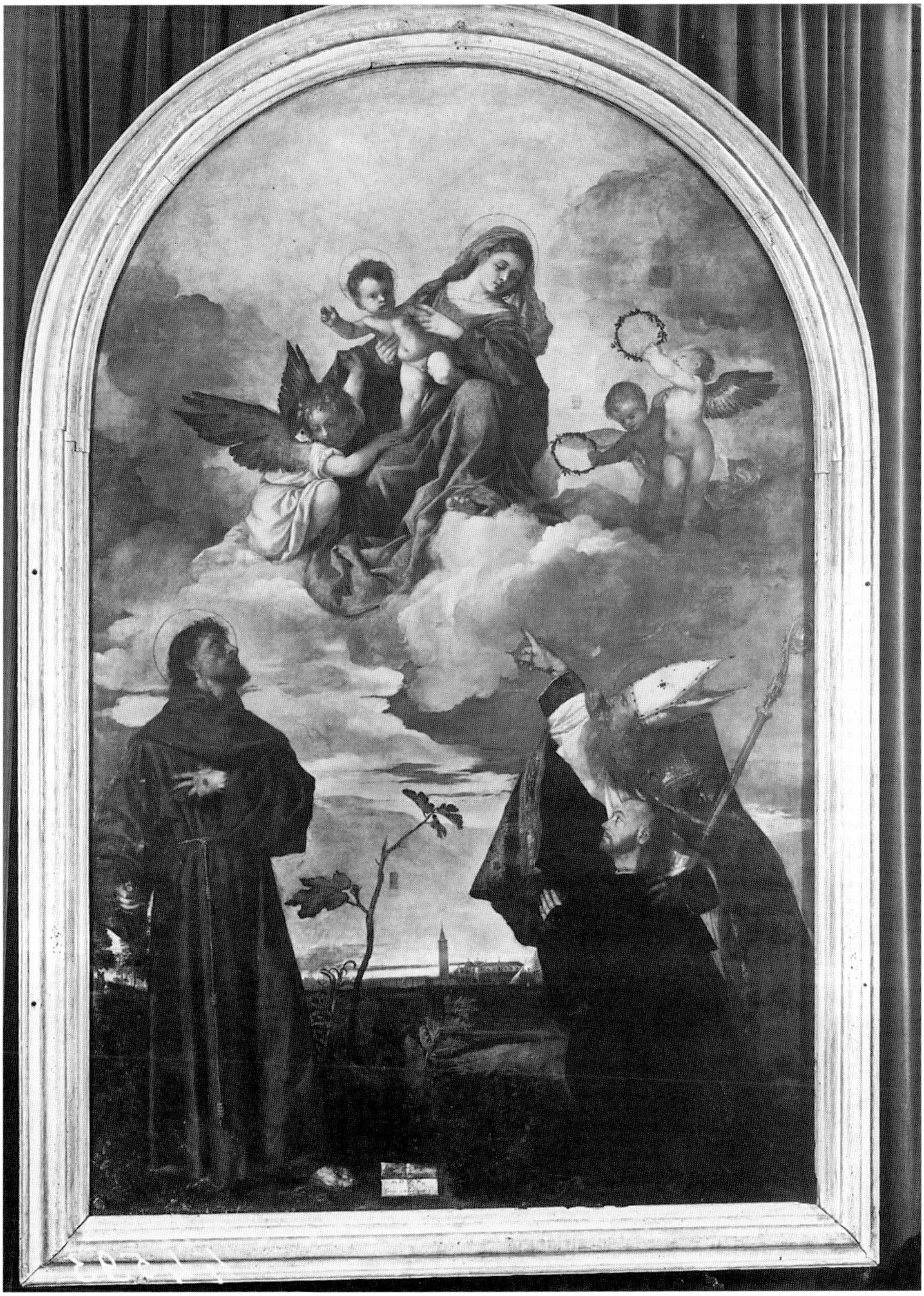

76. Titian, *Virgin and Child in Glory with Saints and Donor*, 1520. Oil on panel. Ancona, Pinacoteca Comunale "Francesco Podesti." Photo: Instituto Centrale per il Catalogo e la Documentazione, Rome.

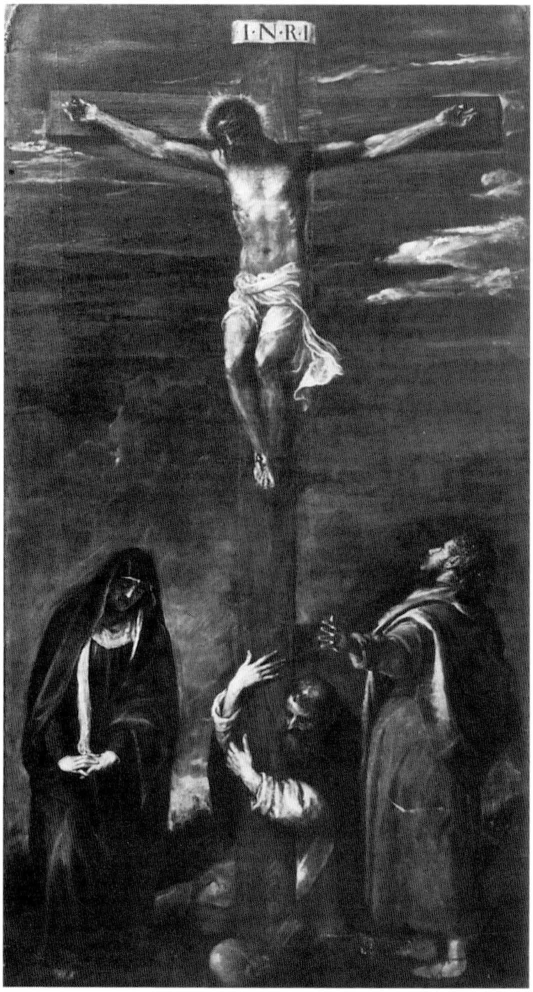

77. Titian, *Crucifixion*, 1558. Oil on canvas. Ancona, San Domenico. Photo: Instituto Centrale per il Catalogo e la Documentazione, Rome.

In the 1568 edition of the *Vite*, Vasari stated that Giorgio Morato, or Georg Mourat in Armenian, brought Pellegrino Tibaldi to Ancona. The first known work by Tibaldi in the Adriatic city is the *Baptism of Christ* with three predella panels, installed in 1556 in the now demolished church of San Agostino (Fig. 79).[10] His move to Ancona was motivated by opportunities for work, and until his departure around 1561 he received all commissions for large-scale, public, pictorial decorations. In his first work he seems to have consciously promoted himself through a *paragone* with the painters who previously had worked in the city. It has been pointed out that Rome is represented in the right background in the *Baptism of Christ*, recognizable from both ancient and modern monuments such as the Colosseum, the Pantheon,

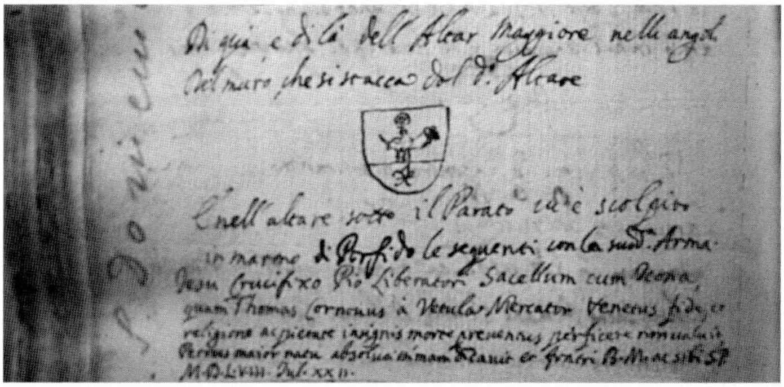

78. Giovanni Pichi Tancredi, *Compendio d'atti, risolutioni et decreti pubblici*. Ink on paper. Ancona, Biblioteca Comunale 'Luciano Benincasa,' Ms. 240, fol. 148v. Photo: Author.

and the complex of Santa Maria in Aracoeli and the Campidoglio, then undergoing Michelangelo's reconstruction.[11] I would propose that through the image of the city Tibaldi was commenting on his pictorial idiom as well as inviting comparisons with other altarpieces picturing cityscapes. With figural quotations from works by Michelangelo, Raphael, Sebastiano del Piombo, and Francesco Salviati, Tibaldi adhered to notions of the arts of Rome as the most perfect, to be continued and revered through imitation. Tibaldi referred to the celebrated inventions of several masters, accommodating them to his graceful, ornamental version of the Michelangelesque *maniera*.[12] The portrayal of Rome points to a *paragone* with the most famous painting in Ancona, Titian's Franciscan high altarpiece (Fig. 76). In the background of this work Titian had painted the Doge's palace and St. Mark's with campanile as a comment on his vernacular, painterly idiom. That Titian made this demonstrative indication of his pictorial 'dialect' outside Venetian territory reveals the artist's concern with the reception of his art abroad.[13] When Tibaldi 'signed' the San Agostino altarpiece with the image of Rome, he entered the *disegno-colore* debate which was played out around differences between north Italian and Roman-Tuscan painting. Even as he made an argument for *disegno* as the highest principle of art in competition with Venetian colorism, however, he also paid special attention to the landscape. It is as if Tibaldi wanted to affirm that even though he imitated Michelangelo, he was also capable of portraying the natural world, thereby challenging the art of Venice on its own distinctive terms. In contrast to the melting contours and golden lights of Titian's altarpiece, Tibaldi produced a sky with cool, dimmed blues. Pink at the horizon indicates a setting or a rising sun, while bright yellow lights and glowing, muted orange are reserved for the areas above surrounding the Holy Ghost and God the Father, holding a globe and carried by angels. Instead of Titian's warm haze, Tibaldi lets contours appear with a higher degree of focus through a clearer atmosphere.[14] That the San Agostino landscape reveals continuity with Emilian traditions of color and naturalism brings to mind the fact that Tibaldi

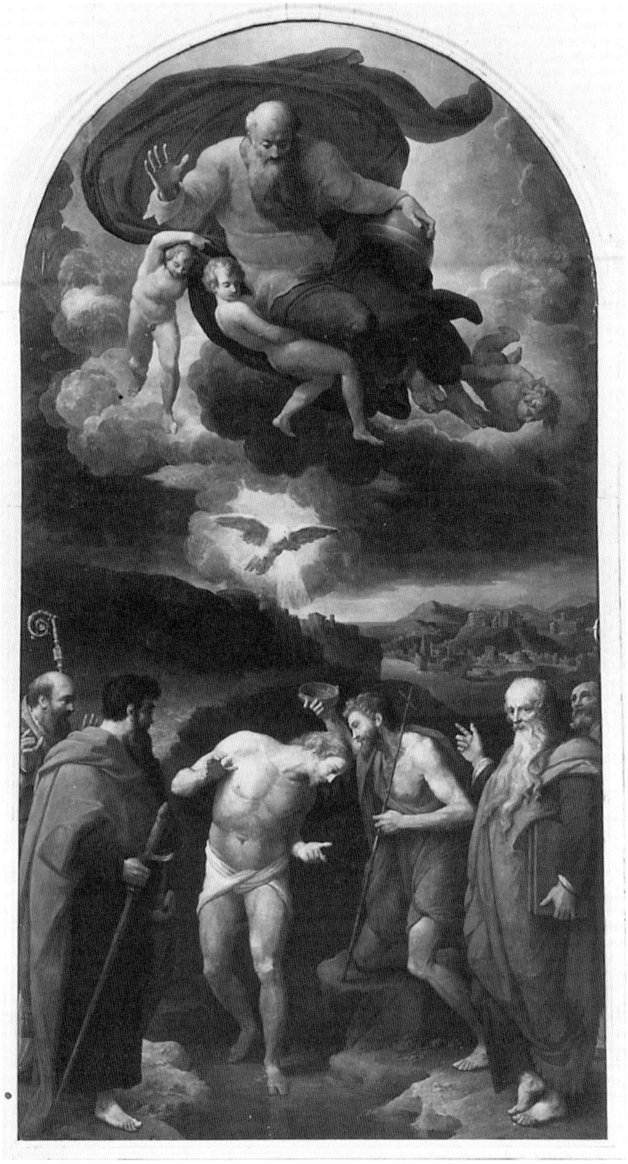

79. Pellegrino Tibaldi, *Baptism of Christ,* 1556. Oil on panel. Ancona, Pinacoteca Comunale 'Francesco Podesti' (on deposit in San Francesco alle scale, Ancona). Photo: Istituto Centrale per il Catalogo e la Documentazione, Rome.

in the sixteenth century was commonly referred to as *bolognese* or *da Bologna* by himself and others.[15]

When Lorenzo Lotto's *sacra conversazione* was placed on the high altar of San Agostino circa 1539–40, it replaced Mariano da Perugia's now lost altarpiece, which was moved to the altar of St. Nicholas of Tolentino. Both altars were under the

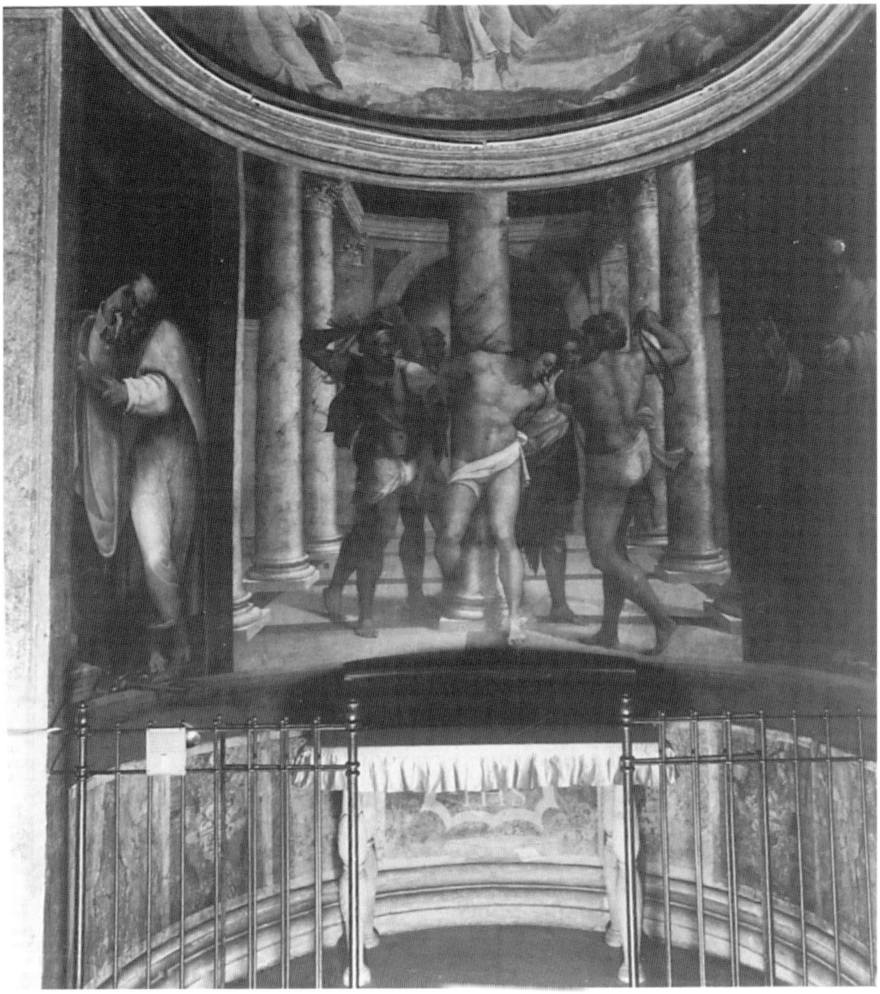

80. Sebastiano del Piombo, *Flagellation of Christ,* 1524. Mural. Rome, San Pietro in Montorio, Borgherini Chapel. Photo: Istituto Centrale per il Catalogo e la Documentazione, Rome.

patronage of the Anconitan Ferretti family.[16] The original high altarpiece had been commissioned by Girolamo Ferretti, and it was installed around 1500. Two manuscript sources describe the lost painting. It contained Mary, Joseph, and the Christ Child with St. Sebastian and another male saint. Kneeling on the right and left sides respectively were Girolamo's sons Angelo and Ciriaco with the city of Ancona 'ritratta dal naturale (portrayed from life).'[17] The inclusion of the cityscape expressed Girolamo Ferretti's hopes for the future prosperity of his heirs in the city (and Angelo Ferretti did indeed become one of the wealthiest and most influential men in Ancona).[18] In this case, the cityscape in the altarpiece (which must have been in the *maniera devota* of Perugino) did not carry any specific references to pictorial style as was the case with Titian and Tibaldi. In January 1554 Morato acquired from the Augustinian friars the right to construct a funerary chapel in their church (Appendix 2).[19] The contract states that it was to be located in the middle of the church between the altars of Sts. Nicholas of Tolentino and Lucy. Tibaldi's altarpiece was therefore placed next to Mariano da Perugia's image. Vasari narrates that Lotto's high altarpiece in San Agostino replaced the older one because it 'did not satisfy much.'[20] As Lotto had previously competed with Mariano da Perugia's altarpiece, so did Tibaldi, as indicated by the cityscapes. Tibaldi thereby signaled the superiority of the Roman style over the *maniera devota* even as he explored the affective possibilities of the landscape, which had been a distinct feature of the older style.

Tibaldi's imitations after Michelangelo included the figure of Christ in the San Agostino altarpiece (Fig. 79). By the mid-1550s Michelangelo had increasingly become controversial as a painter of sacred subjects following the unveiling of the Sistine *Last Judgment* in 1541. Among his designs attacked for lack of decorum was the *Flagellation of Christ* in the Borgherini Chapel in San Pietro in Montorio in Rome (Fig. 80). Executed by Sebastiano del Piombo, it was known from the 1550 edition of Vasari's *Vite* that Michelangelo had provided the drawing and would therefore have been recognized as the author of the invention.[21] Giovanni Andrea Gilio in his dialogue *On the Errors of Painters,* published in Camerino in 1564, had asserted that the flagellation should depict the Savior as ugly and mutilated, whereas Sebastiano had portrayed a beautiful, ideal Christ.[22] In his dialogue Gilio rehearsed arguments circulating in Roman ecclesiastical circles, and no doubt artists were familiar with them as well. When Tibaldi imitated Sebastiano's painting for his Christ figure, who humbly receives baptism, he made a controversial design by Michelangelo decorous and thereby provided a defense of the artist on whom he had based his *maniera.* Tibaldi's imitation of Michelangelo was also a correction, because he transposed the placid and beautiful figure of Christ from a context in which it was found to be incongruous into one which was deemed more appropriate, according to new standards of decorum now prevailing in the Papal States.

Morato's next two commissions also involved artists whose pictorial styles were associated with Rome. In 1559 he received permission from the Consiglio Generale, Bishop Vincenzo de' Luchi (1556–85), and the canons to construct a high altar in the cathedral of San Ciriaco as well as a tomb for the Armenians of Ancona, who could be buried there without charge, except for costs of candles and money to the priests.[23] When I previously published these contracts, I believed that the work originally was commissioned from Prospero Fontana, but I have since realized that the commission was to Daniele da Volterra. When Daniele subcontracted it to Pellegrino Tibaldi, once his assistant, it was stated that the monument had to be carried out according to the former's design. As the author of the splendid stucco figures on the walls of the Vatican Sala Regia and as an associate of Michelangelo, Daniele would have

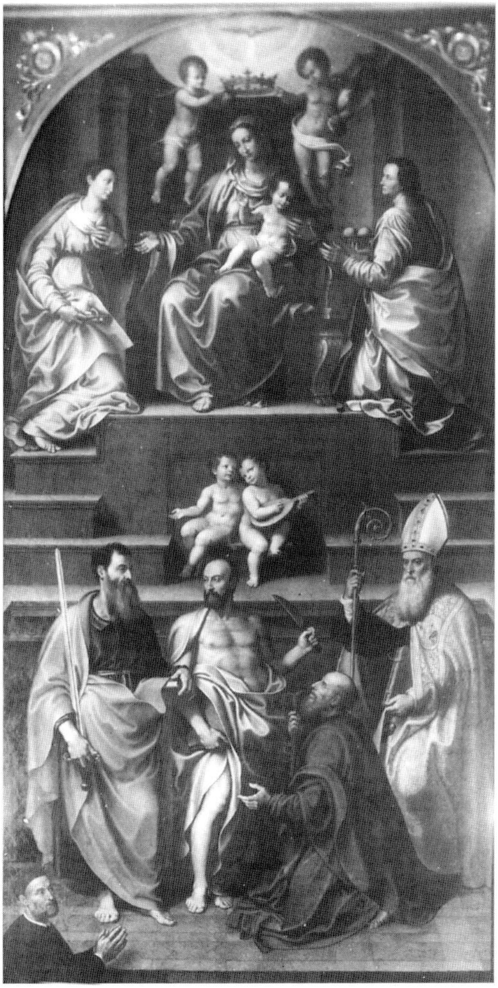

81. Girolamo Siciolante da Sermoneta, *Sacra conversazione with Donor (Pala di San Bartolomeo)*, 1570. Oil on canvas. Pinacoteca di Brera, Milan, on deposit in Santa Maria Assunta, Calcinate). Photo: Use authorized by the Italian Ministry of Cultural Heritage and Activities.

been the ideal choice for Morato's commission. Perhaps for the same reasons the patron permitted that the work was shared with – and probably almost exclusively executed by – Pellegrino Tibaldi. The high altarpiece in stucco was installed in the cathedral of San Ciriaco in 1560. Known from descriptions predating its destruction in the eighteenth century, it consisted of a Resurrected Christ in a Corinthian frame with angels above, placed in a niche in the wall above the high altar and supported by a base. An inscription on the wall in golden letters marked Morato's dedication of the monument to God.[24] Morato's last altarpiece, installed on the high altar of the now destroyed church of the nuns of San Bartolomeo, was signed and dated by Girolamo Siciolante da Sermoneta in 1570 (Fig. 81).

In his religious patronage Morato asserted the union between Armenian Christianity and Roman Catholicism. Although all three commissions included inscriptions referring to Morato as 'the Armenian,' they were placed in Western churches. He chose artists, pictorial styles, and saints associated with Rome while including references to Armenian hagiography. Tibaldi's Trinitarian *Baptism of Christ* is flanked by four saints (Fig. 79). Moses (and not Peter as otherwise presumed) with the tablets of the law and St. Paul stand on the right and left respectively, with two bishop saints behind them. The left one of these expresses his attention to the divine event by lifting his hands in a gesture of pathos. The second bishop saint, who wears red gloves, turns his gaze ecstatically upward. Morato's contract for the chapel states that the patron was to choose to whom the altar should be dedicated (Appendix 2). Two inscriptions once framed the altar. They mention St. Cyriacus, God, and John the Baptist:

> GEORGIUS MORATTUS ARMENUS/ET HOC ET ALIUD IN L[O]DE/ DIVI QUIRIACI OPUS FACIENDUM/CURAVIT AD DEI AC/DIVI JOANNIS/BAPTISTE GLORIAM/ANNO DNI M.D.L.V.I.[25]

Because of the convention of placing the titular saint on the right, it is likely that St. Cyriacus, Ancona's primary patron saint, is pictured on that side.[26] The bishop saint on the left is a reversed and dramatized imitation of St. Augustine in Raphael's St. Cecilia altarpiece in Bologna, and I therefore propose this to be the same saint. Moses points toward the baptism scene and to the Baptist, who stands next to him. His gesture visualizes St. John's status as the culmination of the law (held by Moses) and the greatest of the Old Testament prophets.[27] St. John rests his right knee on a rock, which symbolizes the Roman Church's authority to distribute the sacraments. The presence of Rome above Moses' head points to his role as *typus papae*. In this capacity the Old Testament patriarch had earlier been represented on the walls in the Sistine Chapel as well as in Michelangelo's tomb of Julius II in San Pietro in Vincoli in Rome. Like Moses' authority, the pope's came directly from God. Both held the office of high priest, and both were leaders of states.[28] As the protectors of Rome, Peter and Paul were commonly represented together. Tibaldi's 'replacement' of Peter with Moses leads the beholder to consider the roles of the prophet and the first bishop of Rome as papal prototypes. Tibaldi enhanced their association by painting Moses in the colors usually employed for Peter with blue and orange robes.[29] In the San Agostino altarpiece Rome is both a source of spiritual authority and of perfect *disegno*.

The Trinitarian message and the representation of the law as a prophesy of the Incarnation were theological commonplaces in both Western and Armenian traditions. Central sources for these notions include *De civitate Dei* by St. Augustine (who is represented in the altarpiece) and St. Gregory the Illuminator's *Sermon* and *Teaching*. St. Gregory, who lived around the turn of the third century was, together with Bartholomew and Taddeus, among the legendary founders of Christianity in Armenia, hence the name of 'Illuminator.' The *Sermon* and *Teaching* formed part of

Agathangelos's *History of the Armenians* written in the fourth century.[30] The combination of Paul and Moses might have been inspired by a passage in Agathangelos, where Gregory's conversion of the Armenian people is compared both with Moses' transmission of faith to the Jews and Paul's spreading of Christianity among the gentiles:

> At that time our land of Armenia was blessed, envied and truly admired. Like Moses, who suddenly became a teacher of the law to the Hebrew camp with all the ranks of the prophets, or like the outstanding Paul with the entire group of the apostles, with the gospel of Christ that brings life to the world, so too did he [Gregory the Illuminator] come and appear and speak Armenian to the Armenians.[31]

Armenians familiar with Agathangelos's *History* could have seen in Tibaldi's altarpiece (significantly representing the Baptism of Christ) an allusion to the Christianization of their nation, which was the first to embrace the new religion.

The contract between Morato and the bishops and canons of the cathedral reveals that the new high altarpiece was erected in honor of God and St. Liberius, a legendary fifth-century Armenian prince who had died in Ancona as a pilgrim.[32] His remains were preserved in the cathedral together with two of Ancona's other patron saints, Cyriacus and Marcellinus. While Morato was alive, the priests of San Ciriaco were to celebrate an annual mass for the salvation of his soul on 4 June, eight days after the feast of St. Liberius.[33] The wording of the document defines the ritual in direct relationship to the cult around the Armenian saint. Morato's patronage in San Ciriaco could be seen as a Counter-Reformation restoration of the ancient cult practices around St. Liberius. Because according to his legend the saint had been venerated in Ancona by Armenian pilgrims traveling through the city on their way from Rome to Armenia, the construction of the high altar in his honor and the tomb for the Armenians gave monumental expression to their ancient devotion to Ancona's patron saint.

Like Tibaldi's *Baptism of Christ*, with its sacramental symbolism, the altarpiece in the cathedral of Ancona also revealed Tridentine concerns. It can be construed in the context of the many Italian high altarpieces from the mid-century with representations of Christ's body on the cross, in death, or resurrected. These subjects enhanced the authority of the Roman Church by pointing to the Eucharist, celebrated and distributed below at the altar. In an Anconitan context Peter Humfrey has called attention to Titian's *Crucifixion* in San Domenico, where the titular saint of the church is reduced to one in a group of worshipers of the cross: the painting's focus is on Christ's body (Fig. 77).[34]

The high altarpiece for San Bartolomeo (c. 5.30 × 2.70 meters) was the largest single picture Siciolante ever executed (Fig. 81).[35] Here, the *sacra conversazione* is separated through the painted architecture into two separate spheres. The Virgin and

Child are enthroned above, flanked by Saints Agnes and Agatha. In the foreground below are four male saints, of which Bartholomew appears as the central figure. Paul with sword and book on the left is countered by a bishop saint on the right. A hermit saint kneels in front of Bartholomew, and the latter turns his head to Paul in reference to their status as Christ's apostles. At the lower left corner the patron in profile folds his hands in prayer. Below center an illusionistic plaque on the painted architecture reads:

> GEORGIVS MORATVS ARMENVS/OPVS HOC DIVO BARTHOLOMEO SA/CRUM FACIENDVM CVRAVIT PINX/AUTEM HIERONIMUS SERMONETA M.D.L.XX.

The display of Bartholomew's skin refers to his flaying. Two naked musician angels at center symbolize the purity and innocence of the martyrs, who reached their sanctity through bodily torments. The almost melancholic expressions of the virgin saints above and the furrowed, dark eyes of the male saints below produce a severe air suggestive of martyrdom. As we shall see later, among the saints only the kneeling hermit was not killed for Christ. The strict organization of the figures in a shallow, austere architectural setting leaves an archaic impression. That effect is played out against the stylized proportions and contours of the figures characteristic of the Tuscan-Roman *maniera*. Difference of scale between the saints in the two registers is downplayed, which enhances the iconic impression. When one considers the notion that flourished in ecclesiastical circles during the period of Catholic Reform that less overtly beautiful or even primitive works of art possessed greater sanctity than certain modern works, then Siciolante's archaisms can be understood as the production of effects of piety.[36] The fully enveloping draperies appeal to post-Tridentine notions of the decorum of the sacred image. Some features of the pictorial organization were motivated by the fact that the image was painted for nuns; hence the top section with the crowned Queen of Heaven and two virgin martyrs, exemplars for the nuns, are separated from the male saints and donor below. The gendered organization of the represented space would have been significant to the visitor of the church, considering the separation of the sisters from patron and laity during mass when all were gathered in the church, as well as the separation of the laity along the nave on the basis of gender.

Martyred in Armenia, Bartholomew was the apostolic founder of Christianity in that nation, as described by the fifth-century Moses of Khoren. A relic of the apostle was preserved in Ancona's cathedral.[37] The kneeling hermit in the painting is, I believe, St. Liberius, who in Ancona was depicted as a brown-clad hermit with a tau staff.[38] The portrayals of Bartholomew and St. Liberius were motivated by the dedication of the church to the former and the latter's status as being among Ancona's patron saints. That Liberius kneels in reverence for the apostle, however, can only be understood if one considers the part played by Bartholomew in Armenian church history and Liberius's origins in that nation. The saints associated with Armenia in Siciolante's high altarpiece were also common in Anconitan piety (a convergence with Alvise Gozzi's use of St. Blase). For this reason I believe that the bishop saint here is Cyriacus and not Gregory the Illuminator as otherwise proposed.[39] Gregory was practically unknown to a Western audience and would not have been an effective agent of the theme of union between the Roman and Armenian denominations. If we accept the identification of St. Cyriacus, then the male saints are arranged as three pairs: the apostles Paul and Bartholomew, Bartholomew and Liberius as associated with Armenia, and Liberius and Cyriacus as Ancona's patron saints.

Morato's staging of the containment of Armenian religion by Roman Catholicism coincided with the contemporary efforts of Armenians in Asia to achieve union with Rome. In 1547 a council in Echmiadzin decided that the head of the Armenian Church, Catholicos Stephen V Salmastezì, should visit the Western powers in the hope of gaining support against the persecutions of the Armenians, which were intensified the following year when war broke out between the Turks and the Persians. With respect to military support the visit was not a success. When in Rome between 1549–50, the Catholicos professed the submission of the Armenian Church to Pope Paul III.[40] When one considers the Armenians' attempt to gain the support from the West on the basis of unity of faith, Morato's patronage becomes an argument for the same principle, and the Armenian community in Ancona would have understood such a gesture.

While the historical situation suggests that the Armenians of Ancona were attuned to the claims set forth in Morato's patronage, local clergy and laity might not have been particularly invested in the fate of the Christians in Armenia. The question therefore remains: what was at stake in Morato's patronage for a non-Armenian audience? The high altarpiece for the cathedral was erected by agreement with the city's secular and ecclesiastical authorities. Granted that the high altarpiece was located on the most privileged site of Christian devotion, its significance for a larger audience can be considered. As we saw earlier, the ritual to be carried out in connection with the high altar amounted to a celebration of the Armenian presence in Ancona through devotion to St. Liberius and through the community sepulcher. To explore this further I now turn to papal politics as they were influenced by eschatological thought and to the relationship between the Consiglio Generale of Ancona and Rome.[41]

Since the later Middle Ages, the eschatological scriptures had tended to be interpreted allegorically in terms of real human agencies and historical events. In Catholic Europe the unrest caused by the outbreak of the Protestant Reformation intensified the sense of living in the last days, which, in keeping with St. John's *Apocalypse,* were characterized by crises and persecutions preceding the universal justice of the eschaton. As demonstrated by Kenneth Stow, the changed historical situation resulted in a new attitude on the part of the sixteenth-century popes toward the Jews. Instead of the previous passive expectation of their baptism, a new attitude became prevalent, which actively strove for their conversion. The Jews' conversion, as part of the universal Christianization, was among the signs which marked the arrival of the Last Judgment.[42] In Ancona the new attitude toward the Jews resulted in the burning of the Talmud and other Jewish scriptures on 1 February 1554 under Julius III. The following year saw the beginning of the papacy of Paul IV, who in particular thought of himself as actively partaking in the 'last times.' He opened the ghettos and introduced a series of restrictions against the Jews.[43] The systematic attempts to destroy Jewish culture were supposed to stimulate their conversion. As part of the 'apocalyptic battles,' Paul IV, the former inquisitor, persecuted heresy eagerly, and in the first year of his papacy measures were taken against the Marranos of Ancona for their reversion to Judaism as acts of heresy. A letter from the Consiglio of 22 December 1555 to the pontiff presented concern over the actions, but to no effect. The Anconitans expressed their support of the pope's decision to eliminate the Marranos from his domains, but feared that his actions in Ancona would be the financial ruin of the city because of the disruptions caused by the imprisonments. After the burning of twenty-four Marranos in the following year, a second letter was sent to Rome dated 10 August 1556 by the now deeply troubled Anconitans, but again to no avail. The public executions resulted in the boycott of Ancona by the Jews resident in Ottoman domains, and for a period it seemed to the Anconitans that papal politics would be the end of their city.[44]

Seen in the light of the events in Ancona preceding Morato's patronage in the cathedral, the celebration of the Christian minority in San Ciriaco was a symbolic step toward the universal church of the millennium. In the sixteenth century the millennium was often interpreted by Catholics as a period on earth before the Last Judgment when all Christians would live under the spiritual leadership of the pope.[45] The commission's eschatological significance signaled harmony between Ancona and Paul IV's politics. Considering the grave crisis then barely over between city and papacy, the Anconitans must have felt the need to express their acceptance of papal overlordship in the hope of facilitating their future relationship after the disastrous interlude. In 1558, the year before the high altarpiece was begun, the Consiglio accepted Pellegrino Tibaldi's design for the monumental vault of the Loggia dei Mercanti. Tibaldi prominently painted at its center an emblem of Justice with the Last Judgment, imitating the Vatican frescoes by Raphael and Michelangelo (Fig. 82). Surrounding the central image were four shields containing the coat of arms of Ancona crowned with papal symbols. Justice was among the symbols utilized in the pope's self-representations, as demonstrated by a bronze medal with Paul IV's portrait and an allegory of Justice on its respective sides.[46] Like Giorgio

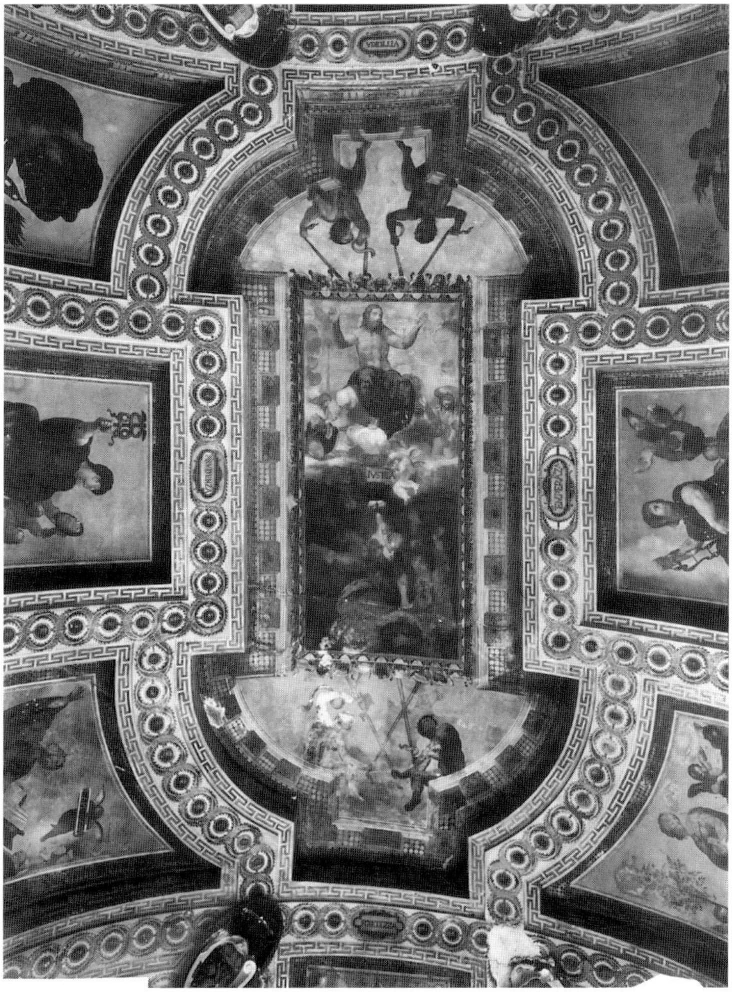

82. Pellegrino Tibaldi, *Vault of the Loggia dei Mercanti*, 1558–61. Fresco and stucco. Ancona (photo predates destruction during World War II). Photo: Istituto Centrale per il Catalogo e la Documentazione, Rome.

Morato's patronage in San Ciriaco, the loggia's vault was a public manifestation associated with the Consiglio, which expressed its reverence for Rome in an apocalyptic context.

The last part of this study returns to the initial question of church patronage as a form of self-fashioning by immigrants in a particular civic context. Titian's patrons certainly negotiated cultural differences, but Morato's situation was more complex because of what might have been a widespread suspicion of the orthodoxy of the Armenians despite the fact that the Armenians honored the papacy. Considering the historical events in Ancona in the 1550s, the question of religious conformity would have been essential to Morato's construction of a pious persona through church patronage, which marked his ideal position in Ancona. As we shall see, he confronted the issue through imagery of conversion.

Historically, in situations when church unions between Rome and Armenia reached the point of implementation, problems had often arisen. Skepticism from the West was based on differences of theology and rite, the Armenians' status as moderate Monophysites (i.e., they denied the dual nature of Christ as defined by the Westerners) and their rejection of the ecumenical Council of Chalcedon (451) being particularly problematic.[47] The Armenians, on the other hand, did not welcome what they saw as attempts to colonize their church, cases in point being the mixed reactions to the Franciscan and Dominican missionaries in the thirteenth and fourteenth centuries and the indifferent reception in Armenia of the delegation which had participated in the Council of Florence in 1439.[48] Even though the Armenians signed the councilliary acts, the results were never codified by an Armenian synod. A sixteenth-century example is provided by the Inquisition's censorship of the Armenian printing press in Venice. The religious writings were considered erroneous and therefore unacceptable, resulting in a limited production of the Armenian texts.[49] In Morato's case a particular wording in the contract between him and the bishop and canons of San Ciriaco suggests the tension:

> The most pious, Christian and Catholic Master Giorgio Morato, Armenian and for many years inhabitant of the magnificent city of Ancona, has decided, for the adornment of the divine cult, to construct an altar and an altarpiece in honor of the omnipotent and great God and also for the celebration and memory of the most illustrious Blessed Liberius, once son of the King of Armenia and one of the principal protectors and advocates of this place where his most sacred body still rests. . . .[50]

The emphasis on Morato's Catholicism and reference to his lengthy residence in Ancona go beyond standard courtesies of notarial prose. The formulations counter potential doubts regarding the Armenian patron's spiritual righteousness.

The notion of the Armenians' strangeness might also have existed on a more popular level, less informed by theological questions. We saw above how Francesco Ferretti spoke of the immigrants' costumes, those of the Armenians included, as beautiful and fantastic. Giorgio Morato, on the other hand, was portrayed in black as was the Italian fashion, just as Alvise Gozzi had let himself be painted wearing the same color in Titian's altarpiece in San Francesco in alto (Figs. 76 and 81). Perhaps these costumes reflect characteristics of the particular ethnic groups, but even so they are strongly reminiscent of local, patrician dress. These 'Italianized' costumes cannot easily be associated with any 'fantastic' native dress. The two donor portraits defy notions of the immigrants' exoticism.

The fact that the Armenian mass was celebrated in a language the Italians could not understand enhanced the sense of their peripheral status. In *L'Acerba* by Francesco Stabili (1269–1327), the beauty of the choir of the angels was ironically contrasted with the 'yelling' of the Armenians during mass. Benedetto Varchi's *L'Ercolano,* published posthumously in Florence in 1570, included Tuscan proverbs which negatively interpreted the Armenian mass, one of which associated it with speaking gibberish.[51]

In two, and perhaps in all three, altarpieces commissioned by Morato, St. Cyriacus was among the *tituli.* In the churches of San Agostino and San Bartolomeo he was represented in paint, while the high altarpiece in the cathedral dedicated to that saint spoke for itself. Jacobus de Voragine's *Golden Legend* narrated the saint's story in 'The Finding of the Holy Cross.'[52] In Jerusalem, when Constantine's mother Helena desired to find Golgotha with the aid of the Jews, one named Judas refused to assist her. To punish him she attempted to starve him in a dried well. After seven days, symbolic of his future creation as saint, he was willing to speak, and when he arrived on Golgotha he converted. The True Cross was then discovered, and Judas became bishop of Jerusalem with the name of Cyriacus before his martyrdom under Julian the Apostate. Ancona's foremost patron saint's status as a converted Jew was foregrounded in Tibaldi's *Baptism of Christ,* where he was placed next to Moses (Fig. 79). The association was emphasized by the fact that positions and expressions of the heads of the bishops imitate those of the saints standing in front of them. Moses looks outward (but, with otherworldly remoteness, not directly at the spectator) while pointing to the baptism scene. His intermediary function between beholder and sacred action expresses his status as forerunner, one who precedes John the Baptist and Christ. God the Father, the three angels supporting him, the Baptist, Paul, and St. Augustine all gaze at Christ. St. Cyriacus looks upward in rapture, and only Moses faces out and away from the central scene. Paul's shaded, inward-turned profile makes his act of looking particularly intense, alluding to his First Epistle to the Corinthians: 'Have I not seen Jesus our Lord?'[53] That Paul functions as a contrapposto to Moses enhances the prophet's lack of visual access to the baptism. The coexistence of Paul and Moses points to Pauline notions of the Old Testament patriarch as set forth in the Second Epistle to the Corinthians:

> [Christ's covenant is a] new covenant, not written but spiritual; for the written law condemns to death, but the Spirit gives life. . . . Indeed, the glory [of the law] that once was is now no glory at all; it is outshone by a still greater glory [which is Christ]. . . . With such a hope as this

> we speak out boldly; it is not for us to do as Moses did: he put a veil over his face to keep the Israelites from gazing at the end of what was fading away. In any case their minds had become closed, for that same veil is there to this very day when the lesson is read from the old covenant; and it is never lifted, because only in Christ is it taken away. Indeed to this very day, every time the law of Moses is read, a veil lies over the mind of the hearer. But (as scripture says) 'Whenever he turns to the Lord the veil is removed.'[54]

In Paul's famous contrasting of the letter to the spirit, Moses appears both as part of Christian prehistory and in reference to the 'blindness' of the Jews after the Incarnation, because they did not perceive the Christological significance of their bible.[55] In Tibaldi's altarpiece Moses' tablets are contrasted with the book held by Paul. The New Testament gives access to the living God, who fulfilled and abrogated Mosaic law. Because Moses does not behold Christ, he recalls the fate of those who continued to live under the law. As in Tibaldi's *Baptism of Christ,* the San Bartolomeo high altarpiece also foregrounded St. Cyriacus's status as a convert saint, here by picturing him as a contrapposto to St. Paul (Fig. 81). Both reached sanctity through dramatic acts of conversion, and both initially as Jude and Saul rejected Christ. Moreover, Paul was the one who, after having been converted himself, eagerly pursued the conversion of others.[56]

Morato's altarpieces argued the perfect harmony between Armenian and Western traditions and the former's containment by the latter. At the same time his commissions were abundant with messages of conversion related to the role played by Judaism in Christian society. As we saw earlier, the union between the Roman and Armenian Church, as solemnly declared by the Catholicos to the pope in 1549, was perhaps more a reality in theory than in practice. The Armenian, religious communities had always been accepted on the Italian peninsula, but on both theological and more popular ground the Armenians occasionally were countered with suspicion and even ridicule from a Western audience because of religious and cultural differences. In Tibaldi's *Baptism of Christ,* the ambiguous representation of Moses next to the convert saint in an altarpiece dedicated to the institution of the sacrament of baptism, abundant with papal allusions, could only evoke the papal policy toward the Jews. Indeed, the altarpiece can be construed as an argument for it. Morato's foremost concern in his first chapel, however, was the representation of his own orthodoxy against negative notions of Armenian Christianity. A sixteenth-century beholder questioning Armenian orthodoxy could in Tibaldi's altarpiece have seen not just an affirmation of Catholic doctrine and papal politics, but also a reference to the patron's own 'baptism' into the Tridentine Church. The fact that Morato's repeated dedications to St. Cyriacus took place in Western churches, and not in the Armenian church of San Anastasia with its 'unintelligible' mass and 'dubious' theology, bore witness to Morato's patronage as symbolic acts of conversion.[57] The references to Judaism as Christianity's 'other' thereby hinted at a second 'other,' that of an unfamiliar version of Armenian Christianity. Morato evoked the stereotype of Armenian unorthodoxy only to distance himself from it.[58]

APPENDIX I

Andrea Bernardini Pilestri, Archivio di Stato di Ancona, Archivio Notarile, vol. 1011, fols. 101v-102r (17 April 1555).

fol. 101 v.

"Concessio cappelle Thome della Vecchia (??). Actum Ancone, in sacristia ecclesie Sancti Dominici de Ancona, posita iuxta dictam ecclesiam, iuxta sua notissima latera, presentibus magistro Dominico Filippi de Camerino, sutore, et magistro Petro Tibaldi, bononiense pictore, habitantibus Ancone testibus etc. Congregato et capitulariter cohadunato, ut moris est, et ad sonum campanelle, capitulo reverendorum patrum ecclesie et conventus Sancti Dominici de Ancona, in quo interfuerunt reverendi patres etc., reverendus prior frater Vincentius de Lugo et vicarius generalis, frater Reginaldus de Faentia subtus prior, frater Remigius de Florentia, bacalarius et rector, frater Thomas de Ancona, frater Micael de Florentia, frater Iohannes de Ausimo, frater Gregorius de Florentia, frater Gratianus de Ancona, frater Antonius de Ancona, frater Zacaria de Ancona, frater Gratia de Senis et frater Iosef de Florentia, in mei et testium supra scriptorum presentia, exposuerent ad eorum notitiam devenisse magnificum virum et fidum et divitem mercatorem dominum Thomam de Vetula, de Venetiis et Ancone comorantem, tabulam seu anconam ad honorem Omnipotentis

fol. 102 r.

Dei erigere et fieri facere, in animo habere ornandi et famosius reddendi gratia templum Dei Omnipotentis et Sancti Dominici in altare magno capelle maioris dicte ecclesie. Propterea dicti reverendi patres concorditer et unanimiter desciderantes [sic=desiderantes] ecclesiam prefatam formosiorem reddi, cultum divinum augeri et dictum dominum Thomam ad dictum pium opus exequendum subinvitari, capitulariter congregati ut supra, per eos et eorum successores in perpetuum, dederunt et concesserunt dicto domino Thome, licet absenti etc., dictam capellam maiorem cum altare maiori in dicta ecclesia Sancti Dominici tenente plenamque et liberam facultatem dictum altare magnum et cappellam ornandi dicto Tome licet absenti, et tabulam seu anconam in dicto altare magno pro se et suis heredibus construendi, actandi, edificandi vel reficiendi et ad eius elipendi eius libitum et voluntatem quicquid ad ornatum ecclesie, capelle et altaris predictorum fuerit gerendi, faciendi et exercendi, dummodo in dicto altari maiori sit sacramentum et eucaristia modo et forma et pro visum fuerit dicto domino Thome et eius heredibus ad ornatum tamen dicte ecclesie. Et dictam facultatem et potestatem dicto domino Thomae et heredibus faciendi dictam tabulam seu anconam durare voluerunt ad annos tres proximos futuros, salvo iusto impedimento. Et promiserunt rata et grata habere premissa ut supra dicte promissa, data et concessa, et illis non contrafacere vel venire, et nemini alii dictam facultatem et potestatem concedere. Que omnia etc. iuraverunt more sacerdotum in posterum etc. omni meliori modo etc. Renuntiantes etc. Iurantes etc."

APPENDIX 2

Girolamo Giustiniani, Archivio di Stato di Ancona, Archivio Notarile, vol. 680, fol. 17r (29 January 1554).

"Concessio loci pro altare et sepulcro construendis Georgii alias Moratti senioris. Die vigessima nona mensis Ianuarii. Actum Ancone, in sacrario sive sacristia ecclesie Sancti Augustini de Plano, adsita in terzerio Capitis Montis, iuxta alia bona eiusdem ecclesie, vias publicas et alia latera. Presentibus Francisco Verchurio, Francisco magistri Thome et Petro Tunoro, civibus et habitatoribus Ancone, testibus etc., convocato et coadunato venerabili Capitulo fratruum ecclesie Sancti Augustini de Plano de Ancona, in numero sufficienti et valido ad sonum campane, ut moris est, de ordine et mandato venerabilis patris et sacre theologie profexoris, fratris Michaellis de Padua, prioris dictorum fratruum et conventus, in quo quidem capitulo interfuerunt infrascripti patres habentes vocem in eo, et ultra duas tertias partes eiusdem, videli, ut dictus reverendus pater frater Michael prior, Magister Aurelius de Lignario regens, magister Augustinus de Ancona, frater Stefanus de Ancona, sindicus, frater Christofarus de Verona, Vicarius, frater Andreas de Ancona, frater Filippus de Ancona, frater Nicolaus de Monte Ulmi, frater Nicolaus de Monte Sancti Martini, frater Marinus de Mondulfo, frater Paulus de Sigillo et frater Iohannes Antonius de Arimino. Qui quidem fratres coadunati ut supra ad sonum campane de ordine et mandato predictis, per eos et eorum successores, omni meliori modo, via, iure, forma et causa quibus magis et melius de iure fieri potest et eisdem licuit et licet, dederunt et concesserunt Georgio alias Moratto prosenete seniori, presenti, recipienti et acceptanti pro se et suis heredibus, unum locum in dicta ecclesia Sancti Augustini, inter altaria Beati Nicolai de Tolentino et Beate Virginis Lucie, causa construendi seu fabricandi capellam seu altarem secundum velle suum, nec non in medio ecclesie predicte, locum pro uno sepulcro respicientem ipsam cappellam, gratis et amore Dei. Quam cappellam et quod sepulcrum ipse Georgius per se etc. promisit et convenit dictis fratribus presentibus, stipulantibus et recipientibus ut supra, facere et construere seu construi facere in dictis locis super descriptis et expressis omni modo et forma providere videbatur omnibus eius sumptibus et expensis, tunc et quando eidem videbitur et placebit de pretio et valore secundum eius velle, dedicanda Sancto seu Sanctis cui seu quibus voluerit. Que omnia et singula supradicta dicte partes et quelibet ipsarum etc., sub pena dupli in quolibet capitulo etc. et obligatione omnium suorum bonorum etc., que bona etc., in quibus bonis etc. iuraverunt; videlicet dicti patres in personaliter, et prefatus Georgius, manu tactis scripturis, ad delationem mei notarii infrascripti etc."

NOTES

1. Reductions of duties were first provided for merchants from Florence and Ragusa (Dubrovnik) in 1499–1500. In 1518 this was expanded to all subjects of the Ottoman Empire. Under Paul III and Julius III the privileges were extended to the Marranos as well. When Montaigne around 1580 visited Ancona, he noticed a high number of Greeks, Turks, and Slavs. Michel Eyquem de Montaigne, *Journal du Voyage*, ed. Louis Lautrey, 2nd rev. ed. (Paris: Hachette, 1909), 293; Peter Earle, 'The Commercial Development of Ancona, 1479–1551,' *Economic History Review*, 2nd ser., 22 (1969): 28–44; Jean Delumeau, 'Ancône, trait d'union entre l'occident et l'orient a l'époque de la renaissance,' in *Sociétés et compagnies de commerce en orient et dans l'Océan Indien*, ed. Michel Mollat (Paris: S.E.V.P.E.N., 1970), 419–33; Shlomo Simonsohn, 'Marranos in Ancona under Papal Protection,' *Michael* 9 (1985): 234–67; Bernard Dov Coopermann, 'Venetian Policy Toward Levantine Jews in Its Broader Italian Context,' in *Gli Ebrei e Venezia, secoli XIV–XVIII*, ed. Gaetano Cozzi (Milan: Edizioni Comunità, 1987), 71, 73–4, 76.

2. For the organization of the Consiglio Generale before and after the papal invasion, see Luigi Franchi, *Benvenuto Stracca: Giureconsulto anconitano del secolo XVI* (Rome: Ermanno Loescher & Co., 1888), 28–35.

3. For Francesco Ferretti, see Marina Minelli, *La famiglia Ferretti di Ancona* (Ancona: n.p., 1987), 98–103.

4. 'et una coppia assai grande di ricchi istrauaganti habiti, greci, arabi, turchi, mori, armeni, ongari, polacchi, boemi, et molte altre sorte vaghissime fantasticarie oltramarine.' Francesco Ferretti, *Diporti notturni* (Ancona: F. Salvioni, 1580), 139–41. All translations mine unless otherwise indicated.

5. Harold E. Wethey, *The Paintings of Titian*, vol. 1, *The Religious Paintings* (London: Phaidon, 1969), 109; Michele Polverari, ed., *Tiziano: La pala Gozzi di Ancona*, exh. cat. (Bologna: Grafis Edizioni, 1988). For church patronage by individual laymen, see Richard A. Goldthwaite, *Wealth and the Demand for Art in Italy 1300–1600* (Baltimore and London: Johns Hopkins University Press, 1993), 121–9.

6. Wethey, *Paintings of Titian*, vol. 1, 85–6; Michele Polverari, *Tiziano: La crocefissione di Ancona*, exh. cat. (Ancona: Confartigianato Provincia di Ancona, 1990), 15–19, with information on the Cornovi della Vecchia family. Polverari published a few lines of a copy of a document in the Archivio di Stato in Venice and referred to the location of the original in Ancona, published here for the first time (Appendix 1). See also idem, 'Ancora sulla committenza della crocefissione di Tiziano nella chiesa di San Domenico ad Ancona,' *Prilozi povijesti umjetnosti u Dalmaciji* 33 (1992): 77–8.

7. Vasari's account of Tibaldi's activities was part of the 'Life of Primaticcio' in the 1568 edition of the *Vite*. Giorgio Vasari, *Le vite de' più eccellenti pittori, scultori e architettori: Testo*, ed. Rosanna Bettarini and Paola Barocchi (Florence: Studio per Edizioni Scelte, 1987), vol. 6, 149. A notarial act of

1605 describes 'figure di stucco' by Tibaldi. A. Leonardi, Archivio di Stato di Ancona, Archivio Notarile (hereafter ASA, AN), vol. 690, fol. 166r. Parts of this document was transcribed by Raffaele Elia, 'La quadreria della famiglia Storani di Ancona,' *Studia Picena* 12 (1936): 85; idem, 'La Chiesa di San Domenico in Ancona e gli artisti che vi operano,' *Studia Picena* 23 (1955): 62–3. Further evidence of Tibaldi's excellence as a *stuccatore* was provided by Anton Francesco Doni. When describing the ideal residence of a lord, the author recommended works by different painters and Tibaldi's 'lavori mirabili di stucchi.' Anton Francesco Doni, *Le ville* (Bologna: Alessandro Benacci, 1566), 7v.

8. Business documents of 27 May 1558 involve Tomaso della Vecchia. A. Pilestri, ASA, AN, vol. 1020, fols. 92r–93r.

9. Leonardi, ASA, AN, vol. 690, fol. 166r, discussed in Polverari, *Tiziano* (1990), 15. The inscription on the altar, preserved in a seventeenth-century manuscript copy, reads as follows: 'Jesu Crucifixo Pio Liberatori Sacellum cum Icona, quam Thomas Cornovus à Vetula Mercator Venetus fide, et religione et pietate ac insignis morte preventus perficere non valuit, Petrus maior natu absolutissimam dicavit et fratri B.M. ac sibi S.P. M.D.L.V.I.I.I. Jul. XXII.' Giovanni Pichi Tancredi, *Compendio d'atti, risolutioni et decreti pubblici . . .*, Biblioteca Comunale 'Luciano Benincasa' di Ancona (hereafter BCA), Ms. 240, fol. 148v, and fig. 3.

10. Vasari, *Vite: Testo*, vol. 6, 149; Paolo Dal Poggetto and Pietro Zampetti, *Lorenzo Lotto nelle Marche. Il suo tempo, il suo influsso*, exh. cat. (Florence: Centro Di, 1981), 423–8. The altarpiece was dated by Massa on the basis of Pichi Tancredi, BCA, Ms. 240, fol. 161v. Marina Massa, 'Appunti per una nuova cronologia delle opere di Pellegrino Tibaldi,' *Notizie da Palazzo Albani* 16, no. 1 (1987): 45–6; Taco D. W. Dibbits, 'Pellegrino Tibaldi in Ancona: Two New Drawings in Red Chalk,' *Apollo* 148, no. 441 (November 1998): 30–2. The first known reference to Tibaldi's presence in Ancona is a payment document of 31 December 1554 mentioning 'mastro Pellegrino pittore in Ancona.' Floriano Da Morrovalle, 'Pellegrino Tibaldi a Loreto,' *Arte antica e moderna* 27 (July–September 1964): 358. Apart from Morato's church patronage our only knowledge of him is that on 6 May 1539 he received from the Apostolic Governor the rights and privileges of the Anconitan merchants. Levon Boghos Zekiyan, 'Le colonie armene del medio evo in Italia e le relazioni culturali italo-armene,' in *Atti del primo simposio internazionale di arte armene*, ed. Giulio Ieni and Levon Boghos Zekiyan (Venice: San Lazzaro, 1978), 864. For the history of the Augustinian church in Ancona: Fabio Mariano, 'La facciata della chiesa di S. Agostino in Ancona e il suo restauro,' in *Arte e spiritualità nell'ordine agostiniano e il convento San Nicola a Tolentino*, ed. Centro Studi 'Agostino Trapè' (Tolentino: Biblioteca Egidiana, 1994), 129–32.

11. Massa, 'Appunti,' 49–51.

12. The sources include God the Father, who combines similar figures from the Sistine *God Separating the Earth from the Waters* and *The Creation of the Sun and the Moon* for his upper and lower body respectively. The central angel, who functions as a throne, quotes Francesco Salviati's *Conversion of Paul* in the Cappella del Pallio in the Cancelleria in Rome. The general style *all'antica* of Paul and Moses derives from the Roman Raphael, and the Christ figure is based on Sebastiano del Piombo's flagellated Christ in the Borgherini Chapel in San Pietro in Montorio in Rome. Christine Baltay, *Pellegrino Tibaldi in Bologna and the Marches* (Ph.D. diss, New York University, 1984), 140; Massa, 'Appunti,' 48. Different approaches to *disegno* in the cinquecento include Wolfgang Kemp, 'Disegno: Beiträge zur Geschichte des Begriffs zwischen 1547 und 1607,' *Marburger Jahrbuch für Kunstwissenschaft* 19 (1974): 219–40; Georges Didi-Huberman, *Devant l'image: Question posée aux fins d'une historie de l'art*, Collection 'Critique' (Paris: Les Editions de Minuit, 1990), 94–103; idem, 'Le *disegno* de Vasari, ou le bloc-notes magique de l'historie de l'art,' *La part de l'oeil* 6 (1990):

31–51; Robert Williams, *Art, Theory, and Culture in Sixteenth-Century Italy: From Techne to Metatechne* (Cambridge: Cambridge University Press, 1997), 29–72. The most perceptive characterization of Tibaldi's *maniera* remains Malvasia's of 1678. Carlo Cesare Malvasia, *Felsina pittrice: Vite de' pittori bolognese,* ed. Giampietro Zanotti et al. (Bologna: Tipografia Guidi all'Ancora, 1841), vol. 1, 134–61.

13. Art historians have proposed political and religious interpretations of the cityscapes of Titian's and Tibaldi's paintings in Ancona, none of which I find convincing. Massa, 'Appunti,' 49–51; Pietro Zampetti, *Pittura nelle Marche,* vol. 2, *Dal Rinascimento alla Controriforma* (Florence: Nardini Editore, 1989), 303, 409; Augusto Gentili, 'La pala Gozzi di Tiziano: Venezia tra Ancona e Ragusa,' *Venezia Cinquecento* 2, no. 3 (1992): 89–97; Michele Polverari, 'La pala tizianesca del raguseo Gozzi ad Ancona. Tre questioni,' in *Marche e Dalmazia tra umanesimo e barocco: Atti del Convegno Internazionale di Studio,* ed. Sante Graciotti, Marina Massa and Giovanna Pirani (Reggio Emilia: Edizioni Diabasis, 1993), 101–11. For a discussion of cinquecento artistic style in the context of the *questione della lingua* with further bibliography, see Charles Dempsey, 'National Expression in Italian Sixteenth-Century Art: Problems of the Past and Present,' *Studies in the History of Art* 29 (1991): 15–24; but see also Enrico Castelnuovo and Carlo Ginzburg, 'Centro e periferia,' in *Storia dell'arte italiana,* pt. 1, ed. Giovanni Previtali, vol. 1, *Questioni e metodi* (Turin: Giulio Einaudi editore, 1979), vol. 1, 283–352.

14. Giuliano Briganti, *Il manierismo e Pellegrino Tibaldi* (Rome: Cosmopolita, 1945), 83–4; Zampetti, *Pittura nelle Marche,* vol. 2, 302.

15. These include a payment document of 20 November 1553, Vasari's *Vite* of 1568, Zanti's description of Bologna of 1583, and Lomazzo's *Trattato dell'arte della pittura* of 1584. Giovanni de Zanti, *Nomi, et cognomi di tutte le strade, contrade, et borghe di Bologna...* (Bologna: Pellegrino Bonardo, [1583]), n.p.; Gian Paolo Lomazzo, *Scritti sulle arti,* ed. Roberto Paolo Ciardi, *Raccolta Pisana di saggi e studi,* no. 33, ed. Istituto di Storia dell'Arte dell'Università di Pisa (Florence: Marchi & Bertolli, 1973), vol. 1, 115; Teresa Pugliatti, 'Un fregio di Pellegrino Tibaldi nel Palazzo Ricci Sacchetti a Roma,' in *Scritti di storia dell'arte in onore di Federico Zeri,* ed. Mauro Natale (Milan: Electa, 1984), vol. 1, 407, 417 n. 14; Vasari, *Vite: Testo,* vol. 6, 148, 527, 532, 535. Tibaldi signed the *Adoration of the Shepherds* of 1548 or 1549 in the Borghese Gallery in Rome with 'Peregrinus Tibaldi Bonon.'

16. Pichi Tancredi, *Compendio d'atti,* BCA, Ms. 240, fol. 163r; Michele Polverari, ed., *Lorenzo Lotto: La pala dell'Alabarda,* exh. cat. (Ancona: Comune di Ancona, Pinacoteca Comunale 'Francesco Podesti,' 1992).

17. The saints were described by Camillo Albertini, *Nota de' quadri migliori delle Chiese d'Ancona,* BCA, Ms. 289. Albertini, probably writing in the late eighteenth century, referred to the work as by the school of Raphael. For portraits and cityscape, see Lando Ferretti, *Dell'istorie d'Ancona in libri dodici,* copy by Giovanni Pichi Tancredi of 1667, BCA, Ms. 239, fols. 248r–v. Vasari commented on the painting's large format. Vasari, *Vite: Testo,* ed. Bettarini and Barocchi (1976), vol. 4, 553.

18. Minelli, *Famiglia Ferretti,* 124–30.

19. Because Morato's contract with the bishop and canons of San Ciriaco of 1559 mentions a sepulcher for the patron it is likely that the tomb in San Agostino never was installed. Riccardo Mazzei, ASA, AN, 836, fol. 280v, published in Hansen, 'Celebrating the Armenian Faith: Giorgio Morato and Pellegrino Tibaldi in the Cathedral of Ancona,' *Analecta Romana Instituti Danici* 24 (1997): 87.

20. 'la quale non sodisfece molto...' Vasari, *Vite: Testo,* vol. 4, 553.

21. Massa in n. 12, this chapter; Michael Hirst, *Sebastiano del Piombo,* Oxford Studies in the History of Art and Architecture, ed. Francis Haskell, Charles Mitchell, and John Shearman (Oxford: Clarendon Press, 1981), 49–65; Vasari, *Vite: Testo,* ed. Bettarini and Barocchi (1984),

vol. 5, 90: 'Fece Michele Agnolo il disegno piccolo di questa opera, e si giudica che il Cristo che alla colonna si batta sia contornato da lui, per essere grandissima differenza da l'altre figure a quello ...'

22. Giovanni Andrea Gilio, 'Dialogo nel quale si ragiona degli errori e degli abusi de' pittori circa l'istorie,' in Paola Barocchi, ed., *Trattati d'arte del Cinquecento,* Scrittori d'Italia, no. 221 (Bari: Gius. Laterza & Figli, 1961), vol. 2, 39–40. For Gilio and the reception of Michelangelo's *Last Judgment* in the cinquecento, see Charles Dempsey, 'Mythic Inventions in Counter-Reformation Painting,' in *Rome and the Renaissance: The City and the Myth,* ed. P. A. Ramsey, Medieval and Renaissance Texts and Studies (Binghamton, N.Y.: Center for Medieval and Early Renaissance Studies, 1982), 64–71, 74–5; Pierluigi De Vecchi, 'Il Giudizio Universale: fonti iconografiche, reazioni, interpretazioni,' in *La Cappella Sistina: I primi restauri: La scoperta del colore,* ed. Marcella Boroli (Novara: Istituto Geografico de Agostini, 1986), 190–4; Bernardine Barnes, *Michelangelo's Last Judgment: The Renaissance Response* (Berkeley, Los Angeles, and London: University of California Press, 1998), passim.

23. 'e morto che sarà, morendo perhò in Ancona o sua diocesi, farlo portare nella predecta chiesa chatedrale accompagnato da tutto il clero et lì christianamente e honorevolmente sepelirlo, con tutti officii et horatione solite della santa madre chiesa, nella sepultura da farsi per esso in decta chiesa doue a lui parrà e piacerà, dandoli piena potestà di potere elegere un loco in decta chiesa per fare una sepultura comuna per tutti quelli della natione armena che volessero essere seppelliti nella prefata chiesa, sanza mai hauere a pagare cosa alcuna o per ragione o per consuetudine di quelli <che> per li tempi illi [*sic*=ivi] serranno sepelliti della decta natione, excepto la cera solita e consueta darsi alli sacerdoti,' Mazzei, ASA, AN, vol. 836, fol. 281r; Hansen, 'Celebrating,' 88. In a forthcoming study, I address Daniele Ricciarelli's authorship of the design of the high altarpiece.

24. The inscription with the coat of arms was first copied by Pichi Tancredi: DEO OPTIMO MAXIMO GEORGIUS MORATTUS ARME/NUS ALTARE HOC MAIUS ECCLESIE CATEDRALIS/EXTRUCTUM SUMMA PIETATE DICAVIT M.D.L.X. Pichi Tancredi, *Compendio d'atti,* BCA, Ms. 240, fol. 123v, reproduced in Hansen, 'Celebrating,' 85. When Saracini copied the inscription for his publication of 1675, it was partly damaged. It is possible that Pichi Tancredi's inscription also is a reconstruction. Saracini's version formed the basis of later reproductions of the text. Giuliano Saracini, *Notitie historiche della citta d'Ancona ...* (Rome: Nicolò Angelo Tinaffi, 1675), 365; Agostino Peruzzi, *La Chiesa Anconitana* (Ancona: Per Gustavo Sartorj Cherubini, 1845), 195; Cesare Posti, *Il duomo di Ancona* (Jesi: Unione Tipografica Jesina, 1911), 210–11.

25. Pichi Tancredi, *Compendio d'atti,* BCA, Ms. 240, fol. 161v.

26. Patricia Rubin, 'Commission and Design in Central Italian Altarpieces c. 1450–1550,' in *Italian Altarpieces 1250–1550: Function and Design,* ed. Eve Borsook and Fiorella Superbi Goffredi (Oxford: Clarendon Press, 1994), 202–3.

27. The nature of John the Baptist was summarized in Jacobus de Voragine, *The Golden Legend: Readings on the Saints,* trans. William Granger Ryan (Princeton: Princeton University Press, 1993), vol. 1, 328–36.

28. Charles S. Stinger, *The Renaissance in Rome* (Bloomington: Indiana University Press, 1985), 207–18. A later but equally representative example is the *Moses Fountain* in Rome, projected by Domenico Fontana in 1587.

29. In Michelangelo's unexecuted project for the tomb of Pope Julius II of 1505, Moses and Paul were placed on the corners of the first cornice. The first published description of the unexecuted scheme came in the 'Life of Michelangelo' in the 1568 edition of Vasari's *Vite.* If there

was common knowledge of the project before Vasari's publication, it would have added to the Roman connotations of Tibaldi's *Baptism*. Vasari, *Vite: Testo,* vol. 6, 27.

30. Leon Arpee, *A History of Armenian Christianity from the Beginning to Our Own Time* (New York: Armenian Missionary Association of America, 1946), 15–20, 58–66; Agathangelos, *The Teaching of St. Gregory: An Early, Armenian Catechism,* trans. Robert W. Thomson (Cambridge: Harvard University Press, 1970); idem, *History of the Armenians,* trans. Robert W. Thomson (Albany, N.Y.: State University of New York, 1976).

31. Agathangelos, *History,* 389, paragraph 854.

32. Mazzei, ASA, AN, vol. 836, fol. 280v; Hansen, 'Celebrating,' 87. For St. Liberius and the history of his relics in Ancona, see Saracini, *Notitie,* 73; Gerolamo Speciali, *Notizie istoriche de' Santi Protettori della città d'Ancona* (Venice: Bartolomeo Locatelli, 1759), 142–59; Antonio Leoni, *Istoria d'Ancona, capitale della Marca anconitana* (Ancona: Dalla tipografia Baluffi, 1810), 254–7; Mario Natalucci, *Visita al Duomo di S. Ciriaco e breve itinerario della città di Ancona,* 3rd ed. (Città di Castello: Unione Arti Grafiche, 1966), 42–3; Reginald Grégoire, 'San Liberio – Ancona,' in *Roma – Armenia,* exh. cat., ed. Claude Mutafian (Rome: Edizioni De Luca, 1999), 244. Bishop Vincenzo de' Luchi attended the last six sessions of the Council of Trent and signed its decrees. On 16 February 1556 he was elected bishop by Paul IV. Mario Natalucci, *Ancon dorica fidei: uomini e monumenti della Chiesa nella storia della città di Ancona* (Ancona: Cassa di Risparmio di Ancona, 1980), 96–7.

33. 'promettano e sollennemente obligano loro e loro successori in detta chiesa, ogni anno in perpetuo, el quarto giorno di giugno che inmediatamente sequita dopo l'octaua del prefato beato Liberio, celebrare o fare celebrare un officio sollenne de tutti Canonici e prefati officianti in decta chiesa per la ⟨sollenne⟩ salute del prefato messer Georgio mentre viverà, dove ogni sacerdote sia obligato specialmente in nelli lochi deputati della Santa Messa e divini officii, fare mentione del predetto, con racomandarlo caldamente a Dio . . . ,' Mazzei, ASA, AN, vol. 836, fol. 281r; Hansen, 'Celebrating,' 88.

34. Peter Humfrey, 'La pala d'altare veneta nell'età delle riforme,' trans. Anna Maria Bagnari, in *La pittura nel Veneto: Il Cinquecento,* ed. Mauro Lucco (Milan: Electa, 1999), vol. 3, 1138–51.

35. John Hunter, *Girolamo Siciolante pittore da Sermoneta (1521–1575),* trans. Nicoletta Coppini, Studi della Fondazione Camillo Caetani, ed. Luigi Fiorani, Studi e documenti d'archivio, no. 4 (Rome: L'Erma di Bretschneider, 1996), 101–5, with bibliography. For characterizations of Siciolante's style, see also Federico Zeri, 'Intorno a Girolamo Siciolante,' *Bollettino d'arte* 36, no. 2, ser. 4 (April–June 1951): 139–49; Bernice F. Davidson, 'Some Early Works by Girolamo Siciolante da Sermoneta,' *The Art Bulletin* 48, no. 1 (March 1966): 55–64; Sydney Joseph Freedberg, *Painting in Italy 1500 to 1600,* The Pelican History of Art, ed. Nikolaus Pevsner (Harmondsworth: Penguin Books, 1971), 339–41; Teresa Pugliatti, 'Girolamo Siciolante da Sermoneta. Considerazione e proposte per una ricostruzione del percorso stilistico,' in John Hunter, Teresa Pugliatti, and Luigi Fiorani, *Girolamo Siciolante da Sermoneta (1521–1575): Storia e critica,* Quaderni della Fondazione Camillo Gaetani, no. 4, ed. Luigi Fiorani (Rome: Fondazione Camillo Gaetani, 1983), 77–108.

36. Gilio let his mouthpiece Ruggiero state that artists before Michelangelo attended more to truth and devotion than to pomp. Vasari, on the other hand, in the 'Life of Fra Angelico' in both editions of the *Vite* regretted those who took a clumsy style for a pious one. See Barocchi, ed., *Trattati d'arte del Cinquecento,* vol. 2, 55; Vasari, *Vite: Testo,* ed. Bettarini and Barocchi (1971), vol. 3, 273–4. See the discussions in Giovanni Previtali, *La fortuna dei primitivi: Dal Vasari ai neoclassici* (Turin: Giulio Einaudi Editore, 1964), 4–40; Charles Dempsey, 'The Carracci and the Devout Style in Emilia,' in *Emilian Painting of the 16th and 17th Centuries: A Symposium* (Bologna: Nuova Alfa

Editoriale, 1987), 75–87; Alexander Nagel, *Michelangelo and the Reform of Art* (Cambridge and New York: Cambridge University Press, 2000), 10–16.

37. Moses of Khoren, *Storia di Mosè Corenese,* trans. Monaci armeni mechitaristi (Venice: Tipografia armena di San Lazzaro, 1841), 166; Richard Adelbert Lipsius, *Die apokryphen Apostelgeschichten und Apostellegenden. Ein Beitrag zur altchristlichen Literaturgeschichte,* pt. 2 (Braunschweig: C. A. Schwetschke und Sohn, 1884), vol. 2, 58–9; Michel van Esbroeck, 'The Rise of Saint Bartholomew's Cult from the Seventh to the Thirteenth Centuries,' in *Medieval Armenian Culture,* ed. Thomas J. Samuelian and Michael E. Stone, University of Pennsylvania, Armenian Texts and Studies, ed. Michael E. Stone, no. 6 (Chico, Calif: Scholars Press, 1984), 161–78. For the relic in San Ciriaco [Camillo Tancredi], *Legenda del glorioso martire santo Ciriaco vescovo Hierosolimitano Avocato della Città d'Ancona* (Ancona: Francesco Salvioni, 1585), 11.

38. One example is the anonymous *sacra conversazione* executed around 1500 in tempera on panel for the cathedral of San Ciriaco, today in the Museo Diocesano in the same city. *Libri di pietra: Mille anni della cattedrale di Ancona tra oriente e occidente,* exh. cat., ed. Giovanni Morello (Milan: Electa, 1999), 45.

39. Brewster identified the bishop as St. Cyriacus, but also suggested the possibility of St. Gregory the Illuminator. Brewster, *Girolamo Siciolante,* 105, n. 14.

40. Ludwig von Pastor, *Geschichte der Päpste seit dem Ausgang des Mittelalters,* vol. 5, *Geschichte Papst Pauls III (1534–1549)* (Freiburg im Breisgau: Herder & Co., 1925), 721; Gregorio Petrowicz, 'Il Patriarca di Ecimiazin Stefano V Salmastetzì (1541?–1552),' *Orientalia christiana periodica* 28, no. 2 (1962): 362–401; Raymond H. Kévorkian, 'La chiesa armena, il Vaticano ed il movimento armeno di emancipazione nei secoli XVI–XVII,' in *Roma – Armenia,* 312.

41. This section develops ideas set forth in Hansen, 'Celebrating,' 85–7. My discussion of eschatology in sixteenth-century Italy is based on André Chastel, 'L'Antéchrist à la renaissance,' in *L'umanesimo e il demonico nell'arte,* Atti del II Congresso Internazionale di Studi Umanistici, ed. Enrico Castelli (Rome and Milan: Fratelli Bocca Editori, 1953), 177–86; Marjorie Reeves, *The Influence of Prophesy in the Later Middle Ages: A Study in Joachimism* (Oxford: Clarendon Press, 1969); Bernard McGinn, *Visions of the End: Apocalyptic Traditions in the Middle Ages* (New York: Columbia University Press, 1979); Richard Kenneth Emmerson, *Antichrist in the Middle Ages: A Study of Medieval Apocalypticism, Art, and Literature* (Manchester: Manchester University Press, 1981); Salvatore I. Camporeale, 'Giovanmaria dei Tolosani o.p.: 1530–1546. Umanesimo, Riforma e Teologia controversista,' *Memorie Domenicane* 103, new ser. 17 (1986): 216–27; Ottavia Niccoli, *Prophecy and People in Renaissance Italy,* trans. Lydia G. Cochrane (Princeton: Princeton University Press, 1990); Richard Kenneth Emmerson and Bernard McGinn, ed., *The Apocalypse in the Middle Ages* (Ithaca and London: Cornell University Press, 1992).

42. The source of the tradition was Romans 11.25, which in the sixteenth century universally was believed to refer to the end of the world. An early formulation of this notion was provided by St. Augustine: 'And so in that judgment, or in connection with it, we have learned that the following events are to occur: Elijah the Tishbite will come; the Jews will believe; Antichrist will persecute; Christ will judge; the dead will rise again; the good and the wicked will be sorted out; the world will be burned in flames and will be renewed.' Saint Augustine, *The City of God against the Pagans,* trans. William Chase Greene, Loeb Classical Library (London: William Heinemann; Cambridge: Harvard University Press, 1960), vol. 6, 451 (book 20, ch. 30). Kenneth R. Stow, *Catholic Thought and Papal Jewry Policy 1555–1593* (New York: Jewish Theological Seminary of America, 1977); idem, 'The Papacy and the Jews: Catholic Reformation and Beyond,' *Jewish History* 6, no. 1–2 (1992): 257–79.

43. For the book-burnings, see Karl Hoffmann, *Ursprung und Anfangstätigkeit des ersten päpstlichen Missioninstituts. Ein Beitrag zur Geschichte der katholischen Juden- und Mohammedanermission im sechzehnten Jahrhundert,* Veröffentlichungen des internationalen Instituts für Missionswissenschaftliche Forschungen, Missionswissenschaftliche Abhandlungen und Texte, ed. J. Schmidlin (Münster in Westfalen: Verlag der aschendorffschen Verlagsbuchhandlung), 53–4; Kenneth R. Stow, 'The Burning of the Talmud in 1553, in the Light of Sixteenth-Century Catholic Attitudes Toward the Talmud,' *Bibliotheque de l'humanisme et renaissance* 34 (1972): 434–59. The convert Alessandro da Foligno assisted the Jesuit Bobadilla and took part in the burning of the Talmud in Ancona and elsewhere in the Marches. Shlomo Simonsohn, 'Some Well-Known Jewish Converts during the Renaissance,' *Revue des Études juives* 148, no. 1–2 (January–June 1989): 36. On 2 June 1554 a commission was ordered to Ancona because the Governor of Loreto had hinted that Jews were still hiding Hebrew writings. Shlomo Simonsohn, *The Apostolic See and the Jews. Documents: 1546–1555,* Studies and Texts, no. 106 (Toronto: Pontifical Institute of Mediaeval Studies, 1990), 2922–3 (doc. 3216).

44. P. Giangicomini, 'Un documento inedito e gli ebrei giustiziati in Ancona (1556),' *Il Corriere Adriatico* (Ancona), 8 February 1929; Stow, *Catholic Thought,* 28–32; Ariel Toaff, 'Ebrei spagnoli nell'Italia ebraica del Cinquecento. Una presenza contestata,' *La Rassegna mensile di Israel* 58, no. 1–2 (January–August 1992): 47–59, with bibliography.

45. See n. 41.

46. J. Graham Pollard, *Medaglie italiane del rinascimento nel museo nazionale del Bargello: 1513–1640* (Florence: Associazione amici del Bargello, Studio per Edizioni Scelte, 1985), vol. 2, 1037–8 (cat. 568); for the Loggia dei Mercanti see John Alexander, 'Documentation of the Loggia dei Mercanti in Ancona, 1556–1564,' *Studia Borromaica* 11 (1997): 193–238. The Christ figure in Tibaldi's painting is flanked by angels holding sword and scales, the same attributes held by Justice on the papal medal. See also *Recht und Gerechtigkeit im Spiegel der europäischen Kunst,* ed. Wolfgang Pleister and Wolfgang Schild (Cologne: DuMont Buchverlag, 1988).

47. Arpee, *History,* 149–64; Karekin Sarkissian, *The Council of Chalcedon and the Armenian Church,* 2nd ed. (New York: Armenian Church Prelacy, 1975).

48. Joseph Gill, *The Council of Florence* (Cambridge and New York: Cambridge University Press, 1959), 305–10; *Decrees of the Ecumenical Councils,* vol. 1, *Nicaea I to Lateran V,* ed. Norman P. Tanner (London: Sheed & Ward; Washington, D.C.: Georgetown University Press, 1990), 534–*59; Thomas F. Mathews, 'The Annunciation at the Well: A Metaphor of Armenian Monophysitism,' in *Medieval Armenian Culture,* 343–51; Thomas F. Mathews and Avedis K. Sanjian, *Armenian Gospel Iconography: The Tradition of the Glajor Gospel,* Dumbarton Oaks Studies, no. 29 (Washington, D.C.: Dumbarton Oaks Research Library and Collection, 1991), 26–31; Claude Mutafian, 'Gli inizi della Chiesa di Roma nel mondo armeno (1200–1350),' in Roma–Armenia, 155–9; Lilit Zakarian, 'Un artista anti-unitore del XIV secolo,' in *Roma–Armenia,* 176–82.

49. In 1565 and 1585 churchmen were sent to Venice from Armenia with the purpose of printing religious literature in the Armenian. Raymond H. Kévorkian, 'Das gedruckte Buch vom 16. bis zum 19. Jahrhundert,' in *Armenien: 5000 Jahre Kunst und Kultur,* exh. cat., ed. Museum Bochum and the Stiftung für Armenische Studien, Bochum (Tübingen: Ernst Wasmuth Verlag, 1995), 284. Vecchio commented on how the Armenians on certain religious matters disagreed both with the Roman Catholic church and the Greeks. Cesare Vecellio, *De gli habii anunchi, et moderni di diverse parti del mondo* (Venice: Damian Zenaro, 1590), 440r.

50. 'Il molto pio, christiano e cattolico messer Georgio Morattj, Armeno e continuo habitatore per molti e molti Anni della magnifica Città de Ancona, hauendo deliberato per honore

dell'onipotente e magno Idio, ad ornamento del culto diuino, e anche in celebre [*sic*] e memoria dell'Illustrissimo Beato Liberio, già figliolo del Re d'Armenia, e uno delli protectori e advocati precipui di questo loco, dove ancora il suo santissimo corpo riposa, e per salute dell'anima di esso messer Georgio e di suo padre e madre e altri suoi consanguinei e attinenti, a remissione di peccati omninamente deliberato fare uno altare e una cona [*sic*=ancona] nella Cattedrale chiesa di questa magnifica città dove riposa il santissimo corpo del prelibato beato Liberio...' Mazzei, ASA, AN, vol. 836, fol. 280v.; Hansen, 'Celebrating,' 87.

51. '*Dire a uno,* egli scrive *il padre del porro e cantargli il vespro o il mattutino degli Ermini* significa riprenderlo e accusarlo alla libera e protestargli quello che avvenire gli debba, non si mutando. Erano gli Ermini un convento di frati, secondo che mi soleva raccontare mia madre, i quali stavano già in Firenze e perchè cantavano i divini ufizi nella loro lingua, quando alcuna cosa non s'intendeva s'usava dire: *Ella è la zolfa degli Ermini.*' From Varchi's *L'Ercolano* printed in Giuseppe Boffito, 'Gli Armeni a Firenze e un passo oscuro dell' *Acerba* interpretato,' *La Bibliofilia* 39, nos. 7–8 (July–August 1937): 283–4, 287–9.

52. De Voragine, *Golden Legend,* vol. 1, 280–3.

53. *The Revised English Bible with the Apocrypha* (n.p.: Oxford University Press and Cambridge University Press, 1989), 1 Cor 9:1.

54. Ibid, 2 Cor 3.6, 3.10, 3.12–16.

55. The association between contemporary Jews and Christian representations of Moses was made by Vasari when commenting on Michelangelo's Della Rovere tomb in San Pietro in Vincoli: 'E séguitino gli Ebrei di andare, come fanno ogni sabato, a schiera, e maschî e femmine, come gli storni a visitarlo et adorarlo, ché non cosa umana ma divina adoreranno.' Vasari, *Vite: Testo,* vol. 6, 29. See also Ruth Mellinkoff, *The Horned Moses in Medieval Art and Thought* (Berkeley, Los Angeles, and London: University of California Press, 1970); idem, 'More about Horned Moses,' *Jewish Art* 12–13 (1986–87): 184–98. The role played by Judaism to Christian image-making is discussed in Herbert L. Kessler, '"Pictures Fertile with Truth:" How Christians Managed to Make Images of God without Violating the Second Commandment,' *Journal of the Walters Art Gallery* 49–50 (1991–92): 53–65; idem, '"Thou Shalt Paint the Likeness of Christ Himself:" The Mosaic Prohibition as Provocation for Christian Images,' *Jewish Art* 23–24 (1997–98): 124–39; Stephen J. Campbell, *Cosmè Tura of Ferrara: Style, Politics and the Renaissance City, 1450–1495* (New Haven and London: Yale University Press, 1997), 99–129.

56. In this vein Agostino Bonucci in his *Conversio Sancti Pauli* of 1545, dedicated to Pope Paul III, wrote, 'you have shown yourself to be the man not only to bring back heretics to the true faith but to convert every last infidel, imitating Paul, who, having first been converted himself by Christ, converted innumerable peoples.' Quoted in Patricia Rubin, 'The Private Chapel of Cardinal Alessandro Farnese in the Cancelleria, Rome,' *Journal of the Warburg and Courtauld Institutes* 50 (1987): 100.

57. Bonardi has argued that Morato's patronage was a means of distancing himself from the local and less affluent Armenian community. Claudia Bonardi, 'Le colonie armene in Italia: Milano, Ancona, Genova, Venezia,' in *Roma – Armenia,* 224. The Armenian *compagnia* of Ancona was dedicated to the same saint as their church. Giacomo Fontana, *La ristauratione del porto de Ancona capo di marca nel mar' adriatico,* Biblioteca Apostolica Vaticana, Vat. lat. 5463, fol. 11r.

58. The strategy of including something in order to displace it was described by Roland Barthes, *Mythologies* (Paris: Éditions du Seuil, 1957), 46–8.

Selected Bibliography

Acidini, Luchinat, and Elvira Garbero Zorzi, eds., *Boboli 90: Atti del convegno internazionale di studi per la salvaguardia e la valorizzazione del giardino,* 2 vols. (Florence: Edifir, 1991).

Mina Gregori and Antonio Paolucci, eds., *Maestri e Botteghe. Pittura a Firenze alla fine del quattrocento* (Silvana Editoriale: Florence, 1992).

and Giorgio Galletti, *Le ville e i giardini di Castello e Petraia a Firenze* (Ospedaletto: Pacini, 1992).

Ady, Cecilia, *The Bentivoglio of Bologna* (Oxford: Oxford University Press, 1937).

Alberti, Leon Battista, *On the Art of Building in Ten Books,* J. Rykwert, N. Leach, and R. Tavernor, eds. (Cambridge, Mass.: MIT Press, 1988).

Allen, Michael J. B., *Plato's Third Eye: Studies in Marsilio Ficino's Metaphysics and Its Sources* (Aldershot and Brookfield: Ashgate, 1995).

Synoptic Art: Marsilio Ficino on the History of Platonic Interpretation (Florence: Olschki, 1998).

and V. Rees, eds., *Marsilio Ficino: His Theology, His Philosophy, His Legacy* (Leiden, Boston, and Cologne: Brill, 2002).

Apfelstadt, Eric, 'The Later Sculpture of Antonio Rossellino', 2 vols., unpublished Ph.D. diss., Princeton University, 1987.

Assmann, Jan, *Moses the Egyptian: The Memory of Egypt in Western Monotheism* (Cambridge: Harvard University Press, 1998).

Baldassari, Stefano Ugo, and Saiber, Ariel, eds., *Images of Quattrocento Florence. Selected Writings in Literature, History and Art* (New Haven and London: Yale University Press, 1999).

Bambach, Carmen, *Drawing and Painting in the Italian Renaissance Workshop* (Cambridge and New York: Cambridge University Press, 1999).

Banker, J. R., 'The Programme for the Sassetta Altarpiece in the Church of San Francesco in Borgo Sansepolcro', *I Tatti Studies* 4 (1991): 11–58.

Bargiacchi, Luigi, *Storia degli istituti di beneficenza, d'istruzione ed educazione in Pistoia e suo circondario dalle respettive origini a tutto l'anno 1880,* 4 vols. (Florence: 1883–4).

Barkan, Leonard, *Unearthing the Past: Archaeology and Aesthetics in the Making of Renaissance Culture* (New Haven and London: Yale University Press, 1999).

Barocchi, Paola, ed., *Trattati d'arte del Cinquecento,* 3 vols. (Bari: Laterza, 1961).

ed., *Il Giardino di San Marco: maestri e compagni del giovane Michelangelo,* exh. cat., Florence, Casa Buonarroti, 30 giugno–19 ottobre 1992 (Cinisello Balsamo: Silvana, 1992).

Baxandall, M., *Painting and Experience in Fifteenth Century Italy* (London and Oxford: Oxford University Press, 1972).

Giotto and the Orators: Humanist observers of painting in Italy and the discovery of pictorial composition, 1350–1450 (Oxford: Clarendon Press, 1971).

Beltrami, L., *Documenti e Memorie riguardanti le vita e le opere di Leonardo da Vinci* (Milan, Fratelli Treves, 1919).

Benjamin, Walter, 'The Work of Art in the Age of Mechanical Reproduction', in *Walter Benjamin: Illuminations,* Hannah Arendt, ed. (New York: Harcourt, Brace and World, 1968), 219–53.

Berenson, Bernard, 'Quadri senza casa. Il quattrocento fiorentino, II', *Dedalo,* 12 (1932): 665–702.

Bertelli, Sergio, Nicolai Rubinstein, and Craig Hugh Smyth, eds., *Florence and Venice: Comparisons and Relations,* 2 vols. (Florence: La Nuova Italia, 1979–80), I: *Quattrocento;* II: *Cinquecento.*

and Gian Carlo Garfagnini, eds., *Florence and Milan: Comparisons and Relations,* 2 vols. (Florence, La Nuova Italia, 1989).

Boas, George, trans., *The Hieroglyphics of Horapollo* (New York: Pantheon, 1950, reprinted with a forward by Anthony Grafton, Princeton: Princeton University Press, 1993).

Bocchi, Francesca, 'Un fonte di reddito dei Bentivoglio: le condotte militari', *Atti e memorie della Deputazione di Storia Patria per le Provincie di Romagna,* n.s. 20 (1969): 429–44.

Borsook, Eve, 'Two letters concerning Antonio Pollaiuolo', *Burlington Magazine,* 115 (1973): 464–8.

Bourdieu, Pierre, *Outline of a Theory of Practice,* trans. R. Nice (Cambridge: Cambridge University Press, 1977).

Brown, Patricia Fortini, *Venice and Antiquity. The Venetian Sense of the Past* (New Haven and London: Yale University Press, 1996).

Bruni, Francesco, ed., *L'italiano nelle regioni: lingua nazionale e identità regionali* (Turin: UTET, 1992).

Budick, S., and Wolfgang Iser, eds., *The Translatability of Cultures: Figurations of the Space Between* (Stanford: Stanford University Press, 1996).

Burke, Peter, *The Italian Renaissance: Culture and Society in Italy* (Cambridge: Polity Press, 1987).

Fortunes of the Courtier: The European Reception of Castiglione's 'Cortegiano' (University Park: Penn State University Press, 1996).

Butterfield, Andrew, 'Verrocchio's Christ and St Thomas: Chronology, iconography and political context', *Burlington Magazine* 134 (1992): 225–33.

The Sculptures of Andrea del Verrocchio (New Haven and London: Yale University Press, 1997).

Caburlotto, Luca, 'Giovanni Rossellino e il monumento a Filippo Lazzàri in San Domenico a Pistoia', *Paragone: Arte* 15–16 (1997): 3–23.

Cadogan, Jean K., *Domenico Ghirlandaio. Artist and Artisan* (New Haven and London: Yale University Press, 2000).

Caglioti, Francesco, 'Sui primi tempi romani d'Andrea Bregno: Un progetto per il cardinale camerlengo Alvise Trevisna e un San Michele Arcangelo per il cardinale Juan de Carvajal', *Mitteilungen des Kunsthistoridchen Institutes in Florenze* 41 (1997): 213–52.

Campbell, Lorne, 'Cosmè Tura and Netherlandish Art', in Stephen J. Campbell et al., *Cosmè Tura: Painting and Design in Renaissance Ferrara* (Boston: Isabella Stewart Gardner Museum; Milan: Electa, 2002), 71–107.

Campbell, Stephen J., '"Sic in amore furens": Painting as Poetic Theory in the Early Renaissance', *I Tatti Studies* 6 (1995): 145–69.

Cosmè Tura of Ferrara. Style, Politics and the Renaissance City, 1450–1495 (New Haven and London: Yale University Press, 1997).

Camporesi, Piero, *Bread of Dreams* (Chicago: University of Chicago Press, 1989).

Canuti, F., *Il Perugino* (Siena: Editice d'arte 'La Diana', 1931).

Cappelli, A., 'Lettere di Lorenzo de' Medici detto il Magnifico conservate nell'Archivio Palatino di Modena con notizie tratte dei carteggi diplomatici degli oratori estensi a Firenze', *Atti e memorie della Deputazione di Storia Patria per le Provincie Modenesi e Parmensi* 1 (1863): 231–320.

Cardini, Franco, 'Il torneo nelle feste ceremoniali di corte', *Quaderni di teatro* 7 (1984): 9–19.

Carl, Doris, 'Der Fina-Altar von Benedetto da Maiano in der Collegiata zu San Gimignano', *Mitteilungen des Kunsthistorischen Institutes in Florenz* 22 (1978): 265–86.

Casali, Giovanna, *San Gimignano. L'evoluzione della città tra XIV and XVI secolo* (Florence: Olschki, 1998).

Castaldi, Enrico, *Santa Fina nelle testimonianze dei coetanei e nei ricordi dell'arte* (San Gimignano: Unione Tipografica, 1927).

Castaldi, Enrico, 'Artefici che lavorano nella Insigne Collegiata ai tempi dell'operaio Onofrio di Pietro', *Scritta per la costruzione della cappella di San Bartolo su disegno di Giuliano da Maiano* (Val d'Elsa: Tipo-Litografico Meoni, 1921), 41–50.

Castelnuovo, Enrico, and Carlo Ginzburg, 'Centre and Periphery', in *History of Italian Art,* E. Bianchini and C. Dorey, eds., trans. E. Bianchini, 2 vols. (Cambridge: Polity Press, 1994), vol. II, 29–113.

Cavallaro, Anna, 'Introduzione alle cappelle maggiore', in *Umanesimo e primo rinascimento in S. Maria del Popolo,* Roberto Cannat, Anna Cavallaro, and Claudio Strinati, eds. (Rome: De Luca, 1981), 75–83.

Celenza, Christopher S., *Piety and Pythagoras in Renaissance Florence: The Symbolum Nesianum* (Leiden, Boston, and Cologne: Brill, 2001).

'Late Antiquity and Florentine Platonism', in Michael J. B. Allen and V. Rees, eds., *Marsilio Ficino: His Theology, His Philosophy, His Legacy* (Leiden, Boston, and Cologne: Brill, 2002), 71–97.

Cennini, Cennino, *Il libro dell'arte,* Mario Serchi, ed. (Florence: Le Monnier, 1991).

Chambers, D., *Patrons and Artists in the Italian Renaissance* (Columbia: University of South Carolina, 1971).

Chastel, André, *Art et Humanisme a Florence au temps de Laurent le Magnifique* (Paris: Presses Universitaires de France, 1959).

Clarke, Georgia, 'Magnificence and the City: Giovanni II Bentivoglio and Architecture in Fifteenth-Century Bologna', *Renaissance Studies* 13 (1999): 397–411.

Roman House – Renaissance Palaces: Inventing Antiquity in Fifteenth-Century Italy (Cambridge: Cambridge University Press, 2003).

Clifford, James, 'The Translation of Cultures: Maurice Leenhardt's Evangelism, New Caledonia 1902–1926', in *Contemporary Literary Criticism: Literary and Cultural Studies,* R. Con Davis and R. Schleifer, eds. (New York: Longman, 1994), 626–41.

Collareta, Marco, 'Testimonianze letterarie su Donatello, 1450–1600', in *Omaggio a Donatello, 1386–1986. Donatello e la storia del Museo,* exh. cat., Florence, Museo nazionale del Bargello 1985–86, Paola Barocchi, ed. (Florence: Museo nazionale del Bargello, 1985), 7–47.

Colombo, Antonio, 'Il palazzo e il giardino di Poggioreale', *Archivio storico per le province napoletane* 10 (1885): 186–209, 309–42.

Comanducci, Rita, 'Produzione seriale e mercato dell'arte: Firenze 1450–1563', *The Art Market in Early Modern Italy,* Marcello Fantoni, Louisa Matthew, and Sara Matthews-Grieco, eds. (Modena: Pannini, 2003).

Connell, S., 'The Employment of Sculptors and Stone-masons in Venice in the Fifteenth Century', unpublished Ph.D. diss., University of London, 1976.

Connell, William J., *La città dei crucci: fazioni e clientele in uno stato repubblicano del '400* (Florence: Nuova Toscana Editrice, 2000).

and Andrea Zorzi, eds., *Florentine Tuscany. Structures and Practices of Power* (Cambridge and New York: Cambridge University Press, 2000).

Copenhaver, Brian A., ed., *'Hermetica': The Greek 'Corpus Hermeticum' and the Latin 'Asclepius' in a new English translation* (Cambridge: Cambridge University Press, 1992).

Corradini, S., 'Parmigianino's Contract for the Caccialupi Chapel in S. Salvatore in Lauro', *Burlington Magazine* 135 (1993): 27–9.

Covi, Dario A., 'Four New Documents Concerning Andrea del Verrocchio', *The Art Bulletin* 48 (1966): 97–104.

Cox-Rearick, Janet, *Dynasty and Destiny in Medici Art: Pontormo, Leo X, and the two Cosimos* (Princeton: Princeton University Press, 1984).

Curran, Brian, and Anthony Grafton, 'A Fifteenth-Century Site Report on the Vatican Obelisk', *Journal of the Warburg and Courtauld Institutes* 58 (1995): 234–48.

'The "Hypnerotomachia Poliphili" and Renaissance Egyptology', *Word and Image* 14 (1998): 156–85.

'De sacrarum Litterarum Aegyptiorum Interpretatione: Reticence and Hubris in Hieroglyphic Studies of the Renaissance: Pierio Valeriano and Annius of Viterbo', *Memoirs of the American Academy in Rome* 43–44 (1998–99), 139–82.

'Cleopatra and the Second Julius: Egyptology and Imperial Inheritance in High Renaissance Rome', in *Cleopatra and Egyptomania,* Margaret M. Miles, ed. (University of California Press, forthcoming).

d'Afflitto, Chiara, Franca Falletti, and Andrea Muzzi, eds., *L'Età di Savonarola: Fra' Paolino e la pittura a Pistoia nel primo '500* (Venice: Marsilio, 1996).

Dal Poggetto, Paolo, and Pietro Zampetti, eds., *Lorenzo Lotto nelle Marche. Il suo tempo, il suo influsso,* exh. cat. Ancona, Chiesa del Gesù, Chiesa di San Francesco alle Scale Loggia dei mercanti, 4 luglio–11 ottobre 1981 (Florence: Centro Di, 1981).

Dannenfeldt, Karl, 'Egypt and Egyptian Antiquities in the Renaissance', *Studies in the Renaissance* 6 (1959): 7–27.

De Benedictis, Angela, *Repubblica per contratto. Bologna: una città europea nello Stato della Chiesa* (Bologna: Il Mulino, 1995).

de Certeau, Michel, *The Practice of Everyday Life,* trans. Steven Rendall (Berkeley: University of California Press, 1984).

Dempsey, Charles, 'Renaissance Hieroglyphic Studies and Gentile Bellini's "Saint Mark Preaching in Alexandria"', in *Hermeticism and the Renaissance. Intellectual History and the Occult in Early Modern Europe,* I. Merkel and A. G. Debus, eds. (Washington, D.C.: Folger Shakespeare Library, 1988), 342–65.

ed., *Quattrocento Adriatico. Fifteenth Century Art of the Adriatic Rim,* Villa Spelman Colloquia, 5 (Bologna: Nuova Alfa Editoriale 1995).

D'Onofrio, Cesare, *Gli obelischi di Roma: storia e urbanistica di una città dall' età antica al XX secolo,* 3rd ed. (Rome: Cassa di Risparmio, 1992).

Draper, James David, *Bertoldo di Giovanni: Sculptor of the Medici Household* (Columbia: University of Missouri Press, 1992).

Du Gay, Paul, ed., *Production of Culture/Cultures of Production* (London: Sage, 1997).

Earle, Peter, 'The Commercial Development of Ancona, 1479–1551', *Economic History Review,* 2nd ser., 22 (1969): 28–44.

Edelstein, Bruce, '"*La fecundissima Signora Duchessa*": The Courtly Persona of Eleonora di Toledo and the Iconography of Abundance', in *The Cultural World of Eleonora di Toledo: Duchess of Florence and Siena,* Konrad Eisenbichler, ed. (Aldershot: Ashgate, 2004), 71–97.

'The *Camera Verde:* A Public Center for the Duchess of Florence in the Palazzo Vecchio', *Mélanges de l'École Française de Rome* (2003).
Elam, Caroline, 'Lorenzo de' Medici's sculpture garden', *Mitteilungen des Kunsthistorischen Institutes in Florenz* 36 (1992): 41–84.
Emiliozzi, Adriana Emiliozzi, *Il Museo Civico di Viterbo: Storia delle raccolte archeologiche* (Rome: Consiglio Nazionale delle Ricerche, 1986).
Esposito, Anna, 'Forteguerri, Niccolò', in *Dizionario biographico degli italiani,* 58 vols. (Rome: Istituto della enciclopedia italiana, 1960–), vol. XLIX, 156–9.
Falletti, Franca, ed., *I Medici, Il Verrocchio e Pistoia. Storia e restauro di due capolavori nella Cattedrale di S. Zeno* (Livorno: Sillabe, 1996).
Farago, Clare, ed., *Reframing the Renaissance: Visual Culture in Europe and Latin America 1450–1650* (New Haven and London: Yale University Press, 1995).
Farmer, Stephen A., *Syncretism in the West: Pico's 900 Theses (1486): The Evolution of Traditional Religious and Philosophical Systems,* Medieval and Renaissance Texts and Studies, 167 (Tempe: Arizona State University Press, 1998).
Ferretti, Francesco, *Diporti notturni* (Ancona: F. Salvioni, 1580).
Ficino, Marsilio, *Opera Omnia* (Basel, 1576; repr. Turin, 1959).
De triplici vita, trans. and ed. Carol Kaske and John Clark (Binghamton, N.Y.: Medieval and Renaissance Texts, 1989).
Field, Arthur, *The Origins of the Platonic Academy of Florence* (Princeton: Princeton University Press, 1988).
Finzi, Claudio, 'Leon Battista Alberti: Geroglifiche e gloria', in *L'Egitto fuori dell'Egitto: Dalla riscoperta all'Egittologia,* C. M. Govi, S. Curto, and S. Pernigotti, eds. (Bologna: CLUEB, 1991), 205–8.
Fiumi, Enrico, *Storia economica e sociale di S. Gimignano* (Florence: Olschki, 1961).
Fontana, Domenico, *Della Trasportatione dell'Obelisco Vaticano* (Rome: 1590; reprint A. Carugo, ed., Milan: Il Polifilo, 1978).
Frommel, Christoph L., *Die Farnesina und Peruzzis Architektonisches Frühwerk* (Berlin: De Grutyer, 1961).
S. Ray, and M. Tafuri, eds., *Raffaello architetto* (Milan: Electa, 1984).
and Nicholas Adams, eds., *The Architectural Drawings of Antonio da Sangallo the Younger and his Circle,* 2 vols. (Cambridge and London: MIT Press, 1994–2000)
Fubini, Riccardo, *Quattrocento fiorentino: Politica diplomazia cultura* (Pisa: Pacini, 1996).
Gardner, Julian, *The Tomb and the Tiara. Curial Tomb Sculpture in Rome and Avignon in the Later Middle Ages* (Oxford: Clarendon Press, 1992).
Gardner von Teuffel, C., 'The Contract for Perugino's "Assumption of the Virgin" at Vallombrosa', *Burlington Magazine* 137 (1995): 307–12.
Garin, Eugenio, *Giovanni Pico della Mirandola: Vita e dottrina* (Florence: Olschki, 1937).
Giehlow, Karl, 'Die Hieroglyphenkunde des Humanismus in der Allegorie der Renaissance', *Jahrbuch der Kunsthistorisches Sammlungen des Allerhöchsten Kaiserhauses* 32 (1915): 1–229.
Gilbert, C., 'What did the Renaissance Patron Buy?', *Renaissance Quarterly* 51 (1998): 392–450.
Glasser, H., 'Artists' Contracts of the Early Renaissance', unpublished Ph.D. diss., University of Columbia, 1965.
Gnoli, Domenico, 'L'opere di Mino da Fiesole in Roma, Parte IV', *Archivio storico dell'arte* 3 (1890): 266–71.

'Miscellanea; Riconstruzione del monumento del cardinal Forteguerri, di Mino da Fiesole', *Archivio storico dell'arte* 4 (1891): 209–16.

Godman, Peter, *From Poliziano to Machiavelli: Florentine Humanism in the High Renaissance* (Princeton: Princeton University Press, 1998).

Goldthwaite, Richard, *Wealth and the Demand for Art in Italy, 1300–1600* (Baltimore: Johns Hopkins University Press, 1993).

Gombrich, E. H., 'Hypnerotomachiana' (1951), in E. H. Gombrich, *Symbolic Images: Studies in the Art of the Renaissance II* (New York and London: Phaidon, 1972, 2nd ed., 1978), 102–8.

'The Early Medici as Patrons of Art', in *Norm and Form: Studies in the Art of the Renaissance,* 3rd ed. (London and New York: Phaidon, 1978), 35–57.

Grafton, Anthony, *Joseph Scaliger: A Study in the History of Classical Scholarship,* 2 vols. (Oxford: Oxford University Press, 1983–93).

'Invention of Traditions and Traditions of Invention in Renaissance Europe: The Strange Case of Annius of Viterbo,' in *Defenders of the Text: The Traditions of Scholarship in an Age of Science, 1450–1800* (Cambridge and London: Harvard University Press, 1991), 76–103.

Guarini, E. Fasano, 'Center and Periphery', in *The Origins of the State in Italy, 1300–1600, The Journal of Modern History,* Julius Kirshner, ed., 67, suppl. (1995): 74–97.

Hall, Stuart, 'The Spectacle of the "Other"', in *Representation: Cultural Representations and Signifying Practices,* ed. Stuart Hall (London: Sage Books, 1997), 223–79.

Hankins, James, 'Lorenzo de' Medici as a Patron of Philosophy', *Rinascimento,* 2nd ser., 34 (1994), 15–53.

Hansen, Morten Steen, 'Celebrating the Armenian Faith: Giorgio Morato and Pellegrino Tibaldi in the Cathedral of Ancona', *Analecta Romana Instituti Danici* 24 (1997): 83–91.

Hatfield, R., 'Giovanni Tornabuoni, i fratelli Ghirlandaio e la cappella maggiore di Santa Maria Novella', in *Domenico Ghirlandaio, 1449–1494: Atti del convegno internazionale,* W. Prinz and M. Seidel, eds. (Florence: Centro Di, 1996), 112–17.

Herklotz, Ingo, *"Sepulcra" e "Monumento" del Medioevo; Studi sull'arte sepolcrale in Italie* (Rome: Rari Nantes, 1985).

Hersey, George L., *Alfonso II and the Artistic Renewal of Naples 1485–1495* (New Haven: Yale University Press, 1969).

Hill, George Francis, *A Corpus of Italian Medals of the Renaissance before Cellini,* 2 vols. (London: British Museum, 1930).

Holmes, Megan, 'Neri di Bicci and the Commodification of Pictorial Values in Florentine Art 1450–1500', *The Art Market in Italy. 15th-17th Centuries,* Marcello Fantoni, Louisa Matthew, and Sara Matthews-Grieco, eds. (Modena: Pannini, 2003), 213–24.

Hope, C., 'Artists, Patrons and Advisers in the Italian Renaissance', in *Patronage in the Renaissance,* G. F. Lytle and S. Orgel, eds. (Princeton: Princeton University Press, 1981), 293–343.

'Altarpieces and the Requirements of Patrons', in *Christianity and the Renaissance: Image and Religious Imagination in the Quattrocento,* T. Verdon and J. Henderson, eds. (Syracuse: Syracuse University Press, 1990), 535–71.

'"Composition" from Cennini and Alberti to Vasari', in *Pictorial Composition from Medieval to Modern Art,* P. Taylor and F. Quiviger, eds. (London: Warburg Institute, 2000), 27–44.

Humfrey, Peter, *Cima da Conegliano* (Cambridge: Cambridge University Press, 1983).

Imbericadori, Iole Vichi, *Fina dei Ciardi* (Florence: Graficalito, 1979).

Iversen, Erik, *The Myth of Egypt and its Hieroglyphs in European Tradition* (Copenhagen: Gad, 1961, reprint Princeton: Princeton University Press, 1993).

Obelisks in Exile, Volume I. The Obelisks of Rome (Copenhagen: GEC Gad, 1968).
Jacobs, L., *Early Netherlandish Carved Altarpieces 1380–1550: Medieval Tastes and Mass Marketing* (Cambridge: Cambridge University Press, 1998).
Jacobus de Voragine, *The Golden Legend: Readings on the Saints,* trans. William Granger Ryan (Princeton: Princeton University Press, 1993).
James, Carolyn, *Giovanni Sabadino degli Arienti: A Literary Career* (Florence: Olschki, 1996).
Kaufmann, Thomas DaCosta, *Court, Cloister and City: The Art and Culture of Central Europe, 1450–1800* (Chicago: University of Chicago Press, 1995).
Kemp, Martin, '"The Madonna of the Yarnwinder" in the Buccleauch Collection Reconsidered in the Context of Leonardo's Studio Practice', in *I leonardeschi a Milano: fortuna e collezionismo,* Maria Teresa Fiorio and Pietro C. Marani, eds. (Milan: Electa, 1991), 35–48.
Kennedy, Clarence, Elizabeth Wilder, and Péleo Bacci, eds., *The Unfinished Monument by Andrea del Verrocchio to the Cardinal Niccolò Forteguerri at Pistoia* (Northampton, Mass.: Smith College, 1932).
Kent, F. W., 'Patron-Client Networks in Renaissance Florence and the Emergence of Lorenzo as "Maestro della Bottega"', in *Lorenzo de' Medici: New Perspectives,* Bernard Toscani, ed. (New York: P. Lang, 1993), 279–313.
and Patricia Simons, with J. C. Eade, eds., *Patronage, Art, and Society in Renaissance Italy* (Oxford: Oxford University Press, 1987).
Kiby, Ulrika, 'Poggioreale: Das erste Nymphäum der Renaissance', *Die Gartenkunst* 7 (1995): 68–79.
Krautter, Konrad, *Philologische Methode und Humanistische Existenz: Filippo Beroaldo und sein Kommentar zum Goldenen Esel des Apuleius* (Munich: Fink, 1971).
Kristeller, Paul Oskar, *Andrea Mantegna* (Berlin: Cosmos Verlag, 1902).
Supplementum Ficinianum, 2 vols. (Florence: Olschki, 1937).
Il pensiero filosofico di Marsilio Ficino, 2d ed. (Florence: Le Lettere, 1988).
Studies in Renaissance Thought and Letters, 4 vols. (Rome: Edizioni di Storia e Letteratura, 1956–94).
Krohn, Deborah L, 'Civic Patronage of Art in Renaissance San Gimignano', unpublished Ph.D. diss., Harvard University, 1992.
'Onofrio di Pietro and the Opera della Pieve in San Gimignano', in *Opera: Carattere e ruolo delle fabbriche cittadine fino all'inizio dell'Età Moderna,* Margaret Haines and Lucio Riccetti, eds. (Florence: Olschki, 1996), 345–70.
Kuhn, Thomas, *The Structure of Scientific Revolutions,* 3rd ed. (Chicago and London: University of Chicago Press, 1996).
Lapi Ballerini, Isabella, and Litta Maria Medri, eds., *Artifici d'acque e giardini: la cultura delle grotte e dei ninfei in Italia e in Europa* (Florence: Centro Di, 1999).
Lazzari, Alfonso, 'Un orazione di Lodovico Carbone a Firenze', *Atti e memorie della Reale Deputazione di Storia Patria per le Provincie Modenesi,* 5th ser., 12 (1919): 187–205.
Lazzarini, V., *Documenti relativi alla pittura padovana del secolo XV,* reprint. (Venice: Arnaldo Forni, 1974).
Lazzaro, Claudia, *The Italian Renaissance Garden: From the Conventions of Planting, Design, and Ornament to the Grand Gardens of Sixteenth-Century Central Italy* (New Haven: Yale University Press, 1990).
Ledderose, Lothar, *Ten Thousand Things. Module and Mass Production in Chinese Art* (Princeton: Princeton University Press, 2000).
Leostello da Volterra, Joampiero, *Effemeridi delle cose fatte per il Duca di Calabria (1484–1491).* Gaetano Filangieri, ed. (Naples: Accademia Reale delle Scienze, 1883).

Maier, I., *Ange Politien: La formation d'un poète humaniste (1469–1480)* (Geneva: Droz, 1966).

Malvasia, Carlo Cesare, *Felsina pittrice: Vite de' pittori bolognese,* 2 vols., Giampietro Zanotti et al., eds. (Bologna: Tipografia Guidi all'Ancora, 1841).

Manca, Joseph, *The Art of Ercole de' Roberti* (Cambridge and New York: Cambridge University Press, 1992).

Martindale, A., 'Luca Signorelli and the Drawings Connected to the Orvieto Frescoes', *Burlington Magazine* 103 (1961): 216–20.

Matarrese, Tina, 'Il volgare a Ferrara all'epoca del Boiardo: Dall'emiliano "illustre" all'italiano "cortigiano"', in *Il Boiardo e il mondo estense nel quattrocento. Atti del convegno internazionale di studi 13–17 settembre 1994,* 2 vols., Giuseppe Anceschi and Tina Matarrese, eds. (Padua: Antenore, 1998), vol. II, 611–47.

Mattiangeli, Paola, 'Annio de Viterbo inspiratore di cicli pittorici', in *Annio da Viterbo: Documenti e ricerche,* G. Baffoni and P. Mattiangeli, eds. (Rome: Consiglio nazionale delle ricerche, 1981), 257–303.

Mazzcurati, Giancarlo, *La questione della lingua dal Bembo all'Accademia Fiorentina* (Naples: Liguori, 1965).

McGinn, Bernard, *Visions of the End: Apocalyptic Traditions in the Middle Ages* (New York: Columbia University Press, 1979).

McGrath, T., 'Color and the Exchange of Ideas between Patron and Artist in Renaissance Italy', *Art Bulletin* 82 (2000): 298–308.

Milanesi, G., ed., *Nuovi documenti per la storia dell'arte toscana dal XII al XVI secolo* (Florence: G. Dotti, 1901).

Milanesi, G., ed., *Documenti per la storia dell'arte senese,* 3 vols., 2nd ed. (Utrecht: Davaco, 1969).

Milner, Stephen J., 'Lorenzo and Pistoia: Peacemaker or Partisan?', in *Lorenzo the Magnificent: Culture and Politics,* Michael Mallett and Nicholas Mann, eds. (London: Warburg Institute, 1996), 235–52.

'Rubrics and Requests: Statutory Division and Supra-Communal Clientage in Fifteenth-Century Pistoia', in *Florentine Tuscany: Practices and Structures of Power,* William J. Connell and Andrea Zorzi, eds. (Cambridge: Cambridge University Press, 2000), 312–32.

ed., *At the Margins: Minority Groups in Pre-Modern Italy* (Minneapolis: University of Minnesota Press, forthcoming, 2005).

'Piero Pollaiuolo's Lost Sacramental Tabernale of the *Corpus Domini',* forthcoming in the *Journal of the Warburg and Courtauld Institutes,* 67 (2004).

Müntz, Eugéne, *Les Collections des Médicis au quinzième siecle: le musée – la bibliothèque – le mobilier* (Paris: Rouam, 1888).

Mutafian, Claude, ed., *Roma – Armenia,* exh. cat., Città del Vaticano, Biblioteca Apostolica Vaticana, 25 marzo–16 luglio 1999 (Rome: Edizioni de Luca, 1999).

Nanni, Giovanni, *Commentaria Fratris Ioannis Annii Viterbensis Ordinis Praedicator, Theologiae Professoris Super Opera Diversorum Auctorum de Antiquitatibus Loquentorum* (Rome: E. Silber, 1498).

Berosi sacerdotis chaldaici, antiquitatum Italiae ac totius orbis libri Commentariis Joannis Annii Viterbensis, 2 vols. (Antwerp: I. Steelsii, 1552).

Natalucci, Mario, *Ancon dorica fidei: uomini e monumenti della Chiesa nella storia della città di Ancona* (Ancona: Cassa di Risparmio di Ancona, 1980).

Negri Arnoldi, Francesco, 'Il monumento sepolcrale del card. Niccolò Forteugerri in Santa Cecilia a Roma e il suo cenotafio nella cattedrale di Pistoia', in *Egemonia fiorentina ed autonomie locali nella Toscnana nord-occodentale del primo rinascimento: vita, arte, cultura,* Convegno internazionale, 18–25 settembre, 1975, Pistoia (Pistoia: Centro di studi, 1978), 11–33.

Neri di Bicci, *Le Ricordanze (10 marzo 1453–24 aprile 1475)*, Bruno Santi, ed. (Pisa: Edizioni Marlin, 1976).

Nieuwenhuizen, Paul, 'Worldly Ritual and Dynastic Iconography in the Bentivoglio Chapel in Bologna 1483–1499', *Mededelingen van het Nederlands Instituut te Rome* 36 (1996): 187–212.

Nova, Alessandro, 'Folengo and Romanino: The *Questione della Lingua* and its Eccentric Trends', *The Art Bulletin* 76 (1994): 664–80.

Oberman, Heiko A., and Thomas Brady, eds., *Itinerarium Italicum: The Profile of the Italian Renaissance in the Mirror of its European Transformations* (Leiden: Brill, 1975).

O'Malley, Michelle, 'The Business of Art. Contracts and Payment Documents for Fourteenth and Fifteenth-century Italian Altarpieces and Frescoes', unpublished Ph. D. diss, University of London, 1994.

'Memorizing the New: Using Recent Works as Models in Italian Renaissance Commissions', in *Memory and Oblivion: Proceedings of the XXIXth International Congress of the History of Art*, W. Reinink and J. Stumpel, eds. (Dordrecht: Kluwer Press, 1999), 803–10.

'Commissioning Bodies, Allocation Decisions and Price Structures for Altarpieces in Fifteenth- and Early Sixteenth-Century Italy', in *The Art Market in Italy, 15th–17th Centuries*, M. Fantoni, L. Matthew, and S. Matthews Grieco, eds. (Modena: Panini Editore, 2003), 163–80.

The Business of Art: Contracts and the Commissioning Process in Renaissance Italy (New Haven and London: Yale University Press, forthcoming, 2005).

Orvieto, Paolo, 'Carnevale e feste fiorentine del tempo di Lorenzo de' Medici', in *Lorenzo il Magnifico e il suo tempo*, ed. Gian Carlo Garfagnini (Florence: Olschki, 1992), 103–24.

Pagden, Anthony, *European Encounters with the New World. From Renaissance to Romanticism* (New Haven and London: Yale University Press, 1993).

Pane, Roberto, 'Le Effemeridi di Joanpiero Leostello', *Napoli nobilissima* 7 (1968): 77–85.

Paoletti, John T., 'Familiar Objects: Sculptural Types in the Collections of the Early Medici', in *Looking at Italian Renaissance Sculpture*, Sarah Blake McHam, ed. (Cambridge: Cambridge University Press, 1998), 79–110.

Paolozzi Strozzi, Beatrice, 'Originale e copia. "L'Adorazione del Bambino" della bottega di Filippo Lippi', in *I restauri nel Palazzo Medici Riccardi. Rinascimento e Barocco*, Cristina Acidini Lucinat, ed. (Milan: Silvana, 1992), 32–49.

Pecori, Luigi, *Storia della Terra di San Gimignano* (Florence: Galileiana, 1853).

Pezzarossa, Flavio, '"Ad honore et laude del nome Bentivoglio": La letteratura della festa nel secondo quattrocento', in *'Bentivolorum magnificentia'. Principe e cultura a Bologna nel rinascimento*, Bruno Basile, ed. (Rome: Bulzoni, 1984), 35–113.

Pigman III, George, 'Versions of Imitation in the Renaissance', *Renaissance Quarterly* 33 (1980): 1–32.

Pinto, Giuliano, ed., *Storia di Pistoia*, 4 vols. (Florence: Le Monnier, 1999), vol. III, *Dentro lo stato fiorentino: dalla metà del XIV alla fine del XVIII secolo*.

Poeschel, Sabine, *Alexander Maximus: Das Bildprogramm des Appartamento Borgia im Vatikan* (Weimar: VDG, 1999).

Poliziano, Angelo, *Miscellaneorum centuria secunda*, V. Branca and M. Pastore Stocchi, eds. (Florence: Olschki, 1978).

Lamia: Praelectio in priora Aristotelis analytica, A. Wesseling, ed. (Leiden: Brill, 1986).

Polizzotto, Lorenzo, *The Elect Nation: The Savonarolan Movement in Florence, 1494–1545* (Oxford: Clarendon, 1994).

Pope-Hennessey, John, *An Introduction to Italian Renaissance Sculpture,* 3 vols., 4th ed. (London: Phaidon, 1996).

Popham, A. E., *Catalogue of the Drawings of Parmigianino* (London: Yale University Press for the Pierpont Morgan Library, 1971).

Puttfarken, T., *The Discovery of Pictorial Composition: Theories of Visual Order in Painting 1400–1800* (New Haven and London: Yale University Press, 2000).

Reiss, Timothy J., *Knowledge, Discovery and Imagination in Early Modern Europe: The Rise of Aesthetic Rationalism* (New York and Cambridge: Cambridge University Press, 1997).

Rosenberg, Charles, *The Este Monuments and Urban Development in Renaissance Ferrara* (Cambridge and New York: Cambridge University Press, 1997).

Roullet, Anne, *The Egyptian and Egyptianizing Monuments of Imperial Rome* (Leiden: Brill, 1972).

Rowland, Ingrid D., *The Culture of the High Renaissance: Ancients and Moderns in Sixteenth-Century Rome* (Cambridge and New York: Cambridge University Press, 1998).

Rubin, Patricia Lee, and Alison Wright with contributions by Nicholas Penny, *Renaissance Florence. The Art of the 1470s,* exh. cat., London, National Gallery, 20 October 1999–16 January 2000 (London: National Gallery of Art, 1999).

Ruda, Jeffrey, *Fra Filippo Lippi* (London and New York: Phaidon, 1993).

Ruggiero, Guido, *Binding Passions: Tales of Magic, Marriage, and Power at the End of the Renaissance* (Oxford and New York: Oxford University Press, 1993).

Sarkissian, Karekin, *The Council of Chalcedon and the Armenian Church,* 2nd ed. (New York: Armenian Church Prelacy, 1975).

Savoldo, *Giovanni Girolamo Savoldo: tra Foppa, Giorgione e Caravaggio,* exh. cat., Brescia, Monastero di Santa Giulia, 3 marzo–31 maggio, 1990 (Milan: Electa, 1990).

Saxl, Fritz, 'The Appartamento Borgia', in *Lectures,* 2 vols. (London: Warburg Institute, 1957), vol. I, 174–88.

Scharf, A., *Filippino Lippi* (Vienna: Antol Schroll, 1935).

Schofield, R., J. Shell, and G. Sironi, *Giovanni Antonio Amadeo: Documents/I documenti* (Como: Edizione New Press, 1989).

Shearman, J., *Andrea del Sarto* (Oxford: Clarendon Press, 1965).

Simons, P., 'Patronage in the Tornaquinci Chapel, Santa Maria Novella, Florence', in *Patronage, Art and Society in Renaissance Italy,* F. W. Kent and P. Simons, with J. C. Eade, eds. (Oxford: Oxford University Press, 1987), 221–50.

Sorelius, Gunnar, and Michael Srigley, *Cultural Exchange between European Nations during the Renaissance. Acta Universitatis Upsaliensis* (Uppsala: Uppsala University, 1994).

Stemp, Richard, 'Cosimo Tura and the Sacrati Chapels in Ferrara', *Musei Ferraresi* 17, (1990–1): 61–70.

Stephens, Walter, *Giants in Those Days: Folklore, Ancient History, and Nationalism* (Lincoln and London: University of Nebraska Press, 1989).

Stow, Kenneth R., *Catholic Thought and Papal Jewry Policy 1555–1593* (New York: Jewish Theological Seminary of America, 1977).

Swartz, David, *Culture and Power: The Sociology of Pierre Bourdieu* (Chicago: University of Chicago Press, 1997).

Syson, Luke, 'Opus pisani pictoris: les médailles de Pisanello et son atelier', in *Pisanello: Louvre conférences et colloques,* 2 vols., Dominique Cordellier and Bernadette Py, eds. (Paris: La Documentation Française, 1998), vol. I, 377–426.

'Ercole de Roberti: The Making of a Court Artist', in Denise Allen, Luke Syson, Jennifer Helvey, and David Jaffé, *Ercole de' Roberti: The Renaissance in Ferrara,* exh. cat., Los Angeles, J. Paul Getty Museum, 1999 (London: Burlington Magazine Publications, 1999), v–xiv.

'Classical Learning and Court Art', in Luke Syson and Dillian Gordon, eds., *Pisanello, Painter to the Renaissance Court* (London: National Gallery, 2001), 86–137.

Thomas, Anabel, *The Painter's Practice in Renaissance Tuscany* (Cambridge and New York: Cambridge University Press, 1995).

Vaccaro, M., 'Documents for Parmigianino's "Vision of St Jerome"', *Burlington Magazine* 135 (1993): 22–7.

Van Marle, Raimond, *The Development of the Italian Schools of Painting,* 18 vols. (The Hague: Martinus Nijhoff, 1931) vol. XIII, 428–64.

Vasari, Giorgio, *Le opere di Giorgio Vasari,* Gaetano Milanesi, ed., 9 vols (Florence: Sansoni, 1906, 2d ed. 1981).

Vasari, Giorgio, *Le vite de' più eccellenti pittori, scultori e architettori,* Rosanna Bettarini and Paola Barocchi, eds. (Florence: Studio per Edizioni Scelte, 1987).

Vauchez, André, ed., *La Religion Civique à l'Époque Médiévale et Moderne,* Actes du colloque organisé par le Centre de recherche 'Histoire sociale et culturelle de l'Occident. XIIe–XVIIIe siècle' de l'Université de Paris X-Nanterre e l'Institut universitaire de France (Nanterre, 21–23 juin 1993) (Rome: École Française de Rome, 1995).

Ventrone, Paola, 'Feste e spettacoli nella Firenze di Lorenzo il Magnifico', in *Le tems revient. 'l tempo si rinuova. Feste e spettacoli nella Firenze di Lorenzo il Magnifico,* Paola Ventrone, ed. (Cinisello Balsamo: Silvana, 1992), 21–53.

Venturi, A., 'Cosmè Tura e la capella de Belriguardo', *Il Buonarroti,* 3rd ser., 2 (1884): 55–64.

Verde, Armando, *Lo studio fiorentino, 1473–1503: Ricerche e documenti,* 5 vols. (Florence: Olschki, 1973–94).

'Studenti e professori fra l'Università di Ferrara e l'Università di Firenze: Fine del quattrocento – inizio del cinquecento', in *'In supreme dignitatis . . .' Per la storia dell'Università di Ferrara, 1391–1991,* P. Castelli ed. (Florence: Olschki, 1995), 75–105.

Vischer, R., *Luca Signorelli und die italienische renaissance* (Leipzig: Veit und Comp, 1879).

von Bode, Wilhem, *Bertoldo und Lorenzo dei Medici: Die Kunstpolitik des Lorenzo il Magnifico im Spiegel der Werke seines Lieblingskünstlers Bertoldo di Giovanni* (Freiburg im Breisgau: Pontos-Verlag, 1925).

Warnke, Martin, *The Court Artist: On the Ancestry of the Modern Artist,* trans. D. McLintock (Cambridge and New York: Cambridge University Press, 1993).

Warburg, Aby, *The Renewal of Pagan Antiquity,* trans. D. Britt (Los Angeles: Getty Research Institute, 1999).

Weinstein, Donald, *Savonarola and Florence: Prophecy and Patriotism in the Renaissance* (Princeton: Princeton University Press, 1970).

Weiss, R., *The Renaissance Discovery of Classical Antiquity,* rev. ed. (Oxford: Basil Blackwell, 1988).

Weil-Garris Brandt, Kathleen, and others eds., *Giovinezza di Michelangelo,* exh. cat., Florence, Palazzo Vecchio, Casa Buonarroti, 1999–2000 (Florence and Milan: ArtificioSkira, 1999).

Welch, E., *Art and Authority in Renaissance Milan* (New Haven and London: Yale University Press, 1995).

Woods-Marsden, Joanna, *Renaissance Self-Portraiture: The Visual Construction of Identity and the Social Status of the Artist* (New Haven and London: Yale University Press, 1998).

Wright, Alison, 'Dancing Nudes in the Lanfredini Villa at Arcetri,' in *With and Without the Medici. Studies in Tuscan Art and Patronage 1434–1530,* Marchand Eckard and Alison Wright, eds. (Aldershot, Hants: Ashgate, 1998), 47–79.

Yates, Frances W., *Giordano Bruno and the Hermetic Tradition* (Chicago and London: University of Chicago Press, 1964).

Zekiyan, Levon Boghos, 'Le colonie armene del medio evo in Italia e le relazioni culturali italo-armene', in *Atti del primo simposio internazionale di arte armene,* Giulio Ieni and Levon Boghos Zekiyan, eds. (Venice: San Lazzaro, 1978), 803–929.

Zeri, Federico, *Italian Paintings in the Walters Art Gallery,* 2 vols. (Baltimore: Walters Art Gallery, 1976).

Ziegler, H. ed., *The Translatability of Cultures. Proceedings of the Fifth Stuttgart Seminar in Cultural Studies* (Stuttgart and Weimar: Metzler, 1998).

Zorach, Rebecca, 'The Matter of Italy: Sodomy and the Scandal of Style in Sixteenth-Century France', *Journal of Medieval and Early Modern Studies* 28 (1998): 581–609.

Zuraw, Shelley E., 'The Sculpture of Mino da Fiesole (1429–1484)', unpublished Ph.D. diss., New York University, 1993.

'The Public Commemorative Monument: Mino da Fiesole's Tombs in the Florentine Badia', *Art Bulletin* 80 (1998): 452–77.

Index